Eccentric
London

the Bradt Guide to Britain's Crazy and Curious Capital

Benedict le Vay

edition
2

www.bradtguides.com

Bradt Travel Guides Ltd, UK
The Globe Pequot Press Inc, USA

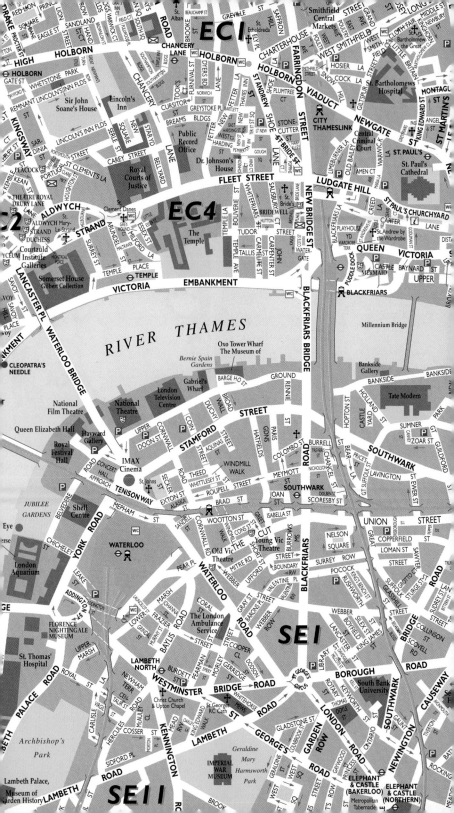

above left Portobello Road has a fabulous antique market, and it's not tricky to work out what this avid collector hoards (DR)

above right You'll never need a watch if this chap's in the vicinity (MK)

left Notting Hill Carnival parades the best Caribbean costumes — and the occasional twerp with flowers on his head

(BoV/JS) page 307

top Beards, perms, umbrellas — the Europride Parade has it all in spades (CH)

centre Eccentric collector Maurice Collins wears a 19th-century hat-measurer on his head and holds a pair of Victorian skates, surrounded by his collection of over a thousand bizarre antique gadgets (JG/Empics) page 50

right Eccentric Hammersmith photographer Scott Thompson detects Tube lines by listening from above, and then photographs the scene (BV) page 261

above   Stainless City traders: the sensational Lloyd's building, inside and out (BoV/BV) page 129

left   The swirling interior of the new City Hall on the South Bank near Tower Bridge is brilliant in a building without any real point, literally if not figuratively (BV) page 132

next page:

above left   An unexpected slice of Japanese tranquility on the South Bank – the Peace Pagoda, built by Buddhist nuns and monks, was the first pagoda to be built in any Western capital (JR) page 116

above right   The old Turkish Baths in New Broad Street, where fatigued Victorians could pop in for a hot bath and sauna for two shillings and sixpence (BoV/EN) page 131

below   Funky footwear covers the roof of this shop in Camden (CH)

top Cosmic, man: Karma Kars, using Indian-built Ambassador cars imported by Tobias Moss, brings the exotic Orient to London streets
(BV) page 85

centre A Fortnum & Mason delivery trots through London; a refreshing change to Tesco vans hurtling along the motorway (BoV/EN)

left If you're a Harry Potter fan, platform 9¾ at King's Cross means a lot to you, as it's there you have to rush at the brick wall with your trolley to reach the Hogwart's Express. Luckily someone has blocked off the wall with this witty sculpture of half a trolley to stop fans trying for themselves (BV) page 95

Author

Benedict le Vay is a national newspaper sub-editor who has worked in four continents but wrote his first book, *Eccentric Britain*, more or less by accident after collecting oddities about his home country. He says he was 'staggered' by the response, which includes media attention from the *Shetland Times* to Gulf Radio, and publicity tours in America and New Zealand. He describes himself as a frankly rather ordinary, happily married father of two, and is hard-pressed to think of anything eccentric about himself. 'At a push, I'd say, yes, I'm Honorary Secretary of the Friends of A272, and I've asked for my ashes to be blasted from the chimney of my favourite steam locomotive at my funeral. Hasn't everybody?'

PUBLISHER'S FOREWORD   *Hilary Bradt*

The first Bradt travel guide was written in 1974 by George and Hilary Bradt on a river barge floating down a tributary of the Amazon. It was followed by *Backpacker's Africa*, published in 1979. In the 1980s and '90s the focus shifted away from hiking to broader-based guides to new destinations – usually the first to be published on those places. In the 21st century Bradt continues to publish these ground-breaking guides, along with guides to established holiday destinations, incorporating in-depth information on culture and natural history alongside the nuts and bolts of where to stay and what to see.

* * *

People still seek me out to talk about *Eccentric London*. 'But it's so interesting,' they say. 'I've lived here all my life and never dreamed there was all this stuff on my doorstep!' Or words to that effect. Ben Le Vay is Bradt's master of eccentricity. His eye and ear for the unusual stems from a journalist's curiosity and runs through all his books. It's a pleasure to be publishing a new edition of this guide.

Second edition published April 2007
First published in 2002

Bradt Travel Guides Ltd, 23 High Street, Chalfont St Peter, Bucks SL9 9QE, England.
www.bradtguides.com
Published in the USA by The Globe Pequot Press Inc, 246 Goose Lane,
PO Box 480, Guilford, Connecticut 06475-0480

ISBN-10: 1 84162 193 5   ISBN-13: 978 1 84162 193 7
British Library Cataloguing in Publication Data
A catalogue record for this book is available from the British Library

Photographs Britain on View (BoV), Johnny Green (JG), Cath Harries (CH), Mark Kerrison (MK), Ben Le Vay (BV), Eric Nathan (EN), James Rice (JR), Deborah Ripley (DR), Jon Spaull (JS), Strange Fruit (SF), Dave Taylor (DT)
Front cover Pierre Vivant's *The Traffic Light Tree*, Isle of Dogs (JR)
Back cover Tattoo studio in Camden (CH), Eccentrically dressed gent with bowler hat in Trafalgar Square (BoV)
Title page Graffito of bikini-clad woman at the beach, Camden (CH), Elvis impersonator at Europride festival (CH), Gold Buddha sculpture at the Peace Pagoda on the South Bank (JR)

Illustrations Carole Vincer, Jo Stearn **Cartoons** Dave Colton, www.cartoonist.net
Maps Steve Munns (Trialzoom Ltd)
Logos The London Underground symbol used in this book is the property of Transport for London

Typeset from the author's disc by Wakewing
Printed and bound in Italy by Legoprint SpA, Trento

Acknowledgements

Dr David le Vay, Hugh Dawson, Jeff Shaw, Jim Garrod, Bill Smith, Flavia Gapper, Ernie McLaughlin, Sue Barnes, Felix le Vay, Martin le Vay, James Levy, Richard Griffin, Kelvin Wynne and many, many other Londoners. Plus the editors and typesetter who tried to keep up with the many changes. The mistakes, however, are all mine!

DEDICATION

For my father, David le Vay, who died while the first edition of this book was being finished. Typically, he'd done a deal whereby I'd buy his last book and he promised to buy this one. I should have known. Meanwhile he knocked off another book about a medieval monk and a radio play at the age of 86. That was the calibre of the man. But at least I can now reveal he's the angry surgeon quoted in the Earl's Court section.

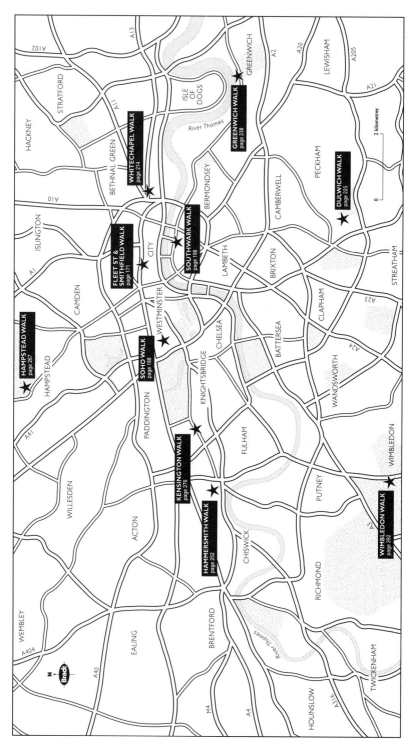

STRATFORD
HACKNEY
A102
A13
A11
BETHNAL GREEN
A10
ISLINGTON
A1
CAMDEN
A41
HAMPSTEAD
WILLESDEN
ACTON
EALING
WEMBLEY
A404
A40
M4
A4
HOUNSLOW
A316
TWICKENHAM
BRENTFORD
CHISWICK
RICHMOND
PADDINGTON
KNIGHTSBRIDGE
CHELSEA
FULHAM
PUTNEY
WANDSWORTH
BATTERSEA
CLAPHAM
WIMBLEDON
WESTMINSTER
LAMBETH
BRIXTON
STREATHAM
CAMBERWELL
BERMONDSEY
PECKHAM
LEWISHAM
GREENWICH
ISLE OF DOGS
River Thames
River Thames
CITY

A2
A20
A205
A21
A23
A24

WHITECHAPEL WALK page 214

GREENWICH WALK page 238

DULWICH WALK page 225

FLEET ST & SMITHFIELD WALK page 171

SOUTHWARK WALK page 198

HAMPSTEAD WALK page 267

SOHO WALK page 188

KENSINGTON WALK page 276

HAMMERSMITH WALK page 252

WIMBLEDON WALK page 292

0   2 kilometres

N

Bradt

Contents

Introduction

London is the greatest big city in the world, and Londoners need reminding of this even if visitors don't:

- Greatest for theatre, with the National and the Royal Shakespeare Company (RSC), the Globe, the thriving commercial West End, the massive widespread fringe and pub theatre scenes: 159 theatres putting on more plays than anywhere on earth;
- Greatest for nightlife and food (every kind and quality imaginable on the planet in 8,500 restaurants);
- Greatest for diversity and tolerance, with more living religions and languages than any other city on the planet;
- Greatest for art, museums and galleries, many of them free or little known (and listed later in this guide), while others such as the British Museum, Dulwich, Greenwich, British Library, Somerset House, etc, have been recently reinvigorated with vast investments of billions of pounds. There is also the dynamic and exciting Tate Modern (already by far the world's most popular modern art museum with 5.2 million visitors in its first year);
- Greatest for layer upon layer of fascinating history in its mellowed, ancient architecture and unique set of churches, ranging from medieval crypts at Westminster Abbey to Wren's fabulous creations;
- Greatest for newspapers, with more and better papers every day than anywhere else on the planet;
- Greatest for daring, breathtakingly modern buildings, with associated provocative sculptures (in Docklands particularly, but in other areas too);
- Greatest for fashion (so that even Paris shops for couturiers here);
- Greatest for cabbies and their 'knowledge' of its reassuringly absurd medieval street plan;
- Greatest for ceremonials – not with a boring president, but a real queen in a real palace with real guards in bearskin hats (but with modern sub-machine guns) parading outside; Gurkhas from the high Himalayas, with their lethal kukri knives; Aussies in bush hats and rifles; or Highlanders in kilts, with daggers in their socks. The world's greatest royal coronations, funerals and weddings, and the unending soap opera that real royalty affords;

- Greatest for classical music, with its unequalled set of orchestras, wonderful concert halls, and incomparable Proms concerts, as well as for rock and pop music and the stars they produce;
- Greatest for shopping, with 29,000 shops;
- Greatest for eccentric humour;
- Greatest for liberty and freedom of speech, with its unarmed police, Speakers' Corner, and Her Majesty's Loyal Opposition;
- Greatest for architectural curiosities and – oddly – for the 'village' charm it somehow maintains within its urban sprawl, giving at its best, and for the lucky few, the most pleasant suburbia on the planet;
- Greatest for transport, with the world's biggest yet clearest Tube network and its renowned double-decker buses; and
- Greatest for its wonderful open spaces, from the unmatchable jewel-in-the-crown royal parks – including the fabulous Richmond Park and Hampstead Heath – to the unique London squares.

But is it greatest for eccentricities and oddities, quirks and queries? This book provides the answer.

... AND THE DRAWBACKS

I had to utter that gushing but deserved paean of praise not only for visitors but for Londoners, who take the place for granted; and yes, I admit London has its downside. For example, the expense of everything if you don't earn London wages; the litter; the graffiti; the inability of the authorities to match up the homeless with the ludicrously priced empty properties (they could have three houses each at the last count); the pickpockets on the Tube; the rudest shop and catering staff this side of Hong Kong (well, not all of them).

But in many of those great claims London just cannot be rivalled. London by the start of the 21st century had undergone another cultural renaissance that nobody predicted. It is far more deeply rooted than the much-vaunted Swinging Sixties era when London was said by some to lead the fashion world. That was a thin, gimmicky-but-colourful veneer consisting of Carnaby Street and the King's Road, mini skirts and Mini cars; the bulk of the city, however, was still poor, grey, straight-laced, sexually repressed, and struggling to recover from the grim, rationed decades of the 1940s and 1950s. Today, the city's rebirth in terms of food, art, architecture etc, isn't limited to isolated efforts such as the Festival Hall (a Fifties attempt to keep culture alive amidst the bombsites) but goes root and branch right across the capital and its population.

And what a changing population! It is the most linguistically diverse city in the world, a polyglot cornucopia of languages and dialects. A recent survey showed that 307 languages were spoken in the city's school playgrounds, with about 100,000 children speaking one of South Asia's four main languages; but up there in the top 30 were Akan (Ashanti) at 6,000 children, Farsi (Persian) at 3,300, and Tagalog (Filipino) at 1,600.

Perhaps the loneliest kids in the playground were those who spoke Mbum (it's from Cameroon, I'm told) – there were only two of them – and the only Pidgin speaker, poor thing. If I ever meet that Pidgin speaker I must try out the Pidgin phrase for 'total eclipse of the sun' which an old sailor told me was, 'Big kerosene lamp in sky him all bugger up'. No, I didn't believe it either.

Against this bubbling background it's perhaps harder to spot an individual eccentric because there's so much diversity. Being odd or different isn't unusual, as you'll soon find if you watch people. Unusual *is* usual in London.

From time to time an obviously eccentric Londoner hoves into view. For example, when Jeff Smith, 60, from Muswell Hill tried to drive two sheep across

Tower Bridge in 1999, City police stopped him. Then he explained that, as a Freeman of the City of London, he had that right. After checking he wasn't pulling the wool over their eyes, Mr Smith, Clover and Little Man were allowed across by the police.

And if you want to drive geese and swine through Dulwich, you will find that eccentric village-within-the-town still has its own arrangements for charging travellers by the sheep or goat.

A constant stream of eccentric explorers sets out from London. In 2001, Jim Shekhdar from Northwood rowed to Australia having spent an astonishing nine months and a day rowing from South America right across the world's biggest ocean. Actually, he didn't row the whole way because he was tossed out in the surf as he arrived. Had he lost his sense of humour? 'I always knew that damned boat wanted to reach Australia before me,' he said as he waded ashore after it. Why did he do it? 'I had to lose some weight.'

But eccentrics arrive in London as well as leave it. Down the Old Kent Road there's a Chinese restaurateur who likes nothing more than dressing up and doing Elvis impersonations. And, no, he doesn't sing 'Brue suede shoes', though he gyrates his hips perfectly. But Paul Elvis Chan is an eccentric all right: his place is called the Graceland Palace.

That eccentricity goes to the top of London society, and colours such mundane acts as answering the telephone, can be demonstrated by the surprisingly complementary tales told by two people about their well-known fathers. One was Tim Healey, son of Denis, later Lord Healey. Apparently, when Denis lived at No 11 Downing Street as Chancellor of the Exchequer, replete with the full panoply of state, red boxes and civil servants, Denis would sometimes answer the phone, 'Aro? Chinese laundly?' Equally, sitting in exactly the same Radio 4 studio with me some months later, novelist Sophie Parkin was discussing her family's eccentric parents. 'My father always answers the phone: "Toad of Toad Hall". He thinks he *is* Toad. He always wears green and has a car that goes "parp, parp" in the same way.'

There are countless examples: there's a crusty old admiral who perfected the very difficult art of sailing backwards down the Thames and persuaded others to do the same annually for a race; and there's a man who drives round in a motorised four-poster bed.

Even the so-called great and good can eccentrically deflate themselves – literally in some cases. Poet Sir Stephen Spender's diary records how one night, thinking himself to be alone, he broke wind after the opera ('It was much louder after five hours of Wagner than I had dreamed possible') causing a group of unseen bystanders in the dark to cheer wildly. He wrote: 'I saw how an incident like this divides people into two categories – those who would laugh and those who would be shocked.' In this book we are in the laughing category.

Talking about humour, or attempts at it, I offer my apologies to those who don't enjoy awful puns and wisecracks. I'm encouraged as I write this book by the occasional bursts of laughter from those reading already completed chapters, but I realise it won't be to everybody's taste.

All I can say is that in buying this book you have shown that you don't want one of those soulless, written-by-committee guidebooks which say 'This is the Tower of London and this is how you get there', but something which gives you more, and tells you something you didn't already know.

I was born in London, have studied and worked and lived all over it for half a century, so I can bring a personal involvement to many places and events. It should bring the real subject – the greatest city in the world and the people who live here – more vividly to life.

SQUALOR AND ELEGANCE CHEEK BY JOWL: SHARP DIVISIONS London fascinates both in how little it changes – the Roman street plan of the City survives, overlaid with those medieval complexities that were not ironed out in the hurried rebuilding that took place after the Great Fire of 1666, despite several grand plans for boring American-style grid patterns being proposed for London's streets – and how much it changes.

In the latter case, consider the now rather posh and respectable area around the Tate Gallery, Millbank. The huge and gloomy Millbank Penitentiary loomed over this area until it was demolished in 1890. A tunnel under the road, still marked by a special bollard, is where the miserable convicts were led down under from the penitentiary to the waiting ships for transportation to Australia. That vast land is hence still known as 'Down Under' (see page 148). Between here and Westminster was 'the Devil's Acre', a teeming, disease-infested warren of brothels, opium dens and gambling haunts, and a no-go area for the authorities. Ironically, it was like this because of the sanctuary rules associated with Westminster Abbey (see page 55). Before that Millbank was where the wind and water mills of Westminster Abbey turned in rural isolation, interrupted only by the horse ferry that gave its name to Horseferry Road. Then again, it is hard to imagine anything more respectable than this rather pompous area today. So the area has transformed itself radically at least twice.

But the geography of London as well as the history is subject to surprisingly sudden shifts. The refreshing thing about wandering about London is how the character of the place can change completely and utterly within a hundred yards. Time and time again when researching this book that has surprised me.

Just a few yards from snootiest Mayfair or bookish Fitzrovia one finds oneself diving into Soho sleaze: a quiet Bloomsbury square full of intellectuals is only a few paces from teeming streets with staggering drunks and hurrying messengers; while the shopaholic bustle of Kensington High Street's designer-label junkies and poseurs soon gives way to leafy Georgian peace and splendour to the south, and in the north to fascinating bystreets.

This, of course, is nothing new. A totally fascinating book, the *History of London in Maps* (see booklist), includes Booth's 1889 Poverty Map. This mapped London by social class, by colour-coding the sides of the streets mapped, and thus divided the capital into classes ranging from 'Upper-middle class and Upper classes. Wealthy' (a nice cheerful yellow) down through six classes including 'Poor. 18s to

21s a week for a moderate family' (blue), 'Very poor, casual. Chronic want' (dark blue) to 'Lowest class. Vicious, semi-criminal' (a gloomy black). It's quite amazing today that anyone should categorise people's wealth and morals like this, although of course many people categorise others to some degree. Whole streets, written off as 'Vicious, semi-criminal', would probably sue today.

Yet to a Victorian world this made sense. People were, on the whole, set in their classes, and the rich were the poor's 'betters', while the poor were either the deserving poor, and worth using as servants, or they were criminals. Many Victorians believed you could spot the criminal classes by the shape of their heads. I remember a hymn at school which included a line about social order being ordained by God: 'The rich man in his castle, the poor man at his gate.'

Today we know that the rich can be idle, drunk and even 'vicious semi-criminals' – I hesitate to mention the last Lord Lucan, who may be innocent of bashing his children's nanny's head in and then disappearing (if he cares to sue me I've got the journalistic scoop of the century) – but you get the idea. We constantly read of such things as the rich fiddling their mortgage applications and aristocrats staging insurance frauds by chopping up supposedly stolen vintage cars.

What's totally fascinating about those old maps is how one end of a street can be one class, while the other end can be five classes above or below it. The book reproduces part of the map showing the Strand and Holborn and shows what was there before the grand curve of the Aldwych and the Kingsway were built. The area was a crawling warren of slums, no doubt stalked by disease. Though the main roads nearby such as High Holborn and Long Acre at Covent Garden were in the second highest social group, just behind them lay the dwellings of 'vicious, semi-criminal' types. This was no coincidence.

THE ROOKERIES: CRIME ON A DICKENSIAN SCALE Another factor in London's astonishing social blend was the existence of the 'rookeries', great, steaming, slum warrens of theft, alcoholism, gambling, prostitution, insanitary diseases, orphans, poverty – the world that Dickens captures pretty realistically, historians agree, in *Oliver Twist*.

The inhabitants of the early 19th-century rookeries, where police dared not penetrate for fear of being beaten senseless by lawless lowlife, and which surrounded London, needed to be near well-to-do respectable districts, or areas in which the rich indulged their pleasures and vices, to have something to prey on. This parasitical relationship explains why, historically, there were sudden shifts in the social standing of neighbouring areas, differences that are still echoed on the ground today.

The Victorian spirit of social campaigning, which found voice in organisations such as the Temperance Society and the Salvation Army, pops up in another map in the *History of London in Maps*, which showed pubs as red dots. 'A modern plague of London, a scarlet fever!' the reformers cried. Pubs were so thick on the ground in Soho that the dots merged into a red mass. Predictably, they are far more common in poor areas (1,059 in Whitechapel and Stepney alone) than rich ones (about 25 in Mayfair), and that's still the case. We have not, it seems, much escaped our social history. You can still make a crime map pretty easily by making a pub map.

Covent Garden, however, is an example of an area whose character has changed radically over time. When it was built in the early 17th century, it was home to many titled families and was the very epitome of elegance. Yet, less than a century later, the constant process of the rich moving westwards – away from London's pollution and towards fresh air and the court at Kensington – left Covent Garden as the main centre of prostitution and drunkenness.

The boom in theatres after the Puritans had been kicked out in 1660 meant that once very smart Drury Lane and its environs became increasingly seedy, with streetwalkers thick on the ground all night, while the development of Covent Garden as London's premier fruit and vegetable market (nicely captured in Hitchcock's film *Frenzy*) meant that a lower class of person thronged the streets. The same streets where once elegant carriages had awaited their titled owners, residents who had fled an area now notorious for stabbings and fights.

Yet the late 20th century saw the Royal Opera House completely refurbished, bringing back the so-called great and the good, with the market banished to Nine Elms on the other side of the river, and the lovely 17th-century buildings being converted for shopping, drinking and the entertainment of the international leisured classes. Re-enter the pickpockets...

LONDON'S WEIRD POLITICS: THE ECCENTRIC CANDIDATES London's politics are riven with eccentricity. What other capital city, when given three official party candidates for the important position of mayor in 2000, would instead vote for a man with no party and, frankly, a pretty mixed track record in running London? I mean, of course, amiable, nasal, newt-fancying Ken Livingstone, once known as 'Red Ken' when his late and unlamented Greater London Council seemed to be throwing money at lesbian handicapped immigrant militant muslim fundamentalist feminist republican terrorists (no offence to any of those mostly worthy categories, but you know what I mean) just to annoy then Tory prime minister, Mrs Thatcher.

Mind you, the other candidates for mayor – a title which has turned out to be even more meaningless than that of the Lord Mayor of London, someone who, confusingly, carries on his or her own sweet way and is considered the 'real' mayor by traditionalists – were 'Dobbo' Dobson, an old Labour carthorse bullied into standing but who clearly wanted the job as much as a hole in the head; Steve 'Shagger' Norris, a Tory sexual athlete who seriously proposed taking over the city's public transport although he had previously said he wouldn't ever use it because of the ghastly people you meet; and some forgettable Liberal woman, whose name escapes me, who was probably the sanest candidate (plus a humorous Indian gent from Dulwich, of whom more later). And you can't get much more eccentric than that.

Of course, Londoners had voted for Red Ken in the 1980s mainly to drive Thatcher insane, and voted for New Ken this time round mainly to take grinning Prime Minister Tony Blair down a peg or two. Blair had foolishly anointed Dobbo as the winner, just as he had already done for leaders of the new assemblies in Wales and Scotland, invented at about the same time.

Just as the Tories had in effect said London could have any council as long as it was Conservative – which is why Tory outer boroughs such as Bromley and Harrow were made part of the old London County Council, which worked for a while, and when it didn't, the GLC (as the LCC had become) was abolished – so New Labour in 2000 effectively said London could have any Labour mayor as long as he (or she) was a Blairite.

Bloody-minded Londoners refused to go along with either, which makes me very proud of them. These are the same people, or about three million of them, who put Middlesex on their addresses although that county was officially abolished more than 40 years ago. They don't get pushed around.

The likeable Ken said, to his credit, when elected: 'As I was saying when I was so rudely interrupted 14 years ago.' Such is London's deeply eccentric political scene.

Meanwhile London continues its own sweet way, bustling with interest, teeming with ideas, stuffed with more odd nooks and crannies than one person can ever see, while in the midst of it all, Old Father Thames keeps rolling along, continuously carrying all our yesterdays down towards the sea – 2,000 amazing years of London history. What a city!

GETTING ABOUT

Although there are maps with the walks in this book, you'll need to refer to a Tube map and ideally for further exploration buy a good street guide, the *A–Z* being the best.

Public transport costs in London are truly, madly, deeply unreasonable. They preach at us to get out of our cars then wallop us heavily for doing so. (Mind you, car drivers are even more persecuted.) It seems you can't win.

But you can! From a visitor's point of view, there are mitigating factors and ways to beat the system. It's not all bad news.

The good news is that it's a superb system – the biggest Metro system in the world, frequent buses often with priority lanes, a really useful night bus network, and a less well-known network of national rail (meaning not Tube) trains which access South London particularly well. Plus ubiquitous, reliable – if not exactly cheap – black cabs. Londoners don't need a car, except in the outer suburbs.

What about beating the fares? Well, don't cheat. The punishments would spoil your holiday.

Let's look at the problem constructively. You really need to take on board the lessons in terms of costs.

ILLUSTRATION DAY OUT AND YOU'D-BE-BONKERS-NOT-TO SAVINGS Suppose a family of two adults and two children (one aged nine, the other 14, say) are staying in Bayswater. At 10am, they go up to Hampstead by Tube for a walk across the Heath to Highgate for a pub lunch. They then go to Trafalgar Square by Tube for a look at Nelson, then take a Tube to Westminster for a look at Big Ben, and then a Tube back to Bayswater, knackered, for a kip. In the evening, they go out to a restaurant in Church Street, Kensington, which they do by going to High Street Kensington Tube. They return by the same route.

A lot of Tube use, OK, but not impossible for a tourist. In fact, that's exactly the sort of exhausting day you have in someone else's city.

Total cost: £60. Arghhhh! How to reduce it?

Saving number one: walk more Visitors tend to see London as isolated pockets of land around Tube stations instead of a real city. It's quicker to walk from Trafalgar Square to Big Ben than catch the Tube, and more interesting. Equally, Bayswater to Kensington. In fact in that case you would have walked part way back to get to the restaurant. So consult a real map as well as a Tube map when planning your journey; your destination may be only an interesting stroll away with better views than a Tube tunnel wall. As you can see, contrary to logic, the two-changes long route such as Bayswater–Hampstead is charged as much as one stop. If you had walked those two short sections: **Total cost: £30. Saving £30.**

Saving number two: Travelcards These are go-as-you-like cards sold for the relevant zones, including red buses, ordinary trains, trams, DLR and scheduled riverboat services as well as Tubes (but not Heathrow Express). They save you a packet, as well as umpteen times queueing up when you could have just waltzed straight through. In fact, remember to keep these until the end of your day – if the 'mechanical rottweiler' ticket gates snap shut at you, it's probably only them trying to be helpful and pointing out you haven't retrieved your valuable tickets. And this approach wouldn't involve walking the short sections as pointed out above (but I'd still do that).

Note you are not able to use Travelcards in the morning rush-hour, but for a visitor, missing this is a bonus. There are more expensive Travelcards for all-day use.

You can buy these tickets in London, or better, if you have time to plan ahead, you can buy three-day or seven-day Travelcards online or at certain overseas tickets agents and have them posted to you ready to use. Go to: www.ticket-on-line.com.

One-day or three-day Travelcards offer worthwhile savings. For instance, a one-day card for this group would have cost £13.40, with the youngest going free. **Total cost £13.40. Saving £46.60.**

If you are staying outside London, you can get your Travelcard incorporated in your return main line train ticket to London, saving a lot of time and money. Again, not valid on trains arriving in the capital before 10.00 Mon–Fri. If you travel in the morning rush, you will have to pay around double the single fare for a return. Illustration: Two adults one-way to London from Liss, Hampshire station £32. Peak hour return £62.20 – ouch!! Plus Tubes, etc, about £80. Off-peak return £34.40. Off-peak return with Travelcard £41.20. **Saving: £38.80.**

Saving number three: Oyster cards These offer great savings (of up to £2.50 single journey), and it seems unfair that Londoners know about this while visitors pay the full whack (£4). You load them up with cash and can even have them topped up automatically from your credit card when they run low, so they cut the hassle. You pay by touching them in and out at readers. However, it involves a little bureaucracy to get one and I don't recommend these unless you are a Londoner, or spending a lot of time here. You can bring them back next year and continue using them, however. You can achieve similar savings with Travelcards, providing you make at least three trips on bus or Tube a day. Apply on line at www.tfl.gov.uk/tfl, which takes only a couple of minutes, or get a form at Tube stations if you do want an Oyster card. One good thing is that if you travel a lot in a day, the cost is limited to what a Travelcard would have cost. Some two-for-one deals at London attractions, such as the London Eye. **Saving: £48.60.**

REMEMBER: You really are being ripped off if you just pay the cash single fare all the time.

Cleopatra's Needle

Part One

ECCENTRIC LONDONERS AND THEIR ODD PURSUITS

Eccentric Londoners

LONDON'S ECCENTRIC CLUBS AND COLLECTORS

There is every kind of collector and specialist society in London. Just a few of the more esoteric ones run by Londoners include: the United Kingdom Spoon Collectors Club; the United Kingdom Belleek Collectors Group (an Irish pottery, it turns out); the Guild of St Gabriel (who collect only stamps with religious aspects); the Spode Society (the English pottery); the Bookplate Society (those printed labels inside books); the Thimble Society; the Indian Military History Society (based, not inappropriately, in Southall); the Great Britain Postcard Club (inquiries by letter presumably not so welcome); the Crown Imperial Society (military medals and badges, Allies only); the Military Heraldry Society (cloth insignia such as shoulder flashes); the Trix Twin Railway Collectors Association (only for the model railways of that brand manufactured 1935–37); the International Map Collectors Society; the International Banknote Society and the Playing-Card Society.

The last three seem to be run by the same person, someone called Yasha Beresiner. With a name like that and hobbies like this, he must be interesting, I reckoned, and I tracked him down in a shop called InterCol in Camden Passage, the antiques alley off Upper Street, Islington.

A CARD-CARRYING COLLECTOR Yasha Beresiner turned out to be a lawyer who had become so involved with his hobbies that they became his whole life. So where did these strange hobbies come from? He started life in Turkey and his father travelled widely for his work, he told me. 'When he came home, he'd empty one pocket of all the foreign coins, and give them to me. I kept them. The other pocket held notes and these went to my elder brother who exchanged them. Now he's a successful commodity trader and I'm still stuck with the coins!' And a lot more, it must be said.

The study and collection of coins, you may know, is numismatics. Of paper money, notaphily. Of bonds and shares etc, scripophily. Of playing-cards, cartophily. And of maps? Map collecting.

But playing-cards? Can they really be interesting? Within five minutes the genial Mr Beresiner has me totally fascinated. 'What is a surprise to most people is their antiquity,' he says. 'They were mentioned in 1377 as being banned by the Church, which suggests they were popular before that. There were four suits from this early date, and there was the moral dimension raised from them, too – cards have often been seen as linked with gambling and immoral behaviour.'

Unlike many others forms of art, playing-cards are printed ephemera – that is, material designed to be thrown away – so few complete sets of 52 survive from antiquity; incomplete sets were usually discarded. The other factor is the relative constancy of the design. 'This is because of the superstition and conservatism of card players, who don't want things changed. A 1450 French queen of spades is the same, essentially, as a new queen of spades by Waddingtons.'

Then there's the meaning of certain cards. Why is the ace of spades the harbinger of death? There was a government tax or duty on playing cards, originally granted in exchange for import controls; each deck would be wrapped in an official wrapper to show this had been paid. Eventually, from 1765, the duty paid was noted on the ace of spades, which was therefore printed in a fantastical and elaborate manner to avoid forgeries. The penalty for forging an ace of spades was death, a sentence carried out at least once, in 1805. The duty on playing-cards, which had then been reduced to 3d, was stopped only as recently as 1967. The six of diamonds, to take another example, is known as the 'curse of Scotland', because a king wrote a death warrant on the back of one of them.

There were educational cards with maths problems on them, maps of England, or historical scenes; there were court cards which were political lampoons; and there were cards which, when held up to the light, revealed pornographic pictures. There's even an odd link between Mr Beresiner's interests in cards and paper money. 'In times of national emergency and war, strange things happen – people hoard, huge inflation, money stops being printed or minted, tokens are given out. In the French Revolution they tried to avoid these problems by making paper money an assignation for a real piece of land – the *assignats*. However as there was a terrific shortage of resources to print money – especially smaller denominations – the authorities printed money on the backs of playing cards. This is a wonderful numismatic curiosity.'

On the map front, what are the rarest? 'The rarest maps must of course be the manuscript maps drawn by individual sailors or explorers so they could return to a place they had discovered. These, known as Portolan charts, were drawn on vellum so they were often re-used as book bindings later. From time to time an old book falls apart and the people rebinding it find a wonderful old chart inside that has been hidden for centuries – fantastic!'

And what of the people who come into his shop? 'There are three types. The browser, who will be attracted by the maps. London's wonderful for historic maps, and they look nice, so everyone is interested. There's the investor, who wants collectibles because of their value. He couldn't care less what they are like, aesthetically, and is concerned only with value for money. Then there's the serious collector. The adrenalin flows with these people when they come in here. They are like gamblers – when they find what they want they are ecstatic, their eyes light up.'

Yasha Beresiner, who has led an interesting life by any measure – he married his sergeant in the Israeli army and says he still salutes her every morning – also offered an insight into the **City livery companies**. These strange organisations – no doubt seen as totally normal by their participants – are part of the deeply eccentric fabric of the City of London. The 101 livery companies are ancient guilds of trades, and often have imposing and historical halls as their headquarters, yet many of the trades they represent are archaic. Watermen, for example. How many people in this day and age get rowed to work by a badged waterman rather than a taxi-driver? Other trades have evolved – for example, the trade of fan maker can now include air-conditioning experts. A 'livery' is a uniform which they are entitled to wear.

Mr Beresiner, when I met him, had just been elected Master of the Worshipful Company of Makers of Playing Cards. 'The livery companies are now a social thing. They have these wonderful dinners in great halls. They don't even have to have anything to do with their trades any more, although they do have tremendous power in the electing of the Mayor of London – the Lord Mayor, that is, not the Ken Livingstone figure.'

One of the rituals in the Worshipful Company of Makers of Playing Cards is to print a specially designed new set of cards bearing the new Master's image, plus special decks for such events as royal coronations, and these special packs, going back centuries, are much prized. In fact, this sense of history and continuity is clearly much valued by Yasha Beresiner.

'If I'm nervous about being Master of the Company, I'll know I have dozens of previous masters looking over my shoulder. It's a fantastic thing for me – an original wandering Jew, if you like – to be honoured with this position. The livery companies have beautiful buildings, ancient silver plate, wonderful people, ancient charters with royal seals attached. Britain has hung on to its history, luckily, when so many other countries have extinguished theirs.'

THE STAMP OF THE TRUE COLLECTOR There are clubs for types of people too: the Left-Handers, the Tall Person Society, the Talbot Association. And there's a lot you can learn from organisations such as the Letter Box Study Group, for example. Did you know that the first British pillar boxes were introduced in the Channel Islands in 1853, or that they were the idea of novelist Anthony Trollope, then a clerk for the General Post Office? Or that the standard Victorian colour for pillar boxes was green, the first red ones not appearing in London until 1874? That air mail used to have its own light-blue boxes – there's still one at Windsor.

TRAINER COLLECTORS: ECCENTRIC TO THE SOLE Pillar box collecting, as Arthur Reeder used to do in Harrow, seems sane to me, in a crazy kind of way, but other equally obsessive collectors leave me cold because the thing collected seems deeply uninteresting. I don't mean things like sickbags – there's a family doctor who has thousands of them (unused) from all over the world – because that's funny, and you get them free on airlines.

But what about trainers? Those unlovely, largely plastic, shoes which the youth of the world would die for but the smell of which would soon make the rest of us die too?

There's a guy somewhere in London called Jeremy. He won't give his last name, he won't give his location, such is his fear of someone stealing his 1,587 different pairs of trainers.

Girlfriends have threatened to leave him over the trainers, but then relationship problems are not unknown for a certain kind of eccentric. 'Shoes don't answer back,' he told the TV crew, tellingly. And one more Jeremy-the-sneaker-freak-geek fact: he has a Nike emblem tattooed on his ankle. 'I'm branded for life.' Now that *is* weird.

There's no logical reason for Britain still having a monarchy except that it works, it's cheaper and less demeaning than a presidency (we make a huge profit on the crown estates), it's admired the world over, and that Hitler and Mussolini were elected. Of course, that's only one side of the argument, but the monarchy epitomises that great British quality, tradition, and this allows for the emergence of eccentricities which politicians would hide.

Take Prince Charles, for example ('and I wish you would', Les Dawson might have quipped). He would make a suitably eccentric king – Prince Charles, for all his other problems, at least talks to plants, meditates in the Kalahari desert, does Goon impersonations, dabbles in alternative medicine, and wears Arab dress in Gloucestershire. Good for him.

Actually, believing in the royals is a bit like a religion. You don't need any evidence for your beliefs, you just need to have them. It's a matter of faith.

PRINCE PHILIP AND THE ART OF THE ROYAL GAFFE Prince Philip's brilliant track record in the royal cock-up quote stakes remains unbeaten. It includes the following:

- He told a Briton in Hungary in 1993: 'You can't have been here long, you haven't got a pot belly.'
- In 1995 he asked a Scottish driving instructor: 'How do you keep the natives off the booze long enough to pass the test?'
- He told British students in China on a 1996 visit that Peking was 'ghastly' and 'If you stay here much longer you'll be slitty-eyed.'
- In 1996 he said British women can't cook.
- He said of Canada: 'We didn't come here for our health. We can think of other ways of enjoying ourselves.'
- In 1996 he outraged gun law reformers who managed to get all handguns banned in Britain after a horrendous school massacre by saying: 'There's no evidence that people who use weapons for sport are any more dangerous than people who use golf clubs or tennis rackets or cricket bats.'
- In 2001 he met a group from the British Deaf Association at the new Welsh Assembly and, because they were sitting near a brass band, said: 'Deaf? If you are near there, no wonder you are deaf.'
- He asked singer Tom Jones: 'What do you gargle with, pebbles?' and said Adam Faith's singing was like bath water going down a plug hole.

All things a politician could never say because they involve a sense of humour or the truth. I don't know about Hungarians' pot bellies but Peking *is* ghastly, Canada *is* sometimes said, by Canadians, to be boring, many British women at the time couldn't cook, on the whole. Scots *did* drink too much (and still do). The handgun ban *was* silly knee-jerk legislation because while it stopped harmless Olympic shooters practising in their own country, illegal handguns became easier than ever to obtain on the streets of South London. No elected politician could say as much because of the public mood. What happens when somebody massacres children with an axe? Ban anything sharp? Or actually deal with the nutters in society?

One of his supposedly offensive remarks was about stress counselling for servicemen in a TV documentary: 'It was part of the fortunes of war. We didn't have counsellors rushing around every time somebody let off a gun, asking "Are you all right – are you sure you don't have a ghastly problem?". You just got on with it.' That was supposed to have offended all kinds of counsellors and wimps. But I just thank God that he, and a lot of men like him, *did* get on with it.

- The royal family's weirdest story: Princess Caroline, page 262
- The complex Diana, and the unpalatable truth: page 288

SERIOUSLY WEIRD, AND WIRED, NORTH LONDONERS

No offence intended, but most South Londoners believe true weirdos start at the river, going north. Of course, there are some normal people up there, but many north-of-the-river types have gone off the scale on the eccentricity meter. They're not on the same planet, Janet (Street-Porter). Just a couple of examples, both marked by plaques of the unofficial sort, will suffice.

ISLINGTON'S FINEST: HOW JOE ORTON BECAME JOE OUGHTN'T Most writers would like to make an impact on their local library; but none has ever done it quite like Joe Orton. The gay Sixties author and playwright used to hang round Islington Central Library and deface other people's books in extraordinary ways.

He and his partner/flatmate Kenneth Halliwell swapped around illustrations, so a gardening book had an extremely ugly monkey where a beautiful rose should be, or they typed outrageously rude reviews carefully to fit in the dustjackets of popular novels. These contained obscenities, and Orton and Halliwell would watch with pleasure as people picked up the respectable volumes and recoiled in horror at the foul language in the reviews. Naturally the library became a little miffed with books being defaced by this rather fifth-form toilet humour and kept watch.

Having worked out it was probably Orton and Halliwell, they – rather clever this, so don't *ever* belittle librarians for lacking imagination – sent the two a fake letter from the town hall complaining about a dumped car near their flat in Noel Road. Halliwell sent back a rude riposte, composed on the same typewriter. It was easy to prove (from the worn-down F, presumably) that the same machine had been used to deface the books, and the pair got six months in jail for stealing 72 books, defacing 44 and removing 1,653 pictures. And 18 shillings and four pence in overdue book fines. Orton, born John Kingsley Orton in 1933, went on to write some hit plays such as *Entertaining Mr Sloan* (1964) and *Loot* (1966). Then, on 9 August 1967, came an abrupt end to his CV. He was murdered by his partner, Halliwell, who then killed himself.

In his book about Orton's life, *Prick up your Ears,* John Lahr gives a rather gruesome description of exactly what Halliwell did. Suffice to say it involved a hammer, Orton's cranium, much exercise and a lot of re-decorating. There's a kind of grim comedy about it. The film of *Prick up* (written by Alan Bennett) has a scene where Orton's sister mixes the ashes of Orton and Halliwell together. As she does so she says: 'I think I'm putting in more of Joe than of Kenneth.' 'It's a gesture, dear, not a recipe,' replies Vanessa Redgrave, playing Orton's agent.

Orton would by now have been a grand old man of literature and, ironically, the same Islington library now carefully preserves those obscene gender-bender addenda as an archive of a local literary great. I know it's wrong of me, but I hope that somewhere, deep in the library's reserve collection, there's an outrageous alteration waiting one day to shock the stuffing out of a little old lady.

A similarly amusing wheeze with books came about in the 1990s when a

London paper, fed up with all the pretentious twaddle that won literary prizes such as the Booker, set out to find if anyone actually read all this claptrap (not all the books, of course, were like this – just most of them). You know the kind of thing: 'A depressed Icelandic lesbian contemplates suicide alone in a beach hut through six months of cold and darkness, only 942 pages'. They snuck into bookshops and inserted between pages 100 and 101 a note saying a fat cheque would be given to any reader who sent the note back to the paper within a year. The note was jammed up by the spine so it wouldn't fall out unless you actually turned the pages. The journalists checked that the books were actually sold and then sat back for a year. Their money was safe.

THE SPOOKY LINKED DEATHS OF JOE MEEK AND BUDDY HOLLY Another North Londoner who met a premature end was Joe Meek, the great record producer of the late 1950s and early 1960s. He inhabited a strange flat in Holloway Road, filled with wiring and half-assembled electronic devices – more like a mad inventor's retreat than a sound studio – but it's fair to say he was Britain's first independent producer with his own sound. He was seriously wired as well as seriously weird. The Chinese restaurant two doors away would rock with the sounds of his playbacks, and the little brown door that led up the stairs to his flat was for a while a place of pilgrimage for would-be rock stars.

Oddly, Meek wasn't very musical, but he was great with the technical side. People can remember amazing lash-ups with old valve amps, biscuit-tin lids held with Sellotape, dangerous uncovered wiring and weird electronic effects that only Meek could create. The arch example of this is the still amazing sound of the hit *Telstar* (which sold five million) and other hits such as *Have I the Right?* It's fair to say that the recording industry was changed by Meek's innovation and high standards, and better-known producers, such as Phil Spector in America, followed in his general direction. Even today, people use some of his revolutionary technical ideas.

But Meek's obsession with American rock star Buddy Holly and Holly's own tragic end was spooky and, ultimately, insane. Meek, a great spiritualist, met Holly in 1958 and told him an earlier Tarot card reading had worked out that Holly would die on 3 February 1958. This was a little after that date, so a relieved Meek told Holly how pleased he was that the cards' figure was wrong. Holly was, of course, killed in a plane crash on *3 February* 1959, exactly a year later than Meek's prediction.

Meek was, as the 1960s went on, not a happy bunny. This Meek was not going to inherit the earth, what with drug addiction, paranoia, low self-esteem, problems in facing his own sexuality, and career failure all prompting him finally to flip and kill first his landlady, and then himself, on *3 February,* 1967!

THE MAN WHO TOOK THE LAST TUBE HOME

We're used to Brits being sentimental about steam engines (with 100 steam lines run by volunteers at weekends it's no small phenomenon) and paddle steamers, but electric Tube trains are hardly up there with the *Flying Scotsman* and the *Orient Express*. In fact many people hate the hot, noisy and claustrophobic things. But not everyone. When London architect Mike Kelly left the City for rural Herefordshire he missed one thing: the Tube trains he had ridden to school, to college and to work. And not just any old Tube train. He was quoted as saying: 'I do have a sentimental attachment to the London Underground and to the 1959 Tube stock in particular.' So he was horrified when he heard all 1959 stock was heading for the scrapyard at the end of the 20th century.

He not only remembered the type of train which was his favourite but the number of one of the favourite cars he rode in as a child: car 1304. He tracked down this very car mouldering in a North London siding, bought it, and had it installed in his Herefordshire garden on a bit of track. It still says on the front that it's going to Finchley Central via Bank (aficionados will know we are on the Northern Line), but it'll never get there again. It makes a great garden ornament, he believes, and a good venue for a party ('Mind the gap, vicar!').

Not that he's alone in loving 1959 Tube stock, as I discovered while checking this wasn't all a leg-pull. There was a website dedicated to the 1959 trains, which included a picture of Mr Kelly's, and was all edged in black. I guessed that this was a symbol of mourning for their demise. But then I read: 'This page remains on a black background, in recognition of the Line on which these wonderful machines ended their days.'

POEM-POWERED TUBES AND A PINT OF BITTER, BITTE Given that the London Tube passenger will famously avoid eye contact with every other person in a crowded carriage (unless he is a foreigner, a loony or a drunk, which increasing numbers are, in which case he may even start a *conversation*, for goodness sake), then the passenger has to look somewhere else. The views outside being somewhat limited, that leaves those curved card advertisements above passengers' heads, which consequently get read far more than they deserve.

One development of this was the series of *Poems on the Underground* which some worthy person suggested – and why not, if it gets people to contemplate a bit of Andrew Marvell instead of 'Buy Biffo's Soap Powder'? In turn, that led to a rather good spoof in the book *Poems Not on the Underground* by someone called Straphanger (see booklist) which included such gems as *Mind the Gap Rap*, or *To his Coy Train Operator*. You get the idea.

The real ads can be funny too, of course. At least, if you understand the Basil Fawlty don't-mention-the-war mentality of many Brits. (In other words, do mention it, but make people laugh.)

The great Kentish brewery Shepherd Neame (they who have a beer, and a pub – the beer is elsewhere too; the pub isn't – in Smithfield, both by the worrying name of Bishop's Finger) were promoting their jingoistically named Spitfire beer with the cheeky slogan: 'Downed all over Kent, just like the Luftwaffe.'

Better was a mock wartime aircraft recognition card with a British pint glass and a German stein in black silhouette, captioned 'Ours' and 'Theirs'. Yet another had a cryptic code message: 'The goat and the marmoset play all night by the river in the spring and later summer.' Certain letters had been ringed by a decoder to spell out 'German beer is pants.'

So the 'Bottle of Britain' went on, with 'Spitfire beer – No Fokker comes near' keeping the tone well-lowered. It ended with the predictable mock German accent creeping in – 'Votz zo funny about zeez posters?' – and an eventual ban from London Underground chiefs who said they failed 'our taste test'. The taste test should perhaps have been applied to Spitfire beer, which is spiffing (as of course are many great German beers in their own way).

Now the offending poster cards have become collectors' items. They've just been driven, well, underground …

One of the biggest causes of eccentric buildings is, ironically, planning controls and their attempts to enforce a dull and boring suburban uniformity. Nothing illustrates this better than the story of Marvin the marlin and his eccentric owner, Croydon businessman John Gladden.

John Gladden was so incensed by Croydon Council's attitude to a mere 14ft plastic marlin stuck on the side of his house, that he stuck a replica Spitfire on the roof. Other features not normally found among the neat privet hedges of St Oswald's Road, Norbury included a Churchill tank, a World War II sea mine on the garage roof, camouflage netting, a hand on a pole giving a giant V-sign visible from the council offices, a 40ft replica of a Scud missile … One could go on, and no doubt the neighbours did. One suspects Mr Gladden doesn't gladden all their hearts, but he rather does mine.

The original marlin – a replica of one he had caught in Hawaii – was what raised the planners' ire, and had they not foolishly made an issue of it, Mr Gladden would probably have been content without all the other clobber. In the end a court trying to make sense of it all (he turned up in a tank with a bagpiper before him) ordered it all removed except the marlin.

Later I heard that Mr Gladden was content to keep the marlin and peace had returned to Norbury – that is, until I checked in 1999.

'We're marching on the council with an army of sympathisers who all own tanks and military vehicles, about 50 in all. We've got our massive Churchill statue, and a huge condom mounted on a tank. When you press a button, it goes whoosh, twice as big. Then we're marching on Scotland Yard to give them a piece of our minds – actually a writ for a million pounds for harassment.'

I ventured: 'I bet they wish they'd never started it.' Mr Gladden agreed, and I couldn't help wishing him the best of British. Come Euro rules or high water, there is some corner of Norbury that will forever be eccentric, and a pain in the backside to nit-picking planners.

So I called Mr Gladden again in 2001 to see if peace had returned to the western front of St Oswald's Road. 'Well I've just taken on the police and won a £4,000 out-of-court settlement, but I'm thinking of moving my business [nuts and bolts, in case you wondered] back to Croydon, which will be difficult as my vehicles are all banned from the borough by injunction.

'That means I've got to take on the planners again. We're thinking of moving in with a column of tanks and a 30ft Russian missile launcher. Plus there's my American police car – there's a giant policeman on top and whenever I brake his pants come down revealing his backside. Marvellous.'

Marvellous indeed, Mr Gladden, and, as I say, I used to think the best thing would be if the council left him alone so he'd be content with Marvin the marlin and his 25ft flagpole. 'They can't stop me flying the national flag, can they?' I imagine Croydon council planners think they can.

But now I realise what an opportunity Croydon is missing. This man is brilliant. He could put Croydon on the map. Give him a bit of Croydon you don't really want – say, Purley – and let him develop it as a military vehicle and mad device theme park. It'd be the best thing since Disneyland Paris. Giant condoms on tanks, mooning policemen – I'd pay a fiver or two to go in.

Oh, and one more thing. You know that bit of grass outside the council office where Mr Gladden once led his troops firing fireworks out of their bazookas in a mock attack? Stick up a statue to him there. Croydon's greatest eccentric – you should be proud of him.

Eccentric Shopping

THE SHOPS THAT TIME FORGOT

GUNS

Holland & Holland 34 Bruton St, W1; ℡ 020 7499 4411

⊖ *Green Park*

Since 1835 this gunshop has been supplying gentlemen with the best guns. Naturally, at this end of the market they are bespoke, tailored to your shoulder and eye. You can specify the engraving and the walnut for the stock, although, at £40,000 a pair, that's understandable. They are all handmade in the firm's own workshops, and only around 100 a year are sold.

HATS

James Lock & Co 6 St James's St, SW1; ℡ 020 7930 8874

⊖ *Green Park*

Hatters since 1676 and birthplace of the British bowler hat. 'A chap called Coke came in and said he wanted a more practical, curved hat for his gamekeepers, so it wouldn't get snagged by branches,' says a spokesman for this family-owned firm. 'He wanted it strong so a blow from a poacher wouldn't do any harm, too. He had a rough design and we made him one. When he collected it, he took it outside on the pavement and jumped on it to test it. It was satisfactory.' Later, a firm called Bowler Bros started producing large numbers of them, hence the name. 'Mad as a hatter' comes from the former use of mercury in the felting process, which made hat-makers a little odd. The days in the 1930s when a man would not dream of going out bare-headed have gone – then it was a flat cloth cap for a workman, a bowler for a tradesman and a topper for a gent. Today, it's mainly top hats for Royal Ascot, panamas for Henley Regatta, and hats for society weddings. Plus a few City gents who still insist on pin-stripes, brolly and bowler.

SHIRTS

Harvie & Hudson 77, 96–97 Jermyn St, SW1; ℡ 020 7930 3949

⊖ *Green Park*

If you want an old-fashioned shirt, with a neck band that takes a separate, stiff, starched collar attached with brass studs (a public school torture you may not wish to revisit), this is the place for you. And starched front shirts for stuffed-shirt gentlemen. Plus more modern, bespoke shirts and ready-to-wear, of course. A splendid mid-Victorian shop-front at 97, by the way. Run by the grandsons of the shirtmakers who started the family firm.

SHOES
George Cleverley & Co 12 The Royal Arcade, Old Bond St; ℡ 020 7493 0443
Green Park

This is where shoes are made by traditional methods using wooden lasts for each customer (stored upstairs like so many feet even though some are unlikely to come back after 100 years or so). You can be shod by the people who made shoes for Rudolph Valentino, Winston Churchill, Lawrence Olivier, Humphrey Bogart, Sir John Gielgud, Gary Cooper, Clark Gable. The last word in shoes.

WIGS
Ede & Ravenscroft 93 Chancery Lane, WC2; ℡ 020 7405 3906
Chancery Lane

Not fashion wigs, or wigs for those who have lost their hair, but full 17th-century-style horsehair wigs for lawyers. It is stark staring bonkers that barristers and judges still need to wear 17th-century wigs, and therefore a good thing. They are curled with old-fashioned curling tongs and last for decades longer than most lawyers. The great eccentric James Crespi would have needed one or two (see page 175).

WINES
Berry Bros & Rudd 3 St James's St, SW1; ℡ 020 7396 9600
Green Park

The rather unprepossessing, battered exterior – understated, one might say – of an apparently small shop hides wine vaults with the best vintages in the world, extending for hundreds of feet. I'd like to recommend the 1928 Petrus at £9,000 a magnum, but I haven't tasted it. There are even late 19th-century vintages which may, of course, be undrinkable. But a tip: if you manage to get hold of one of them and it's as wonderful as it should be, drink it all straight away. It will go off rapidly after opening. More on page 92.

LONDON'S MOST ECCENTRIC BOOKSHOPS

BLACK
New Beacon Books 76 Stroud Green Rd, N4; ℡ 020 7272 4889
Finsbury Park

Said to be Britain's oldest specialist black bookshop, global in its coverage – Africa, America, Caribbean, Britain, you name it – and with a good children's section.

COOKERY
Books for Cooks 4 Blenheim Crescent, W11; ℡ 020 7221 1992
Ladbroke Grove

A recipe for success, founded in 1983 by Heidi Lascelles. Covers every possible cuisine around the world. Small, and crowded at weekends. Sometimes cooks sizzle that wok for the customers.

CRIME
Murder One 76–78 Charing Cross Rd, WC2; ℡ 020 7539 8820
Leicester Square

It's a crime, really, how few small-publisher murder fiction books get to most bookshops, which prefer to make a killing, so to speak, with the big names. Murder One permits more people to have a stab.

FAR-OUT NEW AGE STUFF
Watkins Books 13 and 19–21 Cecil Court, Charing Cross Rd, WC2; ☏ 020 7836 2182
✪ *Leicester Square*
Not just the usual new age stuff about pyramids, tarot cards and ley lines, but also comparative religion. Plus crystals, gems, esoteric and alternative therapy. Plus at No 13 from time to time, in-store tarot card reading, palm reading, clairvoyants, author and expert talks. It's all there, man.

Mysteries Ltd 9–11 Monmouth St, WC2; ☏ 020 7240 3688
✪ *Tottenham Court Road*
Says it is 'the leading metaphysical resource centre in the UK', and that psychic readers are always available. They'll of course know that you're going to call…

GAMBLING
High Stakes Gambling Bookshop 21 Great Ormond St, WC1; ☏ 020 7430 1021
✪ *Holborn*
Fifteen to one you can find this interesting. It's a wide field (and good going) when you consider card magic, horse racing, and the boom gambling of recent years, poker. This is where the serious boys go for tips and systems on a habit that could leave you skint, or make you millions.

GAY
Gay's the Word 66 Marchmont St, WC1; ☏ 020 7278 7654
✪ *Russell Square*
One of the first and biggest in the gay and lesbian field.

LEFTIES
Bookmarks 1 Bloomsbury St, WC1; ☏ 020 7637 1848
✪ *Tottenham Court Road*
I don't know how much longer the communist London daily paper, the *Morning Star,* will survive when even Russia doesn't believe in it, but then you get Maoist guerrillas popping up in Peru and Nepal when the Chinese have long since exposed Mao as a mad wrecker of lives. But someone's got to hold the torch. Better read than dead.

LEGENDARY BOOKSELLER
Foyles Charing Cross Rd; ☏ 020 7437 5660
✪ *Leicester Square*
A bookselling legend, founded by the Foyle brothers in 1904, this great, rambling collection has been at times shambolic. In the past, some of the staff have been deeply odd, and you would have more success addressing telephone enquiries to deaf mutes on the planet Tharg. However, this quirk aside, the enthusiasm and range of books has always been awesome. One of the original Foyle's daughters, Christina, wrote to Hitler when she heard he was burning unsuitable books in the 1930s and asked if she could rescue them from the flames. He replied that if the books were bad influences for Germans, they would be bad for the British too, so he'd rather not lead British readers into a moral morass. A couple of years later, however, he was bombing the stuffing out of those same Brits and a huge bomb blew open the road right in front of Foyles. To keep the capital moving, the Army threw a bridge across the crater and it was named Foyles' Bridge.

MAPS
Stanfords 12–14 Long Acre, WC2; ☏ 020 7836 1321
⊖ *Covent Garden*

Some people read a good map like a book, others use them just to find things like this place near Covent Garden. Some of the maps are pretty specialist. Like a magnetic map of Antarctica, Mongolian geology, that kind of thing. Plus Penge in close-up. Or the London Underground as it really is. Anywhere that gave *Carry On* star Kenneth Williams – 'Infamy, infamy, they've all got it in for me!' – his first proper job can't be that bad.

OBSCURE LANGUAGES
Grant & Cutler 55–57 Great Marlborough St, W1; ☏ 020 7734 2012
⊖ *Oxford Circus*

Literature of more than 200 languages, from Albanian to Uzbek via Kirghiz and Tagalog. Here are 100,000 books, mainly in the more common languages; the emphasis with the rare languages is on textbooks about them. You'll find dictionaries here too.

OCCULT
The Atlantis Bookshop 49a Museum St, WC1A; ☏ 020 7405 2120;
www.theatlanticbookshop.com
⊖ *Holborn*

Why does St George's Bloomsbury round the corner have 'sacred geometry' behind its construction – not to mention two very strange beasts slithering down its truly weird spire? As you troll about this shop such questions and other spooky stuff on divination, numerology, fairies, freemasonry, feng shui, vampires and werewolves leap off the nearest page – or off the nearest pagan, more likely. Unique.

PHOTOGRAPHY
Shipley Photography and Cinema 70 & 72 Charing Cross Rd, WC2; ☏ 020 7240 4157
⊖ *Leicester Square*

Branches in Whitechapel, Barbican. Long-lens lovers can do no better than peruse this shop which explores the image in media, fashion, photography, art and film. Founded by Anton Zwemmer in the 1920s.

PSYCHOANALYSIS
Karnac Books 118 Finchley Rd, NW3; ☏ 020 7431 1075
⊖ *Finchley Road*

Handy for the Freud Museum, and popular with those couch-addicts who live by a system which seems to have about as much scientific and anatomical reality as astrology or tarot card reading. Still, you're only Jung once. Psychoanalysis and psychotherapy, and counselling too.

THEATRE
French's Theatre Bookshop 52 Fitzroy St, W1; ☏ 020 7255 4300
⊖ *Warren Street*

Here drama lamas can find scripts, plays and books about dramatists, some of which are published here. Actually, this is the world's top script shop with branches in New York, Hollywood and Toronto. You might bump into Joan Collins or Whoopi Goldberg looking for material. Their *Guide to Selecting Plays* which will, for example, give you all plays written for three women or one man, or 12 young and old men.

TRANSPORT
Motor Books 33 St Martin's Court, WC2; ℡ 020 7836 3800
✆ *Leicester Square*
Cars, trains, planes, you name it. How to fix them, what they're like. Big picture books, little manuals.

TRAVEL
Daunt Bookshop 83 Marylebone High St, W1; ℡ 020 7224 2295
✆ *Oxford Circus*
Daunt's, like the Orient Express, is an experience for itself as much as where it takes you. The original Edwardian long oak galleries and light and airy glazing gives this rather special shop with a deep expertise of travel books an elegance and calm. It's on Marylebone High Street, a strangely 'villagey' High Street tucked away an arrow's flight from bustling Oxford Circus. If you follow Marylebone Lane up north from Oxford Street, west of the Oxford Circus Tube, you'll see what I mean about a lost river dictating that road's course. Note also the elaborate clock outside Waitrose, an establishment started by a Mr Wait and Mr Rose.

FANCY A WHIP-ROUND? FETISH AND EROTIC LONDON

Don't read this section if you're easily shocked. Perhaps that just makes more people read it, like those signs warning 'wet paint' – you just have to touch it to find out. Such is the perversity of human nature. Talking of which, for some people the fascination of these shops might be figuring out what really goes where. Others might enjoy all the black leather hoods, rubber corsets, chains, whips, etc, but be the nicest people in the world enjoying a harmless dressing-up fantasy, like the middle-aged bank manager I can think of who just loves wearing a tutu. If you really are a sadistic, mass-murdering torturer, you don't need to dress up as one, do you? Well that's my comforting theory. The mad axeman on the Tube is probably the ordinary guy next to you, not the nipple-pierced, purple-haired, tattoo-covered, rubber-trousered freak show swaying to its own insane rhythms across the aisle. And as we know from recent MPs' and pop stars' misadventures, fetishes can be fatal. Nevertheless, these people are definitely eccentric. So here we go with shops that are more S&M than M&S.

Clone Zone 64 Old Compton St, W1; ℡ 020 7287 3530
✆ *Leicester Square*
Fairly tame on the ground floor but, woof, check out the basement. Devices, leather hoods and belts of all kinds and coloured hankies for 'signalling'. Signalling? We might be talking camping equipment here, but not Boy Scouts.

Expectations 75 Great Eastern St, EC2; ℡ 020 7739 0292
✆ *Old Street (Exit 3)*
A huge rambling shop filled with rubber, leather, strange equipment and bondage furniture.

Prowler Camden 283 Camden High St, NW1; ℡ 020 7284 0537
✆ *Camden Town*
Sex toys, fetish videos and mags.

RoB LONDON 24 Wells St, W1; ℡ 020 7735 7893
✆ *Oxford Circus*
If you've ever needed a rubber straitjacket in a hurry, this is your dream shop. Plus chastity belts with padlocks.

SH! 57 Hoxton Sq, N1; ☏ 020 7613 5458
❸ *Old Street* (Exit 2)
Erotic women's shop. Rainbow-coloured unmentionable gadgets, strap-ons and enough vibrators to lay Heathrow a new concrete runway. Or so I'm told. This one's for women.

BITS AND BOBS

BUTTONS
The Button Queen 19 Marylebone Lane, London W1; ☏ 020 7935 1505
❸ *Oxford Circus*
If you thought buttons were just a case of sewing one on occasionally, you couldn't be more wrong. People collect them and cherish them, and this shop pushes all the right buttons for aficionados, with horn, shell, brass, leather, Bakelite, celluloid, wood and plastic jobs of all sizes and colours. A rare one could be worth £130, but more humble buttons are available.

CAKES
Konditor & Cook Cornwall Rd, Waterloo, SE1; ☏ 020 7407 5100
❸ *Waterloo*
This is cake creativity at its most fun. No staid royal icing swags, Corinthian columns or sugar rosebuds, but vibrant colours, zany designs, bright and delicious. And all hand made, many to the order of people such as Madonna and Jerry Hall. Irresistible. The cakes, that is. There's also a branch in Borough Market.

FABRIC
Joel & Son 75 Church St, NW8; ☏ 020 7724 6895
❸ *Edgware Road*
Have you noticed how crazy economics have turned the concept of the homemade on its head? Even as recently as 30 years ago, those needing to save money made their own jumpers, jam, dresses and furniture. Now it's far cheaper to have it made by someone else on the other side of the planet. It's still part of the middle-class dream, exemplified by *Country Living* magazine, to make pretty pots of pickles with gingham tops, but today even the empty jar costs more than a ready-made pot. Similarly, only the well-to-do would consider making dresses, etc now you can buy a ready-made one for the price of a couple of packets of fags, and this extraordinary shop is where they go to get the world's most gorgeous fabrics. Of course, the 'society wedding' types bring their dressmaker-designer or whatever with them – you don't want Mummy running up the stuff at anything from £40 to £2,000 a metre. Yes, £2,000 a metre, encrusted with crystals. Of course, you can get sari cloth that's pretty over-the-top for a few quid a metre in Southall or Whitechapel Road, but this is the top-of-the-range stuff. Fascinating.

MUSIC
Chappell 50 New Bond St, W1; ☏ 020 7491 2777
❸ *Bond Street*
Probably has the most comprehensive stock of music in the world. Sheet music, that is. Full orchestral range of instruments from triangles to bassoons, and from cor anglais to French horns.

SPICES
The Spice Shop 1 Blenheim Crescent, W1; ☏ 020 7221 4448
❸ *Ladbroke Grove*

It must have required enormous self-control to come up with that name. Not something corny like Basil & Rosemary's, Hot Stuff, Spice Odyssey 2001 or whatever. It's hard to imagine a spice or herb that isn't here. Dozens of chillis and paprikas. Also a market stall in the North End Road, which runs from Fulham to West Kensington, on Fridays and Saturdays.

SPY SHOP

Spymaster 3 Portman Sq, W1; ☎ 020 7486 3885
➋ *The name's Bond. Bond Street, actually*
A kind of surveillance supermarket. Covert cameras, phone bugging stuff, listening equipment, shredders, body armour, etc. Great fun and none of it illegal. They'll get you an armoured car if you want one.

TEA

Twinings 216 The Strand (not near Trafalgar Square but up the other end, opposite the Royal Courts of Justice and therefore nearly in Fleet St); ☎ 020 7353 3511
➋ *Temple*
Infused with history, Twinings have been here since 1717. How this gem of a shop survived the Blitz, etc, one wonders – with a good cup of tea to steady the nerves, I expect. Note the extraordinary figures above the door and the ancient fittings inside, where more can be learned of this ancient firm.

TRIMMINGS

V V Rouleaux 6 Marylebone High St, W1; ☎ 020 7224 5179
➋ *Green Park*
This shop, founded by Annabel Lewis, specialises in passementerie, which the dictionary defines as 'a decorative trimming of gimp, cord, beads, braid, etc.' It's an Aladdin's cave of ribbon, braids, feathers, buckles, brocade, tassels, cords and fringes: a mad dressing-up box for grown-ups. 'Sex on a spool,' as one customer put it. Rather good that.

A SHOCK IN STORE AT WHITELEY'S

An eccentrically brilliant London shopkeeper who has left his name writ large on the capital was **William Whiteley**. As you approach central London up the A4 from the Heathrow direction, and rise over a humped bridge near Earl's Court, you notice his name on the old furniture depository on the left. And in Queensway, Bayswater, his name is still used for the flashy shopping centre on the site of his pioneering department store.

Whiteley (1831–1907), invented the modern department store. He boasted that he could get anything for his customers, and when he was tested by being asked for a pint of fleas and an elephant, he produced them in 24 hours.

His radical approach was to provide what the public wanted, not what the store wanted to sell. He had come to London from Yorkshire with less than £10 in his pocket, but having learned the trade in another shop, soon bought his own, and by buying adjoining houses gradually built up his shop with more and more departments until it covered everything from building work to wedding dresses – a concept he called 'the universal provider', but which we now call the department store.

Not that this made him popular with other traders. Local butchers who were undercut by his service burned him in effigy on 5 November. Several fires started in his stores during these years and no doubt some of these were arson. The other traders no doubt wished he would drop dead – a wish that would come true sooner than they imagined.

On 24 January 1907, the great William Whiteley, merchant prince of London as he was known, was shockingly shot dead in the very store that had made him famous. He was not popular as an employer – apprentices weren't paid at all in their first year. He made his 6,000 staff live in dormitories and enforced 176 draconian rules, expecting them to work from 7am to 11pm six days a week. Whiteley also had a habit of taking attractive females to Paris, promising them the earth, but delivering perhaps more direct signs of his desires.

On that January day, a young man, Horace Raynor, had turned up at the store claiming to be Whiteley's illegitimate son. He asked to see the store owner and demanded money for his studies in America. Whiteley refused, and called the police. Raynor drew a gun and shot him dead, but was easily detained. The 29-year-old tried to kill himself shortly afterwards but recovered in hospital and was then charged with the murder in court.

The criminal was sentenced to be hanged, but was reprieved and served just 12 years, a sign, perhaps, that the authorities believed his yarn about his parentage.

Meanwhile, Whiteley had bought himself immortality. Not in the names on the side of the department store and the furniture depository, but in an idyllic woodland retirement village of Surrey almshouses he provided through his will with uncharacteristic generosity in Surrey, and furnished with a statue of himself, all at the then huge cost of £1,000,000. And the name of that village? Whiteley, near Walton-on-Thames.

One of Whiteley's employees, **John Barker**, left to start a small shop in Kensington High Street which became the great Barker's store whose magnificent art deco pile is still at the bottom of Church Street, although not used as a department store any more.

Another famous not to say deeply posh, London store, **Fortnum & Mason** (at 181 Piccadilly for the past 300 years) has survived, thankfully, and has a curious history. A Palace footman, William Fortnum, was entitled to remove the candle ends from chandeliers and candelabra, and sold them on. This was at a time when poor people couldn't sew or read at night because they couldn't afford whole candles, so even a stub end would be welcome. He eventually became rich enough to start up in business.

The store was famous for delivering post anywhere before the penny post stamp was invented, and for feeding the homesick British around the Empire with familiar fare while bringing those countries' spicy, exotic recipes home to tingle the Londoners' palates. A certain young Mr Heinz lugged several cases to this shop all the way from the United States and introduced the British to perhaps their greatest love: the tinned baked bean. Which might be – who knows? – why the store has more royal warrants than just about anywhere on earth. 'More beans, Your Majesty?'

3

Murderous and Battlefield London

SITES OF THE CAPITAL'S MOST MACABRE KILLINGS

BLEEDING HEART YARD At the Bleeding Heart Restaurant (*Bleeding Heart Yard, Greville St, EC1;* ⟍ *020 7242 2056*) you can savour your bloody steaks, bloody Marys or other food in the knowledge that on the very cobblestones where your dining table stands a most gruesome killing took place. As Charles Dickens recalls in *Little Dorrit*, the case involved the 17th-century society beauty Elizabeth Hatton, who in 1626 had jilted the Spanish ambassador. The couple were seen at a ball just after this, whirling round most energetically, and then disappeared. The ball guests speculated that they had made it up, and were entwined limb-to-limb. Actually, Lady Hatton was being ripped apart. As Dickens relates, 'At dawn the body of Lady Hatton was found in the courtyard behind the stables torn limb from limb with her heart still pumping blood on to the cobblestones.' This offal history doesn't seem to put people off dining at this rather good, rather old-fashioned restaurant.

MOSSLEA ROAD, PENGE Penge in South London has, to outsiders, a rather comic name, particularly if spoken by Frenchmen. But what happened in Mosslea Road was so unfunny it shocked respectable Victorian London to the core and caused the name of the road to be changed out of shame. It is a macabre murder tale, but a crime whose solution came about because of two factors: that the centre of this road was then the boundary between the counties of Kent and Surrey, and a million-to-one chance encounter in a post office on, of all days, a Friday the 13th.

The victim was Harriet Staunton, born in 1841, who when she was 33, being rather plain and weak-minded, accepted the proposal of marriage from Louis Staunton, a lowly clerk. He was better-looking, and ten years younger, so why did he do this? She had an inheritance of £4,000 (ten years' pay for some people) and was expected to inherit more. Louis Staunton, under the laws of that time, took possession of this money.

He also had a mistress, and his aim seemed to be to get rid of his wife fairly quickly and enjoy her money. They married in 1875 and settled in Brixton. Louis Staunton quickly moved his mistress, Alice Rhodes, into the house under some pretence. Harriet had a son, born in 1876, and the household employed a servant – as middle-class families did at that time – who was Alice's cousin. Attempts by Harriet's worried family to see her were continually rebuffed.

By the end of 1876, Harriet was imprisoned in a cottage in Cudham, Kent, and given nothing to eat in an attempt to starve her. The doors were locked and the windows nailed shut so she could not cry for help and her clothes taken away to discourage her from running away. And with no heating, that bitterly cold winter would have hastened her weight loss. Louis Staunton, who steadfastly refused his miserable wife's pleas for a crust of bread, lived with his mistress in the same village. The baby boy was also being starved, but it is thought the servant fled with him to save him.

By April, the formerly healthy Harriet weighed just five stone (70lb or 33kg). Her ruthless husband realised that her death would attract attention in a small village, so, seeing the end was near, he hurriedly moved the deeply sick woman by train to a house in Penge – in Forbes Road, as Mosslea Road was then called – where he had rented rooms. She died the day afterwards.

Louis Staunton was unsure about whether that house, an even number, was in Kent or Surrey, so he visited the corner post office to ask where to register a death. Standing in the queue behind Staunton was a certain Louis Victor de Casabianca who just happened to be in the area and needed a postage stamp. He was married to Harriet's sister and knew her family were frantically trying to contact her at Cudham.

The man in front of him in the queue at the post office gave the deceased woman's age and said she came from Cudham, Kent, which aroused Mr de Casabianca's suspicions. He found the name of the doctor who had just signed the death certificate and visited him, discovered it was his sister-in-law Harriet who was dead, and called in the police. He identified the body which, according to the Press, was reduced to skin and bones, and crawling with lice.

Louis Staunton, Alice Rhodes, and Staunton's brother and his wife (who seemed to have gone along with the plot or done nothing about it) were all found guilty of murder. The judge donned the black cap and sentenced them to 'be hanged from the neck until dead. May God have mercy on your souls.'

The Press had a field day, the illustrated papers using engravings to recreate the scenes of the thin, dying woman begging for bread, and the baby, with its ribs showing, strapped to the table by the monster Staunton.

Oddly, the death sentence was never carried out. An appeal was launched and Louis Staunton was sentenced instead to 20 years in prison. His brother had died by then in jail, the brother's wife served just a few years and Alice Rhodes was released.

It was too late for poor Forbes Road. The lurid Press coverage had done its damage and house prices plunged in notorious Penge. The road name was changed to Mosslea Road in an attempt to shake off the gloom. But for the astonishing coincidence of Mr de Casabianca's need for a stamp that day – Friday 13 April, 1877 – Louis Staunton could have enjoyed a comfortable early retirement instead of the grimy hell-hole of a Victorian jail.

WHITECHAPEL The cheap end of the Monopoly board and the location of a grisly end for many, including the victims of the Kray gangsters in the 1960s and, in the 1880s, the blood-spattered ground for incredible mutilations by Jack the Ripper. For more details, if you can stand it, see Whitechapel, page 208.

HILLDROP CRESCENT, TUFNELL PARK AND THE NOTORIOUS DOCTOR CRIPPEN A

quiet suburban road which in 1910 fascinated and horrified the whole country. Here was the home of Dr Hawley Crippen, responsible for the particularly gruesome murder of his wife, and, after a dramatic transatlantic chase and some unlikely disguises adopted by the fugitive's mistress, the first man to be caught as a result of Mr Marconi's newfangled wireless telegraphy on ships. The key characters in this case were:

- Dr Crippen, an improbable lothario or murderer, being a respectable, short, meek, balding 48-year-old dentist who had come from America to promote his medicines;

- his wife Cora, a former music hall singer and dancer;
- his mistress, the strange Ethel le Neve.

It seems sexy Cora, who danced under the name Belle Ellmore, wasn't the woman Dr Crippen had thought when he married her. She was unfaithful with various entertainers and taunted Dr Crippen about this. So Crippen began an affair with Ethel, the typist at his Oxford Street offices.

In January 1910, Crippen ordered hydrobromide of hyoscine, a deadly poison, but a sedative if used in tiny quantities, from his chemist. Being a dentist, this was easily done.

On 31 January, Dr Crippen mixed his wife a hot toddy to drink, including the poison, it was later surmised, because Dr Crippen never admitted to his actions. Cora, once sedated, would die peacefully and then he could call a colleague – whom he had primed with stories of Cora's supposed illness – with the shocking news of her death the next morning.

However, hydrobromide of hyoscine is a sedative only in small doses. Dr Crippen, had he been any good at his job, should have known that in larger doses it causes hallucinations, violent fits, vomiting, hysteria and screaming. It's not the behaviour you want from someone you are trying to murder discreetly.

He panicked, grabbed a pistol and shot his ranting wife through the head. This rather ruined the plan for calling a colleague to check the corpse. Unfortunately, although neighbours heard the sound, they did nothing. His next problem was how to dispose of the large corpse of a stout woman. Here, Dr Crippen's medical training came in handy and this is the macabre bit that absolutely fascinated Edwardian Britain.

He put her in the bath to prevent the blood going everywhere and filleted her as a butcher might, taking out the bones and burning them in the kitchen stove. He could then pulverise the ashes later. Left in the blood-filled bathtub was a floppy 'rubber woman', like a deflated balloon. He cut out the torso and buried it under the stone flags of the cellar. He put her limbs, organs and head in a box in the yard. Having fallen asleep, he woke early and burned his bloody clothes and cleaned up any other traces, then went to work as normal.

That evening, he dropped the box of internal organs in a nearby canal, weighted with bricks. His troublesome wife was gone. But how to explain her disappearance? On the next day he told his mistress Ethel that his wife had left him, and surprised her even more by giving her Cora's jewellery. She chose some and he later pawned the rest in Holloway, near his home, for £3,195 – a heap of money then.

At this point Dr Crippen started making silly mistakes. He asked Ethel to deliver a letter to the local Ladies' Guild, of which Cora was the honorary treasurer.

Purporting to be from Cora, it informed the society that she had been called urgently to America by the illness of a relative, and would therefore be resigning her post and returning their books. The Guild members suspected it was not her handwriting, nor her likely actions.

The next mistake was to use the spare ticket for the Guild's ball on 20 February to take Ethel. Dr Crippen said that as Cora was out of town, he might as well bring his secretary. Clearly as they danced it was evident that this was more than a professional relationship, and suddenly the eagle-eyed Guild ladies noticed Cora's favourite brooch on Ethel's dress. The scandal grew.

In March, Dr Crippen told friends that his wife had been taken ill in California, and that he was expecting very sad news. On 24 March he further telegraphed them that Cora had died. He was, in fact, in Dieppe, having a weekend with Ethel.

Dr Crippen's next mistake was to tell the Ladies' Guild that there would be no funeral as Cora had asked to be cremated. They knew, as she was a Catholic, that this was quite impossible. The doughty matrons of the Ladies' Guild were less than convinced and swung into action like so many Miss Marples.

The Guild members tracked down the only shipping company that had a ship that should have sailed on the date Dr Crippen gave for Cora's departure to the States. The ship was out of action on that day, under repair in dock. They then contacted the Californian authorities about the date of death Dr Crippen had given. No such woman had died on that day either.

They sent for the police who called on Dr Crippen, and he told them it was indeed a fabricated story, to cover up his runaway wife's unfaithfulness. The detectives were, oddly, convinced. The Ladies' Guild didn't give up that easily. They inquired after the doctor at his Oxford Street surgery and found that he and Ethel had both suddenly disappeared. They had in fact taken a train to Harwich in Essex, intending to take a ferry to Rotterdam and meet a liner going to Canada. Ethel claimed in her later memoirs that she still did not know Cora was dead, and was told it was to escape the malicious gossip.

The police called again at Hilldrop Crescent and, at long last, made a search of the house, and, while poking the flags of the cellar, found one of them could be easily raised.

They dug a hole and soon came across what appeared to be revolting animal remains. On examination by a pathologist, however, it turned out to be a woman's torso, minus its bones. Traces of the poison were also found. An operation scar matched one Cora was known to have had.

Now an arrest warrant was issued for Dr Crippen and Ethel le Neve. This is another extraordinary part of the story. They disguised themselves as father and son, Mr and Master Robinson, travelling on the SS *Montrose* to Canada.

But the ship's master, Captain Harry Kendall, was suspicious about the 'boy' in his ill-fitting clothes. The feminine sway of 'his' hips was not right.

By chance, the captain had a newspaper featuring pictures of the two suspects. When he was well past Land's End, going into the Atlantic, he sent the world's first radio message to result in the capture of a fugitive to his base in Liverpool. The Morse code message read:

> Have strong suspicion that Crippen London Cellar Murderer and accomplice are among saloon passengers. Mustache taken off growing beard. Accomplice dressed as boy. Voice manner and build undoubtedly a girl. Both travelling as Mr and Master Robinson. Kendall.

The rest of the story reads as if Arthur Conan Doyle had written it. Scotland Yard's Inspector Walter Dew, a sergeant and two female prison warders were put on an overnight express for Liverpool. There they had some luck. A faster ship was just leaving for Quebec and would probably arrive a day earlier, a real cliffhanger which the Press followed with verve. The 'Robinsons' sunned themselves on the deck unaware of the meaning of the buzzing of the Marconi aerial strung over their heads. (Wirelesses were a recent invention and you had to hire Marconi men to operate them. Not many months later one such machine would play a crucial role in the *Titanic* disaster.)

The story got even better. Ethel became a heroine when a little Belgian boy playing on the deck slipped through the rails and would have fallen to his death had not Ethel grabbed his ankle. The scream 'Master Robinson' gave, officers noted, was definitely that of a girl.

Dr Crippen seemed to suspect the game was up. As the ship approached Quebec, a launch met it, and Crippen was stopped by a tall man saying: 'Good morning, Dr Crippen.' He replied at once: 'Good morning, Inspector Dew.'

Crippen was brought back, tried, and condemned to 'be taken from this court to a place of execution and there hanged by the neck until dead'. He tried to make an appeal and sought a reprieve through the Home Secretary, Winston Churchill, but the execution was set for 23 November 1910. Crippen, his belt and laces taken away to prevent suicide, nevertheless tried to cheat the hangman by smashing his glasses and using the fragments to slash his wrists, but the warders took the pieces away.

A curse seemed to follow those involved. Captain Kendall's next ship went down in 1914 at the exact spot where Crippen was arrested. In the same year the *Montrose* sank by the white cliffs of Dover. And the house in Hilldrop Crescent was blasted to rubble by a Nazi bomb in World War II.

Inspector Dew was so upset by the case that he resigned, aged only 47, before Dr Crippen was hanged. Ethel returned to Canada, and worked there until 1916, when she came back to England under a new name and married a Croydon accountant who looked like Dr Crippen. She had children and her husband eventually died, never having known her part in the most notorious killing of the era. She lived at Addiscombe, Surrey, as a quiet, respectable, needleworking grandmother until she died in 1967.

THE FIRST RAILWAY MURDER The **Top o' the Morning** pub at 129 Cadogan Terrace (✆ 020 8985 9917, nearest station: Hackney Wick) might seem like an ordinary sham-shamrock Irishfied local, but – you knew a but was coming – the pub hides a macabre secret. It was here that Thomas Briggs, victim of the first railway murder in England, was brought to die of his wounds in 1864. At the time, the story was an absolute sensation, not least because of the dramatic transatlantic chase that ensued. In this respect and others it was a strange precursor of the Crippen case (see page 20).

Given the pessimism the rapid spread of railways in the previous 40 years had brought – with doomsayers predicting murder, rape, suicide, theft of luggage, etc, plus the transport of the lower 'criminal classes' to areas where they had been hitherto rare – it is perhaps surprising that this was the first recorded murder on a train, particularly as they were, by the 1860s, conveying many millions of people per year. And particularly when you consider that passengers were conveyed in compartments without connecting doors or corridors – the terms coach, guard, etc, had after all been adapted from the horse-drawn variety whose design was simply copied – and there was no emergency communication cord with which panicking passengers could stop the train.

On the evening of 9 July 1864 there was still some light in the sky as the 9.50 North London Railway service left Fenchurch Street terminus. By the time it arrived at Hackney at 10.11 there were just the last glimmerings, and two bank clerks got into an empty first-class compartment. One of them put his hand on a seat and felt something damp. It was blood. They called the guard who checked the compartment, and found blood all over the cushions and the further door. He locked the compartment and telegraphed ahead to Chalk Farm Station, where the carriage was detached for police examination. There was also a black hat, a stick and a bag as clues.

Meanwhile, an alert driver travelling in the opposite direction from Hackney to Bow Station spotted what seemed to be a body between the tracks. He stopped the train and the severely injured man, whose head had been battered in – and who turned out to be a 70-year-old bank clerk, Thomas Briggs – was carried to a nearby pub, where he died of his wounds. The murder – which had obviously involved robbery, as Briggs's gold watch and spectacles were missing – caused outrage at the lack of protection for railway passengers. An official reward was offered.

The first help resulting from this publicity came, oddly enough, from a Mr Death – a jeweller who had been offered some of the victim's belongings. This in turn led to a cabbie who knew a German tailor called Franz Muller who became the suspect. Muller had a jeweller's box marked – a macabre touch – Death and had fled across the Atlantic on 15 July aboard the sailing ship *Victoria*, bound for New York, as the hue and cry over Briggs intensified.

Warrants were issued and the newspaper-reading public was agog as detectives boarded a faster steam ship on 20 July. This meant, as with the Crippen case (see page 20), that they were able to overtake the fugitive and arrest him on arrival in America. Muller was brought back, tried – his alibi of being with a prostitute at the time led to the judge's observation that 'little reliance should be placed on a clock in a brothel', which leads one to wonder how the judge knew – and publicly hanged on 14 November of the same year. So many drunks crowded and fought to see the hanging, and there were so many robberies in this thick crowd in the Old Bailey outside Newgate jail, that this contributed towards the end of public executions in 1868. At least 50,000 people attended the hanging, and one of the beneficiaries of such macabre fascination was, ironically, the railway companies, which ran special excursion trains.

The case had another consequence. The public clamour for more protection aboard trains led to the communication cord. This, older readers may recall, was a cord or chain running inside the roof which any passenger could pull to apply the brakes. Severe warnings were posted as to fines for misuse – as a prank, or if you missed your station, for example. Later versions had a little flag on the carriage end that popped up to show where it had been pulled, and today there are red handles for such use, although nowadays no-one is forced to travel in a completely isolated compartment as on Thomas Briggs's last journey.

CRANLEY GARDENS AND THE BOILED HEAD MURDERS One of the most macabre serial killers in London's history was uncovered by an unpleasant drain problem. I suggest you read no further if you are squeamish.

In February 1983, tenants at flats in Cranley Gardens, between Highgate and Muswell Hill, complained of their toilets not flushing and vile smells. A drainage clearance company was called. Their employee discovered rotting meat and bits of flesh with hair on it in the drain and discussed this with the tenants. Police looked at the drain the next morning, by which time most of the evidence had been cleared away but enough traces were left to confirm their human origin.

When Dennis Nilsen, who was born in Scotland but had a Norwegian father, arrived home from work in a Soho employment office, he was questioned by waiting detectives, who must have found their task unexpectedly easy. One of them said: 'Don't mess me about, where's the rest of the body?' The first great surprise was that Nilsen said straightaway: 'In the wardrobe. I'll show you.'

The second great surprise came in the car back to the police station. Nilsen was asked casually by a detective how many bodies were involved. 'One or two?' Nilsen calmly replied: 'About 15 or 16.'

It transpired that he was preying on young male gays or vagrants whom he picked up in public toilets and offered a warm meal and a bed for the night in exchange for sex. He murdered them at his flat by strangling them. The first one was killed at his previous address in Melrose Avenue in 1978 and, quite some time later after being hidden under the floorboards, burned in the garden. There followed several similar victims – one was a Canadian tourist.

After moving to a flat with no garden – here's a 'gruesome bit' warning!! – Nilsen resorted to using the butchery skills he had learned in the Army, boiling down the flesh in cooking pots so it would go down the drains. Evidently this plan did not entirely work. Nilsen was there when the drain clearance man arrived and knew he was likely to be exposed. On the day of his arrest, he told a colleague at work: 'If I'm not in tomorrow, I'll either be ill, dead, or in jail.' They laughed like drains.

Later that year, Nilsen, who pleaded not guilty to murder on grounds of insanity was found sane and convicted of six murders. He was sentenced to life imprisonment with a minimum of 25 years, which means in theory he could be out soon. In such a notorious case, however, early release is politically impossible. He is not encouraged to do the cooking in prison, but his stove and favourite head-boiling pan are preserved as they were found in Scotland Yard's Black Museum, open only to the police.

THE GOAT PUB AND THE ACID-BATH MURDERS John George Haigh, who had a polite, impeccable English manner, committed a series of grisly murders in London which horrified and fascinated the public, when the facts came out, because he thought he had the perfect way of disposing of bodies. Like Dennis Nilsen, he was proved wrong. John George Haigh, born in 1909, had a very strict Christian upbringing (he later said he had nightmares about forests of crucifixes dripping blood). He moved to London in the 1930s and was involved in the car trade and petty scams, taking him in and out of prison.

He was a chauffeur for the McSwann family before one such term in jail and bumped into William McSwann again in 1944. The two went for a few drinks at the Goat, still a popular pub in Kensington High Street today. Haigh took McSwann under some pretext to one of his nearby workshops where he smashed his skull in. He put the body in a barrel full of acid. After trying to fool McSwann's parents for a while that their son was hiding from military call-up, he murdered them too, then impersonated William Donald McSwann in order to gain control of their property.

In 1947 he meted out the same treatment to a wealthy couple called Henderson whom he'd met during a property transaction. He gave them 'acid baths' at his new workshops at Crawley, Sussex. Haigh came undone with the case of widow Mrs Olive Durand-Deacon, 69, who in 1949 lived at the same boarding-house as Haigh, the Onslow Court Hotel in South Kensington. Haigh met her at mealtimes and had told her he was an inventor. When she wanted to demonstrate an idea of hers, Haigh took her to the Crawley workshops in his impressive grey Alvis sports car and shot her too. After taking her jewellery and fur coats, she was dumped into an acid barrel and Haigh returned to the Onslow Court Hotel for a relaxed three-course dinner.

Other guests were soon anxious about Mrs Durand-Deacon, and Haigh said he had failed to meet her and was worried too. He offered to accompany one of the others to Chelsea police, who were also unconvinced.

The next day Haigh drove to the Crawley workshop and dumped the acid sludge into the yard. He also made the mistake of taking Mrs Durand-Deacon's jewels to a Horsham valuer. When he returned to the hotel, the police – who had

A hard choice, but a hot favourite concerns the kidnap in 1991 of a former Bangladeshi politician in Poplar, East London by someone with, presumably, a grudge. The criminal inserted an extremely hot chilli pepper in the man (not in his mouth, however) – and this is the truly eccentric touch – then photographed him as he hopped down the street half-naked in agony. No lasting damage, but truly bizarre.

traced his full criminal record – were waiting to question him. He maintained his story but the police had also discovered the address of the Crawley workshops, where they found heavy rubber gloves, empty acid jars, a gas mask and a cleaning receipt for a fur coat like the victim's. Plus a recently fired army revolver.

Faced with this evidence, Haigh confessed, adding in the McSwanns and the Hendersons, and saying he used acid baths to dispose of the bodies. But he added chillingly: 'How can you prove a murder if there is no body?' He also claimed to have drunk some of his victims' blood, but this was never proved and was regarded by some as an attempt to escape the noose by pleading insanity.

He had not reckoned with the mute testimony of normally insignificant parts of the human body: gallstones. That and the painstaking, if gruesome, work of Home Office forensic pathologist, Dr Keith Simpson. Simpson found an acid-proof hatpin in one barrel. In the yard, he was looking around the messy sludge when he noticed what he thought might be a gallstone from a human or an animal. He had the pool of sludge collected and taken to police laboratories. Here analysts found a set of dentures and two more gallstones. The dentures were identified by Mrs Durand-Deacon's dentist. Justice was swift. Haigh's trial at Lewes, Sussex, lasted just two days in July 1949, the jury taking around ten minutes to find him guilty on all charges. The famous hangman, Albert Pierrepoint, was waiting for Haigh at the trapdoor in Wandsworth Prison, South London, on a fine morning in August.

GHASTLY CRIME AND WORSE PUNISHMENT

GOING WEST, BEING ON THE WAGON AND PERVERTED POSH LADIES When Newgate prison stood where the Old Bailey now is, many a prisoner, be he highwayman, Catholic martyr or whatever, was forced to walk the three miles to Tyburn, now Marble Arch, to be hanged on the 'Tyburn tree' (see also *Lost Rivers*, page 98), or was taken there by cart. Thus they would pass St Giles's High Street (before St Giles Circus, the junction of Tottenham Court Road and Oxford Street). Here a strange ceremony would ensue. Matilda, queen of Henry I, had founded St Giles as a leper colony (he is their patron saint) and left money in her will for a cup of charity to be given to the condemned marching in chains to Tyburn (the origin of 'going west'). By the end of the Middle Ages, it had become the custom for the Bow Tavern to give the condemned a pint of ale and they would sit there being cheered on by all the leering

low life of London. Another custom of this time was that if the executioner rode in the cart, he didn't get off to drink alcohol, hence the phrase being 'on the wagon', a term for someone abstaining. Usually, the condemned would dress well and walk with a swagger, a practice recorded with complete astonishment by foreigners. The standing joke of the condemned was that they would pay for the drink on the way back.

Jonathan Swift pictures in his poem *Clever Tom Clinch Going To Be Hanged* (1726) another example of the criminal being executed as a kind of popular hero – with more than a frisson of excitement for the ladies:

> As clever Tom Clinch, while the rabble was bawling,
> Rode through stately Holbourn, to die in his calling;
> He stopt at the George for a bottle of sack,
> And promis'd to pay for it when he'd come back.
> His waistcoat and stocking, and breeches were white,
> His cap had a new cherry ribbon ty't.
> The Maids to the doors and the balconies ran,
> And said, lack-a-day! He's a proper young man.
> But as from the windows the ladies he spy'd
> Like a beau in the box, he bow'd low on each side…
> And when his last speech the loud hawkers did cry,
> He swore from the cart, it was all a damned lye.
> The hangman for pardon fell down on one knee;
> Tom gave him a kick in the guts for his fee…

I record elsewhere how society beauties would swoon after highwaymen (see page 99), but there was a more macabre, even perverted, scramble at Tyburn once the horses had been whipped to pull the carts clear and leave the prisoners dangling and twitching on the infamous Tyburn tree (they died slowly of strangulation, by the way, the trapdoor and slip noose which breaks your neck being more modern). When the bodies were cut down, there was an unholy scramble to get at them. For one thing, the common people believed the touch of the newly dead would cure anything.

The London Encyclopaedia records how one young woman, a beauty 'all pale and trembling … submitted to have her bosom uncovered in the presence of thousands of spectators and the dead man's hands placed upon it.' The hand would have been still warm, if not twitching. Even today's Channel 4 would find that seriously weird.

As well as those wanting to touch the corpse, there was a ready market for freshly hacked-off hands of the dead (for curative purposes) and of course, good prices were paid for fresh corpses by medical schools. It reminds me of a macabre event at a certain northern university in the 1970s where a student was struggling to mend his car in the medical faculty car park. A pal shouts from a window: 'Do you want a hand?' 'Yes, please' says the student. Thud, one lands next to him.

THE HANGINGS THAT APPALLED DICKENS AND THACKERAY
The abolition of executions at Tyburn in 1783 wasn't because of any great moral squeamishness about bunches of people dying before thousands of cheering, jeering, laughing onlookers, but – typically, in terms of priorities – because the rich people moving into Oxford Street and Mayfair in the late 18th century objected to the crowds of common people turning up in their droves to pack Mother Proctor's pews, a specially constructed grandstand next to the infamous Tyburn tree.

After Tyburn's black role was ended, hangings took place right in the Old Bailey outside Newgate prison, making the last journey of the condemned across London unnecessary.

The Old Bailey

Peter Ackroyd's brilliant though wordy book, *London: The Biography* (see booklist, page 312), records not only Dr Johnson objecting to the Tyburn executions being stopped, but, in the following century, Charles Dickens spotting William Makepeace Thackeray at an Old Bailey execution. Both Dickens and Thackeray were utterly appalled, less than a century after Dr Johnson's comments, at the public's enjoyment of the killing.

The Old Bailey, properly the Central Criminal Court, stands in the road of the same name that was wide enough to accommodate the thousands who wanted to watch a public hanging. In fact, moving from Tyburn did not decrease the crowd's appetite for macabre spectacle, only the space available to them, so that sometimes on a hanging Monday, more people died underfoot than on the gallows. Around 100 people died or were seriously hurt at a double-hanging in 1807, for example.

The aristocracy were not above such voyeurism – they rented rooms at the adjacent Magpie and Stump pub to watch the hangings. A novel, *The Bride Of Newgate* by John Dickson Carr, describes the scene more fully if you need it.

The last public hanging at Newgate was of Michael Barrett in 1868, an Irish terrorist convicted of blowing up six people. After that, executions were carried out within the jail.

Dickens was instrumental in getting public executions stopped. He wrote a letter to *The Times* in 1849 complaining of the 'atrocious bearing' of the spectators at the double-hanging of a Mr and Mrs Manning at Horsemonger Lane Prison in Southwark. The present 19-court Old Bailey on Newgate's site was opened in 1907 and hosted some of Britain's most notorious and spectacular trials, including that of Dr Crippen (more on page 20) and Peter Sutcliffe, the Yorkshire Ripper. There are few better free shows in London than that to be had in a good murder case by queuing at the Public Gallery entrance from 09.15. Not as much of a crowd puller as a really good hanging, of course.

More in *Fleet Street walk*, see page 171.

BURNING, BIGOTS AND BOILING IN BLOODY GRUESOME SMITHFIELD

Before Tyburn became the place of common execution, Smithfield in the City was where most hangings took place, not far from where they ended up at Newgate (the Old Bailey). In the 16th century Smithfield became known for religious persecution: Roman Catholic 'Bloody' Mary I's vicious suppression of Protestants, well remembered in Lewes, Sussex, by an annual march on 5 November to commemorate the 11 men she had burned there, also included 49 burned in Smithfield for refusing to acknowledge the Pope.

Mary's final tally, according to Foxe's *Book of Martyrs*, was 314, including widows, labourers and even two blind girls and two infants. How infants could be Protestants and how anyone burning them could be Christian is a question even the worst bigot would find hard to answer.

Perhaps they were among the 16 he records who died in prison or the 12 who were buried alive in dunghills.

Earlier in the 16th century a poisoner called Richard Rose was boiled to death in a cauldron here. Cruelly, like the best boiled eggs, he was cooked from cold, so it took two hours to kill him.

Smithfield was also the site of the execution of Scottish leader Sir William Wallace, lionised as Braveheart in the film of that name. He was hanged, drawn and quartered (castration thrown in for free) here in 1305. But not burned or boiled.

THE LAST HANGINGS THAT MADE HIT FILMS: BENTLEY AND ELLIS The last few hangings in London – by then taking place in various jails – were deeply controversial and included that of Derek Bentley in 1955. He was a simpleton hanged for being with a youth who, during a burglary, shot a policeman after Bentley allegedly said: 'Let him have it'. The only problems were that Bentley could have meant 'give him the gun', that there was little evidence he ever said anything of the sort, and that his accomplice who fired the fatal shot, being too young for the rope, was merely imprisoned while the mental-defective Bentley was hanged for being party to the crime. His family have been campaigning for his posthumous pardon ever since. See the excellent film *Let Him Have It*.

Also in 1955, Ruth Ellis, a much abused victim who had shot dead her cheating lover outside the Magdala pub in Hampstead, swung for it at Holloway, despite huge public sympathy. The lover was David Blakely, and she got him good and proper with four slugs from a Smith & Wesson revolver. The whole sorry story was made into a rather good film, *Dance With A Stranger*, starring Miranda Richardson and Rupert Everett. Ruth Ellis was the last woman in Britain to go to the rope, amid some protest, although one voice which dissented from the general sympathy expressed in the newspapers (see the *Daily Mirror* clipping inside the Magdala pub) was the woman passer-by who had bullets whizz past her. She thought it quite right that Ellis was hanged.

Hanging finally ended in 1964, to the regret of some judges who were not in favour of the abolition of capital punishment, and who were supported by a sizeable proportion of the public – at times a majority.

THE KNELL OF DOOM The most unwelcome sound in London's history was not, contrary to popular belief, Des O'Connor at the London Palladium but a church bell. A very particular church bell. If you look in St Sepulchre's church, off Snow Hill and Holborn Viaduct in the City, there is an old bell mounted in front of the pulpit. This was used on the eve of an execution at the nearby Newgate Prison, where the Old Bailey now stands. The St Sepulchre bell-ringer would visit the condemned at midnight and rouse them with this bell and urge them to make their peace with their Maker while time allowed. So there you are, having bribed the guard to get you a bottle of cheap booze to send you to sleep after your last supper, despite all your nerves, and some nincompoop from St Sepulchre's comes in and makes an awful din.

To make matters worse, they often intoned a corny dirge-like verse:

All ye that in the condemned hole do lie
Prepare ye, for tomorrow ye shall die
Watch out and pray: the hour is drawing near
That ye before the Almighty must appear

Examine well yourselves, in time repent
That ye may not be to eternal flames sent
And when St Sepulchre's Bell in the morning tolls
The Lord above have mercy of your souls
BONG BONG! PAST TWELVE O'CLOCK! BONG BONG!

Bloody racket. It might be enough to make you blaspheme, I should imagine, rather than beg the Almighty's mercy.

As I recount in the Fleet Street walk (page 171), to add insult to injury, on the way to Tyburn the next morning the procession would stop outside St Sepulchre's so that the condemned could be presented with a nosegay (just when they were looking forward to a free pint). I imagine it was not unknown for a priest to get a good kick in the conkers from the condemned man for his troubles. After all, what could the authorities do? Hang him twice?

WHIPPING HALF-NAKED WOMEN, A TOP
SPECTATOR SPORT On the west (left) side of New Bridge Street, which leads to Ludgate Circus from Blackfriars Bridge, can be seen the old gatehouse of Bridewell Prison. This House of Correction was opened in 1555 and eventually replaced in the 19th century by Holloway Prison in North London.

It was a House of Correction aimed at the chastisement of mischievous apprentices, unruly orphans and loose women who broke the law. A popular amusement for Londoners was to see the inmates being whipped in a black-draped cell, particularly the women, who were stripped to the waist before being thrashed. So many wanted to watch this that a gallery was built to accommodate them. It all seems a bit perverted or primitive today, but there are probably still a few who would favour football louts and 'gipsy' beggars being thus treated.

This and various other barbaric punishments are exactly the kind of thing we have condemned the Taliban for performing in Afghanistan, yet we are within just a few generations of behaving in the same way ourselves. How short memories can be.

ROTTING HEADS ROLLED DOWN THE STREET
The gates of London, including those at London Bridge, were equipped with spikes to take the parboiled heads of traitors. The principle was something like gamekeepers putting up dead foxes or vermin: to discourage others. Temple Bar in Fleet Street, a deeply inconvenient ornamental stone arch and gate which pressure of traffic eventually caused to be moved, had spikes covered with heads too.

Occasionally, in a storm, the decayed head of a traitor would blow off and roll past the feet of shrieking ladies. By the 19th century, the spikes had been removed, which is just as well, as the Queen has to stop at Temple Bar (or where it stood) before she may enter the City. I don't suppose Her Majesty would ever shriek at a rolling head, but let's not put her to the test. The spot is marked by a particularly fearsome griffin statue (see Fleet Street walk, page 171).

INSTRUMENTS OF TORTURE AND GRUESOME DEVICES
Torture still holds an odd fascination long after it was ended in London. I have often wondered why – children in particular love macabre stuff – and there are some truly frightening psychological thoughts behind all this.

Is it because we fear being victims of torture? Or do we fear being the torturers, of which despots find there is never any required? With that deeply disturbing thought, there's no denying that the instruments are interesting. They range from the relatively harmless 'scold's bridle', a metal plate that depressed the tongue to stop women nagging, to various leg irons and thumbscrews.

Probably the worst hell-hole in London's history of such brutality was the White Tower at the Tower of London, where every possible instrument of torture was collected, and used. There was the rack for stretching victims until the ball joints dislocated like a barbecued chicken leg being snapped off. Another demonic device was 'Skeffington's Daughter', named after a 16th-century governor of the Tower, which compressed the prisoner's body within boards until blood spurted from every orifice and, ultimately, the skull cracked. Nice. Or as an alternative, you might just possibly, conceivably, confess to something you hadn't done.

Then there was a particularly vile punishment, a cell called 'Little Ease', in which you could neither stand up nor lie down at full-length. If you've ever suffered a 14-hour flight in economy class, imagine that going on for 14 months without being able to get up and walk around the cabin. You'd end up looking like Danny de Vito.

No wonder many of those who were finally beheaded on Tower Green – a blessed relief – needed help to ascend those last few steps. Skeffington's Daughter, by the way, recalls a punishment common in the Royal Navy during the 18th century – 'Kissing the Gunner's daughter', where you were tied to a gun and lashed with a whip. Other nautical favourites included being put on a never-ending series of half-watches, that is two hours on duty, two hours off, so you never fully got to sleep. It drove the victim insane after a while. We're back to that 14-hour economy class flight.

LAST LAUGH FOR LOVAT The great but not-so-good – that is, those of rank – could expect to be beheaded on Tower Hill. In 1745 the Jacobite (that is, a Scottish rebel who preferred a Catholic Stuart king to a Hanoverian Protestant one) Lord Lovat was about to have his head hacked off when a grandstand collapsed, killing 12 people. This may have helped Lord Lovat laugh his head off, but he was one of the last to suffer public beheading.

Oddly, beheading after hanging continued in certain cases. This was often so that traitors' heads could be impaled on spikes, or for medical dissection. Probably the last was outside Newgate in 1820 when the five Cato Street conspirators had their heads removed with knives after being hanged. (It all seems deeply macabre, but I suppose it would be very difficult to hang someone after beheading them. My boss once said to me when I recounted the news of some people being machine-gunned and then crucified in an Arab country, that it was pointless and would be more of a deterrent the other way round. I think he was joking, but some people are never satisfied.) The Cato Street conspiracy was a rather amateur attempt at revolution in the early 19th century. A small group of conspirators believed that if they assassinated government ministers and paraded their heads on poles around the poorer districts of London, a popular uprising would put the conspirators into power. Their bid to put their plan into action was known to the police who surprised them as they were preparing their hopeless attempt in a Cato Street apartment. They killed a police officer while resisting arrest, so four of the conspirators were executed at Newgate on 1 May 1820.

THE PILLORY AND THE GIBBET The pillory was where you were chained to a post and pelted with refuse by the public. It was what trendy museums today would call 'a hands-on interactive experience with public input in a positive urban feedback scenario'. The trouble was that if the public felt the courts had been over-lenient, they could convert the pillory into a gallows by using stones, as happened in London. The gibbet was where a hanged villain would be left on view, the idea being to deter others, or maybe to make the public feel protected by law enforcement. Corpses would be left on the gibbet, initially bloated with gas and then shrunken, for months, even years, until the flesh fell off their bones. (For examples see Hampstead, page 265, and Greenwich, page 249).

BLOODY BRENTFORD

Brentford is a total oddity within West London. Surrounded as it is by genteel Kew with its royal associations and elegant gardens, by posh Syon Park – London home of the Dukes of Northumberland, an ancient family that makes the royals seem new kids on the block – trendy Chiswick and the well-kept suburban sprawl of Ealing, shabby Brentford sticks out like a sore thumb.

It has a hint of the inner-city, of docks and run-down cockney pubs, of a certain industrial grimness, a bit of the East End magically transported out west. It could be the influence of the Grand Union Canal, but whatever the reason, it's well worth a poke around for its unique atmosphere. There are certainly a few real eccentrics among those who live in houseboats along the canal. Walk downstream (south) from the High Street towards the Thames to see them. There's a tidal lock to enter the Thames and the most eccentric boat dwellers – water gipsies, almost, some of them – are moored beyond the lock and are best seen by boat. Upstream from the High Street you pass the Gauging locks and a rickety swing bridge before reaching miles of towpath which leads you initially through industrial wasteland but then through pleasant greenery.

One thing any such foray to this very different bit of West London might not straight away reveal is this place's exceptionally blood-soaked history, which is what concerns me here.

Yet Brentford seems rather proud of its gory past. Outside the County Court on the High Street there's a Battle of Brentford pillar (it used to be in Ferry Lane opposite, which hints at Brentford's strategic location as a river crossing). It recalls how Cassivellaunus and his men repelled Julius Caesar and his centurions who were trying to ford the river at this point in 54BC, plus another battle fought by King Edmund 'Ironsides' against the raping and pillaging Danes in 1016 and the Civil War Battle of Brentford in 1642. My researches soon discovered a possible fourth Battle of Brentford (see below) at the end of that century, but that didn't come off, so another one is overdue. Watch out if you go down there.

COCK-UP, CANNON BALLS AND CANNIBALS The 1642 Battle of Brentford, actually nearer today's Turnham Green, part of the Civil War struggle between Parliament and the king, was more an exercise in bloody cock-up (like most war) than a demonstration of great military skill. Luckily there are records of what happened from both sides.

The witnesses were on the one hand a brave London 'prentice defending Parliament's rights, probably simply dressed in the Roundhead style, and on the other a Royalist cavalier officer, probably flamboyantly dressed and regarding war as a dashing adventure.

Prince Rupert's forces came 'sweeping down like a torrent' and camped on the flat river plain. The 'trained bands' of Londoners barred his way and opened fire with their guns. Rupert, not being the usual total dipstick, didn't suffer his men to stand there and take it. Or as the 'prentice said: 'As the prince is cunning enough to save himself, opening his ranks wide, the artillery did not so much execution on them as was desired.' Rupert's guns replied but fired too high.

Then the Royalist horse charged and were met by the trained bands' pikemen, who stood firm. Rupert was said to have fought 'like a Devil but not a man', but in the nick of time some Parliamentary horse arrived, followed by the red coats of the regular army breathless from London. The Royalists were driven off the Green and camped for the night at some small distance.

The contrast that night in the styles of the opposing camps told a lot. In the Cavalier camp:

> There was nothing but drinking, damning, and horsemen laying all the blame on the footmen, calling them cowards, for that they came up no faster, but said they were afraid of boys and Roundheads: we in the meantime after carefully setting our sentinels, and laying out our perdues, fell to our prayers, giving God hearty thanks for our deliverance from those cannibals.

A partial account, to be true, but prayer seemed to work better than carousing.

Next morning, after a feint attack, Rupert withdrew to Brentford and over the river to Surrey. He left four valuable cannon behind, and 800 dead, while the Parliamentary forces lost only 120.

THE NON-BATTLE OF BRENTFORD Another Battle of Brentford, or perhaps Chiswick, was arranged for 15 February 1696. King William III, hated by Irish Catholics for suppressing them and loved by Protestants in that country for the same reason, was in the habit of going down every Saturday from Kensington Palace to hunt deer in Richmond Park. He would drive by coach with bodyguards through Turnham Green to Brentford, then cross by boat to the south side where another coach and more bodyguards would await. His return by the same route, including the muddy lane now known as Wellesley Road, offered a good chance of an ambush. Sir George Barclay, a Scottish supporter of the Catholic-leaning line of kings which Parliament had thrown out in 1688 (ie: a Jacobite), gathered 40 like-minded men to attack this convoy. As the historian Macaulay noted:

> In the 17th century it was a quagmire, through which the royal coach was with difficulty tugged at a foot's pace… On that day the Forty were to assemble in small parties near the Green. When the signal was given that the coach was approaching, they were to take horse and repair to their posts. As the cavalcade came up to the lane, Charnock was to attack the guards in the rear, Rookwood on one flank, Porter on the other. Meanwhile Barclay, with eight trusty men, was to stop the coach and do the deed.

But a Catholic who disapproved of the tactic betrayed the plot, and most of the conspirators were arrested. Barclay fled to the Continent. King Billy was to die in 1702 by the means of a gentleman in a velvet waistcoat. Thus the fourth Battle of Brentford has not – yet – happened. So don't hang around, it's overdue.

- Round London canal trip, including Brentford: page 87.

Wormwood Scrubs. Relish it, roll it round your tongue, spit it out, growl it with sinister intent. It's a name a Hammer Horror writer would make up for a grim, rain-swept prison, or a blasted heath on the edge of clanking railway yards and grimy industrial scrapyards. Tatty gangland streets where merciless shootings take place, a grim Cold War venue for treachery and escaping spies.

In which case the writer would be dead right. That is exactly what the Scrubs is, or at least has been. But that's not the whole story of the fascinating Scrubs.

If it feels a bit of a geographical no-man's-land, then history has certainly given that impression. It currently belongs to the Borough of Hammersmith and Fulham, the latter place being a million miles away socially and not a few literally. Immediately to the east of the open space of the Scrubs, there's North Kensington, which is a detached and wholly different experience from other parts of Kensington.

It is somewhere many posh Kensington or South Kensington types wouldn't be seen dead in, or perhaps fear they *would* be seen dead in. (You think I'm exaggerating about Kensington types? Someone from Kensington, talking about gardening, sneered: 'Pampas grass … how Croydon!' Perhaps they grow pompous grass instead.)

West Kensington types are not so snobby, but still don't really know where North Kensington is. The A40 expressway flyover marks the rough boundary – the emphasis being on the rough – between shabby North Kensington and the deeply trendy Notting Hill where all kinds of stars, trust-fund trendies and politicos such as David Cameron have to be seen to hang out. The contrast between haves and have-nots is so extreme that straying across the boundary has, from time to time, led to gruesome results.

To add to the confusion, this area was long ago a detached outstation of Chelsea, another area as different from here as chalk from cheese, and was known as the Chelsea Outlands. It was a forest for pigs to root for acorns. Not a lot of people know that.

Linking the Scrubs to North Kensington is the wonderfully named North Pole Road, and nearby there was an old-fashioned railway signal box called North Pole. I'd always wanted to get a picture of it in snow, or take a children's Santa Special train there for a treat.

Actually the Scrubs is besieged by railways, and a canal, on all sides and defined by them. It should be an anorak's paradise ('anorak' being mocking British slang for the supposedly gormless types who hang out on railway platforms writing down the numbers of the locos, with railway badges all over their woolly bobble hats. They are sensitive to being mocked, hence *anoraksia nervosa*.)

The Great Western main line from Paddington to the West Country here almost crashes into the West Coast main line from Euston to Scotland with only Kensal Green Cemetery between them at one point. In fact the line to Scotland contrives to be running south at this point.

Just north of the Scrubs is the hallowed ground of **Old Oak Common**, where the Great Western Railway people and their successors have kept their trains since Brunel's day. Once a year, the gate opens and tens of thousands of railway fans pour down the road to see the latest, and oldest, trains. These eccentric Brits, eh?

Talking about Kensal Green Cemetery (well worth a tour, see page 60), the brilliant creator of the Great Western Railway, Isambard Kingdom Brunel, lies here between the railway lines and alongside the canal, as does his father, Marc Isambard Brunel, the engineer of the first tunnel under the Thames (for more on them, see their home at Cheyne Walk, page 121).

The whole North Pole thing is because of a pub of that name, but is not inappropriate as the Bible refers to bitter wormwood at the end of the world. Back to Wormwood Scrubs. What a great name, roll it round your tongue once more and spit it out again. Can you imagine a developer nowadays coming up with a place-name like that? Shepherd's Mead, Green Acres, Fair Lawns, Palace View … give me good old Wormwood Scrubs any day. One authority says the Wormwood name originates in a snake-infested forest, not the wormwood at the end of the world. Perhaps it was the serpent at the beginning of the world and this was once the Garden of Eden. If so, it's changed.

The Scrubs was put on the map in a big way when the Army built Wood Lane up to here from the south and leased the land so the Life Guards could exercise in the open space, something they have done ever since. Some of that land, 20 acres, was sold in 1873 to the Director of Convict Prisons where the jail, built by convict labour, still stands. It was designed by Sir Edmund Du Cane, the penal reformer, so the prison stands in Du Cane Road.

Another major step in the story of the Scrubs came at the turn of the 20th century when local people were scandalised at the sight of poor men and women, often more than 100 of them, sleeping in the open on Shepherd's Bush Green because they had nowhere else to go.

The Guardians of the Poor were impelled by the outrage to open a new hospital near Wormwood Scrubs in 1905. It was so well appointed that it was nicknamed the 'Paupers' Palace'. Eventually that became the famous **Hammersmith Hospital** that stands there today.

Another landmark for the area came with the 1908 Olympic Games which were based at White City, which still has its own Tube station on the Central Line (haven't they all gone home yet?). Later the BBC Television Centre was built on the site.

Crowds again flocked to Wormwood Scrubs for the start of the famous London to Manchester aeroplane race in 1910. Urban myth has another aviation link, in that the reason why the goalposts are taken down at the public soccer pitches at the Scrubs is that a plane heading for Heathrow and suffering a sudden loss of power could plonk itself down here.

(In fact a jumbo did land once a little further along the A40 at Northolt military airbase. It wasn't a breakdown, just a dozy pilot. He just managed to bring his plane to a halt on the short runway and when it took off again, minus puzzled passengers sent on by bus, for the two-minute hop to Heathrow, all the seats and fittings had to be taken out to get it off the ground. It was a good thing that the A40 at the end of the runway features shortened lampposts. Now there's a bloody great arrow on top of the giant Southall gasholder nearby saying 'Heathrow this way, stupid', or words to that effect.)

Other claims to fame, or infamy, of the Scrubs have included the Braybrook Street shootings in 1966, which took place on the west of the Scrubs, and the escape of spy George Blake a few months later.

THE BRAYBROOK STREET SHOOTINGS

The Braybrook Street shootings were particularly horrifying and this was one of those crimes that transfixed the whole country from the day it happened to the end of the villains' trial. Indeed, as I write 40 years later, public anger still seethes and letters to newspapers still pour in when the release of the gang from jail is discussed. The brutal killings came at a time when hanging had just been abolished and arming the police was being discussed, so the crime was politically explosive too.

A monument in Braybrook Street marks the place where, in August 1966, a car carrying a gang of three low-lives on their way to commit an armed robbery was stopped by three policemen doing routine checks for such minor things as expired road tax discs. The police were, of course, unarmed and it was, for them, appalling luck to have stopped this Standard Vanguard car. No mercy was shown to PC Geoffrey Fox, Sergeant Christopher Head and Detective Constable David Wombwell who were, one by one, shot dead.

People were appalled that our unarmed bobbies could be murdered like this. This was long before American TV had saturated our screens with programmes showing a dozen or so policemen being killed as being no big deal. Scotland Yard received 50,000 letters and calls of sympathy from the public and the then huge sum of £70,000 was raised within days to help the grieving families.

The murder hunt obsessed the nation as, one by one, the villains were hunted down. The capital's cab and lorry drivers vowed collectively to find the Standard Vanguard car and it was soon located in a railway arch in South London.

The names of the suspects were published and one newspaper headlining the story '50,000,000 detectives' was not far off the mark. Fellow criminals, disgusted by the gang's callousness, handed the police information and within weeks two of the gang, John Duddy and Jack Witney, were arrested. The last of the villains, Harry Roberts, was tracked down in a forest near East London, living rough in a camouflaged makeshift shelter. He didn't dare show his face, such was the intensity of the public's anger. Roberts was unearthed by armed police who combed the forest with dogs from end to blockaded end.

Many of those who had opposed the recent abolition of capital punishment doubted if the criminals would have shot the policemen if a noose had been waiting for them. We will never know that, but Duddy died behind bars while Witney was found in a pool of blood at his Bristol home just after being released on licence after serving 25 years. He had been released earlier because he was the gang's driver and had not fired the guns. Even so, he was by the law of the time just as guilty of murder because he knowingly went out with a gang of armed men to commit crime (shades of the Derek Bentley case).

At the trial, Mr Justice Glyn-Jones told the three: 'I think it likely that no Home Secretary, regarding the enormity of your crime, will ever think fit to show mercy by releasing you on licence. This is one of those cases in which the sentence of imprisonment for life may well be treated as meaning exactly that. Lest any Home Secretary in the future be minded to consider your release on licence, I have to make a recommendation.' He recommended 30 years.

These three never showed any genuine remorse; in fact one of them had a tattoo boasting of the killing. Roberts was interviewed by a London *Evening Standard* reporter in 1995 and, according to its report, expressed no personal remorse for what he had done: 'I had to do what I chose to do.' He thought he should spend his 'retirement' fishing. What a pity a retired PC Geoffrey Fox, Sergeant Christopher Head and Detective Constable David Wombwell couldn't go fishing.

Make your own mind up from Roberts's own account, published in a book and several newspapers. It records that:

DC Wombwell was talking to Jack through the window of our van. He was shouting and trying to get the door open. Jack said, 'Let the slag have it, Harry.'

Instantly, I raised my arm and, with the Luger Jack had just handed me, I shot Wombwell point-blank. The bullet whizzed past Jack's nose and hit Wombwell just below the eye.

He slumped to the ground. I could hear my heart thumping. I jumped out of the car still holding the gun. Sergeant Head turned and started running back towards the police car. I aimed, fired, and got him right in the middle of his back. I ran up and aimed at his head. I pulled the trigger. It misfired. I pulled the trigger again. It misfired again.

He got up and staggered to the [police] car, but fell down in front of it. PC Fox tried to drive off but he jammed DS Head under the wheels. Then Duddy shot PC Fox in the head.

COLD WAR SPY ESCAPE: AN ECCENTRIC WAY TO RUN ESPIONAGE Wormwood Scrubs was the scene of one of the most sensational spy stories of the Cold War, putting this grim bit of northwest London on the map with around-the-world front-page news. Double agent George Blake, who had worked for Britain's MI6 monitoring spying in eastern Europe while all the time passing top secret information to the Russians, was caught. He escaped dramatically from Wormwood Scrubs prison in October 1966. The sequel to his escape was totally bizarre too, in the treatment meted out to two British men who had 'sprung' him from the jail.

The seriousness of Blake's treachery has been debated by pundits ever since he was caught. Some said the 42-year jail sentence he received reflected just one year for each agent killed as a result of his revelations. Blake, speaking in Moscow later, denied he had killed any agents personally, but admitted he had passed their names to the Soviets. So what did he think the KGB would do? Give them tea and biscuits or torture or murder them? Any guesses, George?

The entire British spy network in the Middle East was also compromised and destroyed because of the work of this – in some ways – James Bond-like man: suave, dark-haired, athletic and charming to men and women alike.

On the day after his escape, the Shepherd's Bush area was swamped with police, and all airports and seaports were closely watched. Was it a top-level Russian-controlled escape?

Well, no. The escape itself was rather like something dreamt up by an amateur. The authorities found the bars of his cell had been sawn through with a smuggled-in file or hacksaw and that a rope ladder made with nylon cord and knitting needles had been thrown over the prison wall from the outside. It later emerged that Blake had been smuggled to East Germany by two British sympathisers in a camper van, aided by an Irish adventurer.

The two men behind Blake's escape turned out to be 'peaceniks' – idealistic peace campaigners who met him in the Scrubs after being jailed for protesting inside an American airbase in Britain. These were the days of the Committee of

100, a forerunner of the Campaign for Nuclear Disarmament, a movement dedicated to mass protest against the nuclear arms race. They believed in direct action, such as sitting down in the way of convoys carrying nuclear weapons.

They 'sprang' Blake with no pressure from the Soviets and no financial inducements, because they believed in the communist system. They were among those whom the Soviets called 'useful idiots'; had Stalin taken over Britain they would doubtless have been among the first to go to the death camps.

After getting Blake out, they didn't know what to do with their hot potato. They took him round a series of the houses of friends who in horror said: 'Isn't that the man hundreds of armed police are searching for?' and moved him on. It was farcical. In the end, with Blake hidden in the floor of their campervan, they got as far as the East German border from where the double agent made his way to Moscow.

So how hard was it for the police to work out who did it? Well one clue came from the unstable Irish adventurer, Sean Bourke, who had helped the escape by actually flinging the rope ladder over the wall and who wanted to go down in history as the escape mastermind who sprung a spy from the Scrubs. He – perhaps surprisingly – told the police the registration number of the getaway car and the address of the house where Blake was first taken. Later, in the 1970s, before he died, Bourke published a book telling of his role and detailing the two men who were involved but giving them pseudonyms. Then the two men allegedly behind the plot, antiques dealer Patrick Pottle and academic Derek Randle, published their own book, *The Blake Escape: How we Freed George Blake, and Why.* Just a wee clue for Scotland Yard, you may think.

The political and press outrage over the book forced clearly reluctant authorities to prosecute. In 1991 Patrick Pottle and Derek Randle were finally brought to trial for assisting Blake's escape, in the same Old Bailey courtroom where Blake had been sentenced 30 years before and sent down for 42 years. During this trial one of the prosecution lawyers was heard to whisper: 'We didn't want to prosecute them, you know.'

Pottle and Randle appealed to the jury's humanity, saying that Blake's 42-year sentence had been excessive when you consider posh 'Establishment' traitors had gone unpunished for long periods. They portrayed Blake as a victim of the system.

Randle told the jury that the steps down from the court led to a sewer connecting it to Britain's terrible jails, 'Can you imagine what it means to go down those steps for 42 years? It means death. I have no apologies for what I did and no regrets.' The jury agreed unanimously and freed the two, to cheers from some and outrage from others. Randle said: 'Thank God for the British jury system.' What do you think?

4

Eccentric Pastimes

LONDON'S ODDEST MUSEUMS

London is famed globally for its fabulous and unbeatable range of mainstream museums and galleries, from the huge British Museum in Bloomsbury (whose courtyard is now covered with what appear to be bulging fishnet tights) to the incomparable South Kensington Group of museums (the Science, the Natural History and the Victoria and Albert being the most famous), from the free National Gallery on Trafalgar Square to the pioneering and also free Tate Gallery, both at Millbank and Bankside. All of these are well known.

But much of the capital's charm lies in around 250 myriad, odd and eccentric museums lurking on backstreets and in quiet suburbs, each with a fascinating story to tell. Here's a selection of just some of them, with how to get there information, phone numbers and 2007 adult entry charges. As usual, because museums can close for changes, etc, I recommend checking before setting out, if you have to travel any distance to get to them.

BITS OF TRAMS AND TUBES
LT Museum Covent Garden, 39 Wellington St, WC2; ☎ 020 7379 6344; www.ltmuseum.co.uk; admission £5.95
⊖ *Covent Garden*
Many people have heard of the London Transport Museum at Covent Garden, and very good it is too, with its ancient Tube trains, buses and trams. But it is a small site and the linked Acton Depot in West London, more a collection of odd junk and memorabilia than a theme park, is equally fascinating. Where else in the world can you see the remains of a spiral escalator, for example? Nowhere, because there was only one. Did it work? How would the steps get back down again? These are vital questions I cannot live without the answers to. The Depot has open days from time to time. The Covent Garden museum is open nearly every day.

BLOOD-SOAKED SURGERY
The Old Operating Theatre and Herb Garret 9A St Thomas's St, near London Bridge, SE1; ☎ 020 7955 4791; www.thegarret.org.uk; admission £3.50
⊖ *London Bridge*
Return to a land of hope and gory, and to a time when still-conscious, screaming patients endured – or not – butchery that often killed them while sawdust soaked up the blood, all this in front of a theatre (as in operating theatre) audience. The Old Operating Theatre and Herb Garret, near London Bridge, dates from 1822 and offers a fascinating insight into surgery before the days of antiseptics and anaesthetics. If this makes you feel faint, there's always the fan museum.

BLOWN-OFF LEG
National Army Museum Royal Hospital Rd, SW3; ✆ 020 7730 0717;
www.national-army-museum.ac.uk; admission free
⊖ *Sloane Square, walk down King's Rd a little way then left on Smith St to end
(10 mins).* 🚌 *11,19, or 22 to Smith St on King's Rd.*
Traces the glorious, muddy, frightened, disciplined, heroic, horrific life of the British
soldier from Agincourt to Afghanistan. Aimed at the general public, not just military
types. One of the odder displays, indeed a somewhat grisly one, must be the scene
where a blood-soaked surgeon removes the remains of the first Marquess of
Anglesey's leg. During the Battle of Waterloo, as the cannon roared, the Marquess
(then merely Lord Uxbridge, but later elevated for his heroism) cried out: 'My God,
sir, I've lost a leg!' The Duke of Wellington, the British commander, remarked: 'Have
you, by God!' and carried on observing the French lines through his telescope. It is
not recorded whether the Iron Duke dismounted to lend a hand, as it were, but
amputation was performed in the field and the aristocratic leg buried under a willow
tree with full military honours. The actual blood-stained saw and a once-white glove
are included in the museum's display. If you like blown-off legs, or this particular
one, there's a museum to the Marquess's artificial leg (among other things) at Plas
Newydd on the Menai Straits in Wales. There's also a monument where the real leg
is buried at the real Waterloo in Belgium. Three monuments to one leg end, not bad.

Royal Air Force Museum Grahame Park Way, Hendon, NW9; ✆ 020 8205 2266
⊖ *Colindale*
If you like military history, there's also the Royal Air Force Museum. Real planes
from the Battle of Britain and more modern times. Tally ho, Ginger!

CANALS
London Canal Museum 12/13 New Wharf Rd, N1; ✆ 020 7713 0836;
www.canalmuseum.org.uk; admission £3
⊖ *King's Cross, walk (5 mins) north up York Way on the east side of the main station and
then right into Wharfedale Rd, then left into New Wharf Rd*
The colourful history of canals, the tunnels, the navvies, the horses, canal art, and
the canal characters, they're all here. Get narrow-minded at the London Canal
Museum. Or you can tie up here if going by boat. The museum's also part of the
history of ice-cream, because this was the ice warehouse of Carlo Gatti, the great
ice-cream pioneer. Before refrigeration, ice was brought from Norway and stored
here for use in hot weather.

CARTOONS
The Cartoon Museum 35 Little Russell St, WC1; ✆ 020 7580 8155;
www.cartoonmuseum.org; closed Mon; admission £3 adult
⊖ *Holborn, cross Kingsway and go west down High Holborn. Turn right into Museum St
and Little Russell St is on your left after crossing another main road. It's close to the British
Museum and next to a rather good Pizza Express (well, they're all the same but the
building's rather good).*
Should be a good draw (groan) and I'm glad someone is taking laughter seriously.
Hundreds of cartoons and caricatures including the earliest and the burst-out-
laughing variety, plus biting political satire some people would rather forget.

CRYSTAL PALACE MUSEUM
Crystal Palace Museum Anerley Hill, SE19; ✆ 020 8676 0700; open Sat, Sun and
bank holiday Mon only
🚌 *3 bus from Oxford Circus and Central London.* 🚉 *Crystal Palace overground*

The Crystal Palace

A local museum with an interesting story to tell – how gardener Joseph Paxton's dream of a giant glasshouse to house all the best things in the world came to fruition in 1851, how it was moved to Upper Sydenham and how it met its dramatic end in 1936. Plus TV was invented right here.

ECCENTRIC COLLECTORS
Cuming Museum, the Museum of Southwark's History First floor, 151 Walworth Rd, SE17; ☎ 020 7525 2163; closed Mon, Sun and bank holidays; admission free
Elephant and Castle

A very unusual museum. Here, you'll find a Red Indian scalp from North America, a bit chipped off the ceiling of the room where Napoleon died in St Helena and part of the waistcoat Charles I wore to his execution. It's all down to two eccentrics, Richard Cuming (1777–1870) and his son Henry Syer Cuming (1817–1902), who collected this remarkable lot of bric-à-brac. Henry left 100,000 objects and the money to display them, and the new museum opened in 1906, covering every field of knowledge in a scatter-gun kind of way. It was billed as the 'British Museum in miniature' at the time. It really is eccentric. I mean, the Cumings not only collected fakes, knowing they were fakes, but also the sawn-off leg of an Egyptian mummy. It was all the fault of Richard Cuming's aunt who gave him three fossils when he was five years old. That was it. The enthusiasm of these people and their boundless curiosity shines through.

ECCENTRIC TEA MAGNATE'S COLLECTION
Horniman Museum London Rd, Forest Hill, SE23; ☎ 020 8699 1872; www.horniman.ac.uk; admission free
185, 122. *Forest Hill overground*

Another absolutely fantastic collection is at the Horniman Museum in South London. Tea magnate and MP for Falmouth, Frederick Horniman, who died in 1906, started this collection which now offers 6,500 musical instruments (the world's best collection, and kept right up to date), 60,000 items from remote peoples, and 250,000 specimens from nature. Five years before his death, he handed over this amazing collection, and a purpose-built museum, to the people of London. Unlike Pitt Rivers (who created a similar museum in Oxford), Horniman travelled the world to collect much of the material himself. Big on Africa and on recreated environments such as river beds and bee hives.

FANS
London Fan Museum 12 Crooms Hill, Greenwich, SE10; ☎ 020 8305 1441; www.fan-museum.org; closed Mon; admission £4
Greenwich overground, from Charing Cross. Included in Greenwich walk, page 237.

Folding, not footie ones, thankfully, and the world's biggest collection of more than 3,000 of them. A special exhibition of rather pretty art nouveau jobs opened in 1999, perhaps permitting the pun 'Fan de siècle'. Plus advertising fans. Teashop with napkins folded in guess what shape.

FASHION SHOWCASE
Zandra Rhodes's Fashion and Textile Museum 83 Bermondsey St, SE1; ☎ 020 7403 0222; www.ftmlondon.org (lots of pink on this one when I looked)
θ *London Bridge*

Yes, darling, Zandra Rhodes's cherished dream to celebrate London's role in fashion over the last half century and also to showcase the newest and best from all over the world has come true.

GREAT WRITERS If you're a great fan of Dr Johnson or Charles Dickens and don't know their London houses have been preserved as museums, check out:

Dickens House Museum 48 Doughty St, WC1; ☎ 020 7405 2127; www.dickensmuseum.com; admission £5
θ *Russell Square*

Dr Johnson's House 17 Gough Sq, EC4, off Fleet St; ☎ 020 7353 3745; www.drjohnsonshouse.org; admission £4.50
θ *Blackfriars (more in Fleet Street walk, page 180)*

MASSIVE GUNS
Imperial War Museum Lambeth Rd, SE1; ☎ 020 7416 5321; www.iwm.org.uk; admission free
θ *Lambeth North*

Guns that could sink a navy threateningly dominate the forecourt of the absolutely fascinating Imperial War Museum in Kennington, near Waterloo (aptly). But it's not just the sexy guns, planes, bombs and torpedoes you'll find here; you'll also find that the experiences of the British Tommy in the trenches, of the jolly Jack Tar in the Royal Navy and of the 'Few', the Battle of Britain air aces, are brought back to life by the memorabilia displayed here. Great for scholars – I wanted to find out about the disastrous siege of Kut in Mesopotamia (Iraq) in World War I, because my grandfather was involved; a typical bit of British humour (or bureaucratic bloody-mindedness) emerged. A letter home said: 'We are camped amidst the [hole cut in paper] palms. We enjoy eating the [another hole].' It transpired that the military censors had been told to cut out all *dates*. Later, British and American bombers in the Gulf War of the 1990s took out the same bridges my grandfather had built.

MONEY
Bank of England Museum Bartholomew Lane, EC2; ☎ 020 7601 5545; closed weekends; admission free
θ *Bank, unsurprisingly*

The amazing confidence trick whereby instead of giving us a pound's worth of gold we were given a note with a promise to pay that amount and then that promise is abandoned so only the worthless bit of paper has a value is a staggering thing when you stop to think about it. Here you can see the early bank notes, written out by clerks in longhand and individually signed by the cashiers, in this, the Museum of the 'Old Lady of Threadneedle Street'. Originally every country bank around Britain would issue its own bank notes but these were only as good as the bank they were drawn on. Whereas the Bank of England's notes were as safe as, well, the Bank of England. Now only a few Scottish banks provide their own notes. Here you can learn about the evolution of devices to prevent forgeries and the success or otherwise of the counterfeiters – the most severe penalty for counterfeiting being, of course, the gallows. They probably won't tell you about the sexy female financial journalist and the high official who had to resign a couple of years ago after headlines such as 'Bonk of England' appeared about their love-making on the Bank's carpets and the leather-topped desks. Ouch – watch out for staplers. But forget mere sex – who isn't fascinated, just a bit, by piles of gold and money?

MOORISH PARADISE
Leighton House Museum 12 Holland Park Rd, W14; ℡ 020 7602 3316; www.rbkc.gov.uk/leightonhousemuseum; closed Tue; admission free
🚌 8, 9 ask for Melbury Rd or Commonwealth Institute ⊖ Olympia (District Line or overground from Clapham and Willesden Junctions)
In here, you will find an Arab fountain tinkling with water, beautiful original Moorish tiles and a shuttered window balcony overlooking it, furnished with plump cushions, fit for a harem. Plus the sensual paintings of Lord Leighton, the Victorian painter. Fascinating and free. Not near Holland Park Tube but off Melbury Road which goes north off Kensington High Street between High Street Kensington Tube and the nearer Olympia. More rave comments in Kensington walk, page 285.

SPORT
Wimbledon Lawn Tennis Museum Church Rd, SW19; ℡ 020 8946 6131; www.wimbledon.org; admission £6.25
⊖ Southfields (cross over and walk down Wimbledon Park Rd for half-mile). More on bizarre tennis history, page 294.

Museum of Rugby Twickenham stadium (Gate L), off the A316 main road leading from Central London to the M3; ℡ 020 8892 8877; www.rfu.com; closed Mon, and Sun after match days; admission £10 inc stadium tour.
🚂 Twickenham, overground from Waterloo

MCC Museum Lord's, NW8; ℡ 020 7432 1033; admission for the Lord's tour inc museum £6.50
⊖ St John's Wood
Places of reverential pilgrimage for serious rugby, tennis and cricket fans must be the museums at Twickenham, Wimbledon and Lord's respectively. If you want to see how Victorian ladies played tennis in long dresses so they wouldn't show an ankle, and the strange things balls and racquets were once made of, plus Pat Cash's sweaty headband, plus videos of the greatest moments of the world-famous championships, Wimbledon's the place. If you'd like to have a go with a rugby scrum machine, tour the stands, and recall how that boy picked up the ball and ran with it at Rugby School, then it's Twickenham for you. And if you'd like to see a painting of how a well-struck six, soaring from the bat in 1936, killed a passing sparrow, plus the actual ball and the stuffed bird, and of course the real Ashes (a burned bail of 1882), then it's got to be Lord's.

TORTURE AND IMPRISONMENT
Clink Prison Museum 1 Clink St, SE1; ℡ 020 7403 0900; admission £5
⊖ London Bridge, then go past Southwark Cathedral or through Borough Market
When you go down the steps into this prison that gave its name as a nickname for all others – into the Clink – you have an uneasy feeling that getting out again might not

have been so easy for some of those who preceded you. Punishment was one of Southwark's biggest industries, and there were major prisons round here which lasted for centuries, but this one features the chains and manacles, and the harrowing stories, recreated, of inmates. You will learn that whereas men could be hanged, drawn and quartered, women were more gently treated: they were just drowned or burned at the stake. One of the most fascinating devices here is the 'scold's bridle', a device that allowed a flat metal plate to be fitted over the tongue of a woman who talked too much, to keep her quiet (watch out Ruby Wax), plus puritan branding irons for prostitutes (a B on the forehead meant Bawd, not a second-rate one).

TERRIFIC TOYS
Pollock's Toy Museum 1 Scala St, W1, near Tottenham Court Rd; ☏ 020 7636 3452; www.pollocksweb.co.uk; admission £3 (imaginary friends go free)
⊖ *Goodge Street*
Full of bizarre 19th-century gadgets for children, great puppets and dolls' houses and the real story of Teddy bears. Plus an Egyptian clay mouse which could be the world's oldest toy.

Bethnal Green Museum of Childhood Cambridge Heath Rd, E2; ☏ 020 8980 2415; www.museumofchildhood.org.uk; closed Fri; admission free
⊖ *Bethnal Green*
This is a branch of the Victoria and Albert Museum. Zillions more toys, pedal-cars, puppets, mechanical toys, spinning tops, lead soldiers, model trains, children's clothes, and toys you can actually play with. Baby and nursery equipment.

A TRUE ECCENTRIC
Sir John Soane's Museum 13 Lincoln's Inn Fields, WC2; ☏ 020 7405 2107; www.soane.org; closed Sun & Mon; admission free
⊖ *Holborn*
Sir John Soane's House is a quite extraordinary testament to the passions and private life of Georgian England's great architect (1753–1837) whose simple, unadorned style can still be seen in his buildings, which include the Dulwich Picture Gallery and the Bank of England. But what interests us here is why this house holds a human skeleton and Roman cremation urns, a three-yard long Egyptian sarcophagus, an eccentric collection of architectural bits and bobs from around the world and the marble tomb of Fanny, his favourite dog. The front of the building, designed by Soane, of course, includes two stone statues made to the indestructible Coade formula for making artificial stone (as in the Coade lion, page 158). The reason for this house being frozen in time is that Soane fell out with his two sons who didn't want to follow him into architecture. When one of his sons wrote an anonymous attack on Soane's architectural style, and Soane found out who'd written it, that was it. He virtually disinherited them, put his money into a trust for preserving this house and even obtained a private Act of Parliament to set the thing up in perpetuity. This decrees that nothing must be changed, so it isn't. Here you can see the models Soane made of great buildings and ancient monuments, and his entertaining rooms, decorated in the original style. Note the experimental use of domed skylights to shed light as required and compare this to his brilliant achievement at the Dulwich Picture Gallery.

SWASHBUCKLER'S TREASURES
Wernher Collection Ranger's Hse, Greenwich Park, SE10; ☏ 020 8853 0035; www.english-heritage.org.uk; admission £5.50
⊖ *Blackheath (main line or DLR, walk ³/₄ mile up through park)*

The amazing Wernher Collection, surely one of the greatest private collections of art ever assembled by an individual, was saved for Britain in 2001 and found a home in the lovely Ranger's House in Greenwich Park. The man who collected the 650 works, now on 125-year loan to English Heritage, was Julius Wernher, a swashbuckling empire builder from the days of Cecil Rhodes. In 1871 the poor young German sailed for South Africa to make his fortune, arriving amidst scenes of violence and filth. He set up business in the rough and tough diamond town of Kimberley and worked hard for a London firm. He married a society beauty and heiress and bought the massive stately home of Luton Hoo in Bedfordshire, meanwhile starting his art collection which, like everything else he did, was done with shrewd success. He ended a remarkable rags-to-riches story with a baronetcy and a remarkable and eccentric collection of gems, fakes, and heavily restored pieces. English Heritage, for once, have vowed to keep the collection in its original flavour, with the odd eccentricities intact telling of a man who seems to have stepped from the pages of a Kipling or Rider Haggard adventure. The 1723 house, once home to a princess, is itself worthy of a visit.

VICTORIAN INTERIORS
Linley Sambourne's House 18 Stafford Terrace, Kensington (a couple of streets north of the middle of the High St); ☏ Mon–Fri 11.00–17.30 020 7602 3316 ext 300, weekends 020 7938 1295; admission £6 by appointment only
✆ *High Street Kensington* 🚌 *9 from Strand, 10 from Oxford Street and King's Cross*
Almost completely unchanged late Victorian interior. Headquarters of the Victorian Society and once home to the famed *Punch* cartoonist Linley Sambourne, an ancestor of another famous Kensington resident, the Earl of Snowdon, who married Princess Margaret (and their son, twelfth in line to the throne, is furniture-maker Viscount Linley). He – the ancestor – drew his cartoons by getting various comely young ladies to pose in position, undressed for reasons we can only surmise. Note this house is open for a guided tour by appointment only, and it's an intimate experience: you feel you really get to know the family. The guide is sometimes a costumed actor speaking in role. They can also arrange joint tours with nearby Leighton House (see previous entry, Moorish Paradise).

THE LONDON LIDOS: ART DECO OASES?

Just occasionally, this windswept island of grey skies and umbrellas and south-westerly gales experiences a heat-wave, when, for a few days, it's too hot to be comfortable and the newspapers run headlines such as 'Phew wotta Scorcha!'.

Better than that is when the hot weather gets stuck in a groove of endless summer days, blue skies, people walking around in shorts and T-shirts, children with no shoes, sunglasses and car windows wide open. It only happens about once every five years, but this is the only time we Poms can risk planning a barbecue more than a few days ahead, as our more fortunate cousins Down Under are able to do.

At these times, an extraordinary London institution comes into its own: the lido. These enormous open-air pools were mostly laid out in the thirties when 'fresh air for health' was promoted across Europe (even for the Hitler Youth), when some art deco houses were built with outside sleeping areas, even in this country (there's one at Amersham).

Many foolish seaside communities have filled in their 1930s lidos, but a strangely large number of them have survived in London. The hard core of serious, up-and-down, 50-length swimmers get an adrenalin rush from the cold on their bodies. They are mostly far too big to heat (the pools, not the swimmers) – but they only really get busy in a heat-wave or a really good summer.

Then the regulars, with their serious Speedo swimwear and rubber hats, look askance at the families pouring in, at the naked toddlers weeing on the pavements and dropping half-eaten ice-creams, screaming while their mums loaf about reading *Cosmopolitan*, smoking or yacking into mobile phones, and teenage boys, with acne-ridden faces like a Braille Tube map hopelessly eye the hourglass figures of girls posing as *Baywatch* extras, where lido meets libido.

Luckily lidos are usually so big that there's room for everyone, so the serious swimmers can carry on. When there is blue sky overhead it's never as unpleasant as a noisy, crammed indoor pool on a hot day.

You'll usually find some eccentric pensioners whose floppy bodies, painfully awkward and slow on land, move gracefully through the water with ease that comes from years of practice and who put the rest of us to shame with their effortless 40 lengths. Mothers-to-be, great with child, find they are in an element which is more forgiving to their whale-like shapes.

Going to the lido was, for many working-class Londoners in the days before package tours, the closest thing to a holiday and an escape from the discomfort of a city heat-wave they were likely to get. Exposing their bodies to sunshine gave them much-needed Vitamin D. This could prevent rickets, a disfiguring bone disease common in the slums just a few years before.

When I was a child at Brockwell Park Lido, between Dulwich and Brixton, I recall the surface of the water stretching endlessly to the horizon, punctuated by floating dead flies and lolly sticks. I couldn't really see the other end – it seemed like an ocean to me. Probably there were some serious swimmers in the deep bit, but I didn't see them. I just saw the small bunch of children who had claimed a small patch of the shallow end as their own, because there was so much of it to go round.

Now I've gone back on a scorching day as an adult and, yes, the pool's only half the size it seemed to be then, and other things have changed too. There's a definitely Caribbean flavour to the poolside, there are brazen teenagers in skimpy bikinis and spotty youths who haven't quite switched from Toblerone to testosterone, there are strutting gays preening themselves, but why not – there's still heaps of room for everyone. It's still bloody freezing when you get in, but on a scorching day that's exhilarating and all the more reason to get out and bask in the sun once more. It's an instant beach holiday.

LONDON'S MAIN SURVIVING LIDOS

Tooting Bec Lido Tooting Bec Common, Streatham, SW16 (off Tooting Bec); 020 8871 7198; open 26 May–end of Sep
Streatham
London's oldest, built 1906. Nice woodland setting, good for picnics. Not heated. Food: Café, picnics possible.

Richmond Pools on the Park Old Deer Park, Twickenham Rd, Richmond, TW9; 020 8940 0561; open all year
/ Richmond (overground from Waterloo and North London line, District Line Tube)
Open air and enclosed pools; both heated. Food: Café, picnics possible.

Walford Sports Centre Bengarth Rd, Northolt, UB5; ☏ 020 8841 0953; open May–Sep
Ⓔ/🚌 *Northolt, then a 10min walk, or buses 140 and 282*
Food: Picnics possible.

Park Road Pools Hornsey, N8; ☏ 020 8341 3567; open May–Sep
Ⓔ/🚌 *Finsbury Park, then a W7 bus drops off at the door*
Heated. Food: Café, picnics possible.

Serpentine Lido Hyde Park, W2; ☏ 020 7706 342; open 27 Jun–9 Sep
Ⓔ *Knightsbridge or South Kensington*
Food: Café next door; canteen on site.

Parliament Hill Lido Gordon House Rd, NW3; ☏ 020 7485 3873 for a recorded message, or 020 7485 4491; open May–Sep usually; admission free between 07.00–09.00
🚂 *Gospel Oak (overground, North London Line) or* Ⓔ *Tufnell Park (Northern Line), then three-quarters of a mile walk*
On the south edge of Hampstead Heath, beneath that hill with unmissable views over London. An enormous 58m by 27m. Not heated. You occasionally spot local celeb politicians and nubile actresses. If you spot them together, even better. Food: Café on site, picnics possible.

Hampstead Heath Ponds Not really a lido, but a very special place. None of the art deco concrete but instead a near-natural atmosphere. Men's, ladies' and mixed bathing ponds, all free. They even swim in the snow.

Hampton Heated Open-Air Pool High St, Hampton, TW12; ☏ 020 8255 1116; open all year
Ⓔ *Hampton, Hampton Court (overground from Waterloo) both about a mile distant.*
Food: Café, picnics possible.

Finchley Lido North Finchley, N12; ☏ 020 8343 9830; open May–Sep (open air); all year (indoor pool)
Ⓔ *West Finchley, then three-quarters of a mile walk.*
Both pools heated. Food: Café, picnics outside possible.

Brockwell Park Lido Brockwell Park, Dulwich Rd, SE25; ☏ 020 7274 3088; open end of May–2nd weekend in Sep (weather depending)
🚂 *Herne Hill (overground from Victoria or Blackfriars)*
This is a particularly enterprising lido, with classes for t'ai chi, on-site massage, scuba diving (obviously not very far, but it's a start), a children's club, floodlit night swimming and barbecues most Friday nights, plus occasional theme-night barbecues. The pool has been used as a location for filming episodes of *The Bill*, fashion shoots, advertisements, pop music videos and documentaries; many a Brixton-based celeb can be spotted here. Food: Café with comprehensive menu and picnics possible.

London Fields Lido London Fields, Westside, E8 3EU; ☏ 020 7254 9038
I am delighted to announce that the tide has turned at last for lidos and this one, closed like so many others, was triumphantly reopened in late 2006 after a spirited local campaign supported by local MP Diane Abbott. Where there was for 20 years a vandalised, derelict eyesore there is now a splendid heated pool. Well done

x

Hackney, and other boroughs, dive in – there are about 30 other lost lidos that need restoring or recreating. I well remember a freezing plunge at Whipps Cross, and Purley Way, both long gone. Bring them back!

THEATRE: A BETTER MOUSETRAP AND OTHER QUIRKS

The Mousetrap is the world's longest-running play, but it wasn't supposed to go on stage at all. The play, which opened at the Ambassadors theatre in 1952 and is now at St Martin's theatre (✆ *020 7836 1443*) and which has thus lasted an incredible half-a-century, staged at several theatres, was originally written by Agatha Christie as a radio play to mark Queen Mary's 80th birthday. But it was received with such acclaim by whodunnit fans that she decided to rewrite it for the stage.

She gave the royalties to her only grandchild, Mathew Prichard, as a birthday present. Some birthday present! When Mathew became captain of the cricket team at Eton, he took the entire side to see the play. It was a gift whose longevity and reward could only be matched by two I can recall – Handel's gift of the *Messiah* to the Foundling Hospital and J M Barrie's wonderfully apt gift of *Peter Pan* to the Great Ormond Street Hospital for sick children, which still receives income from Disney for its various versions.

The **Theatre Royal**, London's oldest, more usually known as the Drury Lane theatre after its location, dates back to the time of Charles II and his mistress, actress Nell Gwyn (see page 112 for her fascinating story), and comes complete with a resident ghost. The man in grey appears to have been a gentleman horserider, for he wears a white wig, a tricorn hat and boots and carries a sword.

The story goes that such a man in the theatre's early days pestered an actress and was asked to leave the premises. A fight ensued, and the man was killed. His body was hastily walled up. In Victorian days, when rebuilding was taking place, a skeleton was found. It had a 17th-century dagger through its ribs …

The diarist Pepys, himself much taken with Nell Gwyn, attended the very first performance at the Theatre Royal when it opened in 1663, after the boring Puritans who had banned theatre were themselves banned and theatres returned to the capital. Though the theatre has been burned down more than once, it has always risen like a phoenix, so the show could go on. The Irish playwright Sheridan owned it at the time of the third fire in 1809, and refused to hurry over, despite hearing the news; when he finally got there he calmly took a glass of port at Covent Garden. When onlookers protested at his composure in the face of the great disaster, he replied: 'Surely a man may take a glass of port at his own fireside.'

Actors are, as is well known, horribly superstitious, and will always refer to Shakespeare's … Scottish play … as 'the Scottish play' and never as … well, it would be bad luck, wouldn't it? They like to talk about 'thespians' and 'treading the boards' instead of actors and acting. They like to keep up old traditions in case of risking bad luck.

Theatre Royal, Drury Lane

One of the less well-known thespian traditions takes place at the Theatre Royal, where on 6 January, a Baddeley Cake is consumed by the cast in memory of actor Richard Baddeley, who was a successful actor here. When he died in 1794, he

left money to provide for a Twelfth Night Cake and wine to be shared amongst the company (but not the audience). So every 6 January, Twelfth Night, just for luck a cake is carried into the Green Room by bewigged attendants dressed in their 18th-century livery for the company, who drink Baddeley's health. After all, one doesn't want to break a leg. Especially not Baddeley.

If you're having a drink in the bar, you can contemplate the fact that Britain's most successful theatre producer of modern times, Sir Cameron Mackintosh, once scrubbed the floors and polished the brass here as a mere cleaner. It was just a stepping stone for the man behind such mega hits as *Les Misérables* which dominated the West End and Broadway for decades. He had wanted to be a theatre producer from the age of eight. (Personally, I thought for many years that 'Les Miserable' was French for Les Dawson.)

Perhaps the oddest thing that's ever existed off-stage in a London theatre was a royal railway which went from the foyer to the Royal Box in the **London Coliseum**, so the pampered princes didn't have to walk that small distance.

It was hard to know whether or not to believe this story, kindly pointed out by reader Jim Garrod, but on prompting he produced two sources of evidence that was certainly more than urban myth. One was an old Coliseum programme that said:

> Through the Grand Salon is the Royal Entry. Immediately on entering the theatre, a Royal party will step into a richly furnished lounge which, at a signal, will move softly along on a track formed in the floor, through the salon and into a large foyer which contains the entrance to the Royal Box. The lounge car remains in position at the entrance to the Royal Box and serves as an ante-room during the performance.

A photograph accompanying this piece, which may not have come from the same source, shows a square box about 10ft long with no apparent wheels. The caption, crucially, says 'The King's Car: on Edward VII's first visit it broke down ignominiously and was consigned to use as a box office in the Stoll Theatre.'

Mr Garrod goes on to point out that in *London's Secret History* by Peter Bushell (Constable 1983) is the following: 'Dominating the southern end of St Martin's Lane is the Renaissance-style Coliseum, opened in 1904 with a roof garden, the world's first revolving stage and a glass train which carried royalty to their box.'

Given Edward VII's predilection for mistresses (one famously being an ancestor of Camilla, Duchess of Cornwall), I am more likely to agree with Mr Garrod who comments: 'In fact it is more likely that it was to hide the identity of the King's companion, since Bushell's description of a glass box is wrong. The photograph shows it to be of wood with small, curtained windows.' I suppose glass could have been tried at some point.

Mr Garrod adds: 'My wife was originally told about it some years ago by a long-serving member of the ENO staff who said the rails were still there under the carpet, at that time.'

Which turns out to be just as unbelievably believable as the London opera house powered by a German submarine. When the **Royal Opera** at Covent Garden was being done up in the 1990s it was decided to chuck out the old diesel engine that provided emergency power. Someone looked in to where it had come from – a member of the orchestra told me – and it turned out to have been removed from a German submarine surrendered at the end not of the Second World War but the First! For 80 years it had chuntered along at low revs whenever required and never needed repairing. German engineering, eh – better than that royal box railway...

A further disaster befell the Coliseum a week after its royal humiliation when it was decided ambitiously to stage a play about the Derby horse race on its flashy new triple-revolve stage. The plan was to use the revolving stage and real horses to recreate the great race. One of the horses fell into the orchestra pit, killing the jockey and injuring musicians. The horse had to be put down. That's why orchestra pits in the West End today have safety nets over the heads of the band in case anything else falls off stage, pantomime or real horses included.

CRACKPOT CONTRAPTIONS AND GREAT GADGETS

Londoner Maurice Collins has a deeply odd collection of weird gadgets, mostly from the Victorian era. They include a skirt-lifter, a hat-measurer and a pre-electric version of the later famous Teasmaid alarm clock, in which the clockwork sets off the alarm, pushes a lever, strikes a match on some sandpaper, lights a lamp, boils the water, pours it out and makes the tea. It's *Chitty Chitty Bang Bang* come to life, and the Muswell Hill-based enthusiast has not only mounted several exhibitions of his fascinating collection but also written books on the subject. Mind you, some are probably not that much use nowadays, such as an 1810 machine that tattoos deserters with the letter D on their foreheads, but they are all ingenious and intriguing.

Ingenious Gadgets: Guess the Obscure Purpose of Over 100 Eccentric Contraptions and *Eccentric Contraptions: An Amazing Gadgets, Gizmos and Thingamambobs*, both by Maurice Collins, are published by David & Charles, each at £9.99.

Career Eccentrics

LONDON'S ODDEST AND OLDEST JOBS

BEADLES The Burlington Arcade, an exclusive and elegant walk of shops – one daren't use such a common phrase as 'shopping mall' – off Piccadilly has uniformed Beadles who patrol the street much as they did 200 years ago. They are all tall, former army officers and their duties are to enforce the rules against singing, dancing, opening umbrellas, carrying large packages or running. But then no-one of any standing would carry large packages, would they? What an outrageous suggestion!

THE EARL MARSHAL, HEREDITARY MARSHAL OF ENGLAND Thanks to William the Conqueror, who created this job, there is always someone to lead the monarch to Parliament at State openings, to the throne at coronations and to the grave at royal funerals. The Howards, Dukes of Norfolk, have just about got used to the task as they have been doing it since 1483, so they have rather more experience of kingship than most kings have. Come to think of it, when the cartoon character Andy Capp said he was a treacle-bender (so the employment authorities couldn't ever find him a job) he might have done better to say he wanted to be Marshal of England. No chance. The Howards have somehow managed to maintain their allegiance to the Roman Catholic church through the periods when this faith was persecuted. One of their most magnificent seats has for centuries been Arundel Castle in Sussex, superbly sited to command a strategically important gap in the South Downs. By tradition, the Duke of Norfolk's eldest son is always the Earl of Arundel. One of the Earl Marshal's little-known jobs is to sit as judge in the Court of Chivalry. This court within the College of Arms has legal jurisdiction over heraldry, the titles and ranks of aristocrats, etc. It is dusted and maintained beautifully but has not been used since 1954, so it's only part time (being convened once every 50 years or so). The Earl Marshal also appoints the King of Arms.

GENTLEMAN USHER OF THE BLACK ROD, SECRETARY TO THE LORD GREAT CHAMBERLAIN & SERGEANT-AT-ARMS OF THE HOUSE OF LORDS This is a rather long-winded way of saying 'doorman' or 'usher', as in cinema usherettes: someone who ushers people in and out of places, opening or closing doors. This particular doorman (traditionally, these roles are combined) has a hell of a lot of history hanging from his short black staff, however. Edward III wanted someone to keep the Knights of the Garter in order, and mind the doors while their annual ceremonial took place at Windsor (as it does today), so an usher was appointed in 1348 and given a black rod made of blackthorn. Pay: twelve old pence a day for life (that's 5p, not allowing for inflation). While he still performs this function, Black Rod is better known for his role at the State Opening of Parliament. Here the tradition is that the Queen arrives by coach and a magnificent procession takes her into the House of Lords, where her throne awaits her. She then sends Black Rod to command the House of Commons to attend and hear her speech as to what 'my Government' has in mind for legislation. Black Rod approaches the door of the Commons, only to have it slammed shut in his face. He then beats his rod on the door with crashes that echo through the building – and presumably dent the woodwork – when he is admitted to the Commons.

He conveys the Queen's command to 'attend upon Her Majesty immediately in the House of Peers'. If she wants them immediately, why do they slam the door in her usher's face? On the answer to this question hinges a lot of blood spilled and heads chopped off, including that of Charles I, in the Civil War between king and Parliament, and the key issue of how democracy can thrive in a monarchy.

On 4 January 1642, Charles I burst into the House of Commons to arrest five Members of Parliament who had disagreed with the king and were therefore, in his opinion, treacherous. He wanted to fling them in the Tower and probably execute them. There was a convention that parliamentary privilege prevented the arrest of any elected MP, but Charles told the Speaker that this did not include treason. The MPs were outraged, and the five wanted members were nowhere to be seen. Charles demanded to know their whereabouts and the Speaker famously, and courageously, replied: 'Your Majesty, I have ears to hear and eyes to see only as this honourable House shall command me.'

A furious Charles said: 'I see all my birds have flown,' left the chamber humiliated, with MPs yelling 'privilege' at him. It was the beginning of the Civil War and years of misery, brother fighting brother, whole towns, armies, churches and castles being destroyed before things got back on an even keel with the Restoration of 1660. One of the first things Charles II did, not being a total prat like his father, was to get himself a Black Rod to summon the Commons for him. It was a lot less troublesome.

GLOVE AT FIRST SIGHT A retired haulier forked out £40,000 in 1994 for the distant prospect of the privilege of presenting the next king with a ceremonial glove at his coronation. John Hunt bought, by auction, the title of Lord of the Manor of Worksop. He therefore has this role at the next coronation; Mr Hunt will not only present the future king with a right-handed glove but will also get to support the regal right arm when the Archbishop of Canterbury hands over the heavy sceptre.

THE KING OF ARMS People who wish to use heraldry, that is coats of arms, etc, to show their titles, lineage and status on their buildings, documents, knickers, carriages or servants' liveries – I know, it's such a chore fixing your servants' liveries – depend entirely on this figure to grant their rights. Otherwise you could have all kinds of bods inventing their own titles and coats of arms, couldn't you? You know what social climbers and how pretentious the *nouveau riche* are. There are also Heralds of Arms and Pursuivants of Arms in Ordinary and Extraordinary. It gets more complex, as you would expect. There are in fact three kings of arms: the chief Garter King of Arms, named after an intimate item of ladies' underwear (see page 304); Norroy, who looks after England north of the Trent; and Clarenceaux, who looks after the south. The Heralds, whose original job was to cry out the names of knights at jousting tournaments) are fairly boringly called Richmond, Chester, Lancaster, Windsor, York and Somerset. But the four Pursuivants are given wonderful names: Blue Mantle, Rouge Croix, Rouge Dragon and Portcullis. (What do you want to be when you grow up, Jimmy? An engine driver? No, dad, Rouge Dragon.) Their quite gorgeous uniform is a tabard of velvet, silk and damask on which the royal arms are lavishly embroidered. Real coats of arms in fact.

THE LORD GREAT CHAMBERLAIN The Lord Great Chamberlain was the royal manager at the Palace of Westminster, which doesn't need him, as it's not really a palace any more, except when the monarch visits, in which case he makes the arrangements. For ceremonial occasions, he wears a golden key on his hip over his heavily embroidered red frock coat to symbolise his housekeeping role, and a sharp sword on his other side, lest the Yeomen of the Guard should miss an attempt on the monarch's life. Or possibly to kill himself if he breaks the great white stick he carries prematurely – a real possibility as he has to walk backwards with all this paraphernalia while leading the monarch to the House of Lords at the annual State Opening of Parliament. The correct time for him to break this thin 6ft-long wand is over the grave of the monarch after a royal funeral. The Lord Chamberlain, a totally different position, is by contrast the full-time manager of the royal household and hence a major employer in a multi-million pound concern. Bizarrely, the Lord Chamberlain was, until 1968, responsible for the theatre though he may not have necessarily been educated to a sufficiently high standard. If he didn't like a play, he could take it off.

PEARLY KINGS AND QUEENS, AND THE FLASHEST BOY OF ALL The Pearly Kings and Queens of London, a tradition much-beloved of cockneys, through which each district of cockney London has its own king and queen dressed in elaborate sequin-, pearl- and button-covered costumes, is an eccentric custom whose origins ought to be lost in the mists of time, started by we-know-not-whom for purposes only to be guessed at. It's that kind of tradition.

Surprisingly, its origin, originator and purpose can be precisely fixed. It's all down to orphan Henry Croft who grew up in the 19th century in Somers Town, a poor district near King's Cross. He was a small lad, born in 1862 without many prospects for the future. He left his orphanage to become a rat catcher in the Somers Town market at the age of 13. Yet he ended his life known and respected across London.

The young rat catcher soon became popular throughout the market with the market traders, or costermongers as they were then known (they knew the coster this, the coster that). Now this is the vital bit. Some costermongers wore special outfits – the 'flash boys' – to make themselves stand out from the others. If you got a good cucumber and a smile from the one with the top hat, say, you'd go there next time. Some of the 'flash boys' would sew pearl buttons down their sleeves or whatever – it became a kind of uniform.

Henry Croft had a brainwave. He'd help all the boys left back in the orphanage by making them a lot of money and he'd do it by being the flashest flash boy ever – he'd completely cover a suit with pearly buttons. It took ages to make, but when he appeared at the local fair, people flocked round him to marvel at him, and the costermongers rallied round to his cause. He became so much in demand for charity fund-raising that soon every borough had its own Pearly King and Queen. By the time Henry died in 1930 he'd collected a fortune for charity. His funeral procession to Finchley, where he is buried, was enormous. The entire Pearly monarchy – some 400 kings and queens – followed the hearse and the occasion made front-page news around the world, as well as going on cinema newsreels.

The tradition thrives with an annual pearly harvest festival on the first Sunday in October which brings them all to St Martin-in-the-Fields church where Henry's statue is displayed, having been vandalised in Finchley in 1995. Most London parades, carnivals and fêtes that might not attract the regular Queen of England will feature a Pearly King or Queen, the titles being handed down within families. The Somers Town Pearly Queen at the time of writing, for example, is Henry Croft's great-granddaughter.

QUEEN'S REMEMBRANCER A shadowy figure involved in various duties such as collecting ancient and bizarre quit rents for ancient properties which no-one can, er, remember, any more. A quit rent is a service or tribute payable when payments of a normal cash rent have been avoided, let off, or forgotten. It's totally and wonderfully absurd. See page 308.

QUEEN'S SWAN MARKER Almost all swans in Britain are royal birds in that they belong to the Queen. There are heavy penalties for harming them, in theory: a year and a day in jail for stealing a swan's egg, and if one is killed, the miscreant must pour sufficient grain on the dead swan, hung from a ceiling vertically, to cover it completely. This grain could then be used to feed live swans, presumably. Personally, considering that when a yob kills a swan, its partner must live alone and palely loitering (because swans mate for life), I'd string the yobs up by their beaks too. Quite why the Queen owns swans is debatable: certainly people used to eat them. Perhaps it's because the lovely bird is simply the grandest in the kingdom and deserves some special protection. But being Britain, things don't stop there, not by a very long chalk.

The Queen's Swan Marker, with his splendid red uniform and a crook on the end of a long pole for catching them by the neck, supervises the astoundingly old and mind-bogglingly complex ceremony known as 'Swan Upping'. This is all down to Edward IV being in money trouble in the 15th century. He had to borrow some money quickly from the wealthy Dyers and Vintners companies in the City, and the price of the 1473 deal was that the Dyers and Vintners could own some of the swans on the Thames.

The trouble was that swans tend to have little swans, or cygnets rather, and the nit-picking ninnies in charge decided these, too, needed to be divided into those belonging to the monarch and those belonging to the Dyers and Vintners. So it is that more than 500 years later, once a year an unbelievable procession of six rowing boats sets off from Sunbury up the Thames towards Abingdon.

Some of these boats are controlled by the Queen's Swan Marker and his swanherds (you just couldn't make it up), and others by the Swan Wardens of the Worshipful Company of Dyers (ditto Vintners). The Royal Swanherd's boat looks particularly fab with two grand flags, the one in the bows with the Queen's initials (her signet, one could say) and a crown upon it so that any oiks swanning about on the river know he is a big cheese, and one at the stern depicting a swan with raised wings. The other boats are allowed only one flag each.

Their task, undertaken with utmost seriousness and requiring great skill to avoid injuries to bird and swan wardens, is to capture these strong and sometimes angry birds, determine the ownership from previous marks in their beaks and mark the offspring accordingly. So it's not just a case of: 'This swan's for you, mate.'

Now the Dyers' birds get one nick in their beaks and the Vintners' get two nicks, punched out rather as railway tickets used to be punched by inspectors. If a mixed marriage, as it were, has taken place, then half are marked with one mark and half with the other. By the way, if you see the funny-sounding pub name The Swan With Two Necks, it comes from two *nicks*. Probably a South African involved at some point. Come to think of it setting a black Australian swan on the river could ruffle a few feathers.

What about the Queen's swans? Well they need no marks as the law states they obviously belong to the monarch, and very majestic they look too. It is possible, by a 540-year-old law, for a person to own the swans on a closed lake or pond within his land (provided the land is worth at least five marks, whatever that is), but not on open water. These are all royal birds.

The whole process takes at least a week and involves not a few visits to the riverside pubs. The former cygnet pies and swan banquets are no longer eaten, as the whole thing is seen as some sort of conservation effort nowadays. But one tradition is upheld: As they pass Windsor Castle the Swan Markers propose a toast: 'To Her Majesty the Queen Seigneur of the Swans.'

In 1947 a member of the Labour government, dedicated to soaking the rich and helping the working classes, asked why on earth the state paid £600 a year – then a good salary – for someone to look after the King's swans, who could perfectly well look after themselves. Poor, naïve fool … as if ancient British traditions need any point to them.

ROYAL RAVENSMASTER His job, at the Tower of London, is to make sure these creatures are content and not likely, by virtue of clipped wings, to leave the Tower. If they ever do, legend has it, catastrophe will strike England.

SEARCHER OF THE SANCTUARY & HIGH BAILIFF OF WESTMINSTER ABBEY The medieval Abbey owned considerable lands nearby, much of it, such as Soho, wild countryside – London was still confined to the City and Westminster was a completely separate place. Certain religious sites were able to offer inviolable sanctuary, for a limited time, for those accused of various crimes. Part of the Abbey's lands were deemed sanctuary, particularly the side towards what is now Horseferry Road and the river. However, if the usual authorities had no jurisdiction here, the Abbey needed to act in their place; hence the job of the Searcher of the Sanctuary was to check through all the sanctuary-seeking miscreants, fugitives, wronged innocents and murderous types to make sure they didn't overstay their welcome. But the concept was abused and gradually the sanctuary, originating as an expression of holiness and mercy, became ironically an area of debauchery, prostitution, gambling and murder known as 'the Devil's acre'. This was an irony much repeated south of the river in Southwark (see page 196), but there is still a red-robed Searcher of the Sanctuary and High Bailiff, just in case you should loiter too long in the cloisters for the wrong reasons. More on Westminster Abbey, page 111.

SILVER STICK IN WAITING Another of those curious ceremonial posts for courtiers, often ex-army, such as Brigadier Andrew Parker Bowles, the man who famously laid down his wife for his country. He shared the anguish of Diana, Princess of Wales, that Prince Charles was more attached to Mrs Camilla Parker Bowles. In

5

The *Cutty Sark*, dry-docked at Greenwich, is immortalised for sail-lovers round the world as the epitome of the great British tea clippers, her rig a thing of beauty. Which is ironic as she carried tea for less than ten years and was in fact Portuguese with ugly, much cut-down rigging for much of her sea-going history.

Launched in 1869 at Dumbarton on the Clyde, the *Cutty Sark* was designed to win the annual race to get the new tea harvest home from the Orient. She had a new hull design that promised well, and 11 miles of rigging carrying enough sail to cover 11 tennis courts.

Her first Master said: 'I never sailed a finer ship. At 10 or 12 knots she did not disturb the water at all. She was the finest ship of her day, a grand ship, and a ship that will last for ever.'

Her strange name refers to Burns's poem *Tam O'Shanter*, based on a Scottish folk story. Farmer Tam came across three dancing witches in a churchyard one night and one of them, Nannie, was young and beautiful, dancing brilliantly and wearing a cutty sark (a short chemise). Tam made the mistake of cheering her and as the three witches turned on him he galloped away. As his horse leapt a stream – witches cannot cross running water – Nannie grabbed part of the horse's tail. So it was that the figurehead of the *Cutty Sark* was Nannie; even today grasps a tail of horse's hair.

But the *Cutty Sark* came into service just as the Suez Canal was about to open and as the new steamships, which didn't have to rely on unpredictable winds, came into prominence. She carried her last tea in 1877, switching to the Australian wool trade. This was when her elegant hull made the world-record runs for sailing ships.

By 1895 she was losing money again, so was sold to the Portuguese whose crews nicknamed her *Pequina Camisola* (little shirt). She worked hard for them, with her rigging cut down after a storm in the Indian Ocean dismasted her. In 1920 she came back to Surrey Docks, near Greenwich, for repairs; before her return to Portugal she was blown into Falmouth by a gale – with unforeseeable consequences.

There a chance encounter changed her history. She was spotted riding at anchor by Cornish seafarer Captain Wilfred Dowman, who as a young sailor 25 years before had seen her slicing through the water under full sail, the finest sight he'd ever seen. That breathtaking vision had made such an impression on him that he bought her from the Portuguese, refitted and rerigged her and once again hoisted the Red Ensign. After a spell as a training ship, by 1951 she was again surplus and sat, unused, at a mooring off Greenwich.

Fund-raising by her now many fans, not least of whom wasthe royal sailor, the Duke of Edinburgh, started in earnest; by 1954 she had moved into her own dry dock where she lies today. Millions of people have since boarded her to examine this , the last of the great tea clippers, and a great collection of ship's figureheads. But no witches.

fact this kind of carry on was totally normal for British royals until around 100 years ago, historians will tell you.

AND THE VILEST JOB IN LONDON... Mortuary assistants and bomb disposal experts? No, it's having to clean the grids in the sewers of a kind of congealed waxy stuff consisting of fat poured down the drains from restaurants blended with human excrement.

6

Dead Eccentric London

LONDON, MORE DEAD THAN ALIVE

THE MACABRE PROBLEM London, more dead than alive, has been literally true at certain points in the city's history. The Black Death of 1348, having marched steadily across Asia and Europe, landed at Dorset and, when it reached the capital, swept through the overcrowded, unsanitary medieval city and killed perhaps 30,000 here. There were not enough living to bury the dead properly, so plague pits were dug and corpses cast in them willy-nilly – then the plague went away for no particular reason.

In 1665, bubonic plague returned, with its grotesque symptoms of swelling under the arms, black patches on the skin and fairly rapid death for most of those infected. Still people didn't understand it was the rats carrying fleas which caused it, for when the rats died the fleas in desperation turned to human fodder. The churchyards were so 'stuft with corpses,' wrote clergyman Dr Thomas Vincent, 'that they are in many places swell'd two or three feet higher than they were before.'

This wasn't enough, as 68,576 died by official figures; the actual total was almost certainly far more than that. Again, plague pits were used. You may have walked over some while strolling round the City of London. There was no time for coffins. Cartloads of people, Defoe writes in his *Journal of the Plague Year*, were shot semi-naked into heaps, rich and poor, young and old alike.

So, when the Great Fire of 1666 helped kill off the plague, London's graveyards were full to bursting. Things got worse for the next 150 years. That picturesque bulge of the churchyard above the level of the paths takes on a sinister appearance: Dickens notes this several times, at St Peter on Cornhill, for example. Some churchyard walls were being overtopped, some complained, as the freshly dead were being shoved in on to the hardly decayed.

It is said that the tiny churchyard of St Martin-in-the-Fields somehow absorbed more than 60,000 bodies. There is a notice at the top of the crypt stairs at this church that reads:

> Ordered that in future no Graves be Dug in any of the Vaults under the Church as a Practice thereof will be Prejudicial to and in time endanger the Foundation of said Church and also ordered at a Vestry Held the 31 Day of March 1774 that in future no corps be buried in any of the Vaults under the church but what are in leaden Coffins.

Inside the churches, where once only the rich and powerful were buried, the dead were increasingly jammed, with flagstones and pews going awry as the coffins and graves gradually collapsed. The middle classes were scandalised: Pepys wrote of going to see the gravedigger about his brother's funeral in 1664:

> But to see how a man's tombs are at the mercy of such a fellow, that for sixpence he would (as his own words were): 'I will jostle them together but I will make room for him,' speaking of the fullness of the middle aisle, where he was to lie.

By the 19th century, the living London poor were stealing coffin wood from recent burials for fuel. Human bones from paupers' graves were being shipped north and ground up for fertiliser. Fresh bodies could always find ready takers, if not undertakers, for use in anatomy classes, and for rich rewards; crooked clerics could sell the bodies of the dead at one gate and their broken-up coffins for firewood at another. The dead were crowding out the living in London.

By the 19th century, Parliament was told in medical evidence presented to it that piles of decomposing bodies were crammed into the vaults of churches just under the feet of living worshippers. At last, in the can-do Victorian era, something radical was done, just as freshwater pipes and sewerage systems were built in that era to improve the city's public health too. These latter measures sharply reduced the pressure on the graveyards by curbing outbreaks of cholera and similar diseases, so that the great graveyard crisis passed – for the time being.

RADICAL SOLUTIONS
Cities of the dead and the fascinating people who reside there
Parliament decided massive new private cemeteries on an unprecedented scale on the fringes of London would provide the answer, and these were built at places such as Highgate, West Brompton (see page 165), Kensal Green, West Norwood, and further out of town still, linked to the capital by an extraordinary railway for the dead, the massive Brookwood cemetery (see below). One of the key figures in all this was Sir Edwin Chadwick (1800–90) who campaigned tirelessly to stop the stuffing of bodies into the bulging churchyards and under the floors of churches. His publication, *The Practice of Interment in Towns*, did much to promote the properly laid out cemetery as an alternative. Ironically, he is laid out in the Old Mortlake Cemetery in South Worple Way, not a particularly good example of what he was on about. But the commercially run cemeteries – shocking, said the clergy, who had been making money out of the death business for years – soon became extremely fashionable, with their sweeping drives, massive tombs, impressive monuments, neatly gravelled paths and leafy green spaces. They put life back into gravedigging. Below are some of the best, well worth a visit for the greenery and wildlife as well as the fascinating monuments to some of our greatest ancestors, after two radical ideas the Victorians considered for the dead.

Brookwood and a death railway
One of the Victorians' solutions to the 19th-century problem of London's literally bulging cemeteries was the macabrely fascinating London Necropolis Railway which started running to Brookwood in Surrey in 1854.

It was exclusive, in that you only travelled once and then only in one direction. The service was run mainly for the dead, so the 'coffin tickets' issued right up until the 1950s were not available as returns. Funeral trains to Brookwood ran from the discreet London Necropolis station adjoining Waterloo (in fact jammed right next to a turntable for locomotives), where steam power hoists would raise coffins to the level of the hearse vans. In the spirit of the age, these vans were segregated between Anglicans and the rest, as were the mourners' waiting rooms and carriages. In later years, the entrance to the London Necropolis station was marked by a discreet stone-built entrance. Everything was done to maintain dignity and avoid the view, expressed by the Bishop of London when the scheme was first floated, that it was improper to convey corpses by anything as fast as a steam train.

At Brookwood, a part of Woking, a vast city of the dead was laid out with every possible nationality and creed catered for; judging by the number of graves marked 'resting' or 'fell asleep', waking Woking might still be a possibility. If today you take the pleasant and fascinating walk along the route of the long siding into which these mournful trains were directed, reversing back from Brookwood station, to two smaller but truly terminal stations (one Anglican, one for the rest), many interesting things will come to light.

Such as why the further station is now home to Orthodox monks, incongruously established with their chickens on a former platform for the dead in deepest Surrey. (They are venerating the relics of the English King Edward the Martyr, an important saint for them, in the nearby special chapel.) There is a fascinating collection of people to discover who finally met their Waterloo, as it were, at Brookwood, so a stroll round makes a happy day out, if you like that sort of thing. There are sections here for every kind of religion and every sort of dead.

Freddie Mercury, rock star of Queen, was born in exotic Zanzibar but ended his days at Brookwood; the deeply eccentric explorer Gottlieb Leitner (see my book *Eccentric Britain*) is responsible for there being a mosque the other side of Woking station; Turkish aviators killed in World War I; American sailors; the feminist author Rebecca West (of whom more on page 275). Great people – but dead people. There is a fascinating book on the subject of this forgotten death railway (see booklist, page 313). Brookwood also pioneered cremation.

🚇 Brookwood (from London Waterloo).

The perils of pyramid selling: five million dead in the sky
One really radical solution for getting rid of London's dead not pursued at the time of the 19th-century crisis was Thomas Willson's pyramid, proposed in 1829. Unlike the pharaoh's pyramid, or indeed the many fascinating smaller ones scattered around the English countryside, Willson's vast pyramid wasn't designed for just one person. It was to accommodate *five million*.

It would have dominated the view from almost every point in London, just as Canary Wharf does today. It was to have been taller than St Paul's and was to have a huge obelisk set on its summit. The vaults would have been brick arches arranged on 94 floors and the whole thing was to be faced with granite. Steam-powered lifts would have been included, but this was not a place in which the poor would have ended up: the cost of a family vault would have been prohibitive.

The profits, had the scheme gone ahead and received public support, would have been many millions of pounds. I can't quite see people visiting the dead up in the skies of north London, somehow, but it would have been a fabulous landmark. In the end Parliament went for the underground option with the massive new cemeteries listed here.

WHERE TO FIND SOME GREAT DEAD PEOPLE

WEST NORWOOD
🚇 *West Norwood, then up Norwood High Street to the north a little and on the right*
Norwood has many claims to fame, such as being the temporary home of impressionist painter Camille Pissarro during the Franco-Prussian War. Or being where I got into an X-rated film at the Norwood Regal when aged about 13 by the odd trick of inserting penny chews in the heels of my shoes until I looked old enough. You can come unstuck like that, you know. But the dead of Norwood are far more interesting. Here lie people who really changed our lives – making them sweeter, tastier, shorter and noisier.

There's **Sir Henry Tate** (1819–99), whose sugar sweetened the Empire, and whose golden syrup still bears that macabre image of bees feeding on a dead lion ('out of sweetness came forth strength', as if golden syrup were made from honey). He collected a good few pictures and founded the Tate Gallery which replaced the notorious Millbank Prison in Pimlico on the Thames. His marketing of cube sugar created the sugar tong industry and it was soon popular all over the world. The eventual merger with someone called '& Lyle' made one of those enduring partnerships like Marks & Spencer or Burke & Hare and gave a lifetime's work to thousands of dentists.

One who doubtless increased the demand for his products, **Mrs Beeton,** as in her *Book of Household Management*, is also here. One imagines her – well I did, anyway – as a stuffy, fussy old matron, in which case one is completely wrong, as her grave shows she died aged a mere 28 in 1865 and was a lively (until that point, obviously) young journalist who published her book as a serial in *The Englishwoman's Domestic Magazine*. A classic case of confusing the messenger and the message. You can't imagine either such a book or magazine being great successes nowadays, but they certainly were then, luckily for her husband, publisher Sam Beeton.

Sir Henry Bessemer (1813–98) changed our lives more than many people realise. Until he perfected his Bessemer process for steel-making, it was more than 100 times slower and far more expensive to make a decent bit of steel. Mass production of this useful metal made possible stronger bridges and railways, ships, cars, fridges and cookers, skyscrapers and all kinds of tools that we now take for granted. He has many a school and road named after him, but then he created much of the modern world.

Dedicated to shortening lives in the most efficient way possible was **Sir Hiram Steven Maxim** (1840–1916), Maine-born inventor of the Maxim gun, plus various military fuses and gunpowders. His primitive machine-gun was good enough to fill quite a few cemeteries in its time.

KENSAL GREEN As I said in my remarks on Wormwood Scrubs, this cemetery, in between the Great Western main line, the West Coast main line and the West London line, is a superb site for the graves of those great London engineers, **Isambard Kingdom Brunel** (creator of the Great Western Railway and much else) and his father **Marc Isambard Brunel** (who built the first tunnel under the Thames). But there's much more to discover in this cemetery which, oddly, has a working canal running alongside it.

There's that chum of Charles Dickens, lawyer-turned-author **Wilkie Collins** (1824–89), who just about invented the detective story and is most remembered for *The Woman in White* and *The Moonstone*. Here too is **Anthony Trollope** (1815–82), writer of the *Barsetshire Chronicles*, the first of which is *The Warden*. He

TAKING A GRAVE EXCEPTION

There's nothing so funny as when a pompous inscription on a grave is wrong. One such is in Westminster Abbey where a slab proclaims gushingly, 'O rare Ben Johnson'. Rare indeed, as everyone else spells it Jonson (unless one is talking about the runner disgraced at the Seoul Olympics, Ben Johnson, not an obvious candidate for Poets' Corner). Or did the stonecarver leave a gap in the Latin word 'Orare', making it 'Pray for Ben Johnson', in which case was he doubly careless in following his instructions?

Elizabethan dramatist Jonson, playwright of *The Alchemist*, is buried upright under here just a stone's throw from where he was educated at Westminster School. And knowing that lot, the stone was probably thrown.

Jonson was always poor, and there is said to have been a conversation between the Dean of the Abbey in which the Dean asked if Jonson had ambitions to be buried in Poets' Corner. Jonson replied: 'I am too poor for that and no-one will lay out funeral charges upon me. No, sir, six feet long by two feet wide is too much for me: two feet by two feet will do for all I want.' 'You shall have it,' said the Dean. There would have been no mark at all of the grave (in fact in the north aisle) had Jack Young not been walking past when the paving stone was being tapped back into place and asked whose grave it was. He gave the stonemason 18 pence to carve the name (wrongly, as it turned out). Later the stone was moved to a wall, where it may be seen, but the grave itself is marked by a small grey stone.

A macabre confirmation of the fact that Jonson was buried standing up came in 1849 when an adjoining burial was being made. Jonson's two legs, or rather the bones of them, were seen sticking into the sand, and a skull rolled down with some red hair visible. It was stuffed back. Alas, poor Jonson, Shakespeare knew him well.

Mind you, how many playwrights can have had Shakespeare in his opening night cast, as Jonson did with *Every Man In His Humour* in 1598? Rare indeed.

had previously been a civil servant with the General Post Office and invented the pillar box.

Here, too, although lost in undergrowth when I looked, is **William Makepeace Thackeray** (don't those Victorian names just roll off your tongue?). Thackeray (1811–63), born in Calcutta, wrote *Vanity Fair* (1847), still much read and recently televised, having dabbled in law and journalism. He wrote regularly for *Punch* and other magazines.

There's also **Charles Babbage** (1792–1871), the inventor of the world's first computer (he called them 'analytical engines' – see Science Museum, for what happened to his brain, see next page), and the last man you'd expect to find here dead of natural causes, **Charles Blondin** (1824–97), the world's greatest ever tightrope walker. It was French-born Blondin who not only astonished the world by crossing Niagara Falls on a tightrope, but who did it again blindfold. Pushing a wheelbarrow, on stilts, in a sack, stopping midway to fry an omelette. He was a great hit in London, performing at the Crystal Palace. Perhaps his greatest feat was persuading a man to be carried on his back across that Niagara rope – would you have done it for him?

For **Brompton Cemetery** at Earl's Court and its fascinating inhabitants, see page 165.

IT'S COOL TO BE CREMATED: GOLDERS GREEN CREM There's one seriously cool place to be cremated, if that's possible, and that's Golders Green Crematorium, pioneer in the once shocking art of taking that ashes to ashes stuff rather literally.

A controversial exhibition at London's Serpentine Gallery in 1995 included, beside a totally naked actress sleeping in a box, the pickled brain of mathematician **Charles Babbage** (1792–1871). Babbage's brilliant ideas on devising calculating machines in the early 19th century laid the groundwork for today's computers more than a century before such machines were actually made to work. But the bizarre preservation of his brain – it normally resides at the Royal College of Surgeons of England – isn't at all unique.

Not far away, the embalmed body of philosopher **Jeremy Bentham** (1748–1832) sits in state within a glass case in University College, Gower Street. In the 19th century his head was replaced with a replica, as disrespectful students had the macabre habit of playing football with the real thing, even if this followed his famed principle of utiliarianism – matters should be arranged to be useful for 'the greatest happiness of the greatest number' (astonishingly, no-one had thought of this before). Well at least he made a few football-crazy students happy.

People get very pompous when writing their wills and Bentham was no exception. He directed how his body was to be displayed in great detail:

> …my executor will cause the skeleton to be clad in one of the suits of black
> occasionally worn by me. The body so clothed shall together with the chair and staff
> in my later years bourne by me he will take charge of and for containing the whole
> apparatus he will cause to be prepared an appropriate box or case and will cause to
> be engraved in conspicuous characters on a plate to be fixed thereon and also on
> labels on the glass cases in which the preparation of the soft parts of my body will be
> preserved … etc etc'

Not only does this suggest the eccentric Bentham's lectures might in real life have been less than riveting, but that he had that delusion of the self-appointed great and the good that the world's fascination with them cannot possibly end with their death. Does that remind us of anyone today?

Neither has Lord Protector **Oliver Cromwell's** (1599–1658) head had a restful time in the three centuries since it was ripped from his remains in the 1660 Restoration and impaled on a pole at Westminster Hall. It supposedly blew down in a storm and was buried in various places, being dug up again by various pro- or anti-royalists, before ending up in the grounds of Sidney Sussex College, Cambridge. Its location is unmarked in case Royalists, still angry after all those years at his part in chopping off another head, that of King Charles I, dig it up again.

Another head which had an unsettling end was that of Catholic martyr **Bishop St John Fisher** (1485–1540), executed at the Tower, and whose head, a witness said:

> being parboiled, was pricked upon a pole and set high on London Bridge. And here I
> cannot omit to declare unto you the miraculous sight of this head which stood up to
> the space of 14 days upon the bridge… daily it grew fresher and fresher, so that in his
> lifetime he never looked so well, for his cheeks being beautified by a comely red.

If they'd left it up any longer, he would have started preaching.

Actually Brookwood (see page 58) pioneered the idea, but Golders Green with its proximity to Hampstead had a ready supply of free-thinking agnostic or atheistic radicals who didn't go along with grave burial, such as **Sigmund Freud**, father of psychoanalysis. ('Sigmund Fraud he should have been called,' a great psychiatrist told me. 'It's amazing that half America goes along with this stuff which is about as scientific as astrology.' Typical Piscean.)

As the underground became unfashionable with the dead North London intelligentsia, so Golders Green became their favourite last stop. Around 300,000 cremations have been carried out here, and the advantage is that the place can never become full.

Among those who went up the chimney here at Britain's busiest crematorium are the following:

- WRITERS: Children's writer **Enid Blyton** (1897–1968), creator of Noddy and much loathed by some North London literati whom she outsold by millions; the creator of Dracula, **Bram Stoker** – jolly good name for a crematorium, really – (1847–1912); **Kingsley Amis** (1922–95), splendidly curmudgeonly creator of great novels such as *Lucky Jim*; sexologist **Havelock Ellis** (1859–1939), whose books were as likely to be burned as he was; **Rudyard Kipling** (1865–1936), writer of Britain's favourite poem for many years, *If*, creator of the *Jungle Book* and chronicler of the Empire.
- COMPOSERS: **Sir Arthur Bliss** (1891–1975); **Eric Coates** (1886–1957), who wrote the *Dambuster's March*; **Ralph Vaughan Williams** (1872–1958), composer of the *London Symphony*. Well at least they're not decomposing.
- DANCERS: Modern dance exponent **Dame Marie Rambert** (1888–1982), who has a blue plaque in Kensington's Campden Hill Gardens; ballerina **Anna Pavlova** (1885–1931), who, like Nellie Melba, was immortalised in a pudding, and was also good at dying swans. Australia and New Zealand both think 'Pav' is their own national dish and unless you like wearing cream and meringue, don't venture an opinion when Down Under.
- SCIENTISTS: **Sir Alexander Fleming** (1881–1955), whose chance discovery of penicillin saved more lives than anyone else in the last century; **Sir James Dewar** (1842–1923), who proved life was a picnic, by inventing the Thermos flask; **Sir Bernard Spilsbury** (1877–1947), the brilliant pathologist who detected the undetectable by discovering the means by which Dr Crippen poisoned his wife. Ironically, in depression, he poisoned himself in his laboratory.
- COMEDIANS: **Peter Sellers** (1925–80), original Goon, Dr Strangelove and creator of Inspector 'Ees it a beumb?' Clouseau; **Tommy Handley** (1892–1949), the man behind the radio smash-hit *ITMA*.

And that's just a selection of the luminaries who have added to the atmosphere – literally – of this special corner of North London. There is no charge for admission; guided tours are sometimes available.

TOOTING'S ODD LINK WITH GANGLAND There were at least two Charles Wilsons in London in the past 40 years, and it was a good idea not to get the two mixed up. One was a Glaswegian editor of *The Times*. The other was a member of the notorious Great Train Robbery gang, who brilliantly yet ruthlessly coshed their way to several million quid on a mail train in 1963. They faked a red signal for the Glasgow–Euston train, slugged the driver and moved the train to where they could unload the mailbags. This **Charlie Wilson** did his time in jail before coming to a sticky end in 1990 in his retirement in Spain. He was murdered by some low life. If you are fascinated by British gangster chic – and the film industry certainly is – you can pay your respects at Streatham Cemetery, Tooting, about half a mile up Garratt Lane from Tooting Broadway Tube. By the way, the star of the TV quiz show *The Weakest Link*, a hit on both sides of the Atlantic, the suitably snooty Anne Robinson, was first married to one of these Charlie Wilsons. It was the rough, tough ruthless one from the gangland city whom no-one dared cross. Yes, the

Perhaps the oddest case of its kind concerns a woman who never reached her grave at all. When the first wife of the king of 18th-century eccentrics, Martin van Butchell, died in 1775, he had her embalmed with turpentine and camphor, fitted with glass eyes, coloured to appear lifelike and mounted in a display case in the front room of his Mayfair home. She was wearing full wedding dress and van Butchell charged the public to see her.

Van Butchell, who made a fortune supplying dentures and trusses to the gentry, although qualified in neither field, refused to visit his rich clients despite, in one case, being sent a horse and carriage and the small fortune of 500 guineas. On the other hand, he regularly visited Newgate jail to treat prisoners free of charge.

His bizarre preservation of his first wife's corpse may have been brought on by her will stating that her fortune was to go to a distant relative 'the moment I am dead and buried'. She had been offered, incidentally, the choice of wearing black or white for the rest of her life on her wedding day – she chose black – and when van Butchell married his second wife (his maid Elizabeth – perhaps so he had no longer to pay her a wage), she chose white.

Still the first wife was not buried. In 1815 van Butchell's son Edmund offered the body to the Royal College of Surgeons. There she remained unburied until blown to bits by a Nazi bomb in the Blitz of 1941. From dust to dust …

newspaper editor. Miss Robinson, now on her second marriage, rather seems to thrive on bitchy comments. The BBC's own website promoting her show called her: 'A cross between Cruella de Vil and Hitler's mother, a dominatrix, a bossy school ma'am, the Creature from the Black Lagoon, and a PoW camp commandant.' Nice …

CITY: ST GHASTLY GRIM AND PEPYS AT THE PAST The ghastliest gate in London is definitely that at St Olave's in Hart Street, EC3. It is grimly festooned with skulls, bones and spikes. The records show this slightly predates, oddly, the churchyard being used for mass burials of 326 people in the Great Plague of 1665.

The explanation is that intimations of mortality, death and decay were then acceptable ornaments and even regarded as a good thing for concentrating the minds of the living on the hereafter. Many a 17th- and 18th-century grave showed Death carrying his scythe, hourglasses running out, skulls, and warnings such as 'Tempus fugit, vita brevis' – 'Time flies, but life is short'.

Further, there's always a certain attraction in repulsion. To quote Dickens, who used St Olave's for a fictional location in *The Uncommercial Traveller*:

> It is a small churchyard, with a ferocious strong spiked iron gate, like a jail. This gate is ornamented with skulls and crossbones, larger than life, wrought in stone; but it likewise came into the mind of Saint Ghastly Grim, that to stick iron spikes a-top of

the stone skulls, as though they were impaled, would be a pleasant device. Therefore the skulls grin aloft horribly, thrust through and through with iron spears. Hence, there is attraction of repulsion for me in Saint Ghastly Grim.

Among those buried here at St Ghastly Grim – I mean St Olave's – is the great diarist Samuel Pepys. He – a ghastly character himself when you get to know him – had his own pew erected so he didn't have to mix with hoi polloi.

HIGHGATE: FREEZE, PARTNER! PRESERVING THE DEAD
Highgate Cemetery, in two sections either side of Swains Lane, is renowned for its rambling Victoriana, celebrity dead and for the kitsch of death – there's a piano tomb – and for the tomb of **Karl Marx**. But Highgate's oddest death was surely that of Elizabethan philosopher, writer, politician and scientist, and some say real author of Shakespeare's plays, **Francis Bacon**.

Bacon, a former Lord Chancellor in the government, was out in a coach with some friends one snowy morning in 1626 when at the top of Highgate Hill he made the coachman stop. He had had a brainwave and wanted to conduct an experiment and, typically, thought there and then the best time for it. He bought a hen from a poor woman in a nearby hovel, disembowelled it, then stuffed the body with snow. He had a strange new idea, laughable to his friends, that freezing could preserve meat.

Unfortunately it was soon a case of frozen Bacon as much as chicken. He fell ill and was taken to the Earl of Arundel's House nearby. There they put him in a bed but it was a damp bed not used for a year or so, and Bacon caught pneumonia and soon died. Hence Bacon's Lane here next to the cemetery in Highgate, and hence, eventually, a whole new industry for people like Mr Clarence Birdseye. There is no record of whether the chicken did, in fact, keep well.

Meanwhile Highgate Cemetery has acquired a seriously spooky atmosphere, and has often been associated with occultism. Tombs have been broken into and bones removed for weird rituals and once, in the 1960s, a local resident opened his car door to find an exhumed corpse in the passenger seat. Not my idea of a joke. By day it has some fabulous monuments to examine and is well worth a visit.

The architecture in the well-laid out grounds is extraordinary. At the top of Egyptian Avenue there is a street of the dead called the Circle of Lebanon. Little family houses line this grassy road with half a dozen people in each. Dead ones, that is.

Famous residents also include **Douglas Adams**, of *Hitchhiker's Guide*, novelist **George Eliot**, scientist **Michael Faraday** and Leftie writer and *Private Eye* stalwart **Paul Foot**.

A STRANGE BREADFRUIT IN LAMBETH
In the eastern part of Lambeth churchyard there is a strange tomb surmounted by a stone breadfruit. Few passers-by suppose that this is the last resting place of the survivor of the Royal Navy's most famous mutiny, Captain Bligh. The tomb mentions that one **William Bligh** who died in 1817 'first transplanted the bread fruit tree from Otahette to the West Indies' and 'bravely fought the battles of his country'. Nothing about a mutiny, then.

Without retelling the whole story which was the basis for the Charles Laughton and later Marlon Brando films *Mutiny on the Bounty*, Bligh may not have been the tyrant Hollywood supposed. In any case his feat in 1879 in navigating a 23ft open boat with 18 loyal sailors across 4,000 miles of the empty Pacific to Tonga and safety in 47 days was unsurpassed even by Shackleton. In fact he faced a second mutiny when Governor of New South Wales – the Rum Rebellion of 1808 (of which he was also absolved of blame). So the tomb should mention mutinies,

London's oddest memorial is a tree in Barnes. It is the one pop star Marc Bolan hit in his Mini in 1976, causing his untimely death. Unlike, say, Jimi Hendrix who died not far away, he didn't become a much bigger star after his death than before. But nevertheless the flowers, photos and loving messages tied to his tree loyally almost every single day since make this London's most enduring and extraordinary unofficial memorial. The effect is a little spoilt by the crash barrier in front of the tree, but given its history, I suppose that's understandable.

There is no footpath on that side of this fast and narrow road, so view the tree from the opposite side unless you wish to join Mr Bolan, formerly of T-Rex, prematurely. Bolan's body was taken to Golders Green crematorium in northwest London, last venue of many a British star of stage and screen; he was joined by Keith Moon of The Who only two years later.

In fact the far side of what was for a long time a place of informal, spontaneous tribute, approached by a path from Gipsy Lane, now has a proper marble memorial and a better view than the main road side. When Marc Bolan's fans aren't putting flowers on this memorial they're sometimes listening to a tribute band featuring, bizarrely, his son Rolan Bolan.

For a while some local people resented the T-Rex pilgrims turning up and there was even a sacrilegious attempt to hack down the tree in question. The great headline writer Willy 'Three Puddings' Bloch punningly headed a paragraph about this 'Tree Wrecks'. Insensitive, some fans may feel, but brilliant in its way.

---

plural. But in 1792, he had successfully transferred the breadfruit from Tahiti to the West Indies and like the sailor who took the rubber plant to Malaya, or the potato to Ireland, its usefulness was huge, so his tomb is rightly decorated with a stone breadfruit.

GONE FOR A BURTON IN DEEPEST MORTLAKE The most eccentric tomb in London must be that of **Richard Burton**. Not the Richard Burton who kept marrying Elizabeth Taylor – admittedly eccentric behaviour in itself – but the great explorer who opened up the vast and unknown lands of Arabia to the eyes of an enchanted Western world. Thus, a full-scale Arab sheik's tent – complete with stone folds of cloth frozen in mid-flap of a desert breeze as if touched by a Narnian witch's wand – stands somewhat incongruously in a sleepy corner of suburban Mortlake.

Aptly, finding Burton's mausoleum is something of an exploration in itself. It is not in the vast municipal Mortlake cemetery, nor in the graveyard of the confusingly named St Mary the Virgin church fronting Mortlake High Street near the Thames. But behind there, through a labyrinth of paths such as Tinderbox Alley lined by Victorian cottages, lies St Mary Magdalen, a Catholic church, where the extraordinary monument can be found by following a well-worn track through the undergrowth.

Close up, one can see an iron star romantically hidden in the foliage above the tent, a well-over-the-top valedictory poem typical of the era and, behind the tomb, its most fascinating aspect: a window in the tent's roof with a handy steel ladder enabling one to peer at the coffins of Burton and his wife surrounded by some of their favourite objects from his explorations, along with some well-withered wreaths, a century of dust and decrepitude having failed to spoil the oddly cosy, domestic scene.

More prosaically, Sir Richard's fascinating tomb is very easy to reach by public transport: opposite the church gates runs the line from Waterloo to Mortlake. Walk back towards Barnes on the north side of the tracks, to find the man somehow always on the wrong side of the tracks for Victorian Britain (see his biography in my book *Eccentric Britain*). Or take a 209 bus from Hammersmith almost to the church gate and walk a bit further alongside the railway. By car, you need North Worple Way from the level crossing in White Hart Lane, Mortlake.

AND ONE LAST SPECIAL PLACE ... ST PANCRAS It was in the old St Pancras graveyard that **Mary Shelley** (1797–1851) plighted her troth to poet **Percy Bysshe Shelley** (1792–1822) over the grave of her mother, **Mary Wollstonecraft** (1759–1797). If that seems a little spooky, then remember the younger Mary wrote *Frankenstein* and the older one was an early feminist whose other daughter poisoned herself. Later, younger Mary dug up older Mary and moved her to Bournemouth, which she might have enjoyed more if she had been alive. Equally, Shelley would have enjoyed swimming there – if he hadn't already drowned.

The other great grave to note here is that of eccentric architect-collector **Sir John Soane**, whose house is mentioned on page 44. The strange, domed roof of the tomb, cut off to make a square base, may remind you of the classic British phone box. In fact it's the other way round: the phone box designer got his idea from here.

One more thing – note the spooky way the old gravestones have been gathered round the dripping, gnarled old tree. The roots no doubt penetrate their forgotten owners' skeletons as the wind howls round … sorry, this Shelley stuff is getting to me.

THE LONDON RESURRECTION MEN AND GRAVE CRIMES

The grave-robbers who by the end of the 18th century were making a healthy £4 per fresh body (less for a 'short', that is a child's body, which would be paid pro rata per foot) were also known as the 'resurrection men'. There is a reference to them in an inscription just off West Smithfield.

They had various ways of getting fresh corpses. One was to mingle with mourners at a funeral and note the grave. Relatives could, as a counter-measure, set markers in the soil to see if it had been disturbed or use watchmen, spring guns and primitive landmines as booby traps – at least one killed a resurrection man. A rare case of the dead killing the living.

The job of digging a corpse up from 6ft under in the dead of night was arduous; the favoured method was to make a small hole using short wooden shovels (metal ones being too noisy) and then crack the coffin lid and pull the corpse up through this, leaving the rest of the coffin lid intact.

Given all this effort, it seemed inevitable that grave-robbers would sooner or later cut out the middle man – the funeral – and kill people to order. In 1831, two known London resurrection men, John Bishop and James May, tried to haggle for the price of a body at King's College Hospital, arguing it was exceptionally fresh. So it was, but as it also had suspicious marks on it, the surgeons pretended to dither while police were called. It was found that the body was of a well-known street urchin who had been seen with Bishop, May and another man, Williams, two days previously. Evidence of murder at the three's homes was quickly found, and it transpired that they had killed and offered for dissection at least three people by first drugging them, thus avoiding the inconvenience of the intervening burial and disinterment.

Bishop and Williams were convicted of the killings and, by a neat bit of justice, were not only hanged but then dissected by surgeons.

This particular crime was instrumental in getting the Warburton Bill against the selling of bodies by grave robbers through Parliament. Previously it had been held that grave robbing was no crime because a body could not be owned as property. Now it was arranged that any body not claimed within 48 hours could be lawfully given for dissection, if no objection had been stated by the deceased, but corpses could not be sold in the previous manner.

The bottom fell out of the corpse market (perhaps not the best choice of words). Thus workhouses, for example, saved themselves the expense of conducting even a pauper's funeral and the grave-robbing era, which had transfixed and terrified a nation, was over. Or was it?

THE STRANGE STORY OF THE MODERN-DAY BODY-SNATCHER AND AN ARISTOCRATIC SCULPTOR

It had all the makings of a really cheesy Hammer Horror film, except that it was true. A nephew of the Duke of Norfolk, Anthony-Noel Kelly, 42, was jailed for nine months in 1998 (cut to three months on appeal) for stealing human body parts to make gruesomely realistic sculptures. Kelly had enlisted the help of an undertaker's embalmer, Neil Lindsay, 25, who worked at the Royal College of Surgeons. It was a landmark case, heard with the grotesque sculptures lining the courtroom, because as before it hinged on whether or not human remains could be owned, have a value and therefore be stolen. Previously Britain's body-snatchers had to be convicted of the lesser common law offence of outraging public decency.

The former sculpture tutor had permission in 1993 to sketch some of the human remains held by the RCS to help his work. But why sculpt the human form if you can just make plaster casts? He paid his accomplice £400 to take preserved medical specimens from glass jars and barrels in the college's basement. They were taken away in black dustbin bags, by Tube or taxi, to Kelly's studio in Shepherd's Bush where Kelly used moulds to copy the body parts. Remember a man with a dripping bag on the Central Line? The used parts were buried in a field near one of his family's mansions.

He was planning to go one stage further and get fresh corpses from the funeral directors where Lindsay was later working. This was too far for Lindsay who refused, saying it would be disrespectful to the dead.

The eccentric but naïve Kelly – a loner obsessed with death, contemporaries at school said – saw himself as heir to the great anatomical artists such as Leonardo da Vinci. He completely failed to see there was far more brilliance in recreating the human form, as with Rodin, or in altering it, as with Moore or Frink or Hepworth. What he was doing was merely making moulds, not art.

Like mass murderer Dennis Nilsen, Kelly was a skilled butcher – he had worked in an abattoir before attending art college – and used this knowledge in preparing dead animals, such as horses, which he had obtained for his 'sculptures'. Kelly was regarded by his high-born family as just a bit of an eccentric.

He made a death mask of his grandmother, and a cast of her hands, within half-an-hour of her death, and this was thought harmless enough. He was hired by a surgeon to make anatomical drawings for a book and this led to the recommendation that he be allowed access to the Royal College of Surgeons' archive of body parts.

Then, in 1996, Kelly exhibited his works at an Art Fair in Islington. They were priced at thousands of pounds and did not sell. But they drew the interest of a newspaper reporter, to whom he unwisely divulged his methods. The resulting article was brought to the attention of Dr Laurence Martin, Her Majesty's Chief Inspector of Anatomy, who informed the police. This subsequently led to Kelly's arrest.

Part Two

THE ECCENTRIC CITY WITH ALL ITS ODDITIES

7

Immortalised London

LONDON ADDRESSES IMMORTALISED

84 Charing Cross Road is the location of the bookstore made famous by Helene Hanff in her romantic book about her real-life correspondence with its manager Frank Dole, and by the feel-good film made of it. This area is still riddled with bookshops (see page 12). Helene Hanff had a witty, acerbic and affectionate 20-year correspondence with the London bookseller whom she never met. Ironically, she was a poor struggling New York writer with barely enough to live on, yet her correspondence – her being brash and demanding, yet deeply sympathetic to the literature she discussed with Dole, at first British and reserved and then increasingly affectionate towards her – was a world-wide hit. He died before she was able to visit London; she died in 1997 aged 80. It's quite a story.

The address of the home of the greatest of all detectives, Sherlock Holmes, **221B Baker Street**, was parodied by Dorothy L Sayers in the address of her hero, Lord Peter Wimsey, 110A Piccadilly. Today there's a museum at a fake 221B (actually at 239) which is a reconstruction of a film set of Sherlock Holmes's apartment, complete with the fire, the violin, the pipe and deerstalker hat. The actual 221B is the headquarters of the Abbey National bank, which receives some 90 letters a week from Holmes fans around the world, including an occasional one genuinely seeking help from the world's most famous detective as if he were real.

If you understand why the almost powerless queen lives in palaces and castles and the prime minister, who has a lot more power, lives in an outwardly tiny terrace house, **10 Downing Street**, you have understood the British constitution (if there were one). George Downing created the street; he must have been a great political survivor, because he worked for Cromwell as a leading republican in the 1640s and 1650s, yet did equally well as a strident royalist after the 1660 Restoration of the Monarchy. Not the last unprincipled two-faced turncoat to live in this street, some may feel. I couldn't possibly comment. For the bizarre story of how his bequest led to Downing College, see my book *Eccentric Cambridge*.

19 Railway Cuttings, East Cheam, is a fictional address immortalised for Brits of a certain age by Tony Hancock in the radio then TV comedy show in which he was paired with South African Sid James. The scripts have been published, but real fans don't need them and can recall Hancock's outraged tone as if it were yesterday – eg: in *The Blood Donor:* 'A pint? But that's nearly an armful!'

10 Rillington Place is a book and a film. This address was where real-life simpleton Timothy Evans supposedly murdered his own baby girl in 1949, leading to his execution by hanging. The discovery that another occupant of the house,

John Reginald Halliday Christie, was a serial murderer led to Evans being pardoned, posthumously, in 1966. Classic miscarriage of justice stuff.

79 Cadogan Place was made notorious nationwide in 1886. The steamy divorce case that centred on this fashionable address caused outrage in the Press (so outraged that they gleefully printed every word of the evidence, day after day) and concerned 'What the butler saw'. It involved Lady Colin Campbell, née Gertrude Blood, a dark and gorgeous Irishwoman (not unlike Andrea Corr in looks). Married in 1881, she soon caught syphilis from her husband and sued him for divorce on the grounds of adultery with a maid. He fought the case on the grounds of her promiscuity and the evidence that fascinated Britain was what went on in the drawing room at 79 Cadogan Place, involving the highborn sons of two dukes. Among her ladyship's male visitors was the Marquess of Blandford who had already been cited in divorce cases, a chief fire officer, Captain Shaw, and a surgeon, Tom Bird. The butler told the court that he was told not to announce these men in the hearing of Lady Campbell's husband, Lord Colin (son of the Duke of Argyll). On one occasion, the butler found Lady Colin with Lord Blandford (heir to the Duke of Marlborough), her dress 'disordered' and her face flushed. Yet again, by spying through the keyhole, he saw her lighting the fire, so to speak, of Captain Shaw.

'I saw Lady Colin lying down with Captain Shaw on the carpet,' the hushed court heard.

'Did you see her bust?' asked his lordship's counsel.

'I certainly saw more than that.'

There were arguments as to whether the heavy metal escutcheons (covers on the keyhole) would prevent this kind of spying, so the jury insisted on seeing for themselves. The court was solemnly taken to peer through London's most famous keyhole. The jury found that not only would the stiff escutcheons stay in any position but that they would not even cover the keyholes. Even more peculiar, the jury found none of the claims of adultery proven, so the Campbells remained married but separated until, unsurprisingly, they both died prematurely of syphilis.

RHYME AND REASON

MACABRE MEANINGS BEHIND WELL-KNOWN SONGS
St Clement's, oranges and lemons and a right old ding-dong New Zealand
crime writer Ngaio Marsh said the first sight of Eros in Piccadilly brings a lump to the throat of an Antipodean raised on images of this so-called 'hub of the world'. (Dame Ngaio's Maori first name is repetitively geographic, by the way, because *Ngaio* is a marshy coastal shrub, or perhaps she prefers its other meaning, 'competent'.)

I prefer the story of another New Zealander, my wife, a journalist who, when first arrived, walked down Fleet Street to where the Strand splits from the Aldwych. There she heard the bells of St Clement's ringing 'Oranges and Lemons', a song sung in school playgrounds around the world. 'It was a nursery rhyme come alive,' she says, 'a magic moment.' And indeed, every March, schoolchildren are given oranges and lemons there.

The shorter version of the rhyme, which has more variations than J S Bach could have dreamed up, goes:

Oranges and lemons,
Say the bells of St Clement's;
You owe me five farthings,
Say the bells of St Martin's;

When will you pay me?
Say the bells of Old Bailey;
When I grow rich,
Say the Bells of Shoreditch;
When will that be?
Say the bells of Stepney;
I do not know,
Says the big bell of Bow.
Here comes candle to light you to bed,
Here comes a chopper to chop off your head;
The last, last, last, last man's head.

It's a rhyme beloved of children in playgrounds many miles from London's bells for many generations because of the simple metre and catchy tune, plus the game where two of the children form arches with their arms and the rest run through in a line with linked hands.

There's a suitable amount of menace – which children love – in not knowing who will be caught by the chopper of the arms coming down and capturing a child. In the oldest versions of the game the trapped child is asked, out of earshot of the rest, which he prefers, oranges or lemons, and then he must stand behind one of the chopping pair who secretly agreed to be lemons or oranges. The process repeats until the children are divided into two teams, who then compete in some other way – such as a tug-of-war.

Why should such a game have evolved at all? It's certainly very old. It was probably long-established when printed in a 1744 book with hardly a word different except one line reading: Ring Ye bells at Fleetditch. It is known that the various London parishes met for sporting challenges in the Middle Ages, including just such tug-of-wars, and a rhyme about the parishes involved may have followed this long-forgotten custom.

On the other hand it is undoubtedly macabre with its reference to execution, the candle to light you to bed being a funeral torch, public executions being a popular event for children as well as adults for many centuries. All such topical events were made into rhyme, just as London's football fans today chant insulting doggerel about their opponents.

So with this ancient rhyme we have children in playgrounds in the 21st century acting out a folk echo of real events more than a thousand years ago. Fascinating.

Which St Clement's is the one in the song is in serious doubt – today it is assumed by most visitors that St Clement Danes in the Strand is the church involved, but St Clement's Eastcheap near the north end of London Bridge in the City could have a better claim. It was here oranges and lemons unloaded from ships would be carried from the river to the market by porters who on New Year's Day gave each tenant a fruit and some more to the church.

St Clement Danes, a wedding-cakey Christopher Wren church, was after all then outside the City, although both churches claim to be the one in the rhyme. Adding weight to St Clement Danes' claim is the idea that fruit porters rested their loads there on their way from the wharves of London to Clare Market nearby.

A clue to the confusion lies in a colourful character called William Pennington-Bickford, minister of St Clement Danes in the 1920s, who installed a fancy new carillon of bells to ring out the famous nursery rhyme tune. He was what would now be called a media-friendly cleric. He started the annual presentations of oranges and lemons to schoolchildren and had the carillon's tune broadcast on radio. Did he then appropriate another church's history and tune for his precious bells? No-one can say for sure, given how old the rhyme is, and the fact the Rev Pennington-Bickford is long dead. Either way, it's a right old ding-dong.

- More on St Clement's: A burned-out church, upside-down thrashed choirboys, pillaging Danes and exploding anvils, page 104.

Ring-a-ring of roses and a horrible death Another apparently harmless childhood rhyme, still sung in nursery schools and playgroups all over the world, is 'Ring-a-ring of roses', and again it is full of the blackest most macabre London history. The version I recall from childhood goes,

Ring-a-ring of roses,
Pocketful of posies,
Atishoo atishoo,
We all fall down.

At the first line the children circle round with joined hands in a ring, at the third they stop and do exaggerated sneezes and at the fourth they fall on the floor. Children of about three or four love it.

There's no need to tell them, until they're well grown, that 'ring-a-ring of roses' refers to the skin discoloration that the Black Death brings, that 'pocketful of posies' refers to the herbs people carried to try to ward off the dreaded plague, that 'atishoo, atishoo' describes its remarkably rapid onset and 'all fall down' the inevitable end, death, then being tipped from carts into pits of quicklime. The poem probably started with the 1665 Great Plague.

One of the ironies of that plague, not mentioned in the poem, is that people thought cats and dogs brought the fast-killing disease, so they killed any they could find. As we now know, it was the rats, or rather the fleas on them, which carried the plague. When it killed the rats, the fleas reluctantly jumped on to humans. And the only thing which might have kept rats out of ramshackle houses of the day – yes, those poor cats and dogs.

- More about plague, page 57.

The Grand Old Duke of York: giant British cock-ups, a Nazi intruder and real heroes Everyone knows the magnificent curve of Regent Street as it approaches Piccadilly Circus. Beyond the brash and vibrant Circus the road continues a little into the rarified air of St James's (yet another example of how the atmosphere of London can change totally in 100 yards or so) and then peters out as it crosses Pall Mall, changing into Waterloo Place. The massive column looking like something out of imperial Rome is, as usual for such overblown things, to someone not terribly important, Frederick, Duke of York, forgettable second son of mad George III, and commander-in-chief of the army.

It was this duke who, in the words of the nursery rhyme, insanely marched his men up and down hills. As well as being fed up with all this marching, the army had to suffer every man having a day's wages stopped to pay for this ludicrously tall monument.

The Grand Old Duke of York,
He had ten thousand men,
He marched them up to the top of the hill,
And marched them down again etc etc

At the time it was said to be built so high to keep the Duke of York away from his creditors, as he owed the enormous sum of £1.9 million at his death. The current Duchess of York, the title denoting her former husband being another second son of a monarch, has also owed a few quid from time to time. I can't imagine the army coughing up for a massive monument to her.

(Her former husband, Prince Andrew the Duke of York, of course, was in the navy, not the army. A naval officer told me of when Prince Andrew was sitting with a bunch of admirals at a dinner and he turned to one and said: 'You can call me Andrew.' The crusty old admiral replied: 'And you can call me Sir.' If it's not true, it should be.)

There is another amusing link between money, this part of London and a previous Duke of York, that is the younger brother of George III. He liked to visit the upmarket courtesan **Kitty Fisher** at her home in nearby Carrington Street, off Shepherd Street north of Piccadilly, in the early 1760s. She notoriously charged 100 guineas a go – £105, an enormous amount of money then – to her gentlemen, mostly married figures of high social standing. When the duke gave her a mere £50, her contemptuous reaction was to stick it between two slices of bread and eat it. (Oddly, it was just about this time that the fourth Earl of Sandwich, gambling near here, ordered thin pieces of meat to be placed between slices of bread so he could continue his game uninterrupted for 24 hours. Just because he was a nob, the thing became known as a sandwich. We could just as reasonably ask for a cheese and tomato Kitty.)

There is yet another secret about this area. It contains the only **Nazi memorial** in London. In February 1934, Giro the faithful hound of the German ambassador Leopold von Hoesch (not, I'm told, a Nazi himself), was buried complete with tombstone near the then German embassy at 7 Carlton House Terrace.

The memorial, with touching epithet *Ein treuer Begleiter* (a true companion), is tucked under a tree at the top of the steps from the Institute of Contemporary Art on the Mall up to Waterloo Place, perhaps somewhat cheekily given that the area is laden with such vast monuments to heroes of the British Empire.

Indeed, the statues show serious bomb damage inflicted by Giro's master's master, Hitler, fewer than ten years later. Giro's tombstone, however, was undamaged – as was the splendid Nazi interior nearby designed by Hitler's architect Albert Speer – and has been encased in glass to preserve it further. Every February someone puts flowers on the little mutt's grave. That the simple love of a faithful dog has survived all this terrible history is in its way reassuring.

But stay and contemplate the quite superb collection of sculpture at Waterloo Place, and what this conveys about British history. That the German bomb went off between the equestrian **Edward VII** statue and that of Field Marshal Lord Clyde, epitomises the end of the most imperial phase of history – look how Edward VII's statue is confidently inscribed Rex Imperator (King Emperor) without a shred of the embarrassment many young Britons feel today. They'd perhaps rather remember the Edward VII cigar or the potato.

The other statues tell of far sadder but far more heroic deeds. There is **Franklin**, who died searching for the North-West Passage from the Atlantic to the Pacific. The sides of the monument are inscribed with the names of the full company of the two ships, *Terror* and *Erebus*, which were lost, including, poignantly, the ships' boys in both cases. It says: 'They forged the last link with their lives.' A noble sentiment, but hardly true. It was a useless, ice-blocked passage.

Then there's **Robert Falcon Scott**, the hero of the Antarctic who was beaten to the South Pole in hellish conditions and died on his way back. It is inscribed with a quotation from his diary:

> Had we lived I should have had a tale to tell of the hardihood, endurance and courage of my companions which would have stirred the heart of every Englishman. These rough notes and our dead bodies must tell the tale.

Of course it stirs our hearts, as much as Oates's well-known sacrifice, 'I'm going out, I may be some time' or, even more wrenchingly in the Oates Museum at Selborne, Hampshire, the note clearly written in agony by a frost-bitten hand, 'For God's sake, look after our people.'

You turn away with a heavy heart from that monument and there, across Pall Mall, is **Florence Nightingale**, the Lady with the Lamp who tended the hundreds of wounded dying through criminal official neglect in the Crimean War *and* a monument to the Brigade of Guards who died so needlessly but heroically in that conflict, of which the Charge of the Light Brigade said it all. If you can bear any more, back down the steps by the Duke of York and across the Mall is a monument to the men simply slaughtered in their hundreds in the **Boer War**.

So the nursery rhyme poking fun at the Duke of York's military ineptitude doesn't even *begin* to tell the tale of military cock-ups and British failures compressed into around half a century. Crimea, Boers, Franklin, Scott – why there's even the Indian Mutiny, another sorry bloodbath, on another statue. I couldn't find Gallipoli or Singapore, but they ought to be remembered in this catalogue of disasters, this vale of blood and tears, somewhere.

Certainly, the Victorians and Edwardians were less interested in success than heroic failure. Yet there is so much more to these stories than shallow melodrama. Scott, Franklin, Oates, Nightingale – will the 21st century ever produce such heroes who even half as much deserve a statue?

London Bridge, pillaging raiders and a virgin's bones

It sounds innocuous enough, you'll remember:

> London Bridge is broken down,
> Broken down, broken, down,
> London Bridge is broken down,
> My fair lady.

Various solutions are tried:

> Build it up with mud and clay,
> Mud and clay, mud and clay etc

and problems encountered:

> Mud and clay will wash away etc

Iron and steel will bend and bow, Silver and gold will be stolen away, but stone so strong will last ages long, the song eventually concludes.

The last part was true if we consider the extraordinary history of this bridge, the one key factor in the whole 2,000-year history of London. The Romans saw how the hills of where the City now stands caused the wide marshy river to narrow and built the first bridge right here. The Romans believed in river gods and would often throw into a river inscriptions aimed at appeasing them, or makes sacrifices to them. In fact in pre-Christian Europe a child sacrifice was thought particularly effective, so sometimes infants were walled up alive in the bridge stones.

The Vikings under Olaf the Norseman managed to pull down the timber London Bridge in 1014 as part of their campaign against the Saxons and it is probably this event that is remembered by the rhyme. Fascinatingly, there are Norse rhymes told to children on the other side of the North Sea celebrating exactly this event a millennium ago.

The stone London Bridge, begun in 1176 by a monk, Peter of Colechurch, took until 1209 to finish and lasted, amazingly, until the 19th century. For nearly all this time it was London's only river crossing and thus its survival was critical to the City.

It is said by various chroniclers that the previous timber bridge had a virgin's bones in its foundations in line with the legend above.

The London Bridge we generally picture was the 1176 stone one, built with stone arches on a series of boat-shaped artificial islands called starlings. These arches had to be repeatedly strengthened, making the channels between them narrower, so when the tide was at full flood, or ebb, it roared through with white water. For boatmen, shooting the bridge was a risky business. It could also slow the water upstream enough, in the right conditions, for the river to freeze deeply enough to hold a Frost Fair on it (see page 202). This bridge lasted, with many repairs and embellishment, until 1830.

Taking it down had two unlikely results. Firstly a cutler on the Strand bought all the steel straps strengthening the steelwork and made the best cutlery of the day out of them, and the elm timbers were made into thousands of souvenir knick-knacks such as snuff boxes. Secondly, two stone shelters on the bridge somehow survived and can be seen even today in Victoria Park, Hackney, by St Augustine's Gate.

The four-pier stone bridge which replaced it was completed by 1831, and it survived heavier and heavier traffic, German bombs and the ebb and flow of the river until 1967, when an American squillionaire bought it to put over a specially created river in Arizona. Famously, and probably apocryphally, he was said to have thought he was buying the medieval bridge with houses on rather than the somewhat boring 19th-century job. This has been denied, but today we have a steel-arched thing which is functional and even graceful but not curious, giving a 330ft clear span. Same place, fewer piers and wider spans sums up the 2,000 years so far.

Now the great and the good are thinking of another bridge nearby with – guess what – lots of shops and houses on it.

Half a pound of tupenny rice

Round and round the cobbler's bench
The monkey chased the weasel,
The monkey thought 'twas all in fun
Pop! Goes the weasel.

A penny for a spool of thread
A penny for a needle,
That's the way the money goes,
Pop! Goes the weasel.

A half a pound of tupenny rice,
A half a pound of treacle.
Mix it up and make it nice,
Pop! Goes the weasel.

Up and down the City Road,
In and out of the Eagle,
That's the way the money goes,
Pop! Goes the weasel.

I've no time to plead and pine,
I've no time to wheedle,
Kiss me quick and then I'm gone
Pop! Goes the weasel.

This strangely pleasing rhyme is probably not all that old and has puzzled generations of children who wonder why weasels should go pop. But, as is fairly widely known, it is a tale of hand-to-mouth working class life in Islington, north of the City, where there's indeed a pub called the Eagle and a City Road. To 'pop' something is to pawn it, to take it to the shop with three golden balls outside (there are still some around London and one opposite the Angel pub, Islington) where money would be handed over for valuables which could be redeemed later, if the person produced the money, plus a little more no doubt, and the ticket. If not, the valuables could be sold. It's much the same the world over.

A weasel was a kind of ironing and clothes-making machine that would have provided an income for a family in the rag trade, as London's famously badly-paid clothing industry was, and is, known. The irony captured by the rhyme was that once the weasel had gone, so had much of the family's income. Hard times.

The last four lines seem to echo Marvel's *To His Coy Mistress*, a very different poem with the same message of don't mess about, get your kit off and let's make love because we'll all be dead and gone soon enough.

8

London's Road to Eccentricity

ABBEY ROAD Everyone's heard of the eponymous Beatles album, but why is Abbey Road in St John's Wood linked to Kilburn High Road by the oddly named Quex Road, with the equally unlikely Mazenod Avenue running off it? Urban myth has it that these road names were the last throw of a desperate council department with a few odd street-name letters left over, like a losing Scrabble player. In fact Mazenod is a Catholic saint and Quex is connected to a stately home in Kent (don't ask me how). A version of Scrabble with London road names allowed would be fun: Mazenod would score 87 on a treble word score.

BATTERSEA The English name ending -sey, or -sea, meant island. Battersea was St Peter's Sey, an island in the marshes where monks from Westminster Abbey of St Peter would retreat. No doubt Chelsea, Marshalsea and Bermondsey are named for similar reasons: long before the Thames was finally confined within Victorian embankments it was a wide marshy estuary (the north shore being where Buckingham Palace now stands).

BELGRAVIA Though the origin of the name of Belgravia, home of thousands of wedding-cakey, white stucco terraces, is well known – the Grosvenor family who owned so much land here had an estate at Belgrave, Leicester – the derivation of neighbouring Pimlico is a mystery.

BLOOMSBURY Named after a Norman noble to whom William the Conqueror gave land here. The Dukes of Bedford still own large chunks of Bloomsbury and the street names recall them and other aristocrats who developed the squares and terraces: Russell Square, Bedford Square, Tavistock Square and Woburn Place. More recently, Bloomsbury has become associated with intellectuals, the British Museum, London University, student residences, bookshops and publishers, and the early 20th-century bunch of writers called the Bloomsbury Group, remembered in the awful schoolboy joke: 'Why did Virginia Woolf? Because E M Forster.' Whether their work would be read if the English literature industry hadn't cottoned on to that title and if they hadn't tolerated some odd sexual arrangements is open to debate. I heard one English student say: 'Virginia Woolf? Over-rated, tedious toff. Best thing she did for English literature was walk into the River Arun with her pockets filled with stones!' Ooo errr, missus.

BROMPTON Incredible though it seems standing in today's Brompton Road (you wouldn't live long if you did) with its Kensington-style house prices, this was once a country lane which crossed common land covered in the yellow-flowering broom. Hence the hamlet along it came to be known as Broom-ton.

BUNHILL FIELDS Bunhill Fields, off City Road, EC1, is actually a corruption of Bone Hill. Not surprising when you consider that 120,000 Londoners are crammed into the cemetery here, including John Bunyan, Daniel Defoe and William Blake, with John Wesley's chapel opposite.

CANNON STREET Cannon Street was originally Candle Street, until the candle makers who boiled their animal fats there were expelled to the countryside because of the vile smell their trade created.

CARTING LANE Talking of pongs, Carting Lane, off The Strand, WC2, was once listed as the less than fragrant Farting Lane. However, this simple typographical error had a whiff of truth about it, for the gas lamps there were once lit by the gases rising from the sewers of the Savoy Hotel.

CHALK FARM Chalk Farm sounds rather nice, but has nothing to do with chalk or farms. Instead, it's named after a large country house once here, Chalcotts.

CLARIDGE'S The London residence of many a king and president (and often spelt without that apostrophe), Claridge's is also the most frequently used and thinly disguised location in crime fiction. According to an excellent book for whodunnit fans, *London: Mystery Reader's Walking Guide* (Passport Books, Illinois) by Barbara Sloan Hendershott and Alzina Stone Dale, it has appeared as Alridge's in Anthony Berkeley's *The Piccadilly Murder* as somewhere 'where the air cost several pounds an hour to breathe' and as Harridge's in Agatha Christie's *The Golden Ball*: 'Who in England did not know Harridge's where notables and royalty arrived and departed as a matter of course.' Complete with apostrophes, of course.

CLOAK LANE Cloak Lane, EC4, sounds pleasant enough but it means 'open sewer street', as in Rome's Cloaca Maxima.

FITZROY SQUARE Fitzroy Square could have been Royal Bastard Square, although perhaps that's not quite so elegant as an address. The prefix Fitz often meant 'illegitimate son of' (not in current holders of the name, *of course*), so Fitz-roy meant the king's bastard. In fact this whole area, known as Fitzrovia, is linked to yet another of randy Charles II's mistresses, the voluptuous and sexually insatiable Barbara Villiers, much fancied by diarist Samuel Pepys, among others. She had many other lovers at court, which Charles didn't seem to mind, and many street names in this area, such as Euston, Warren, Grafton, and of course Fitzroy are taken from titles created for the offspring of this most fruitful woman's loins.

FRYING PAN ALLEY, EI A City name which probably has more to do with its shape than its function.

GLOUCESTER ROAD Gloucester Road in South Kensington was originally the rural, winding Hogmore Lane or even Hogmire (pig pooh) Lane. But it was felt this was too lowly a title when the Duchess of Gloucester moved there in around 1800, so it was changed to something posher. Oddly, during the boom in recreational gardens of around 40 years before – with Vauxhall Gardens being the most famous of them – there was one here in what were semi-rural surroundings. Florida Gardens, situated where Stanhope Gardens is now, was a popular pleasure ground for ladies and gentlemen who weren't always quite the ladies and gentlemen they should have been. The Legoverland of its day.

HA HA ROAD, SE18 A ha-ha is a boundary for country estates. It's a dry, grassy ditch in which the side of the ditch nearest the house is built up with brick or stone. The idea is you get a fenceless boundary that makes the view from the house more pleasant: you can't see the join between the lawns which surround the house and the fields beyond where deer or cattle graze, and it stops them from straying on to your lawn. And if anyone comes across the ditch unexpectedly, they would say: 'Ha ha!' Well, they might have in the 18th century.

HAYMARKET Yes, once the place to get hay for the capital's thousands of horses, but later a highly disreputable part of town. Even Dostoevsky was appalled by how the Haymarket prostitutes put their young daughters to work: 'Little girls, aged about 12, seize you by the arm and beg you to accompany them.' Haymarket was notorious for its louche drinking salons until the late 19th century.

HERNE HILL An island occupied by a heron, or herne, once stood in the lost river Effra at the bottom of this hill.

HOUNDSDITCH Just what it says: a stinking ditch, notable for dead dogs floating in it.

KENSINGTON GORE This slightly vile-sounding name for a rather posh road turns out to be completely innocent. There was a triangle of land, whose apex was near the Knights Bridge (see opposite) and covering where the Albert Hall now stands, which was seized by King Henry III, when it was said to be worth 12 pence per acre per annum (now, of course, it's some of the most valuable real estate on the planet). A 'gore' is a triangular piece of cloth, so this triangular piece of land became known as the 'Kinggesgor'. So a gore is a sewn-on patch of cloth. They're lucky it isn't called Kensington Gusset.

KEW The earliest reference to Kew is in a 1440 court case involving 'Richard Hunte of Shene and his wife Alice in Kayowe'. It has also been called Kayhough, Kayhowe, Kaio, Kaw, Keyhowe, Keyo, Kayo, Cayo, Kaw, Cewe and Kewe. They probably all derive from 'quay' or 'key', a landing place. It's the home of the fabulous botanic gardens, once a royal park popular with the unpopular Georgian kings and princes beginning with Frederick, Prince of Wales in the 1730s, who had popular composer Handel pop over to play for him. Once, writer Alexander Pope brought him a gift of a dog. On the dog's collar Pope had engraved

> I am his Highness's dog at Kew,
> Pray tell me, Sir, whose dog are you?

This Frederick, part of a bitterly divided family of squabbling Hanoverians, was to die young in 1751 after catching a chill walking at Kew and from an abscess which developed after he was hit by a tennis ball. But his wife's closest companion played an interesting role: Lord Bute. He was always hanging around the Princess, and the Prince, who took a mistress himself, once said: 'Bute, you are the very man to be employed at some small proud German Court where there is nothing to do.' But Bute didn't take the hint, and after the Prince's death, Horace Walpole recorded bitchily of Bute and his scandalously indiscreet relations with the Princess:

> The favoured personage, naturally ostentatious of his person, seemed by no means desirous of concealing his conquest… the beauty of his legs was constantly displayed before the poor captivated Princess. The Prince [so he could have a quick one with his mistress] used to bid the Princess walk with Lord Bute. As soon as the prince was dead, they walked more and more, in honour of his memory.

The widow devoted herself to her son George, future mad King George III, and to Bute who lived at King's Cottage near the church and who was appointed to the ancient office of Groom of the Stool. This, literally, means cleaner of the king's excrement but someone more lowly usually actually carried out the royal potty. Still, some thought it an apt job for Bute. And whatever you think of that Prince of Wales and his wife, they left some amazing gardens at Kew; it was stuffed with far more pagodas, temples and follies than survive today. But there's still one superb pagoda left.

KING EDWARD STREET, EC1 This sounds better than its two previous names: Blowbladder Street after the unsavoury practice among crooked butchers of inserting bladders into the orifices of dead animals and inflating them to make them look bigger. You got your turkey big enough for six home, it passed wind like the cowboys in *Blazing Saddles* and suddenly you had only a chicken big enough for two. Charming. Then it became Stinking Lane because of the awful offal the butchers left around. No wonder they changed it to something more fragrant in time for King Edward VII to open the General Post Office here.

THE KING'S ROAD Famously fashionable sixties egalitarian hang-out of hippies and nobs alike, this road was until 1830 an entirely private road for the King to reach the countryside without having to share his road with hoi polloi.

KNIGHTSBRIDGE Knights heading off for the Crusades or whatever had to ride to the Bishop of London's Palace at Fulham (hence today's Fulham Palace Road) and cross the Westbourne stream at this point, hence Knights' Bridge. Actually, given its extreme Harrods-and-Harvey-Nicks poshness nowadays, it is odd to recall what a scummy low-life dump Knightsbridge used to be. For one thing, it was all mud and it was difficult for people to wade through to the village of Kensington. There were rich pickings for highwaymen this close to London, so every night in the late 18th century a convoy system would operate, with pedestrians waiting at Hyde Park Corner to run the gauntlet to Kensington in large enough numbers to put the blackguards and cut-throats off. There was a leper colony where the French embassy now is and the High Road was once condemned for its immorality and having 'a succession of music halls, taverns, beer stores, oyster saloons and cheap tobacconists'. Sounds more fun than snooty Sloaney department stores, some may think, but the complaint went on: 'The nightly meeting place of disorderly men and women whose behaviour makes the area quite as unseemly as the Haymarket.'

LITTLE BRITAIN, EC1 Little Britain actually refers to the Bretons who lived here.

MAIDEN LANE, WC2 Again, this sounds nicer than it was. It's named after middens: rubbish and dung heaps.

MAGGIE BLAKE'S CAUSE Sounds like a truly ancient name whereby hangs a tale. Actually rather recent. By the 1980s and 1990s the great Victorian wharves and warehouses on the South Bank of the Thames just east of Tower Bridge had received their last cargoes and fallen into disuse. Smart property developers grabbed their chance and they are now trendy riverside apartments, many with balcony views of the river and the City. Part of this process was the insertion of achingly trendy restaurants – some of which have gained international reputations and have had Tony Blair and François Mitterrand as diners – and these meant walkways or promenades in front of the old wharves. Not surprisingly, some of the developers wanted these walkways to be for the rich and powerful using the cool restaurants and the fashionable flats; equally predictably, local people led by Maggie Blake wanted to share the access to the wonderful river views being created. In the end they won and without going all socialist on you, this is what town planning should do. Let the rich and powerful make money, but on the terms that suit the people, not exclude them. Anyway enjoy the walk east from the south end of Tower Bridge and when you are in Shad Thames – itself a fascinatingly Dickensian path between former warehouses and crossed by frequent bridges above you – look out for the passage to the left marked Maggie Blake's Cause. Tip your hat to the lady as you go through to share some of the best riverside views in the world.

THE MALL AND PALL MALL Does any tourist think these parallel roads are shopping centres? Pall Mall is named after a French game once played there, *paille maille*. The Mall is the grand royal processional route from Admiralty Arch to Buckingham Palace, an area laid out in a brief period of imperial pomposity that thankfully didn't spread throughout the whole of London. Lesser countries with less well run, smaller, less useful and more corrupt empires, flattened entire cities to lay out imperial boulevards giving views of self-important temples to national grandeur and commemorate battles of little consequence, and sometimes to create useful fields of fire to mow down potentially hostile populations. All very well with new cities, such as Washington and New Delhi, but here, not very British, in my view, and not very eccentric. It would have deprived us of the fascinating medieval rabbit warren of a maze that is London, warts and all, as would have Wren's grand plan for the redevelopment of London after the Great Fire of 1666.

MAYFAIR The poshest corner of the Monopoly board game and an area to which snobbish words such as 'exclusive' could apply. Odd to recall that the original May Fair, moved to open ground east of Park Lane (now Curzon Street), was so raucous and raffish that it was banned in the late 18th century. Maybe it was just the snobbery of the rich and powerful, for it was about this time that London's aristocratic centre of gravity shifted westwards.

NEWGATE STREET Well, it was new in the second century. Compared to Aldgate (old gate), that is.

PARK ROAD You'd think someone would have tried to avoid repetition of London road names. This one takes the biscuit for confusion, there being 62 of them.

PETTY FRANCE, SW1 'Petit' being the French for 'little', this area was a hang-out for Huguenots driven from France by Louis XIV.

PICCADILLY A piccadil was a collar or ruff.

PORTOBELLO ROAD, W10 A farm here was renamed Porto Bello in 1739 to celebrate the British capturing a town of this name in the Gulf of Mexico.

PUDDING LANE, EC3 Famously where the fire of London started; the spot is marked by the monument. Again, 'Pudding Lane' sounds a lot nicer than it was. 'Pudding' was the slang name for the butchers' offal that slopped down here.

SCOTLAND YARD Great Scotland Yard was where kings of Scotland would stay while visiting kings of England. When James VI of Scotland became James I of England in 1603, this became unnecessary, but its name lives on, spreading to New Scotland Yard when the police moved there from Great Scotland Yard.

SEETHING LANE, EC3 A more interesting name than its origin, this time. Seething comes from an Anglo-Saxon word for the chaff blown across here from a nearby cornmarket.

SEVEN SISTERS ROAD, TOTTENHAM Robert the Bruce, King of Scotland, had seven daughters and asked them to plant seven elm trees here. The trees, and then the road, and then the Victoria Line station, became known as Seven Sisters.

SHERBORNE LANE This street in the City is nothing to do with the fragrant West Country town, but is a cleaning up of its medieval name, Shitteborwe, ie: the public bog, khazi, longdrop, loo, outhouse, or whatever.

SHRAPNEL CLOSE Not the most friendly address, but then this road in Charlton is close to Woolwich's historic Arsenal and nearby roads are called Gun Park, Master Gunners Place, Ordnance Road and Artillery Place, so it fits in. British soldier Henry Shrapnel was the inventor of the artillery shell which blew up on impact into many lethal fragments, shredding anyone nearby.

SOHO Sohoposedly named after a hunting call, for these were hunting grounds before London spread west. But the only hunting round here for the past century or two has been for two-legged quarry. More on Soho, see page 187.

SPITALFIELDS Unusually, less horrid than it sounds. The 'spital was a hospital for mental patients set up in 1197.

TURNAGAIN LANE, EC4 Nothing to do with Dick Whittington, but an alley which turns back on itself and crosses the Fleet river.

TURNHAM Despite featuring in a rude schoolboy's ditty about London which ends with the place names 'Turnham Green and Peckham', Turnham Green probably originates as the rather boring 'Turnum' or medieval court of the hundred, a unit of local government. (Battle of Turnham Green, or Brentford, see page 33.)

XX COURT Supposed to be in the City of London somewhere, but I've never seen it. Let me know if you spot it.

ZETLAND STREET, E14 Zetland is a variant spelling of Shetland, the Scottish and once Norwegian island. Or is that Zcottish? Hence the Marquess of Zetland.

8

THE CAPITAL'S ROADS

- The first London bus service, from Paddington Green to the Bank, was by horse-drawn coach and cost one shilling. Newspapers were included, for the journey could take three hours.
- Savoy Court, the road that joins the Savoy Hotel to the Strand, is the only road in Britain where, because of its angle to the Strand, you are required to drive on the right.
- Under many London crossroads lie the corpses of those who committed suicide. Suicides were buried according to a most gruesome ritual. Suicide was a mortal sin, which meant that victims could not be buried in consecrated ground, and custom had it that they be buried in a pit under a crossroads, covered with quicklime to eat away their flesh, and even, sometimes, with a stake driven through their hearts à la Count Dracula. De Quincey wrote about one such burial, at the junction in Wapping of Cable Street and Cannon Street, in his gruesome essay *On Murder Considered as One of the Fine Arts*.
- The Adelphi is the area south of the Strand, going down to the Embankment, and as it was developed by the Adams brothers, it is appropriately named ('adelphi' means 'brothers' in Greek).
- London's first toll gate was in Highgate; the last is in Dulwich (see page 234).
- Juxon Street in Lambeth was the home of the first motorised taxi, which was registered in 1897. So that was the destination of two Japanese taxi drivers who made a 12-week, 30,000 mile pilgrimage to mark the centenary which made the *Guinness Book of Records*. They were greeted by 32 London black cabs sounding their horns. These taxi drivers saw London as the birthplace of the world's history of the taxi.

LONDON'S SIX FREAKIEST ACCIDENTS

Woolwich In 1929 an electricity generating station in Woolwich suffered a freak accident. The load on a Bellis & Morcom high-speed steam engine was disconnected so the thing oversped. The heavy flywheel flew apart due to enormous centrifugal forces and a large lump of it smashed through the roof and soared across the Thames in a graceful parabola, landing with a crash in North Woolwich Gardens. No-one was hurt.

Silvertown A few years before, there was a massive explosion at a Silvertown chemical factory nearby which was processing TNT for use in World War I. It flattened the factory, killing workers and destroying nearby homes. Careful detective work proved it was not the explosives that had gone up, however, as their handling had been carefully controlled, but a little understood by-product of the manufacturing process that was given off as vapour, then crystallised in the roof space as a highly explosive and unstable danger which the slightest knock could set off.

Macclesfield Bridge Macclesfield Bridge on the Regent's Canal near London Zoo is supported by massive cast-iron pillars higher and broader than a man. These have grooves in them, like all canal bridge pillars, where thousands of tow-ropes pulled by horses have rubbed against them. But why do the pillars have grooves on the landward side? An amazing gunpowder barge accident blew the place to pieces in 1874, and threw the pillars weighing many tons aside. To even up the wear, they put the massive pillars back the wrong way round. Hence its nickname, Blow-Up Bridge. See Round London canal trip, page 87.

Harrow on the Hill It didn't take long for the newfangled motor car to produce its first fatal crash in 1899, and Harrow on the Hill, with its steep roads, seemed as good a place as any for it to happen. The accident interested the army's top brass, because they were in the car. They had hired the eight-seater Daimler wagonette, which came with driver Edward Sewell, and thought a test run from Whitehall to Harrow for a spot of lunch would make an excellent trial for the horseless carriage, as it did, but only because it showed the car's weakness. Refreshments at the King's Head went well enough – too well, possibly – and they set off down Grove Hill so they could test the brakes. Reaching the dizzy speed of perhaps 20mph, Sewell hit the brakes at the corner. The car's wheels collapsed under him and it turned upside down. Sewell and a brass hat were killed.

Crystal Palace Not that this was Britain's first horseless carriage fatality. Three years earlier a Mrs Bridget Driscoll was knocked down and killed in the grounds of Crystal Palace where the Anglo-French Motorcar Corporation had been invited to demonstrate its machine in August 1896. Crowds of curious sightseers flocked to see the machine. The driver insisted he had been keeping to the regulation 4mph and had rung his bell furiously but Mrs Driscoll had seemed bewildered and froze to the spot in his path. Some backed the driver, Arthur Edsel, and others said he'd been driving recklessly. There were notices all around to warn the public of the new hazard, but no-one had yet decided whether motorcars should drive on the right or left, so he kept to the middle (a policy some South London drivers still seem to adhere to today). The driver was cleared of any blame and Mrs Driscoll became the first of hundreds of thousands of road victims, human hedgehogs flattened by human road-hogs.

Waterloo One of London's most bizarre railway accidents was when a locomotive fell down a lift shaft. It involved the Waterloo and City Line, a one-stop Tube route owned and operated by the main line at Waterloo until 1994. Because there was no inter-connection here with other Tube railways, and no sloping entrance to it, access for new trains, etc, is via a huge lift shaft. One carriage at a time can be hoisted to the surface. Unfortunately, a shunting locomotive once over-ran the siding it was connected to at the top and plummeted down the shaft. The wreckage was recovered with cranes.

TRANSPORTED TO ORIENTAL HIPPIEDOM Decades after the hippie counter-culture, Carnaby Street, oriental gurus and all that befuddled London with its joss-sticks and dresses for men, something of that era is returning to the capital's transport system.

8

I don't mean the official London Transport system, although frankly you might at times imagine dope heads run the Tube. 'Wow man, signals problem at Baker Street. Heavy stuff – better close the Circle, Metropolitan and Jubilee lines. I can't handle this. Freaky!' Actually my favourite saying about the sixties is: 'If you can remember the sixties, you weren't really there, man.'

Be that as it may, those who miss – or completely missed – the hippie culture can travel around London in laid-back style with **Karma Kars**, a strangely alternative cab company. Never mind the old joke about 'my dogma has been run over by my karma', it seems inconceivable that you could come to harm in the inner peace of a Karma Kab.

For one thing, the interior is opulent, covered in embroidered silks, etc, with satin cushions, joss-stick incense and twanging sitar music to lull you into deep relaxation.

For another, an effigy of the Hindu god Ganesh sits on the dashboard. He – the remover of all obstacles – is the same god painted on the front of thousands of lorries in India which hurtle down the potholed, buffalo-strewn roads with apparent impunity (even though many of their drivers, one study has shown, could be registered as blind in Western countries).

And third, you can't imagine the main driver and man behind the idea, Tobias Moss, ever reaching a speed which would create a crash. 'Motorways are too fast. I won't go to Gatwick or anywhere like that,' he says. Creating an impact with the populace, however, is what his old Ambassador cars – an Indian reincarnation of the 1950s British Morris Oxford – certainly do as you pass it serenely by. Not drug-induced serenely, of course. 'I've been there and wasted enough time on that,' says Tobias. So, I ask, the slogan on the Karma Kars calendar, 'All Trips Considered', doesn't mean what it would in the hippie heyday? He laughs.

We tour Notting Hill, making a sedate, not to say snail-like, progress squeezing through the crowded Portobello Market. Children gawp, tourists raise their cameras, workmen wave and shout, people give the 'peace' sign in salute, others rush over to talk to Tobias who chats happily oblivious of the cars behind (this part is like a Bombay bazaar). It is more like being royalty, in that nobody, but nobody in the street ignores our car, named *Mosaica*. As well as being gaily decorated with flowers on the outside, it has a fantastic mirror mosaic on the ceiling that wouldn't look out of place in a top-class Bombay brothel (or so I imagine).

One of the other cars, *Kama Sutra* – designed by Tobias' fashion designer girlfriend Heather Allan – is more anonymous outside and more exotic inside. He jokes: 'She made a good job of the car, so I've decided to marry her.' The third car, *Scherezadze*, was designed 'by an Egyptian princess'.

Where did the idea come from? 'I was sitting in a bar in South India with Robin Brown, author of a book about travelling around India on an Enfield Bullet motorbike [another great British design still made in India]. He said: "As you love India so much, Tobias, you shouldn't be driving Mercs around London, you should use these Indian cars." It was one of those moments where everything clicked.'

What about karma in a religious sense? 'We are on this earth to redeem ourselves for a past life,' begins Tobias. Hang on a minute, isn't that a bit well, weird, for a 56-year-old North London Jew? 'Well, I was raised as a Jew, but I first went to India when I was 24 and have lived in both Buddhist and Hindu temples. You could say I'm confused, but I'm not into dogma and rituals.'

Well that's cleared up that then. But how laid back and hippie *is* Karma Kars, and what is it for? 'I don't like going fast, motorways and so on. I'm not interested in airports apart from Heathrow. We're not really a cab company, we're a form of entertainment, and experience. If someone rings up wanting to get somewhere in a hurry, I tell them to get a taxi.' So, at £40 an hour, and if he likes you – 'I refuse a lot of people, you don't have people you don't like in your home, do you, and this is my home, not just a job' – Karma Kars will take you in style to wherever you like, within the M25. The Orient, for example – Leyton Orient, that is. Nirvana, if it's within the M25. But the destination is not the thing, says Tobias. 'The journey is more important than arriving,' says Tobias. 'Life's a journey.'

On another day I could have argued that this philosophy arises from Indian buses and trains, where you must forget any possibility of arriving to endure the longest journeys. But the whole experience has at last got to me and I mutter: 'Cosmic, man' and sink back into the cushions...

• Karma Kars can be contacted on 020 8964 9700.

HAIL A RICKSHAW WALLAH Another Indian method of transport doing well in London is rickshaws. Not the running man sort that poor, sweating, short-lived rickshaw wallahs pull in steamy Calcutta, but modern pedal-powered ones, or pedicabs. Or – if you can bring yourself to say it – **Bugbugs**, the rather cutesy brand name under which they have been brought to London.

They are a fun way to get to a restaurant, show or just have a ride around the West End, and the place to pick one up is Old Compton Street in Soho, or by phoning 020 7620 0500. Being 21st-century pedicabs, Bugbugs are equipped with mobile phones, and are made in the US, or Manchester in the case of the four-wheeled model, which is truly bug-like. 'We get lots of bookings for hen nights and stag nights, but some people just want to cruise around without causing pollution,' says manager Liz Harrison. 'Everyone loves them and it adds a bit of fun to a night out.' But are they safe in modern traffic? 'We think so because in the 18 months since the first one went out we haven't had an accident, and the drivers are trained and insured. Maybe because they're bright yellow, motorists give them a wide berth.' That and disbelief that anyone would ride one of these things up Park Lane.

SAILING PRIVATE RYAN Fancy a tour round London where the driver has to obey not only the rules of the road but the rules of navigation too? Where the bus has lifebelts? Amphibious trips using London streets and the River Thames are run by **London Duck Tours** (✆ *020 7928 3132; www.frogtours.com*) using a World War II-style amphibious military vehicle, adapted for carrying passengers.

The organisers say the yellow-painted 'frogs' (old military types call them Ducks, or DUKWs) are tested and certificated by both the rules for buses and for the river, which must be a headache. The 80-minute tour leaves from behind County Hall and goes round the streets before driving, lemming-like, down a ramp into the river. The tour company had about a dozen of the vehicles last time I checked, but was intending building a more modern version. Perhaps they should go the other way, and go for authenticity. Give customers tin helmets to wear and dummy rifles to hold while coming ashore through fake explosions....

LONDON'S FORGOTTEN TRANSPORT SYSTEM

Amazingly, it is possible to get round London even slower than on the Circle Line: you do the London Ring canal trip, which takes at least two-and-a-half days, and it's a totally different way to see a city you thought you knew, underside and all.

If canal boating brings to mind images of chugging along in chocolate-box picture scenery where thatched yokels go 'ooo-aar', delete them. This is utterly different – a demanding weekend crammed with the unforgettable. Come with me on such a trip.

We start from Southall, West London, on a Friday afternoon on the Grand Union Canal and head towards Birmingham for half a mile, then turn right (east) on the Paddington Arm, heading for Little Venice. This section includes, as it nearly all does, wonderful wildlife and the children were soon spotting herons just a few feet away, cormorants drying their wings, and avocets dipping for silvery fish. I lost count of the times that the youngsters up on the bows about 70ft away (we had a ten-berther but you can get smaller) shouted to 'slow down because there's a coot sitting on a nest.' Even in the grimmest city sections I see more wildlife here than in all my boating trips to the Norfolk Broads and other supposed wildlife reserves.

There are long quiet stretches along the backs of factories to look at, as well as the greenery. You can see anglers, a few children messing about, the odd drunk with a can of Special Brew, but the most remarkable thing about the whole system is how under-used and empty it is, a massive resource all but ignored ever since the railways made it more or less redundant shortly after it was built in the early 19th century. How else could you cross a city of eight million people and meet perhaps four of them in an afternoon?

This is illustrated by a surreal moment, crossing the North Circular (bumper to bumper with traffic) on a double aqueduct designed for busier times. We were the only boat in sight, or rather out of sight, in a parallel universe Londoners obviously know little about.

Having tied up to Kensal Green Sainsbury's for the night (ship's victuals quickly taken on board), we head next morning down to the impossibly pretty Little Venice, one of the few patches where people and money have clearly been attracted to the canal, and where dozens of plush houseboats jostle with bijou restaurants, but for a summer Saturday there is strangely no sign of anyone actually going anywhere on their boats, although there are no locks to put people off. If it had been the Solent we would have passed a hundred moving boats an hour.

We pop through Maida Vale tunnel (272yds) where boats were once legged through by crew lying on the roof of their boat and 'walking' on the roof of the tunnel, while tow horses were led through the streets above (and still are, occasionally) to pick up the boats on the other side. Then it's past Regents Park. We look up to see a horny couple copulating furiously. Luckily, they are antelopes and so this must be London Zoo.

On this section, which includes Blow-Up Bridge (see page 85), you only meet a few tourist canal buses, and at Camden there's our first lock, which the novice crew fumble with while zillions of tourists gawp and offer helpful advice in several languages.

Legging boats through such a long tunnel as Islington's was too time-consuming even by canal standards, so in 1826 a rather natty steam tug was devised, which pulled its way along a chain lying on the canal bed, and the canal boat behind it. This unlikely contraption worked well for more than 100 years.

On in silent, empty canals weaving under and over the road and rail routes thrumming with traffic, we note the wittiest boat name, *Onion Bargee*, and contemplate the longest tunnel, at Islington (960yds).

It is a bizarre thing to be half a mile into a dark tunnel which has been flooded with water, no footpath if anything goes wrong, while London double deckers and the antiques market bustle overhead. The presence of thousands of tons of hill all around you can be felt in your bones. You checked before entering that there's no oncoming traffic (as if there could be, we thought) but to our surprise at the other end there's a boat with its tunnel light on, engine revving, impatient to go in. I tell him there's another boat coming half a mile behind us but he goes in anyway. If the boats are traditional narrow boats, they can squeeze past.

Our journey now takes us towards East London, and more industry and dereliction. This section, the **Regent's Canal**, was opened in 1820 and not much has changed since. Though some gates have been replaced, we used locks (now frequently) that are far older than the railway system that replaced the canals, built, in fact, before our New Zealand crew member's country had even been founded. This is real industrial archaeology.

It helps, of course, if you see romance and interest in abandoned viaducts, soaring brick chimneys and rusting power stations. I much prefer them to ones done up with billions of tourists, dinky souvenir shops and soiled unmade bed art exhibits, but perhaps I'm a little eccentric.

Victoria Park at **Bethnal Green** is a nice place to stop, but after a brew-up we decide to plug on. Here the dereliction becomes a little less picturesque – we tie up at one spot and emerge at street level for a moment to see a gang of youths stoning in the windows of the chip shop we want to visit and a junkie lying unconscious on a bench. While it isn't quite a case of 'pull down the armoured shields and man the starboard gun turrets', we decide not to stay the night there but plug on to Limehouse where, after a heap more locks, we arrive just as the light is fading. We pretend we're in *Apocalypse Now*, cruising through hostile Vietnamese jungle. Actually you're never remotely threatened on the canal itself, as long as you don't stop, but we watch out for 'gooks' in the gloaming. We hurried really because you're not supposed to travel at night.

Limehouse, reached through the beautiful long low arches of the Docklands Light Railway viaduct, is completely different. Futuropolis meets Yuppieville, with amazing skyscrapers, swanky penthouses and a posh marina in which, exhausted but delighted, we found a berth for the night.

Various boats gather this side of the Thames lock on Sunday morning and are called forward into a ship-sized powered lock. The gates open like the start of the Grand National and you're off. Wham! After all those hours of being narrow-minded, as it were, on the canals, you are in a heaving great river with far horizons and large ships passing by. You're in with the big boys and it is for this reason that the London Ring is not for totally inexperienced boaters (who could nevertheless have a great weekend trip to Islington, or a week up the Grand Union towards Tring and the Chilterns from the same starting point). While you don't quite need a duffel coat and binoculars and no-one's chucking water over you and yelling

'Enemy sub, range 4,000 yards, whoop, whoop, whoop!' you do need to secure the breakfast washing-up, shut the side hatches, fit the crew with life-jackets, and inform Woolwich radio of your presence by mobile phone. Plus you can yell all that stuff if it makes you feel better. You can do this trip only with the tides as advised, so not every weekend. You could not possibly beat the tide in a canal boat.

What follows is the highlight of the trip. Before you is Tower Bridge and the **Pool of London**, and your eyes are drawn to hundreds of fascinating buildings and monuments seen from a new angle, and in the case of many such as Somerset House and the Houses of Parliament, the side they were supposed to be seen from. There's a side to the city few Londoners ever consider – the River Police in their blue-lamped motor launches looking out for terrorists and suicides, a river fire station with floating fire engines, a river fuel filling station.

This must be the best river ride on earth. Unbeatable, for you pass not only under Tower Bridge (inexplicably, it fails to open in salute and the RAF flypast doesn't happen either), but also under every other London bridge, from the spider's-web-thin Millennium Bridge and the candy-coloured, far-too-pretty Albert Bridge, all the way to Kew rail and road bridges, where you have to look out for Brentford Aits (Thames speak for islands).

If you pass behind them you will see a completely different type of houseboat owner: water gypsies, their hulks piled high with junk and lashed-up generators thrumming away. Old hippies and counter-culture types who didn't want to get on the property ladder and now never will. Chaps growing herbs – I think they were herbs, man – on their cabin roofs, listening to the Grateful Dead while the ship's cat snoozes at their feet. Rainbow windows, stained glass, Middle Age Travellers if you like, some probably going nowhere. At least this huge city has somewhere for fringe people who don't want to push and shove their way through life.

We now go back into the canal system and, under the unyuppified Brentford High Street, we soon head northwest. There's a short stretch of canal here disfigured by a disgusting amount of floating litter, explained by the fact that here the River Brent joins the canal, along with northwest London's entire output of plastic bags and water bottles; but after that it's back to tranquillity and yes, the chocolate-box rural beauty of the **Hanwell flight of locks**. The crew were by now deft at running from one filling lock to empty the next one, and we made it back to Southall by 19.00. We're soon back in Southall, India's new northwest frontier with its temples, fabulous and cheap food and exotic clothes. In fact the traditionally hand-painted roses and castles on the woodwork of a narrow boat remind me of nothing so much as the gods and flowers painted on the wooden cabs of trucks in India. Exhausted but satisfied, we're glad we tackled London's forgotten transport system and hugely impressed by all we saw. What a trip!

9

Beneath the Eccentric City

DIFFICULT-TO-BELIEVE TUBE EXPERIENCES

It may be inconceivable, looking at today's Tube, to imagine on that system a dining car rolling past with waiters serving gents in tail coats sitting at tables covered in white damask, the glint of heavy silverware reflecting the glow from gilt table lamps. But this Pullman level of luxury could be regularly seen passing Baker Street in the early days of the Metropolitan Line as wealthy commuters from leafy outer suburbs such as Northwood and Rickmansworth – the gin and Jag belt today, or Metroland, as it became known in the 1930s – tucked into full English breakfasts on their way to the City. The staff knew their regular gents so well they'd have the table laid for certain customers and serve their eggs or kippers just after they sat down to peruse *The Times*. The cars were given names such as *Galatea* and were just as luxurious as those on the British version of the Orient Express.

Mind you, the Metropolitan Line was quite unlike any other. Its cranky creator, Sir Edward Watkin, dreamed of great things – he actually started building a Channel Tunnel to take it to Paris, and his line reached out to remote Verney Junction near Buckingham in its attempts to reach the Midlands. Another branch snaked across country to end at Brill, a sleepy hamlet which became a sleepy terminus for the rambling country tramway – people would load pigs for market here, while Londoners would bring their horses for hunting by the train – perhaps the Met dreamed of reaching Oxford but never quite got there.

Of course the Met lines run mostly on the surface or just below it, so its carriages are as big as normal railway trains. How much more difficult would be catering on the tiny trains of the deep-level Tubes?

Yet this happened – and was done well – in the extreme circumstances of the World War II Blitz, when people sheltering from the massive German bombing campaign forced the authorities to open more and more of the Tube as shelters. Previously only disused bits of the system were being used as shelters. Here, people could sleep relatively safely; I say relatively, because if a bomb did penetrate the crowded tunnels, the results could be horrifying. One bomb that fell on Bank Tube in January 1941 killed 111 people.

An excellent book on this period called *The Shelter of the Tubes* by John Gregg (Capital Transport, £16.95, 2001) quotes a Hungarian doctor who was called to the horrific scene at Bank station:

> You English people cannot appreciate the discipline of your own people. I want to tell you I have not found one hysterical shouting patient. I think this very important, that you should not take such things as given – because it does not happen in other countries. If Hitler could have been there for five minutes with me he would have finished the war. He would have realised he has got to take every Englishman and twist him by the neck – otherwise he cannot win this war.

In October of the previous year a bomb caused a tunnel collapse at Balham – you may have seen the almost comical picture of a London double-decker which drove into the crater but you may not have realised that 68 people died down below.

But for the hundreds of thousands sleeping in the deep-level Tubes during the raids, the London Underground had suddenly to provide lighting, fresh air, water, toilets, and food. Six catering trains were hastily organised and ran all night, bringing hot drinks and food to all stations, with the American aid committees stepping in at Christmas and loading trains with a toy for every child huddled in the tunnels.

Something of the spirit of those days is conveyed by a contemporary poster headed: 'Tube Refreshments'. It read: 'This Depot supplies Service Points, Stations and Feeds People. They rely on us for food and drink night and morning. We must not let them down.' And they didn't, even when damaged tracks meant they had to carry the food through the blazing streets.

It's all food for thought as we ride the same tracks today. How petty all our troubles seem compared to the lives of the heroes who were Londoners' parents and grandparents.

TEN FASCINATING BITS OF UNDERGROUND LONDON

Ministry of the Interiors The wine cellar to Cardinal Wolsey's London palace, York Place, renamed Whitehall Palace after Henry VIII dumped Wolsey and seized the building for himself, survived the great fire that destroyed the palace above in the 17th century. In the 1940s this area had to be cleared for the building of the new Ministry of Defence and road widening, but the royal wine cellars were saved by ingenious engineering. The entire structure was exposed to foundation level, a concrete collar inserted, the resulting 1,000-ton block being rolled sideways on rails and lowered into a pit. Now the 60ft by 30ft structure is in the middle of the much bigger basement of the new ministry, and not a stone was dislodged.

Unfortunately, security means we civilians can't pop in for a look at any old time. But the London Open House weekend (see page 308) offers a tour.

Tardis wine vaults The Tardis, you will need to know if you are not a fan of TV's *Dr Who*, was a time machine which was as small as a phone box on the outside but as big as a house on the inside. Berry Bros & Rudd, the long-established wine merchant in St James's which has supplied the crusty old gentlemen's clubs in that area for decade after decade, manages the same trick. On the outside, it is a small, worn-looking shop but inside, hundreds of feet of cellars stock perhaps quarter of a million bottles of wine, including the rarest 19th-century ports and Cognacs. The explanation is the network of cellars under adjoining properties that the burrowing Berry Bros borrowed over three centuries, accessed through a trap door in the shop. You can walk at street level around the corner into Pickering Place, or as far as Pall Mall, and still be above rows of dusty bottles – maturing nicely.

King William Street Tube There are more disused Tube stations in London than many a city has on its entire network – an amazing 48 in all where only ghost trains call. Some of these were little more than above-ground halts that were later closed or moved, or stations on the annoyingly cluttered Piccadilly Line, which has, thankfully for passengers heading for Heathrow, lost Brompton Road and Down Street in central London, plus six other suburban stations. Not all trains stopped there, but 'Passing Brompton Road' became such a familiar cry for passengers (like today's 'Mind the gap') that a play called *Passing Brompton Road!* became a surprise hit at the Criterion Theatre in 1928. Older people may remember British Museum station on the Central Line.

Other ghost stations are on sections of line completely abandoned, the first and oldest being at King William Street in the City. The City and South London Railway, the world's first electrically-operated Tube, opened from Stockwell in South London in 1890. Because of Parliament's insistence that the newfangled Tube should not burrow beneath buildings, even in the tightly packed City, the King William Street terminus was badly laid out and its approach was so steep and twisting that trains sometimes had to have several runs at it; access for passengers was poor too.

Nevertheless, such was the success of this railway that an extension from Borough to Moorgate (now the City branch of the Northern Line) was opened in 1900, making 1,267yds of former track to King William Street redundant. In World War II, as Nazi bombs rained down on London, it was obvious that it would make an excellent air-raid shelter and large new entrances were provided for workers from adjoining office blocks to pour in. Bunks were erected in the tunnel, but signals and a signal box remained from the station's short life 40 years before. After the war, these were sealed up again. Twice in the more than a century since the station closed, the building above, Regis House, has been replaced, but the station slumbers on with wartime posters warning 'Careless talk costs lives' recalling its short revival as a bomb shelter.

Aldwych Tube's theatrical history That such abandonments of whole sections of expensively built Tube railway in good working order can still take place was shown in 1999 when the relatively new part of the Jubilee Line from Green Park to Charing Cross was closed, to enable the south and east extension of the line through Westminster to Greenwich and Stratford to open.

A little-used branch line, which nevertheless ended right in theatreland and which closed in 1994, had a very peculiar history. It was the Aldwych branch. If you get a chance for a station tour – arranged occasionally through the London Transport Museum – it's well worth it. Because the station was on a sleepy, one-station branch of the Piccadilly line at Holborn, it was relatively unaltered by station interior revamping diktats and retains much of its original art nouveau style tilework.

First, its history. It opened as the Strand station in 1907, and was to have been the terminus for the Great Northern and Strand Railway, linking the river to King's Cross and Finsbury Park. That line's merger with the Brompton and Piccadilly Circus Railway made a through route, giving rise to the even more cumbersomely named Great Northern, Piccadilly and Brompton Railway (now thankfully the Piccadilly line), leaving this station on a dead-end branch. It was for a while intended to make a river crossing to Waterloo from here, but it never happened.

The station served a few hundred people each day, and was closed for seven years during World War II, becoming a bomb shelter for Egyptian mummies, etc, from the nearby British Museum. Early on, from 1917, one of the sets of tracks was ripped up, so the through theatre trains from the suburbs could come in, but not leave again (not rejoin the 'main line' in one movement, that is) which was daft. So the service was reduced to a shuttle from Holborn, usually just two coaches, which was plenty.

The kind of architectural detail Tube history buffs love is typified by the lifts here, original wood-panelled Otis jobs with art nouveau ventilation screens designed by Leslie Green. (Ironically it was the need to spend £3 million replacing these lifts that led to the station's closure in 1994.)

I can see the appeal of this place, and the lovely tilework that gives it such period charm. But some of the arcane details the buffs get into are quite amazing. Take the directional arrows on Tube walls, for example. Now a *real* Tube buff knows you can date these arrows in disused stations by the number of feathers (flights) they have. Four flights means 1920s–30s; three flights, 1930s–40s, two flights, late 1940s–50s; one flight, late 1960s–early 70s; no flights from the late 1970s onwards. It may be staggering – or sad – that people know stuff like this, but it's certainly eccentric. For more information try www.ltmuseum.co.uk.

5 **London's Eiffel Tower went loco** Wembley's famous soccer stadium, old and new, has had a steam railway locomotive buried under its pitch for 80 years. It's all to do with an all-but-forgotten scheme dreamt up by eccentric visionary railwayman Sir Edward Watkin to transform London and Wembley in particular. In 1893 he started building a Wembley rival to the Eiffel Tower (known of course as the Watkin Tower), designed to be 170ft taller, and this monstrosity reached the first stage by 1895. Because of financial problems the tower never went any higher, although thousands of people ascended the bit that was there. It was demolished for scrap in 1907, and the land levelled for redevelopment. During this process the locomotive either fell off the tracks into a muddy morass, or being beyond repair was tipped in as part of the landfill, depending on whom you believe. But it's definitely been there all these years, through dozens of FA Cup Finals, buried deep under the hallowed turf.

6 **The Underground line for ghosts** London has the world's most complex underground railway, but there's a whole mothballed separate system down there on which no-one ever rides, or in fact ever rode. Until 2003, 50 trains ran 19 hours a day along 23 complicated miles of track, yet no member of the public ever travelled on them, heard them or saw them.

This was Mail Rail, the Post Office's own 2ft gauge system of driverless trains, opened in 1927, for more than 70 years carrying four million letters a day that would otherwise have been in little red vans snarled up by London's traffic. One end is at Paddington, and the other at Whitechapel, and it is still there. It mostly runs 70ft (21m) underground, although it ducks and soars from time to time to pass normal Tube lines and other underground features.

There are a couple of battery locomotives in siding tunnels for emergency and repair staff to use, so in truth a very few people *have* actually travelled through this unique system, and one lady who braved the darkness from one end to the other said how very bumpy it was. But plans to extend it to the east and west, raised from time to time, have been scotched on grounds of cost. Another radical suggestion was to make loops into the basements of the major Oxford Street stores, such as Selfridges, under which it runs, to supply goods to the stores from warehouses outside the city centre without generating road traffic.

Yet in 2003 the system was closed down and consequently the little red van population of London was redoubled, and the once totally reliable mail system was further eroded. Meanwhile, the London Mayor, nasal newt-lover Ken Livingstone and his expensive talking shop of bossy bureaucrats at the London Assembly, were implementing the congestion charge system to reduce traffic. You couldn't make it up, frankly.

7 Boadicea's grave and Harry Potter The grave of Boadicea (or Boudicca), the great warrior queen, is located under platform nine, or perhaps ten, at King's Cross station. There is a fab sculpture of her in full charge on her chariot at the north end of Westminster Bridge. Talking of fearsome old British queens, you can find some modern-day versions lurking round King's Cross late at night along with ladies daubed in strange colours (not woad, of course), but they aren't the sort you'd want to meet. There is a Boadicea Street just north of here, off Copenhagen Street.

Another legend had it that a barrow (burial mound, that is!) on Parliament Hill, Hampstead, was Boadicea's last resting place after her death in AD62. But a thorough investigation of it by archaeologists at the end of the 19th century failed to find any trace of her, and anyway, such barrows were old long before Roman times. Perhaps a classic case of a legend being moulded to fit the landscape. (My favourite is the '12 Apostles' standing stones near Dumfries in Scotland; it was clever of those ancient Brits to name them after people who weren't born for another 2,000 years or so.) Oddly, that queen of children's fiction, J K Rowling, used a platform 9¾ for the departure point of the Hogwarts Express from the station here in her globally successful Harry Potter series. And so it was that platform 9 was temporarily redesignated 9¾ so that a steam engine representing the Hogwarts Express could draw in a promotional train carrying Ms Rowling, rattling old Boadicea's bones. Ah, these indomitable British women … Meanwhile, some wag has put up a platform 9¾ sign with a trolley half-way through the wall.

8 Secret spare tunnels One of the most apparently ludicrous of the myths and legends of secret bunkers and tunnels under London – and of course there are plenty of both – seemed to be the one about various Northern Line station tunnels having duplicate tunnels underneath them. I mentioned this once to an LT press officer when I was preparing a newspaper article and received a nervous laugh, as if they had been asked about UFOs at Uxbridge or trolls at Turnham Green. A couple of days later, I received the oddest call back from the press officer. 'You know those duplicate tunnels under Northern Line stations such as Belsize Park? Well they *do* exist, it's just that I didn't know and didn't believe it either. Something to do with air raid shelters.' I'd like to find out more, so if you recall sheltering in one of them in World War II, for example, drop me a line. The idea might have been that the trains could continue to use the existing tunnels, while people sheltered beneath in spare tunnels. If these tunnels are indeed there, why not join them up with each other, creating a non-stop express route in from Golders Green to Camden Town to speed rush-hour commuters from the outer suburbs past slower stopping trains?

9 The Tube station that never was Insanely, there is one station on the Tube that never made it to the surface, although it *was* constructed underground. Still known unofficially to Underground staff as the Bull & Bush after the pub (which inspired the song), North End station would have been near that pub, between Golders Green and Hampstead on the Northern Line. You can still see a widening of the tracks where the platforms should be. This bizarre state of affairs is usually blamed on doughty philanthropist, Mrs Henrietta Barnett, an eccentric battleaxe who realised that the new Tube would logically mean housing sprawl extending over Hampstead Heath, one of London's premier open spaces. She was in the process in 1903 of securing 80 acres north of the station as an extension of the heath and wasn't going to let the Charing Cross, Euston and Hampstead Railway spoil things. Politicians at the London County Council were unimpressed by her munificence, thinking no doubt that well-to-do types at Hampstead already had enough green space and that ordinary people needed houses.

The doughty Mrs Barnett – who wasn't opposed to the Tube as much as to urban housing sprawl – then changed tack and proposed the construction of Hampstead Garden Suburb, an estate laid out on land nearer the Finchley Road and on the revolutionary 'garden city' principles then being tried out in Letchworth, Hertfordshire. This would be an improving and healthy environment for the 'industrial classes', she argued. This did the trick and the Garden Suburb was laid out, although the chances today of any industrial type getting a home there among the millionaire celebs without winning the Lottery first are as remote as their chances of finding a way out of the Tube station that never was. The Tube bosses, having dug out the station tunnels and cross passages, gave up on the station because there wouldn't have been enough custom to pay for the expensive lifts. Its above-ground site became a house, No 1 Hampstead Way. Perversely, in recent years a small lift *has* been installed, for maintenance access.

10 **Greathead and his Shield** Just near the Bank of England, in Cornhill, is a statue of the Victorian, James Greathead, the man who made tunnelling under London's rivers and gravel beds possible. It's appropriate that he's standing on what seems to be a vent for an Underground line. His invention was a framework with a top shield which was pushed forwards from the tunnel sections behind with rams as the digging progressed, when new sections were bolted in. You can see near here a 19th-century Greathead shield used in the digging of the Waterloo and City Line. Take the Waterloo and City to Bank, then follow the signs to the Docklands Light Railway, and you'll see it in the former Waterloo and City overrun tunnel. There's the shield, painted red.

• Greenwich's underground mystery and the tunnel of flatulence, page 237.

THE LOST RIVERS OF LONDON AND THEIR LEGENDS

TRACKED BY GHOSTS AND DISEASES There's something truly fascinating about London's lost rivers. Most of the seven to the north, and the seven less interesting ones to the south, are entirely forgotten even by Londoners, until one floods, collapses or blows up (as the Fleet did once, because of sewer gas, demolishing a few houses).

Yet even today you can plot their sources, their routes and their outfalls by a number of methods. Controversially, a London hospital doctor once showed you could plot their courses by the incidence of disease on the ground above, particularly respiratory problems brought on by dampness and sewers. It is also claimed that you can plot them by the incidence of ghosts – there are supposedly more murders and suicides by water than in dry places.

More concretely, their old courses are given away by the road names above – Brook Street, Bridge Road, Bourne Street ('bourne' meaning stream, and revealing the former presence of the Celts here), etc – or by the river names being directly incorporated into the street map, as in: Effra Road in Brixton; Fleet Street in the City; and Westbourne Grove in Notting Hill.

Also, if you can get a vantage point high enough, you can see how the hills and valleys of London's landscape, difficult though they are to see today, still reflect the hidden watercourses below, Farringdon Road on the course of the Fleet being a clear example. And yet there are places where the authorities don't know where their rivers go, except that they reappear further along. Another, eighth, river seems to have formed itself under Soho after the area was built up, although experts debate whether the so-called Cranbourn exists or is just an abandoned sewer which has made a new route for itself. All of these rivers carry a lot of strange history with them, swirling in the darkness, much forgotten, much not. The lost rivers of North London are:

The Fleet – Frozen corpses and exploding filth
One of London's lost rivers that has much influence on today's landscape is the Fleet. It rises near the Jack Straw's Castle pub in Hampstead, goes into the Vale of Health and into the ponds, disappearing underground at South End Green. It is soon joined by a tributary from Highgate ponds, which starts at Kenwood House. In fact, if you climb Parliament Hill on Hampstead Heath for the excellent view, you will be standing between the two branches of the Fleet. The Fleet flows under the Regent's Canal at Camden Town, past King's Cross and along the obvious river valley that is Farringdon Road, discharging into the Thames beneath Blackfriars Bridge. The Saxon *fleete* is said to mean 'float', a navigable river, so pedantically the upper reaches of the Fleet should take the river's other name, the Cent or Cant.

Holborn viaduct which bridges this Fleet valley (over Farringdon Road) shows how steep it really is; the name 'Holborn' itself means 'stream in a hollow'. Eventually, the river, or the Fleet Ditch, as it became known, became so choked with sewage sludge that people who fell in would suffocate, not drown, as frozen corpses with their legs up in the air sometimes revealed the next day. In 1862 so much foul gas had collected in the covered-over river that it blew up, throwing brickwork all over the place and causing traffic havoc.

Its contribution to the Great Stink of London's summers was in no small way responsible for the pressure to build London's great sewerage systems, the work of Victorian geniuses such as Bazalgette (see *Hammersmith Bridge*, page 256).

The Fleet was once a wide river, 60ft wide at one point in Camden Town, discharging into a massive basin 500ft wide below the bridge which stood where Ludgate Circus now is. Ludgate was once at the western edge of the City, so as it was necessary for the professions of journalism and law to be outside but near the City, shunned as they were by nobility and the Church who found them somewhat vulgar no doubt, their position across the Fleet was ideal. No doubt some cynics will believe a sewer full of rats, vermin and parasites fed by fetid gutters of filth was the ideal spot for journalists and lawyers. As a Fleet Street journalist myself, I couldn't possibly comment.

The Tyburn – Walking to doom
Tyburn is a fascinating area, forever associated with death, crime, retribution and martyrdom thanks to the Tyburn tree, a three-sided gallows which stood at the junction of Tyburn Road (now Oxford Street) with Edgware Road, near where the Marble Arch now stands.

Before the gallows were taken down in 1783, an estimated 40,000 people met their ends here. Tens of thousands of people would turn out to see a murderer strung up. Tickets would be sold for stands: the nobility would book the best spots in overlooking houses. The deaths would have been slow because the modern noose and trapdoor were not used. Instead people waited for 'the turning off' where the prisoners would be turned off their ladders or carts if they refused to jump and then choke to death agonisingly slowly.

But during the Protestant Reformation, and the associated paranoia about Popish plots, the Tyburn tree saw more than 100 Catholic martyrs go to their deaths here, sometimes on the flimsiest of pretexts.

Not that it was *all* Protestant paranoia. The Catholics enthusiastically burned Protestants during their brief return under Mary and their supposed treason of supporting the Pope was certainly true in the 1605 Gunpowder Plot, and various plots and rebellions up to the last big one, the 1745 Jacobite Rising, had an undeniable Catholic element.

Later attempts to blame everything on Popish plots were, however, often unfair – the inscription on the Monument in the City to the Fire of London blaming it on Popish plots has now been chipped off as ludicrous, and the last Catholic martyr, Primate of All Ireland, Oliver Plunket, was hanged at Tyburn in 1681 for taking part in a plot that probably didn't exist.

The Tyburn convent was established early in the 20th century off Bayswater Road and although the main chapel is public, there is also a shrine to the Tyburn martyrs, the more than 100 Catholics who met their deaths here as a result of Protestant persecution, complete with a replica of the triangular gibbet.

Each year, on the last Sunday afternoon in April, the Tyburn walk led by a Catholic bishop retraces the three-mile last walk of the martyrs from Newgate prison in the City to the Tyburn shrine for a special service.

Neither was the Tyburn tree the end of the humiliation for those condemned to death. Many would be cut down and taken to the anatomy theatre of the Company of Barber-Surgeons at the Barbican, back in the City. There was little demarcation between barbers and surgeons until the 17th century, and indeed that's why a real barber in London still has a striped pole outside his shop, the red stripe running down it denoting the blood associated with his profession. You could be bled by a barber who kept leeches for such purposes and Samuel Pepys records going to the anatomy theatre to watch a still warm body being cut open by barber-surgeons and then enjoying a hearty beef dinner afterwards.

Surgeons didn't form their own company until 1745, eventually becoming today's Royal College of Surgeons, and so the barbers' anatomy theatre – a fine oval job by Inigo Jones – was eventually demolished.

Maps of early 18th-century London show Tyburn Road (now Oxford Street) as being on the north edge of London, with open fields towards Marylebone to the north, and Tyburn Lane (now Park Lane) facing open country (then, as now, Hyde Park), so what is now Marble Arch was the very northwest corner of London.

The Tyburn rises on Haverstock Hill which leads up to Hampstead from Chalk Farm. It flows down through Swiss Cottage, over the Regents Canal in a large conduit pipe near the northwest corner of the Park. Authorities disagree whether it feeds the Regents Park lake or not, but the Tyburn certainly continues under Marylebone High Street and beside the consequentially winding Marylebone Lane (the village of St Mary's by the bourne), across Oxford Street (further east than the Tyburn tree), Mayfair, Berkeley Square, under Buckingham Palace and eventually falls into the Thames off Grosvenor Road, west of Vauxhall Bridge. So much of it leaks into the Tube near Victoria that a pumping station sucks out a million gallons

of water a day. On the other side of Vauxhall Bridge, on the south side, is the outfall of the **Effra**, one of the lost rivers of South London.

Once, long before manmade embankments narrowed the Thames, a wide marsh surrounded the river and the Tyburn entered this marsh at the edge of the firm ground where Buckingham Palace now stands, Westminster Abbey was built on an island in the Thames, as was Battersea on the other side (see *Place names*, page 78). There's an amusing record of a Victorian boating trip up the Tyburn: when the boatman said that they were now under Buckingham Palace, the passengers stood up and sang the national anthem. Lucky they didn't fall in the pooh.

The Tyburn also carries with it the history of the dashing French highwayman, Claude Duval, the very handsome, young, courteous and honourable (apart from being a thief) terror of the rich in the 1660s. He stalked the lonely hills near Hampstead village, often right at the Tyburn's source and, having held up a coach at gun point and with many apologies relieved the gentry inside of their baubles, he would then sometimes ask the ladies to dance in the moonlight, with much bowing and courtesy. He was arrested while blind drunk in the Marquess of Granby pub in Chandos Street, Covent Garden (or rather in its predecessor, the Hole in the Wall). He was hanged at Tyburn in 1670, and his lying in state, as it were, at a pub in St Giles drew huge crowds, many of them fascinated females. His subsequent funeral at St Paul's, Covent Garden (see also page 107) was attended by several society beauties. What his connection with these ladies was is something we have to guess at, but a stone once said to be at St Paul's perhaps points us in the right direction:

> Here lies DuVall:
> Reader if male thou art
> Look to thy purse;
> If female to thy heart.

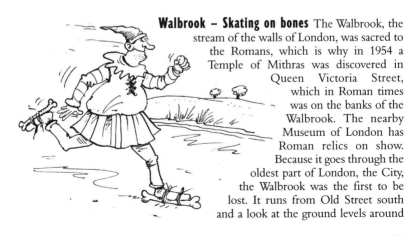

Walbrook – Skating on bones The Walbrook, the stream of the walls of London, was sacred to the Romans, which is why in 1954 a Temple of Mithras was discovered in Queen Victoria Street, which in Roman times was on the banks of the Walbrook. The nearby Museum of London has Roman relics on show. Because it goes through the oldest part of London, the City, the Walbrook was the first to be lost. It runs from Old Street south and a look at the ground levels around the Bank of England shows that it runs under the skirts of this the 'Old Lady of Threadneedle Street'. A similar dip in Cannon Street reveals its course, now much diminished, although in the 16th century still strong enough to carry away a youth who was trying to ford it and drown him when he hit a cartwheel at Dowgate, where the river then poured into the Thames. In the 12th century the river was recorded as flooding Moorfields, then freezing, when City apprentices tied animal bones to their shoes and skated on it. Moorfields was so marshy that the road name Finsbury Pavement records a causeway that was the only firm footing here. The river itself is remembered in a City street name, Walbrook, which still leads into Dowgate, and a lovely, light and airy Wren church, St Stephen's, Walbrook. It runs unseen a few feet beneath Cannon Street Tube. This church, by the way, contains the grave of the 18th-century playwright and architect Sir John Vanbrugh (died 1726) who was good but not brilliant at either career. His tombstone, now gone, was inscribed by rival (and better) architect Nicholas Hawksmoor, who said pithily:

Lie heavy on him Earth! For he
Laid many heavy loads on thee

Counter's Creek – Up the creek in a forgotten canal

A once-clear stream edged with healthy watercress, and rising near Kensal Green, Counter's Creek flowed down the west edge of Kensington, forming its boundary, as it still does, unseen. The stream was once crossed (by what is now Fulham Road) by a sand ford, later bridged, hence Sandford Bridge, now **Stamford Bridge**. It became known as Chelsea Creek by the time it hit the Thames.

After hundreds of years of trickling along in rural peace, during the 19th century Counter's Creek underwent several huge revolutions. First, Lord Kensington, impressed by the canal boom of the preceding 30 years, canalised the creek from the Thames to the Grand Union Canal at Paddington not with a mere narrowboat canal but with one capable of taking 100-ton freighters. There were locks to allow for the change in height, one being at Cromwell Road. It was opened with a stately barge procession, brass bands, a banquet and much pomp in 1828, just in time for the railway boom to make it completely redundant. Later, with the development of the huge Brompton Cemetery alongside the canal, there was a suggestion that funeral parties could arrive by boat, but with the speeding up of roads and railways, this notion was soon, er, dead in the water.

By 1839 it had switched to being a carrier of sewage, which it did for around 20 years until, condemned because of an outbreak of cholera in Fulham which might have been caused by the creek, it was ordered to be filled in. Soon afterwards, in 1863, railway tracks were laid over it. Now known as the West London Line, the route still forms the boundary between Kensington and Hammersmith.

The Westbourne – Deaths and Peter Pan

The Westbourne is another of London's lost rivers which rises on Hampstead Heath, in a small detached part of it near Whitestone Pond, flowing under Branch Hill as an infant rivulet.

Curvy West End Lane towards Kilburn was once a rural route beside this wandering stream which was also known as the Kilburn. (More plausible than the violent thoughts which may have prompted a possibly drunk late-night station announcer at St Pancras to declare once that a train was going to Kilburn, Luton, Pillage – you have to say it out loud.) Eventually it goes into the **Serpentine** and then underground again. This pleasant lake, named because of its snake-like shape, was once a scene of Victorian horror when dozens of people skating on it were drowned when the ice gave way. After that it was supposedly filled in so you can stand up all the way across – but don't take my word for it.

Oddly, thousands of commuters unknowingly pass daily under the Westbourne at **Sloane Square** station, where it passes over the tracks and platforms in a massive pipe which thrums with a gentle vibration when the river is in full flood. Eventually it reaches the Thames by Chelsea Hospital.

Incidentally, Sloane Square station not only has its own lost river but also a sad link with the 'lost boys' of *Peter Pan* fame. The author of this famous children's work, J M Barrie, had adopted five boys when their parents died; one of them was Peter – Peter Llewelyn Davies – who became a publisher. Barrie first met the orphaned boys in Kensington Gardens which are inextricably linked with the book and where there is a monument to Peter Pan.

When I say Barrie adopted the boys after their parents died, in truth he informally adopted them well before that – which led to tensions between the families who lived either side of Kensington Gardens (Barrie's wife couldn't or wouldn't have children).

Barrie had grown up in Scotland always mourning his dead brother David. He dressed up as David to appease his mother's grief from time to time, which sounds distinctly unhealthy. He said he always looked wistfully back: 'When I became a man, he was still a boy of 15.' Surely this is the origin of the boy who would never grow up.

Even more interestingly, there are some stones in **Kensington Gardens** which look like miniature tombstones, one of them actually marked PP. Barrie told children there that these were the graves of babies who fell out of their perambulators while their nannies weren't looking, and were left to die in the park. Their souls lived on and flew round the Gardens at night, he supposed, well before the Peter Pan play was written. In fact the PP stood not for Peter Pan but for, I believe, Paddington Parish, for these are parish boundary stones which one can see tucked away here and there all over this part of London.

Those who are reared on the Disneyfied *Peter Pan* are always surprised on reading the original to their children how bleak and black it is, and how almost malevolent Peter is. Barrie said he was dissatisfied with the statue of Peter Pan in Kensington Gardens, for example, 'because it doesn't show the Devil in Peter'. The world wanted Peter to be a benign, happy boy. He isn't, and now you know why.

Back to the macabre link with London's lost river, the Westbourne. But one more bit of Pan trivia – no-one was called Wendy until this book was published, and since then millions of girls have been given the name.

Peter Llewelyn Davies grew up feeling oppressed by the legacy of being labelled, rightly or wrongly, as the model for Peter Pan and hating the book. No doubt an unstable personality, he threw himself under a train here at Sloane Square in April 1960, more than 20 years after Barrie himself had died. In fact three of Barrie's adopted boys died terrible deaths: George, Barrie's favourite, was killed in World War I; Michael, perhaps Barrie's second favourite, drowned in the Cherwell while an undergraduate at Oxford; while Peter died under a Tube train, and under the Westbourne as it happens.

On a lighter note, Barrie dedicated the royalties from his story to the Great Ormond Street Hospital for Sick Children so, however many times people remake soppy versions of this great yarn, the great hospital always benefits, at least until the Barrie copyright ran out in 2007. And while we're on the subject and in the Sloane Square area, Mallord Street, Chelsea, is where A A Milne wrote *Winnie-the-Pooh* for his son Christopher Robin, who was born here in 1920; another boy who grew into a man not always delighted to be constantly reminded of his eponymous fictional character.

Stamford Brook – Running with blood Probably the least substantial of North London's seven lost rivers, Stamford Brook not only has a road in Hammersmith named after it but a whole Tube station of its own on the District Line. It was also the site of a bloody battle in the Civil War (see page 32).

Kew's pagoda

10

Eccentric Churches

LONDON'S STRANGEST CHURCHES

SECRET CHURCHES AND HIDDEN PUNS Many London churches are so hemmed in by later development that they are accessible only by narrow passages, and located in secret churchyards, or tiny courtyards, and so are easily missed. The discovery of these treasures is all the sweeter for it.

One such is **St Mary-at-Hill** off Eastcheap in the City, although the church is not as old as its churchyard, being a modern rebuild after a fire.

Another not visible from the road, **St Bartholomew the Great**, is accessed through a curious medieval gate, surmounted by a Tudor beamed building, from West Smithfield, also in the City. St Bartholomew's was a priory before Henry VIII destroyed the monasteries, but its name lives on in the famous Bart's hospital nearby.

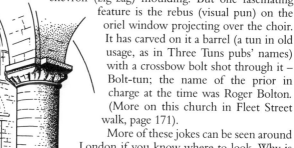

The interior of St Bartholomew's is pure Norman (no pointed Gothic arches here) with massive pillars, romanesque arches and chevron (zig-zag) moulding. But one fascinating feature is the rebus (visual pun) on the oriel window projecting over the choir. It has carved on it a barrel (a tun in old usage, as in Three Tuns pubs' names) with a crossbow bolt shot through it – Bolt-tun; the name of the prior in charge at the time was Roger Bolton. (More on this church in Fleet Street walk, page 171).

St Bartholomew the Great

More of these jokes can be seen around London if you know where to look. Why is the famous statue of Eros at Piccadilly shooting his arrow downwards, as if to *bury* the *shaft* of his arrow in the roadway? Because it was a monument to the Earl of Shaftesbury. Not convinced? There is a tomb in Westminster Abbey, of the last Abbot of Westminster, showing a man slipping from a tree. Did he die like this? No – but his name was I slip – John Islip in fact, and there's a road nearby named after him.

Still not convinced? Try the puzzling rebus milestones between London and Eastbourne on the A22. These give mileages but no written destination at all except a bow and some bells. Bow bells … the bells of the church of St Mary-le-Bow, which was the traditional measuring centre of London. Freaky or what?

COCKNEYS WITH BELLS ON It would be no exaggeration to say that, **St Mary-le-Bow** (Bank Tube, walk down Poultry to Cheapside) has an impact on the aural, and oral, heritage of London, the nation and even Europe.

For one thing the Bow Bells define who is and who is not a cockney. Those born within hearing of the bells – the biggest being a two-ton job called the 'Great Bell of Bow' – are by definition cockneys. This means that a lot of luvvable cockneys born in the outer suburbs, or dare I say it, beyond the M25, either have superb long-range hearing or are fakes. (The worst of the latter type are the public school-educated toffs who reinvent themselves for the media in a kind of reverse Eliza Doolittle process, moving effortlessly from 'Actually, mother, I would awfully like some Perrier' to ''Ere, Darren, gotta glass o' wa'er' in a few months. I name no names, but we know who you are. It is so well-known a phenomenon nowadays that the accent is known as 'Mockney'.)

It was these same Bow Bells that famously called back Dick Whittington, the real medieval lad who came to London to make his fortune, failed and set off home dejectedly. He reached Highgate Hill – the spot is today marked with a stone – when he heard the Bow Bells saying:

> Dick Whittington, Dick Whittington, Thrice Lord Mayor of London

Well, he did become Lord Mayor of London, three times, but I'll have a pint of whatever he was drinking because the rhythm of the bells could have just as well have been saying:

> Dick Whittington, Dick Whittington, You useless dozy half-wit.

More seriously, recently, accurately and poignantly, the sound of Bow Bells was broadcast in World War II to the peoples of Europe enslaved by Hitler. How much this meant to them can be seen from the Norwegian chapel in the church, a beautiful place that recalls how the sound of far-off bells could keep alive the hope of liberation.

And, lastly, that name. Is it anything to do with the district of Bow in East London? No. It is an ancient church, destroyed at least twice, once by the Great Fire of 1666 and once by the Blitz of the 1940s. Yet part of the original medieval church remains undamaged – look in the crypt for the arches, or bows, that gave the church the nickname that has stuck for a thousand years. Just as in Bow Street, a bow means simply a curve.

THRASHED CHOIRBOYS, PILLAGING DANES AND EXPLODING ANVILS Another
church whose bells have gone into legend is **St Clement Danes**. St Clement Danes (Temple Tube, walk up Arundel Street) is a most unusual church for many reasons, not just its role in the ancient rhyme 'Oranges and Lemons' (see page 71). Not only does it stand isolated, hemmed in by rushing traffic like a rock in a torrent, but it looks to the sky – it's the church of the Royal Air Force. The men and women of the RAF, and the thousands of them who perished during World War II, are remembered here.

St Clement Danes was gutted in that war and left a blackened shell. Of Sir Christopher Wren's fabulous legacy of 51 churches, built to replace 98 destroyed in that earlier disaster, the Great Fire of 1666, just 27 remain more or less intact. Much of the City of London was reduced to rubble, thanks to the 417 high-explosive bombs, thousands of incendiaries, 13 parachute mines and 2,498 oil bombs that were dropped on it.

A sea of yellow ragwort grew in the roofless interior of the bombed-out church, although Wren's lovely steeple survived. The bells, rehung after World War I and used in the carillon beloved of the rector in the 1920s, the Rev William Pennington-Bickford, had been taken down and stored in a pile of sand at the bottom of the tower for safety during the Blitz as so many churches were being hit. Sadly, when the firemen fighting the fire that destroyed the roof of the nave played their hoses on the tower to save it, the cold water cracked the hot bells. Having been destroyed by aerial bombardment, it was apt that the church was restored as the RAF's church, when this parish was merged with that of the almost adjacent church of St Mary-le-Strand, now also stuck on a traffic island.

Yes, that's Strand as in shoreline – St Clement Danes was indeed once at the waterline. Its squat tower had cannon on it for firing at sea raiders or unruly mobs. It is claimed that, even further back, when the Danes were finally driven out of England by the Anglo-Saxons, those who had married Englishwomen were compelled to live between the isle of thorns (now Westminster) and Ludgate – in other words, here. But no-one knows the origin of the word 'Danes' in its name for sure.

St Clement Danes was a few hundred yards west of the line where the Great Fire stopped, so Wren helped rebuild it – for which he charged no fee – because it was decrepit, not because it was burned down as were so many other ancient churches destroyed at that time.

One great loss from all these changes was the ending of St Clement Danes' version of the ceremony of beating the bounds, surely one of the very best versions of this ancient custom. **Beating the bounds**, which still goes on in many a British parish, involves the clergymen on Ascension Day taking young people such as choirboys to the boundary stones of the parish and beating them – usually the stones – to drum into the next generation exactly where the parish boundary lay. (No wonder children don't know where their parish boundaries are any more, you may think.)

St Clement Danes had one of the most colourful versions of these ceremonies. Its parish line on one side went right down the middle of the Thames, so the boys were bizarrely taken out to thrash the water with willow wands. On land the boys thrashed various markers on the ground – you can still see an ancient iron anchor mark with 'SCD' on it in Strand Lane, and there are more in nearby Devereux Court. I'm told one of the marks was in a building that had been raised higher than the old street level so a choirboy had to be lowered headfirst into a dark hole and bumped on the relevant stone. It's the sort of eccentric tradition that the British usually cherish, and it's a shame that small matters such as the Danes raping and pillaging, the Black Death, Great Fire, Plague and the church being destroyed by Nazi bombs and the parish disappearing, should have allowed a good tradition to lapse.

And why *do* the remaining parish marks have an anchor on them, including the one you can see on the side of the tower? Because it was a shoreline parish? Not a bit of it. It's because St Clement, the patron saint of blacksmiths, was martyred in AD100 by being thrown into the sea with an anchor tied to him.

• St Clements, oranges and lemons and a right old ding-dong: see page 71.

FASCINATING FEATURES AND MARVELLOUS MARBLES The most over-the-top Victorian church, festooned with layers and layers of decoration for its own sake, can be found at **All Saints** in Margaret Street, W1 (near Oxford Circus) where the walls positively drip with colour. The multi-coloured stone pulpit is just insane. It is as if you'd tried to paper your house using pages torn from hundreds of wallpaper sample books – there's every kind of marble imaginable here in architect William Butterfield's psychedelic 1850 creation.

This is High Church Anglo-Catholicism at its most decorative and about as far as you could possibly get from the plain, whitewashed simplicity of the Puritans' churches 200 years before.

Staggering out into the sunshine I had a sensation similar to that of coming out of richly decorated Chinese temples in Hong Kong or Singapore and straight into a modern city. But then I walked across the road and by chance into the Fo Guang Temple (see below, page 117).

WEIRD NAMES WHICH TELL GREAT STORIES You couldn't make up names like those of some London churches: St Vedast; St Mary le Stocks; St Peter Ad Vincula (St Peter in Chains, appropriately in the Tower of London); St Cyprian (Clarence Gate, Marylebone); and St Lawrence Jewry-next-Guildhall. St Alfege's, Greenwich, has a better claim to its name than anywhere else, as this is the very spot where rampaging rapacious Vikings who had come up the Thames in their longboats slew Alfege, Archbishop of Canterbury.

Near Blackfriars, a few paces up Victoria Street, is the quaintly-named **St Andrew-by-the-Wardrobe** which sounds like something out of a Narnia story. There's been a church here since at least the 13th century but it's been through a few upheavals, to put it mildly. Formerly known, only slightly less eccentrically, as St Andrew juxta Barnard Castle after the old fortifications nearby, its name changed when the royal apparel stores were moved nearby. It was destroyed by the Great Fire of London in 1666 and rebuilt by Sir Christopher Wren. It was then gutted by bombs in 1941 and its interior rebuilt in the 1960s.

Other churches in the City with unusual names include St James Garlickhythe, St Margaret Pattens and St Ethelreda's Chapel (Roman Catholic). Going without is perhaps saintly, but we have a St Botolph Without Aldersgate, St Botolph Without Aldgate, and a St Botolph Without Bishopsgate. Their names simply refer, of course, to their position outside the old City gates. Ditto St Giles Cripplegate. Equally, the distinction between St Bartholomew the Great and St Bartholomew the Less refers, of course, not to two saints, but to the relative status of these two churches, both in the Smithfields area.

Oddly, few of the City churches are open on Sunday. The population has shifted and City workers, since the advent of the train, tram and bus, now live further afield and go to their own local Sunday churches, while the few working-class inhabitants of the City have moved to estates in the surrounding boroughs. The City is largely a ghost town at weekends.

So what do all these 47 churches (about half the 109 crammed in here in 1665) actually *do*? They are in fact at their busiest during the week when the City population is huge. Services, prayer meetings and concerts thrive. On a Sunday only around eight churches – including St Paul's cathedral, of course – need to open.

The reason why there were originally so many churches in the City is not entirely clear, as they must have always exceeded in capacity the number of worshippers. Perhaps rival monastic orders pushed their own churches, like competing half-empty supermarkets do today. And then there was the medieval Catholic cult of the saints. People believed – some still do – that contact with, worshipping and touching relics of saints would bring protection and admission to heaven in the afterlife. A great city's insurance policy, as it were, would include churches dedicated to all the powerful saints in the Christian calendar.

So why did having 109 churches fail to protect the City from the Great Plague of 1665 and the Great Fire of 1666? Some would say the sinners of the City brought these disasters upon their own heads. And remember that the Puritans and republicans who took control of the City in the Civil War about 20 years before, chopping off the king's head, also banned the cult of the worshipping of the remains of saints, chopping off the heads of their statues and obliterating their paintings and names from churches. Asking for trouble, you may think.

Among the City's lost churches, but remembered today as a street name, was **St Mary Axe**, which displayed the axe with which St Ursula and a bunch of virgins were said to have been martyred. (Could rebuilding it be another opportunity for Sir Richard Branson's Virgin brand? If Virgin cola and Virgin trains, why not Virgin virgins?)

• St Alfege's Greenwich, the ghastly truth: page 239.

THE HANDSOME HIGHWAYMAN AND THE HANDSOMEST BARN It was at **St Paul's, Covent Garden** (Covent Garden Tube), the actors' church, not the other grander one, that Samuel Pepys made the first recorded mention of the great Mr Punch puppet in Britain, and thus it is here that the annual Mr Punch service takes place, which sees the extraordinary spectacle of numerous Mr Punches and their professors sitting in rows while another Mr Punch interrupts the sermon (see page 304).

Talking of professors, it is here that Shaw's Eliza Doolittle meets Professor Higgins in *Pygmalion*, the play which became the hit musical *My Fair Lady*.

The area in front of the church also figures in Hitchcock's horror film *Frenzy*, notable for the way its killer says *'lovvly'* as he strangles women, just as cockney flower and veg sellers used to say 'lovely caulis', or whatever, until the Covent Garden flower, fruit and vegetable market was moved to a different part of London.

Many a famous 'luvvie' is buried or commemorated here, including Vivien Leigh, Noel Coward, Charlie Chaplin, Terence Rattigan and, strangely, Claude Duval, the handsome highwayman who became a darling of high society (see page 99). Plus a certain William Henry Pratt, better known as Boris Karloff of horror film fame (he died in 1969 although not until after I bumped into him in Barclays Bank in Midhurst, Sussex, where he was convalescing and I was a startled schoolboy).

He is not forgotten today, for one of the funniest soubriquets attached to our recent British politicians is that of Tory heavyweight hardwoman, Ann Widdecombe, dubbed 'Doris Karloff'. Not that it's so unfair to tag her so – wasn't it she who said memorably about creepy Home Secretary Michael Howard (and he was supposed to be on the same side!), 'He has something of the night about him.' It was brilliant because Howard is far more Vincent Price than Boris Karloff.

Samuel Butler (1612–80), satirist, left instructions that he should be buried here in the churchyard with his feet touching one of the outside walls. Is there a joke there somewhere I have missed? We can be sure of this because his friend, John Aubrey, recorded it:

> His feet touch the wall. His grave, 2 yards distant from the pillaster of the dore (by his desire) is 6 foot deep. About 25 of his old acquaintance at his Funerall. I myself being one of the eldest, helped carry the Pall.

He should perhaps have been buried at Westminster Abbey with the other literati, but died in poverty so had to be buried locally. He eventually got a rather heartless monument in the Abbey:

10

The Poets Fate is here in emblem shown:
He asked for Bread and he received a Stone.

The history of this rectangular, spireless building that is St Paul's, Covent Garden, is that when Francis Russell, Earl of Bedford was developing land at Covent Garden (formerly the garden of a convent, which the Reformation had put into the Russell family's hands) into an Italian-style square in the early 17th century, he asked the superb architect of the day, Inigo Jones, to build him a church. He warned that it had better be a barn-like structure to keep the costs down. Jones responded: 'You shall have the handsomest barn in England.'

The great Tuscan portico facing the piazza shows how the whole building is the wrong way round. Jones wanted this to be the entrance and the altar to be at the far, western, end. But the church authorities insisted that the altar should be, as usual, at the eastern end, that is nearest to Jerusalem, so the entrance is round the back. There is something Italian about the massive eaves, but when all's said and done, Russell was right. If you prefer your churches Gothic, with a steeple, you might well think this is just a blooming big box.

Perhaps the most unlikely memorial round here is at the Jubilee Market Hall and it is to donkeys. About 2,000 of these humble beasts toiled here for three centuries until about 1970, pulling carts laden with produce about and adding to the malodorous niff of the neighbourhood. Oddly, they sometimes appeared on stage in nearby theatres. Their carts were often gaily coloured and the beasts themselves festooned with their headpieces and horse-brasses gleaming brightly. On the other hand, a good many of them were tatty, drab and miserable, which donkeys do rather well.

CLASSIC DING-DONGS AND A GOTHIC HORROR SHOW But, at least St Paul's, Covent Garden, is honestly classical (ie: not Gothic) and therefore doesn't have a spire, which is from the Gothic tradition. Greek and Roman buildings didn't have spires, did they? Did Sir Christopher Wren take the medieval spire of old St Paul's Cathedral and stick it on his new classical replacement after the Great Fire? No, he gave it a dome, a properly classical topping.

The severest possible contrast between these two styles can be seen in the difference between Westminster Abbey's supremely Gothic soaring heights and the Methodists' Central Hall opposite, which is in the classical style. To many eyes, it doesn't look like a church and could have been a railway station or a bank. In fact one end of it *was* my bank, at the time of writing. I suppose there's Methodism in their madness.

But it was felt that many of the rest of London's hundreds of classical churches (such as St George the Martyr, Southwark, see page 198) should have spires despite their not fitting in with classical-style porticos and so on, and some very odd hybrids resulted, but then at least it was somewhere to stick the bells.

The oddest spire in London could be the stepped pyramid at **St George's, Bloomsbury** (Holborn Tube), which is said to be based on a classical mausoleum described by Pliny, the Roman writer. It's almost as if architect Nicholas Hawksmoor is desperately saying, 'It IS classical, honest!' while breathing a sigh of relief at having found something resembling the steeple most English people demand of a church. Hawksmoor's efforts at **Christ Church**, Spitalfields, is a much more honest and successful attempt to stick a Gothic spire on a classical building.

Actually, Wren wasn't immune from this problem. Those in his fabulous set of City churches which don't have square towers often feature spirish things which are a fancy attempt to marry the two frankly almost incompatible traditions.

Talking of marriage, it is not surprising that Wren's tower of **St Bride's**, **Fleet Street** (Blackfriars Tube, walk away from the river, up New Bridge Street, left on Fleet Street), looks to us today the very image of a wedding cake. All the tiered wedding cakes in the world were modelled on this inspired creation of Wren's, perhaps because of the aptness of the name of the saint to whom the church is dedicated.

St Bride's

The elaborate 230ft spire of Wren's **St Mary-le-Bow** is beset with pillared drums as if to apologise for its existence. They almost hide the spire within, rather like those prim Victorians who allegedly put trousers on table legs because they thought bare legs rather rude.

Absolutely fabulous, though, is the much more honest effort at **All Souls, Langham Place** (Oxford Circus Tube), in front of Broadcasting House, at the top of Regent Street. A clean cylinder of columns that could have come straight from ancient Greece is given a needle sharp spire right through the middle, wallop. Architect John Nash makes no apologies for putting the two together. Brilliant. The contrast with the plain rectangular body of the church behind is to my mind deliberate and geometric. But one website church fan imagined Nash saying after building the superb foyer: 'I've had enough of this now. Stick a big box on the back for the rest of the church. I'm off down the pub.' It makes you like Nash all the more.

SMOG, PEA-SOUPERS AND LONDON PARTICULARS: AN INTERESTING IRRELEVANCE CONCERNING CHURCHES AND POLLUTION

No-one should miss seeing for themselves the interior of **Westminster Abbey** (Westminster Tube), known to millions through numerous televised royal services and funerals (sometimes on a summer weekend it feels as though they've all turned up at once). But the Abbey is neither church nor cathedral but a 'Royal Peculiar'.

This reminds me of the Dickensian term for a pea-souper fog: a 'London Particular'. It is hard now to imagine how bad these fogs were even if you lived through them (thousands died from chest problems in the worst ones). Every London house burned cheap, sulphurous coal up until the 1960s. Look at those rows of chimney pots on old buildings, and the metal plate coalholes in the pavements before them, and imagine every chimney churning out black or brown clouds of coal smoke. All London's factories belched smoke; every district had its gasworks which burned thousands of tons of coal to make poisonous coal gas, another vital fuel; every London rail terminus was attended by dozens of coal-fired steam engines putting up monstrous clouds of pollution; and steam tugs and freighters made the sky black above the river. No wonder our great churches were blackened quickly.

The last London Particular before public outrage brought in the Clean Air Acts was in 1963. I remember it well. Bus conductors would get off and walk in front of the driver shining a torch to find a way as it crawled forward. In suburban Dulwich, as a not-very-tall schoolboy in broad daylight, I found I could not even see my feet. I felt the kerb of the road with the front wheel of the bicycle I had to push and, unaware of a gently curving side road, soon found myself way off track.

That particular London Particular also saw off the poet T S Eliot (he was rushed to the Brompton Hospital but took a long while to die). An irony perhaps, as he describes London fog so well in 'The Love Song of J Alfred Prufock':

The yellow fog that rubs its back upon the window-panes,
The yellow smoke that rubs its muzzle on the window-panes,
Licked its tongue into the corners of the evening,
Lingered upon the pools that stand in drains,
Let fall upon its back the soot that falls from chimneys,
Slipped by the terrace, made a sudden leap,
And seeing that it was a soft October night,
Curled once about the house, and fell asleep.

Another writer who produced a memorable description of London's smog was the writer Charles Dickens. In this extract from *Bleak House*, he sees it as a metaphor for the dead hand of the lazy, inefficient, unjust and greedy legal system of the day run by vainglorious Lord Chancellors (not much change there, then, you may think, but it was even worse 200 years ago):

Smoke lowering down from the chimney pots, making a soft black drizzle, with flakes of soot in it as big as full-grown snowflakes – gone into mourning, one might imagine, for the death of the sun. Dogs, indistinguishable in mire. Horse, scarcely better; splashed to their very blinkers .... Fog everywhere... in the eyes and throats of Greenwich pensioners, wheezing by the firesides of their wards; fog in the stem and bowl of the pipe of the wrathful skipper, down in his close cabin; fog cruelly pinching the toes and fingers of his little shivering prentice boy on deck. Chance people on the bridges peeping over the parapets into a nether sky of fog, with fog all around them, as if they were up in a balloon and hanging in the misty clouds.

Before my time, in a particularly bad fog in December 1952, the smog was so thick in London that it asphyxiated prime cattle at the Smithfield Show and, entering buildings, caused the abandonment of a ballet performance at Sadlers Wells theatre. Thousands of old people with chest problems died in such London pea-soupers: the coffin makers and grave diggers were working non-stop.

The railways had the occasional foggy crash (including a really bad one in 1952 at Harrow) but were actually rather good in fog; the Tube lines that run overground still have fog repeater signals they hardly need today, and a pretty well foolproof system for applying the brakes if the train ran past a red light.

Although no-one yet talked of the environment or knew what ecology was, London set about cleaning itself up with the help of North Sea gas for house heating, which burns much more cleanly (and more conveniently) than coal gas and of course didn't need smelly, poisonous gasworks. The thousands of steam trains that chuffed all over town were replaced with electric and diesel ones.

At about this time, the River Thames, a poisonous evil soup without a living thing in it, was cleaned up to the point where crabs now happily wander the mud flats by the Tower of London and many species of fish and even dolphins have been seen gambolling outside Parliament, just as they did in the Middle Ages. Then in the 1980s, the ecological brigade of spotty teenagers came along and said how terrible things were getting and our air and water was all doomed and getting worse, save the planet and all that. If only they knew, if only they knew …

THE PECULIAR ABBEY HABIT AND THE PERILS OF KEEPING TALLY Just building **Westminster Abbey** on the Isle of Thorns in the empty, soggy marshes alongside the Thames, west of London, was a deeply eccentric decision, but one which decided the shape of London for all time.

Edward the Confessor was, on 3 April 1043, the last king to be crowned at Winchester, capital of England under the Saxon kings. He had a vision in which St Peter told him to build the Abbey on this boggy island, and a palace as well. The building of the Abbey took up the rest of Edward's life, and he was buried there in 1066, his death sparking off the Norman Conquest by William the Bastard. After this all monarchs have been crowned in this massive Abbey, which – as recorded above – is a Royal Peculiar, a church decreed by the royals to be neither a church nor a cathedral. You can visit part of Edward the Confessor's church, although the main structure is of an obviously later date.

In fact the brand-new Abbey had two coronations in its first year – Harold's being followed by that of William the Conqueror on Christmas Day 1066. The Norman guards asked the surrounding population to acclaim him as king, whereupon some reluctant Saxons half-heartedly cheered. Other Norman troops took this strange noise to be rebellious resistance to the Coronation and promptly burned down the Saxons' homes all around. It was an ominous start to Norman rule. So much for Norman wisdom.

But what of Edward the Confessor's plan to build a palace at Westminster too? It was indeed built and soon became home to the Norman kings. William's son, William Rufus, planned to extend it to gigantic proportions but he managed to build only **Westminster Hall** – the great medieval barn of a place still survives – before fate, in the form of an arrow ricocheting while out hunting in August 1100, intervened. Revenge for Saxon king Harold, some said, and you can visit the Rufus Stone where it happened in the New Forest of Hampshire. (Incidentally, Rufus, red-haired, openly gay, anti-Christian, was not the most popular king. Once he ordered a critic's eyes to be pulled out and his testicles cut off and watched this being done with glee. The very day before the stray arrow hit him, the Abbot of Shrewsbury had called for divine vengeance to strike the king for his sins.)

That this great hall of history has survived fires, the Blitz, modernisers, etc, to be the scene of tragedy and treachery – with the trials of Guy Fawkes and Charles I, as well as the lying-in-state of Winston Churchill and the Queen Mother – is partly luck, and partly down to repairs. Regarding the latter, I caught a fascinating radio broadcast in which an official recalled how the great hammer-beamed roof needed some new oak in the early 20th century. The only problem was that the exact size and shape of tree was hard to find. Experts scoured the southern counties, but it seemed all the suitable great oaks had been felled for the Royal Navy's great wooden ships in the six centuries since Westminster Hall was built.

They came to an estate near Wadhurst in East Sussex, where a stand of great oaks of exactly the right dimensions marched up a hill to a great house. They hastened up to the home and knocked on the door. The owner himself answered and the conversation – if I remember rightly – went something like this:

'We're very sorry to bother you, but it's about your oak trees. They are rather special, aren't they?' started the official.

'Oh, you'll be from Westminster Hall, then.'

'What?'

'Westminster Hall, am I right?'

'How on *earth* did you know that?'

'Well my ancestor supplied the original oaks, so he planted some more. He said they would need some more in about 600 years, when they would be ready, and here you are.'

'Yes,' said the staggered official, 'here we are.'

I have since another version of that extraordinary story, which confirmed that the trees came from the Courthorpe family estate. In that version, however, a despairing official looked up the original records to see where the original timber had come from all those centuries before and therefore this led them to Wadhurst, where a similar conversation took place. Either way, the centuries and centuries of foresight must be almost unprecedented anywhere on earth.

The rest of the **Palace of Westminster** became a government building, and the seat of Parliament, after Henry VIII moved his court to nearby Whitehall Palace. Westminster Palace was to fall victim to taxation, but not in the usual way. In the Middle Ages, taxes collected were recorded on a 'tally stick', a stick with notches cut out to show how much tax had been paid. The idea was that you could split the stick lengthways so that both the Government and the taxpayer would have a record or receipt. Any argument, and the two halves could be joined again. It's a bit like indentures, where an apprentice's contract was cut with jagged, indented edges so both parties get a half that matches only the right document.

All very well, but what to do with the tens of thousands of tally sticks? Being civil servants, they filed them away in bundles under the Palace of Westminster for nigh on a thousand years. Eventually, in 1834, someone decided the tally sticks would probably not be needed to settle 800-year-old tax disputes.

Charles Dickens retold what happened with one of his usual caustic observations: 'It would naturally occur to any intelligent person that nothing could be easier than to allow them to be carried away for firewood by the miserable people who live in that neighbourhood. However, they never had been useful, and official routine required it that they never should be, and so the order went forth that they should be privately and confidentially burned.'

That part rings true by modern civil service standards. The sticks were confidential documents so people couldn't be allowed to see one even 800 years later and let's get rid of them quietly without fuss.

This last objective wasn't achieved, however. The sticks were burned in a furnace under the House of Lords but the fire soon spread to the mountains of crisp, centuries-old sticks all around. The Palace burned down that night, 16 October 1834. The glow was visible all around London, and one man who spotted it from the North Downs was Charles Barry, travelling towards London in a coach from Sussex. He wondered what it was. In fact, it turned out to be the greatest architectural job of that architect's life: he was awarded the contract for designing the new Palace of Westminster, the sublime Gothic masterpiece that is today's Houses of Parliament.

A SMALL ROUND TOTAL One of the treasures of London, now a little better known thanks to the *Da Vinci Code* book and film, is the round **Temple Church** off Fleet Street (Blackfriars Tube, walk away from the river up New Bridge Street, left on Fleet Street, footpath to church signposted on left), the church of the Knights Templar, and a rare example, one of fewer than half-a-dozen (another is in Cambridge), surviving from the fashion for copying the round design of the Church of the Holy Sepulchre in Jerusalem, the avowed destination of the Knights Templar and their Crusades.

NAUGHTY NELL, ROYAL WHORES AND EXPLODING CLERGYMEN St Martin-in-the-Fields (Trafalgar Square Tube) is a church known around the world by the broadcasts and recordings of great classical music made by the famous orchestra, the Academy of St Martin-in-the-Fields. More down-to-earth, literally, are the characters buried here, who include the highwayman Jack Sheppard, King Charles

II's mistress the actress Nell Gwyn, and William Hogarth, who chronicled London's whores, drunks and pickpockets with such humour in his 18th-century cartoons.

Jack Sheppard was so bad that he was rather good. Born in 1702, and brought up in a City workhouse, he took to crime to satisfy the demands of his loose-living wench, Edgeworth Bess. He was soon robbing people almost daily around London and, in the extraordinary year of 1724, he was captured twice and escaped twice, captured a third time and tried at the Old Bailey but escaped again with Bess's help, caught again and chained to the floor in Newgate jail, escaped up the chimney, was caught again when blind drunk and quickly hanged at Tyburn hardly before he could sober up enough to escape again. He was still only 22 when he died. He has stayed put since he came to St Martin-in-the-Fields … he won't escape now.

There are two very curious connections between those buried here and outside town, beyond the northern M25. Salisbury Hall between Hatfield and St Albans in Hertfordshire, is where **Nell** 'buy my lovely oranges' **Gwyn** and the king would spend naughty weekends together. She gave birth to their bastard son in this house, and as the baby took its first breath and yelled, Nell asked the king to give him a title. He refused, so Nell hung the mewling infant outside the bedroom window, threatening to dash his brains out in the courtyard below if he wasn't worthy of a title.

The panic-stricken king looked past her at the mighty St Albans Abbey on the sky-line, and blurted out 'Someone catch the Duke of St Albans!' Feisty girl … but a risky way to start a dukedom. Nell, who is buried here at St Martin-in-the-Fields, not far from where she was born in an alley off Drury Lane, is remembered by the Nell of Old Drury pub near the great Drury Lane theatre with which she and the king were associated.

She had started as an orange-seller but soon became a great hit on the stage, as Pepys records several times. 'Pretty, witty Nell,' he enthused in his diary. She was also popular with Londoners, partly because she was 'one of us' and partly because she was not French and not Catholic, unlike Charles's other main mistress, Louise de Keroualle, a voluptuous woman who was placed in Charles's gaze by the French government.

This led to an amusing Nellism at Oxford in 1681 when, during the anti-Catholic unrest known as the Popish Terror, she sought to reassure the mob who stopped her coach of her good character: 'Pray, good people, be civil. I am the *Protestant* whore.' A huge cheer went up.

One more ring of the old Nell. The descendant of that infant she gave birth to the Duke of St Albans, and heir to the dukedom at the time of writing, is the Earl of Burford. Whom did the noble Earl marry but a rather buxom, rather risqué, outspoken actress-come-singer called Louise Robey? Sadly, the marriage foundered in 2001. Check out some of the truly bizarre websites with which she is connected. On one of them, the Countess of Burford – or the raunchy Ms Robey – was said to have quipped that the next time she marries someone called Earl, she's going to make damn sure he's black. I don't believe a countess said any such thing, but it's a good joke. She was a bit of fresh air in a stuffy old world, some might say, and yet another case of London history repeating itself.

On his deathbed in 1685 Charles begged his brother, about to succeed him as James II, 'Let not poor Nell starve'; she was given enough of an estate to keep her in style, with plenty of oranges, for life, which was not long. She died in 1687 aged just 37, so Nell never had the chance to grow old disgracefully, as she surely would have. One legacy of hers was that the only house on the south side of Pall Mall which was not a Crown Estate freehold was hers, because she cannily levered the title to the land out of the besotted Charles. I'd have loved to have heard the sermon preached on this hugely popular Londoner by the vicar of St Martin's, Thomas Tenison, in the 17th century, given her life of non-stop adultery.

St Martin's also has a strangely explosive link with a small Bedfordshire village. In **Fenny Stratford**, near Woburn, cannon fire rings out each 11 November as the vicar of St Martin's church here, and the verger and churchwardens, take part in firing the Fenny Poppers – three salvoes of miniature, tankard-shaped weapons which the churchwarden primes with gunpowder.

The tradition, every St Martin's Day, was started by Dr Browne Willis who founded St Martin's in 1730 in memory of his grandfather who worshipped at St Martin-in-the-Fields, and died on St Martin's Day in St Martin's Lane. *(That's enough Martins, Ed.)*

LOST AND WANDERING TOWERS, A CRYPT ASCENDING TO HEAVEN Not a few London church towers are lost like orphans or even wander around by themselves, it seems. Besides the isolated towers like that at **St Anne's**, Soho (see page 194), and towers that have become homes (at Wood Street, City of London and Gipsy Hill), some of them have actually moved.

The tower of **All Hallows** in Chertsey Road, Richmond (the A316, the main road linking the M3 to London; overground to Twickenham from Waterloo, right out of station, follow Whitton Road to the end, turn right), must strike many motorists heading for the M3 as looking surprisingly like a classic Wren City of London job. It is. It was moved from All Hallows, Lombard Street, in 1938, when that church was demolished. Although the main body of the later church is not even slightly Wrenish, it contains many of the original fittings (panelling, ceilings, that kind of stuff) from its predecessor.

Another church tower that has moved, unbelievably, from its original location, is the 14th-century tower and 12th-century crypt of **St James-in-the-wall**, now in Mark Lane, EC3 (Tower Hill Tube), moved in 1873 because they were in the way. Even the brash Victorians sometimes had a conscience about knocking down such treasures.

But how do you move a medieval church? Get lots of bubble wrap and string? I once had a slightly surreal demonstration. I was in the men's lavatories high up in the old *Daily Mail* building off Fleet Street, looking out of the window over the ground where the *Sun* building had just been knocked down, and discussing the world with the chap at the next urinal, ace headline writer, Willy 'Three Puddings' Bloch. It had been a beery lunch – such things were possible before computers – but even so we were aghast to see a medieval crypt, complete with arches and pillars, rising past our window. An angel or two would have helped us cope with the concept.

It was the old 13th-century crypt of the **Whitefriars monastery** which famously was located in the bowels of the *Sun* and *News of the World* building's printing works. It had always been a trick up the sleeve of a desperate rival news editor that he could covertly send a religious-looking reporter to demand to see the crypt (and, hopefully, the rival paper's next day's front page) at any time. Even more bizarrely, real Carmelite monks would occasionally turn up to look at the crypt, maybe inadvertently catching sight of pictures of naked *Sun* page three girls in the process.

The crypt had been forgotten about for a few hundred years after the destruction of the monasteries that covered the area before Henry VIII's time. Then in 1867 someone rediscovered the lost crypt, a damp, decaying haunt of rats and skulls. It was used as a coal cellar for 30 years but in the 20th century was conserved, though the presses thundering overhead probably didn't do it much good. Eventually, as the Murdoch newspapers fled to Fort Wapping, redevelopment of the site loomed. The crypt was protected, yet the foundations needed to be rebuilt. How to solve the two problems – lift it out and rebuild, then put it back again.

So the 13th-century crypt was lifted out in a steel cradle high into the heavens above the office blocks and later returned to its original position. But the heart and soul of old Fleet Street, sadly, has never been craned back into position since the great papers left.

AND FINALLY, A RATHER POULTRY EFFORT Another City church you won't find in its right place is **St Mildred's, Poultry**. It's actually in Lincolnshire, but it might be a bit difficult to recognise, because, while parts of it are piled up in a field at South Elkington awaiting re-assembly like a Lego kit, many others have been used in neighbouring building projects or to make a fine swimming-pool terrace for Thorpe Hall.

It was at Thorpe Hall that the Rev John Lewis Fytche lived. He had no church of his own, although he used to preach locally for other ministers. He was well-to-do, and when strolling through the 'over-churched' City of London one day in 1872, he saw the Church Commissioners were proposing to demolish St Mildred's. The opportunity seemed heaven-sent.

He had the whole thing taken carefully apart and laboriously shipped in barges down the Thames and up the North Sea to near his home, then lugged in carts to Thorpe Hall. Then an economic downturn hit, and the Rev Fytche was bankrupted. The pile of stones was lost in weeds.

LONDON'S MOST EXOTIC PLACES OF WORSHIP

Amid London's truly wondrous heritage of mainstream Christian churches, there are here and there some astounding, beautiful, surprising or just curious edifices constructed by other religions. Here's just a selection:

THE SWAMINARAYAN HINDU TEMPLE, NEASDEN
Road: Between North Circular A406 and Brentfield Road. ⊖ *Neasden (Jubilee line). Car parking available.* ⋒ *Stonebridge Park (from Euston).*

Swaminarayan Hindu Temple

Built on a cathedral scale, this stone and marble edifice stands out like an exotic oriental gem in this, the dreariest of North London suburbs, with its vast, shining pinnacles rising incongruously near the North Circular road. Built by Indians using traditional methods (and traditional rates of pay, one of them pointed out), this is a rather special place. The most unlikely way to construct a building like this would be to quarry a load of Bulgarian marble, ship it to India where it would be carved, then ship it back across the world to Britain where it would be painstakingly reassembled like a monstrously complicated Ikea kit temple (we are yards from the Ikea furniture store here, after all). So that was exactly how they made it. Has to be seen to be believed. Believers in the Swaminarayan sect, a division of Hinduism, say the building will last more than a thousand years because it is all stone, with no steel or wood.

THE BUDDHAPADIPA TEMPLE, CALONNE ROAD, WIMBLEDON

Road: Signed off Wimbledon Parkside, which is south off A3 at Tibbetts Corner, Putney Heath. ⊖/🚃 *Wimbledon station (District Line or mainline from Waterloo) then bus 93 through Wimbledon village. Included in Wimbledon walk, page 295.*

Only a good lob away from the tennis courts, this beautiful, glittering building sits serenely in a bubble of unlikely oriental tranquillity. The exquisite murals inside are fascinating in their blend of Buddhist teaching and the Western environment.

RUSSIAN ORTHODOX CATHEDRAL

⊖/ 🚉 *Gunnersbury Park (District Line).*

An incongruous and definitely unorthodox sight for visitors to London arriving up the M4, this onion-domed cathedral is tucked in beside the M4 flyover at Chiswick. Finished only in 2000, with its gold and blue decoration, it adds a completely new dimension to this patch of West London.

PEACE PAGODA, BATTERSEA PARK

Road: Between Chelsea and Albert bridges on south bank of Thames. 🚉 *Battersea Park station (from London Victoria one stop) then cross park to river.*

This startling riverside apparition makes the point that those on the receiving end of the ultimate warfare weapon, at Hiroshima, wish to promote global peace. The pagoda's elegant constructions bring an exotic yet peaceful style to their waterside locations.

REGENT'S PARK MOSQUE

⊖ *Baker Street (Circle Line, etc).*

The glittering gold dome of this cathedral of Islam, or the London Central Mosque, to give it its proper name, with its 140ft minaret, is one of London's most stunning landmarks. Often you will find people who are willing to show you around this 1969 building which arose from a suggestion that the Islamic troops who found themselves in London during World War II should have somewhere to worship. It is austere but beautiful.

ST ARKIS ARMENIAN CHURCH, KENSINGTON

⊖ *High St Kensington (Circle and District Lines). Also featured in Kensington walk, page 276.*

This is a little gem of a building, so prettily perfect it is almost like a divine jewellery box. Built in 1922, and with that peculiar Armenian script above one entrance, and English above another, it is tucked away a few yards off Kensington High Street, down Wright's Lane, and right into Iverna Court.

FO GUANG TEMPLE

✛ *Oxford Street (Central, Bakerloo, Victoria lines). Also in Soho walk, page 188.*

Situated off Oxford Street on Margaret Street near All Saints church, this is a most surprising and rather wonderful Chinese Buddhist centre. As you enter, you notice that the building was dedicated in the 1970s as All Saints Christian Study Centre, by the Archbishop of Canterbury no less, so the fact that the Fo Guang (founder the Most Venerable Master Hsing Yun and based in Taiwan) are now resident shows some things change quickly in religion.

It is an extraordinary experience, having removed your shoes on the stairs and sought permission, to enter the Main Shrine, dedicated to the Sakyamuni Buddha, with its three large statues, in total tranquillity – yet we are only a hundred yards from Oxford Street's incessant commercial bustle.

The walls and ceilings are covered with the Buddhas of Five Directions and Eight Tathagatas respectively, with the lighting designed to highlight this. You can see from name plaques attached to these hundreds of Buddhas that individuals have sponsored them. It is a friendly yet intense atmosphere.

BEVIS MARKS SYNAGOGUE, CITY OF LONDON

✛ *Liverpool Street or Aldgate (Circle, Metropolitan Lines).*

Britain's oldest synagogue, for although Jews and this country go back to Roman times, their expulsion in the late Middle Ages meant that their history began again only when they were allowed back during Cromwell's 17th-century interregnum. These were Jews mainly from the Spanish and Portuguese traditions. This building was put up in 1701. The Quaker architect waived his fee rather than profit from the building of God's house, and Queen Anne gave a massive oak beam from one of her warships. It is not, today, the busiest synagogue in London but it is the most interesting. The 12 columns of the gallery are said to represent the 12 tribes of Israel. Bevis Marks is also the name of the road.

SOUTHALL, WEST LONDON

Road: Just south of A4020 (from Shepherd's Bush to Uxbridge). From M4 J3 take A312 north, then A4020 east (right). ☒ Southall from Paddington.

Not so much one place of worship but a collection of temples where one can be the only chap not wearing a turban in a busy street (if one is a chap and one doesn't wear turbans, that is). If you visit the area, the authentic Indian food at authentic Indian prices, the shops glittering with gaudy Indian brassware, spices, carvings, over-the-top Ali Baba shoes and endless Indian clothes, will make this a cultural experience.

Note: If you are reading this book you have clearly got considerably more than the usual two brain cells to rub together (flattery gets you everywhere), but even so I feel compelled to remind you that these sites are not tourist destinations, or theme park ornaments, but places of worship. Make sure you have permission to enter any grounds or buildings; observe rules about removing shoes, taking photographs, etc. I've seen enough Westerners – and other tourists in our own churches too – wandering in chewing gum, smoking, showing off bare flesh or with screaming brats who fiddle with sacred ornaments, or photographing people praying, to be thoroughly ashamed of them. Don't be like them…

10

London: Home of Eccentrics

PLAQUE TO THE FUTURE

Immortality here on Earth is available to Londoners through the medium of official oval blue plaques, those 'Joe Bloggs lived here' things that are stuck on the exteriors of many a house. Candidates are selected by a special committee and English Heritage. They must have been dead for at least 20 years, which at least frees us from the tyranny of the self-appointed great and good of the moment.

The official plaques are made by, and at, Armitage in Staffordshire (spiritual home of the modern lavatory) and unveiled in a small ceremony at the rate of about 12 a year. So in about 300,000 years, every house in London will have one (if some don't have two or three, which they already do).

In fact they're not all 'official oval'. Older ones are rectangular, even brown (as in Dr Johnson's at 17 Gough Square off Fleet Street and Thackeray's in Young Street, Kensington; Thackeray raises the question of the need for more than one plaque; having another one on a house in Palace Green just across Kensington High Street.

Unofficial ones are in Perspex, round, or whatever. There's a strange one to George Orwell in Pond Street, Hampstead, which has the writer of *Animal Farm*'s face coming out of the wall. The Dead Comics Society had one up for Frankie Howerd in Edwardes Square, Kensington, almost before the old chap ('titter ye not') was cold; they put another one up not far away in Eardley Crescent, Earl's Court, to commemorate *Carry On* star Hattie Jacques who lived there.

(Talking of Frankie Howerd, he died on the same weekend as another British comic, Benny Hill. A certain newspaper managed to print a eulogy from the one who turned out to have died first, to the one who died second. Not that the papers make things up, of course. The comics would have laughed.)

The interesting thing about plaques is: how much will the people they recall matter to future generations? I mean, and I parade my ignorance here, who was Ugo Foscolo, commemorated on the other side of the above-mentioned Edwardes Square? An Italian nationalist, apparently. Yes, perhaps it's good to remind us of people who really mattered once to Londoners. But if these nationalists need to be remembered, why don't they leave us a decent biscuit, like Garibaldi did? (Aptly, he fought against the Bourbons.)

In fact Foscolo, who turns out to be a once-famous Italian patriot and poet, was buried at Chiswick churchyard where there is a rather flash cenotaph with a pompous inscription about how his remains were transported later to Florence 'From the sacred

guardianship of Chiswick … honoured custody for ever held in grateful remembrance by the Italian nation.' Flowery tosh. Actually he was an ineffective bore when in Kensington and the nobs at Holland House soon grew tired of extending him endless hospitality, so irritable and irresponsible did he become.

Does it increase the value of a property to have a blue plaque on it? This may not have been the motive, but a property developer stuck a blue plaque looking remarkably like the real thing on 64/65 Glebe Place, Chelsea, recently. Only by looking closely do you see the usual endorsement English Heritage is missing – as well as, sadly, the final 'S' of the name Sir Alfred Munnings, an artist already commemorated by another unofficial plaque at Beldon House, Chelsea, as English Heritage rather sniffily pointed out.

There's the very peculiar story of a house on Bankside, just south of the river, which makes two impressive claims on a plaque that are both total fantasy, yet should have two real ones, which are missing, on page 204.

Nevertheless, genuine plaques are thicker on the ground north of the Thames than south. This is doubtless because most of South London has a history of only a century or two. But a Radio 4 wag, Arthur Smith, has another theory, less flattering to South Londoners:

> Up in North London we have blue plaques to mark where famous people lived. Down in South London they instead have those yellow boards – you know, murder, stabbing, rape, appeal for witnesses, that kind of thing.

Charming.

STAMPS OF HEROISM COLLECTED IN POSTMAN'S PARK
Other people have suggested different ways of commemorating heroes. For example, at the Postman's Park off St Martin's le Grand, near St Paul's Tube (Central line), in the City, there is a rather moving and extraordinary wall of plaques to 53 people who gave their lives trying to save others. The idea of a Victorian artist G F Watts and opened in the 1880s, it caught on only for a decade or so.

> Daniel Pemberton, aged 61, foreman LSWR, surprised by a train while gauging the line, hurled his mate out of the track, saving his life at the cost of his own, Jan 17 1903.

> Thomas Simpson died of exhaustion after saving many lives from breaking ice on Highgate Ponds, Jan 25 1885.

> Frederick Alfred Croft, Inspector Aged 31, Saved a lunatic woman from suicide at Woolwich Arsenal Station but was himself run over by the train, Jan 11 1878.

More than a hundred years later lunatic women are still jumping on the tracks, workmen are still surprised by trains on railways, and people still fall through thin ice – I've done it myself. Such is human frailty.

Actually the memorial, which features some rather splendid tilework, is a typically British Victorian concept: the mawkish, melodramatic celebration of dead heroes: people who jump into lakes, save loads of people and then die themselves, trying to save just one more. The only sure way to British hearts was to die heroically failing to do something, such as Scott of the Antarctic. Shackleton, who achieved far more without losing one of his men, was clearly not dead enough to achieve immortality when he returned and was almost ignored by the population when he returned from his own Antarctic expeditions.

We Brits love our failures. (At the peril of sounding smug, when we were marking the 60th anniversary of the defeat of the British Army at Dunkirk during World War II, another heroic failure, I wagered we were making far more fuss

11

about that than we would for the 60th anniversary of its victory at El Alamein the following year, where the British and Empire troops turned the whole course of the war, without the Americans having arrived yet. It was the end of the defeats and the beginning of the victories. And come that anniversary, I was right. Hardly a word was said about it.)

Going back to memorials to those who died for others, halfway across Hammersmith Bridge (see page 256) is a memorial to a man who jumped in to save someone in the Thames, and who somehow managed to save the other person but died himself. Heroic and poignant but, as Mr Spock would say, not very efficient.

LONDON'S MOST BRILLIANT ROAD

Some locations in London positively thrum with genius past and present. **Cheyne Walk** (pronounced 'chainey'), in Chelsea, for example, is stuffed with an astonishing heritage of great people. What a creative pantheon, what a cornucopia of talent is revealed by a blue plaque attack of measles-like proportions! What stories they tell, of brilliant engineers, wonderful artists, mad Irish barbers, eccentric millionaires, recluses, pop stars, saints, sinners, and a possible living link to Jesus Christ.

It is said to be the street with the most blue plaques in Britain, and achieves that on only one side too – the other side suffers from a slight damp problem, as estate agents might say. That side is, of course, the River Thames, either side of Battersea Bridge's north end.

In numerical order of their addresses, the blue plaques are:

4 George Eliot (1819–80), novelist, wrote *Middlemarch*, *Mill on the Floss*, etc; the name George, although odd for a woman, was helpful at a time when some considered no lady should write novels. Jane Austen, for example, at the beginning of the same century, published her books initially without her name. Painter Daniel Maclise had this house before her.

16 Dante Gabriel Rossetti (1828–82), poet and painter. This house is also known as the Queen's House and is judged the finest in the row by some. Rossetti kept an odd menagerie of animals in the garden – strange ones for Chelsea – such as armadillos, a raccoon and a kangaroo; a fountain nearby is dedicated to him.

16 Algernon Charles Swinburne (1837–1909), poet. Swinburne is greatly underrated, an Oxford poet tells me, but the latter poet's ex-wife's family included one who stood next to Swinburne in the urinals at the Athenaeum club and found he had virtually no penis. Hmmm, curious. He was also a right menace if you were a baby, poet Robert Graves recalled (see Wimbledon, page 299).

93 Mrs Elizabeth Cleghorn Gaskell (1810–65), a novelist who proved it was all right for women to write novels under their own names after all, as long as they had silly names like Cleghorn. Her first book, *Mary Barton*, drew the admiration of a certain Charles Dickens, who then employed her to write for his magazines.

96 James Abbott McNeill Whistler (1834–1903), painter and etcher, was buried at Chiswick church. American-born Whistler painted Battersea Bridge (well, pictures of it; workmen painted the actual bridge) which is within sight – not the present rather ugly 1887 structure but the previous wooden bridge of 1772. This area owes much to Sir Joseph Bazalgette (1819–91), the civil engineer, who created this whole fine Chelsea Embankment from a swampy, disease-ridden shore, though aesthetes agree Battersea Bridge is not his finest. There was a very funny court case in 1878 in which Whistler claimed he had been libelled by writer John Ruskin over a picture of Battersea Bridge at night. Ruskin had said it wasn't a correct representation at all. The case, which included long evidence about a waterman who rowed Whistler about in the moonlight, featured some classic exchanges between the artist and the judge:

> *The judge, Baron Huddleston, shown the picture:* 'Which part of the picture is the bridge?'
> *(Much laughter in court.)*
> *His Lordship earnestly rebuked those who laughed…*
> *Judge:* 'The prevailing colour is blue?'
> *Whistler:* 'Perhaps.'
> *Judge:* 'And those figures on top of the bridge are intended for people?'
> *Whistler:* 'They are just what you like.'
> *Judge:* 'Is that a barge beneath?'
> *Whistler:* 'Yes, I am much encouraged at your perceiving that.'

Whistler was always good for a pithy quotation. Hearing a witty remark, Oscar Wilde sighed: 'How I wish I had said that.' Whistler retorted: 'You will, Oscar, you will.' Another time, when Ruskin was appalled at Whistler asking a huge price for a work, Ruskin said: 'For two days' labour, you ask two hundred guineas?' Whistler replied: 'No, I ask it for the knowledge of a lifetime.' One more Whistler quote, about painting: 'Nature is usually wrong.'

98 Sir Marc Isambard Brunel and Isambard Kingdom Brunel (1769–1849 and

1806–59 respectively), engineers. This brilliant engineer father and son duo who contributed much to London, including its first under-river tunnel at Rotherhithe (the first underwater tunnel through soft soil in the world) and the Great Western Railway and Paddington station (son). Although the Brunels were of French Huguenot extraction, the name 'Isambard' comes from Germany and appropriately means 'man of iron'. Isambard Kingdom Brunel was both brilliant, taking, for example, the chains from the Old Hungerford Bridge across the Thames near Charing Cross and creating the spectacular Clifton Suspension Bridge in Bristol out of them, but also a little crackpot. His atmospheric railway in Devon (where trains were sucked along by a vacuum) didn't work too well, and his method of laying railway track (with longways sleepers attached to piles) was disastrous and had to be abandoned, as – eventually – was the broad gauge rail track he insisted on. On the other hand, his billiard-table flat GWR is still the best laid out railway in Britain. There was a certain haughtiness about the GWR. For example, their horse drinking troughs were marked with the warning that only GWR horses might drink there. Another favourite episode concerns a GWR train waiting at Reading for a branch train from Newbury to pull in at a nearby platform. A GWR director leans out of the carriage in his top hat and suggests to the guard that he blows his whistle to hurry up the passengers crossing to the London train. The guard replies: 'Sir, one does *not* blow whistles at people from Newbury.' Isambard Kingdom Brunel was picked in 2000 as Man of the Millennium (admittedly by readers of *Railway Magazine*) and I borrowed his name for my son (not all of it, just the first bit). For the Brunels' apt gravesite, see page 60.

104 Hilaire Belloc (1870–1953), poet, essayist and historian. He wrote *Cautionary Tales* and a lot about Sussex, which he loved sincerely despite being half-French. He once featured in a radio show about someone who pronounced 'E's as 'O's as

| |

Hilairo Bolloc. He wrote about himself: 'When I am dead, May it be said, His sins were scarlet, But his books were read.' He is, it isn't, they weren't, but they are.

104 Walter Greaves (1846–1930), artist. A great follower of Whistler (see above) and a painter of Thames scenes. He once said: 'I never seemed to have any ideas about painting – the river just made me do it.' Honest, Guv.

108 John Tweed (1863–1933), sculptor. Forgettable.

109 Philip Wilson Steer (1860–1942), painter. Forgotten.

120 Sylvia Pankhurst (1882–1960), women's rights campaigner. For more on the Pankhursts' graves see page 160.

FLOATING VOTERS AND THE CELEBS TOO NEW FOR PLAQUES The other, river, side of the road does in fact have a few residents, at the west end, but these are the truly floating voters of Chelsea, with nothing more to affix blue plaques to than houseboats, which may not even last as long as the inhabitants (although I like the idea of beplaqued boats; one of them could be for politician Dr David Owen, now Lord Owen, who lived there for a while, and tried to make a home for the whole country's floating voters in his short-lived Social Democrat Party – which has since sunk with all hands. Boats such as these which took part in the miraculous evacuation of Dunkirk in 1940 did actually acquire plaques to say so).

Given that blue plaques usually don't go up until 20 years after the death of the great person, the present status of more recent inhabitants of Cheyne Walk may well lead to yet more plaques. It's still an intriguing mix, although being well-heeled is of course now more of a qualification than being a genius. Not that this makes all recent inhabitants of Cheyne Walk, all too fresh to have blue plaques, boring. Far from it.

Residents over the last few decades have included the following:

- Rock superstar **Mick Jagger** (in his **Bianca** years). No need to explain him to anyone except perhaps a High Court judge.
- One of the Rolling Stone singer's neighbours was **J Paul Getty II,** son of the famous American billionaire, who ended up here in the early 1970s after taking the sixties permissive thing rather to excess. He was in quite a bad way – let's not go into details – and rarely went out. He recalled later how his salvation was neighbour Mick, who survived the sixties with less damage. Mick kept popping in for cups of tea – how English – and would chat to Getty, but put the cricket on the TV while he was there in case he missed anything in the Test matches.

Getty recalled: 'I'd have to watch too.' Eventually, while Mick patiently explained the finer points (such as when you're out, you come in, and someone else goes out to be in, and when they're all out, you're in, that kind of stuff), Getty became hooked: 'I started watching even when Mick wasn't there. That was the turning point, the day I found myself watching cricket when no-one else was there.'

It's so unlikely that it *has* to be true. Getty, deeply troubled, was reborn as an eccentric English gentleman with the help of Mick Jagger, cups of tea and cricket. He turned out to be a great philanthropist and built a wonderful cricket ground at his later home, Wormsley Park in the Chilterns, where he bred red kite birds of prey, and famously became so British that he was knighted to become Sir J Paul Getty in later life. Amazing.

- Saintly rock person and Live Aid inventor and all-round good egg, 'Sir' **Bob Geldof.** The 'Sir' is in quotes because he, unlike Getty, has retained his nationality, in this case Irish, and so cannot be awarded an honour.
- The late Aussie rockstar **Michael Hutchence** of INXS.
- Aussie pop kitten **Kylie Minogue**, formerly of *Neighbours* soap opera.
- **Paloma Picasso,** the model-perfume person and daughter of the great painter.
- Labour luvvie and novelist **Ken Follet**.
- **Sir Jocelyn Stephens**, English Heritage new broom and newspaper supremo.
- Spy writer **Nigel West**, not, in fact, the brother of John, the tinned tuna magnate, but really an MP called Rupert Allason.
- **Jane Asher**, actress for whom a new career in baking was the icing on the cake.
- **Gerald Scarfe**, the great cartoonist, who drew Asher down the aisle.
- Former pop star **Simon le Bon** and his model wife **Yasmin**, if you include the adjoining Apollo Place. The le Bons are not the only ones on this list to be connected.
- The late **Paula Yates** was famously connected at one time to Bob Geldof and another time to Michael Hutchence and was deeply eccentric in her choice of children's names: Fifi Trixibelle, Peaches Honeyblossom, Pixie and, the best of the lot, Heavenly Hiraani Tiger Lily. This led to the unkind joke Londoners told at the time of her mysterious death in 2000. 'Did you hear about Paula Yates? She was found dead with Tri-Sulphate Lysurgic Dinucleorubinic Acid by her bed. But the other children were at Bob's.' Paula's too short life was never boring, even though it included selling ice-creams in Bognor as a teenager. She thought she was the daughter of entertainer Jess 'the Bishop' Yates but it turned out not long before she died that she was in fact the daughter of the late, insufferably smarmy gameshow host, Hughie Green.
- But if we are flexible enough to include the le Bons, that truly great painter of the Thames, **J M W Turner** (1775–1851), must be included too (the river hereabouts is called Turner's Reach). He lived here anonymously at No 119 Cheyne Walk on and off from 1846 to his death in 1851 (he has an unofficial plaque). Joseph Mallord William Turner (who, like Shakespeare, cleverly contrived to be born on April 23, St George's Day, England's national saint's day) was indeed a little eccentric. There is, by the way, just the other side of King's Road, a Mallord Street in Chelsea (and a plaque there to artist **Augustus John** and *Winnie the Pooh* author **A A Milne**); and Turner has a plaque of his own elsewhere.

Turner was a great impressionist about 50 years before the French think they invented it, and was very reluctant to sell his paintings, which he regarded as his children. Indeed, he would go into a sulk if one did sell.

His subjects include the Great Western Railway – the creation of another Cheyne Walk resident, Isambard Kingdom Brunel – in his superb painting 'Rain, Steam and Speed'. Like Brunel, he sometimes got things wrong and in that painting, to be seen at the National Gallery at Trafalgar Square, Turner seems to have thought the loco's firebox was open at the front. Even Brunel would never have allowed that. Perhaps it was a flag or a coat-of-arms, but I'm

11

sure it was supposed to be the fire. Have a look. Only a pedant would feel this negates the atmosphere of the picture. By the way, this bridge at Maidenhead, built by Brunel, has daringly wide and low brick arches, and the authorities were so worried that they insisted wooden arches be put beneath them for safety. This Brunel did, but he made sure the wooden supports didn't actually touch his superb engineering by leaving an unseen gap, so eventually they rotted and fell down, unlike his daring arches which are in their second century still holding up thundering express trains heading for Bristol and South Wales.

In fact Turner often really studied his subjects with devotion. He once paid a fisherman a great deal of money to take him to sea in a storm, with him, the artist, lashed to the mast. It nearly cost him his life, but his raging seascapes are magnificent. At other times Turner was known to inhabit a room in St Mary's church, Battersea, and spend hours gazing at the Thames. Perhaps his most famous work is set on

the surface of the Thames, 'The Fighting Temeraire', the sad, stately hulk of a sailing era man-of-war (once captured from the French, hence her name, or maybe one named after such a prize) being towed to the breaker's yard by a symbol of the exciting, brash new era, a smoke belching steam tug.

Late in his life the reclusive Turner – who had a very secretive private life, and no real friends except his father and who never married – fell ill and disappeared from his London home. After several months of searching, his housekeeper found him here in Chelsea, where he died the next day in December 1851.

Thanks to his possessive feelings towards his works, he was able to leave the nation 300 paintings, plus thousands of watercolours and drawings, many both brilliant and popular. Those two adjectives would seem to be a disqualification for the winners of today's **Turner Prize**, an annual prize worth £20,000 for the assiduously avant-garde who relentlessly try to shock a jaded public with such creations at the tediously risquée Tracey Emin's unmade bed (including, apparently, her soiled underwear – how flipping fascinating). The media, always short of a story at that time of year (therefore known as the silly season), always go along with the hype and pretend to be shocked, thus creating another instant celeb out of this year's enfant terrible. Not one of them will be remembered long enough to get a blue plaque, of course.

One might reasonably suspect, given the calibre of artist the Turner Prize produces, that it may have been named after Tina Turner, the raunchy rock star, or possibly Anthea Turner, the vacuously grinning TV presenter, not J M W Turner, and that Turner the painter's last wishes have gone out of the picture.

One would suspect rightly in the latter regard. Turner left money for a Turner Medal, not a Turner Prize, to be awarded each year by the Royal Academy, not the Tate. Turner's fan club, of which I am a fervent but inexpert member, point out that his last wishes have been largely ignored. He left his beloved pictures to be shown as a whole in the Turner Gallery, now part of the

Clore Gallery, which has quite a few, but others have been split off and lent abroad then stolen (and did the insurance money go to the collection?). The Turner Medal was presented by the RA until around 1990 but then the money left for it was merged with many other such bequests and the Medal quietly forgotten. Shame on them.

A BIT OF SPANISH BLARNEY AND A RECLUSIVE MILLIONAIRE Back to Cheyne

Walk, and that strange propensity for encouraging eccentric genius which the area around here seems to have. What about the unsung eccentrics of the Walk who have no plaque but should have?

One such must be **James Salter** who ran a coffee shop here, at No 18, in the 1720s and who called himself 'Don Saltero'. A bit rum for a skinny, small Irishman, but why not? He was known as a great wit and a philosopher, and as well as providing excellent coffee for his customers, would extract their teeth, play the fiddle to them, shave them and generally entertain them with the extraordinary collection of curios and oddities he called his museum. The exhibits included, he claimed, a petrified crab from China, a pair of nun's stockings, several pieces of the True Cross, a starved cat found in the walls of Westminster Abbey when they were being repaired, and one of Elizabeth I's chambermaids' hats. Among his customers were Jonathan Swift and Benjamin Franklin.

In modern Cheyne Walk, one of the most massive eccentrics, in terms of what he will leave to future generations, must be multimillionaire **Christopher Moran.** Supposedly very rich at an early age, he is a brilliant but highly controversial performer at Lloyd's insurance market, and a complex, intelligent and equally controversial character (let's leave the personal stuff aside here, but don't expect some genial old buffer to invite you in for tea and biccies). Moran has, with the rebuilding of Crosby Hall, achieved in a home – surely the most remarkable private residence in London – something on the scale of the recreation of the Globe Theatre or perhaps the restoration of Somerset House, at an outlay of tens of millions of pounds (one estimate was £25 million). It has window arches around 70ft high, 30ft oak portals, a fireplace big enough to live in, and a glorious Tudor painted and scissor-beamed ceiling.

Moran, whose business acumen from an early age was such that he sold cigarettes and the *Financial Times* at school and had a Rolls-Royce by the time he was 20, acquired the freehold to the 15th-century hall, once home of 16th-century Lord Chancellor and later saint, **Thomas More** (see the play and film *A Man For All Seasons*), in 1989 for a reported £100,000.

The incumbent Association of University Women, who had the leasehold, soon moved out. The Hall then underwent a massive restoration by the finest craftsmen, who releaded its oriel windows and cupolas, and gilded the weather vanes on the Tudor cupolas, taking down the 15th-century brickwork and replacing it with authentic materials, and building further matching wings. It took years.

Now, as you can see even from the exterior, it is a thing of real beauty, and it seems impossible that such a structure could have survived the ravages of London's fires, plagues, wars, and the pressures of development and whatever intact right here.

Well it didn't. In the 15th century, Chelsea was miles outside London and this house, built by a wealthy wool merchant and lord mayor, Sir John Crosby, in fact stood at Bishopsgate in the City of London. Crosby died in 1475 and is buried at St Helen's, Bishopsgate.

Threatened with demolition, Crosby Hall and its beautiful Tudor timber roof was taken apart beam by numbered beam and stone by numbered stone by London

11

County Council in 1908, and re-erected on the embankment here, the clear intention being to save it for the public good. The stone hall itself, now on the right, was the only medieval part which survived 17th-century fires in its previous site, according to one source. I have seen it suggested that most of the convincingly Tudor-looking stuff at the front dates from 1927, built by a certain Walter H Godfrey. And of course substantial parts are brand new, so detailed has been the restoration.

In the complex history of the next 90 years of its development, the public access part of the original plan for the relocated building has somehow gone by the board, although it is undeniable that the building has been saved in a remarkable operation. A curt notice on the side door of Crosby Hall when I revisited it warned away those who think they may have a right to have a look.

Like other driven and indeed slightly obsessive perfectionists, the reclusive Mr Moran is to some degree building a monument to himself. He is reported as saying he wants to be buried at Crosby Hall. After his efforts he can be sure this remarkable building will be here in Cheyne Walk many more centuries. It is quite a staggering thing to be undertaken by, and apparently for, one man and most surprising to find in Chelsea a massive medieval building the size of an Oxford college, looking virtually brand new.

MORE MORE AND A STRANGE HOLY RELIC There is a lot more More to the right of Cheyne Walk as you look at Crosby Hall (that is downriver). What was once Thomas More's orchard next door is now a sunken garden and if you are a Londoner of a certain age and see a garden obviously laid out in the late 20th century in a gap in a row of houses, you say to yourself 'bomb site'. Either you saw the smoking ruins or, if a bit younger like myself, you played in the marvellous weed-filled lands of adventure that such ruins offered. Mostly they've now gone, giving way to some ghastly fifties or sixties block stuck incongruously in a row of older houses, but occasionally the gap was retained for public use as in Roper Gardens here, offering peace and tranquillity – odd when you think of the violence that created them.

In the middle of this one is a fine statue of a girl – *Awakening* by Gilbert Ledward. She is looking up, perhaps watching for another parachute-mine like the one that flattened this place in 1941. At the other end of the garden is a much more cryptic sculpture by **Jacob Epstein** whose former studio here was redistributed by the Luftwaffe. His brilliance, along with that of so many other great Jewish artists and musicians, we ought to remember, would have been extinguished for ever had the Nazi campaign succeeded, when all their works would no doubt have been destroyed.

Just a bit further on is a fine statue of **Sir Thomas More** in front of the Chelsea Old Church, looking not unlike the fine picture of him in the National Portrait Gallery, apart, of course, from the skin tone. The statue bills him simply as 'statesman', 'saint' and 'scholar'.

More's saintliness was, as I have mentioned, not only brilliantly portrayed by Paul Scofield in Robert Bolt's 1966 film, *A Man For All Seasons*, but was also confirmed by the Pope who canonised him in 1936. However, others think the above monument should have added to it: 'scheming politician, arrogant extremist and enthusiastic torturer'. At least, that's what a not-very-convincing BBC documentary tried to argue in 2001.

I think I prefer the original so the programme may just have been the creature of bored TV executives saying, 'Let's see what hero we can debunk this time', curiously expecting 16th-century people to have 21st-century values.

More wrote a good epitaph for himself shortly before his head was chopped off for refusing to agree that Henry VIII was now head of the Church. On the scaffold

Sir Thomas, by the way, pushed his beard to one side with the words 'Well, at least my beard has not committed treason.' His head, as was usual for those judged traitors, was stuck on a pole on London Bridge for a few weeks; when it was taken down it was pickled in spices by his daughter. He had expected to be buried in the church here with his first and second wives, but was buried (minus his head, of course) at the church within the Tower of London, where he was executed in 1535, St Peter Ad Vincula (appropriately, St Peter in Chains).

And More's own epitaph? It was 'The King's good servant, but God's first'.

Not a bad CV and commendably concise too – unlike the gushing monument to **Sir Hans Sloane** at the right-hand side of the churchyard behind him.

Sloane (as in Square and by extension Ranger) may not have been a saint but was President both of the Royal Society and of the College of Physicians 'who [the monument tells us] in the year of our Lord 1753 the 92nd of his age without the least pain of body and with conscious serenity of mind ended a virtuous and beneficent life.' Sloane's house nearby was flattened by the construction of Beaufort Street, running north from Battersea Bridge, but his collection of antiquities became the nucleus of the British Museum, a finer monument still. Sloane is crucial to the Cheyne Walk story because he bought the land from a Lord Cheyne and hastened the development of the area.

Of that inscription, you may think 'Pass the sickbag', but, yo, way to go Hans, baby, I'd say (if I were in an American film): 92 then kazoom! Straight out. Anyway, it was put up by his daughters and who nowadays wouldn't be happy to live to 92 and still have the respect of their daughters?

Don't miss, at the other corner of the churchyard (that is left as you look at Thomas More), an apparently insignificant-looking sapling. This just could be the most significant thing in Cheyne Walk, or in London, or indeed in your whole life. It could just be a living link to when Jesus Christ was on earth. Not convinced? Well, hear this. It's quite a story.

It was planted in 2000 to commemorate the second millennium of Christ's birth. It is a piece, I am told, of the **Glastonbury Thorn**, a legendary tree of that epicentre on Glastonbury, Somerset, of British … British what? Spirituality? Sacred myth? Folklore? Hippiedom? Rock festivals? (Tick the box that says 'All of the above'.) This undoubtedly extraordinary place is linked to King Arthur, the past and future king who will return, it is said, and which is the focus of ley lines. (Ley lines? I haven't time to go into all that, but if you believe in astrology, corn circles, UFOs, pyramid power and Atlantis, you'll love them. If not, you won't.)

The important bit of the story they tell you in Somerset is this. When Joseph of Arimathea, having arrived in Britain carrying the Holy Grail, first saw the Isle of Avalon (now Glastonbury Tor), he directed his boat there and thrust his hawthorn staff into the ground, where it took root and flowered.

It *is* possible for a piece of wood to root like this, but then miracles, if it was one, don't need to be possible. (I hate all that stuff newspapers blather on about; for example, 'Well, the Red Sea could have parted if there was a very strong tide and the wind was from the east, etc, etc.' If it's a miracle, it's a flaming miracle, for God's sake.)

A church was built there, St John's, Glastonbury, and when the monumentally po-faced Puritans came along in their inane, humourless republican way, smashing stained-glass windows and decapitating statues of saints (they went on to create whole cities across the Atlantic which some less fair people than myself still label 'irony-free zones'), they of course chopped the tree down as idolatrous.

They hadn't reckoned with a faithful priest who kept a cutting and replanted it. One thing that lends credence to this whole story – and I am merely telling you what is said – is that each reigning monarch takes care to have a sprig from this tree on his or her table each Christmas time. This very tree in Chelsea is one such sprig.

Chelsea Old Church itself was badly damaged by that parachute-mine in 1941 (what was the point of the parachute, why didn't the Germans just fling the thing out? Is this the teutonic sense of humour?), but parts, such as the south chancel rebuilt by More in 1528, were undamaged. There are more More monuments, plus a rather good one with effigies of Dacre of the South (died 1595) with his wife, and an unusual monument to Sara Colville (died 1631).

• For the Dacre Beasts, linked to the Dacre of the North, see page 155.

THE MISERABLE COUPLES AND A WRITERS' BLOCK
Back to the plaques. Between Cheyne Walk and King's Road, there are some fascinating streets and footpaths, mostly on an agreeably small scale and dotted with welcoming, if not cheap, pubs.

The main road north from the ludicrously pretty Albert Bridge is Oakley Street, home of heroic failure **Captain Robert Falcon Scott** (of Antarctic fame) at No 56. And in Cheyne Row, a small street running north from the river just east of here, is the home of the 'sage of Chelsea', author and philosopher **Thomas Carlyle** (1795–1881), who wrote histories of recent great events such as the French Revolution. Others thought him not quite as fascinating as he did. Samuel Butler wrote: 'It was very good of God to let Carlyle and Mrs Carlyle marry one another and so make only two people miserable instead of four.' The house is now owned by the National Trust, having been bought by Carlyle's admirers in 1895, so you can inspect his study, the kitchen where he would smoke with Tennyson, and the grave of Nero, Mrs Carlyle's dog, in the garden.

At 21 Carlyle Mansions, a block at the river end of this street, American novelist **Henry James** breathed his last in 1916. He wrote about London in his *Notebooks*: 'It is difficult to speak adequately or justly of London. It is not a pleasant place; it is not agreeable, or cheerful, or easy, or exempt from reproach. It is only magnificent.' His funeral was held in nearby Chelsea Old Church (see above) where he was a regular; **Rudyard Kipling** was one of his mourners. Other literary greats who lived in this block included another American, poet **T S Eliot,** and author **Ian Fleming**, creator of James Bond. Fleming lived like a would-be playboy while Eliot lived like a monk, sleeping in a bare cell of a room lit by one unshaded bulb. But then his poems aren't a bundle of fun, either.

I know it's frightful of me, but there's a great deal of pleasure to be had in contemplating the publication of Eliot's at times impenetrable *The Waste Land* by the equally over-serious Leonard and Virginia Woolf at their Richmond home press in 1923. This is because it was full of printing errors, but nobody noticed, least of all the entirely eccentric Eliot who was supposed to check it. Now wouldn't it be obvious if any normal poem were full of errors? Someone has written in my copy of *The Waste Land* a quotation from Byron: 'I wish he would explain his explanation.'

12

Eccentric Buildings

ELEVEN ECCENTRIC LONDON BUILDINGS

1   **The Ark** This superb apparition next to the thundering A4 flyover in Hammersmith offers changing and different vistas from any direction. It is brilliant, elegant and avoids that cigarette-pack-shape cliché of most modern offices. Oddly, when a newspaper where I worked asked readers to nominate the ugliest building in Britain, this one made it into the top few. It's a matter of taste, I suppose, but there's no denying it is eccentric. I think it's a brilliant breath of fresh air in a jaded era. For full details, see Hammersmith walk, page 252.
↔ *Hammersmith*

2   **The Lloyd's Building** Leadenhall Street, the City. Centre of London's insurance market, the building was designed by Richard Rogers but is much better and more durable than his Pompidou Centre in Paris, which by comparison looks like some relic from a 1970s Habitat store, the chief fault of the Centre being, in my view, its trashy colours, which are avoided in this rather effective building. The basic Rogers idea was that you don't have to hide all the ducts, lifts, escalators, etc inside the building, but could instead put them on the outside, freeing up the interior and offering an exterior that is sculptural yet functional. Everything but the kitchen sink is visible on the outside (actually it would make about two million kitchen sinks if they demolished it).

The steel boxes on the outside are mostly lavatories, a humorous touch when you think how Victorian and 20th-century architects mostly hid these unmentionable things away in the bowels of a building. Actually it's more of a return to the medieval approach to the lavatory – garderobes were tiny chambers projecting from the outside walls of castles and great houses. But, standing beneath Lloyd's one hopes that the affluent effluent doesn't just drop out of holes in the floor and streak the walls as in those malodorous days.

Lloyd's had a wobbly lip moment in the 1980s when a huge bunch of insurance claims from disasters such as the *Exxon Valdez* tanker crash put pressure on the individual 'names', well-connected people who put up cash for insurance syndicates, hoping to get stonking rich if things went well – if there were no big insurance claims against them. Unfortunately, they are personally liable for those claims and some lost their homes and their fortunes. Sad for some, but it was hard for the ordinary Joe to get too upset about a lot of rich people using their connections to try to get much richer without doing a stroke of work.

Hence the joke in London at the time: 'At Lloyd's they call people names – such as greedy git, that kind of thing.' Lloyd's has, however, weathered the storm, learned its lessons and will likely sail on for centuries yet.

⊖ *Tower Hill*

3 The Albert Memorial and the Royal Albert Hall

The Albert Memorial and the Royal Albert Hall Kensington. Londoners may think they don't need to read this, so well-known are these landmarks. But how many have considered this pair in their extraordinary detail? First, the overall scheme of things. I suppose you would expect the memorial to Albert, the much-loved consort of Queen Victoria, the Empress of the greatest empire the world has ever seen (well, she was about to become empress when he died) to be noteworthy. After all, wasn't the lovely Taj Mahal in India built by Shah Jahan in mourning for his wife? But here in Kensington these two structures of astounding contrast bedazzle the eye – the Memorial, a soaring arch-Gothic Victorian fantasy with every fantastic embellishment; and the Hall – across the road, epitome of restrained, unadorned and even severe classicism, neatly summarising the two incompatible roots of British architecture, Gothic and Roman, which are usually kept well apart, or horribly watered down to make them live together.

The **Albert Memorial**, recently restored at huge expense, was designed by Sir George Gilbert Scott (1811–78), great architect of the fantastic Midland Grand Hotel at St Pancras – and grandfather of Sir Giles Gilbert Scott (1880–1960), creator of the classic red phone box, Battersea Power station and Waterloo Bridge.

Sir George, when he designed this structure, evidently had in mind the Eleanor crosses, soaring Gothic spires put up by the grieving King Edward I at every spot where his beloved Queen Eleanor's coffin rested overnight on its 12-day journey back to London (see page 139). The Albert Memorial, a soaring pile of expensive stonework, with hundreds of sculptures on it, is the same idea taken to ridiculous extremes.

Revealingly, two other ideas for the Albert Memorial were rejected. One was an obelisk, similar to Cleopatra's Needle, located on the Victoria Embankment. Another was a great monolith, a massive slab which, *The Times* complained, would cost as much money as half an ironclad frigate. Both ideas were sarcastically attacked as 'England may show she can do in the 19th century what the Ancient Egyptians, and even the painted Britons, were able to accomplish in the Sphinx and Stonehenge.'

This is the nub of it. What the Albert Memorial reflects above all was the sheer confidence of the British at the time: confidence in their industry, their navy, their empire, their history, confidence that they were better than other ages or countries. That's why 20th-century Britain found the Albert Memorial in such bad taste. Demolition was considered seriously in the 1960s, while restoration had to wait for the very end of the century.

The Albert Memorial

The **Royal Albert Hall**, opened in 1871 and designed to hold 8,000 people, would not have looked out of place in ancient Rome as a place for gladiators to hack each other to bits, or, in its almost industrial severity, as a Victorian roundhouse for servicing giant steam locomotives. Victorian virtues are listed around the top of the outside walls of the building.

Of course this pair of royals is linked for ever to high-minded Victorian moral values. Queen Victoria, typically, was said to have refused to include lesbians in laws against homosexuals because she didn't believe such behaviour was possible. Equally typically of our age, if you travel to Earl's Court where many of the said homosexuals (now entirely legal) hang out, you'll find the term 'Prince Albert' refers to a rather less edifying aspect of body piercing for males. If you don't know, don't ask.

↪ *High St Kensington, turn right out of station, walking east along Kensington High Street for just over half a mile.*

4 A lost Sultan's bog? Off Bishopsgate. When Ali Baba rubbed his lamp, a genie appeared and said: 'Master, what is your will, for I can perform any task you desire?' Ali thought for a moment and said: 'Take the money-changer's harem from the great bazaar at Baghdad and transport it on your magic carpet to an infidel city beyond the sea called London.' 'It shall be done, master.' Well that's a plausible explanation of how this eccentrically oriental building came to be in its incongruous surroundings. What else could it be? Has Brighton pavilion slipped up to London and pupped? Is it a lost Sultan's bog? Actually, it's a restaurant, but its origin in 1894 was as a Turkish bath, so builder Harold Elphick made it utterly Ottoman. It's still charmingly here, blending into the background as well as a bowler-hatted City gent at the Taj Mahal would. Wonderful.

↪ *Liverpool Street*

5 Trellick Tower If you're going to have tower blocks, the Trellick Tower is the tour de force. No quarter is given to convention here, no pussyfooting around with apologising for being a concrete tower. God knows how it was ever permitted to be built. Wallop! It punches into the air near Paddington to remind us of the new brutalism of the sixties. Generally, we came to hate the people who ripped the heart out of towns and terrace streets to make these brutal blocks. Being an old age pensioner on the 17th floor wasn't fun when the urinated-in lifts broke down while elsewhere unseen thieves and vandals rampaged. We thought the architects monstrous hypocrites and blew up a lot of the towers (memorably, one in east London, Ronan Point, blew itself up).

This one was different. Far more radical than the boring boxy blocks elsewhere, it is so tall it would bridge the Paddington main line or the Grand Union Canal (Paddington Arm) were it ever felled. Architect Erno Goldfinger, unlike the usual bunch of architect-hypocrites, actually lived in one of his towers for a bit, although he preferred his low-rise modernist house in Hampstead, now a museum (see page 272). He scorned the whitewashed stucco art deco style of some houses then being built: 'I want to be remembered as a classical architect, not a kasbah architect,' he said.

Now that trendy Notting Hill is colonising the former combat zone that is North Kensington, flats in the tower are becoming sought-after by those who fit the uncompromisingly trendy radical profile. What a stonking place for a minimalist look! Most of Goldfinger's urban renewal stuff has – in my view rightly – been blown up or refurbished. Trellick House is different. It is, on a somewhat Soviet or fascist monumental scale, an unashamed, powerful piece of sculpture. Long may it remain.

↪ *Westbourne Park*

6 The NatWest Media Centre Lord's Cricket Ground, St John's Wood. Have the Martians landed? Is the War of the Worlds about to start in exclusive St John's Wood? I don't know of any other building in the world which looks like this spaceshippy thing – but then its monocoque aluminium shell was built in a shipyard. It has suitably large sloping windows on the cricket side (ball proof?) but

to the outside world it is exciting, alien, about to take off – and they say Lord's and the MCC are stuffy. For hallowed turf of dead cricket legends' graves, see page 168.
⊖ *St John's Wood*

Peckham Library Unlikely in that it is in Peckham and done on the cheap, this library, designed by Alsop and Stormer, avoids both the stamp of council mediocrity and the clichéd emblems of post-modernism. It's different and it works. In 2001 Peckham and design were in the news again when Angel of the North sculptor, the otherwise brilliant Antony Gormley, created some immensely phallic bollards for the streets. What was that rude schoolboy rhyme ending 'Turnham Green and Peckham'? Answers in a plain brown envelope please.
⌖ *Peckham Rye (from London Bridge)*

The Gherkin Fast becoming an icon for modern London, the Gherkin is instantly recognisable from its fat cigar – well all right, gherkin – shape. The gherkin is an ugly pickled cucumbery thing sold in British fish 'n' chip shops, and not to everybody's taste (although if you haven't tried pickled eggs, also in jars in such shops, you haven't lived). Gherkins are like the French cornichons, only bigger, and if you cut the curved end off one and set it with the other end upright, you would have the perfect Gherkin building shape (but the smell would be rather different). It might seem an eccentric name for a building, but it's an unofficial one, the proper address being 30 St Mary Axe, and the official building name at the time of writing 'the Swiss Re'. Both of which are frankly considerably dafter names than the Gherkin. They could have dubbed it the Rocket or the Pine Cone but that wouldn't have been humorous. It is nevertheless a fantastic building, designed by Norman Foster, and uses far less power to run than a normal office building. Not the tallest tower by any means, at 180m it is slightly outranked by the nearby Tower 42 (which used to be the NatWest Tower) and 237m Canary Wharf in the Docklands (but how much more fun is the Gherkin?). And soon, across the river, it will have a rival for startlingness in the Shard of Glass, the 303m London Bridge Tower. That should be the tallest building in Europe, or will be until the French notice.
⊖ *Aldgate or Bank*

The Glass Helmet – City Hall Recognisably part of the Norman Conquest of London (Norman Foster, that is), City Hall near Tower Bridge looks like a vast alien has put down his helmet, or is perhaps buried whole deep in the riverside. Despite the curved glass on a fishnet signature of Foster's work – which might become a horribly dated cliché one day but may have bought a few glaziers a nice holiday home – this tilted building is eccentric because of its spiral interior ramp that goes up around perhaps ten storeys like a demonic apple peeling. This design is said by the usual know-alls to 'symbolise openness, accessibility, democracy and transparency'. It could equally well be said to symbolise a huge waste of space, uneccessary and profligate duplication (we had a perfectly good County Hall, and needed another layer of government like a fish needs a new bike), elitist disdain for our culture and gesture politics. Anyone in a wheelchair who really takes that right-on ramp to the top deserves a medal. Be good for skateboarding, however. Well I really like it, although cyncial Londoners who came up with the Gherkin for the tower have called this the Testicle. It's on the South Bank in Southwark, close to Tower Bridge. Another Foster triumph you must see is the indeed great **Great Court at the British Museum**, where the gap between the circular reading room and the surrounding building has been covered by another set of bulging fishnets. And as you look up, consider again the work for glaziers – are any two of those glass panes the same shape?

10 **Halls of residence** University of East London. Great examples of clean, functional attractive modern architecture. They are also an antidote to those increasingly common riverside developments on the Thames which look as if they are what happens when rich people and Lego kits collide without an architect. These halls, situated in Docklands, are dramatic truncated cylinders, whose roofs are shorn off at an angle to shed London's rain (whatever fool thought flat roofs would work in this climate?). They are bold and clear about what they are doing, and don't pretend to be anything else or from any other period. The student rooms inside them are arranged, like pizza slices, in a long triangle, 12 to a floor. Economy is achieved by linking two such blocks so the stairs, etc can be shared. They are brightly painted; like most organic and efficient things (and unlike most buildings), they are curved, not square like a mortarboard, presumably representing a well-rounded education. Great for spotty plane-spotters, too, as it is located opposite London City Airport on Royal Albert Dock. ⊖ *Royal Albert (DLR). Not open to the public.*

11 **Launching Ramps** Vauxhall Cross. Well they might be a bus station canopy, but this building (or sculpture) is deeply eccentric, with its undulating roof ending up in a pair of ramps which look suspiciously like those used for launching the V1 doodlebug rockets at London during World War II. When you bear in mind they could swivel round to aim directly at the MI6 Secret Service headquarters across the road, should we be worried about elderly teutonic types who want revenge? Vauxhall Cross was known as the world's most unpleasant road junction before it was tarted up with this insane structure, and it has improved the area a little. Oddly, all Russian railway stations are called Vauxhall because the main line from the south-west ended here before Waterloo was built and the Tsar, being shown round, said the Russians should get a Vauxhall for themselves. That may be apocryphal, but if so, the Russians probably named stations after the Vauxhall pleasure gardens nearby, because a pleasure park was called a Vauxhall in Russia at the time, and the first railway there went to one. Meanwhile, the James Bond film *Die Another Day* features a secret Tube extension to the MI6 headquarters, a concept derided by rail buffs as no such line crosses under the river. Well, if it were secret you wouldn't know would you, thickos, that's what secret means. What do you mean, James Bond *isn't real*? Anyway, we've heard of MI5 and MI6. But who admits to working for MI1, MI2, MI3, MI4? Ha! They must be the real Secret Services.

- If you're a fan of modern architecture, then the 20th Century Society (*www.c20society.demon.co.uk*) might be for you. Originally called the Thirties Society, it saved a few art deco masterpieces, and failed to save a few more, such as the Firestone factory on the Great West Road, which was scandalously demolished just before it could be listed for preservation, and on a bank holiday Monday too. The Society then found itself fighting to preserve fifties, and even sixties, architecture, which was confusing, so it changed its name to the 20th Century Society. Of course, as the 21st century continues, the same problem will arise but, like 20th Century Fox in films, they haven't got round to dealing with that one yet. Perhaps they should be the Not Before World War I But Anything Modern After That Is Pretty Well OK By Us Society.

ART DECO, DREAM PALACES AND RECOGNISING A SUCKER

For the greatest quality art deco architecture, people go to Miami, perhaps to Napier, New Zealand ... and to Perivale, West London.

Here on Western Avenue the extraordinary **Hoover building** stands testament to that confident era when pseudo-Tudor suburbs sprawled unrestrained, when

12

grand arterial roads for the newly popular motorcar were being laid out, along which sprang up buildings in this astonishing architectural style which looked forward to the supposedly bright future of the rest of the 20th century, and not at all backwards. It's a matter of taste, of course, but I think the Hoover building, with its odd glass angles and the tilework over the door is superb.

The Hoover building

This example of art deco, on Western Avenue, is surely one of the best. Hoover products are no longer made here, but the building is part supermarket, part offices.

At a similar distance out of London on other roads can be found other examples of art deco buildings, the architecture that threw every previous notion out of its curved windows. They can be private homes, still with those strange bits of curved glass, often in ribbon development which would now never be allowed, or cinemas, such as the **Regal** in nearby Uxbridge, or factories and offices, also situated along or near the A40 (the road that leads out of London to Oxford).

If it stands out now, how must it have seemed to 1930s Britain with its predominantly Edwardian and Victorian stock of buildings? A bombshell.

Art deco fans may have spotted its frontage, cast as a cinema supposedly in Doncaster in the TV film of Agatha Christie's Poirot story, *The ABC Murders*. The interiors of such splendid cinemas often survive too (and don't miss the old Arsenal Football Club building in Highbury, North London).

While we're on **cinemas**, the twenties and thirties saw the great dream palaces of this, the golden age of cinema, being finished with some very eccentric interiors. There was the elaborate Venetian palace interior of the Granada Tooting (1931); while the New Victoria (1928–29) had, and has, not only a striking modernist exterior but also a fabulous underwater-palace-style interior complete with scalloped everything and fantastic lighting.

Then there were the Astorias, of which two have survived, at Brixton and Finsbury Park. The latter, which enjoyed a resurgence as a top rock venue in the later 20th century as The Rainbow, has a fountain court foyer and an elaborate moorish interior, with lions on pillars either side of the stage, and a silhouetted-oasis roof-line of palm trees, minarets and houses set against a sky cleverly lit from below so that it faded through various blues and pinks to black, revealing twinkling stars set in it. Superb.

Other exotic themes used in these dream palaces included an ancient Egyptian temple at the Carlton, Islington (1930), and the wacky, Chinese-pagoda-style Southall Gaumont (1928) and the completely over-the-top Tsarist Palace interior of the Kilburn State (1937) – its exterior was art deco with tower. The cinema changed the face of architecture in London as surely as the great railway stations had 50 years before.

With their electrically driven trains, **Tube stations** were particularly suited to reflect the art deco vision of clean, suburban living – from the radical modernist boxes that are the Tube stations at Sudbury Town, Sudbury Hill, Acton Town, Turnpike Lane, or the marvellous drums that are the stations of Chiswick Park, Arnos Grove, Hanger Lane (just before Perivale on the A40 heading out from London), or, one of the best in terms of detail, Southgate.

These still look modern today – in the 1930s they must have resembled science-fiction spaceports. To put it another way, the ultra-modern Jubilee Line extension, opened in 2000 – that is, the bits that run from Westminster eastwards – features some superb modernistic stations which, on first glance, look not unlike the art deco or modernist counterparts of 70 years before.

So back to Perivale and the Hoover art deco palace, a landmark in London's architecture. Actually it should be called the Spangler Building. The inventor of the vacuum cleaner was an American boffin, Murray Spangler; William H Hoover was merely the canny businessman who recognised a great sucker – literally – when he saw one, and really cleaned up. So after a party, one should really say: 'I'm just going to Spangler the carpet.'

• Art deco style in swimming pools, see page 45.

TOWERING ECCENTRICITIES AROUND LONDON

Eccentric towers – follies, indeed – are usually associated with the remote country estates of barmy barons, delinquent dukes and mad marquesses. But if you know where to poke around, there are some darned odd buildings around London too.

One rather strange triangular tower not only gives a superb view over much of southeast London, but tells of a swashbuckling fight against pirates in the exotic east. **Severndroog Castle** in Castlewood Park off Shooters Hill, near Blackheath in southeast London, was built in 1784 for the widow of Sir William James as a tribute to the heroic attack led by Sir William, with four ships and thousands of men, on the original Severndroog Castle, a nest of pirates on the Malabar coast of India. That castle was taken in 1755. This one's still here.

A whole set of strange towers puzzles travellers going southwest from London along the line of the A3. They look as if Rapunzel might let her hair down from them. They are in fact **semaphore towers** for sending messages quickly back and forth from the fleet at Portsmouth to the Admiralty in London, in the days before the electric telegraph was invented. They say a message could be got from one end of the system to the other in about 20 minutes. There's one you can visit at Wisley, where the road crosses the M25, and, I was delighted to discover, one converted into the Telegraph pub between Wimbledon Common and Putney, on the edge of **Roehampton**. Again it's on a hill, so it's a logical location – in fact in Telegraph Road, Putney Heath – and again it's next to the modern A3, which takes a similar line because it's also making for Portsmouth. Go on down this road far enough and you will find Tower Road in Hindhead, Surrey, and a little further another Tower Road in Liphook, Hampshire. Coincidence? I think not. There were a chain of these things.

To visit the **Wisley** one, in fact called Chatley Heath Semaphore Tower, take the A3 to the M25 junction, about ten minutes out of the edge of London, and go on the roundabout as if you were leaving the A3. In fact rejoin the A3 southbound and immediately take the little lane to the left, marked Semaphore Tower. Note that you cannot safely do this directly by staying on the A3 across the M25 (but if you come by the M25 you will be fine). Then take the second car park on the left (not marked particularly) after a few hundred yards. It is about half a mile of clearly marked paths through woodland to reach the tower which is open and functioning on summer weekends, with its wooden arms flailing about transmitting messages, although a somewhat lonely task as no-one is receiving them.

The tower is 60ft high, built in 1822, and could do six words per minute, the 15 stations taking about 20 minutes to reach Portsmouth.

Perhaps this system wasn't unique. The novelist C S Forester has his Royal Navy hero, Hornblower, notice a French semaphore tower on an island annoyingly waggling its arms around giving away the position of British ships to admirals ashore. So he rows ashore in a small boat and burns the thing down. That would certainly stuff it up for a bit.

12

In fact further investigations show that the French had 155 of these towers in Napoleonic times, so much so that they thought Morse's electric telegraph unnecessary when it arrived. But the semaphore towers were expensive and slow compared to Morse's system. They were also easily spied upon, and didn't work well at night with lamps. And one further thought – the first railway signals of the waving-arms type appeared on the Brighton line in the 1840s and sprouted from the roofs of signal boxes just like the semaphore towers. They must have been influenced by the semaphore chains of only a few years before.

Don't hang around at Wisley after dark as your car will be towed away, and the other car park is by local legend associated with nefarious practices I really don't want to discuss (but they probably also involve arms flailing about).

The fascinating thing about another little-known piece of architectural eccentricity in London is that no-one has a clue why it's there. Near King's Cross, where Gray's Inn Road and Pentonville Road converge (we're on the blue corner of the Monopoly board), there's what's known as the **King's Cross lighthouse** which sits on top of a plain four-storey building. Some claim it was once a fairground helter-skelter tower but it would have to have been, impossibly and improbably, moved up there. How? Why? Inspections of the interior, say Camden council, show that it can't have been a clock tower or a camera obscura.

A sham, on the other hand, is a building that pretends to be what it isn't. In country estates, for example, that would be to improve the view from the big house by the function of a folly making a barn or a cottage look like a ruined castle or a chapel, eg: the **Sham Chapel**, in Blackfen Road, Sidcup.

One sham in central London you could pass every day without noticing. If you deal with anyone who gives a London address at 23 or 24 **Leinster Gardens** – such a respectable street – you may be dealing with a con artist. The two houses appear there in the right sequence, but they are a thin sham without foundations or substance, even the windows being painted on.

When the gracious, wedding-cake-style five-storey terrace was broken in 1865 to make way for the South Kensington extension of the newfangled Tube railway, property owners demanded that instead of a yawning gap over the railway track, a phoney frontage be erected to continue the line of the buildings. At first glance, you hardly notice the join, though from the back – it is between Bayswater and Paddington stations – the thing looks like a film set. An utter sham, in fact.

13

Monumentally Eccentric

THE HISTORIC STONES OF OLD LONDON

STONE OF SCONE You might think the veteran Rolling Stones, bless 'em, are the most ancient stones in London, but there are some even more ancient rock stories, that's real rock with legendary, mystic, king-making properties.

One of these you will no longer see in London, except at a coronation. The ancient and much-travelled Stone of Scone was the coronation stone of Scottish kings and has had quite a history.

Legend has it that this very stone was where Jacob rested his head in the Bible story. St Columba used it to crown Aidan in 574.

Eventually, this 'Stone of Destiny' ended up at Scone Palace in the Scottish lowlands – where Malcolm goes to get crowned at the end of Shakespeare's *Macbeth* – from where it was seized in 1296 by England's Edward I, the 'Hammer of the Scots'. It was then incorporated into the base of the nation's Coronation Chair in Westminster Abbey. All English (and, after 1603, British) monarchs since have been crowned at Westminster Abbey over this Stone of Scone.

Even the republican, and hence anti-royalist, Oliver Cromwell sat on it in Westminster Hall when he was installed as 'Lord Protector', as if the stone had magic powers to legitimise him. Interestingly, when Charles II had himself crowned in 1651 at Scone during the Civil War but without the Stone, it didn't count.

Then on Christmas Eve 1950 a bunch of Scottish Nationalist students removed the Stone from Westminster Abbey and took it secretly back to Scotland – gaining much publicity for their cause. But it was back in Westminster in time for the coronation of Queen Elizabeth II in 1953.

In 1996, the Stone of Scone was taken back to Edinburgh, where it was installed with much pomp in the castle, with three of those 1950s students present to see their aim fulfilled. It may be brought back to Westminster for the next coronation, so it has not finished travelling yet. The Scone of Stone, on the other hand, was the name of a cake on offer in Dundee University Student Union from 1973 to 1975.

ENGLAND'S FORGOTTEN CORONATION STONE Outside Kingston-upon-Thames Town Hall, completely forgotten except by local people, stands a massive stone which was the coronation stone of the Saxon kings of England. Kingston means 'king's stone', after all. The old kings of Wessex who were crowned on it, or perhaps next to it, included Edward the Elder, Edward the Martyr, Ethelred the Unready, Hagar the Flatulent, Ethelstan the Unreasonable and Geoffrey the Hysterical. I made up the last three of course, but the others were real; what is remarkable about these coronations that took place between 900 and 978 is how very little is known to historians about them.

A MAD MILESTONE IN LONDON'S HISTORY
The **Brass Crosby Milestone** that is neither brass nor tells accurate mileages from where it is, despite distances shown on it being detailed down to the very last foot, can be found in St George's Road, London, SE1, right outside the Imperial War Museum. But it does tell a rather fascinating story.

It is named after the Lord Mayor of London, Brass Crosby, who became a national hero in 1771 when he refused Parliament's order to jail a printer who dared to report Parliament's proceedings in the press. Brass Crosby was thrown in the Tower but public outcry assured his release, and he eventually won his campaign for the free reporting of Parliament.

The milestone – more of an obelisk in size – was set up in St George's Circus, south of the Thames, where the roads from Blackfriars, Waterloo and Westminster bridges converge, as a memorial to him but was removed during rebuilding in 1905 to its present site. This may be only a few hundred yards southwest, but it does make the rather precise measurements it displays singularly and totally useless. The present spot may have been chosen because during Crosby's life, the War Museum was the original **Bedlam** (a corruption of 'Bethlehem') lunatic asylum. Crosby was appointed president of the asylum in 1772, helping the process of its reform.

So when people say parliamentary debates sound 'like Bedlam' on the radio, they are paying tribute to two different major steps forward in British life where Brass Crosby went the extra mile. Milestones, in fact.

AN UN-ROYAL RELIC
Another obscure, obsolete obelisk is **Cleopatra's Needle**, located on the Thames embankment near to Embankment Tube. It's a strangely moving pillar but it had nothing to do with Queen Cleopatra. It is a fascinating 1400BC Egyptian relic, which survived being moved by the Romans in 14BC then being taken to England in 1878 in a sort of submarine and being nearly sunk in a storm in the Bay of Biscay, only to be covered in pollution and then damaged by German bombs after it arrived. You can see the shrapnel marks on it today. Its twin was erected in Central Park, New York, in 1881.

HOW TO MAKE BEAUTY OUT OF COAL AND WINE
In 1851 London was ringed by hundreds of Coal Dues obelisks and markers in four different designs to mark the point – you can't avoid the word – on every road, railway or canal at a distance of 20 miles from the General Post Office in St Martin's-le-Grand in central London. It's all the fault of the Great Fire of London in 1666, which led to the City of London Corporation being empowered to levy tax on coal or wine brought within a certain distance of London to pay for rebuilding.

In 1851, because of the sprawl of London, an Act laid down that the distance should be that 20-mile radius, still marked with four types of iron pillar, post or obelisk, all bearing the City's coat of arms or at least their main elements: the crusader shield, red cross on white with a dagger.

To complicate matters, some of these markers were moved slightly in 1861 to coincide with the boundary of the new Metropolitan Police area, so posts such as that on Watling Street, Radlett, still have a function today ... it marks where the Mr Plods of the shires take over from the Old Bill of the Met.

More impressive are the 14ft stone Coal Dues obelisks such as the one alongside the London–Norwich main line at Chadwell Heath on the boundary of Barking and Havering boroughs, or that beside the main line at Watford which refers on its inscription to the Coal and Wine Duties Act of 1861 (which must have updated the earlier Act) and which demanded a duty of 11d (4½p in today's coin, but then a week's pay for some) for every ton of coal which rolled past southwards.

Like most taxes dreamed up for a specific purpose, the Coal Dues carried on long after the original point of the obelisks was forgotten, and were finally abolished in 1889, although we have the splendid heritage of Wren churches such as St Paul's to thank them for.

MORE BLOODY OBELISKS Even the dullest London suburbs are riddled with obelisks, if you know where to look, to testify to blood-soaked history and other excitements that once happened there. A foggy Sunday morning in **Barnet** doesn't sound too dramatic, but an obelisk at nearby Monken Hadley tells of the desperate struggle of 14 April 1471, when the Earl of Warwick's waiting army in the Wars of the Roses between the houses of York and Lancaster attacked under the cover of mist and drove Edward IV's men right back into Barnet town centre.

A swift cavalry counter-attack had the Lancastrians retreating; Warwick was caught on foot and slain close to where the obelisk stands. Some 1,500 men died. The next Tube station to High Barnet on the Northern Line, by the way, is **Totteridge and Whetstone**. The latter takes its name from the high number of whetstones found there, discarded by soldiers after sharpening their swords and daggers before the Battle of Barnet.

More than 200 years later a very different rebellion, the Jacobite rebellion, was crushed in 1715 and the Earl of Derwentwater executed for taking part. An obelisk to his memory stands incongruously in the suburbia of Churchfield Road East, **Acton**, in a small park.

Even nearby quiet **Brentford** seems anxious to stress its blood-soaked history with a monument to a whole series of battles there (see page 33).

LOVE FOR A DEAD QUEEN IN SPIRES When the funeral of Diana, Princess of Wales, in 1997 followed a route through North London up the M1 to Northampton, many were surprised by the crowds and flowers that lined every available bridge over that road. But these were soon all gone, with surprisingly few permanent monuments, unlike the tributes to a dead queen who passed this way, in the opposite direction, 600 years previously.

The grieving Edward I, first Prince of Wales and 'Hammer of the Scots', whose beloved and beautiful queen Eleanor died suddenly aged 46 at Harby in Nottinghamshire, didn't just order one monument but a whole set of **Eleanor Crosses**, 12 of them; these intricate, Gothic, free-standing spires were to be erected at every spot where the funeral cortège stopped for a night.

The king – who had taken his popular bride, Eleanor of Castile, to war with him and even on a Crusade where she had one of their 16 children – also ordered that candles be burned non-stop beside her tomb in Westminster Abbey 'for ever'. The order was obeyed for more than 200 years but then lapsed.

Only three of the original dozen elegant and richly carved spires, now much weather-worn, survive – at Geddington and Hardingstone, near Northampton, and at Waltham Cross, Hertfordshire. The latter place is named after its Eleanor Cross, as is London's **Charing Cross**. The soaring spire outside the station of that name is in fact a 19th-century reproduction of a long-lost original, but it perhaps gives a better idea of the original.

Towns and cities along the route, such as St Albans and Stamford, when considering how to enhance their high streets, could do worse than copy Charing Cross's example and replace their missing Eleanor Crosses.

13

1 There's a beguiling **water tower sculpture** in the middle of the diamond-shaped roundabout at the east end of Shepherd's Bush. When it's working properly at night, the water flowing within it is a strange fluorescent blue; it must have puzzled and intrigued thousands of drivers coming down the motorway spur from Westway.

2 Pierre Vivant's strange and unexpected work, a **traffic light tree**, is at Heron's Quay in East London just south of Westferry Circus gateway to the Isle of Dogs (see front cover). It features more than 75 sets of traffic lights and seems designed to give oncoming drivers apoplexy. Unveiled in February 1999, the strange sculpture seems at its best at Christmas time when its red and green lamps going on and off look rather festive. The world's first traffic lights, for horse-drawn traffic, were at the corner of Parliament Square and were gas-powered. Sadly, they eventually blew up and killed the policeman operating them.

3 **East Finchley Tube Archer**. This clean-looking lead-covered archer, located at one end of the station, combined with the elegant lines of East Finchley's modernist station, evokes the best of 1930s style. The station, with its ship-like curved glass walls, was designed by Charles Holden and opened just before the outbreak of World War II. The Archer was by Eric Aumonier and has since become the district's emblem – the community newspaper is called *The Archer*. The 10ft-high sculpture aims its massive bow at the mouth of the Northern Line tunnel which goes all the way to Morden right across town in South London and was, until the building of the Channel Tunnel, Europe's longest. There should be a matching sculpture at the other end – a warrior holding up a shield with an arrow stuck in it, perhaps.

4 **Bronze commuters**. At Brixton station, which stands at rooftop level in this vibrant Caribbean-cockney community, stands a surprising pair of passengers on opposite platforms, endlessly waiting for trains (you know the feeling). One looks a relaxed dude, the other a young housewife with her shopping bags. They know no colour bar – they're both bronze, after all – but they endlessly eye each other up, waiting for their trains that never come. Like many excellent sculptures, it seems a real moment frozen for ever.

5 **The Window Cleaner**, 1990, is at Capital House, Edgware Road, London. It's by Allan Sly and besides having a comic, almost Laurel and Hardy jauntiness, it has the guy looking quizzically up at the vast expanse of glass above, a daunting prospect. Or maybe it's pride at having finished them. We'll never know.

6 **Goldsmiths College of Art roof sculpture**. This is called Scribble, an honest name. On first sight it looks like a scrap metal merchant has dumped a load there. In fact it reminds me of the politically incorrect joke – 'Did you hear about the Jewish kamikaze pilot? He crashed in his brother-in-law's scrap yard.' What we have is a medium-sized office block style building of several storeys in the usual boring cigarette-packet-on-its-side shape. But someone seems to have cut a two-storey-deep square out of one on the top corners, and in this hole stands this sculpture (that is if someone didn't just blow up that corner, leaving a twisted wreck, which may be an explanation). A student there tells me that the college wasn't allowed to block someone's view otherwise the building would have been a complete box. The sort of thing students say, but why would anyone prefer a view of *this* to an office building? Anyway, for a college that produced *enfant* yawningly *terrible* Damien Hirst – the pickled shark guy, about whom the less said the better – then perhaps it is a fitting attempt to shock and produce a kind of high-level advertising hoarding saying: 'We're arty but not artistic, we're really rebellious but not so rebellious you stop giving us all that money.' Make up your own mind: The building is in New Cross Road, SE14. Perhaps I just don't get it, like I don't get why a dead sheep or an unmade bed is considered art at all and is 'worth' many thousands of pounds, and don't get why we no longer transport such annoying people to Australia in chains. However, I do get that Goldsmiths has produced some brilliant artists over recent years, including Antony Gormley, who made the *Angel of the North* and many other wonderful things. The architects of this sorry structure, Alsop and Stormer also produced the jolly creative nearby Peckham Library (see page 132). We all have off days.

7 Is a clock a sculpture? The most delightful **clock at Fortnum and Mason's**, the royal family's grocery shop in Piccadilly, has, on the hour, little figures of Mr Fortnum and Mr Mason which come out to the tune of the 'Eton Boating Song'. If the clock were new, it would be pronounced totally naff, kitsch or whatever, but as it isn't, it isn't. Afternoon tea here is one of those very English things, but be careful to whom you chat. For Sir Thomas Beecham's very odd encounter here, see Soho walk, page 191.

8 Definitely a clock rather than a sculpture, but worth mentioning because it's little known, being stuck on a traffic island in front of Victoria Station, is Big Ben's counterpart, **Little Ben**. Big Ben, pedants will tell you, is correctly the name not of the tower at the Houses of Parliament, but of the deep-toned bell whose sound starts the news on millions of radio sets around the world. And if you thought you saw an identical Little Ben in the Seychelles, you were right.

9 **Sentimental statues of children**. There's an odd statue of a boy behind the London Planetarium, and another of a child on the Victoria Embankment. Several old schools are decorated with children in archaic uniforms, such as the Blewcoat School, Caxton Street, Westminster and high up on the wall beside Kensington church, on the intriguing footpaths north of the High Street Kensington Tube, and at St Andrew's, Holborn.

The Blewcoat School, a lovely building, is now a National Trust gift shop. Is this endless commercialisation unavoidable or would it be much better as a restored 18th-century school where today's schoolchildren could come and learn lessons as in days gone by? Another charming pair of statues of children at St Botolph's church hall, Bishopsgate, are made of that indestructible Coade stone that the Coade lion is made of (see London beasts, page 158).

10 **Wellington Arch**, Hyde Park Corner. This massive monument to the Iron Duke who made Europe safe for, well, Europeans, by defeating Napoleon at Waterloo in 1815, a huge arch surmounted by the biggest bronze sculpture in the country, is ignored by millions of people every year rounding this busiest of road junctions. But it is neither what was first intended or constructed, nor is it even where it was first put, yet it has a fascinating history, marked with bitterness of architects and sculptors. In fact it was once topped with one of the world's ugliest sculptures, so much so that the embittered architect of the triumphal arch left a huge amount of money in his will to get the blasted thing taken down. Let's start in 1825 when the great architect **Decimus Burton** designed the arch which was finished in 1828. It was aligned with the Hyde Park screen, making a processional route into Buckingham Palace, then being tarted up for George IV (he whose adulterous affair as Prince of Wales, despite the popularity of the Princess of Wales, had led to her funeral with emotional violence at this very spot – see page 262).

Burton had envisaged the arch being adorned with complicated sculptures and a quadriga (a four-horse job as in St Mark's Cathedral in Venice), but to his complete consternation an immense statue of a mounted Wellington was instead erected with great difficulty there in 1846. This stiff, lifeless, clumsily colossal equestrian effort reduced the arch to a mere plinth or pedestal – the combination was ugly indeed.

When Burton died in 1881 he left £2,000 – a huge amount then – to have the statue removed. Queen Victoria, however, was careful of the elderly Duke of Wellington's feelings (after all, he lived at Apsley House nearby) so nothing was done until he died. Even then, the real impetus was the opening of Victoria (the railway station not the Queen) in 1874 when the thing just had to be moved out of the way of the traffic to its present alignment. The opportunity was taken to whip the horrid horse off to Aldershot, where it remains in a more military setting. In 1891 another Prince of Wales, later King Edward VII, revived the four-horse idea having seen an excellent smaller work on these lines by sculptor **Adrian Jones**. Jones was set to work but his magnificent creation, 'Peace Descending on a Chariot of War', wasn't placed on the arch until 1912, two years after King Edward had died. Perhaps Edward was lucky to miss the irony of the spectacle of this sculpture featuring Peace ringing to the sounds of the bloodiest conflict in our history just two years later. As a result, Peace is now an odd bedfellow to other sculptures at Hyde Park Corner, such as the massively military Machine Gun Corps Monument, the Australian and New Zealand memorials and the Royal Artillery Monument.

Poor Jones the sculptor lived on unrewarded and forgotten. The monument, his greatest work, was never even given an official unveiling, and he died embittered in 1938, not having even been fully paid for it.

Neither do many people know that during this era the arch housed London's smallest police station, complete with 18 officers and a cat called Snooks. One of them was a sergeant, but the police cat had no recorded rank, other than perhaps PC for 'police cat'. This station was closed in the 1960s with the building of the road underpass leading from Piccadilly to Knightsbridge and the need to put a huge ventilation shaft through the arch's north side. From this point to the end of the century, the arch and sculptures suffered an ignominious period, both decaying slowly and in danger of collapse. It was only the massive intervention of English Heritage, when they'd finished the nightmare job of restoring the Albert Memorial outside the Albert Hall, that saved it; by November 2000 the Wellington Arch was restored to its full glory, with creative

floodlighting dramatising the sculpture at night. Now the arch's interior is open to the public for the first time which gives the public a chance to enjoy the fabulous views over London once enjoyed by PC Snooks.

11 Head of Newton. This sculpture, located at Butler's Wharf in East London, outside the Design Museum, is by Eduardo Paolozzi (1990). Does it suggest there's something mechanical about Newton, the man who reduced the orbits of the heavens, until then inexplicable, to mere natural laws of motion? Or perhaps it is a joke that, if he famously 'discovered' the laws of gravity by an apple falling on his head, this is what would result: a cracked nut. Either way, Newton's fame lives on in other ways too: if you have a £2 coin in your pocket (and aren't they satisfying things?) you'll see some of the great man's words around its rim. Heaped with praise, he said he achieved what he did because he was 'standing on the shoulders of giants'. There's another good Paolozzi bust of Newton at the British Library at St Pancras.

12 La Delivrance, Finchley Road. This naked woman is so full of youthful sexual energy that it was inconceivable that it could have been unveiled in the early 20th century, which it was, unless it was by a Frenchman, which it also was. It was supposed to symbolise the joy at the defeat of the Germans by the French and the British at the Battle of the Marne in September 1914 and was paid for by the first Lord Rothermere.

LONDON'S LOST AMERICAN CONNECTIONS

What could be more American than Pocahontas, Mark Twain, Harvard and Texas, for example? Here, you'll find the oddest connections with all of them, and more, and some strange stories to go with them.

First **Pocahontas**, if you can forget the Disneyfied version (why do all cartoon heroines have the same kind of dumb, doe-eyed, big-boobed gormlessness and the heroes the same lantern-jawed, broad-shouldered creepiness? Why don't they supply sickbags in the video boxes?). She was that American Indian princess who famously saved the life of Englishman, Captain John Smith, who had been captured by the Indians and was about to have his brains bashed out; many people assume they fell in love with each other. She also conveniently came to stand for the empowerment of women and the proudness of native American culture. Thus the much misunderstood Indians themselves ensured the survival of America's first settlement by Europeans. Or so the popular misunderstanding of the legend goes, at least on this side of the Atlantic, encouraged by that rather catchy song and at least six monuments in London.

The truth was as extraordinary as, and more interesting than, the smoothed-out, politically correct version.

What most people forget is that she actually became Mrs John Rolfe, not Smith, became a Christian, called herself Rebecca, and came to Britain. She's still here, having met her grave end in Gravesend from some ghastly English disease she was ill-equipped to resist. And that John Smith was more Danny de Vito than Keanu Reeves to look at.

There's very little evidence that the thing with Smith actually happened in Virginia in 1607, but then there wouldn't be. The scepticism arises only because he wrote one account not mentioning at all her role in saving him from the wrath of her father Powhattan, and then much later in 1622 wrote another which included it. Perhaps there was a good reason for this. Maybe he was embarrassed. Or maybe he had thought of a good yarn to immortalise himself. He was a known fantasist when it came to his adventures, although he was certainly a ruthless, wideboy adventurer who didn't balk at chopping off the heads of three Turks he captured on an earlier voyage.

Neither is there any evidence the legendary event did *not* take place. It was certainly the kind of hostage-taking and tit-for-tat stuff that went on, and still does in some countries. What we do know is that in the years following 1607 Pocahontas was often seen in Jamestown, Virginia, and did a great deal to reduce friction between settlers and Indians. By 1614 she had indeed become a Christian, called herself Rebecca and married John Rolfe with whom she had a son. The family arrived in London in 1616, where she was a great favourite at court. Legend had it that she bumped into John Smith again while staying at the Belle Sauvage ('beautiful woman savage') pub in Ludgate Hill. Ironically, she died suddenly at Gravesend in 1617, victim to a disease her background had not prepared her for, just as she was about to return to her homeland; she is buried at St George's Church in that town on the Kent side of the Thames estuary. There is a statue of her there, erected by the people of Virginia. There is another, rather sexy, statue of her in offices in Vincent Square, SW1.

Not that Captain John Smith, one of the founders of Virginia, is forgotten. There is a statue of him in the City of London, in a garden once the churchyard of St Mary-le-Bow. He is also remembered in the Church of the Holy Sepulchre Without Newgate on Snow Hill, Holborn, where there is a memorial plate to him (he died in 1631) and a stained-glass window to him and Pocahontas.

This window makes Smith look like William Shakespeare, but in 2001 an extraordinary sequel emerged when crime novelist Patricia Cornwell declared she would erect new windows in the church to tell the full story. Cornwell lives in Virginia and had been in London to research her novel based here (in the Isle of Dogs).

John Rolfe, who had returned to Virginia, was killed in a surprise attack by the same tribe of Indians in 1620. They had pretended to be friends with the settlers, sharing their tables and playing with their infants, yet massacred hundreds of them that day, infants, women, children and all. So the story of the Indians ensuring the colonists' survival are a little off the mark. Their son, Thomas Rolfe, survived only because when his mother died, he had been put ashore at Plymouth to be brought up by his uncle in England.

There is also a riverside monument in Blackwall to the first settlers who departed from here to America on 20 December 1606.

Second, there's a little bit of London that is, or rather was, **Texas**. In the somewhat exclusive gentlemen's ghetto that is St James's, there was some real Lone Star Texas territory. If you go through the narrow timbered entrance on St James's Street, next to Berry Bros, you can enter Pickering Place, a hidden tiny 18th-century square that not many Londoners have ever seen. No 3 was the embassy of the Republic of Texas in the 1840s.

The founder of Pennsylvania. One of the baptisms at All Hallows by the Tower in 1644, in the Civil War era, was of a William Penn who, when he grew up, went on to found Pennsylvania. His father, Admiral Sir William Penn, was instrumental in saving this church in the 1666 Great Fire of London by blowing up houses around it to create a firebreak; he had also lent the cash-strapped King Charles II a great deal of money. In return, in 1681 the king gave Penn's son, William, a licence to set up Pennsylvania which he did, along Quaker lines. He also founded Philadelphia (without which we Brits wouldn't know what to call cream cheese), now one of Pennsylvania's principal cities, but he was regularly in trouble with the government in London over his radical religious non-conformity. He was as relentlessly serious as Quakers, bless 'em, sometimes are. 'No pain, no palm; no thorns, no throne; no gall, no glory; no cross, no crown,' he wrote in a cheerful 1699 pamphlet. He died in 1718 when Pennsylvania was well on its way and is buried just west of London at Jordans, the Quaker Meeting House near Chalfont St Giles, Buckinghamshire, a lovely part of the country. His tombstone is plain and assiduously self-effacing, as you'd expect from a broad-brimmed hat Quaker (apart from naming an entire state after yourself, of course). I've always respected Quakers whom I've met (as if my opinion mattered a jot) but I can't resist one more friendly poke at their seriousness. Victorian cleric Sydney Smith, told of a Quaker infant, retorted: 'Quaker baby? Impossible! There is no such thing, there never was. They are always born broad-brimmed and in full quake.'

Harvard's origins were humble. What could an inn-keeper's son do apart from enjoy a life of wassailing and brawling? Well, quite a lot judging by publican Robert Harvard's son, baptised in 1607 at Southwark Cathedral, then a mere parish church in the notorious South Bank district (for more about Southwark, see page 196). The infant Harvard's name was John, and his achievement was to found the first and most famous university in the New World. Or rather to bequeath half his estate and his entire library of 320 books for the foundation of such a college, for he died in 1638 of consumption, only a year or so after arriving in Boston. Most of his family had died from the plague in 1625, but he is remembered by a chapel and a library in Southwark.

In its heyday *Punch* magazine at its offices in Bouverie Street off Fleet Street used to host literary lunches at which the guests of honour would traditionally carve their illustrious initials in the huge dining table. When writer and humorist **Mark Twain** attended one such lunch and was invited to carve away, he spotted WMT, the initials of William Makepeace Thackeray and said: 'Two-thirds of Thackeray will do for me.'

A spot of possible pilgrimage for Americans is 10 Hertford Street, Mayfair, where **General John Burgoyne** lived. He was the British general who managed to lose the Battle of Saratoga to the colonials' Benedict Arnold.

In Fashion Court, Spitalfields, lived the young **Abe Saperstein**, founder of The Harlem Globetrotters. He was born in 1902 to a couple of the 100,000 Jewish refugees who had fled the pogroms of Poland, Central Europe and Russia. His family, with ten children, struggled in poverty and so they migrated to America in 1905. You might not associate a 5ft 3in Jewish lad with basketball – a natural home for lanky black guys – but he was excellent at it. In 1927 he took over the management of a struggling team called the Savoy Big Five and gradually the team – they were not allowed to play everywhere because of race segregation – fought its way up, winning the world title in 1940 and, arguably, making a major step forward in the battle for black people to be treated with equal respect around the world. It wouldn't have happened without, as he put it, 'the poor little Yiddish boy from the East End who made good.' Abe died on 15 March, 1966 and is buried in Chicago.

In 1860, the eccentric but aptly-named American, **George Francis Train**, set up the world's first street tramway along Bayswater, running from Lancaster Gate to Marble Arch. Londoners weren't ready for railway lines on roads yet, so the huffed Mr Train puffed back to America, where he decided to prove a man could live on peanuts alone. He died shortly afterwards.

One of the most under-valued writers of the last century was surely **Jack London**, the fearless, San Francisco-born explorer-journalist-novelist who gave us such wonderful reads as *Call of the Wild*. His courage in penetrating the most inhospitable and perilous wastes of the world came in handy when in 1902 he took a trip into the worst of London's East End; his resulting book, *People of the Abyss*, revealed to a wider world the desperate poverty, the over-crowding, the slums and the starvation of this area. Children starved (the word means 'to death') on the street just as they do in Third World disasters today, and with just as little need for it to be allowed to happen. His words rightly shocked the complacency and pride of Edwardian Britain. Just read this, describing a walk he took with a couple of London workmen up the Mile End Road, still, 100 years later, London's most deprived area:

Both kept their eyes upon the pavement as they walked and talked, and every now and then one or the other would stoop and pick something up, never missing the stride all the while. I thought it was cigar and cigarette stumps they were collecting, and for some time took no notice. Then I did notice.

From the slimy, spittle-drenched sidewalk, they were picking up bits of orange peel, apple skin, and grape stems and were eating them. The bits of greengage plums they cracked between their teeth for the kernels inside. They picked up stray crumbs of bread the size of peas, apple cores so black and dirty one would not take them to be apple cores, and these things these two men took into their mouths, and chewed them, and swallowed them; and this, between six and seven o'clock in the evening of August 20, year of our Lord 1902, in the heart of the greatest, wealthiest and most powerful empire the world has ever seen.

That was great writing and it was anger such as this, anger that the success of Britain's economy meant great wealth for a few and grinding poverty for many, that fuelled the country's great 20th-century social advances, such as the introduction of the 'cradle to the grave' Welfare State, the National Health Service, better schools, pensions, sickness benefits, etc. How soon we forget how much the world has changed since our grandparents were young. Today a family, even what we would consider a poor family, takes for granted things like hot water, heating, free medical help, colour TV and a DVD player, all of which were far in the future for most East Enders then, crammed at times 12 to a bed as they were (there are photos of this in social history books).

Around London there are many homes for working people proudly labelled **Peabody Buildings**. These are a memorial to a truly great man, American banker and philanthropist George Peabody, saviour of the state of Maryland, the man who put the United States on the international financial map, improver of the lives and education of thousands.

George Peabody, born in 1775 in what was then South Danvers, Massachusetts, a very rich and prosperous merchant and banker, was a philanthropist.

Eventually, he moved to London and set up a soon-thriving merchant bank, helping the young United States enter the world's financial stage and rapidly making a vast fortune of $20million which he rapidly spent on others. He built libraries, museums and art galleries at Baltimore, Yale and South Danvers. In 1862, appalled at the slums and poverty in London, he gave $2,500,000 for the building of tenement blocks for working people. Many of these survive today.

He was the first American to be given the freedom of the City of London and at his funeral in 1869, the carriages of Queen Victoria and the Prince of Wales followed the hearse containing his coffin to Westminster Abbey. Vast crowds lined the streets, showing the respect Londoners held for Peabody. The Prime Minister was among the mourners.

George Peabody statue

After the funeral service his coffin was taken to his burial in the US at Danvers (by then renamed Peabody) by the Royal Navy's latest ship, such was the esteem in which this man was held. As he envisaged, his good works have survived into the 21st century, with 24 organisations on both sides of the Atlantic, including those housing 26,000 Londoners. A statue of him stands near the Bank of England in Threadneedle Street in the City of London.

Benjamin Franklin, that splendid fellow who wrote the opening part of the American Declaration of Independence, wouldn't be a chap you'd expect to have skeletons in his closets. Certainly not ten of them. Yet the remains of four adults and six children were found at his London home in 1998 and they date from around the times he lived there: from 1757 to 1762 and again from 1764 to 1775.

The skeletons were found at 36 Craven Street, next to Charing Cross station, when it was being refurbished and restored. So what is the answer to the mystery? This building, after all, was, de facto, the first American Embassy in Britain, so it has a place in both countries' history. Could the founding father of American independence have been involved in some gruesome crime?

The answer, strangely, involves the eccentric bull-wrestler, buffalo collector and surgeon we meet in the Earl's Court section of this book, John Hunter (see page 162). A clue lay in the skeletons themselves – most bones had been sawn, drilled or chiselled. This suggests anatomy classes for would-be surgeons, not to mention grave-robbing, whose purpose was to supply bodies for those classes, that was rife at the time.

Franklin's landlady – the full details of their relationship are a little cloudy – had a daughter, Polly, who married a promising young surgeon, William Hewson. He was a close colleague of the anatomist, John Hunter. It seems that Hunter and Hewson may have run an anatomy school in part of the house while Franklin was in America or living further up the street.

The fact that the remains of the bodies, presumably dissected for students, were disposed of so surreptitiously suggests that those corpses were supplied, illegally, by 'resurrection men' – grave robbers. The punishment for the crime of grave robbing was hanging and in some cases, bizarrely, drawing and quartering – a form of dissection – as well. At the very least, those convicted of supplying or receiving stolen bodies could expect to be transported to some tropical hell-hole where life was short, hot and brutish. So under-floor burial must have seemed a sensible option. Whether the great philosopher and humanitarian Franklin knew of or condoned such activities is not known, but it seems unlikely. Hewson was a pioneer in several fields of anatomy and must have learned his trade somewhere. In the end the dead got their revenge – he cut himself while dissecting a rotting corpse and contracted septicaemia, dying in 1774 aged 34.

Oddly, one of Franklin's visitors at this address included libertarian author Thomas Paine, whose bones also came to a peculiar end, this time in a pub (see page 282). Franklin's house is now fully restored and can be visited for studies by arrangement or as part of a 'historical experience', a re-enactment, at a cost of £8 per adult. Details from Benjamin Franklin House, 36 Craven Street, London

WC2N 5NF; ℩ 0207 930 6601; www.benjaminfranklinhouse.org; or from the New Players Theatre round the corner which acts as box office; ℩ 0207 839 2006.

- An astonishing story of a Red Indian chief – a native American, that is – buried in Earl's Court, see page 169.
- For Americans, authors Henry James and T S Eliot, painter Whistler, and amazing billionaire J Paul Getty II who was saved by cups of tea, the rules of cricket and Mick Jagger, see Cheyne Walk, page 120.
- For the Liberty Bell's origins, see Whitechapel, page 216.
- For Canadian links, see Wolfe in Greenwich, page 240.

THE ORIGINS OF DOWN UNDER

Australia, of course, has its historic links in London too. On the formal side, the church of St Mary-le-Bow in the City's Cheapside has a bust of **Admiral Arthur Philip**, founder of Sydney in 1788. There is also a banner of the Order of Australia here. That's the official stuff, but the arrival of many in what was to be their home country, Australia, was a lot less comfortable than his, and undertaken rather more reluctantly: they were transported for life for, sometimes, quite trivial offences.

Millbank, on the Thames where the Tate Gallery now stands, was once the site of an area of brothels and drinking dens known as the 'Devil's Acre' plus a grim jail, Millbank Prison. Near the Tate Gallery, on the waterfront, Australians might ponder a squat bollard which marks the spot where thousands of prisoners in clanking chains passed 'Down Under' in a special tunnel under the road from Millbank Prison to barges which carried them downriver to ships waiting to take them to the other side of the world. This sad traffic ended in 1867.

If you're interested, the sister book to this one, *Eccentric Britain*, tells of the Red Sign Post in Dorset where other transportees were chained up for the night on their grim march to the prison fleet.

Their plight was all the worse since Arthur Philip and co had named the site for where Sydney was to be built 'Botany Bay' because they visited it after the rains, when it was all temporarily green and blooming. They thought the rest of Australia would be lush and green too, full of fruit and rich meadows able to grow anything. It wasn't quite that easy.

So if it's that simple to find the origins of the expression 'down under', how come nobody seems to know why Aussies call the Brits 'Pommies' (or just 'bloody Poms')? The least convincing argument is that new arrivals would be Prisoners of Mother England, hence POMEs. Anyway, that would make Aussies the real Pommies, not those who stayed in Britain. I tried explaining that once in a rough drinking den in Kalgoorlie in Western Australia. The hospital food there is excellent.

- Australia and New Zealand have striking war memorials at Hyde Park Corner. An ANZAC Day ceremony takes place on 25 April each year. For another New Zealand memorial, see Greenwich walk (page 244).

14

Eccentric Boozers, Beasts and Bogs

PECULIAR PUBS AND THEIR STRANGE STORIES

London was alcohol-soaked in the 18th century. Pickled in the stuff. For one thing, the water was not safe to drink so even infants were given small beer, even for breakfast. The gin was cheap and strong, so much so that Hogarth's famed cartoon of Gin Lane, with its drunken mother dropping her baby, was very close to the truth.

A survey of 1746 said there was one tavern to every five dwellings, and that at least one of the remaining four was a gin shop. Some 36 gallons of beer was brewed for every man, woman and child that year, while a barely comprehensible seven million gallons of gin were consumed. This was before laws limiting the strength of booze, the hours it could be served and the age of the customers allowed into pubs and gin shops. Pub landlords boasted that they could have you drunk for tuppence, so of course regular customers made it a point of honour to consume twice as much. Free straw was provided for the unconscious in the back rooms.

So when people complain about drunken yobbery and debauchery nowadays, they haven't seen the half of it. Our ancestors would be astonished, and probably appalled, at our sobriety. It was not until World War I that the necessity to maintain munitions productions meant that pub hours and the strength of drink were strictly controlled.

Of course you don't have to get three sheets to the wind to appreciate London's wonderful collection of pubs, many of them deeply strange in their ways. Here's just a few of them:

The **I Am The Only Running Footman** in Mayfair is unusual on three counts. First, it is Britain's second-longest pub name – the longest being the Green Man And Black's Head Royal Hotel in Ashbourne, Derbyshire – and London's longest. Second, its name is initially totally incomprehensible (actually, that isn't that unusual for pub names). Third, it has been taken wholesale for the title of a book by Martha Grimes, a murder mystery no less, which starts with a dead hitch-hiker in a Devon wood. In the book, another victim is found outside this pub in Charles Street near Berkeley Square, and the rest … well, you'll have to read it.

The pub itself eluded my attempts to track it down for some years until one day in desperation I said to a cabbie: 'Take me to the I Am The Only Running Footman in Mayfair.' 'Yer wot, Guv?' 'A pub in Charles Street.' 'There ain't no pub there, Guv.' 'Well let's go anyway because I need to prove it doesn't exist.' The cabbie gave me a sideways look and probably thought about diverting to the nearest funny farm at this point but gamely went along with my delusions. 'Here we are, no bleedin' pub, Guv.' 'What's that down the end?' 'Er … looks like a pub, dunnit?' To my chagrin, the door merely had 'Running Footman' over it, losing the longest name in London title, so I went inside for a consolatory few pints and to read about its history.

149

Difficult though it is to imagine today, the nobs of Mayfair in early days required that a footman, dressed in full livery, should run before their coach or sedan chair, opening gates, paying tolls or whatever. Of course, the real reason for the presence of these 'running footmen' was to increase the pompous self-importance of their employer: 'Make way, here comes the Duke of Bombast! Make way!' That kind of thing. There was also a group of liveried footmen whose job it was to walk behind the bigwigs to emphasise their importance even more. These equally pointless characters were known by down-to-earth Londoners as 'fart-catchers'. You get exactly the same kind of thing in big business nowadays – toadying executives hovering behind the big cheese, laughing noisily at his every joke – but not his inferior's jokes.

Anyway, the fashion for running footmen declined until there was only one poor sweating booby left, whose Mayfair master would not change with the times. Hence the pub name.

Fortified by this knowledge and its ale, I burst out into the adjoining street and was delighted to see the swinging sign still proclaiming in its full glory: 'I Am The Only Running Footman.' Saved!

Dickens lived in Bloomsbury, among other London addresses, and his house at 48 Doughty Street, WC1, can still be visited. His favourite pub, the **Lamb** in nearby Lambs Conduit Street, a perfect example of a Victorian pub, has a bar equipped with small pivoting glass shutters designed to enhance drinkers' privacy, and, the last time I visited, truly excellent ale.

If you're interested in medical history and booze, try the **John Snow** pub in Broadwick Street (✆ *020 7437 1344*). John Snow solved the mystery of cholera by taking off the handle of the water pump outside. Now the pump handle inside is more interesting. Pictures and explanation upstairs. This is said to be Soho's oldest pub, but not vastly ancient by London standards. See Soho walk, page 194.

Talking of sedan chairs, those rather ridiculous boxes on poles in which rich people somehow incapable of walking were carried about by poor people (quite fast too, by all accounts), there are several pubs named the **Chairmen** or **Two Chairmen** – I can think of one off Dean Street in Soho and another at the end of Queen Anne's Gate in Westminster. Naturally, you think of the wrong sort of chairman until you see the signs. There are also several pubs around Soho called the **Blue Posts**. This is to do with the blue posts located outside pubs, etc, where one waited for a chair in those days. (Why walk to a blue post when you could walk to wherever you were going? Perhaps the people who used sedan chairs were disabled by gout. Perhaps they couldn't be seen to be using their own legs to walk.)

Packhorse and Talbot, Turnham Green. Many pub names conjure up links with the past and this is simply one. Goods coming into London, in this case along the old Great West Road, before the revenues raised by turnpikes allowed the roads to be improved, would often be carried on packhorses. The talbot was a hunting dog used to protect packhorsemen from the highwaymen that plagued this route. So when a traveller stopped to drink and eat at this inn, he would have left his packhorse and talbot outside, guarding the goods.

The Old Mitre, Ely Place, EC1. I hesitate to direct you to a pub that is (a) difficult to find and (b) may not be in London at all but in soggy Cambridgeshire, but it's worth it. Let me explain. In Holborn Circus are gates leading to Ely Place. This is so-named because it was the London residence of the Bishop of Ely so that, once past these gates, one was technically in Ely, so pickpockets and others escaping justice would head this way and nip inside during a hue and cry; the officers pursuing had to catch them before they entered or wait outside. Having said that, you didn't see the Kray brothers or the like using this supposed sanctuary in their gangster careers, so perhaps it wouldn't work today.

Armed with that information and the assurance that the Old Mitre was in Ely Place, we marched up that road. And down again. And up again. No sign of it, although there were a lot of French people who, when asked, gesticulated in the direction of the Cheshire Cheese (see below) and shrugged several times. We gave up and walked around the corner into Hatton Garden, home of the nation's jewellers.

We soon noticed that one of the lamp-posts there is completely different from the others (first clue). On the glass of this old gas lamp was painted in large letters 'The Old Mitre' (second clue). We plunged into the murky alleyway and found our little gem.

It has a poky, smokey but cosy bar at the front, a larger one round the back and another one above that. That the Mitre refers to a bishop's hat rather than the thing for cutting corners accurately in woodwork (they both look the same from above, of course) is clear by the wonky angles of some of the ancient beams. Maybe they did indeed cut a few corners, but you know what I mean. More on this pub in the Fleet Street walk, page 178.

Prospect of Whitby, Wapping Wall, Wapping. Few Londoners have not heard of this pleasant-sounding pub (named after a collier – a coal-carrying ship which brought coals from Newcastle past Whitby) but the pub's old name, the Devil's Tavern, gave a more accurate idea of its clientele. Pirates, cut-throats, spies, loose women, coachloads of tourists, you name it. Nearby is Execution Dock where some of the pub's customers would end up being hanged; their bodies were then left in chains, tied to piles at low tide, for the tide to wash over them three times before they were buried. One such pirate, caught in the Americas, who was thus executed here has a new pub round the corner named after him in Wapping High Street: **The Captain Kidd**.

The Prospect was visited by Dickens and the painter J M W Turner, both – in their own way – fascinated by the murky shadows of the river hereabouts and both of whom brilliantly captured something about the murky depths of Old Father Thames.

The **Mayflower**, Rotherhithe, recalls the founding fathers' ship that set sail from here in 1620 to found the New World (calling at Plymouth in Devon on the way, of course). The fact that John Smith had got to Pocahontas a few years before (see page 143) wasn't the point. This was the big one. The pub's wharf was the starting place and this building which dates from 1560 was then called The Shippe. The commander of the *Mayflower*, Captain Christopher Jones, brought his ship safely back in 1621 and its timbers were later used in rebuilding the pub, so it's not so much that the pub's part of history, but more that history is part of it. Captain Jones himself was permanently berthed in St Mary's churchyard in 1622.

The longest bar in London – and, it is said, Europe – is a 50-yard monster at **Zander's** in Buckingham Gate. It's upmarket, as the location suggests, but it won the accolade of Evening Standard Bar of the Year for 2001. The great length of the bar gives heaps of room for snacking on the wide range of food, and snazzy cocktails at not-so-unreasonable prices, that are a speciality here. I thought it best, on the whole, not to describe the oddities of cool-dude bars in this guide because

14

unlike the pubs in these pages, which have mostly been around for hundreds of years, there's no guarantee that any trendy bar will be around for even a hundred days. Plus the fact that if you're a cool dude, reading this book with dark shades on is impossible. But no-one's going to remove this successful 50-yard bar in a hurry. A zander, in case you're wondering, is *Stizostedion lucioperca*, otherwise a pikeperch fish which is rather tasty, if a bit bony. And, no, it's not 50 yards long. By the way, don't worry if a Hungarian offers you crap for dinner. It's carp, apparently.

The World's End pub, Camden, was called the Mother Red Cap for some 250 years; the histories tell the very strange stories of the first of the two Mother Red Caps who ran this house. The first Mother Red Cap had a child at 15 by a man called Gipsy George, hanged not long afterwards at Tyburn for stealing sheep. She then took up with a man called Darby, who disappeared after a few months of drunken quarrelling and was never seen again. Then her parents were convicted of killing a girl by black magic and were hanged. She took up with a third lover call Picher, who before long was found in her oven, burned to a cinder.

She was tried for his murder but acquitted after a witness declared that he often took refuge in the oven to escape her cruel tongue, and could well have been burned by accident. She then became something of a recluse, but was occasionally seen in the lanes and hedgerows, collecting herbs and berries.

During the Civil War (1642–49), she gave shelter to a fugitive, who knocked at her door one night begging for shelter. He had money and stopped with her for a few years, even though, from time to time, they were heard quarrelling. When he died there were whispers that she had poisoned him, but nothing was ever proved.

When she went out, she always wore an ugly grey cap and a grey shawl, and her huge black cat was never far behind. By this time people were convinced she was a witch, and most were too frightened to go near her, her only visitors being Moll Cut-purse the highwaywoman, and a few brave souls wanting their fortunes told or to be cured of some ill by one of her strange brews.

The night she died, people declared that they saw the Devil walk into her cottage, but no-one saw him come out. She was found the next morning, sitting by a pot on the fire, her cat beside her. When the cat was given some of the contents to drink, its hair fell off in two hours, and it died soon afterwards.

The second Mother Red Cap was far more cheerful. She turned the place into an inn and brewed a rather potent ale there.

Dirty Dick's, Bishopsgate EC2, City of London. One Nathaniel Bentley, an early 19th-century ironmonger who lived near here, was all set to marry a veritable beauty. He turned up at the church only to discover that his intended had dropped dead the night before. Desolate, he preserved the wedding feast that had been intended for the guests on the tables, spending his life in broken-hearted squalor, the cobwebs and dust gathering on the dining table as his wedding clothes turned to rags. Locally, he became known as Dirty Dick and was something of a legend. His dead cats were allowed to dry and become mummified, unburied, and eventually Dirty Dick died too. That was the opportunity for the landlord of this pub, who bought the decaying contents of this strangely fascinating, nightmarish house and put them around the pub – even the dried cats. Sadly, they eventually fell to dust and were cleaned away. However, one Charles Dickens thought the macabre story worth reusing in *Great Expectations* (probably his best book – I can't decide), where Miss Havisham is the one who never gets to eat her wedding breakfast.

The Old Red Lion, High Holborn, Bloomsbury. Another pub connected to gruesome dead stuff. When the English realised that, like royalty, republicanism sometimes stinks (and was even worse) and invited King Charles II back in 1660 for the Restoration of the Monarchy, this pub decided to do its loyal best. It exhibited the freshly dug-up corpses of some of the chief characters in the interregnum: Oliver Cromwell, or Lord Protector as he was styled; Henry Ireton, a relative of his; and John Bradshaw, the man who had issued the order to behead the new king's father, Charles I, just 11 years before. The bodies, which certainly pulled in the curious punters for a pint or three, stank not a little, and were the next day dragged off to Tyburn to be hanged and decapitated (the sort of penalty they have in mind for parking on those new red lines, I expect). Cromwell's head was to suffer further indignities (see page 62).

The Anglesea Arms, Selwood Terrace, South Kensington. This is where the plot was laid for Britain's most infamous – but not biggest – heist of the 20th century, the Great Train Robbery. Bruce Reynolds and an associate met here to decide how to rob a train. It appears they didn't intend to rob a mail train at all, originally, and not on the mail line from Euston where they eventually succeeded so famously. Their preferred target was a train taking a ton of gold shipped from South Africa to Southampton to the Bank of England. Exactly how they would have stopped it was not exactly clear, but when they arrived at the main line near Weybridge in the early hours, when the train was due to arrive there they found the area swarming with police, also intent on keeping an eye on the train. But when the gang did stop a train, their plan was efficient and ruthless. They covered up a green signal on the main Glasgow–London line near Leighton Buzzard, wired up a battery to the red signal and brought the train carrying valuable mail to a halt. When the driver climbed down from his cab to phone the signalmen, he was coshed over the head and nearly killed. The gang then drove the train to a bridge over a lonely track where they threw out all the mailbags to waiting accomplices.

The Bucket of Blood, Covent Garden. This is the nickname for the Lamb and Flag (its modern name) where bare-knuckle fights used to see gore-a-plenty in times gone by. Today it can still be a bit of a bare-elbowed fight to get to the bar on a Friday night. The timber-fronted pub, where Floral Street meets Garrick Street and Rose Street, is said to be Covent Garden's oldest. Low beams, wood floor. Talking about fights, in 1679, the poet John Dryden was given a good thrashing just outside the Bucket of Blood for writing scurrilous stuff about the Duchess of Portsmouth. If only that habit had continued – 'Look here, T S Eliot, you jumped-up Yankee scoundrel, my man here will give you a damned good hiding if you don't explain what the hell all this Waste Land nonsense is about.'

14

London's rudest landlord, you may be relieved to know, retired in 2006. Norman Balon was the legendary and not-so-genial meinhost (more of mein führer, frankly) at the **Coach and Horses**, Greek Street, Soho. His intellectual, writer, artist and actor regulars absolutely loved it. Here's some sayings from the great man:

'You're barred, you're too boring to be in my pub.'

'I don't care if you are a man or a woman, you can go now.'

To American tourists seeking sandwiches: 'Leave now and don't come back.'

'You're so ugly you're upsetting my customers.'

The attraction of the pub for a certain kind of grumpy English intellectual was huge in the second half of the 20th century. It was an extension of the nearby office of *Private Eye*, the satirical magazine, which held weekly lunches upstairs. It was the basis for the magazine's cartoon strip *The Regulars*. The pub interior became the setting for regular Keith Waterhouse's play *Jeffrey Bernard is Unwell* in 1989. Peter O'Toole, another customer, was the star.

Serious drinkers and thinkers drank at 'the deep end' on the Romilly Street side, while the Greek Street 'shallow end' was said to be inhabited mainly by Italians, conmen, spivs and shoplifters. In between was poured a generous serving of students from the nearby St Martin's School of Art, (one of whom inspired a Jarvis Cocker song *Common People*). Jeffrey Bernard also used the Coach, as it was known, as an office whence he produced the celebrated *Spectator* column, *Low Life* (or rather didn't when he was too drunk, in which case the unwell line would go in the magazine). His favourite Senior Service cigarettes (strong as they come) were kept in a special cupboard.

Balon wasn't and isn't really rude: he was adopting a persona that his clientele enjoyed, and the affection seemed mutual on the day he retired to go home to Golders Green (where he could run the Kosher Horses, presumably) one day in May 2006. *The Daily Telegraph* caught him sitting outside while the party went on and saying somewhat out of character: 'I couldn't have wished for a better life.' Then he happily went back in the pub and returned to his role as London's rudest landlord.

Typical eccentric customers, besides painters Lucian Freud and Francis Bacon, were a man who invented cat racing and a deaf poet who spoke after a particularly noisy slanging match across the bar: 'Why's it so quiet today?'

One more Jeffrey Bernard story. He'd been drinking far too long and heavily with the comedian Tony Hancock, who had urinated in his trousers, as drunks sadly do. Bernard held Hancock up in the street while they persuaded a taxi driver to take them. In the cab Hancock slid to the floor and spent ages fumbling around trying to get something from all of his pockets. Eventually he retrieved his card, which he handed to Bernard saying: 'If you ever need my help, jusht call me.'

Bernard replied: 'Why on earth should I want help from you?'

'Becaushe,' Hancock replied in all seriousness, 'becaushe I think you might have a drinking problem.'

William Butler did for constipation what Vlad the Impaler did for human rights, and is rightly remembered in a London pub name. A medical quack and physician to James I, his legacy was for years known widely as Dr Butler's Purging Ale. This evil concoction was made by hanging a thin cloth bag containing senna, polypody of oak, very strong spices, agrimony, maidenhair and scurvy grass in a barrel of strong ale. It had a violently laxative effect likened by its victims to the largest cannon used in the Navy. Who knows, if the Richter scale had been invented, maybe it could have measured the arsequake involved. It was sold at pubs or shops with the sign, 'Butler's Head'. One survives in

Mason's Avenue, in the City of London, EC2, now known as **Old Doctor Butler's Head** in memory of this man.

Dr Butler probably wouldn't have come to much had he not been approached by King James, who was suffering from an agonising bad back his doctors could not cure. Butler prescribed a barrel of his purging ale – as he did for most patients – and whatever happened to the king, he forgot entirely about his back. In gratitude he conferred a degree upon Butler and appointed him Court Physician, which went down with the other doctors like a dose of something very unpleasant.

His eccentric treatments were deeply unorthodox. For the relief of epilepsy, he would ask a patient to sit still and close his eyes, then fire a pair of pistols either side of his head, inches from his ears. For malaria or the ague, then common, he would throw patients into the Thames head first. For opium overdose he had a man inserted in the belly of a freshly killed cow. They loved it, and the rich queued up to be maltreated, as they still do.

(Old Doctor Butler's Head, ☎ 0207 606 3504, Mason's Avenue, EC2, tiny, charming, hidden down an alley, gas lighting, well worth a visit, excellent Sheperd Neame beer, collection of politically incorrect Spitfire Beer ads – see page 8 – nearest Tube Bank, or Liverpool Street, or Moorgate, follow signs for The Guildhall.)

TO DRAUGHT FROM OVERDRAFT A lot of London banks have been converted into pubs, whatever that says about Londoners' priorities.

In the days when bank managers were respectable, disinterested professionals one was in awe of, the banks provided suitably impressive, confidence-building premises, many of them marbled halls that make rather atmospheric pubs or wine bars (better than being demolished or subdivided into offices). One such in Southwark is the **Barrowboy and Banker** in Borough High Street, the proximity of both the market and the City across the river giving the pub its name. But 'barrowboy' has a wider meaning now than merely one who works in a vegetable market shouting 'luvvly mush, luvvly caullies'. It means any cheeky chirpie cockney chappie who, nowadays, may even have his own TV or radio show and earn more than most of us. But he's still a barrowboy at heart and proud of it.

Across the river is another cavernous former bank, the **Hung, Drawn and Quartered** in Great Tower Street off Tower Hill. This particularly vile form of punishment would be suitable for certain classes of traitor or rebel. Samuel Pepys records this happening outside the Tower of London in 1660 but, of course, as a literary giant he should have said (well he did write in code) 'Hanged, drawn and quartered.' Being well hanged and well hung are completely different. As a heartless toff once remarked, one is for peasants, and the other's for pheasants.

The Banker, in Cousin Lane, EC4, wasn't a bank at all. It was, and is, a railway arch beneath Cannon Street Station, and there's no rhyming slang about the name. Another truly great bank-turned-into-boozer is the **Counting House** in the City's Cornhill.

LONDON'S MOST UNLIKELY BEASTS

THE DACRE BEASTS These fabulous four, 7ft-high, carved creatures stood menacingly in Naworth Castle, Cumbria, for 485 years until 1999, when they were unceremoniously ousted by the castle's owner, Philip Howard, who declared financial necessity the reason for such a break with the building's heritage. They are now in the care of the Victoria and Albert Museum.

The creatures – a Red Bull, a Black Gryphon, a Crowned Salmon and a White Ram – look as if they had stepped out of Lewis Carroll's mad poem *Jabberwocky*.

14

But they would be particularly menacing to Scots, given that their original job was to proudly hold aloft the battle standards captured in Lord Dacre's thrashing of the Scots at Flodden in 1513.

Thomas Dacre was a formidable soldier who, when he earlier took to the field at the Battle of Bosworth in 1485, helped Henry Tudor get rid of Richard III, and so become Henry VII. Richard, of course, was the king who died, according to Shakespeare, shouting: 'A horse, my kingdom for a horse.' He definitely wasn't yelling: 'My kingdom for a crowned salmon or a black gryphon!' What Dacre was yelling was his battle cry: 'A red bull, a red bull, a Dacre, a Dacre!' Pretty frightening, eh? (I don't suppose at the moment the hated king popped his clogs that anyone said: 'Hey, what do you know, the Middle Ages just ended!' but that's when they did, the history books say.)

It turns out, like all the heraldic nonsense, that the Dacre Beasts mean something. The Crowned Salmon represents the crest of Elizabeth de Greystoke with whom Lord Dacre eloped as a randy young man; the Black Gryphon represents Dacre's ancestor Ranulph de Dacre who fortified Naworth Castle in 1335; the White Ram represents Ranulph's wife (charming); while the Red Bull was Dacre's family emblem. They were all carved from a single oak tree in 1520 and are splendidly unique. Hollywood might consider turning this ripping yarn into a film starring Mel Gibson as Dacre and Kate Winslet as Elizabeth de Greystoke. See the glorious beasts in the new British Galleries at the Victoria and Albert Museum, South Kensington; ☏ 020 7942 2000.
➌ *South Kensington.*

GOG & MAGOG Traditional guardians of the City of London, these giants have headed the Lord Mayor's Show procession since the times of Henry V. They are ugly and enormous but basically benevolent (a kind of wooden John Prescott, you may think). They are legendary pagan giants from so far back in British history that their origin is shrouded in the mists of deepest bulldung. In fact the story is so totally ludicrous it might just be true, because if you were inventing it, you'd want to make up something faintly credible, wouldn't you? Judge for yourself.

Diocletian – the Roman Emperor – had 33 wicked daughters, for whom he selected 33 strict husbands to curb their wilful and unruly ways. The daughters, ungrateful wretches, were not happy about this, and the eldest, Alba, hatched a wicked plot to slit the 33 throats of their husbands with 33 knives as they slept, presumably having 33 nightmares. 'Daughters, eh, who'd have 'em?' sighed the Emperor, no doubt. For this vile crime they were set adrift in a boat with six months' food. So far so good.

Now comes the incredible bit – they chose Britain as their destination. I mean there you are, 33 gorgeous princesses, nothing to do, a good boat and six months' grub and where would you head? Nice? Monte Carlo? Capri? Nope, Gravesend. Yes, instead of Miami or Mustique they chose some rainswept island in the north, inhabited by miserable rude pagans with vile manners (and that was just the taxi drivers). Mind you, it might just have been their map reading – I don't want to be sexist, but you know, lots of girls holding it up the wrong way and arguing. They renamed the island Albion after the eldest sister, which has remained the poetical name for this country ever since (hence the various football teams and pubs named Albion).

These 33 foxy ladies then chose not to move in with the Druids, too busy not building Stonehenge presumably, or the hunky woad-painted animal skin-wearing Mel-Gibsonesque ancient Brits, but shacked up instead with 33 of the ugliest giants they could find. This produced a race of the most evil giants ever seen in the history of the world. Two of them, however, came to London and befriended the City (it must have been the beer). They were chained to the Guildhall to guard the place. Hence Gog and Magog have remained giant guardians of the City since time immemorial.

Or there's another angle, version B, involving Brutus, son of Aeneas, escaping from Troy and his champion Corineus, another giant, slaying Gogmagog (just one giant in this version). As a reward, Corineus is given that end of England which he calls Cornwall after himself while Brutus sets up New Troy, or London.

OK audience, vote A or B now. No, there's not a 'none of the above, you credulous dipstick' button.

AN OUTBREAK OF WYVERNS A wyvern, a sort of winged dragon, if you have never met one, is a mythical medieval heraldic beast of the sort that adorns the badge of every Vauxhall car, including the splendid Vauxhall Wyvern of the fifties, a car that looked to me more like a battleship. London, however, has a coven of wyverns at St Pancras station, for it was the adopted heraldic beast of the Midland Railway which spent the equivalent of £300m on building this insanely eccentric Gothic palace, which also has Indian mogul detailing, if you like that kind of thing. Wyverns don't like to be confused with...

GRIFFINS Please don't talk about the City of London *dragons*. It upsets them, apparently. Dragons are for the Welsh and Chinese. The City's beasts are *griffins*. There's a totally rampant, cosmic and fearsome version in Fleet Street to mark where the Temple Bar stood and a monarch visiting the City must stop (see Fleet Street walk, page 186).

DRAGONS A 9ft dragon (or is it a griffin?) surmounts Wren's huge spire at St Mary-le-Bow on Cheapside in the City of London. It wasn't on the cheap side, as it happened, the church in fact being the costliest of Wren's post-Great Fire reconstructions, the huge tower being, to my mind, a strange architectural mishmash, no doubt accounting for some of the huge cost, but this wonderful dragon is the icing on the cake. Cheapside the road, on the other hand, is well-named for a cheap which was, quite logically, a market in medieval times, as in Eastcheap and those West Country towns such as Chipping Norton, Chipping Sodbury (don't ask) or whatever.

BEASTS UNDER YOUR FEET One of the loveliest and simplest of London's churches is the round Temple Church of St Mary, a 12th-century gem of a building located in that lawyers' warren south of Fleet Street (see page 184) and now a star of *The Da Vinci Code*. The Purbeck marble effigies of crusading Knights Templar, or their supporters, show them often with their sleeping dogs curled up under their feet, a charming detail. Another interesting detail about crusaders and knights' tombs is that if their legs are crossed it indicates that they died in action, or possibly while waiting for the toilet. Romantic stuff of course – nowhere does it mention that the Crusades were usually a complete cock-up, with the armies diverted into attacking Christian Constantinople instead of the Muslims in the Holy Land, because there was more money in it for the Venetians.

LANDSEER LIONS, AND DOGS The most splendid lions in London sit proudly around Nelson's column in Trafalgar Square; they were created by Sir Edwin Landseer in the 19th century. There's a painting by John Bollantyne of Landseer working on the enormous beasts in 1864. A little more homely are his cast-iron dogs on each side of the porch of St George's Church, Hanover Square. They would have been a little late to see the wedding of Emma Hart and Sir William

14

Hamilton in that church in 1791, but there is a connection because the naughty Lady Hamilton later became the object of Nelson's affections, his greatest love. After the Navy, of course.

FOREST BEASTS Lurking in the park at Crystal Palace is an unlikely set of concrete dinosaurs which emerge from the undergrowth as one wanders round the park, terrifying generations of children. Some would emerge spookily from the lake as water levels changed. It's a kind of Victorian Jurassic Park (not to be confused with the railway restaurant car favourite, Jurassic Pork). The park adjoins Crystal Palace railway station and was home to Joseph Paxton's 1851 revolutionary glass and iron Great Exhibition building, brought to the site from Hyde Park but later destroyed.

THE COADE STONE LION This lion at the south (County Hall) end of Westminster Bridge is the cause of more urban myths than most sculptures. It is made of Coade stone and many a London guide will tell you that the formula for this strangely indestructible artificial stone has been lost; no-one knows where the lion came from and why there are no similar statues elsewhere. Well, its source is easy enough: it was one of a pair that adorned the Lion brewery that was cleared away for the Festival of Britain in 1951 (like the Millennium Dome but much more successful); one was moved here, the other to Twickenham, home of the English rugby team. Far from being indestructible, the Westminster Bridge lion's male appendages were thought shockingly enormous now it was at ground level, so they were trimmed back. The formula for the kind of cement that is Coade stone was invented by Mrs Eleanor Coade in the 1760s in Lambeth and a great many Coade stone statues decorate London houses, the Royal Opera House at Covent Garden, cemeteries and country estates too. The formula was not lost – some Coade stone was made in a university laboratory in recent years. And on the subject of the rubbish that bored guides spout, a colleague heard a coach PA system announce near here: 'And this is the world's oldest hole-in-the-wall cash machine; Henry VIII used this.' More than one of the tourists on the bus turned and took a picture of it.

CORNHILL DEVILS These three grotesque adornments which decorate the building at 54–55 Cornhill, EC3, seem to be bearing a grudge against the adjacent St Peter's Church, as indeed they do. The architect of this 19th-century building had infringed the church's land by a few inches and instead of letting it go, the rector insisted that building work was stopped and the plans redrawn. The three Devils continue to scowl at anyone entering the church, the one near the street bearing a particular resemblance to the unfortunate cleric. Next door is the splendid Counting House pub.

THE NAZIS' FAVOURITE GIANT BUTTERFLY The Camberwell beauty has long been an object of affection in southeast London. A 20ft x 14ft mural on Wells Way Library, SE5, honours the butterfly first recorded in Camberwell in 1748. Consisting of 231 tiles, the mural was assembled from separate ceramic tiles made in the 1920s at the Royal Doulton factory in Lambeth. During World War II, the Nazis' pet traitor Lord Haw-Haw, William Joyce, said on his propaganda radio programme, *Germany Calling*, that the butterfly was aiding Luftwaffe navigation. Winston Churchill had it blacked out within hours, so when Lord Haw-Haw repeated his claim, Churchill replied: 'What butterfly?' Lord Haw-Haw was unable to go and check at the end of the war due to a prior appointment with a bit of rope.

THE STRANGEST LOOS OF LONDON

Loos, the twee middle classes call them. In fact nearly every name for the bog is a euphemism that refers to cleaning: lavatory, toilet, bathroom, washroom, etc, which isn't what you go there for. Ditto the euphemistic restroom. How on earth can you rest with people trumpeting all over the place? More honest is the French pissoir, the colonial long-drop, or the American outhouse (when it was). Other terms are comical: khazi, throne, great white trumpet, bogs, thunderbox. Technically accurate (although absurd used, as it is, in French) is WC for water closet, the wonderful invention that cleans everything away and shuts off the stink too. Oddly, the WC was the cause of London's worst disease outbreaks because until it became popular, it was illegal to deposit human manure into watercourses so it was, theoretically at least, emptied into cess pits and earth closets, or taken away by 'night soil men' for fertilising fields. Increasing wealth meant everyone wanted a WC, so the affluent society became the effluent society. The stuff was then flushed from those cess pits right into the same river from where many water companies drew their supplies. Only the arrival of the great Victorian engineer Bazalgette, who created sewerage systems separate from the rivers and drains, saved the situation.

The main early producer of the 'syphonic' bog that sucks the stuff through a U-bend, thus preventing the pongs returning to the house, was Victorian inventor Thomas Crapper. His grave may be inspected at **Elmers End** cemetery in South London. It was recently rededicated with several happy Crappers in attendance. (I expect the local paper had a headline Flushed With Pride.)

Thus we had the splendid spectacle of elaborate Victorian cast-iron and porcelain bogs proudly branded 'The Crapper'. Incidentally, I've heard many an intelligent person say that is the origin of the eponymous verb, but I have to pooh-pooh the idea, as the said verb appears in medieval literature. It's a fascinating subject; someone should open a London loo museum, because there'd be a lot to go on. Anyway, here are just a few of London's finest bogs:

It may not have been a question that ever occurred to you, would a view of anteaters make your visits to the loo more interesting? The men's lavatories at **London Zoo** have a special porthole for such a purpose. Or maybe it's for the anteaters to watch what humans do…

The urinal in the **Warwick Arms** pub in Warwick Road, Kensington, has a daily paper framed dead ahead of men's gaze. Many bars have followed suit. Some North London wine bars have scenic views behind glass on their urinals, so you can pee on Austria or whatever.

The mind-boggling prospect of a **female urinal** came to pass in 2000 with the Standolet, a thing shaped like an upside-down racing bike saddle. One was installed in the Soho bar, Pop, but I gather they haven't taken off. Some people may try to wash their hands in them. Women tell me what they want is more bogs, not less privacy and wet shoes.

14

The **Roof Garden**, Kensington High Street, formerly Derry & Toms department store, features the most fabulous urinals, in a room whose brilliant lighting is typical of this, a most modern department store when it was built in the 1930s. The urinals are of the Adamsex Radio brand: I have a Radio ceramic hot water bottle from this era which could perhaps be explained in that it radiates heat, but what exactly does a urinal radiate? Don't answer that.

Princess Louise in Holborn. This splendid Victorian pub has some splendid Victorian bogs; time was – I'm told – when the glass cisterns had goldfish swimming about in them. They must have got swirled around a bit when flushed, and may have provided the odd flash in the pan if they were very unlucky. The thing is, can anyone remember this or is an old drunk pulling my leg? An urban myth, possibly.

Notting Hill Florist, Westbourne Grove. A new building that contains a florist at one end and a public bog at the other has to be something of a challenge, fragrance-wise. It's hard to see any connection between florists and lavatories, their purposes being somewhat divergent. Of course there's a fine plant called *Helleborus fetidus* (the much-maligned stinking hellebore) but a florist is unlikely to stock the humble dandelion, known to Shakespeare as the piss plant and to the French as *piss-en-lit*. This is because of the severe diuretic qualities of the dandelion. The odd leaf in a salad is all very well but don't try serving all your dinner guests dandelion root coffee as I once did before attending a *Missa Solemnis* at St Albans Abbey. Everyone was bursting for relief by the end of the first part. And the second part? Well … back to Notting Hill, where this modern building serves two rather different necessities rather well. Why not?

London's most famous mayor, Dick Whittington, when he wasn't passing political motions, gave some thought to the need for public loos and came up with a typically practical solution. Every City ward (an administrative division) then had at least one public latrine (I think things were so much better run in the Middle Ages), but this wasn't always enough. In 1419 he had built at his expense the most sociable super-bog in London, the **Long House**, roughly at the northern end of Southwark Bridge. There were places for 60 men and 60 women and the thing was purged twice a day by the tide. There were even almshouses for five pensioners above the stalls. Hopefully the oldsters' sense of smell had gone by the time they took up residence, but, sadly, this rather nice place for an afternoon chat was destroyed by the Great Fire of 1666.

Robobogs. Having laughed at the 'filthy froggies' for having hole-in-the-floor bogs for many years, we now face their revenge. Yes, they have out-bogged us while we weren't looking. *Voila*! The French-designed, self-cleaning, vandal-proof, fully automatic Gallic thunderbox, which I have dubbed Robobog. You enter these things, half sanitaryware, half machine, all bog, through a sliding door that hisses shut as if preparing you for a moon mission. After you leave, they go through some mysterious cleaning cycle whereby the thing is probably turned upside down and blasted with death rays or something. Has anyone ever been trapped in one during the cleaning cycle? Could this explain disappearances in London? These Schwarzeneggers of sanitaryware are all over London; some enlightened authorities (such as Hammersmith) have even made them free. *Formidable*!

Part Three

BIZARRE BITS OF INNER LONDON

15

Earl's Court

Earl's Court – a great place for gunshot wounds, female nutcases, venereal disease and asylum seekers. Not today, when the place bustles round the clock, but in the 18th century, when it was still an isolated farm surrounded by market gardens. The farm is shown on a 1787 map, reached by a turning north from a crossroads on Brompton Lane, as you still can, if you don't mind being killed by one-way traffic hurtling south.

From early times it had been the principal farm in the area and thus a manorial court. A tenants' charter of 1610 says: 'By custom any tenant may call a court, at his own charge, without suit unto his lord, the stewards and tenants to have their dinners provided and the steward to be pleased for his pains.' How you pleased a steward in those days wasn't specified.

But by the 18th century, Earl's Court House was a substantial mansion. ('Barons Court', by the way, was just a bit of snobby, or possibly humorous, fiction to call the next stop on the District Line. It's just lucky they didn't carry on the line to Little Chalfont, which by my reckoning would have been 'Lord High Panjandrum Supreme Emperor of the Entire Galaxy's Cosmic Court'.)

Here at Earl's Court lived the strangely eccentric but pioneering anatomist **John Hunter**, who was fascinated by the bodies of exotic species, and had first refusal on all the beasts that died in the 'London Zoo' of those days – the menagerie at the Tower of London. In fact he started a small zoo of exotic species at Earl's Court, where buffaloes, cattle, exotic goats, zebras, leopards, ostriches, eagle owls and snakes lived.

His oddest habit was wrestling with bulls, even odder when you find he was small in stature, so much so that the queen gave him a small one that was his favourite opponent. He was once trapped under a beast that had got the better of him and would have died if a manservant had not bullwhipped the beast.

Hunter made a name for himself by treating gunshot wounds and venereal diseases (separately, one sincerely hopes), although some said he was not properly qualified. He picked up his knowledge working for the army in the Seven Years War and made a good living while at Earl's Court, although he refused to charge any fee for treating authors, artists or priests, who seem to have accounted for a good proportion of the population nearby.

He accumulated almost 14,000 stuffed animals or skeletons that added greatly to knowledge of

comparative anatomy. He secretly bought the body of the then famous 8ft-tall Irish giant, Brian O'Brien, and, buying an especially huge pot for the gruesome purpose, boiled down the body and reassembled the bones into a remarkable skeleton which joined the other exhibits in his museum. What happened to the rest of this horrendous Irish stew is not recorded.

Eventually, after Hunter got rather angry at a meeting at St George's Hospital and dropped dead in 1793, his amazing collection was accepted by the Royal College of Surgeons of England. The Irish giant's skeleton still occupies pride of place in a glass case, and a portrait of Hunter hangs there too. The picture shows him at his desk with a book on skulls, a ghoulish specimen in a jar and part of a huge creature's skeleton hanging behind him.

Following his death the house became a lunatic asylum for posh ladies. The private asylums were much in demand from those who wanted to escape the public provision at Bedlam, and there was another one on Old Brompton Road at Cowper House, where Melton Court now stands.

I asked an eminent British surgeon and medical author whether he'd heard of John Hunter and received the following explosion worthy of James Robinson Justice in the *Doctor in the House* films:

Heard of him? John Hunter? Of course I've heard of John Hunter! He is one of the all-time British medical greats. Don't you know anything? His collection at the RCS was bombed in the war but a lot of it remains. I don't know whether the giant is still there. They would willingly let you in if you ask nicely – mention my name, I'm a Fellow. When he was investigating VD he courageously inoculated himself with infective material and may or may not have got syphilis as a result.

He had an only slightly less famous brother, William, who was also a physician and ran an anatomy school in Windmill Street near, or actually at, where the Windmill Theatre famous for dancing girls now stands, or stood. There's a joke in there somewhere about living and dead anatomy! Ha ha!

His name is held in the greatest reverence by us surgeons and there is a very old Hunterian Society. He had angina and knew that emotion was bad for him and said that any scoundrel who made him angry held his [Hunter's] life in his hands, but he persisted in fierce internecine politics at St George's and died therefrom. He was a genius.

Earl's Court House was demolished in 1886 and Barkston Gardens built on the site.

The Victorian and earlier amateur anatomists, ornithologists, dinosaur hunters, etc, were often far from complete crackpots and their work led directly to the creation of the great museums we enjoy today, or to smaller personal museums such as the Horniman's, Pitt Rivers, or Soane's (see index). Nevertheless there is something odd about people who wrote letters to the Natural History Museum. One opened: 'Dear Sir, I am extremely interested in anatomy and – you must have plenty – will you please send me one horse's clavicle and a pair of sparrow's kneecaps.'

EARL'S COURT TODAY: BLADE RUNNER AND DWARF-TOSSERS The unique character of Earl's Court – which, to overstate it a tad, gives it a seedy 24-hour rootlessness reminiscent of the film *Blade Runner* – is connected with the transience of its population and the multi-occupation of its large houses. It has been described as a reception centre for whatever ethnic group or desperate refugees are currently arriving at Heathrow, as the road and Tube from the airport lead to the capital through this district. This might be true now, but the neat explanation evaporates historically when you realise that the district featured cheap boarding houses from

15

long before Heathrow and the refugee ghetto idea goes back at least to World War I when a million Belgian refugees fled the German invasion for fear of atrocities (very wisely, as it turned out) and several thousand ended up right here.

In the 1960s, the arrivals were largely Australians of the Rolf Harris or Clive James variety and the place was nicknamed 'Kangaroo Valley' or 'Dingo Gulch'. I can forgive Clive James anything for his brilliant description of the late Barbara Cartland's eye make-up: 'Like two crows that had collided with a chalk cliff.' But I'm not sure about Rolf Harris.

Even today you can find the odd stuffed kangaroo in a pub or chundering dwarf-tosser (an eccentric Australian sport) outside but generally the backpackers and asylum seekers are now a little more varied.

On the plus side, this makes the place constantly cosmopolitan, tolerant and interesting – didn't Bob Dylan play at the Troubadour? Isn't there great jazz from time to time? Where else can you get Iranian groceries at 2am? Or a gay hang-out with no hang-ups? How much less boring than snooty Brompton just down the road, you may think.

You might imagine the great houses in the area have gone to seed in this process, but the truth is that the poshness that spread like golden syrup oozing through silver cutlery, from Mayfair's top drawer sterling silver into Knightsbridge and Kensington's silver plate, never quite reached slightly tarnished Earl's Court, made of baser metals – and not entirely stainless.

Yes, the huge wedding-cake terraces of smarter bits of West London were ideal for well-to-do Victorian families of perhaps nine children and four servants, but how many people live like that nowadays? Even then there were many people who were neither servant nor master but just wanted temporary accommodation – a problem for snobs in the neighbouring upmarket wedding-cake terraces.

Even as close to Earl's Court as Gloucester Road, multi-occupancy of a building was often seen as lowering the tone. In Queen's Gate Gardens, near Gloucester Road, a woman who wanted to use one of these large houses as a boarding house in 1906 was reluctantly granted permission by the freeholder on the condition that no-one called or whistled for a cab nearby and that windows were constantly curtained in such a way that no-one in the street could see people seated inside.

Less snobbish Earl's Court itself – although part of that borough – has always been less worried about lowering the tone and has lustily embraced these changes. Houses have been divided up from the earliest times (that is, the 1870s) if not built as flats. Or just rooms for letting.

A GREAT CARRY ON, AND MORE IRISH ECCENTRICS Thus generations of students and struggling actresses (struggling on the floor with MPs in Chelsea strip, in at least one case) have leavened the mix.

The social change brought by the building of the Earl's Court area was rather sudden. The place was utterly re-invented in less than 20 years.

There is a charming photo in the borough archives of Earl's Court Farm in the 1860s, showing chaps sitting around in farm carts, wearing straw hats, with market garden produce growing in the foreground. This was demolished in 1875 to make way for the railway station and associated housing. The coming of the District Railway changed everything.

Roads were laid out rapidly, some, such as Kempsford Gardens and Eardley Crescent, ingeniously cramming houses into the curve made by the railway junction, giving them the pleasing architectural unity they have today.

But Eardley Crescent, despite its orderly layout, has seen a few real characters. The great *Carry On* film star, **Hattie Jacques**, who was also the matron in the above-mentioned *Doctor in the House* films, lived here.

Earlier, 58 Eardley Crescent was home to John Butler Yeats, an Irish painter, and his sons **William Butler Yeats** and Jack B Yeats. The Yeats, particularly Mrs Lily Yeats, hated Earl's Court, or rather their cramped home, and later moved to leafy Bedford Park.

W B Yeats went on to become poet laureate, and not such a useless one as they often are. (Odd, when you think about it, how, when England's greatest heroes and intellectuals – such as Shaw, Yeats, Wilde, Swift and the Duke of Wellington – were in fact Irish by origin or connections, people used to tell jokes about Irish people being stupid. That's what I'd call really thick.)

Anyway, Jack B Yeats became a painter and died in 1957 having written a rather good epitaph for himself:

Under no stones
Nor slates
Lies Jack B
Yeats.
No heaped up rocks.
Just a collection box,
And we thought a Nation's Folly
Would like to be jolly
And bury in state
This singular Yeat.
But they were not so inclined
Therefore if you've a mind
To slide a copper in the slot
'Twill help to sod the plot.

So is this carved in the adjacent Brompton Cemetery? Not a bit of it. He's in Mount Jerome Cemetery, Dublin, and as for sods, they didn't even carve his bit of doggerel on the tombstone. Mind you, his poet brother's painting was bloody awful too. Which leads us neatly to perhaps the very best bit of Earl's Court across the road from the southern end of Eardley Crescent, on the south side of Old Brompton Road…

THE DEAD CENTRE OF EARL'S COURT

The most interesting residents of Earl's Court will definitely be in if you call round, for they are all dead. The massive **Brompton Cemetery** offers fascinating encounters, marvellous monuments, real heroes and villains, peaceful strolls and a surprising amount of greenery and wildlife.

As detailed in *Chapter 6*, London's church graveyards were literally bulging with the dead by 1800 and radical measures were needed. Great new cemeteries were opened with private capital behind them after the cholera outbreak of 1831. One of them was the West London and Westminster Cemetery Company which opened these grounds, then outside London, in 1840. In fact, not enough people died (blame the new sewerage) – fewer than 100 customers in the first year, and London wasn't near enough. Soon, with the rapid spread of London up to and past the cemetery, more people were falling off their perches and the project became dead successful.

Not just quantity, it must be said looking round this slumbering city of the dead, but quality too. The cemetery is positively brimming with artists, actors, singers, engineers and businessmen (two still familiar names among the last are **Samuel Sotheby**, who went for the last time in 1861, and **Sir Samuel Cunard**, who docked here in 1865). The great journalist and *Times* correspondent in the Crimea,

W H Russell, dubbed the world's first war correspondent, reached his final deadline here in 1907. The doctor who helped conquer cholera, **John Snow** (d1859), is here too. He also pioneered anaesthetics, using ether or chloroform, which must have been a great relief to those facing sawbones surgery in those days (see operating theatre museum, page 39). It was certainly a relief to Queen Victoria, who took chloroform from Snow in 1853 at the birth of her son Prince Leopold – the first royal to use anaesthetic.

The founder of Chelsea Football Club, whose stand is just the other side of the railway tracks, **Sir Henry Mears** (d1912), is here; his bones perhaps gently vibrate to the chants of 'Chelsea' on weekend afternoons. The great boxer **'Gentleman' John Jackson** (d1845), champion of England for many years, whose tomb is marked by a lion, once taught Lord Byron to box at his boxing academy. **Percy Lambert** is here, first person to drive faster than 100mph, and who died … guess how.

The great suffragette leader, **Emmeline Pankhurst**, was buried here in 1928, having won votes for women. Her daughter Sylvia lived in Chelsea (see page 122) and carried on her work but is buried, I'm told, in Addis Ababa. Emmeline was force-fed in her hunger strikes before World War I, but once the war started put her energies into recruiting women for munitions work. Her rather beautiful grave records her, possibly rather oddly by modern feminist thinking, as simply 'Wife of R M Pankhurst'. She died after the aim of her life's work, the second Representation of the People Act, was passed.

Heroes are here too, such as Flight Sub-Lieutenant **Reggie Warneford**, VC, who in 1915 brought down one of the much-feared Zeppelins over Ghent. This is particularly relevant here, as German bombers violently raised the dead in Brompton Cemetery in World War II, as the shrapnel marks on monuments near the north gate show. It was even suggested they blew up people previously blown up in World War I. If so, that's Teutonic thoroughness for you. On the other hand, perhaps they wanted to get old Warneford again, just to make sure.

DEAD ZEPPELIN'S GREATEST HITS How long does it take nowadays for a courageous soldier, sailor or airman to be given a medal for bravery in battle? Months? Years?

Consider then this announcement from June 1915:

His Majesty the King has sent the following telegram to Flight Sub-Lieutenant Warneford:

I most heartily congratulate you upon your splendid achievement of yesterday, in which you single-handed destroyed an enemy Zeppelin. I have much pleasure in conferring upon you the Victoria Cross for this gallant act.

GEORGE R.I.

This was from King George V, Rex Imperator (King Emperor) straight to the ordinary airman and the speed of his recognition of Warneford's feat indicates one thing: how desperate the British were to combat the German Zeppelin menace.

Aircraft with wings were then most primitive, made of wood and cloth with puny, unreliable engines, difficult to control and likely to crash at any time. The Zeppelin was a more reliable hydrogen-gas-filled cigar-shaped balloon that enabled the Germans to go high above the reach of British guns and bomb London with impunity. There was little that could be done about these great silver menaces in the sky and even at this early stage there was little pretence that military targets were being aimed at. The German press published gleeful cartoons of men, women and children being blown to pieces.

So although the amount of bombs the Zeppelins were carrying was small, the British were desperate for countermeasures. In fact my father's cousin, by then a very elderly man in New Zealand, told me of running through the streets of South London as a boy with this huge silver thing in the sky dropping bombs, seeming to chase him.

On that day in 1915 Flight Sub-Lieutenant Warneford – the RAF had yet to be formed, so he was in fact a sailor – was flying a Morane aircraft over Belgium and saw a Zeppelin, L37, returning from bombing Britain. Single-handed, he flew to 6,000ft and then manually tossed bombs on to the enemy while trying to control the unstable aircraft at the limit of its altitude.

At least one of the bombs exploded, and those who have seen that amazing film of the German civil airship the *Hindenberg* crashing, will know what happened next – a huge unstoppable conflagration as the hydrogen inside caught fire and escaped from the plunging Zeppelin.

Warneford's plane was caught by the blast, said the *Times* man in a dispatch, and turned upside down so all his remaining petrol fell out of the tank. Warneford calmly landed Biggles fashion on a Belgian road behind German lines, filled up his tank from a spare can, restarted the engine and took off for home.

The Dutch newspapers carried a different account which hints at civilian casualties on the ground, but perhaps would have said explicitly if there were any, and has the action at a lower altitude. On 8 June 1915, *The Tyd* wrote:

> Yesterday, at dawn, a Zeppelin appeared near Ghent, pursued by two Allied airmen. The German guns posted on the parade-ground and at other points in the town opened a terrible fire on the aeroplanes, which were trying to cut off the Zeppelin's return. The airship was flying over St Amandsberg and attempting to escape the airmen by descending. The Zeppelin had already had a skirmish with its pursuers, as it was listing to the left side. Shots were exchanged with the pursuers, of whom one was daring enough to approach close to the dirigible in an attempt to fly over it. After a sudden bold swoop this airman was seen to drop some explosives on the Zeppelin, which was at once enveloped in flames. The balloon covering was fiercely burning, and, after some minor reports and one big explosion, the dirigible dropped on the convent school of St Amandsberg.

Not that this stopped the Zeppelin menace overnight. The night raids continued and of course the things could drift silently over a town and attack without warning. Hertford, for example, hardly a military target, was blitzed in October 1915 with great loss of life.

But the aircraft sent up to meet them were improving, and forward-firing machine-guns with incendiary bullets were not good news for Zeppelin owners. In September 1916, the first Zeppelin to be shot down over England fell at Cuffley, Hertfordshire, just north of the M25, after being attacked by Lt William Leefe Robinson of the Royal Flying Corps. He, too, became an instant hero; he was awarded the Victoria Cross, a rather good monument was built by newspaper readers at Cuffley and a pub, the Leefe Robinson, was named in his honour, at **Harrow Weald**, Middlesex (northwest London).

And Warneford is far from the only VC holder in this fascinating cemetery. There are 11 more, including five who won the award during the Indian Mutiny of 1857–58. Another, intriguingly, is Alice Mary Adamas, a clergyman's wife awarded the VC during the Afghan War; yet another is Private Parkes of the 4th Hussars, decorated for his part in the Charge of the Light Brigade.

Other notables connected with this cemetery include:

- **John Wisden**. Cricket fans will need no introduction to this chap, for they will read Wisden's cricket almanac regularly, the bible of the sport. Here his grave is aptly marked with bat and ball. It was Wisden who said on seeing the mountainous waves of the Atlantic Ocean for the first time: 'What this pitch needs is ten minutes of the heavy roller.' While we're on the theme of cricket legends, it's worth noting that the greatest of them all, **Dr W G Grace**, who lived in the 19th century but scored by the double century, is buried in South London. At Elmers End cemetery, Beckenham, may be found his grave also inscribed with bat and ball. Fans of the thwack of leather upon willow (if you're American, you probably haven't got a clue what I'm on about) who marvel at the first man to reach a hundred centuries (over a century ago, in 1895) can slake their thirst in the nearby W G Grace pub. Actually it's not entirely true about Americans being ignorant about cricket. The extremely rich American-born Sir John Paul Getty, who lived over here, was a great fan and knew more about it than I do (see page 122). On the other hand, would we Brits want them to understand it? Look what happened when we told them about tennis. Big mistake.
- **George Godwin**. Local boy, born in Brompton, who contributed hugely to the area's architecture. A prodigy who won a medal for his treatise on concrete aged just 20, he campaigned for better housing for the poor and had an eccentric obsession with chairs. He collected those belonging to the famous – Shakespeare, Pope, Napoleon, Thackeray, Byron, etc. His memorial has two mourning maidens and a lamp of learning, as well as his portrait – but no chairs.
- **Beatrix Potter**. The legion of fans of the creator of Peter Rabbit, Jeremy Fisher *et al* will, having spotted her name on this page, be dashing to their old-fashioned typewriters to tell me she's not buried here, and they are right. Not that they know where she's buried either, for the eccentric Miss Potter desired her shepherd Tom Storey to scatter her ashes on her favourite spot on her Cumbrian farm after her death in 1943. He revealed its location to no-one except his son, who died in 1989, so we shall never know. However, she was raised in London around the corner from here and a fascinating bit of literary detective work in 2001 suggested she may have got the inspiration for naming her characters from Brompton graveyard rather than her beloved Lakeland. Her 23 animal stories with those lovely colour plates of her watercolours were published from 1902 onwards, and if you ever loved these books you will agree it is no coincidence that these names can be found in the cemetery: Peter Rabett, Jeremiah Fisher, Mr Tod, Mr Nutkins, Mr Brock and Mr McGregor. Amateur sleuth James Mackay even found an early version of the Jeremy Fisher stories in which Potter had named her character Jeremiah, as on a headstone here. I'm convinced, Mr Mackay, although if you find a Flopsy, Mopsy and Cottontail I'll eat a row of soporific lettuce. Either way, I still haven't forgiven her for having Tom Kitten wrapped up in pastry and shoved in an oven by a bunch of rats, if I remember rightly.

THE INDIAN HERO LONG WOLF, AND THE FALLING STAR Far more exotic a tale is that of Brompton's most extraordinary burial, that of a Red Indian brave, a chief in fact, whose life and death have proved equally dramatic and turbulent.

His bullet-scarred and sabre-slashed body lay here in Earl's Court for a century but has now gone. Long Wolf was undoubtedly a great warrior and the evidence suggests he took part in the Sioux people's greatest victory, the wiping out of Custer's 7th Cavalry at the Battle of Little Big Horn in 1876.

It was a last act of defiance on the part of a proud people standing in the way of the unstoppable juggernaut of history; the settlement of the Indian hunting grounds by millions of immigrants went ahead, ending their way of life. The humiliated American government could not let the Indian triumph stand (any more than the British felt the mutiny by real Indians in the same era could go unpunished). The Red Indian culture was subjugated, their fighting prowess destroyed, historic freedoms lost – and replaced with different ones – and the proud chief could not bear it. He was told there was a great opportunity in London for a man of his romantic standing (to Londoners) and rather than exist in some reservation by permission of his former enemies as a second-class citizen, he came to London.

Here, in Colonel 'Buffalo Bill' Cody's Wild West Show at Earl's Court exhibition centre (see below), he was a huge success. He was no mere foreign curiosity put on display like a caged animal; he was respected and even a little feared by the awed crowds. He was the real thing, every inch a great Chief.

Sadly, as with Indian Princess Pocahontas (see page 143), such a proud Indian could defeat the white man's guns and swords, but could not cope with his common diseases. Long Wolf died of a cold that developed into pneumonia in 1892. A post-mortem examination at the West London Hospital described a body 'covered in gunshot wounds and sabre cuts'. So much for anyone who doubted Long Wolf's story. At around the same time a 17-month old Indian performer, Star, had died at the Wild West Show in a fall from a horse. They started them young and dangerous in those days.

Long Wolf's grieving wife and his daughter, Lizzie, could not afford to take his body back to America, although he expressed a wish to return to his homeland on his deathbed. They buried him in Brompton Cemetery with little Star and left for a lonely sea voyage home. For a century, that was the end of the story, the grave forgotten as wars, kings and queens came and went.

A dusty book and an extraordinarily persistent Worcestershire housewife were instrumental in changing all that. Plus Lizzie's daughter, Jessie Black Feather, who was not content to leave grandfather Long Wolf's grave forgotten 'somewhere in London'.

The housewife was – according to press reports at the time – one Elizabeth Knight who stumbled across a dusty book about Long Wolf, written by explorer and MP Robert Cunningham Grahame, in an antiques market. It told of the forgotten grave of Long Wolf. Mrs Knight then spent six years, it was reported, trying to track down Long Wolf's details and his people in America, resorting to advertisements in the American press.

One of these was at last seen by Jessie Black Feather, who had been searching for years for a clue to the whereabouts of her grandfather's remains.

There followed negotiations between the US State Department and the British Government, an exhumation from West Brompton, a horse-drawn funeral procession through London, a flight to America and a combined Christian and Indian burial ceremony at Pine Ridge Reservation, South Dakota, near the site of the Wounded Knee massacre, the ancestral burial ground of the Oglala Sioux.

Jessie Black Feather, then in her 80s, was quoted as saying that her grandfather's soul would not have been at peace until his body had come home. Perhaps Jessie, and that extraordinary woman from Worcestershire, both gained some kind of peace.

The main reason for Earl's Court being known to the outside world must be the huge exhibition centre which fronts Warwick Road. This vast building is a West London landmark and is visible from vantage points for miles around, the roof looking like the upturned hull of some gigantic ship that has somehow come to grief here.

You could say cathedral-like space for both buildings, but you'd be wrong. Cathedral builders didn't have steel and concrete and couldn't span these immense halls without interruption. Here one might see an entire fishing village, complete with harbour and boats floating in it, constructed for the Boat Show in January, or mini mountains of real snow at the annual ski show. The Royal Tournament (before it was banned for effectively being too British by New Labour) featured realistic battles with real cannon fired across the arena. Massive crowds greet the megastars of pop, rock and opera here too – Madonna and Pavarotti, for example.

Yet the siting of this extraordinary asset is entirely down to a side-effect of Victorian technology. Earl's Court station is on a straight bit of track, perhaps half-a-mile long, between two triangular junctions. Being railway triangles, these are large with inwardly curved sides.

When the building boom followed the railway in the second half of the 19th century, at first the roads simply curved to fit in with the tracks behind (Eardley Crescent on one side and Philbeach Gardens on the other). The question arose for the Metropolitan District Railway Company of what to do with the vast triangle within the railway junction.

Enter entrepreneur **John Robinson Whiteley**, who in 1886 was travelling in the United States and decided to bring a Wild West show to London. His instincts as to what Europeans wanted to see of America – sharp-shooting cowboys, wagon trains, bareback-riding, headdress-wearing whooping Indians, and feats of knife-throwing, archery, fire juggling, etc – were absolutely spot on. The massive site, located then as now between four railway stations that could rapidly deliver thousands of customers, was rapidly transformed by masses of labourers over that winter, many of them railway navvies, to include a large arena and stand, an exhibition building and extensive pleasure gardens, built with the aid of bridges over the tracks at all angles.

It opened in 1887 and was a rollicking success, and secured the future of this site for the more than a century that has passed since.

Colonel 'Buffalo Bill' W F Cody was in charge of the acts that Whiteley had encouraged to come from America, and the public loved them. It was the beginning of the fascination that continues today in Europe for Western films and novels, and Britons, led by Queen Victoria herself, flocked to see it. The crowned heads of Europe made visits while supposedly in London to pay their respects to the old Queen Empress who was, at Earl's Court at least, amused at last.

The theme of the shows changed over the years with varying success, but memorable hits were made with what we would today call theme park rides: the first 'Water Chute' (in which you rode down a railed track in a kind of boat and shot across an artificial lake with great sheets of water and much screaming from nervous passengers) and a Great Wheel at the end of the century which, several people have pointed out, was a more massive ancestor of the London Eye wheel on the South Bank erected 100 years later. London history repeated yet again.

16

Fleet Street

FLEET STREET AND SMITHFIELD WALK

A circular walk of less than 2 miles, 3 hours. Start and finish: ❷ *Blackfriars. Optional halt halfway at Farringdon station.*

EXPLODING FILTH AND NAKED WOMEN BEING FLOGGED The River Fleet, one of London's seven lost rivers north of the Thames (see page 96 for a brief history of them), was once a pleasant rural stream, and at this end a river big enough to float a boat – hence 'Fleet' – in the lower reaches. But since the Middle Ages it has carried so much of London's filth and muck that people who fell into it were sometimes found asphyxiated, legs in the air; on one occasion the by then covered-over river blew up from the accumulation of evil gases, destroying a few houses.

Today we will cross and recross it and never be far from it, yet will not see it. But it is silently slipping through the darkness under our feet towards Blackfriars Bridge, where it has an outfall you can really see only from a boat on the river. Its unseen presence explains the geography of the whole district.

Leaving Blackfriars Tube station, take the tunnel under the road, leaving by Exit 1, and take a look at the quite extraordinary decoration of the Black Friar pub, a rare gem of a place, and our first contact with the monastic heritage that once dominated this area.

If you walk to the corner of the Black Friar, you'll notice the tiny wedge of cheese-shaped land that it occupies. As I say in the Southwark walk, which ends here, the builders also had a railway line at first-floor height to contend with behind the pub, so the site was very restricted, and is only about 4ft wide at one end. Look at the rich ornamentation, the bronze signs and the mosaic detail. The architect did a good job in 1875, as can be seen by the interesting exterior, but the real treat is inside, and clearly dates from the early 20th century, with heavy art nouveau influences in its whimsical interpretation of the life of monks.

A NOTE ABOUT WALKS

The rest of this book includes several walks around districts of London that I love. Unlike certain other authors, I have actually done these walks and thoroughly recommend them. However, they vary in length and are also just a convenient way of telling you some rollicking good yarns you would equally enjoy sitting in an armchair in Arkansas. Walking ain't compulsory! As you can't easily read while you walk, one approach would be to read them first and see what interests you and just visit those bits, or take breaks at the suggested watering holes and have a good read there. There are often escape routes at halfway points to help the less energetic. Just enjoy it and don't treat it as a Death March that must be endured while cursing the author ...

16

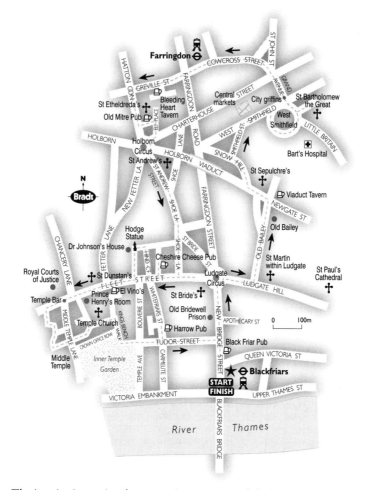

The interior is a national treasure, in my view, and the beer isn't bad either. But we are at the start not at the end of this walk, so save your thirst and check out the interior later.

We go on up the right-hand side of New Bridge Street, with tantalising glimpses of **St Paul's** to the right and **St Bride's** pretty spire, the model for the world's wedding cakes, on the left. When we pass Apothecary Street on the right, we are almost opposite the old **Bridewell** prison, where people would pay to see semi-naked women flogged in a special chamber.

The major junction here is **Ludgate Circus** and I recommend crossing to the further corner (straight across) to get our bearings, and one of the finest views in the land. Standing on the corner and looking back towards Blackfriars and the river, it's worth realising that a dock as wide as the street reached up here from the Thames before the new road bridge (Blackfriars) was built. Ships and even river pirates lurked here. Looking in the opposite direction, this is the valley of the Fleet and the bridge over it in the distance is Holborn Viaduct, a road we'll encounter later. Holborn means 'hollow bourn' or 'valley of the stream'.

Looking east (that is to your left if you're facing back to Blackfriars) there's a magnificent view of St Paul's – actually, its best view. The contrasting slender black bulb of a spire in the foreground is almost too perfect a part of the composition to be a happy accident. In fact Sir Christopher Wren, the masterful architect of St Paul's – whose tomb inside the cathedral is marked *Si monumentum requiris, circumspice* or 'If you require a monument, look around you' – also had to fix a new spire on this church, **St Martin within Ludgate**, in the aftermath of the 1666 Great Fire. So he made it a perfect foil for his cathedral without telling the parishioners why he chose the odd steeple.

Looking in the opposite direction up Fleet Street – and the hill on each side reveals that we are in a river valley and that Ludgate Circus was once a bridge over the Fleet – is the soaring Gothic majesty of St Dunstan in the West, and a glimpse of further splendours beyond. Isn't this a fabulous perspective? If it's been so good for hundreds of years, why haven't more people painted it?

Because the perspective *wasn't here*. From around 1672 until 20 years ago the perspective was obscured either in Fleet Street by the ugly Temple Bar, a massive arch that blocked the view and much of the traffic, or to the east by a railway bridge which carried trains from south of the river (crossing next to the Black Friar) heading for Smithfield market and by tunnels to Farringdon and the north which crossed over the road on a bridge not far from here. Or, for a short period, by both. The railway now goes under the road, using old tunnels to the market. We are, strangely, the first generation to enjoy this splendid view unhindered.

A word about the 'within' and 'without' names around here: they mark places inside and outside the old city walls which ran down near the Fleet on the City side (unlike the present City boundary which includes Fleet Street). From Roman times the City of London was up on the hill where St Paul's is and the Romans' wall still exists in odd places. The Fleet ditch was the obvious defensive line. The various gates such as Ludgate here and Newgate which we shall encounter soon were fortified entrances from the Middle Ages on. The road over the Fleet Bridge to the swampy thorn-infested island of Westminster and the West was where those who were not welcome within the City itself had to make their business as close to the City as possible – lawyers and writers, still Fleet Street's stock-in-trade.

Naturally, with this combination of people, the area boasted not only its share of eccentrics but a good number of drinking places for them to meet. Note the gilt sign of the **Punch Tavern** opposite, recalling the magazine of that name once based here.

We go up Ludgate Hill towards St Paul's a few steps, passing Seacoal Lane, reminding us of the harbour once here, and left into Old Bailey.

SPIES, MURDERERS AND NOVELISTS The **Old Bailey** – or rather the Central Criminal Court which stands at that address – is another globally famed institution and nearly every major criminal has been dragged in here. I walked past when there were satellite TV vans with their dishes pointed to the heavens, (and reporters and cameramen with their eyebrows likewise) following the Jeffrey Archer trial inside. The world-famous novelist's private life had turned out to be far more interesting than the plots of his books, so Fleet Street – meaning the press in general – was having a ball. Entrance to the public galleries is free and it can either be the best, or the most boring, show in town. Spies such as George Blake, gangland murderers such as the Krays, and Dr Crippen – all detailed in this book – have trodden through these courts whose history is soaked with blood, suffering and, of course, lawyers getting rich.

The old Newgate jail was housed in another city gate at this point and was so overcrowded and vermin-infested that it was a death sentence for some just being admitted there. As I recount in the gruesome chapter on crime and punishment , the condemned were forced to walk from here all the way down Tyburn Road (or

16

British judges absolutely reek of eccentricity. Many see them as ignorant of modern culture, completely out of touch, and having a flippant attitude to their powers. Their blindness to the feelings of female victims of crime is legendary. They are traditionally old, white, upper-class males (many have continued working until well into their 70s) who are insulated from real life in their chauffeured cars with police escorts and special houses with servants. This caricature may be unfair, but judges can't complain because they often play up to the legend.

Thus unbelievable questions – such as that of one judge who had to ask 'Who are the Beatles?' – receive unbelievable answers – 'a popular beat combo, m'lud.' There have been others: 'Who is Marilyn Monroe?', 'What are a woman's boobs?' When a judge asked from the bench, 'What does "humping" mean?', he had to order a young woman out of court for giggling.

Some play to the gallery. Particularly brilliant at this was High Court judge Sir Jeremiah LeRoy Harman, an Old Etonian, who seemed to make a point of not knowing anything common people might know. He once asked: 'Who is Bruce Springsteen?' But his tour de force came during a case involving Paul Gascoigne, then Britain's best-known soccer star, known as Gazza and on every front page twice a week.

The upper classes from posh schools follow rugby football, and sneer at soccer or 'association football' as they would call it. Told that Gascoigne was a very well-known footballer, Harman asked: 'Rugby or association football?' He was informed Gazza was a Tottenham Hotspur star, and had played in the World Cup. He replied: 'Isn't there an operetta called *La Gazza Ladra*?' The Press fell off their bench. 'Batty old judge asks: is Gazza an opera?'

Mr Justice Melford Stevenson was the epitome of an eccentric British judge. He was once sitting in the Court of Appeal with the Lord Chief Justice, the most famous judge in the land, and another prominent legal figure.

He called the usher over and said: 'Can you give me the names?' The usher said, 'You've got them, m'lud, on your sheets,' and he said, 'No, no, not the counsel! The names of these other judges.' During another case he refused to believe the evidence of a witness because he chose to live in Manchester, 'a wholly incomprehensible choice for a free man'. He told an epileptic who had tried to kill himself in remand cells he should have done it with more efficiency 'to save us all the bother and expense', and said raped hitchhikers were asking for it.

During one high profile case at the Old Bailey, Judge Leslie Boreham told the jury to learn from the statue of Justice on the roof. 'She is blindfolded not because a jury should be blind when they are looking at the evidence,' he told them. 'She is blindfolded so she

Oxford Street) to the infamous Tyburn tree at what is now Marble Arch, where the triple-sided gallows could dispatch up to 20 at a time.

Later, when snobbish Mayfair began to object to the crowds of common people and aristocrats who would jostle to see the hangings at Tyburn, they were instead held here in the broad space known as the Old Bailey, and Newgate jail had by then been rebuilt (it was where the courts now are). The entire space was packed with people eager to see a good hanging. Quite often far more people were killed in the crush than on the gallows.

Moving on, notice on the opposite corner the **Viaduct Tavern**, a splendid Victorian gin palace with completely over-the-top interior which had its own cells in the cellar for rowdy customers. This pub name serves to remind us that the main road to the left, **Holborn Viaduct**, is an artificial level and the road used to plunge down to Farringdon Road, with difficult access to Newgate.

takes no account of race, creed, colour, political parties or nationalities.' The jury who could see the statue was not blindfolded were left deeply puzzled.

Another judge, asked by a woman lawyer to explain why he told a criminal not to worry because 'it is a woman's function to upset men', retorted, 'What lesbian group are you from?' He also told lager louts to try bitter.

Mr Justice (Ian) Starforth Hill told a young joyrider: 'To my mind it is a thousand pities that you didn't damage yourself in the crash.' On another occasion he proposed that those who claim unemployment benefit and get drunk on it should have their ears cut off. An eccentric measure by any standard, but it has the merit of being cheap and quick I suppose.

In another case – obviously not in the Old Bailey or the High Court but priceless nevertheless – a judge said: 'You leave the court without a stain on your character – except that you were acquitted by a Welsh jury.'

Such wit, if that's what it is, isn't confined to judges but affects barristers and solicitors in these courts. There was a terrific barrister, James Crespi, who famously got blown up when the IRA attacked the Old Bailey. He was pictured covered in blood, but it wasn't long before he was back in El Vino's in Fleet Street, where he spent every evening, saying: 'I thought I would put my person between the bomb and the Old Bailey to protect it from the blast, but it didn't work.'

True, if anyone could protect the Old Bailey with his body, the portly Crespi was the man. He was so Falstaffian that he'd take a taxi to travel 200yds to El Vino's; sadly he is no longer with us. One of his quips in court came when his chair collapsed under his enormous weight and a pathologist who was giving evidence rushed to help him. Crespi said: 'My dear boy, thank you, thank you, but not just yet.'

Neither is the public in British courts immune from eccentricity. There was a case in a magistrate's court – or so the story goes, as I haven't found the case myself – where a German tourist was accused of shoplifting. The defendant made out he couldn't understand English, so the magistrate asked if anyone in court could speak German. A man in the public gallery volunteered, and came down to the well of the court.

Magistrate: 'Ask him his name.'

Man, shouting in mock-German: 'VOT IS YOUR NAME?'

They were both jailed.

And even cases that never come to court can go eccentrically. For instance, a motorist in a London suburb was snapped by a speed camera and police sent him the usual picture of his car speeding and a demand for £60. The motorist sent them a photograph of £60 in notes. However, he paid up pretty quick when police replied with a picture of handcuffs.

We cross to the church of **St Sepulchre's**, an apparently meaningless name and a suitably gloomy church for one so associated with premature doom. The church still has a bell which would be rung outside the cell of the condemned at midnight before they were hanged (just in case they were trying to grab some sleep). On the morning of the execution, prisoners were given a nosegay and a blessing by the priest as they passed on the start of their terrible journey to Tyburn. I fancy a fast horse and a pair of pistols would have been a lot more welcome.

By the way, get a good look at the gilded statue of Justice on top of the Old Bailey from here. Yes, she carries a balance of justice and the sword of retribution (fat chance nowadays) in either hand, but she is not blindfolded as nearly everyone seems to think, including some of the dafter judges working below her (see box above).

St Sepulchre's faces the problem that there was no such saint; its name is actually an abbreviation of St Edward and the Holy Sepulchre. St Teddy's would have done as well. It's far older than the Wren churches we pass (and therefore not as handsome), being a Saxon church from the three-figure dates and having been last rebuilt in 1450. It's interesting to Americans because of its connections with Captain John Smith and his saviour, Pocahontas (see page 143).

SMITHFIELD: BEEF ENCOUNTER OR BOEUF OF A NATION, PLUS STONKING BREAKFASTS, TESTICLES AND SHAKESPEARE IN LOVE We turn right down **Snow Hill** beyond the church, past Snow Hill police station which was once

the rowdy Saracen's Head pub. Drunken toffs used to roll down Snow Hill in barrels for sport in the 19th century, and the steepness of the road as an approach to the City explains why someone thought the Holborn Viaduct a good idea. It was here that at the Duke of Wellington's funeral in 1852, the horses slipped on the wet cobbles and couldn't haul the enormous 12-ton funeral carriage manufactured out of the metal from French guns captured at the Battle of Waterloo, his greatest victory.

His escort of soldiers took hold of ropes and assisted the vast iron juggernaut, which may still be seen at the Duke's country seat, Stratfield Saye in Hampshire, up the hill to St Paul's so he could be buried near Nelson, the other great hero of the Napoleonic Wars. The weather was suitably awful for a grief-stricken nation and Wellington's hearse had already overturned in the floods – the 'Wellington flood' it was known as locally – at Maidenhead on its way to St Paul's. It was the only maidenhead the Duke had ever had much trouble getting past, the soldiers' joke went. The slippage on Snow Hill is why state funerals since, such as Winston Churchill's wonderful one in 1965, have included servicemen pulling the hearse on ropes. Thus are barmy British traditions made.

Turn right into **Smithfield Street** halfway down Snow Hill and we rapidly approach the giant Victorian meat market that dominates the area. Of all the great London wholesale markets, such as Covent Garden and Billingsgate, this is the only one that has stayed put in its splendid setting.

Just like those other markets, this one is at its busiest at about 6am. Pubs such as the **New Market** on the right, or the **Fox & Anchor** at the far corner, are thrumming in the early morning and don't follow normal licensing hours. In fact many a top-hatted heartless toff has ended up here after a night ravishing innocent chambermaids (or whatever they do) because you can get a damn good breakfast and a drink before dawn. The New Market serves a spanking breakfast indeed for around a fiver, a bloody marvellous one for a little more, and an insanely good one for about £30 for two including champagne (must be those heartless toffs again). Just don't be heard to ask for the vegetarian option unless you want 400 cleaver-carrying butchers to take offence.

Of course there are other pubs all round the market as we come into the open space known as **West Smithfield**, with glorious names such as **The Bishop's Finger** (don't ask, but the Shepherd Neame is a good pint) or **the Butcher's Hook & Cleaver** (ditto the Fuller's). I wonder if young women being eyed up by

top left   On a cathedral scale, the astounding Swaminarayan Temple, with its shining white pinnacles, has put the suburb of Neasden on the map — somewhere east of Mumbai, by the look of it (BV) page 115

top right   This Russian Orthodox onion-domed cathedral provides a startling sight from the A4 at Chiswick. All we need now is a lot more snow, decent vodka and a sledge to Heathrow being chased by wolves (BV) page 116

bottom left   'St Ghastly Grim' in the City is in fact St Olave's near Tower Hill (BV) page 64

bottom right   Just yards from Oxford Street is the surprisingly tranquil Fo Kuang Temple. Please ask permission and remove shoes to view the splendid interior (BV) page 117

above   Some funky graffiti on the wall of a Camden carwash (CH)

below   The surreal sculpture *Out of Order* by David Mach sits in Old London Road, Kingston. It's what you feel like doing when the umpteenth phone box has swallowed your 30p for no service... (BV)

top — Strange Fruit is a performing-arts company whose exhibitions include people swaying on 4m-high poles (as here in Docklands) or emerging from illuminated orbs: wacky, but brilliant (SF)

right — Chiho Aoshima's painting of anthropomorphic skyscrapers entitled *City Glow, Mountain Whisper* gives commuters at Gloucester Road something to look at other than their papers (JR)

below — Salvador Dalí's sculpture *Nobility of Time* in front of the London Eye (JR)

top left Deadline gone on an art-deco clock on a former newspaper building in Fleet Street (BV)

top right Surely this little 'gravestone' in Kensington Gardens gave J M Barrie the idea for Peter Pan. But what does the stone really mean? (BV) page 101

below Does Frying Pan Alley's name derive from the custom of ironmongers to hang a frying pan outside their shop as a means of attracting business? Theories on a postcard please. (JR) page 79

top left   A spooky monk stares down from the London Dungeon at London Bridge, always visible from afar by its queue. Actually London has plenty of genuine cemeteries, catacombs and murder sites for the more courageous to explore, as detailed in this book (BV)

top right   Self-described 'art terrorist' Banksy likes to try the councils' patience : in this case, by creating a designated graffiti area (CH)

bottom   Lanterns for sale at Greenwich's fabulous but pricey market (BoV/DT)

top What would really cheer up grey commuters trudging to the station in rainy London? I know, how about a sculpture of grey commuters trudging to the station in rainy London? *Rush Hour*, by George Segal (1987), near Liverpool Street Station (BV)

left The metal men at Royal Arsenal will certainly confuse archaeologists in years to come CH)

top left   Dale Chihuly's 30ft-high blown-glass chandelier is suspended over the entrance to the Victoria and Albert Museum, and probably makes visitors wonder if someone slipped something in their tea before they arrived (JR)

top right   These cast-iron Victorian lamp posts along Embankment were adorned with sculptures of sturgeon, though you won't find many of those in the Thames today (JR)

bottom   A small slice of Egypt on Embankment: these bronze sphinxes lie either side of Cleopatra's Needle, a 3000-year-old obelisk brought to London in the nineteenth century (CH)

London's pubs offer all manner of eccentricities:

top left   The wedge-shaped Black Friar, on the site of a Dominican priory until the mid-16th century (JR) page 206

top right   Dirty Dick's, Bishopsgate, named after a man who became so distraught after the death of his bride-to-be that he forsook tidiness for ever (JR) page 152

bottom left   The Cutty Sark in Greenwich, whose name is written big enough for sailors to spot from the Thames (BV) page 246

bottom right   The Thames-side Barmy Arms, Twickenham (BV) the blokes in these Smithfield pubs have ever said: 'This place is just a flaming meat market.'

West Smithfield is certainly worth a stroll round (and includes excellent public bogs). In the far right corner, next to the imposing and surprisingly original entrance to **Bart's Hospital**, is the half-timbered entrance to **St Bartholomew the Great** (as opposed to the nearby St Bartholomew the Lesser). Not only is the medieval entrance a gem, but the church itself is really special and well worth including, as the makers of the hit movies *Shakespeare in Love* and *Four Weddings and a Funeral* agreed, with crucial scenes set here.

The curve of the romanesque arches is unusual and striking, and elsewhere I mention the rebus, or visual pun, in the overlooking oriel window, which has a crossbow *bolt* through a barrel, or *tun* as they were called in those days – a memorial to *Bolton*. William Bolton was the last prior of the order of monks here and this same rebus can be seen on a house in Canonbury near Islington, named because it belonged to the canons of St Bartholomew.

Other treasures in this wonderful building include the eccentric banner of the 'Worshipful Company of the Art or Mistery of Butchers of the City of London' (oh to be a member of such a grand organisation), which depicts their arms supported by a particularly well-endowed pair of bulls, a very unlikely angel-bull and a pig's head and a pair of cleavers. A vegetarian's nightmare, no doubt, but splendid too.

(As we're in the Fleet Street area, I must tell you of the funny story of a particularly prudish newspaper which would never show a white woman's nipple – tribal types were all right – or pubic hair or anything like that. The paper once published a picture of a West Country prize bull but a nervous executive ordered that the beast's enormous wedding tackle be cut out of the picture. As a result the outraged farmer sued the b★★★★★★s off them, as his bull's income depended on that equipment being in full working order.)

Also in St Bart's, I'd recommend the memorial to Edward Cooke, who died in 1652 aged just 37, for its fine bit of tombstone doggerel:

Unluce your briny floods, what can ye keepe
Your eyes from teares, & see the marble weepe.
Burst out for shame: or if yee find noe vent
For teares, yet stay, and see the stones relent.

Back out into Smithfield, which the historians tell us was probably 'smooth field' originally. It was the biggest open space near the City and used for jousting, the famed Bartholomew Fair (banned in 1850 because of public rowdiness – so much for Victorian standards) and for public executions before Tyburn and Newgate took their turn. As I recount in the crime and punishment section, here 'Bloody' Mary burned a good few Protestants in her brief attempt to force England back into Roman Catholicism, a poisoner was slowly boiled to death and William Wallace, or Braveheart played by Mel Gibson as Hollywood has it, was hanged, drawn and quartered. They also ripped his testicles off. Nothing personal, guv, just doing my job. Monuments in the frontage of Bart's hospital tell of these bloody events.

Talking of blood, back to Smithfield Market. Before we plunge through the central Grand Avenue opposite, take a look at the fearsome **City griffins** perched high above the entrance. They guard the City as surely as nine invisible Chinese dragons guard Kowloon, but we prefer ours visibly terrifying – more fang showy than feng shui.

Unless you're here early in the morning, this vast Crystal Palace-like cathedral to carnage will be all quiet. A very different kind of slaughter is remembered on the fine war memorial to Smithfield men on the right.

Crossing Charterhouse Street at the bottom and passing the Hope pub, we move into **Cowcross Street** (they were driven through here to Smithfield on the hoof) and it's worth noting first the **Castle** pub on the right with its three different signs. One shows a cockfight, another the Tower of London, and the last depicts three golden balls signifying, unexpectedly, a pawnbrokers. There's a strange story behind this.

King George IV, the deeply unpleasant and greedy monarch whom we will meet in Hammersmith (page 262), was enjoying a night out cock-fighting (hence the cockfight sign) in a nearby cockpit when he ran out of money. So the king went into the pub and asked the landlord to pawn his gold pocket-watch and give him some cash. The landlord, bold as brass, said he could do so only if he had a pawnbroker's licence. The king granted him one then and there (hence the golden balls) and the landlord claimed to be the only person licensed as a publican and a pawnbroker. They prefer money for a pint nowadays, however. The Tower sign refers to the pub's official name, the Castle.

Another oddity worth a look, further down on the right, is the deeply eccentric brickwork above the Pizza Express on the right. Superb.

And talking of expresses, here is **Farringdon Station** which we would have reached in two minutes if we'd taken the Thameslink train from Blackfriars under Smithfield. Oddly, if we'd taken the Circle Line between these two it would have been about as slow as walking with eight stops and according to the misleading Tube map we would have crossed London.

Here we cross Farringdon Road – the course of the Fleet river under our feet – and Holborn Viaduct is down to our left. We go straight up **Greville Street** (noting the sign of the One Tun pub on the right confirming my earlier remark about barrels and crossbow bolts).

You'd thought we'd left all the blood and gore behind, but on the left is the **Bleeding Heart Tavern** and down through the yard to the left, one of the hardest restaurants to find in London, the **Bleeding Heart Yard**. As I recount in the section on murders (page 19), this was the scene of a most gruesome killing recalled by Dickens, involving the 17th-century society beauty Elizabeth Hatton (a big name round here). The lady was found here 'torn limb from limb with her heart still pumping blood on to the cobblestones'. Black pudding, anyone?

PAST THE NARNIAN LAMPPOST Carrying on up Greville Street, we turn left into Hatton Garden. Talk about diamond geezers, this place sparkles from end to end, with enough diamonds and gold to keep hundreds of Elizabeth Taylors in sparklers. Along with Amsterdam, it's a world centre in diamond dealing and it's hard to find a shop that isn't flogging gems or gold.

But there's another gem of a pub tucked away near here, and you'll never find it on your own. You need a bit of Narnian magic, for in some ways it is in a different land. The wonderful Narnia stories of C S Lewis, you may recall, hinge on the strange fact that when the children pass a strange, wonky lamppost in the forest, they are crossing from one reality to another, from fir trees to fur coats in the wardrobe or back again. And what do we see on the pavement ahead of us near the end of Hatton Garden but a wonky lamppost? Plunge into the unpromising gloomy alleyway to the left and we find a pub, and a very singular pub, the **Old Mitre**.

Ignore the actually fascinating pub for a moment and come out at the other end of the path in **Ely Place**. This was the residence of the Bishops of Ely, and therefore part of Cambridgeshire. Hence the lodge and the gates at the end of the road to the right and, if you don't believe me, the lack of an EC1 district number on the street names, because they don't have district numbers in soggy Cambridgeshire.

Many a petty pickpocket has escaped the clutches of the law down these passageways because once behind these gates you were no longer in London.

The pub was built in 1546 by Bishop Goodrich, although it was completely rebuilt in 1772. In the small bar there is a fragment of cherry tree that formerly grew here which apparently has much significance.

For one thing, the tree formed the original boundary between the bishop's garden and the garden of Sir Christopher Hatton – yes, as in Hatton Garden and as in bleeding heart ripped out. As a young girl, Queen Elizabeth I danced around this tree while having an affair with Sir Christopher. Sir Christopher was still a favourite of hers when she became queen, so when he coveted the Bishop of Ely's house and gardens, and the bishop refused to sell, the queen intervened. She threatened to defrock him if he did not sell up, so a deal was done for ten quid, ten carts of hay and a red rose every year. Seems reasonable. (More on this pub, page 150)

A relic of the former bishop's palace is the chapel and crypt of **St Ethelreda's**, now a Roman Catholic place of worship. Funny thing about Catholics, they can always look at an Anglican church from before the 1530s and say, 'Oh yes, that was one of ours' and it's hard to argue with them.

Leaving Ely Place at its only exit into **Holborn Circus**, we cross Charterhouse Street (again) and pause to look left along the top of Holborn Viaduct (I only say this to help you get your bearings – St Sepulchre's is by the trees down on the left and we're heading south, back to Fleet Street). We cross the road, with the statue of Prince Albert to our right and pass the church, **St Andrew's**, on our left. This one didn't burn down in the Great Fire which stopped near here but Wren did it up anyway (he was like that).

Note that the bottom of the church tower features a blue boy and blue girl in statues. These are surprisingly common all over London and denoted a school. I mean, if they needed to go to school there was no point sticking up a sign saying 'School', was there, because they couldn't read! These are far more charming and follow in the illiterate tradition which saw, for example, a wooden boot hanging outside a bootmakers.

This road, St Andrew's Street, rapidly becomes **Shoe Lane**. The road soon sloping off to the left is St Bride's Street and leads back to Ludgate Circus, but we go on down Shoe Lane noting the Cartoonist pub on the right and enter a kind of tunnel into what was, until around 15 years ago, the heart of newspaperland.

RATTED JOURNALISTS AND THEIR WATERING HOLES As you come out into Fleet Street the *Daily Express* used to stand on your left with, bizarrely, the *Standard* upstairs somewhere even though it was owned for many years by the *Express's* greatest enemy, the *Daily Mail*. On your right was the *Daily Telegraph*. Opposite was Reuters and the Press Association, and on the other side of the road were narrow lanes hemming in the *Sun* and the *News of the World*, as well as the *Mail*. No wonder, as I describe in the box on newspapers, the place was seething with activity come late evening.

Luckily, someone has preserved the quite amazing lobby of the **Express** building, nicknamed the 'Black Lubyanka' after the Moscow prison, and you must take a few steps to your left to see this utterly extraordinary art deco black-and-chrome fest through the front windows. On reaching the end of the Express building, you will be able to see Wren's elaborate tower of the journalists' church, **St Bride's**.

16

In films, it is Hollywood. In food and fashion, it used to be Paris. In newspapers, the best place in the world to work is Fleet Street, meaning the London daily press which used to occupy that road, but is now scattered around the city. Your Australian reporter, your Canadian photographer, your South African sub-editor all dream of working here – or they do if they're any good.

Nowhere else in the English-speaking world is there the cut-throat competition of a dozen or so dailies slogging it out.

Newspaper editors and proprietors tend to become strange because they have absolute power. They can build up and destroy at a whim the lives of the hundreds of people who work for them, and can often do the same for the characters in national life. They can call on huge resources, spending – and losing – millions of pounds if they get it wrong.

In among the cut and thrust of Fleet Street, there was one proprietor who instantly sacked everyone on one side of the central newsroom carpet in order to make savings. He didn't care if they were any good or not. There was the tyrannical *Express* owner, the Canadian, **Beaverbrook**, who, when he was called by an editor who had displeased him, pretended not to know him. 'You know, I'm the Editor,' the confused man explained. To which Beaverbrook retorted: 'You were,' and slammed the phone down.

If Beaverbrook's Rolls-Royce was held up for a few moments, he would phone his editor and demand a hard-hitting leading article on the necessity for a new underpass on the A3, and it would be in the first edition.

A newspaper boss's abuse of power can sometimes backfire, however. **Cap'n Bob Maxwell**, tyrannical and crooked giant that he was, was apt to make the odd mistake while he controlled the *Daily Mirror*. He was once overheard in the Old Mitre pub (see page 178) making some arbitrary rule banning the wearing of jeans on one floor of the *Mirror* building. One day, he was striding through the building smoking his fat cigar when he spotted an unfortunate who had not heard of this rule. 'Hey, you! Didn't you hear I've banned jeans on this floor?' He peeled a bundle of £50 notes from the fat wad he always carried and gave a pile estimated at £5,000–£10,000 to the humbled young man. 'Now f*** off and don't come back!' The man left without a word. All very impressive and macho. Except the 'sacked' man could be seen dancing a jig in the street below. He didn't even work for the *Mirror* but was merely delivering a message.

Evelyn's Waugh's wonderful comedy about Fleet Street, *Scoop*, revolves around the story of two writers on the same paper with the same name – a gentle, nature-notes writer from a remote village and a hard-bitten war reporter – whose assignments become mixed up and the nature guy gets sent to some inexplicable war in Africa. Far-fetched?

Just a few years ago, a new editor was put in charge of the troubled *Daily Express* and in the ritual blood-letting that takes place on such occasions, one hapless hack was summoned to the managing editor's office, given a fat cheque and booted out of the

Turn around and go back up this north side of Fleet Street, past Shoe Lane and under the extravagant art deco clock of the old *Daily Telegraph* (why some prat has taken the name of the paper out I don't know, it's obviously made for it).

We should pay our respects to the creator of the first English dictionary in 1775, Dr Johnson, if only by popping into the legendary **Cheshire Cheese** pub, which is not, of course, up Cheshire Court but up Wine Office Court. This is a labyrinth of a building, with more bars and private dining rooms and more levels than you'd ever guess from the outside. Even after many visits and private dinners here, I still find new bits. Or maybe because of the visits, I've forgotten them.

door. In Fleet Street you know it might happen any day, so anyone remotely employable banks the cheque, takes a few days off and starts work elsewhere.

This individual was relaxing in his garden deck-chair the next day when the phone went. It was the normally mild-mannered *Express* editor. 'Where the hell are you?' he thundered.

'At home, sunning myself, because you sacked me.'

'No I didn't. Now get into the office right away, we need you.'

It transpired, as life imitates art, that there was someone else of the same name who should have been sacked.

Another colourful Fleet Street boss of the late 20th century was *Sun* editor **Kelvin MacKenzie**, who, when judged by newspaper sales, was the greatest of his era. To journalists, the brilliant but eccentric MacKenzie was feared and revered equally in the great tradition of barmy but witty British press barons and editors. He sacked an astrologer with a letter beginning: 'As you already know ...'; he also sacked the entire showbiz department, followed shortly by the replacements, as he was still cross.

People generally judge newspapers harshly. My favourite quotation is Adlai Stevenson: 'An editor is one who separates the wheat from the chaff, and prints the chaff.'

In the age before computers made lunchtime drinking impossible, boozing was de rigueur. You couldn't get a job, or your stories, without it, and Fleet Street hacks knew all the bars where after-hours drinking was rife.

The drink-related tales of old Fleet Street are endless. Veteran columnist **Keith Waterhouse**, creator of the inimitable *Billy Liar*, recalls taking the ashes of a departed colleague in a cardboard box for a last pub crawl – 'it's what he would have wanted' being the refrain on such occasions. The rainy evening wore on, and on, as every watering hole was visited. Eventually, standing in Fleet Street in the rain, someone noticed that the bag and cardboard box containing the ashes was sodden, and the remains of the departed were swirling down the gutter. 'It's what he would have wanted,' they choloused.

Cue for two quotes, a century apart, about the gutter press:

Journalists belong in the gutter because that is where the ruling classes throw their guilty secrets.
Writer Gerald Priestland (died 1991)

We are all in the gutter, but some of us are looking at the stars.
Oscar Wilde, in *Lady Windermere's Fan* (1892)

There's always been a Dr Johnson legend based here, with his chair and even his chipped soup bowl available to the gullible to lap from. Actually there's no record of his ever having been here, but there is to his having visited nearly every other old pub within five miles.

One must assume that as this was his 'local', he didn't bother to mention it. Or it could be the old Fleet Street advice: 'When the facts conflict with the legend, print the legend.'

Johnson was the smart aleck who thought up the risible idea that if you didn't know how to spell a word, you could look it up in a book where you needed to know how to spell it to find it. Of course, it was easy for him as none of the spellings had been fixed yet – look at the Americans, for example.

He was scathingly funny about the Scottishness of his companion Boswell (and I write as part-Scot and not at all English by blood). For example: 'The noblest prospect which a Scotchman ever sees, is the high road which leads him to England.' Or 'Much may be made of a Scotsman, if caught young.' And an entry in his dictionary for the word 'oats' reads: 'A grain, which in England is generally given to horses, but in Scotland supports the people.'

He wasn't vain about his work, as two further entries make clear:

Dull To make dictionaries is dull work.
Lexicographer A writer of dictionaries, a harmless drudge.

The most relevant quotation for this book is one I reluctantly drag out, because you must know it: 'When a man is tired of London, he is tired of life.'

Dr Johnson's House is accessible a few steps further up Fleet Street, through Hind Court to Gough Square, and here we see a statue to Dr Johnson's great companion – no, not Boswell, but **Hodge** his cat. Johnson's house, a museum to the great lexicographer and boozer, is opposite. Turning left in front of the house brings you through Johnson's Court back into Fleet Street, where we turn right.

You will have noticed that although the journalists have scattered from here, the lawyers – held in a similar regard by the public – are thick on the ground, the bundles of documents tied up with ribbon (how quaint) being hurried back and forth. The two breeds would meet at legendary venues such as **El Vino's**, which we'll cross to opposite, perhaps to discuss the day's events at the Old Bailey or the Royal Courts of Justice at the top of Fleet Street (The High Court). It wouldn't admit women at all until recent years and I remember coming a cropper of its 'no tie, no drink rule'. The barman lent me one.

The press's top columnists – or calumnists – would bore the pants off each other while getting seriously ratted, go back to the office, abuse their underlings, write a load of piffle and fall asleep. Of course, it didn't always read like piffle by the time it got in the paper, but you get the idea. In fact one admired as sublime professionals those who could write an almost meaningful column which would move the readers to tears while almost incoherent with alcohol, but the need to operate computers has put an end to all that daytime drinking. Now things are far more civilised. And women are admitted.

GIANTS, A SNARLING GRIFFIN AND THE WAY TO A DIFFERENT WORLD Going on up Fleet Street, don't go too fast. Look left for the many picturesque courtyards of the legal profession whose patch this now is, such as Old Mitre Court, and upwards at the fascinating clutter on the buildings, which Londoners hurrying by will miss. For example, the golden bottle hung high as the sign of Hoare's Bank, or the plaque marking the site of the Devil's Tavern.

Across the road we get an excellent view of the tremendous tower of **St Dunstan's-in-the-West** and the two giants which, although 18th-century, still bong their bells on the hour. To the right of them is a fine figure of Mary Queen of Scots (head not yet chopped off) and beyond them a reminder of Fleet Street's newspaper glory days with the mosaic titles of D C Thomson's newspapers, endowed with names such as *People's Friend*. But this Dundee-based publisher should include its far more famous – and more interesting – publications, children's comics the *Beano* and the *Dandy*.

On the left, before the arch at the bottom of Chancery Lane and up some stairs, is an extraordinary little museum: **Prince Henry's room**. It is free, it's small (and therefore quick) and it tells some amazing stories. Prince Henry was the eldest son of James I, hence the Prince of Wales feathers and Duchy of Cornwall crest in the stained-glass window, and the 'PH' in the plaster ceiling. This was the promising prince's London office, as it were, and had he not died aged 18, the troublesome Charles I would not have come to the throne and there may have been no civil war. The best king we never had, some say. But the interest is as much in the room itself, with its fine Jacobean plaster ceiling and original panelling, because the Great Fire of London didn't quite reach this far. Everything east of here is necessarily younger – a change of wind saved this house.

This quirky little museum is open only 11.00–14.00 and is actually used as part of a legal office the rest of the time. I was delighted to find the guide on duty was former Fleet Street printer, Len Hall. He told me how this ancient room had survived another conflagration and many other bizarre changes.

> After Prince Henry's death the building was a pub and a coffee shop. Eventually, by the early 19th century, it was Mother Salmon's Waxworks. Dickens has Little Nell come here for work after the Old Curiosity Shop closes in the book.
>
> The waxworks had huge advertising hoardings falsely claiming it to be a former royal palace, but also offering haircuts for 6d!

At length the London County Council bought the derelict building for £1,000, intending to demolish it. They pulled down the Waxworks frontage and were amazed – hey presto! – to find an entire Jacobean frontage behind. Len says:

> I was a messenger boy during the 1940s Blitz, and three hundred tons of high explosive fell in this area. So much was flattened, Fleet Street workers used the bomb sites for car parks for years afterwards. Yet again this little room escaped, and the ceiling didn't fall in the huge shocks – I think the horsehair and plaster mix makes it so strong.

On up Fleet Street just a little more to where the High Court's massive bulk becomes visible on the right and you see the snarling black griffin of the City of London in the centre of the road. This was the site of the **Temple Bar**, Wren's ceremonial entrance to the City. The griffin, guardian of the city, is spectacularly aggressive but don't miss the amazingly detailed frieze along the side of the monument facing this pavement (see box on page 186 for more).

On the left, another gem not to be missed is the marvellous marbled foyer of Lloyds bank – it's insane, frankly. What was the architect on? LSD?

Ahead in the distance, in the middle of the road, lies **St Clement Danes** church with its fascinating oranges and lemons history (see page 104). There are public toilets in the middle of the road there too, if you need them.

But we go left down **Devereux Court**, a footpath, to visit the startlingly different world that is the **Middle Temple**, an ancient Inn of Court named after the Knights Templars who held sway round here until they were suppressed. We zigzag along the court past more pubs until the end where we turn left into the

The atmosphere in the old Fleet Street was unique, as was the atmosphere at the old Covent Garden market, and now the great newspapers have left the street, I'll have to conjure it up for you.

The newspapers were like massive warships. During the day, things were quiet as ammunition supplies – giant reels of paper – were hoisted aboard to fill the magazines for the coming battle. As day turned to night, things became increasingly frenetic as reporters and photographers rushed back aboard from their assignments. Sub-editors, the midshipmen of newspapers, who until now had had a fairly relaxed day, reported to their battle stations as things began to hum. The wire machines chattered relentlessly with intelligence from every corner of the globe. Pictures were coming in from all quarters, some by wire, some dripping wet from the darkroom.

Up on the bridge – as it were – the key officers planned the battle. Which way would the enemy – the other papers – go? Would they lead with so and so's story? Would they obey influential Mr X's pleas to hush up such-and-such an indiscretion? The spies in the enemy flagships were approached: did they have a whopper to blow the rest of Fleet Street out of the water? If so, a cunning paper would produce a dummy first edition with a boring story on the front, make sure the agents of all the other papers had got a paper, and then bring the big guns to bear, printing a massive scoop in the second edition. The hapless rivals would sink with all hands, trapped in this carefully-sown minefield, befuddled by the enemy's smokescreen.

Down in the bowels of the building, the massive print works, shoe-horned into the ground floors and cellars of these medieval building plots, were the equivalent of the engineers and stokers – the blue-overalled print workers. They would be tending their massive, gleaming machines, oiling and inking, ready for the bell that indicated full steam ahead.

On another floor, the gun deck, as it were, hot metal typesetters would be working full tilt in the deafening row of the composing room. They produced metal lines on Linotype machines and these were rapidly clamped together by 'comps' with picture blocks and headlines.

A skilled sub-editor would read the text back-to-front, and possibly upside down,

---

Middle Temple. Note the building on its left at the corner has anchors and SCD on it, to mark the boundaries of St Clement's parish – St Clement having been tied to an anchor and drowned. We enter the Temple on sufferance, it not being a public right of way, but as the notices explain if we don't bring dogs or make a noise the porters won't haul us out.

To the right is a scene a million miles from the hubbub of Fleet Street. A fountain restfully tinkles in a circular pool beneath beautiful trees, a scene marked by Dickens in *Martin Chuzzlewit*, perhaps his best work (I still can't decide on that). Rest on the curved benches or walk on to the left past the hall (note the lamb and flag, the temple's emblem, all over the place) and across the road into the arch, past another garden, up the steps and through some cloisters into a square. Here is the strange, circular **Temple church** (the original part) of the medieval Knights Templars, and inside you will find their ancient burial effigies, glowing in the light from stained-glass windows as they have for so many centuries since they returned from the Crusades. Outside, a sculpture of a couple of knights is somewhat newer – it dates from 2000. (More on that church, page 157).

MONKS, GHOSTS, SKULLS AND THE LAWLESS ALSATIA Leaving the church door and going left we progress into the huge space that is **King's Bench Walk**, which feels trying to catch any cock-ups. A story that was too short was 'leaded', not as today with a computer instantly spacing out the lines a bit more, but with a skilled compositor sliding ultra-thin bits of lead between the lines so fast you couldn't see his fingers move.

A bell sounded and, just as in the old black and white films, the mighty presses began to whirr, slowly at first, then gathering speed until the pages were just a blur. Upstairs, in the 'tween decks, where reporters and sub-editors worked, you could feel the whole building lurch when the presses started. A humming vibration grew as the machines ran faster and faster.

When a late story broke that really mattered, bells would ring, lights flash, the presses would be stopped, the whole place would lurch and hurrying crews of writers, sub-editors, comps and printers would rapidly make good the damage – as in a warship which has taken a hit. The top brass would pace the deck nervously until that reassuring hum of the engines meant the moment of sudden vulnerability had passed.

Outside in the tiny streets such as Bouverie Street, Tudor Street, and Shoe Lane, hundreds of vans in rival liveries would push and jostle for space, like sampans and lighters eager for trade round a great ship in Hong Kong harbour. The presses disgorged thousands, nay millions, of bundled papers right on to the narrow pavement.

The van drivers, having cut up the rivals in their own queues as many times as possible with the usual cockney insults, would tear off up Farringdon Road, racing the other companies' vans at hell-for-leather speeds, to Euston, King's Cross and St Pancras and the other great railway stations where long trains of vans stood behind a simmering express engine. Tipsy lords and fur-coated ladies heading for the sleeping cars of the Scottish night trains after a night at a West End show would try to catch a glimpse of the next day's headlines.

Soon doors slammed, the platform-end signal clanged upwards, whistles blew and the monstrous snorting locomotives sprinted faster and faster into the night, towards thousands of darkened towns and villages where newsagents and paperboys slept soundly, ready for the final link in the chain.

At least, that was how it was supposed to work.

more like a donnish old university or cathedral close than a part of central London. Angle to the right somewhat to find the gap in the houses marked 'No Exit' (for cars) and proceed past the porter's lodge and through an arch into **Tudor Street**.

We are now nearing the end of this walk and back in the former newspaper territory, the 'Lost Valley of the Inkers'. Bouverie Street, next on the left, was the home of the *Sun* and the *News of the World*, and *Punch* before that. It is named after the family that owned all this land before it was built up. We go straight down Tudor Street (named because Henry VIII grabbed some of this land when he destroyed the monasteries) but pause at the corner of **Whitefriars Street**. There's just one more story, of monks and ghosts.

A few steps up Whitefriars Street (what with Carmelite Street, we are obviously in monastic territory once more) is the **Harrow** pub, haunted by the ghost of a tailor whose workshop was absorbed by the pub (his treadle machine can be heard running sometimes, I'm told). It was certainly haunted by journalists from the old *Daily Mail* opposite, who found they could drink there way past the licensed hours in the old days.

Opposite, up some steps, is Ashentree Court where the only remaining part of the medieval Whitefriars monastery, a vaulted cellar, remains in the basement of a modern office block. You can look at the outside by following the steps or go round

Wren's arch stood here where the snarling griffin sculpture now stands from 1672 to 1878, a splendid entrance to the City, sometimes adorned with traitors' and murderers' rotting heads or other body parts on its spikes. This arch replaced an earlier wooden structure – a literal wooden bar at one point. As the Victorian City boomed, the narrow arch became hopelessly constricting for traffic.

Here's Dickens on the Temple Bar in *Bleak House*:

> The raw afternoon is rawest, and the dense fog is densest, and the muddy streets are muddiest, near that leaden-headed old obstruction, appropriate ornament for the threshold of a leaden-headed old corporation: Temple Bar.

For him it perfectly symbolised the obstructiveness, sloth, greed and self-interest of the legal system. Nothing like today, then…

So in 1878 it was taken down, stored in pieces and later moved to Theobald's Park in Hertfordshire, where it served as a grand gate for a brewery magnate's country estate for a while, then was forgotten and left to moulder in woodland, neglected and vandalised.

Finally, in 2004, after more than a century in exile and a £3 million restoration, it was brought back to the City and rebuilt next to St Paul's cathedral, where it can be seen – the last gate of the city of London, although in the wrong place – and even hired as a banqueting venue. The statuary has been restored, although 95 per cent of the original stonework has been saved, so it is not a mere replica.

Meanwhile, the Temple Bar in Fleet Street still exists as a concept, and has a meaning. A reigning monarch must still halt here, thus acknowledging the hard-won independence of the City, and is given a sword by the Lord Mayor and granted the freedom to enter the City.

to the front and demand to see the interior. (For how this vault once gave hardened Fleet Street hacks a shock, see page 114.)

The crypt had been forgotten about for a few hundred years after the destruction of the monasteries which covered the area before Henry VIII's time. Then in 1867 someone rediscovered the lost crypt, a damp, decaying haunt of rats and skulls. It was used as a coal cellar for 30 years but in the 20th century was conserved. Eventually it was lifted out in a cradle while foundations were dug for the new office block to be built here and returned intact.

The few stones also relate a tale of sanctuary, for after the monastery disappeared in the 16th century the right of sanctuary from the law remained. It was much abused by criminals, and the area – called Alsatia, after the lawless borderland between France and Germany – became a lawless den of narrow streets, brothels and drinking dens where law officers would not dare enter. That the teeming refuge of criminals, prostitutes and other low life stood next to the Temple, citadel of the law, was ironic indeed, and fights ensued between the two communities, especially when the lawyers sought to brick up the arch at the end of Tudor Street we have just come through. After one particularly bad fight, the Alsatians' leader, Captain Francis White, was hanged here in Fleet Street. So dense were the crowds that you could walk across Fleet Street on the shoulders of onlookers. The sanctuaries were suppressed by Parliament in 1693, just as the monasteries had been a century and a half earlier.

Well, all this blood and history is exhausting, so it's down to the end of Tudor Street and turn right for **Blackfriars** station, or a well-deserved drink at the Black Friar with its own unmissable interior (both detailed on page 206).

17

Soho

Just as the snobbish centre of London's wealthy classes has been gradually moving westwards over the centuries, to get away from proles and pollution and nearer to the Kensington court, so the centre of vice and sleaze has been tracking northwest. From Elizabethan Southwark to 18th-century Covent Garden (which the upper classes had just left, going towards Mayfair) it had reached Soho by the 20th century and King's Cross by the 21st. At this rate, by the 25th century posh Radlett in Hertfordshire will be the home of all-night strip joints, transvestite dens and table dancing. Can't wait.

But of all these disreputable places it is Soho that has retained its agreeable, raffish quality. It has somehow maintained the cosy building height typical of scruffy poverty without imitating the massive tower blocks or pompous stuccoed terraces which surround it. Indeed, it is a refreshing antidote to those neighbouring districts. Intellectually, it is the closest thing London has to the Left Bank or Greenwich Village.

The vice and drugs are still here, but are not nearly as prominent as during the fifties, when gangs were rampant. Instead of shootings, garish neon signs offering rip-off sex shows are about as threatening as it gets. And of course where Soho was once unique in offering such services (remember the famous double entendre cards in corner shops – 'French lessons', 'large chest for sale', 'young lady requires challenging position', 'stocks and bonds advisor' and no, I'm not going to decode them for you), today just about everywhere in Europe except frumpy Frinton has such sleaze. Far less subtle cards drop out of phone boxes in the most hoity-toity districts of London.

So Soho has gone on its own unsavoury way, reinventing itself occasionally. Jazz clubs and restaurants come and go, but musically the area has always been at the leading edge. Rock and roll bands have, since the fifties, lived and died in venues such as the Marquee Club in Wardour Street, the 2is in Old Compton Street, or the hot 'n' sweaty 100 Club in Oxford Street. Jazz veteran George Melly, remembering Soho in the atmosphere of post-war austerity, said: 'Soho was like another land, full of eccentric drunks. I discovered Soho when I was in the navy – sailors were very welcome.' The sixties saw the amazing outbreak at the now-vanished UFO Club in nearby Tottenham Court Road, with Pink Floyd, Arthur Brown, Fairport Convention and Procul Harem all appearing here within 12 months. Later the emergence of punk saw Poly Styrene strutting her stuff here. Doubtless today there's someone who's going to be huge playing somewhere in Soho, unknown to all but a few insiders.

The film and TV industry has taken root in Wardour Street, where the many thriving independent production companies are based. Whether it's a new drama series, an independent movie or the sexually deviant TV show Eurotrash, it will have been thrashed out in Wardour Street. Equally Soho has been a haunt for interesting literary types – the more Bohemian ones at any rate – for a hundred years. Now you can hardly move without stepping on a publisher, independent film-maker or whatever. So although the area – named after a hunting call in what were wild woods, and now better known for hunting two-legged quarry, as I remark elsewhere – has a charm and a history well worth exploring, it is still alive, humming and free from the cloying clutches of the heritage industry.

The area is bounded by commercial Oxford Street to the north, elegant Regent Street to the west, theatreland's Shaftesbury Avenue to the south and bookish Charing Cross Road to the east. Ambling across this small patch need not be too organised, but here's a short walk with some highlights pointed out. I've bunged in a corner of Fitzrovia too for the mildly energetic. To keep to just the Soho part, simply go to Tottenham Court Road Tube station and walk west on Oxford Street to pick up the walk at Wardour Street, soon on the left (and skip to page 191).

FITZROVIA TO SOHO WALK: ARIEL TO CALIBAN

⊖ *Oxford Circus, ends Piccadilly Circus. Distance about 1 mile but it'll feel like 3. Time taken more than an hour.*

If you walk north from Oxford Circus up Regent Street, preferably on the right-hand side, you soon come to the kink in the road where **Broadcasting House**

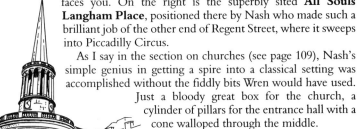

All Souls

faces you. On the right is the superbly sited **All Souls Langham Place**, positioned there by Nash who made such a brilliant job of the other end of Regent Street, where it sweeps into Piccadilly Circus.

As I say in the section on churches (see page 109), Nash's simple genius in getting a spire into a classical setting was accomplished without the fiddly bits Wren would have used. Just a bloody great box for the church, a cylinder of pillars for the entrance hall with a cone walloped through the middle.

Broadcasting House is the centre of the BBC, and BBC radio in particular. It is a classic thirties building, with its Reithian high-mindedness and art deco motifs. Its symbol is Ariel, the girlie, wispy thing from Shakespeare's *Tempest*. Broadcasting House was built with massive sound-proofing so that a symphony orchestra could belt out Elgar next to a *Woman's Hour* studio.

Of course, in the early days announcers would wear dinner jackets and bow ties and speak in ludicrously plummy accents. Now if you see an apparent cockney oik

STAN, YOU WERE RIGHT ALL ALONG

One of Soho's great eccentrics – Oxford Street's, to be precise – was a man that anyone who shopped there between 1969 and 1994 will recall: Stanley Green. They won't remember the name, but they will remember the sandwich-board placards he carried preaching his message that proteins caused lust and passion.

He warned that 'fish, meat, bird, cheese, egg, peas, beans, nuts and sitting' caused unhealthy desires and would sell leaflets denouncing the 'Eight Wicked Passions of Proteins'. He wasn't treated as a nut – he denounced them, after all – but was liked and recognised the length of Oxford Street. Drivers would toot and wave, tourist buses would stop and salute him, shop-workers would greet him as they passed.

Stanley lived in Northolt and in his flat there would print off the leaflets and then cycle into London with his placard on his back. Later, when he got too old, he took the bus. He must have been around 75 when he died, so he didn't do too badly on his recommended diet of steamed vegetables, fruit, grains and home-baked bread. Hang on a minute, isn't that what health watchdogs tell us to eat nowadays? Stan me old fruit, you were right all along! His placard and leaflets are preserved in the Museum of London.

There was another eccentric character in Kensington High Street – a black man with a white mac, who sweated buckets in hot weather as he carried a full-sized white fold-up cross, with metal hinges at the joints so he could take it on the bus. Sadly, I can't tell you who he was or where he is now.

The great landlord of Soho's **French House** pub, Gaston Berlemont, born upstairs in the pub to his French parents in 1914, and who died in 1999, had exaggerated Gallic charm. He would say to a customer who'd had too much to drink: 'One of us has to leave, monsieur, and it cannot be me. Come back tomorrow morning and we'll drink a glass of champagne.' Or to a lady, with a raised-eyebrow *double entendre*, 'Madam, I cannot wait to see more of you.'

He would not serve pints, only the demi, not so much out of Frenchness but because there was more money to be made out of wine in those days. Plus he didn't fancy the beer-swilling types.

He would patiently indulge the Bohemian clientele, cashing cheques that were as bouncy as Barbara Windsor's frontage. Of one man who entertained a number of young women in the upstairs restaurant, he said: 'I've never known anyone with so many nieces.'

He was no snob and among the great writers and film makers could be found prostitutes and tramps – one of his customers famously slept in a hollow tree on Hampstead Heath. A celebrated customer after the war was Pierre Labric, who had ridden a bicycle down all the stairs of the Eiffel Tower.

When Gaston retired in 1989, the pub was packed – as was the street outside – with hundreds of fans of this contradiction, a true British pub with a true French patron in charge. For more on the French House, see opposite page.

or Liverpudlian lout in shabby old jeans shuffling past the steps of All Souls, he's probably a top BBC presenter. Nation Shall Speak Unto Nation, the old high-minded building says, and that now includes yer actual efnics speaking wiv yer yoof, innit? Still good and ludicrous, then.

MORE SOULS AND I CAN'T BELIEVE … IT'S NOT BUDDHA? Between All Souls and Oxford Circus take Margaret Street running east, and you will come to a completely contrasting church, called **All Saints**. As I say in the church's section (page 105), instead of classical simplicity we get the most over-the-top Gothic revival decoration for decoration's sake. It's virtually psychedelic, as if you tried to decorate your home from hundreds of pages torn from wallpaper sample books. And it is amazing to stagger out of this rich sensation only to cross the road and find yourself in the **Fo Guang Temple**, a Chinese Buddhist centre most unexpected in the heart of London (although we are not far north of Chinatown in Soho).

Here, having removed your shoes and sought permission, you can enter the amazing Main Shrine, dedicated to the Sakyamuni Buddha, with its three large statues, in total tranquillity. The walls and ceilings are covered with hundreds of Buddhas amid an atmosphere of serenity that is hard to credit only a few yards from Oxford Street's commercial bustle.

Going right and then left at the end of the street we come into Eastcastle Street, and then right into Berners Street we face Oxford Street and our entrance into Soho. Fitzrovia, that unofficial patch of London, is up the other end of Berners Street and past the Telecom Tower. The best bit of it, if you're interested, is the beautiful Fitzroy Square, setting for Ian McEwan's brilliant recent novel, *Saturday*. (More on Fitzrovia, page 79).

FRENCH CONNECTION, TOP MARX AND GREAT LITERARY DRUNKS Crossing Oxford Street, pickpocket centre of the universe, we enter Wardour Street, home as I said above to the independent film-makers, publishers and media hangers-on. The most interesting bit of Soho is really this and the parallel streets also running south to your left (that is, east) – Dean Street, Frith Street and Greek Street – so there's no harm in just blundering around, taking odd paths that suggest themselves to you. After all, it's a bohemian place so let's not be too organised.

But if you survive the raffish pubs and clubs with no ill effects (needless to say some of the sleazy red-lightish clubs are there to rip tourists off), there are some fascinating nooks and crannies to mention.

A literary landmark, or rather a set of literary landmarks, are the connections with Charles Dickens's *A Tale of Two Cities*, that evocative drama set between Paris and London during the French Revolution and for me perhaps his best book (I can't make my mind up). In Greek Street, the Pillar of Hercules pub features in the book as the Hercules Pillar and the nearby House of St Barnabas, a hostel, is said to be the model for the house of Dr Manette. In which case it's not surprising to find Manette Street nearby.

Incidentally, there's a French church in Soho Square at the top (north end) of Greek and Frith streets, but this square, to be honest, is less interesting than it looks. I'm told the statue of Charles II appears to talk occasionally because the park-keepers in their pseudo-Tudor lodge hide a walkie-talkie in it, to play tricks on tourists, but I've never heard it. And dang, I've spoilt it for you now.

In Dean Street, the **French House** pub is legendary for literary connections, bohemian lifestyles and odd eccentricities. The Idiots' Club, which met here in recent years, was run by someone calling himself Baron Peter de Massenbach, who greeted potential members with 'An idiot, I presume'.

And the French House has countless theatrical and literary connections, from Peter O'Toole to Keith Waterhouse to Auberon Waugh. Dylan Thomas once drunkenly left the manuscript for *Under Milk Wood* here, to be rescued by the landlord. (Incidentally, he created the Welsh-sounding place name for that 'play for voices', Llareggub, perhaps to mock the English for taking Welshness so seriously, until they spelled it backwards. Last time I looked on the internet I was pleased to see a Llareggub & District Railway in California, which seems a real operation, and a Llaregub Hill School in Iowa, which seems unreal.) When drunk, Dylan Thomas would play his rather puerile game called Cats and Dogs in which he would crawl round the pub on all fours biting the ladies' ankles, much to their surprise if they weren't regulars.

Here the blind poet John Heath-Stubbs and the deaf poet David Wright hit upon the idea of *The Faber Book of Twentieth-Century Verse* in 1953. Also, the writer Daniel Farson first met the painter Francis Bacon here, starting one of Soho's great friendships.

A wonderfully embarrassing moment at the French House in recent times occurred when a certain TV critic and fragrant hackette – I'd better not give her name – was in a deeply 'relaxed' mode. She went up to some fanciable bloke and said: 'You're awfully Ewan McGregorish. You could be in films if you play your cards right.' The chap decently explained that he *was* Ewan McGregor and therefore was already an actor. Exit red-faced fragrant hackette, although at least she had the balls to tell the story herself later.

Actually, this was the complete reverse of the situation another great British eccentric of the 1930s, the conductor **Sir Thomas Beecham**, found himself in

17

Soho today has a reputation for sleaze and sex, but the scale of the industry was once very much larger, and conducted more openly, in those days when one in eight London women worked in the sex industry. In 1796, for example, it was estimated there were 25,000 'ladies of the night' in London.

Nor were they all living in squalor and poverty. One survey said that in Marylebone alone, 1,700 houses, mainly elegant terraces, were inhabited by upmarket courtesans. Some charged phenomenal amounts of money and became rich property owners in their own right.

These sophisticated creatures made vast sums of money and helped account for the boom in property and building. There was even a printed directory of prostitutes, Harris' Lists, giving revealing descriptions.

There were specialist services on offer: what the French called the 'English perversion' was catered for at Mrs Jenkins' Flogging Establishment, on the spot La Bohème Restaurant in Covent Garden now stands, where a sound thrashing with birch twigs would be applied to naked bodies.

Some brothels, as recorded in Hogarth's cartoons, were presented as Turkish baths or bagnos or bagnios. Couples would take hot and cold dips before retiring to discreet rooms. One old bathhouse, said to have been Roman but modernised during the 18th-century vice boom and used for this purpose, can be seen at 5 Strand Lane, WC2, through a display window or inspected by arrangement with the local council (✎ 020 7641 5264; ➓ Temple, District and Circle Lines).

Society courtesans, royal mistresses and working-class prostitutes worked fairly openly up until the late 19th century when Britain underwent a convulsion of morality which, despite the loosening of the bonds by the 1960s era, has never entirely gone away.

For example, there's a blue plaque at 15 South Street, W1, honouring Catherine Walters, 'the last Victorian courtesan'. The word 'last' tells of the change in moral standards during that reign as much as it tells of the long life of this woman, known as Skittles, who survived well into the 20th century. She had a ravishing face, by all accounts, a stunning hour-glass figure which she displayed to great effect, tumbling tresses of red hair, and a Liverpudlian street-girl's way with words. The flame-haired temptress would put on her tightest corset with revealing decolletage, grab her riding crop, and go for a gallop along nearby Rotten Row in Hyde Park, where society men would be out riding. Once, when complemented by a gentleman on the pink flush on her cheeks after a gallop, she retorted: 'You should see my arse.'

Some of them did, but she was aiming higher. She became entangled with the heir to a dukedom and was soon provided with this house and a lavish income for life. In 1867 she befriended the Prince of Wales – before he met the actress Lily Langtry – and soon her civilised soirées were frequented by the great and the good of the age, such as Gladstone, Lord Kitchener, and leading artists and poets. She had reinvented herself as a society lady, but never disguised her past.

near here, at Fortnum and Mason's store. He said to a woman he'd just greeted, and whose face he vaguely recognised but whose name escaped him – we all get in this pickle occasionally, I'm sure – 'And what is your husband doing nowadays?' The lady replied frostily: 'He's still king.'

Beecham was forthright as a conductor. He once brought his orchestra to a halt mid-score and bellowed at some poor woman cellist: 'Madam, you have there between your legs that which could give pleasure to thousands, and all you do is sit there and scratch it.'

Back to Soho and the French House. The pub was originally the York Minster and was in the control of Frenchman Victor Berlemont from 1910. It was a base for the French Resistance and Free French during World War II and their leader Charles de Gaulle came here for cloak-and-dagger wartime meetings. Or so they say…(Gallic shrug).

At 28 Dean Street the father of communism, **Karl Marx**, and his family took lodging rooms upstairs amidst dreadful poverty in 1850. They had no money, apart from what his bit of writing earned, and some hand-outs from Engels. Eventually they inherited some money and moved to a more, er, bourgeois location in Hampstead. Eleanor Marx was born at this impoverished flat and went on to become a political firebrand in her own right. She was involved in the matchgirls' strike of 1888 and the dockers' of 1889.

Marx while living at Soho liked nothing more than a stiff walk across Hampstead Heath and a stiff drink at the Jack Straw's Castle pub. See, he was almost human. Nothing on American humorist Groucho Marx, of course. He was a *real* revolutionary.

Which brings us neatly to **Groucho's**, a discreet club for media luvvies at 45 Dean Street. Here editors, writers, people from the nearby film centre of Wardour Street and others meet, launch books, raise funds and generally get sloshed. According to one member, everyone is constantly looking over the shoulder of whomever they're talking to, to see if there's someone more important to suck up to. They then cut the first person dead in mid-sentence as they go off to praise the big cheese and shout with laughter at his, or her, jokes. If you think that's cynical, I'm sorry, but I see it almost every day. However, anyone preferring Groucho to Karl Marx can't be all bad. The club took its name from Groucho's famous dictum that he wouldn't join any club that would have him as a member. Just so long as they don't forget his other one: 'I've got a good mind to join a club and beat you over the head with it.'

MYSTIC VISIONARY AND ECCENTRIC PRAT Soho's greatest eccentric was probably poet-artist and mystic **William Blake**, his birthplace being marked by a plaque in nearby Marshall Street. His poem 'Jerusalem', now set to music as an alternative national anthem and celebration of Englishness, was in fact a radical protest against what the industrial revolution was doing to the country and an attack on the system.

He and his wife used to sit naked in their garden, pretending to be Adam and Eve, and were frankly a complete puzzle to contemporaries. One suspects he was a combination of stocky cockney artisan, visionary and prat. His pictures and poems seem simple yet are easily made complex by English literature bods. (For example, the poem about the big cat, 'Tyger, tyger burning bright', is said to be about the French Revolution. Why doesn't he flaming well mention it then?) Blake was surely naïvely direct about things, un-luvvie-like, and deeply attached to innocence. He once pointed to a group of children playing nearby and said with feeling: 'That is heaven.' His visionary poems live on in unpredictable ways. For example, he wrote: 'If the doors of perception were cleansed, man could see things as they truly are: infinite.' In the 1930s, Aldous Huxley borrowed the phrase for his book about drugs, *The Doors of Perception*. Then in the 1960s Jim Morrison took that for the title of his band, The Doors. You probably couldn't find a more different artist, but another one of Soho's finest was **Canaletto**, who lived at 41 Beak Street, towards Regent Street, where he has a blue plaque.

MURDERS, WHODUNNITS, A VAMPIRE AND A ROTTEN KING An area like Soho ought to be good for a decent murder, and one that is still remembered as a sensation, partly because it involved a dramatic chase across the Atlantic and the first international arrest aided by Mr Marconi's newfangled wireless telegraphy, was that of Soho dentist Dr Hawley Crippen. He worked on the corner of Soho Street and Oxford Street, at No 59. (For the full fascinating story, see page 20.) Oddly, the same surgery had produced another medical scandal just a few years before. A Dr Talbot Bridgewater had set up a huge forgery business involving stolen postal orders and cheques obtained by the simple method of levering open the doors of pillar boxes. He was jailed for seven years in 1905.

Wardour Street, as I mentioned at the start of this section, has had a huge role in the film business in the last couple of decades as well as rock music with the Marquee Club one of its landmarks. But other landmarks tell of half-forgotten characters and their links with Soho.

In Broadwick Street, which is off Wardour Street to the west, Dr John Snow made a discovery which has since saved millions of lives. In 1854 there was an outbreak of cholera here, caused – contemporary thinking would have it – by air-borne vapours. He was convinced that pollution of the groundwater by sewage meant the disease was carried in drinking water. He persuaded the authorities to take the handle off the pump here at the centre of the outbreak and the epidemic suddenly stopped. You can find out more upstairs in the **John Snow** pub, Broadwick Street, said to be Soho's oldest. For Snow's grave and more on him, see Earl's Court, page 166.

Halfway down Wardour Street is the pub **The Intrepid Fox** at No 99. This refers not to the hunting background of the name Soho, but to the great radical politician Charles Fox who once offered a kiss from a great society beauty to anyone who'd vote for him, and won by a landslide. The walls and ceiling look like a crack-crazed junk-merchant's yard, festooned with memorabilia and musical clutter, some connected with famous customers.

At the far end of Wardour Street, as you leave Soho, is the remarkable stone, brick and copper churchless tower of **St Anne's** with its strange bulbous shape. A Russian onion-dome in a foreign land. The church was destroyed by World War II bombing. Services are held in a building in the street to the rear.

The ashes of whodunnit writer **Dorothy L Sayers**, creator of Lord Peter Wimsey, are in the floor of the Sayers Room in the tower, where one can see her portrait. Sayers (1893–1957) was a churchwarden here. There is also a dead deposed king here, Theodore of Corsica, a debt-ridden wastrel by all accounts (not like any of our royals, then). He may have been a rotten monarch. (He certainly is now.)

The churchyard still makes a peaceful place to rest, if not a particularly peaceful last resting place for the hundreds of people crammed into it to the point where the ground level is well above the surrounding streets. Dorothy L, a great discusser of death and bodies, would have been amused by this.

Another local who would have known St Anne's was the author of *The Vampyre* (1815), John William Polidori, who lived a few streets west at Great Poultney Street. He was Byron's doctor and would have been with the group in Italy when Mary Shelley wrote *Frankenstein*. Spooky.

Emerging from Soho proper onto Shaftesbury Avenue, London's Broadway in terms of theatreland, you can turn right towards Piccadilly. Or plunge straight across into **Chinatown** – which replaced the opium dens of Limehouse, London's first Chinatown near the Docks – and Leicester Square if you like showbizzy crowds.

The area simply fizzes in the early evening with bright-eyed crowds heading for the shows, and Leicester Square is where filmstars appear for premières on a regular basis, to be whooped at by adoring fans. Theatres have their 'nutty devotees' side too. One of the strange things about London's theatreland is the side passage which leads to the stage door at many of these splendid old buildings. Theatre groupies will hang around after the shows to catch a glimpse of the great stars of the stage, strangely ordinary out of the limelight and sans make-up, wigs and costume, perhaps hoping for an autograph on a programme or a word. Some people will attend these doors for all 14 nights of a show's run and are well known to the bemused actors.

Back to **Piccadilly Circus** and the Tube. As I say elsewhere, the supposed statue of Eros is in fact a clever joke, and Piccadilly is named after a strange garment (page 78). But as you look one way past the garish neon signs and back into Soho, don't forget to see how London completely changes character in a few yards by looking down Lower Regent Street to the frightfully restrained St James's area (for a guide to the intriguing mad monuments at the far end of this street see page 73). And if you have never seen the magnificent sweep of the bottom end of Regent Street proper (curving right away from Piccadilly opposite Shaftesbury Avenue), you *mustn't* miss it. This is the other end of the road from All Souls at the start of our walk and it is Nash's brilliance yet again. Look at the garret windows, the magnificent way Air Street intercepts the grand sweep. Wonderful.

18

Southwark

Southwark, being just across the river from London, was home to every evil the medieval City could not tolerate within its walls but could not do without – brothels, bear-baiting, cock-fighting, gambling, theatres, fleeing criminals and unspeakably cruel jails. It was a medieval Soho or Las Vegas.

Some of this murky but fascinating history can be retraced by the inquisitive visitor today, as we shall see, and the atmosphere has been soaked up by dozens of film-makers precisely because it's not fake.

Dickens couldn't have created the insane, illogical world that he portrays in books like *Little Dorrit* without Southwark. It has never been anything like smart or fashionable, but today, with the Bankside's new Tate Modern and the wobbly Millennium Bridge, it's drawing some crowds across the river again, as it did for very different reasons for five centuries up to the Civil War.

The Millennium Bridge takes pedestrians across on a route many a lustful man used to take by boat from Stews Lane in the City (the 'stews' were the whorehouses) to the Bankside brothels that lined the stairs at the other side. The watermen who rowed you across were themselves often drunk and often as bloody-minded as the worst of today's cockney cabbies and were suitably lampooned in the hit film about this area, *Shakespeare In Love*. London may seem odd in some regards today, but in previous centuries it was a seething mass of insane and eccentric contradictions like a Gormenghast made real.

For example, the **brothels at Bankside** were regulated by the government, owned by the Church (for much of their 400-year history), and the normal rule of law was set aside under the paradoxical term, the Liberty of the Clink. How the Clink – the very prison after which all others are nicknamed – could offer liberty was a typically contradictory eccentricity of medieval London.

Certain institutions around and near the City had their own jurisdiction, meaning normal law and regulations were suspended therein. They had their own powers and laws over their small patches of land, however inefficient and corrupt they may have been in enforcing them. The medieval manor of the Clink was one such, with its own manorial court (such as existed throughout rural England) and its own jail for wrong-doers, the Clink. Hence 'being in the Clink', British slang for being jailed, doesn't relate to the noise of the chains as I had assumed. Such an area of private jurisdiction was known as the Liberty. This particular one, a 70-acre patch along the South Bank, was owned by the Bishops of Winchester from 1107, and the operation of the stews was regulated by a law introduced by Henry II in 1161, although they had obviously been in existence for many years before that. Those who caught venereal disease from the Bankside brothels were said to have been 'bitten by the Winchester geese'.

Fair play for customers was ensured by a law from the 12th century ruling that 'no single woman to take money to lie with any man but she lie with him all night till the morrow'. We know little about the lives of the 'Winchester geese' beyond this, but they were not allowed to be buried in consecrated ground such as churchyards. There are masses of them buried a little way south of here at Cross Bones Ground near an old crossroads on Redcross Way.

Brothel-owning may seem a bizarre occupation for a bishop. The attitude of Catholic church and king seemed to be that such things were better regulated than otherwise, but these were the only London brothels ever to be legalised. And it has to be said that before the Reformation the Church was about big business, property and money as much as anything else.

It was not until the rise of Protestantism, partly in reaction to the Church's greedy commercialism, that another Henry – Henry VIII, hardly a moral paragon in his own private life – banned the Bankside stews in 1546. This forced the sex industry into backstreets and behind unmarked doors, where it has been ever since. It was not long after this that the City took over part of this area, making it the South Ward, or Southwark.

The area was by that time already booming as it serviced London's other pleasures and vices, with gambling, bear- and bull-baiting and theatres doing well by Shakespeare's time a few decades later. The **baiting of animals** involved setting vicious dogs upon other beasts for the amusement of the public who paid to get into a sort of theatre, and laughed as they watched enraged horses, bulls or bears being torn apart as they struggled with their tormentors. One show that made people laugh was a horse with a monkey on its back, the monkey trying to keep out of the way of the leaping dogs but eventually being killed when the horse was brought down.

Another factor in Southwark's notoriety is the existence of the small **sanctuaries** where fugitives could hide from justice. These generally had some kind of religious origin but became completely abused as they were used to evade the law or cheat people. One of these was known as the Mint, behind where Borough station now stands, and thousands of debtors lived here to escape imprisonment. Oddly, this sanctuary never had any legal status but it took several Acts of Parliament to close it down.

Another sanctuary was the Paris Garden, just upriver of Bankside, where bear-baiting and gambling thrived in the 16th century without the restriction of legal rules, despite the land being owned by a church order in the first place.

The British who today collectively tut-tut at the Spanish with their bull-fighting and the Chinese with their various cruelties involving dogs or bears seem to have conveniently forgotten that such 'sports' were enjoyed here by commoners and royalty alike – Elizabeth I loved to see such bloodsports (and Elizabeth II isn't averse to seeing the odd pheasant blown out of the skies). The greatest actor of Shakespeare's time, Southwark's Edward Alleyn (more on him in Dulwich, page 228), was Master of the Royal Bears, Bulls and Mastiff Dogs, so close was the connection between theatre and bloodsports.

All these pleasures were banned by the rather boring Puritans who took control during the Civil War of the next century, but bull-baiting and dog-fighting returned with the Restoration of the monarchy in 1660. However, with theatres once more legalised and the growth of both pleasure gardens and theatres to the west of the City, Southwark was soon eclipsed by the emerging West End around the then new Covent Garden, and pleasure gardens elsewhere soon attracted crowds for pleasures both innocent and illicit.

The other aspect of Southwark's seedy past was the presence of several **prisons**. Not so much the visible evidence on the riverside of the already-mentioned Clink, which offers excellent visions of medieval hell-holes and grisly instruments of torture, but the massive debtors' prisons further south, around Borough High Street.

The Marshalsea Prison where Dickens's father was imprisoned for debt was one of these, and no wonder he felt angry about imprisoning people who could not pay bills and thereby making the situation worse. In *Little Dorrit* the heroine is born in the Marshalsea, which Dickens describes as 'an oblong pile of barrack building, partitioned into squalid houses standing back to back, environed by a narrow paved yard hemmed in by high walls duly spiked on top.' As Dickens wrote, whole families lived and died in prison because one of them, not even a criminal, had once got into debt. The King's Bench Prison of earlier centuries stood nearby (and features in Dickens's *Nicholas Nickleby*), as did the White Lion jail, one of Surrey's main prisons for serious criminals. Further south, at Newington Gardens, stood yet another prison, Horsemonger Lane jail. Dickens's account of a gruesome husband-and-wife hanging there was instrumental in getting public executions stopped. The gloomy sombreness that this once massive and miserable population cast over this part of Southwark has never entirely dissipated. It's part of its charm.

A TOUR OF SOUTHWARK'S SUFFERING AND HORROR

✪ *Borough, ends Blackfriars. Time taken: 2 hours and 2 miles approx. Plenty of refreshment stops. Or just read it and visit what interests you without walking!*

ANCIENT INNS, SECRET BIBLES AND BLOODY SURGERY We start at Borough station on the Tube's Northern Line City branch. This section is the world's oldest Tube railway. (For its history and the forgotten buried terminus, closed for more than a century but still there, see page 92). Today we'll stay above ground but it'll still be gloomy in spots because that's what we've come to see: the simultaneously grim and cheerful Southwark, historical warts and all. It starts in Dickensian – even Chaucerian – picturesque grimness but ends with the most sublime views possible.

The sites of the many prisons (discussed above) are around here, and the name of the road on our sharp left, Marshalsea, is the most famous, thanks to Dickens. When the Thames was bordered by a wide swamp, the place names ending in '-sea' or '-sey' denoted an island, so we also get Bermondsey, Battersea and Chelsea along the river.

Leaving the station and crossing Borough High Street, we're confronted with **St George the Martyr** church, one of Dickens's settings for *Little Dorrit*. The clock is lit on the three Borough sides but dark at night on the far Bermondsey side because, it's said, the parishioners in the latter district were too tight-pursed to fork out for the new church, so they can blunder around in their own time. This road junction is still where two great national roads meet – the A2 from Dover and the A3 from Portsmouth - and this is a reminder of Southwark's past and present role in transport.

We walk quickly up the first bit of Borough High Street, the odd bit of fifties and sixties architecture hinting at bomb patterns of the 1940s. At one of these points, on the left note **Little Dorrit Court** which leads to a school. Actually Southwark was riven, and still is, with hundreds of these little walkways through to the criminal sanctuaries and liberties of prisons. Evading the law through this network was all the easier.

We rapidly see on the right ancient names, many linked to inns and taverns: Chapel Court, Mermaid Court, St Christopher Inn, Mermaid Yard, Talbot Yard. The **St Christopher Inn**, still there in a rebuilt form, was where up until the railway age travellers from London would gather to board the Dover stage. A good spot to catch those fleeing to France, and choice pickings for the highwaymen up

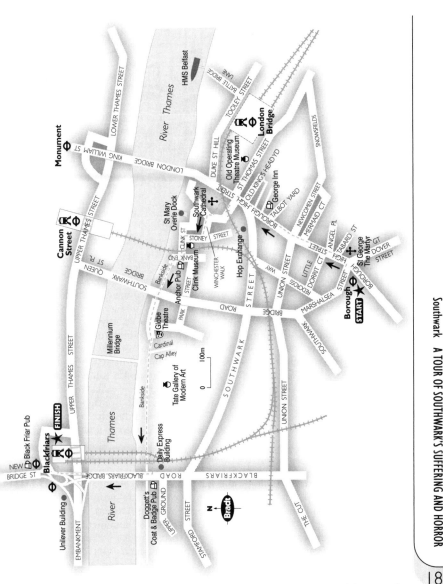

on Blackheath. In an earlier era the famed Tabard inn was the assembly point for the Canterbury pilgrims walking the Pilgrims Way through Kent, recorded with such ribaldry and colour by Chaucer in the 14th century. (The Tabard was in Talbot Yard and is remembered by Tabard Street beside George the Martyr church.)

This was Southwark's great *raison d'etre*: where the stage routes from the south and abroad converged close to London Bridge – the only Thames crossing – which travellers could walk across, or take a sedan chair over. We can see how close the City is from the tower blocks ahead, across the river. Hence the stagecoach-sized-entrances to many of these little lanes. One of the greatest of these old inns that really shows how things used to be is the **George**, again on the right. This is said to be London's last great galleried inn and is massive, yet is only a fraction of its previous size, this being one side of a huge rectangle of land it once occupied. It's owned by the National Trust and leased to Whitbread pubs. Shakespeare, Dickens, Pepys and Johnson would have known this place, as it dates from at least the 16th century (Stow's *Survey of London* of 1598 mentions it), although this rebuilding is a mere 330 years old, being of 1677. In its heyday this one pub received perhaps 80 coaches a week, and was just one of

The George Inn

many great galleried inns in Southwark. They were the railway termini of their day, or the airport terminals and departure gates. And the fact that the City gates, including London Bridge, were locked at night meant there was a great deal of accommodation in demand from travellers arriving late.

Two easily missed details to see here: on the right a splendid shop front of W H & H le May, hop factors. You have to crane your neck or cross the road, but high up there's an ornamental front. Hops for beer brewing famously come from Kent so would have arrived in London on this road. To see just how important they were, go back ten paces and look across the street through a narrow walkway called Counter Alley. You will see a glimpse of the magnificent **Hop Exchange**. Counter Court, the narrow walkway you are looking through, is named after yet another prison, and it is soon apparent that the grand-looking HSBC Bank next to it is shaped like a slice of cake, perched on an odd bit of ground, a pattern we will see in a yet more extreme form in a truly splendid pub later in the walk. (You may wish to pop through to see better the splendidly ornamented frontage of the Hop Exchange, or the interior, which you may ask the chap on the left as you go in for permission to view. It is a cast-iron cathedral to hops, decorated with the white horse of Kent.)

Staying on the right of Borough High Street, you can appreciate the defining characteristic of this part of Southwark: a great convergence of roads, and a great convergence of railways overlaid on this medieval muddle giving a pleasing chaos to the geography as the lines, like the roads, twist and turn at different levels to make junctions and gain access to the bridges over the Thames. Ahead can be spotted through the railway bridge the golden ball of the Monument to the Great Fire in the City, from which Southwark was spared by the Thames. Note the Borough Market front on the left, which we will soon enter.

There are yet more pubs or signs of them: **White Hart Yard** on the right was mentioned by Shakespeare in *Henry VI* and by Dickens in *Pickwick Papers*. Particularly atmospheric is **Old Kings Head Yard** again on the right. You can go through the arch and see an effigy of the old king high up on the wall, together with a date showing this is not the old Old Kings Head but a new Old Kings Head. Beyond it are the buildings of Guy's, one of the two great teaching hospitals historically based here.

We cross St Thomas Street, and on the right just before the massive railway bridge is a grey stone church-like building. This is the old St Thomas's hospital – the other half of this area's great medical history. If we had turned right down St Thomas Street, we would have seen the church of St Thomas Apostle, where the hospital started in 1215. Today the **Old Operating Theatre Museum and Herb Garret** offer a fascinating glimpse of the bloody days when screaming patients endured saw-bones surgery in front of audiences (see *Museums*, page 39). Or perhaps they didn't endure it.

The old hospital building near the railway bridge on the main road is also the site where the first English Bible was printed in 1537. Until then it was heresy for Bibles to be in anything other than Latin, the exclusive medium of the monopolistic, corrupt Catholic church, stopping ordinary people from understanding a word of it. As Protestantism spread in the 1520s, great pioneers such as William Tyndale printed copies in English and smuggled them into England hidden among other cargoes. He risked being burned for heresy if caught, and in fact was caught and executed by Catholic authorities in Europe in 1536, just one year before Bibles were printed here. Tyndale, as a student at Cambridge, had horrified a senior clergyman by vowing: 'If God spare my life, I shall cause the boy that driveth the plow to know more of the Bible than thou dost!' And so he did. St Thomas's hospital is now further upriver, in Lambeth.

MURDER BY GASLIGHT AND A BISHOP'S BROTHEL If we cross the main Borough High Street just by the railway bridge, we can plunge left through an archway in the bridge supports into the spooky and Dickensian atmosphere of Green Dragon Court, which rapidly takes us into **Borough Market**. This is murder-by-gaslight territory, and there's plenty more, often used for films, around London Bridge too, where entire streets are under the arches. It gets a lot more sinister after dark. Among recent films to use this setting are *Bridget Jones's Diary, Lock, Stock and Two Smoking Barrels, Keep the Aspidistra Flying, Wings of a Dove, Entrapment* and, of course, all kinds of 1950s British B movies. It's a black-and-white kind of place, really.

The market – 'London's larder' it boasts – opens early, and so do the pubs, from 6am, as they still do at Smithfield the meat market. So a night on the town could end here, if you wish to keep drinking.

One of these pubs, the **Globe Tavern** on the left, is neatly dovetailed into the railway viaduct above, and if you walk past it the view back from Bedale Street is typically jumbled: the ornamented pub, the chaotic market under the railway and **Southwark Cathedral** serene behind all that.

The cathedral somehow totally avoids the soaring inspiration of many such churches and squats low on the ground, girded by the railway viaduct and riverside buildings. It was, after all, just a large parish church until 1905; its low-key sombreness suits the place, and the poor neighbourhood it has served. It is not, architecturally, in the top one hundred. There are a few fine monuments inside, including ones to local star Shakespeare, to John Harvard (as in university), and a strange one to a pill-merchant, John Lockyer. There is also a trendy exhibition/museum next to the shop but I didn't find it worth the admission fee.

Between the cathedral and the riverbank is **St Mary Overie Dock** with its floating replica of the *Golden Hind* in which Drake circumnavigated the world. Here, also, the legend is told of the miserly ferryman who used to control the crossing before the bridge was built. He was so tight with his money that one day he pretended to be dead so his family and servants would stop eating and save him a few pennies. Instead, however, they started celebrating with his best wine. As he rose angrily from his 'death bed', they assumed the Devil had got into the corpse and struck him really dead. His daughter's greedy fiancé, rushing over to claim the dead relative's property, fell off his horse and was killed. Not a good day for the daughter, Mary Overie. In disgust at the meanness and greed of them all she set up a monastery dedicated to aiding the poor; she eventually became a saint, while her monastery became St Thomas's Hospital.

Now, continuing along the line of Green Dragon Court through the market or Winchester Walk (it's those naughty brothel-keeping bishops again) we reach

Stoney Street and turn right. The atmosphere here is definitely of riverside wharves and warehouses, and although Old Father Thames is not yet visible, you can already smell him. If we go left at the end we're in **Clink Street** and the high wall on the left is the only surviving part of that original prison which gave its nickname to all others. Nevertheless, there is a rather good Clink museum here on the left and various authentic instruments of torture may be seen (see page 43). There are also more of the same nearby at the London Dungeon at London Bridge.

Soon we go under another railway and reach, on the riverbank, the **Anchor** pub. Park Street was the real site of Shakespeare's Globe Theatre, the recreation of which is coming up. For 800 years a pub has stood here. But this is undoubtedly the site of the Castle stewhouse, one of the biggest brothels, and as discussed above, owned by the Bishop of Winchester. The diarist Pepys sat here and watched the Great Fire of London rage across the river in September 1666. Sir Christopher Wren sat here a few years later and watched his magnificent dome of St Paul's rising as a consequence. The river walls were not so high then, and there's a plate recording the highest flood level four feet up one of the walls of the pub to show why they are so high today. Now you have to go upstairs or cross to the riverside terrace to enjoy the view.

SUPERB VIEWS, HEROIC TALK AND AN ECCENTRIC RACE And the view along this riverbank is simply superb. To the right, downstream, is London Bridge and Tower Bridge plus the 'museumified' World War II cruiser, *HMS Belfast*, Europe's largest surviving armoured ship of that conflict. In front is the City, with the best possible view of St Paul's and so many other landmarks to admire – the steeple of St Bride's on Fleet Street being just one, and roughly where we are heading.

Following the riverside we approach Southwark Bridge – the office on the left is that of the *Financial Times* and should be faced in pink really – and plunging under the arches there is a slate mural depicting the great Frost Fair of 1564. The building of the narrow-arched London Bridge in 1169 (the one with houses on) had enabled the Thames to freeze over, and in 1564 it froze so thoroughly that a fair was held here. Oxen were roasted on spits, sports and games were played and the river did not thaw for weeks.

Beyond the bridge the newest wonder on the Thames is the **Millennium Bridge**, a strange contraption making a footbridge from St Paul's to the Bankside and its new tourist honeypots, particularly the Tate Modern. The idea behind the bridge seems to have been to make it appear as thin as possible when viewed from the side, the result being that it swayed like one of those plank bridges over canyons. It has since been stiffened somewhat. I didn't mind the swaying. In fact they shouldn't fix it but make it *worse*, and add holes in the decking, apparently unravelling support ropes and automated monsters lurking in the river below – the *Disbelief of Suspension Indiana Jones Bridge Experience*. People would flock to it. Make a virtue of your cock-ups.

One path up from the river here is Cardinal's Cap Alley, which commemorates an early 15th-century Bishop of Winchester (one of those famous brothel owners) who went to Rome to be made Cardinal Beaufort and landed here to parade his red cap of office through the Liberty of the Clink, which he owned. Others suggest it was where the Cardinal's mistress lived and the road should be Cardinal's Tart Alley. Or Cardinal Sin Alley possibly.

First on the left is Shakespeare's **Globe Theatre**, which is of course not Shakespeare's Globe but a complete and beautiful replica built thanks to the vision and drive of American actor and film-maker Sam Wanamaker, who died during its construction, having fought for 25 years to get the project off the ground (or on to the ground). The thatched building is as faithful as possible a replica and one can tour the structure when no plays are showing. Before this, the only representation we knew was in films such as the wartime *Henry V*, starring Laurence Olivier. Shakespeare refers directly to the theatre building and to what literary types call the 'suspension of disbelief' – the way in which you let him take you out of the theatre into his imagined lands – in the prologue to that play:

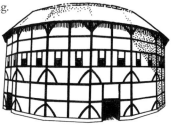

Globe Theatre

> Then should the warlike Harry, like himself,
> Assume the port of Mars, and at his heels,
> Leashed in like hounds, should Famine, Sword and Fire
> Crouch for employment. But pardon, gentles all,
> …Can this cockpit hold
> The vasty fields of France? Or may we cram
> Within this wooden O the very casques
> That did affright the air at Agincourt?

And a little later:

> Suppose within the girdle of these walls
> Are now confined two mighty monarchies,
> Whose high upreared and abutting fronts
> The perilous narrow ocean parts asunder.

Marvellous stuff, Will. It is not his greatest play for sure, but Shakespeare's talk in it of the heroic few taking on the many must surely have been ringing in Churchill's ears when he spoke of the 'Few' in another such battle over the same narrow sea centuries later.

Leaping on (or, as Shakespeare put it so much better in that prologue, 'jumping o'er times, / Turning th'accomplishment of many years / Into an hour-glass'), we come to the **Tate Modern**. Housed in the former Bankside Power Station, it is judged to have been a great achievement and in some ways recalls the French recycling of an old railway station, the Gare d'Orsay, on the banks of the Seine for a similar role. This one dwarfs the Parisian one for scale, if not content, and much of the space is courageously left open. Either you like modern art or you don't, but, hey, at least it's free. Actually, I preferred it as a power station with those vast turbines humming away, but I'm a little odd. Even for old fogeys, there is a benefit in that it enables the old Tate at Millbank to clear out all the pretentious piles of bricks etc and put some real art from their stores back on the walls. There was a joke doing the rounds in London in 2001: 'You know there are two great disused power stations on the South Bank. One is an empty shell, full of any old rubbish, and the other is near the dogs' home.'

Don't let my poking fun at this cathedral of cool put you off. Plenty of people whom I respect have come back enthused about the Tate Modern.

Then past the Founders Arms pub to Blackfriars Bridge. We go under the railway bridge – properly called Alexandria Bridge but no-one ever does – and up on to the road bridge. The black office to the left as we reach it is that of the *Daily Express* newspaper, a pale imitation of the superbly black old *Express* building on Fleet Street. The *Daily Express* is a pale imitation, too, of its broadsheet heyday when Canadian dictator Lord Beaverbrook was in charge and the masthead boasted 'World's Biggest Daily Sale' of perhaps five or six million a day, printed here in Fleet Street and in plants at Manchester and Glasgow. In the fifties, before television really got going, the *Express* maintained a massive pack of foreign

18

When you walk by the obviously ancient, battered and unpretentious house at 49 Bankside, opposite St Paul's and in a few of the original properties crammed between the reconstructed Globe Theatre and the former Bankside Power Station, now the Tate Modern, you will be astonished to see a plaque on the front wall boldly announcing its double claim to fame:

> Here lived Sir Christopher Wren
> During the building of St Paul's Cathedral
> Here also, in 1502, Catherine
> Infanta of Castile and Aragon
> Afterwards first Queen
> Of Henry VIII took shelter
> On her first landing in
> London

Oddly, both claims are complete tosh. Having once been invited into this charming Queen Anne house (it is a home, not a museum, so don't knock), I could well imagine Wren relaxing in the upstairs sitting room with a first-class view of St Paul's going up across the river. Sadly, it's balderdash because when this house was finished, so was St Paul's, more or less. As for the Infanta, that notion should have been strangled at birth – infantacide – because the house is 200 years younger than her arrival. There was a tatty inn on the site, true, but Spanish princesses with their enormous retinue do not stay in tatty inns in an area known for brothels, gambling and bear-baiting. The plaque was a jape by an eccentric owner, who copied the idea from a nearby house, now long gone, where Wren *did* stay. Even odder, as I stood among the Mary Poppins-style chimney pots on the roof drinking in the quite marvellous view, was to find out that the building could reasonably have two plaques to other more probable events. One, as it was a Tudor tavern and close to the Globe Theatre – although not as close as the rebuilt one suggests – it is inevitable that Shakespeare drank there and probably characters such as Marlowe too. The other – and this is a certainty – is that mid-20th-century silver screen siren Anna Lee lived there. There are pictures of the blonde bombshell reclining gracefully (frankly, she didn't do any other kind of reclining) where Wren didn't in Gillian Tindall's fascinatingly detailed biography of this property, *The House Beside the Thames*. See *Further reading*, page 313.

correspondents, with the picture desk alone employing 50 photographers around the world. How many would it employ full-time overseas today? Don't ask, it's too depressing. One chance to see an old-style editor of the *Express* is to watch the old movie *The Day the Earth Caught Fire* where Arthur Christiansen, a great *Express* editor, plays himself.

Across the road is one of London's odder pub names, **Doggett's Coat & Badge**, which refers to a prize offered in a strange annual Thames boat race which ought to be as well-known as the Oxford & Cambridge race but is forgotten by most people. Comedian Thomas Doggett launched the race in 1716 to celebrate the accession of George I to the throne, and every July (the precise date depends on tides) the race is held between London Bridge and Chelsea Bridge. Prizes, funded by Doggett's legacy, include a splendid full-length red coat with a tight waist and a silver badge. So the winner looks like a right ninny, giving comedian Doggett the last laugh.

The architecture of the pub, and of the flats behind, is, however, less prepossessing, and it gets worse along this river bank. As feet may now be tired, I suggest crossing Blackfriars Bridge to a pub of utterly superb architecture and the Tube home. If you agree, skip the next section. Or just read it for fun in the pub.

THE SOUTH BANK OPTION However, if you're still full of energy or if heading for Waterloo station, you could continue along the river bank, in which case there's that galaxy of cultural institutions of increasing size all the way to Westminster Bridge, an area collectively known as 'the South Bank'. To this the intelligent tourist needs no guide, as it's all well known to culture vultures and well signposted. Or you could make a trip on another day to stroll through this lot.

A brief reminder of how very much is here, in order from Blackfriars Bridge: **The Museum of** (it's not a printing mistake, what it's 'of' varies enormously and randomly and aims to be not the usual museum stuff at all), the **Oxo Tower** (restaurants, hopefully serving thick brown gravy, and arty stuff), **Bernie Spain Gardens** (low-key arty-crafty stuff), and **Gabriels Wharf**, past the IBM offices to the **National Theatre**.

By now the buildings look like Nazi bunkers and gun emplacements from World War II. No, that's totally unfair. Some of those Nazi concrete works were quite attractive, if you forget their purpose. Does anybody think the bleak designs of these two buildings, and the even more dismal **Hayward Gallery** and **QE Hall** around the corner, have anything to contribute besides alienation? I suppose it's a generational thing and someone out there thinks they are brilliant (that guy with a white stick possibly?). If so drop me a line and put me right, when you're out of therapy.

Meanwhile I suggest that the Mayor of London arranges for the guns of *HMS Belfast*, just up river, to be used to blow these monstrosities to hell. They have a 30-mile range, and were used to attack just such Nazi gun emplacements, so it should be easily possible, providing they miss the Tate Modern's chimney (or even if they don't).

Around the rather elegant Waterloo Bridge are the **National Film Theatre**, the Hayward Gallery and the Queen Elizabeth Hall, all built in the same ghastly Nazi-bunker style. This is not to denigrate the often world-class offerings within these buildings, of course. Oh no.

The **Royal Festival Hall**, on the other hand, the sole large remnant of the 1951 Festival of Britain that cheered up grim post-war Britain, has aged rather well. (Not that I'm suggesting the concrete bunkers alongside will also mellow with age. Their total removal would greatly improve views of the RFH. In fact some of the ghastly concrete walkways have been chopped off at the rear of the RFH, so the authorities have in effect admitted they are vile.)

By the way, if you are going to a concert at the RFH you will be unlikely to obtain a ticket for seat 26B. It's been occupied almost every night since the hall was opened 50 years ago by eccentric Yvonne Peglar, a great fan of music of all sorts and of the Royal Festival Hall in particular. So much so that she started going as a 13-year-old schoolgirl, and now as a retired civil servant she's still a regular. The booking office staff reserve her seat automatically, so, like the Queen, she doesn't have to book. She just rings to say when she *doesn't* want to come. Not that she's away for holidays much; she spends so much on concert tickets that she can't afford many holidays.

But does she see each show more than once? Yes, if they're any good. She told a reporter: 'When Otto Klemperer was playing, I went on 23 consecutive nights. He was my god.' On Maria Callas's last appearance in London, Yvonne was invited backstage to meet the world's leading soprano. She estimates she's seen 14,000 concerts from this seat. Incredible, and how broad-minded her musical tastes must be.

Plus – I'm still listing the astounding South Bank cultural cornucopia – one can turn down towards Waterloo station and find the **IMAX** surround cinema and Britain's oldest theatre, the **Old Vic**.

Past the Festival Hall comes the world's biggest observation wheel, the simply superb **London Eye**, and County Hall with its various visitor goodies. You can easily find signs to Waterloo station nearby,

BACK TO BLACKFRIARS AND A NATIONAL TREASURE Meanwhile, if you stayed back on Blackfriars Bridge, don't miss (almost opposite Doggett's Coat and Badge) the enormous colourful brackets marked with the arms of the London, Chatham and Dover Railway and featuring that Kentish White Horse and 'Invicta' the white horse we saw at the Hop Exchange. It splendidly holds nothing, as do a fine set of piers across the river, the railway tracks having been found unnecessary at some point and removed (a cast-iron guarantee that they will soon be needed, of course). *Invicta*, you may know from school Latin, means 'the undefeated ones', and the people of Kent who use this emblem insist they were never conquered by William the Conqueror, or the Norman bastard, in 1066, but met his army and agreed terms for his taking over from Harold. Or so they say.

Crossing the bridge we might recall with a shudder that under one of these spans the body of 'God's banker' Roberto Calvi was found hanged in June 1982, his pockets stuffed, bizarrely, with cash and bricks. One of those Mafia things, it was suggested, but how the hell did they get poor Calvi up there?

Another unpleasant thing under our feet is the outlet of the **Fleet**, once a freshwater river but for about 1,000 years a foul-smelling open sewer and then rescued as a river by the great engineer Bazalgette in the 19th century who diverted the vile stuff into proper sewers. You can't see it except by craning out from the steps up to the bridge on the upstream side and I don't recommend that dangerous option, especially not if you had a few pints in the Founder's. It's better seen from a boat if you must. See *History of the Fleet*, page 96 and *Fleet Street walk*, page 173.

At this side of the bridge there's some grand architecture to behold. The curved building opposite is the Unilever headquarters and don't miss its absurd sculptures up high and the grand pieces at the sides. The Unilever company makes soap so perhaps the building is carved from the stuff.

Further round the corner towards the river is the beautiful City of London School (on the left of it, looking from the bridge), like part of a French château spirited here from the Loire.

We go ahead, into the subway (pedestrian underpass) and up out of exit 1 to the **Black Friar** pub, small but perfectly formed. The name Black Friar comes from medieval monasteries and priories around here.

First regard carefully the outside, the tiny cheese-shaped wedge of land that it occupies. As I've noted elsewhere, the rebuilding of the City after the Great Fire of 1666 was so rapid that plans for a boring American-style gridiron pattern of roads were thrown aside and the daft medieval street pattern lived on – thankfully, in my view. Here the builders also had a railway line at first-floor height to contend with behind the pub, so the site was very restricted, and is only about 4ft wide at one end. Second, look at the rich ornamentation, the bronze signs and the mosaic detail. Certainly, the architect did a good job in 1875, as can be seen by the interesting exterior, but the real treat is inside, and clearly dates from the early 20th century, with heavy art nouveau influences in its whimsical interpretation of the life of monks. I think that the interior is a national treasure, and the beer isn't bad either. I can't describe it fully, so see for yourself. It'll be crowded at City lunchtimes, but soon thins out at around 14.15 so you can have a proper look round. Superb, and definitely eccentric.

Here you can sample what Brits call 'real ale', the living beer made with live yeast, water, hops and malted barley. If you are from a poor, benighted land where chilled lager is the only brew, I have to warn you that it's a bit of an acquired taste. Like sex and cigars (or both at once in former President Clinton's case), it gets better. The fourth pint is probably the best. You can return to **Blackfriars** station, across the road, for a train home via the subway and don't miss a final detail in the station's booking hall. The ornate blocks, which formed part of the façade of this station before some blockhead removed it, were engraved with places the aforesaid London, Chatham and Dover Railway could take you to via its suburban lines but also via Channel ferries. These blocks were saved and put here. Thus we have prosaic Bromley ludicrously next to Bremen as alternative destinations, St Petersburg next to Westgate-on-Sea, and Beckenham next to Baden-Baden. I had hoped to see Penge next to Peking, but they seem to have lost that one.

Whitechapel

LAND OF GROPE AND GORY

MURDER, MAYHEM AND MASALA Half the English-speaking world seems to watch a BBC TV soap opera called *EastEnders*. It would be called 'gritty' if it were about northerners, for all the characters are dysfunctional and constantly having affairs, abortions, fights, prison sentences, etc, and I can't remember the last 'normal' couple who merely brought up their own children and actually worked for a living. Perish the thought. And a 'gay outing' isn't a trip to Clacton.

But it's all far too tame compared to real life in the East End, which to judge by events around Whitechapel is far more dramatic, murderous and violent than in the fictional Albert Square. In fact, I wouldn't read the next section at all if you are squeamish. For those who have a horrified fascination with Hannibal Lecter and such like, however, it's worth taking a look at the area around Whitechapel, which offers:

- Jack the Ripper's amazing killings
- A shoot-out involving mad anarchists and Winston Churchill
- The place where the bigots of the 20th century's worst 'isms' – communism and fascism – came to a bloody battle on British streets
- The Kray brothers' merciless executions
- Layers of rapid cultural reinvention worthy of New York, as completely different waves of immigrants move in and out

And that means there's fabulous and cheap Indian, or rather Bangladeshi, food. There's also the origins of Philadelphia's famous bell and a radical art gallery.

WHERE THE RIPPER STRUCK The Ripper, a serial killer of women who exhibited revolting perversity and brutal ferocity and who has never been identified, has been well documented in a mountain of books which have put forward many fantastic theories about who he was and why he did it. Let's just stick to what he did and where. That's bad enough. In fact SKIP TO THE NEXT SECTION IF YOU CAN'T TAKE GRUESOME DETAIL.

He picked up prostitutes in the streets around Whitechapel and took them to dark corners, as many did for standing-up sex (a 'quick knee-trembler', they'd say) in Victorian times. He then strangled them, cut their throats right through and carried out the bizarre mutilations which earned his great notoriety. Six such killings are attributed to him, although the first, of **Martha Tabram** on 7 August 1888, was possibly by someone else, because although she was stabbed around 40 times, there were none of what would become the Ripper's trademark macabre mutilations. She was found off Wentworth Street in Gunthorpe Street and was last seen leaving the White Swan pub for sex with a soldier. On the 31st of that month, the body of **Polly Nichols** (née Walker), 42, a drunk and a prostitute, was found in Buck's Row (now called Durward Street) by a policeman. Her throat had been cut so severely that her head was only just connected to her body. Her skirts had been lifted and her abdomen ripped open. She is buried in the City of London Cemetery, Manor Park, and her gravestone is a flat marker.

A few days later, on 8 September, **Annie Chapman's** body was found in the yard of a house in Hanbury Street with her intestines ripped out and her womb missing. The neighbour who found her said: 'I found a female lying down, her clothing up to her knees and her face covered in blood. What was lying beside her I cannot describe – it was parts of her body.' She is buried in the same cemetery in unmarked grave No 78.

Then on 30 September, **Lizzy Stride** (née Gulafsdotter) was found in what is now Henriques Street with her throat cut. It is thought she escaped further mutilation because the Ripper was disturbed, so within an hour another woman was killed to satisfy the madman – **Cathy Eddowes** in Mitre Square. Her face had been hacked about, and her womb and a kidney were missing. Stride was buried at East London Cemetery, West Ham, with a white marble frame around the grave but no marker. Eddowes was buried in Manor Park, near Polly Nichols' grave. By this time Victorian London was transfixed with terror and the police poured men into the area. Nevertheless, on 9 November a 25-year-old Irish prostitute, **Mary Jane Kelly,** was killed in her room in Dorset Street. Body parts were scattered around, hung up like Christmas decorations some said, her breasts had been cut off and her heart was missing. Police officers slipped on the revolting gore on the floor. Several internal organs were displayed on nearby tables. Her body was empty, and he left her with both hands tucked up inside the empty abdomen. What remained of her was buried at St Patrick's Roman Catholic Cemetery, Leytonstone, in row 67, grave 16, although thanks to ghoulish souvenir hunters there is now no marker. This seemed to end the reign of terror, but Jack the Ripper was never caught (unlike the Yorkshire Ripper of the 1980s who committed a series of similar crimes in that county). A whole industry has been spawned speculating on who he really was, but the one thing we can safely say is that he is dead today. By the way, one of the detectives working on the Ripper case was to crack the equally macabre Dr Crippen case a few years later (see page 20), and perhaps the most unlikely suspect on his Ripper list was philanthropist Dr Thomas Barnardo, simply because he had campaigned to help young prostitutes. Dr Barnardo is buried, aptly, in the grounds of one of the children's homes he founded at Tanners Lane in Barkingside.

WHITECHAPEL'S BATTLES: THE SIEGE OF SIDNEY STREET

Whitechapel's first great gun battle of the 20th century was the Siege of Sidney Street, involving the unlikely combination of Peter the Painter, Latvian anarchists and Winston Churchill directing fire in his top hat. In fact, knowing Churchill's amazing subsequent life, perhaps it wasn't all that unlikely.

The gang of anarchists had come into Britain in the rush of immigration after the failed Russian revolution of 1905. Their leader was Peter Paiktow, who worked as a painter while in London.

In 1909 the authorities became aware of the dangers posed by these types when two Latvians staged an armed robbery in Tottenham and two people were killed and 27 people injured during the ensuing shoot-out and pursuit.

In 1910, Peter the Painter's gang rented a Houndsditch shop with the aim of tunnelling into an adjacent jeweller's shop. Neighbours were made suspicious by the noise and when an unarmed constable entered the building, he was immediately shot dead. This was on 23 December 1910, the year after the 'Tottenham Outrage'. Three further policemen called to the scene were also killed.

19

One of the gang was accidentally shot by a colleague as they made good their escape, and he was left here to die with a nurse, who bizarrely was also a gang member (it's turning into a kind of Latvian Bonnie & Clyde – certainly not the kind of thing decent British robbers ever got up to, at least not until the Krays came along). The police soon found the injured man and arrested various connected people.

By the New Year, the police learned that two of the gang were holed up at 100 Sidney Street in Whitechapel. On 3 January, as armed officers cordoned off the street, a gun battle broke out and it soon became clear that the gang, with their machine-guns, could outshoot the police, who were armed just with revolvers.

The police asked the Home Office to call in the Army. The Home Secretary at the time was Winston Churchill, the larger-than-life figure who had already escaped from an armoured train in the Boer War, and who was later to lead the troops personally in the defence of Antwerp, introduce the tank in World War I, mount the daring but disastrous Gallipoli campaign, and then face down the might of Nazi Germany when Britain stood alone during World War II. Asking him if he'd mind summoning armed help was like asking Dawn French's Vicar of Dibley if she'd mind eating a cream cake.

Churchill arrived and took charge, sheltering behind a wall as the bullets flew. He called in the Scots Guards who were nearby. He was probably showing restraint in not calling in heavy artillery or a dreadnought battleship to come up the Thames and flatten Whitechapel with 15-inch shells. The Scots Guards riddled the building until it looked like a colander. It caught fire, but Churchill ordered the Fire Brigade to let it burn and let them die.

The two gunmen were indeed dead in the ruins, but neither turned out to be the leader, Peter the Painter. He was never traced. Neither was the criminal trial of the gang members who had been caught a great success. It couldn't be proved who had shot the policemen in Tottenham, and the case collapsed. The key members returned to Latvia and one of them, Jacob Peters, became a top Bolshevik and a high official in the communist government after the Russian Revolution. In the 1930s he, like hundreds of thousands of others, fell victim to one of Stalin's purges and received the customary shot in the back of the neck.

Having avoided a shoot-out with Churchill, one giant of the 20th century, he fell victim to the megalomania of another, so this might have been a kind of justice. Better Latvian than never, perhaps. But Peter the Painter, an altogether cleverer kind of anarchist, lived on, although no-one is ever likely to find out where.

THE FRONT LINE OF HISTORY AND THE BATTLE OF CABLE STREET There have, of course, been tensions between the previous residents here and the latest wave of arrivals, from the French Huguenot silk workers undercutting the local men and then gaining a virtual monopoly to the Jewish rag trade easing out their rivals a century or two later.

And, while during all these hundreds of years of various groups arriving the overwhelming experience has been of peace and tolerance, there have been flare-ups. **Brick Lane** has been the front line between the newcomers and those who wanted to resist them.

In 1901, angry cockneys would meet near here in the British Brothers' League to try to push back the advance of the Jews, driven from Russia and Central Europe by vicious pogroms over the previous 30 years. The man behind the League was Stepney MP, Major W Evans-Gordon, and this period saw the introduction of Britain's first immigration control, the Aliens Act of 1905. Before that you didn't really need a passport at all.

In the 1970s, it was the National Front and 'Paki-bashing'. But outbreaks among

For over a hundred years, the East End has meant the 'rag trade' – tailoring at its posh end, sweat shops at its cheap end. In adjacent Spitalfields, near Petticoat Lane, there's Fashion Street, and nearby Weaver Street and Vallance Road. The thriving clothing trade – carried on by French Huguenots, then Jews, and now Bangladeshis – has given the street names real resonance. French, Yiddish, Bengali, Sylheti (a related language), and of course cockney have been the weft and warp of this place. Eventually each robustly working-class group did well and moved to middle-class suburbs, making room for the next wave of immigrants.

In Fournier Street, Spitalfields, there's a religious building which has seen these tides of people come and go. Built for the French Huguenots in 1743 it has been a Methodist church, a synagogue and is now a mosque. Like the mosque in Whitechapel Road, it is packed to overcrowding for Friday prayers.

Around here not only has halal food become more common than kosher, with the delicious sweets well worth a try, you can see the traditional dress, the bilingual shop and street signs, the books, CDs and videos and newspapers in Bengali. The culture is alive.

But then, like the Jews before them, the Bangladeshi community is hardly a minority. In Spitalfields it's said to make up 60 per cent of the population; in London as a whole one estimate is 123,000, mostly in the borough of Tower Hamlets. Like their Huguenot and Jewish predecessors, these people are tight-knit and hard-working. Who knows if they too will move on into the more comfortable strata of British society to make room for another wave of the dispossessed.

cheap power-seekers using the basest tribal emotions to attack people who looked or worshipped differently were usually short-lived and linked to economic hard times.

But between these two dates, back in the 1930s, while the Nazis were blaming the Jews for the economic troubles in Germany, the East End came the closest Britain has ever got to embracing this intolerant politically organised race hatred, this blind worship of political '-isms', that ruined hundreds of millions of lives in the 20th century.

In those days, just as fascism had not yet been exposed to the wider public as the evil it was, so communism was held up by British intellectuals such as George Orwell and the working class of the East End as an ideal way of life. No-one would have believed that what was going on in Stalin's Russia was as terrible as in Nazi Germany. There were communist MPs and councils in the East End. Times were hard and the great -isms seemed to offer a simple answer. Nor is this so remote from our own lives. My own father, son of a Walthamstow shoemaker, was a Trotskyite sympathiser for a time.

On Sunday, 4 October 1936 would-be fascist demagogue, Sir Oswald Mosley, and around 3,500 would-be fascist Blackshirts tried to march into the East End, shouting: 'Get rid of the Yids'. They had put up stickers saying that Jews were taking jobs that 'white workers' should have, trying to drive a wedge between the two economically hard-pressed groups. The event had been well-publicised among the Left, and thousands of communists, socialists and Spanish Civil War veterans converged on the scene, as did the fascists.

The police tried to clear the way and used baton charges on horseback when the going got rough. And it *did* get rough. The battle was almost entirely between the police – who in upholding the Blackshirts' right to march seemed to be on their side – and the Left, who adopted the Spanish Civil War slogan '*No Pasarán*' (they shall not pass). There was huge support in East London for the Left – far stronger than for the fascists, in fact. On this day, perhaps 300,000 communists, Jews, socialists and anti-fascists gathered to block the Blackshirts in what became the **Battle of Cable Street**.

The police started using baton charges and the whole mounted division to clear the crowds from Leman Street, but at Aldgate they came up against a tram immobilised by an anti-fascist driver. More trams joined, forming a massive road block surrounded by tens of thousands of people – some papers said half a million, some 100,000. Plans for the Blackshirts to march down Commercial Road, going east from the City, were scuppered.

The Blackshirts could have pressed eastwards down The Highway, further south, but there were no Jews there to intimidate and attack, which was the whole point of the operation, only Catholics, so the only route left to the east was Cable Street. The police tried to force their way through.

The Left had a plan ready. A lorry was turned over and a builders' yard ransacked to make a barricade. All the way along the road the inhabitants pelted the police – rather than the Blackshirts who never really got going from their start in Royal Mint Street – with bottles, fruit, bricks and the contents of chamber pots. Every time the police cleared a barricade a new one sprang up. A witness quoted in *The Battle of Cable Street 1936* (see *Further Reading*, page 312) described the women throwing down everything they had – beds, chairs, tables – to build the barricades. 'I can remember the old girls with their aprons and shawls on … and glory on their faces.'

A whistle blew and someone shouted: 'The dockers are coming' and they swarmed from a side street in their hundreds, carrying pick handles. They prised up the cobblestones to use as missiles. Another eyewitness said: 'The most amazing thing was to see a silk-coated Orthodox Jew standing next to an Irish docker with a grappling iron. This was unbelievable.'

Police were getting seriously hurt and getting nowhere. After three hours battling, the police advised the fascists that they could not march through and, humiliated, they dispersed westwards, never to pose a major threat in British politics again. Whether the dreaded political -isms would ever have taken hold in Britain as a whole is doubtful. But to treat the Battle of Cable Street as some kind of exaggerated silly scuffle is to under-estimate the volatile rip-tide of history flowing through here at the time. Many of those on either side at Cable Street were also volunteers in the Spanish Civil War where Left and Right fought to the death. Those people, if not the wider public, understood what fascism meant.

Similarly provocative marches through Jewish areas were exactly what Hitler's bullies were doing. If the mass of the people there had also resisted and defeated them in the early days, would the agony of global war and the Holocaust have been avoided?

In the late 20th century, there were still plenty of people around who had been at the Battle of Cable Street. Leading trade unionists of the 1960s such as Jack Dash had won their spurs fighting for the Left in Cable Street, and the battle was of course lionised by the far Left who need such conflict and suffering to thrive as much as the extreme Right does. Another East-Ender I can think of still boasted – long after World War II exposed such attitudes for what they were – of 'having knocked down six Jews that day'. Amazing.

As a postcript, the last throw of the trade unions that had been so strong in the East End for most of the 20th century, often bringing the docks, railways or buses to a halt, came with a 1980s battle just a couple of streets south of Cable Street – the **Battle of Fort Wapping**. This was when the labour movement tried to stop 'scab' labour under Rupert Murdoch putting out his newspapers in a new fortified printing plant without the print unions. By this time the unions weren't on the side of starving children, oppressed races and Spanish liberty, but were behaving like spoilt brats who scream every time they pass the sweets at the supermarket checkout and always get their way. Much of the public was fed up with their stupid stoppages of essential services. Margaret Thatcher's Conservative government was right behind the Australian news magnate, and the unions were smashed amidst much stone and mud slinging, never to recover their stranglehold on the Press. And here again, the poor police became the enemy on the ground for the protestors.

THE KRAY GANG'S KILLINGS AND THE STORY OF THE BLIND BEGGAR The **Blind Beggar** pub in Whitechapel Road (left out of the Tube) has seen, so to speak, more than one killing. Before World War I the pub was home to a gang of pick-pocket ruffians, heirs to vicious Bill Sykes of *Oliver Twist*. One of them, 'Bulldog' Wallis, got into an argument and killed a man by pushing the tip of his umbrella through his eye into his brain, a macabre method of execution at the best of times, but particularly in a pub with 'blind' in its title. And in the Blind Beggar's tradition, no-one saw *nuffink*, as they told police and Wallis had to be released from police custody. He returned to the pub accompanied by cheering supporters. What happened to the gruesome umbrella is not recorded.

When Ronnie Kray, one of the merciless Kray Twin gangsters, protection racketeers and would-be Al Capones of London, killed George Cornell here on 8 March 1966, again the police found no-one in the Blind Beggar had seen anyone at all. *We ain't seen nuffink, guv, 'onest.*

Later, after the gang began to be rounded up, people's memory suddenly improved and the police put together what happened.

Cornell had made the mistake of calling Ronnie Kray a 'fat poof' ('poof' is British slang for 'homosexual'). This had the virtue of accuracy on both counts, but all the wisdom of Bambi's mum picking a pack of starving rottweilers as baby-sitters. He was doomed. Kray could not let such loss of face go unchallenged without his hold over the East End being weakened.

Cornell was sitting by the bar on 8 March, drinking a light ale (a bit of a 'poofy' drink, it could be argued) when Ronnie Kray and one of his thugs marched in. Cornell turned to face Kray and, ever lippy, said: 'Well look who's here.' Kray's answer was to shoot him through the eye with a 9mm pistol. The other drinkers ran for it. In the commotion the juke box, playing, appropriately for Cornell, *The Sun Ain't Gonna Shine Anymore,* was jolted and played the 'any more' over and again. It's the kind of detail film-makers like.

Kray got away with this one for a while but was jailed for life at the Old Bailey four years later. But not until Ronnie had spurred twin brother Reggie into being a bit more villainous and shooting another minor criminal, Jack 'the hat' McVitie. That was the one that got the Krays into the dock.

Many years later, a Fleet Street newspaper printed a smuggled picture of Reggie Kray enjoying a cup of tea behind bars. Referring to a well-known British biscuit, the headline was: 'I could just murder a McVitie…' Brilliant.

Another pub well-used by the Krays was further along the High Street, the **Grave Maurice**. The nemesis of the Krays, Inspector Leonard 'Nipper' Read, sat himself here once to observe Ronnie Kray arriving for a TV interview.

He recalled seeing a brash American car pull up, a hefty man in a suit get out, look up and down the street, feel in his pocket for, doubtless, a gun, go in the pub to have a look, come out again, check the street and then open the door for Kray to step out. Similarly ostentatious precautions worthy of an American president took place at the end of the interview. The hapless interviewer was frisked by

19

Kray's thugs, although presumably they weren't, on this occasion, too worried that he might be wearing a wire.

There is a story that the name Blind Beggar comes from the great medieval warrior Simon de Montfort. Blinded in battle, and supposedly killed, he in fact returned incognito to London to beg on the streets, a broken man, and was found by his followers who had refused to believe he was dead. Or something like that. There's a 16th-century ballad entitled *The Blind Beggar of Bethnal Green*. It's a great yarn, but some people put it back a few more centuries and make it King Harold, he who got one in the eye from William the Conqueror.

There was another Kray, Charlie, who was not so directly involved in the gang killings but was given 10 years' jail for helping dispose of Jack 'the hat' McVitie's body (and the hat, presumably). This Kray once had an affair with a certain Barbara Windsor, the bubbly and buxom star of *Carry On* films. They carried on while her husband, another villain, Ronnie Knight, was in jail. She, TV soap fans will know, became Peggy Mitchell, mistress of the Queen Vic pub in the *EastEnders* TV series. So perhaps I was wrong to say the TV East End and the real one weren't connected. When Peggy's son Phil was shot outside the Queen Vic on TV, was it so different to how George Cornell got to stain the Blind Beggar's carpet so red?

Today the Blind Beggar's carpet is still crimson (just in case) but it's a friendly enough place with cheap food, souvenir T-shirts and books about the Ripper. While I was there, a chap came in and ordered three pints of strong lager. I assumed they were for his mates on the way from the market outside, but no, he just sat there and drank them off, and it wasn't quite noon. Funny old world, innit?

A SHORT WALK ABOUT WHITECHAPEL

❷ Whitechapel, ends Aldgate. Distance about 1¹/₂ miles, time about 1¹/₂ hours with stops … permanent ones for some people. Having read Whitechapel's horrible history above, you will find today's Whitechapel both pleasantly fascinating and surprisingly unchanged from its poor East End origins despite being cheek by jowl with one of the world's richest financial centres. It's less dangerous than most inner cities. But then these busy pavements have had a lot of blood washed off them – all really gruesome detail is in the sections above, not in the walk, so don't worry.

Coming out of the Tube, there's a great street market in front of you (except on Sundays). There are Asian stalls with saris and glittering cloths of all descriptions, the wonderful vegetables favoured by the sub-continent such as *brinjals* and *okra* (aubergines and ladies' fingers), plus stalls run by cockney costermongers selling tools or unbelievably cheap gadgets such as, when I visited, those aluminium micro-scooters for £15.

Here was a cockney chappie without a stall selling 'lovely hankies, five for a pound'. How Victorian – don't people use paper tissues nowadays? In Oliver Twist's day the silk handkerchief was the prime object of pickpockets and it was said that you could have your pocket picked at one end of such a market and buy it back at the other. Whether it had been washed and … no, let's not go down that road.

In front of us as we leave the Tube is the London Hospital. Over the road, if you're interested in the social history of the East End with its communism and the Battle of Cable Street, is a rather good Lefty bookshop, **Eastside Books**.

Take a quick excursion to the left (east) to the **Blind Beggar** pub to check if the carpet where the gruesome gang killings took place is still crimson (I'm assuming you've read the sections above throughout this walk). The bullet-holes in the pub ceiling have gone, however, but the food is cheap. At the major road crossing here,

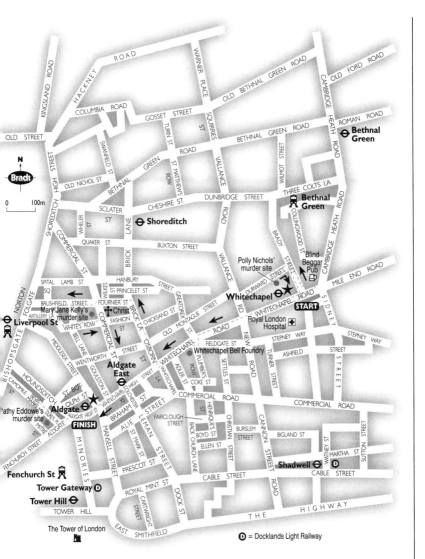

D = Docklands Light Railway

the road to the right (south) is **Sidney Street**, where the amazing events of the Siege of 1911 unfolded at No 100 on the left, although the bullet-riddled house has been replaced at least twice, so I don't suggest going to look.

Turning back down Whitechapel Road towards the Tube, we are close to the spot where Jack the Ripper's victim **Polly Nichols**'s body was found on 31 August 1888. If you want to reach the actual spot, take a short deviation by turning right into Brady Street after the Sainsbury's entrance and go left into Durward Street. Down here, on the left, you are soon faced with an old school, now converted into flats. At the nearest corner of this school's redbrick wall, there used to be a gate where a newer wall now stands. Here, half on the road and half on the pavement, Polly's body was found at about 03.30, her head almost ripped off.

She was a drunk and a prostitute. That night she made three times the money needed to pay for her vermin-infested 'doss house' lodgings in Thrawl Street but

215

If you went to school outside the USA, you might not know that the foremost symbol of American independence is the Liberty Bell of Philadelphia, made right here in Whitechapel in 1751. That's the one which has cast on it: 'Proclaim liberty throughout all the land unto all the inhabitants thereof.'

But as for why it's cracked, there's a gap the width of the Atlantic in the historical record.

The thing was hoisted into the Philadelphia State House steeple and was said to have cracked the first time it was used. The ship that brought it refused to return it and certain Americans tried to recast it. This is where it gets complex. They thought the metal too brittle, so they added different metals, and the result was a very poor bell. The Whitechapel Bell Foundry, frankly not at all sure the bell was undamaged when it was hoisted up in the first place, was horrified. Bell metal must be brittle otherwise it won't ring true, they argued. You can crack the biggest bell in the world with a 2lb hammer, they said. You just don't wallop the thing.

The Americans recast it again with the correct blend of metals. Again it was hoisted and again it was cracked although there is a story of a bunch of untrained lads – I think at this point, but I may be confused – being left to make a noise with it and running off home when the crack developed. Of course that yarn could be a British fabrication (they make those even better than bells).

In 1978, a bunch of 30 demonstrators from the Procrastinators Society of America protested outside the foundry in Whitechapel bearing placards saying WE GOT A LEMON and WHAT ABOUT THE WARRANTY? They paraded round in circles in the way that American protestors always do. Are they not allowed to stand still, or are they providing more of a challenge for the cops trying to shoot them, like toy ducks at the fun fair?

The Bell Foundry, to be fair, responded magnificently. Despite the Americans having recast the bell twice, mishandled it by letting youths bong it (and thus totally invalidated the warranty as surely as if you'd used a golf club as a fence post) and certain other outstanding bills over Boston tea shipments they could have mentioned, they offered to replace the thing at once. Without charge. If it was returned in its original packaging.

Of course the Americans don't really want it replaced or the crack fixed, because they love it how it is. But in that same year a new bell was presented, the Bicentennial Bell. It was inscribed 'For the people of the USA from the people of Great Britain. Let freedom ring.' Not bad – I can't see Chrysler giving a British customer a new car 200 years after he broke the last one. And it wasn't cracked when it left the premises.

---

drank the lot and was turned away, and was last seen looking for more custom in Whitechapel Road at 02.30.

Return to Whitechapel Road, turn right and walk back past the Tube. Keep an eye out for No 259 on this side of the road, now an ordinary shop but once home to one of Whitechapel's weirdest stories. Here the **Elephant Man**, with his hideously deformed skull, was exhibited in a typical Victorian freak show and people paid to see him. When he was rescued (see page 219), he was taken to the Whitechapel Hospital opposite. The more modern bits of the hospital, by the way, replace those bits bombed to hell in the 1940s. Hospitals weren't avoided in the indiscriminate Blitz, and that war also destroyed the White Chapel that gave this area its name.

On a happier note, we soon see on the left the massive **East London Mosque**, heart of the Bangladeshi community round here, with its distinctive crescents where a church's crosses would be. And, of course, minarets wailing for Friday's prayer rather than bells tolling in steeples on Sundays.

That's ironic, for the world's oldest bell foundry is on the left. The **Whitechapel Bell Foundry** is Britain's oldest manufacturing business and must be one of the world's oldest. There are records of Richard Chamberlain, 'bell founder of Aldgate', in 1420, and the business may be a lot older than that.

It's well worth popping into the office at 34 Whitechapel Road and looking at the display in the foyer of the offices. Opening the door rings a bell, of course, like an old-fashioned sweet shop and as you enter you step through the bell-frame (the stencil-like thing that gives the contours) of possibly the world's most famous bell, Big Ben.

This 9ft high, 7ft 6in wide, 13½-ton job cost £572 2s 0d – you can see the bill – and rings the hours at Parliament's clock tower. It's heard from one end of the earth to the other on the BBC radio news.

If it's a business day you can probably get a glimpse into the workshops from the side street and no doubt there will be several bells on the ground, the church names chalked upon them: St Mary the Virgin, St Botolph's, etc.

One of my favourite obscure saints in Cornwall, a county of obscure saints, was St Disen. He had been revered for a hundred years, with people assuming he was a weird Irish saint, of which they have plenty around there, and a mythology of his life began to grow up. But not long ago it turned out that he was a typoijg error (sorry, a typing error): it should have been not St Disen but St Denis. As for new bells, I rather liked the approach of a benefactor of Selborne in Hampshire. When his new bells were delivered, he had them set upside down and filled with punch and the whole village got blind drunk.

Of course Americans would disagree that Big Ben is the most famous bell in the world, as they've got their own candidate (read box opposite to see if it's all it's cracked up to be). But it also came from Whitechapel. Tours of the foundry are possible by arrangement, and there is sometimes an annual open day on the first Saturday in September (for enquiries, ☎ 020 7247 2599).

We go on down Whitechapel Road and it's worth recalling that on the British version of the Monopoly board, this is the poorest (brown) end of the game while Mayfair (royal blue) is the richest. Some things never change.

At Brick Lane (or Osborn Street) we turn right, although the constantly radical **Whitechapel Gallery**, with a rather cool frontage, if that's an object of your visit, is just a few yards further straight ahead, on the right-hand side.

Let's wander up fascinating Brick Lane, where Whitechapel's ethnic tidal waves came ashore over the centuries, bringing Huguenots, Jews, then Bangladeshis. This road, named after a brickworks here, has a great market on Sundays and an annual festival (see *The Eccentric Year*, page 308).

CHAOS AND BANGLATOWN As I turned the corner here, I noticed some hopeful bureaucrat had put up a Red Route (no stopping) sign on a lamppost. These are supposed to be far more draconian than mere yellow lines and frighten the doodoos out of would-be parkers. Terrible penalties await anyone who even *thinks* of stopping in these zones. They will go to your home and disembowel your cat with a rusty tin opener, then shred your car into 1,000 pieces, encase them in plastic, label them 'Souvenir of Whitechapel' and mail them to remote addresses in 200 countries. Or something pretty serious.

The reality, I was kind of pleased to see, was three parked white vans, a minicab, a taxi, a hearse, two flash cars and a motorbike. Transit vans were hooting and shoving trying to get through the gap like blood trying to get through a fat man's coronary arteries. It's the antidote to the law-abiding Swiss, one of whom once told me that if he saw a car parked illegally, he'd stop at the next phone box and call the police. He might have been pulling my leg, but I think I'll settle for the chaos. Let freedom hoot.

Further up Brick Lane the road signs become bilingual, as in Chinatown, and the food consequently becomes better and cheaper (if, like most Brits, you love food from the subcontinent, and no jokes about subcontinence, *per-lease*).

But hang on, we're near another murder site, the killing of **Martha Tabram** in George Yard tenements, Gunthorpe Street (see page 208). If you're interested, turn left down Wentworth Street and it's an alley on the left, leading back to Whitechapel Road

But scurrying on up Brick Lane, enjoying the rich sweets and colourful garments, and noting a small outbreak of trendy 'loft living', we soon reach Fournier Street on the left. The building on the right as we enter has had several religious incarnations (Huguenot, Jewish and Muslim, none of which believe in reincarnation, but never mind) and halfway down on the right there's a chance to see another Ripper murder spot. If you wish, take a right along Wilkes Street to Hanbury Street at the end and find where No 29 was, opposite Nos 28 and 30. Here, in the backyard, was found the body of **Annie Chapman** (see page 209). By the way, No 3 Fournier Street was the location for the 1992 film *The Crying Game*, starring Miranda Richardson.

Christ Church

Continuing along Fournier Street, whose architecture is much the same as in the Ripper's time (and indeed long before, to judge by the French Huguenot-style window shutters) we find at the end Hawksmoor's spectacular masterpiece – in some eyes – of **Christ Church**, Spitalfields.

On the opposite corner of Fournier Street, the **Ten Bells** was where Annie Chapman had her last drink before leaving with a man, presumably the Ripper. It was also a regular drinking place for the customers of most of the victims, so here we are closer to the Ripper and his victims than anywhere.

He, whoever he was, and his victims would have stood here occasionally and looked up at this spire just as you do. It was built in 1714–29 and, unlike Wren, Hawksmoor made no bones about adding a 225ft Gothic-based spire to a classical temple-shaped barn of a church. Wallop, like sticking a giant ice-cream cone on a shoe box. But then Hawksmoor, associated with great classical churches such as this and St Alfege's, Greenwich (see page 239) – both built under the Fifty New Churches Act of 1711 and both paid for partly by coal dues – was also a master of Gothic style. Probably the first bit of flamboyant Gothic people think of in London, the West front of Westminster Abbey, is also by Hawksmoor, and is not medieval at all.

The Elephant Man, greatly deformed though he was, was perhaps a natural for Whitechapel Road in the 1880s. Then, as now, a market stretched along here and it included fun-fair elements trying to catch the attention of travellers using this artery eastwards – which in the Victorian way of thinking could mean paying to see the two-headed chicken, the amazingly fat naked girl, the world's ugliest dwarf, that kind of thing.

In November 1884 showman Tom Norman brought to a shop he had hired at No 259 a number of attractions, including the professional freak Joseph Merrick, the Elephant Man. He was so called because his skin hung in folds like that of an elephant. His head and face were extremely disfigured so he didn't look human at all, with random growths akin to huge fungal bodies on a dead tree. The show included waxwork representations of other ghastly freaks. This one, at least, was real, and a money-making possibility.

The humiliating circumstances in which Merrick performed are probably difficult to understand nowadays. He was kept in a darkened cage (for maximum shock value) and when punters paid their pennies he had to take off his hood and clothes and stand naked in front of them. He was ordered around like a dog, not because he couldn't speak, but because it made a better show. He had to stand naked in front of the appalled or jeering crowd.

Sometimes the Elephant Man stood in the shop window, with his hood on, to entice passers-by, and there was a lurid representation of him on the outside of the building with sensational promises about the hideous ELEPHANT MAN prominently displayed.

As you have noticed, we are opposite the London Hospital, and a surgeon-pathologist from there, Dr Frederick Treves, saw Merrick posing in the window one day and visited him. Dr Treves believed Merrick was suffering from Proteus Syndrome and, because of the way he was treated, expected him to be a simpleton. He was appalled, given Merrick's treatment, to find a highly intelligent and sensitive young man beneath the horrible appearance.

Merrick had learned to read using the only book he'd ever seen – a copy of the Bible. Treves had drawings and photographs taken to record his condition, but for a year or two Merrick remained in the freak show.

Merrick was then taken temporarily on show in Brussels, and on his return to Liverpool Street his sudden appearance caused a near riot. Dr Treves was called by the authorities and he 'bought' Merrick – paid off the showman Norman – and took him into the London Hospital. He spent the rest of his life there in an isolation room in the attic, at that time part of the nurses' accommodation.

Nurses who initially wanted to run shrieking from him found he was, underneath it all, a reasonable and even likeable young man. Many society figures, fascinated with what they had heard, came to visit him here, including the then Princess of Wales. He was famous, but for the wrong reasons.

His head was so deformed that he was told that to sleep on his back would be dangerous, although he expressed a longing to be able to sleep like other people. One night in 1890 he went to sleep on his back – whether with suicidal intentions, we shall never know – and died aged 28.

In 1980, a movie, *Elephant Man*, was made of his story, which moved many of its viewers. Anthony Hopkins played Dr Treves and John Hurt was Merrick. His key-line was: 'I am not an animal … I am a human being … I am … a man!'

There's a difficult-to-read inscription on the corner stating 'In Case of Fire, apply for the key of the engine house at No 1 Church Passage Cottages etc' and I think dated 1843. In which case it was understandable, as the tower had burned down in 1836, on Ash Wednesday, appropriately, so the parish had to pay for it to be rebuilt. The original tower had more Gothic detail than the rebuilt one, incidentally. Even so, it's an amazing structure, starting with four absolutely massive Tuscan columns and then going through various stages to the top.

Across the road is **Spitalfields Market**, which like Smithfield shows direct lineage from gardener Joseph Paxton's glass-and-iron Crystal Palace of 1851. They're just overgrown cucumber frames, really, these Victorian markets, railway stations and glasshouses. There's food, drink and toilets in here, plus an indoor market. This place was a Fruit Exchange and Wool Exchange. Go up Brushfield Street, beside the market, more or less straight on from Fournier Street, and as you start up here, the site of the Ripper's most gruesome murder, that of **Mary Jane Kelly,** is a few yards on your left, the actual building having disappeared.

We want Gun Street, at an angle on the left. Go down here to the end, and take a look at Artillery Passage on the right, truly an ancient bit of the East End, a real feel of Ripperian or Dickensian times – imagine it in the dark and the fog, ooo err – and in fact much, much older. There were warrens of such passages and streets in the East End where the law dared not enter – the so-called rookeries where characters like Dickens's Fagin held power.

Going not right but left into Artillery Lane we come down to Crispin Street, where on the left is the Providence Night Refuge and Convent, still a home for the poorest and most desperate but also where Ripper victim Annie Chapman spent her last night alive.

Crossing Crispin Street, and going down White's Row, we come to the place where Mary Jane Kelly was killed on the left.

We emerge back on to Commercial Street and cross over. We don't go down Fashion Street (ahead) but have a look before turning right.

Again not much has changed from 100 years ago, although the use of the houses and their interiors certainly have, from lodgings for the poor to posher homes and businesses. Fashion, and the rag trade, is still in evidence here with almost every shop in Commercial Street connected with it in some way. The other striking thing about this area is how we are next door to the millions of billions of pounds the City handles, yet we have the poorest and meanest streets in the capital.

We go on down Commercial Street going south (away from Christ Church, that is). At the corner of Whitechapel High Street, as Whitechapel Road has become, you have a chance to escape down Aldgate East Tube, and why not? I'd recommend it, frankly, but read the rest in case you want more, or rather so you feel you know the whole Ripper story.

If you turn right (west) down Whitechapel High Street, you can soon reach another Ripper murder site. You go past Aldgate Station (the road becomes Aldgate High Street) and about the same distance again (across Houndsditch) you'll find Mitre Street on the right, leading to Mitre Square, where **Cathy Eddowes** was killed. She was found still warm by a policeman shining his lamp into dark corners of the square, just 20 minutes after she'd been seen alive, yet she had been expertly butchered like the others. The policeman blew his whistle to summon help (there were always police within earshot, unlike today) and a crowd of appalled onlookers gathered. Even today, locals say, a ghostly woman is seen late at night sometimes lying across the cobblestones. I haven't seen it myself, but then I wouldn't dream of being here late at night.

If we go through Mitre Square and out the other end into Duke's Place, we have the choice of looking at Britain's oldest synagogue in Bevis Marks to the left, or going right and back to Aldgate High Street and left to the Tube.

And what, you may ask, of **Lizzy Stride**, the Ripper victim whose murder site we have missed? This is in another direction, south of the rest, but can easily be reached by an energetic walker. You go back down to Aldgate East (not Aldgate) Tube and turn right down the main road, Leman Street, then the third left into Cable Street where the eponymous battle took place. The fascists wanted to come from Royal Mint Street on your right at the junction.

Go down Cable Street, left up Christian Street a couple of blocks down, left into Fairclough Street and right into Henriques Street. At this end of the street on the opposite side there's a gateway, almost opposite Baron Bernard House. This is where Lizzy Stride was killed. Then go to the top of the road and turn left on Commercial Road, which quickly brings us back to the major junction with Aldgate East Tube on it, to the north (the right).

Well that's it. Actually there were at least two more gruesome murders on this walk, but we don't want to give an area a bad name …

Part Four

VILLAGE LONDON

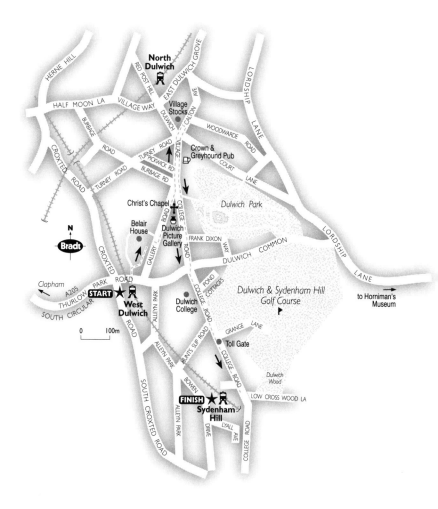

20

Dulwich

A CRAZY MIXED-UP PLACE

Dulwich, picturesque and peculiar though it may be, is geographically rather confused – fittingly, for the home of so many eccentrics. East Dulwich is north, not east, of West Dulwich, while North Dulwich is southeast, not northwest, of East Dulwich. South Dulwich is called Sydenham, as far as I can make out, but Upper Sydenham is mostly known as Crystal Palace after a Palace that wasn't crystal, or a palace and doesn't even exist any more.

Dulwich also contains what should be the National Gallery of Poland (more of that below plus an amazing museum created by an eccentric tea magnate). Borough-wise, some smart aleck leftie put Dulwich under the control of Southwark, which some felt made about as much sense as putting the posh bits of Long Island in the hands of the Bronx.

None of this geographical nonsense matters, but being England, the social divisions certainly do. **Dulwich Village** (as if a city of millions can have a real village in it) is the prettiest, oldest, poshest and most interesting part. **West Dulwich** retains some of this cachet and is a hang-out for professionals.

(I recall when there were eight psychiatrists or psychologists on one side of Alleyn Park alone. Of course, their children were mostly bonkers – I was one of them – in the same way that social workers' children are often delinquent, teachers' illiterate, vicars' sex-crazed, policemen's trouble-makers, etc. Another of them, a school chum of mine, had a strange game called Russian Brick which consisted of throwing a whole brick in the air and standing there, waiting to see if it landed on your head, a sort of poor man's Russian roulette. Eventually, the inevitable happened – a trip to casualty at King's College Hospital in Denmark Hill. The boy was still daft as a brush afterwards. Ah, what japes.)

East Dulwich, on the other hand, used to be rather good for other kinds of violence: murders, rapes, police stabbings, that kind of thing. I thought this was mere West Dulwich snobbery until I analysed newspaper files for the past 20 years and found a horrendous litany of crime in East Dulwich.

The records of crime in the area go back a fair way. In 1334, one Richard Rolf at the old manor court (where Court Lane now runs) alleged that William Hosewood 'at Dylwysh had carried off Edith, his wife, together with one cow worth ten shillings, clothes, jewels and other goods'. No change there then, apart from the value of the cow.

But East Dulwich has outgrown its rough past, and is now said (by estate agents, mainly) to be becoming gentrified. This is all too possible as it has even become trendy among the chattering classes with not quite enough money to live in Fulham; and indeed some utterly lovely people and posh celebs (not always the same thing) already live, with their upwardly mobile lifestyles, Volvo estates, nannies, whatever, in East Dulwich.

This guide will, however, concentrate on Dulwich Village and its environs, because it is far more interesting. To put it another way, East Dulwich may have had crooks and nannies, but Dulwich Village has nooks and crannies.

VILLAGE PEOPLE AND THE CRYSTAL PALACE The 'village' tag for Dulwich isn't really such a joke. With its pond, archaic 'finger' signposts, pubs, toll gate giving prices per pig, and leafy green roads without formal edges, you could think you were somewhere in the Chilterns. Well, you could if it were five o'clock on a June morning, with no-one around.

In medieval times the place was Dilwihs, the meadow where dill grows; being surrounded by wooded hills it must have seemed – and still does just a little – a rural paradise, if less than half-a-dozen miles from Charing Cross.

Even in Victorian times this isolated bliss was still to be found. The essayist and philosopher John Ruskin who lived at nearby Herne Hill, wrote affectionately:

> The crowning glory of Herne Hill was that, after walking along its ridge southward
> from London, through a mile of chestnut, lilac and apple trees, hanging over the
> wooden palings on each side – suddenly the trees stopped on the left, and out one
> came on the top of a field sloping down to the south into Dulwich valley – open
> fields animate with cow and buttercup and below the beautiful meadows and high
> avenues of Dulwich, and beyond, all that crescent of the Norwood hills; a footpath,
> entered by a turnstile, going down to the left …

Something of that remains, making Dulwich special.

On the other hand, things were changing. The Crystal Palace, that famous conservatory-like shed built by Joseph Paxton (hence the pub named after him) for the 1851 exhibition in Hyde Park, was relocated here after that show and burned down in the 1930s. I can remember from childhood West Dulwich old folk saying: 'Oo yes, dearie, I can remember molten glass flowing down the hill as if it was yesterday.' This I didn't believe, for how anything made of iron and glass could burn was a puzzle. Anyway, we were expecting a nuclear attack on London at any moment so it didn't seem too important at the time.

However, today there's such nostalgia over Paxton's creation, the forerunner of the great railway station arches around the country, that nothing less than a replica would seem to satisfy some campaigners.

So have the people always loved the Crystal Palace?

Well, let's hear what Ruskin had to say in the 1880s about the newly arrived Crystal Palace, which stood on the hill across Dulwich's wooded valley, opposite his vantage point.

> … the Crystal Palace, without ever itself attaining any true aspect of its size, and
> possessing no more sublimity than a cucumber frame between two chimneys, yet by
> the stupidity of its hollow bulk, dwarfs the hills at once; so one thinks of them as
> three long lumps of clay, on lease for building.

And later in the same essay (from *Praeterita*, 1890), he goes on:

> Then the Crystal Palace came, for ever spoiling the view through all its compass, and
> bringing every show-day, from London, a flood of pedestrians down the footpath,
> who left it filthy with cigar ashes for the rest of the week: then the railroads came,
> and expiating roughs by every excursion train, who knocked the palings about, roared
> at the cows…

I don't think he liked it. As it turned out, the Crystal Palace didn't spoil the view for ever (not as much as the two Eiffel Tower-like transmitters that now crown this, London's highest point, do).

Ruskin was a bit strange. He was appalled to discover on his wedding night that his bride Effie Gray had, unlike sculptures of women, pubic hair. The marriage went unconsummated.

WALK: PICTURESQUE DULWICH

Starting at West Dulwich station and finishing at Sydenham Hill station (both on the same line and about 10 minutes from Victoria), taking in places to eat and drink, with an opt-out to cut the walk short, and with an optional extension to take in Horniman's museum. Time taken: 2 hours, plus stops. The car- or bike-borne can trace the same route.

West Dulwich station bestraddles Thurlow Park Road, which is also the South Circular A205 (a rather eccentric road for a national trunk route, come to think of its total lack of main roadness at some points). Cross the road on the pedestrian crossing, noticing the monogram 'EA' high up on the bridge, and the first of many archaic wooden fingerposts beneath pointing vaguely to Norwood. The monogram is that of Edward Alleyn, a 16th-century chum of Shakespeare, who dominates the Dulwich story (his monogram, name or coat of arms is just about everywhere. We are near Alleyn Park, one of three roads named after him).

Alleyn coat of arms

Going east a little from the station (that is, turn right out of the entrance) you soon take a turning to the left, Gallery Road. Or you can cut through the small gate across the road from the station into the grounds of Belair House, an elegant 18th-century (1785) white mansion which you should aim for. On the right through the trees (if it is winter and the branches are bare), you may glimpse the spires and the backside of Dulwich College public school, where many famous backsides have been tanned over the years. Brits will know that 'public' means definitely not public, but private, and that 'college' means not college but school. More on the school, sorry College, and its extraordinary old boys (sorry, Old Alleynians) when we come to it.

When you reach Belair House – which, thanks to death duties in the 20th century, is no longer the preserve of the rich but now serves rich preserves as a posh restaurant – leave it to the left and come out on to Gallery Road. Walking down this leafy country road, we reach on the right Dulwich Picture Gallery.

THE STRANGE STORY OF DULWICH PICTURE GALLERY This surprising, world-class gallery located in a sleepy London suburb, is stuffed with works by Poussin, Rubens, Watteau and Canaletto, and has a bizarre history. In fact, it should have been the National Gallery of Poland, for the greatest part of the collection was put together for that country.

In the 18th century, the Dulwich collection was greatly enhanced by art dealer Noel Desenfans (1745–1807), who had been collecting by order of the King of Poland, Stanislas Augustus. When Poland was partitioned in 1795 (as, sadly, it often has been), that was the end of Stanislas's dreams and Desenfans was left with dozens of Old Masters and nowhere much to hang them. To his credit, he suggested they should become the nucleus of Britain's own national gallery, a concept novel at the time.

Desenfans and his wife Margaret lived with a painter called Sir Francis Bourgeois, and when Desenfans died, the odd couple inherited the collection and passed them on to become, in effect, Britain's first national gallery at Dulwich. The three in that unlikely ménage-à-trois are buried in a mausoleum right here at the gallery. Actually they're not buried but are in sarcophagi – well, boxes – in an odd little hall, dimly lit by amber glazing. Restful and not at all spooky. But who is the fourth box for?

Margaret Desenfans gave the college a £500 silver dining service in 1817 so it could entertain visiting dignitaries, Royal Academicians in particular, in suitable style. The service was used until 1820, after which it was deemed extravagant to lay on such feasts, and then not for another 170 years until a dinner was laid on for Lord Sainsbury who had helped raise a whopping £20 million for the gallery. It was felt that, at last, the best silver could be got out again, so the trustees dined off this now very valuable Georgian silver, using equally valuable silver cutlery.

But why did Bourgeois and the widow Desenfans choose the unlikely village of Dulwich, then some miles from the edge of London, to be the recipient of their hugely valuable collection?

Re-enter the great actor manager, **Edward Alleyn**, a friend of Shakespeare, of fellow playwright Marlowe, and an even bigger friend of Dulwich. He and another actor called Cartwright had gathered several hundred pictures in the 17th century, which were bequeathed to Alleyn's other great legacy, Dulwich College.

These early pictures are valuable sources of information on the life of the stage in Shakespeare's time (before the Puritans closed the theatres) and the Dulwich gallery thus contains the only picture of the great actor Richard Burbage (1567–1619), the greatest of his age, for whom Shakespeare wrote the parts of Hamlet and Richard III. To the left, just beyond the gallery, is Burbage Road, named in memory of this giant of the original Globe theatre.

In 1811, Bourgeois was contemplating the gallery that the College would need to house Britain's first national collection, and commissioned the great eccentric collector **Sir John Soane** (see page 44) to build a combined gallery, mausoleum and set of almshouses for poor widows.

Soane, architect of the Bank of England, was honoured to be asked to contribute to what he considered a noble project and refused to be paid for this work. He designed a radical yet brilliant scheme.

Soane knew that the governors of the College were hardly awash with cash, so he eschewed the fancy Portland stone porticoes and pillars that were at that time de rigueur. He opted instead for plain but strong London brick in starkly modern and simple outlines – daring even by today's standards. In those days, the exterior severity was shocking to many, but in the late 20th century taste caught up with Soane and his work was widely praised and imitated.

Instead of spending money on outside grandeur, Soane concentrated on making the galleries inside work. He did this brilliantly by using ingenious natural-light-gathering rooflights which threw masses of light on to white supporting walls, which then diffused this light over the paintings. This meant there was no need for any side windows, which create too much reflection and damage the paint colours with direct sunlight, and also little need for artificial lighting even today.

The only hint of grandeur comes in the antechamber of that mausoleum constructed for the munificent dead. Here is the portentous atmosphere which Soane assiduously avoided in the rest of the gallery, yet it avoids total gloom with the aid of amber lighting.

Much extended, and restored after a World War II German 'doodlebug' landed nearby and caused severe damage, the Dulwich Picture Gallery lives on, a testament to these three's eccentric vision.

And the odd story goes on. Around ten years ago, a mysterious stranger, acting like someone out of a John le Carré spy novel, turned up with something for the gallery.

With his Panama hat pulled down so he could not be recognised, a coat and scarf covering him, the mystery man walked up to the reception desk and gave the puzzled staff a package, which he said had been found on a bus. He disappeared without giving his name and has not been seen again.

When the parcel was unwrapped, the astonished experts at the gallery found three valuable English 17th- and 18th-century miniatures, worth tens of thousands of pounds.

A letter accompanying the gift said:

> I am dying and have asked a dear friend to deliver the enclosed three miniature portraits to the trustees of Dulwich Art Gallery as my anonymous gift, because I have lived in obscurity into old age and wish to remain so in death.
>
> If they are unsuitable for display at Dulwich, it is my wish that they be given to a gallery where they blend in. May God be with you. Anon.

A poignant note indeed, but why if the deliverer was the 'friend' described in the note did the man in the Panama hat come up with the story about the package 'being found on a bus'? Staff at the gallery suspect the man in the overcoat was the anonymous dying benefactor. Yet again Dulwich had benefited from a very strange circumstance.

In fact the Gallery has often been in the headlines, the 'takeaway Rembrandt' of the late 20th century being the centre of Pink Pantheresque shenanigans. This small portrait of the engraver Jacob de Gheyn, worth an estimated £5 million, was stolen no fewer than four times in 20 years.

Raiders entered through skylights, drilled through reinforced doors or simply stuffed it under a macintosh, and the painting ended up in the oddest places: in the back of a black cab, under a tree on Streatham Common, tied to a bicycle in Dulwich and in a left luggage locker at a German railway station. They certainly get around, these Rembrandts.

Yet again in 2001 a Polish aristocrat who claimed descent or connection with Stanislas Augustus turned up to say: 'Can we have our paintings back, please?' The Gallery authorities politely asked him to come to Dulwich and view the pictures, but I suspect the words 'chance', 'snowflake' and 'hell' may have been privately constructed into a well-known phrase.

THE MASTER OF THE KING'S BEARS AND HIS ARMS Beside the Gallery is Chapel

Close and Christ's Chapel, which has a massive Alleyn coat of arms above the door and underneath a huge plaque extolling in Latin how Edwardus Alleyn had set up his college.

Just in case you missed that, there's another coat of arms at the far end of the grounds, above the gates to Chapel Close, with his monogram in stone on either side. The richly-ornamented Chapel where Alleyn was laid to rest is private, sadly, although the Dulwich College boys who troop down here on Founder's Day, 21 June, wearing blue cornflowers, may not be so enthusiastic to see its interior again. (In fact, I'd keep out of Dulwich churches altogether. They've burned three down in recent years – St Barnabas, All Saints and one in Gipsy Hill. Probably a coincidence, but you can't be too careful.) The school colours, by the way, are black and blue, so the cornflower is perfect.

Edward Alleyn, mini-biography: Born 1566, son of City innkeeper, married into theatre family, became a great actor and owner of Fortune theatre, and Master of the King's Bears. By 1605 Alleyn was rich, bought Manor of Dulwich. Vowed to create a home 'for six poor brothers and six poor sisters' and a school 'for 12 poor scholars'. On 21 June 1619 King James I gave Alleyn his royal charter to found the college, and so Dulwich College celebrates each 21 June as Founder's Day. Alleyn died in 1626.

The 20th century saw an amazing flowering of literary talent in Dulwich College's old boys, or Old Alleynians as they are correctly called.

Where else could two authors as different as P G Wodehouse and Raymond Chandler have rubbed shoulders, for instance? Or C S Forester and Michael Ondaatje, who wrote about the same war from such different angles? Dulwich also contains fascinating clues to the origins of several of these writers' heroes.

Actually, I was disappointed to learn on investigation that Wodehouse the prefect couldn't possibly have thrashed pipsqueak Chandler for running in the North Block ('contravention of the Block Rules, Chandler you oik') because their time at Dulwich was separated by a summer holiday.

If **Wodehouse**, creator of the ever-funny Bertie Wooster, Jeeves, Lord Emsworth and his pig, seems a bit comfortable, even smug, for some tastes, the answer lies right here.

As the relentlessly cheerful Wodehouse wrote:

The three essentials for an autobiography are that its compiler shall have had an eccentric father, a miserable, misunderstood childhood and a hell of a time at his public school, and I enjoyed none of these advantages. My father was as normal as rice pudding, my childhood went like a breeze ... while, as for my schooldays at Dulwich, they were just six years of unbroken bliss.

Wodehouse is immortalised at the College Library by a display of his typewriter, desk, pipe and manuscripts. He worked for a while at some indescribably boring job at the Bank of England (where another employee was Kenneth Grahame, author of *Wind in the Willows*, the children's classic).

As for **Chandler**, the great crime thriller writer and creator of the quintessentially American gumshoe, Philip Marlowe, his completely contrasting life was far from charmed.

He was always on the move, never putting down roots. By the time he joined Dulwich in the autumn term (sorry, Michaelmas term at Dulwich) in 1900, the 12-year-old Chandler had already lived in Waterford, Nebraska and Chicago, Illinois. After he left Dulwich, he moved on average once a year, owning barely any furniture, his restlessness always driving him on to another rented address. In this case a disturbed life did produce great writing.

One bit of Dulwich may have stayed with Chandler. At the College new boys are put into houses for sporting purposes which they stay in throughout the school. They are named after Elizabethan heroes: Spencer, Sydney, Drake, Grenville ... and Marlowe. I wonder which house Chandler was in.

More literary detective work can be enjoyed with **C S Forester**, creator of the eponymous swashbuckling hero Hornblower. When at Alleyn's School, which he attended before Dulwich College, Forester would have had to attended St Barnabas Church in the village. In that church there's still a war memorial a possibly bored young

THE VILLAGE HEART AND A PUB WITH A DICKENSIAN HISTORY Continuing down the road, into what is now known as Dulwich Village, notice Pickwick Road on the left for a Dickens connection. Soon we reach a number of rather olde worlde shops, many Victorian or Georgian.

On the right is the imposing **Crown and Greyhound**, a splendidly convivial meeting place, not merely a 'chat-room', as internerds call them, but one with real ale, real food, real people, real voices and comfortable chairs.

Not that it's really the Crown and Greyhound, for a variety of reasons. One is

Forester may have gazed upon during the sermon; it has the name 'Hornblower' carved upon it. It cannot be a coincidence, can it?

Other authors include **A E W Mason**, author of *The Four Feathers*, and **Michael Ondaatje**, author of the powerful novel *The English Patient*, which was made into a hit film in the 1990s. Plus **Dennis Wheatley**, thriller writer, expelled after a short stay. And much-missed comedian **Bob Monkhouse**, who said: 'When I was young they laughed at me for saying I wanted to be a comedian. Well they're not laughing now!'

Not that all Dulwich's success stories have been literary. For many years a small open boat called the *James Caird* lay here almost unnoticed by the boys straggling back from choir for double Latin. Had they but investigated they would have found that it was in this boat that the greatest of Antarctic heroes, **Ernest Shackleton**, made his almost unbelievable escape across hundreds of miles of terrible seas to get help for his men after his ship the *Endurance* was crushed by ice.

It was heroism of the highest order, and all the *Endurance*'s men were saved, although by the time they got back to Britain, years later, World War I was in full spate and no-one was interested in live heroes any more. For by far the best account of his journey – and I've read the lot – read *Shackleton's Boat Journey* by F A Worsley.

Before that last terrible journey, Sir Ernest had taken part in Scott's first expedition. After returning a hero, Shackleton gave a talk to Dulwich schoolboys. He put up a slide of frozen wastes and snow and left it without commentary. After a while the boys began to fidget, and Sir Ernest said: 'Well boys, you've stuck it for 45 seconds, we stuck it for five weeks.'

Sir Ernest had been particularly bad at his lessons at Dulwich and was said to have been thrown out of the place for climbing the clock tower, from the outside. If so, it was just a rehearsal for far, far greater feats of daring.

If Wodehouse and Chandler didn't meet, Wodehouse and Shackleton certainly did. Wodehouse was made a German prisoner-of-war in World War II and famously and unwisely made radio broadcasts from his camp which were seen as collaboration with the enemy, although they were perhaps more his being typically and naively genial. His reputation never quite recovered from this so he spent much of the remainder of his life in America.

While a German prisoner, Wodehouse wrote: 'Under certain conditions, the mind is bound to dwell on food. Shackleton once told me that when he was on the Polar high seas, he used to dream every night he was running about a field chasing those three-cornered jam tarts which were such a feature of our life at our mutual school. And if that is how Shackleton felt, I am not ashamed of having felt that way myself.'

the British irreverence for titles, so it's more convenient to call it The Dog or simply The Greyhound. But what have Crowns and Greyhounds got to do with each other anyway? These were once two ancient Dulwich taverns. The Crown, on this site, was a very unpretentious alehouse, popular for thirsty farmworkers. Maybe they had real ploughman's lunches there. The Greyhound, then across the road, was a much posher inn, and banquets and balls were held here. Here, too, Charles Dickens attended the snooty Dulwich Club. Eventually the businesses were merged in today's grand establishment.

There is a strange old bench inside marked 'When you bee wearie reste' which is nice, if a little obvious. Why not reste before getting wearie? More of such village nonsense in a minute.

There are several grand 18th-century houses here, but a particularly charmingly tiny one on the left at the crossroads ahead, where more quaint fingerposts point all over the place. Turn right at the junction and take just a few steps up Calton Avenue and on the left before the petrol station is a stone marked 'It is a sport to a Fool to do Mischief to Thine Own Wickedness shall correct thee'.

This marks the site of the **village stocks** where wrongdoers would be chained up and pelted with dung, etc, but does that engraving make a lot of sense, if you read it again? Are you doing mischief to Thine Own, or is Thine Own Wickedness correcting thee? It's bad enough being chained up and having chamberpots poured over thy head without this kind of grammatical inexactitude facing thee. I just hope the poor criminals couldn't read. The Calton family, recalled in the road name, bought the land from Henry VIII after he dissolved the monasteries, and the Caltons sold it to Alleyn.

Retracing our steps, we cross Court Lane, a reminder that in the old manorial system the main landowner, here Court Farm, dispensed justice as well as collecting the rent. Hence several London names, such as Earl's Court. On the corner of Court Lane and the high street – Dulwich Village, as it is called – lie many of the inhabitants of those fine 18th-century houses in the old cemetery.

(If you are 'wearie' after visiting the Greyhound, you could continue through Dulwich Village for a few hundred yards, across a road junction and reach North Dulwich station, with frequent trains to London Bridge. If so, note the eccentric ornamentation in the old station master's house just before the station and the totally over-the-top coats-of-arms on the bridge opposite.)

But if we turn back through the village towards the gallery, there is much more to see.

CYCLE LOGICAL PROFILES AND PICKWICKIAN TYPES On the same side as the Greyhound there are some particularly fine 18th-century houses at 103 and 105. Taking the left fork, College Road, and leaving the gallery to the right, you pass the Old College Gate of **Dulwich Park** on the left. This rambling park, where the lines of old oaks show the old field shapes, has four impressive gates, a lake and an aviary, and also offers the oddest bicycling in the form of London Recumbents, a literally laid-back version of cycling that its fans believe should be more widespread. It looks odd but it's really cycle logical.

The man at the heart of it is cycling crusader, not to say fanatic, Nigel Frost, who has even bought a fantastic £8,000 machine called an Octos which bizarrely seats seven and on which one can have civilised face-to-face conversations. Mr Frost believes they should become widespread to combat the evils of pollution, noise, unfitness, etc.

That's if you can handle maintaining 14 pedals, three brakes and nine chains and can always find half a dozen people wanting to go in the same direction.

The latter question isn't a great problem, Mr Frost believes. He enthuses: 'It's the most sociable vehicle around – you set off alone but begin to pick up onlookers within 100 yards. Everyone can have a face-to-face conversation, except of course the driver.'

'As well as being pollution-free, it carries more passengers than most cars and can be used by people with special needs, including the blind, as it requires only one person to steer.' I'm beginning to think I want one. I just need to get six blind cyclists.

Staying on College Road, past the park gates, is the impossibly pretty **Bell Cottage** on the left, looking a bit like a New England clapboard house, with a fire mark above the door. These marks date from before proper fire brigades, when insurance companies operated horse-drawn fire engines but would put your fire out only if you had a fire mark showing your house was insured. Otherwise it was: 'Tough, burn to death, suckers!' Mind you, being about the only wooden house around here, I expect Bell Cottage's owners were more nervous than most.

Then there's the very pretty **Pickwick Cottage** on the left. Charles Dickens liked Dulwich and used to stay in the village. His great affection for Dulwich was such that he had his most affectionately-drawn hero, Mr Pickwick, retire to live here. He writes of him: 'Somewhat infirm now', he 'may still frequently be seen, contemplating the pictures in the Dulwich Gallery, or enjoying a walk about the pleasant neighbourhood'. Even today there are several Pickwickian types bumbling about in the village.

Soon we cross the road called Dulwich Common, the busy South Circular road again. This is a point of decision. The feeble-hearted or weak of body could go right and quickly return to West Dulwich station, but it's not much further to continue on my route. The very strong of heart, or bike- or car-borne, could go left (and then right at Lordship Lane) to take in the extraordinary tea magnate **Horniman's Museum** (see page 41), but that is perhaps a mile away and worthy of a day out on its own.

The best option is to go straight on, up College Road, as we are now more than two-thirds through our walk. Dulwich College hoves into view on the right, its three massive Victorian-Italianate blocks by Charles Barry, Jnr, layered like massive gateaux and set off by the landmark clock tower. The gates, of course, are larded with Alleyn's arms.

THE COLLEGE, GREAT IMPRESSIONISTS AND TUNNEL VISION Dulwich College is
the grand replacement for Alleyn's original school down in the village (confusingly, not for Alleyn's School or even James Allen's, nor the College's grammar school set up in 1842 opposite the art gallery to educate 'local boys' – the scholarly soil of Dulwich is fertile indeed). By the mid-19th century the governors, who could hardly afford to host the picture gallery a few years before, were rolling in cash thanks to the incursions of railway companies, who were snapping up land as suburban London spread, and for some reason running all over the Dulwich estate in various fairly random directions. But the College landowners insisted on the railway companies putting posher bridges in Dulwich than elsewhere, including Edward Alleyn's monogram and sometimes, as at North Dulwich station, the whole caboodle of Alleyn's arms and those of the railway companies not just once but three times more.

The style of the College is Italianate, but the Great Hall in the centre block is completely different in style, obviously influenced by ancient Westminster Hall (see the Palace of Westminster, page 111), hardly surprising as Charles Barry supervised the restoration of that medieval building.

The college grounds are massive and, what with the park, various sports grounds, the golf course and ancient woodland nearby, contribute to the remarkably rural feel of this otherwise town-locked area. That and the charming row of old cottages facing the **Mill Pond** on the left.

The view from the pond was immortalised by Camille Pissarro, the French impressionist who fled the 1870 Franco-Prussian War to live in nearby Norwood and painted many local scenes. Contemporaries, not yet up with the play about impressionism despite Turner's best efforts, assumed his painting was unfinished, poor French chappie.

- One of the characters livening up the sometimes tedious race to be the first Mayor of London in 2000 was Dulwich chemist **Ashwinkumar Tanna** (his shop is in Lordship Lane) who wanted to run as an independent. His best quote was: 'There are too many chiefs and not enough Indians.' He said, 'I am the only Indian left.' He managed a creditable 51,000 votes despite being virtually ignored by the mainstream media.

- East Dulwich estate agent, **Nigel Skelton**, arrested by Irish police for strolling naked along a Cork street, said: 'Well, it's just what you do, isn't it?' He was on a stag night and was so overcome with emotion to see that he was in Caroline Street (his fiancée was named Caroline) that he peeled off. Let's just hope he doesn't have to visit any properties in Caroline Close, Croydon or Caroline Road, Wimbledon.

- Among Dulwich's plethora of schools is one for butlers, set up by **Ivor Spencer**, president of the Guild of International Toastmasters and head of his International School for Butler Administrators. Some 750 of these gentleman's gentlemen have been turned out from Alleyn Park, appropriately just a stone's throw from the alma mater of P G Wodehouse, creator of Jeeves, butler par excellence.

- Bright young British actor **Jude Law** went to Dulwich's Alleyn's School, and lived in Lewisham at the time, so was immersed in all aspects of 'sarf Lunnon' culture. He told one interviewer that it amazed him when he saw the film *My Beautiful Laundrette* because to talk with that Sarf Lunnon accent was suddenly all right. (Not that that film's star, Daniel Day Lewis, got stuck with it. He was right posh again in *A Room with a View*.)

- Another alumnus of Alleyn's School is the great tabloid newspaper editor **Kelvin MacKenzie**, who famously left with not many O-levels (one) and went straight into reporting as a teenager (the best way). His reign at the *Sun* was famed for (naked) Page 3 girls, provocative headlines such as 'Gotcha!' over the sinking of the Argentine cruiser the *Belgrano*, and 'Stick It Up Your Junta' in the same Falklands War, plus the more surreal 'Freddie Starr ate my hamster'. On the French banning British lamb: 'Hop Off You Frogs'. More in Fleet Street section, page 181.

By the way, my admittedly ignorant assertion when writing about Turner that he influenced the French impressionists is backed up by a letter to English impressionist painter Wynford Dewhurst (1864–1941) from Pissarro:

> In 1870 I found myself in London with Monet. Monet worked in the parks, whilst I, living at Lower Norwood, at that time a charming suburb, studied the effects of fog, snow and springtime … The water-colours and paintings of Turner and Constable certainly had influence on us.

Dulwich College has certainly had more than its share of characters (see box on page 230) but the survival of Dulwich's special village feel has been largely down to the school too, or rather the landlords of the Dulwich Estate, properly the Estates Governors of Alleyn's College of God's Gift.

Certainly one of the oddest survivals in their control lies ahead on College Road (having left the College and its boarding houses, such as Blew House, behind): the **toll gate**.

London was once surrounded with roads that became impassable morasses in the winter and, given the rain, at other times too. (They say the Devil, tossing the damned to the eternal fires, chucks some aside in a heap. These, he explains to those waiting to be judged, are the English, too wet to burn.)

The solution to the road problem was turnpike roads, properly drained, with

- In late 2000, Dulwich pensioner Bob Talley read his 100th-birthday telegram from the Queen, proudly announced 'I've made it', then dropped dead. The party planned for him at his nursing home with friends and relatives went ahead as a wake.
- Boxer and bemonocled and caned dandy (I didn't say that, Chris, honest) **Chris Eubank** was born in Dulwich. Comedienne **Jo Brand** lived here. Mrs, now Baroness, **Thatcher** had a house there for a while in Hambledon Place, Dulwich Gate. She was much mocked by her many enemies for the Barratt Homes architecture of her home, but then someone paid £595,000 for it when she moved out so it can't have been that bad. **Charles Dickens** lived in Dulwich, and in a great number of other places. Actor **Tim Roth** of *Reservoir Dogs* film fame grew up in West Dulwich. Not enough killings, presumably. A large number of great authors attended Dulwich College (see box, page 230).
- Quintessential castaway and great eccentric, **Gerald Kingsland**, who repeatedly set himself up in remote desert islands in the Pacific, Indian Ocean and anywhere hot and empty, usually with a young lady in tow, came home to less exotic Dulwich to die in 2000. He had famously advertised for a Girl Friday in *Time Out* magazine and secured the young and naïve Lucy Irvine, half his age, who in the event beat him to a publisher when their ordeal ended. The book *Castaway* and the film of the same name starring Oliver Reed and Amanda Donohoe, made Lucy Irvine a celebrity, but Kingsland carried on with his experiments, fathering the odd child. When he became seriously ill in Samoa with his fifth wife and seventh child, he returned to his London family who were surprisingly forgiving. Irvine was quoted as saying he had lived the life of four men, but he had already written his epitaph: 'In memory of Gerald Kingsland. He caused a lot of damage.' He didn't really prove his thesis that a man and a woman could live most happily in a Garden of Eden state of paradise, merely what a lot of women already knew: that many men are often ready to walk away from their responsibilities and find the grass greener on the other side of the hill, no matter how old they are.

macadam stone dressing on top, which sped the booming stagecoaches of 1750–1840. In many parts of London if you look carefully you can spot the old toll-houses, sometimes octagonal single-storey lodges too close to the road for modern comfort, sometimes not much more than a shed. This toll gate is the only one surviving in use in London, and the road it's on is still in the hands of the Estates Governors.

The road up to what is now Crystal Palace was in fact built in 1789 by leaseholder John Morgan, who charged the people, and even the sheep or pigs, who used it. On his death, the freeholders, the Governors, continued to collect the tolls, now 50p for a car, though prices for hogs, donkeys, sheep or whatever are still listed.

Passing through the toll gate and up the hill, we reach on the right, just before the handsome spire of **St Stephen's**, Sydenham Hill station, the end of our walk. If you fancy another pub, you can instead go left here at Low Cross Wood Lane, and climb steeply to the **Dulwich Wood House**, a tavern which reminds us that the woods on the hillside are ancient and still full of wildlife such as foxes, badgers, bats, etc coming out at night.

The sylvan setting of **Sydenham Hill station** was once described by the architect Ian Nairn as the 'quintessence of true suburbia due to its rural nature'. The deep cutting contains a nature reserve, a partnership between London Wildlife Trust and Network Rail.

The platforms are deep in a cutting, being at the mouth of the South's longest railway tunnel which burrows right under Crystal Palace hill to Penge East, and (since they built the Channel Tunnel) Warsaw, Moscow and Vladivostock. You need the further platform for your return to London.

You can see right through the straight tunnel today, which you rarely could in the days of steam, and it is a good example of recycling. The clay extracted from the boring of the tunnel was dragged out at either end and baked into the millions of bricks that line the tunnel. The last time I visited there was a heap of flowers on the platform in memory of some misguided boy who tried to walk through the tunnel. Don't bother – the tracks are electrified.

As you ride back past the College grounds, you could until late 2007 have seen a sleek Eurostar on these tracks, looking like a Darth Vader train with its dark glass nose, taking its strange, double drone (and about 800 people) to Paris or Brussels in around three hours. They were so frequent that the boys playing cricket down below hardly bothered to look.

But many a catch may have been dropped here 50 years ago when a steam whistle sounded and the glorious *Golden Arrow* London–Paris train hoved into view just once a day. It had a French tricolour and a Union Jack fluttering on its front buffer beam. A massive golden arrow attached to the side of the loco bore the proud legend '*Golden Arrow*' or '*La Flèche D'Or*'. It towed a rake of immaculate brown and gold Pullman carriages, all named, and manned with uniformed flunkies who greeted you as you joined the train at Victoria station and polished the brass handrails as you climbed into the interior of marquetry woodwork, deep pile carpet, starched tablecloths and heavy silver, and diplomats, spies and filmstars resting in the deep red armchairs.

FURTHER INFORMATION

Dulwich Picture Gallery ☏ 020 8693 5254; www: dulwichpicturegallery.org.uk; closed Mon; admission: £4.
Dulwich history and society www: dulwich.co.uk
Dulwich park odd bike hire London Recumbents; ☏ 020 8299 6636; e recumbents@aol.com.
Belair House Gallery Rd, SE21; ☏ 020 8299 9788.
Crown and Greyhound pub ☏ 020 8299 4976.
Horniman Museum See page 41.

21

Greenwich

That Greenwich is truly special is undeniable. The place is a World Heritage Site for its fabulous maritime history on show. Architecturally it is rightly famed too. The atmosphere of the place is unique, with its back alleys and strange little shops, its creaking pubs soaked in history, its sweeping views dominated by Old Father Thames sliding past in a superb bend in its millennia-old, seabound meanders. The tides and fogs have brought heroes, pirates, murderers and kings and queens to this little place.

But it's not all history – there are modern follies such as the **Millennium Dome**, and new transport links such as the Docklands Light Railway and the Jubilee Line extension, the latter provided with fabulous stations in innovative styles, trendy shops and a buzzing craft market plus some strange sculptures very much of the 21st century.

Talking of transport, there was a myth put about in 2000 that the Dome would fail because transport to its North Greenwich peninsula site was impossible. Greenwich was presented as an obscure backwater no-one from the rest of the country could ever reach. Balderdash! Greenwich has tunnels under the Thames galore – foot and road – two new rail routes to East London; good road and bus links; new rail links to South London, and surprisingly good rail links to central London. Plus the traditional route along the river from Charing Cross pier, which is fun but far from quick.

Nor is the line from central London, which links Greenwich in around 15 minutes to not one but four London termini (London Bridge, Waterloo East and Charing Cross or Cannon Street), anything new. Far from it; it is the oldest main line in the capital, dating from very early in the railway age. As it snakes across Southwark in the most convoluted series of intertwined viaducts, you may wish to discover what goes on in the Dickensian gloom below. For that, see the Southwark walk, page 196.

The first part of this, the **London & Greenwich Railway**, was opened astonishingly early in the railway age in 1836; it was finished in time for Christmas 1838. The world's first purpose-built commuter railway, it was also the world's longest viaduct, because the whole route was, bizarrely, built on arches – 978 of them – not so much anticipating the at times spivvy car dealers who would eventually rent out the noisy caverns in the arches beneath but to cross the numerous roads and creeks en route.

Many a strange business is located within the cave-like arches of London's railways: a lobster breeding farm for gourmets in Battersea, a golf range for top City types beneath Cannon Street, a garden centre, wine cellars, sound-insulated offices and a security vault, to name a few. Later railways into the capital resorted to the much cheaper method of using earth embankments.

So if you come to Greenwich by mainline train, the route you ride on is a lot older than some of the relics, such as the *Cutty Sark*, that you are coming to see.

Seven modern celebs who live or have lived in Greenwich/Blackheath: Churchman/Beirut hostage Terry Waite, *Changing Rooms* presenter Laurence Llewyllen-Bowen, or Lawrence Bowen as he was known at school, comedian Malcolm Hardee, musician Jools Holland, raunchy actress-turned government minister Glenda Jackson, pop stars Marty Wilde and Manfred Mann.

And if you are visiting Greenwich via this route for the first time, look left soon after leaving London Bridge station for an unusual longways view of Tower Bridge.

WALK: THE BEST, AND ODDEST, BITS OF GREENWICH

Distance (basic walk) 2¹/₂ miles, or about 2 hours plus stops, plus two interesting add-ons of half an hour and half a mile each, and an optional diversion to end instead at Blackheath station. Or just read it and visit the bits you want. With all add-ons and much browsing in junk shops, pubs, etc I took 6 hours. And that was without going, on that occasion, to the National Maritime Museum, or the Cutty Sark or the former Royal Naval College, all well worth several hours, so you could easily spend all day here with visits to some of the many pubs and restaurants. I recommend doing the walk on one fine day, visiting a selection of the indoor treasures on another, perhaps less fine one.

Emerging from Greenwich station, we are already confronted with the strange mixture that is Greenwich's real charm. Here you can see working-class London's shabbiness in the unpretentious row of shops opposite which, however, include an excellent second-hand bookshop (first of many), Halcyon Books, and a fascinating junk shop that sells the oddest architectural details to the Greenwich yuppie incomers; an ancient almshouse is to the right of this, while to the left is the staggering shaft of the modernist-art deco town hall, beyond which a classical church and some ship masts beckon.

The **almshouses** opposite have a pretty courtyard, which blows with a snowstorm of cherry blossom in May. Called The College of Queen Elizabeth, they were set up by philanthropist William Lambard in 1576, early in the popular Virgin Queen's reign and before she had done her Churchill bit, so to speak, with the defeat of the Spanish Armada. In fact, the neat row of homes you are looking at is an 1819 rebuild.

Walking left towards the town centre and waterfront, we pass evidence of another remarkable philanthropist; a Carnegie library is marked as such on its weather-worn front. This West Greenwich library is one of dozens of Carnegie libraries that have enriched the lives of Britons for more than 100 years thanks to the Scots-born billionaire (1835–1918) who became America's greatest steel magnate. The human face of capitalism.

The inhuman face of socialism, some may think, is evident in the massive **Town Hall** block jammed up against the Carnegie and extending round the corner into Royal Hill. Severe, bereft of all adornment, it would in fact sit well with a massive red star and portrait of Joe Stalin on top, or Nazi banners unfurled, for a film backdrop, or would do well as Orwell's faceless Ministry of Truth in *Nineteen Eighty-Four.*

Yet in its way this 1939 building by Clifford Culpin is brilliant and daring. That it works is thanks to its crowning glory – the superb and improbable clock tower that looks as though it stabs down from the sky, much as if God had angrily thunked down a carving knife into a bread board. Don't miss – it is easy to do so – the underside of the entrance canopy near the corner, which makes up for its lack

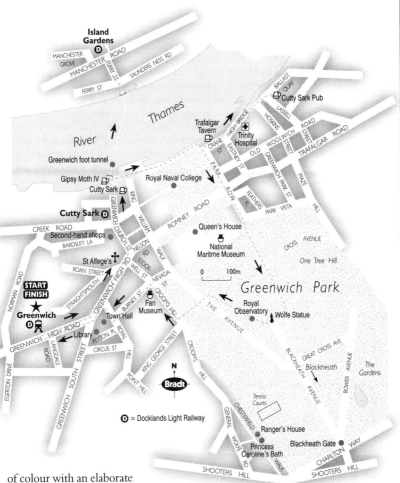

of colour with an elaborate
mural (well, whatever you call
a ceiling mural). As architectural
high drama it reminds me of the Bank of China building in Hong Kong, built in
the 1980s at a time when the Brits still ran that place, a
glittering dagger shaft higher than anything else with which
Red China said: 'That's ours and you're not having it.'

Onwards down the High Road, past the oddly named road
called Straightsmouth, we reach the rather extraordinary **St
Alfege's church**, which despite its restrained elegant classical
exterior contains more dramatic and wondrous history
than a dozen normal churches.

Greenwich
Town Hall

GREENWICH PILLAGE: SAINTS, HEROES AND BRILLIANT CREATORS
St Alfege's is a wonderful
church, but built on spilt blood. **Alfege** was a
medieval churchman, greatly loved and more
Christian than most. When he was Bishop of
Winchester there were no beggars in that city, the

histories say. From 954–1012 he was Archbishop of Canterbury at a time when rampaging Danes were raping and pillaging their heathen way across country. The Danes landed here at Greenwich several times in their longboats and struck inland in search of riches (had there been newspapers at the time, doubtless an editor would have yelled: 'Hold the front pagan'). No messing about seeking asylum in Kent in those days, they simply laid siege to Canterbury.

Alfege was urged to leave and save himself but he sat in his cathedral calmly awaiting the battle's outcome. He was seized by the Danes who demanded: 'Give us gold.' He replied: 'The gold I give you is the Word of God.' The Danes dragged Alfege back to their landing place at Greenwich and pelted him to death with stones, meat and bones.

Moving on a few centuries – all these great characters are remembered with monuments and stained-glass panels in this church – we come across the extraordinary composer and musician **Thomas Tallis** (1505–85). He was organist here, something to do with the proximity of Greenwich's royal palace, no doubt. Nothing more beautifully haunting had then yet been devised – nor has since, some would argue – in church music than his complex harmonies rooted in the chants of medieval monks. His 40-part motet *Spem in Alium* is emotionally overpowering.

Look at the turbulent periods his amazingly long career spanned:

- Henry VIII, so loyal a Roman Catholic that the Pope called him Defender of the Faith (hence FD on our coins), and later an aggressive Protestant who suppressed the monasteries;
- the Protestant ascendancy under Edward VI, who clobbered Catholics;
- then back to Catholicism again under 'Bloody' Mary who burned hundreds of Protestants at the stake; and finally
- Elizabeth, who persecuted Catholics once again.

Few people in high position could weather such violent storms, yet Tallis the survivor lived through the lot as a royal musician and composer, to a succession of monarchs of different religious persuasions, adjusting his music to the times. He is the Wren of church music, the Shakespeare of sound. But Christopher Wren isn't the architect who comes to mind as you look round this elegant creation, for it was one of his followers, **Nicholas Hawksmoor** (1680–1740), who rebuilt this church as part of the Fifty New Churches campaign of the government of the day (of which around a dozen were actually built).

Another notable parishioner was **John Flamsteed** (1646–1719), Astronomer Royal at the nearby Greenwich Observatory, whom we shall encounter later. He said his mapping of the heavens was a way of understanding the mind of God. While I can manage neither of those feats, doesn't this recall looking upward from a dark place into a starry night with a billion stars stretching away to infinity? When you realise that it is as likely you are looking down as up, it's not so much awe as terror.

Back on earth we meet one of Greenwich's greatest heroes, **General James Wolfe** (1727—59). You can see his home at Macartney's House at the top of Croom's Hill on the west side of Greenwich Park later in the walk. Wolfe not only squashed the ambitions of the French in Canada, making that huge country British for many years, but also had the great merit of dying heroically at the moment of victory (as did Nelson), thus cementing himself in the public's affection. (If only Wellington had had the sense to get cannon-balled at Waterloo.) We will come across two other suitably dead heroes later.

Aged only 32, Wolfe captured Quebec, the French-held city in Canada, in 1759 in a surprise attack by storming the Heights of Abraham up steep cliffs. He was killed in action and was buried here at St Alfege's. We will encounter a statue of General Wolfe in Greenwich Park later; the view from there is even better than from the Heights of Abraham.

Canadian visitors (well, maybe not French Canadian visitors) and other Wolfe fans may want to make the pilgrimage to Quebec House, at the eastern end of Westerham, Kent, just outside the southern M25, to see Wolfe's charming childhood home, where memorabilia and an exhibition about the Battle of Quebec are on display. A magnificent painting, *The Death of Wolfe*, hangs in the library of Ickworth, a stately home in Suffolk.

Back to Victorian times, when Dickens knew and loved Greenwich and this church. In *Our Mutual Friend*, perhaps my favourite Dickens novel, he goes all sentimental at the end, as ever, when Bella is married to John Rokesmith:

> … the church porch, having swallowed up Bella Wilfer for ever and ever, had it not
> in its power to relinquish that young woman but slid into the happy sunlight Mrs
> John Rokesmith instead.

A real Victorian hero from Greenwich is remembered here too: **General Gordon** (1833–85), he who was slain at Khartoum in the Sudan and was portrayed in the film *Khartoum* (1966) by Charlton Heston. Oddly Gordon of Khartoum was known as Chinese Gordon at the time, more famed for putting down a rebellion in China than his work suppressing slavery in the Sudan. And as Christians are enslaved in the Sudan and civil war rages in the 21st century, his memorial raises the question of whether the Pax Britannica that the old British Empire sought to impose was always a bad thing. (Mind you, sometimes sailors took with them pox Britannica, but that's another question.)

Anyway, Gordon didn't get any pax out of the Mad Mahdi so he ended up suitably dead, thus becoming a lasting Victorian hero. There were several pubs and a railway engine named after him.

Then in 1941 Nazi bombers blew in the roof of St Alfege's, possibly aiming for London Docks, or maybe just blowing the stuffing out of any Londoners they could hit. It was not until 1954 that the building was fully restored.

There you are: exactly 1,000 sweeping years of dramatic history, blood, war, love, art, heroism all within one building. Amazing.

SHOPPING AND CHANGING Now, thank God, the arrival of the Danish means a delivery of delicious pastries. Tourists from all the countries mentioned in this turbulent history are welcomed in peace to poke around Greenwich and find its historical nutty bits, the architectural icing on the cake and perhaps in a junk shop, the occasional cherry.

Going on down Greenwich Church Street one can glimpse through an archway to the right an intriguing view of pubs and treasures beyond. Leave it for a moment and turn the corner left into Creek Road to check out a couple of rather strange shops. The first is **Emporium**, dedicated to the clothes of the 1950s, 1960s, 1970s and 1980s. It's well known by film companies who come here for period costumes; some of today's big-name designers have even been seen browsing the shelves, according to proprietor Jonathan Hale, who set up here in 1986.

Is it nostalgia? 'No, not really. For one thing, a lot of the people who come in here don't remember those times because they were too young. It's about style and originality – being different from the designer pack.

'Say you're going to a big do. Does a woman want to meet someone wearing the same outfit? They will if they go to one of the big designer chains,' says Jonathan. 'And some of this stuff is real quality – or it wouldn't have lasted. Not like today's stuff made to throw away after one season. And this stuff is cheaper.' A good sales

21

pitch. It's irrelevant but I'm reminded of that old East End rag trade saying: 'Never mind the quality, feel the width.'

But did sane men really wear huge check flared hipsters and sit in burned orange chairs? Just how awful was sixties taste?

Further down a shop called **Flying Duck** answers this, with its range of 1950s, 1960s and 1970s design and kitsch objects. Spindly metal chairs with pastel-coloured plastic seats. Elliptical cane chairs. Chopper bikes. Squeezy tomato-shaped tomato sauce bottles, like you used to get in Wimpy bars.

Back on Church Street, a step or two further towards the masts of the *Cutty Sark*, there's a cockney cultural checkpoint, a pie and mash shop (complete with liquor and eels, the sign reassures us). **Goddard's Pie House** has been run by the same family since 1890, so they must be doing something right. Every possible type of pie *except* eel pie – apple, steak, cheese – seemed to be being eaten when I popped in, but I expect someone eats eels. (Hence the cockney song: 'Eel meat again, don't know where, don't know when.')

Over the road is another gem of a shop, **Unique Collections**, which on my visit is stuffed with strange firemen's helmets, a Rochdale County Borough Police badge, a Memphis police captain's regalia, plus more model cars than I've ever seen in one place. Matchbox, Dinky, Corgi – you had to have grown up in those days to really love them. And model Thunderbirds and Thunderbird dolls. Heaven for some people, and immensely collectable.

Now, if you like this kind of thing you could peek into **Greenwich Charter Market** by walking a little way up College Approach. It's a colourful place and my only hesitation in recommending it is that if you like shopping and browsing in old bookshops, you may never complete the walk. That's up to you – there's always another day.

The market runs on Wednesday, Friday and Saturday until 17.00 selling arts and crafts and on Thursday selling antiques and collectables. Note over the College Approach colonnaded entrance the cast-iron proclamation:

A FALSE BALANCE IS ABOMINATION TO
THE LORD BUT A JUST WEIGHT IS HIS DELIGHT

Try that on the poltroons of Sunderland council, who recently prosecuted a man for selling a pound of bananas rather than a hectolitre or whatever it's supposed to be. If Sunderland folk had any guts they'd refuse to pay a penny in council taxes until that man is recompensed and all the officials put in stocks and pelted with the same rotten fruit.

The market is still worth a look on non-market days, all the better to examine the interesting surrounding arts, craft, antiques (we're too posh for mere junk by now) and book shops and the cobbled lanes

connecting it to the rest of the town, which is hemmed in against the lush grounds of the former Royal Palace rather in the way that many a crammed medieval village huddles against spacious castle walls.

Back to the waterfront and the *Cutty Sark*, a beautiful, fascinating ship whose name lives in the hearts of any Briton with salt in their blood as surely as that of the *Victory* at Portsmouth. Actually a better comparison is with the *Flying Scotsman* or the

Mallard steam engines, for this is a sleek racer, the fastest of the clippers. Aptly, given Greenwich's interest today in fashion, the ship is named after a girl's garment (it was a short petticoat). For its history, and why the figurehead is holding a bit of hair, see box on page 56.

THE TUNNEL OF FLATULENCE AND THE BEST VIEW IN LONDON Over to the left of the *Cutty Sark*, or on her port beam (splice the mizzen wench, me hearties, etc), there lies another Greenwich dome. Across the river you'll see a matching one, reached by the Greenwich foot tunnel, a fun and free experience I recommend to all except claustrophobes.

Just before we plunge down into the tunnel, there's an isolated yacht nearby in a dry dock, like *Cutty Sark* but tiny in comparison. This is *Gipsy Moth IV*, centre of the nation's attention in 1967 when Francis Chichester arrived back from a solo voyage around the world, tracking the route of the big tea clippers. It was a big deal at the time, as Chichester (who had earlier pioneered aviation round the world in Gipsy Moth planes) knelt before Queen Elizabeth II to be knighted with the very sword that the first Queen Elizabeth used to knight another Sir Francis – Drake – after arriving back from his trip round the world in the *Golden Hind*. I was standing by this tiny ketch while a cockney gent was reading aloud this information to his family. He paused and said: 'Best bloody queen we ever had. Bit cheeky mind.' Which Elizabeth he had in mind I'll leave it to you to decide.

Elizabeth I, or Good Queen Bess as some called her, was born here in Greenwich at the palace where the massive naval college now stands on the waterfront, as were her sister, Mary, and her father, Henry VIII. Her grandfather, the first Tudor king, Henry VII, had made the Palace of Placentia, as it was then called, the great royal palace it was throughout the Tudor era.

Back to the **Greenwich foot tunnel**, created to help workers reach the then booming London Docks in 1902. You can take the lift, built for dozens of workers but now taking a handful of people, still operated by a man on a stool (As in: 'Second floor, ladies underwear and surgical appliances'), or be a big kid and race it down the steps as I always did as a child living in Greenwich. Racing up is a bit harder. At the bottom you appreciate its 1,217ft length and the 200,000 glazed tiles that line it. We are told it is 33ft under water at low tide and 53ft at high tide. They must mean the top of the water, which doesn't worry me. How close is the bottom of the water?

Well this isn't entirely academic, as when Marc Brunel (see page 121) pioneered the first tunnel under the Thames at Rotherhithe, the water burst through several times before they could get the lining up, drowning the workers within. And they say you can hear the beat of ships' propellers above you in that tunnel, so it's quite a thin riverbed.

However, this tunnel is quite safe (it's a century old) and I've always enjoyed the walk down to the dip in the middle and up the other side. What they don't tell you is that the reinforced and therefore narrowed bit on the far side, just before you leave the tunnel, is like this because a German bomb landed on the foreshore, damaging the tunnel, in the 1940s.

And they also don't tell you about the opening day's big embarrassment. When top-hatted mayors and officials emerged from the champagne banquet held in the tunnel below they forgot about the slight decompression effect, exaggerated by champagne, and they all began to fart and burp uncontrollably. If you merely walk through, such effects are unlikely. But stay off the fizz while you're down there. On the other side we're on the **Isle of Dogs**, so called because hounds for the Greenwich hunt used to live here (well, so they say, but did they swim across?).

GREENWICH PALACE, THE HOSPITAL AND LONDON'S FINEST VIEW The trip under the river is well worth it for the utterly splendid view it gives you – London's finest, many say – of Greenwich from the waterfront on the other side, which gives you a good chance to place everything in your mind. The pair of buildings in front of us directly on the waterfront opposite is the **Old Royal Naval College**, built by Sir Christopher Wren as a naval hospital from 1694. It was not finished until the middle of the next century by Wren's successors, Hawksmoor and Vanbrugh.

It replaced Greenwich Palace, which stood here in Tudor times but the architects cleverly not only kept the elegant Queen's House behind but also preserved views between there and the water.

The **Queen's House** by Inigo Jones is a gem of a building and now forms the centrepiece of the National Maritime Museum. (The architect was not Indigo Jones as the naughty *Daily Telegraph* had it recently – is that why they call Welshmen 'Dye'?) This was the first mathematically disciplined classical building in England. At first glance it looks to be 18th century, by which time every architect was copying Jones. In fact it was built between 1616 and 1635 and was revolutionary at the time.

Looking beyond up the hill is the **Royal Observatory**, start of all the world's longitudes and birthplace of modern timekeeping. If you have very good eyes you will see at the top of this hill a black statue of General Wolfe.

You can return via the foot tunnel but more fun and less tiring is to stroll a couple of hundred yards inland to the **Docklands Light Railway** station (it's signposted) and catch one of the frequent tram-like trains back to the *Cutty Sark*. If you choose to do this, note that your Travelcard, if you have one, will cover the fare; sit near the front for a view of how this rail tunnel dips under the river, like the foot tunnel.

Back on the South Bank, go past the *Cutty Sark* and along the waterfront footpath outside the grounds of the former Royal Naval College. This building, now turning into colleges plus a major heritage site, is worthy of several hours; you can find out more about it at the tourist information at the nearest corner to the *Cutty Sark*. I don't propose to describe it, or the National Maritime Museum, or the Royal Observatory in full detail here, where we are supposed to be looking for eccentric bits ordinary tourists would miss. But the interior of the Naval College is amazing. Most astounding is the **Painted Hall**, the ceiling of which took Sir James Thornhill nearly 20 years to paint.

It was here that Nelson's body was brought following the Battle of Trafalgar in 1805 when his fleet destroyed a much larger Spanish-French fleet after he hoisted his famous signal: 'England expects every man to do his duty.'

The national grief that followed his death was a bit like when Princess Diana died. This quotation from *The Times* about that day his body lay in state in the Painted Hall captures the nation's overwhelming grief and gratitude:

> Before eight in the morning, every avenue from the metropolis to Greenwich was crowded with vehicles of every description … the approach to Greenwich Hospital Gate a little before that hour must baffle the conception of those who did not witness it. When the gate was thrown open, above ten thousand persons pressed forward for admittance.

Passing along the front of the College on the riverside path we see two fine obelisks, wonderfully useless things except in one regard – they remind us of things we would otherwise forget, making a point in every sense. The one nearest the *Cutty Sark*, within the grounds of the Naval College, is by Hardwicke and remembers sailors from here who died in the New Zealand war of the 19th century. The rights and wrongs of that war are another story but suffice it to say that, as with the Boers in the Boer War, if the British thought the Maori would be a push-over they were sorely disappointed. The military were so impressed by the Maori fortifications that they sent experts to study them at the end of the war. As with the Gurkhas and the Fijians, the Brits made sure they were on the same side in future.

The second obelisk recalls one M Bellot, a heroic Frenchman whose efforts to find Sir John Franklin (1786–1847), the British explorer who went missing in the Arctic (see page 74), ended up with his sharing the same fate in the frozen wastes of the north. You can read the story on the landward side.

Next is the **Water Gate**, the elaborate entrance where monarchs would have landed to enter the previous palace, and to visit the later buildings. Notice how one of the great domes – you can't get away from that word round here – tells the time while the other tells wind direction, both then vital for mariners.

The statue of George II was put up by some crawling creep so the monarch would see it first when he arrived at Greenwich and grant the man some vast amount of money. The grovelling git got his dosh, as cockneys might have it.

THE MOST FAMOUS PUB, WORST HANGOVER AND WISEST LITTLE FISH At the end of the riverside path walk we come to the **Trafalgar Tavern**, Greenwich. This pub has a special memory for me because in the late 1950s, my father took a lease on a flat upstairs. I remember how up-and-down the floor was, as well as running along the riverside walk to the *Cutty Sark* and the foot tunnel under the Thames but, do you know, I didn't once stop to look at the river view or even appreciate the architectural splendour around me. The only issue then was if they would have pink ice-cream across the water. Today, at these same windows, one sees a

fascinating, inspiring sweep of ever-changing view that could keep me mesmerised for hours (and that's even before having a pint). Funny things, children … I wonder if some metal detector nut has retrieved my Dinky Riley 1.5 police car (with bell on the front bumper, if I remember rightly) from the river mud and taken it to that Greenwich collector's shop?

This graceful building dates from the 1830s, a tribute to Lord Nelson's then recent victory giving it its new alliterative name. Famed for its whitebait suppers (those tiny fish that you get fried by the hundred, eyes and tail and all) which were a big hit with Dickens and his chums. Didn't Dickens say there is no hangover like that following a Greenwich supper? Many Victorian politicians such as Gladstone dined here. Perhaps the best advice came from Lord Palmerston during one such whitebait supper:

Let us all imitate this wise little fish, and drink a lot and say nothing.

21

THE BALLAST QUAY EXTENSION AND A QUESTION OF PHILOSOPHY After the Trafalgar Tavern (or tshlaugar tashern if you've enjoyed too many drinks), we strike inland straight up Park Row. But if you're a good walker, and haven't drunk too much, dive down Crane Street first for an interesting half-mile there-and-back extension. (Otherwise skip to *Mad tunnels* below.)

You pass the **Yacht** pub, again with splendid riverside views, and a couple of rowing clubs before coming to a beautiful little almshouse, **Trinity Hospital**, built in 1616. This place – really quite exquisite if you look through the gates at the courtyard fountain – is 'for retired Greenwich gentlemen'. Well, I hope to qualify on one of those counts eventually.

Don't miss on the river wall behind you the high tide marks from certain Thames floods. London is now protected from the North Sea tides and winds by the 1982 Thames Barrier at Woolwich around the corner of the river – you can take boat trips from Greenwich. Nicknamed the 'drowning nuns' because of their cowl-like appearance, a set of massive gates shaped like gas taps lie in the river bed ready to be swivelled upright when needed.

Next to the Jacobean almshouses, which sit on the meridian line, by the way, stands a massive power station that dwarfs the place. The juxtaposition is astounding, like that of the Carnegie Library and the neo-Nazi Town Hall mentioned earlier. No-one would dream of allowing it today, which makes it all the more delicious. It's insane. Surreal. Walk past the slumbering giant - it was built to power trams and is now a stand-in for tube power - and its old loading jetty and we're in industrial docks mode. Keep straight on a few more yards and there's yet another gem of a riverside pub, the **Cutty Sark**. This was used as a location for the film *Original Sin*, a P D James detective story featuring Roy Marsden as Adam Dalgliesh. In the distance as you sup a riverside pint you can hear the clanks and bashes of gritty southerners earning a real living by the sweat of their brows, a real rarity in a London of estate agents, hairdressers, restaurateurs and 'meeja' people. On the other hand it could just be tape-recorded gritty northerners, an astute move by Greenwich tourist authorities.

Am I being an inverted snob or is there something starkly noble about a power station (or coal mine or dock or engine shed) that filling it with meaningless arty twaddle and souvenir shops and cafés where thin people push food around without actually eating it, and designer-clad people kiss the air next to each other's cheeks, would somehow demean? A choice between the wreckage of reality or living in a theme park?

I knew I shouldn't have had that last pint. Quick, back to the Trafalgar Tavern before this philosophising gets out of hand.

Oh yes, it was called **Ballast Quay** because those clipper ship crew, poor beggars, had to load the empty hulls of their vessels after their cargo had been landed, with hundreds of tons of gravel or stones – by hand – to make them stable enough for the long sea voyages back to China or Australia. If your ballast shifted in a typhoon, as authors Conrad or Eric Newby or Alan Villiers probably say somewhere, you'd had it.

MAD TUNNELS, A GHOST ON THE STAIRS AND TUMBLING LADIES Heading away from the river up Park Row, over the pedestrian crossing on the main road that slices between the Naval College and the **National Maritime Museum**, the latter building becomes obvious by the parade of anchors on our right. The first of them, a rather modern, black and evil looking job, is from a nuclear submarine. It's funny to think these sinister, unseen high-tech Darth Vader machines which could end the world (or prevent it being ended, arguably) could need anything as prosaic as an anchor, but they do; this one's odd shape is so that it can be retracted exactly flush with the hull of the submarine, so no undue swirling of water is created that might be detected when the vessel is in motion.

The museum, superb for content and container alike, cannot be detailed here. The elegant **Queen's House** (1637), which forms the centrepiece, is a perfect gem of its time, with its splendid hall, a perfect cube, and haunted Tulip Staircase. It was here that retired Canadian clergyman the Rev R W Hardy took an extraordinary picture. With witnesses watching, he waited until the staircase was entirely clear of people and, with his Zeiss camera, the best there was, took a picture. When the picture was developed and printed, a shadowy hooded, monklike figure could be seen climbing the stairs, his white left hand clearly grasping the banister. The film was examined by Kodak and the museum authorities but no hint of any fraud was detected.

We enter **Greenwich Park** – a royal park like those in Central London and Richmond – through the gate ahead. If you hear the bellow of a train whistle as you approach the gate, don't worry. The trains approach from the east in a deep cutting where the trees are to the left and must whistle before they pass between the Maritime Museum and the Naval College in a tunnel. Thank God someone sane insisted on the railway being hidden here and what a pity they didn't do the same with the infernal road we have just crossed.

Entering the park, you can check the time on a massive sundial on the left. This sundial is slap bang on the Greenwich meridian, so it should be right.

Up the hill from the boating lake there is a small feature which looks like a bricked-up tunnel. There are extensive tunnels, medieval in origin, throughout Greenwich, for which no plausible explanation has ever been devised. They are far too large to have been water supply conduits for the former royal Greenwich Palace, as has often been suggested. There are repair bills for these tunnels dated 918 and 1268. So what were these mysterious tunnels running perhaps 40ft under your feet for?

My theory is that they are not that old but were excavated by a team comprising Erich von Daniken, Thor Heyerdahl, and Col John 'Blashers' Blashford-Snell who were trying to prove that tunnelling cockneys, guided by alien gods in flying saucers, created the lost civilisation of Atlantis. Well, at least it's an idea; with newspaper serialisation rights, it could just make my fortune.

Joseph Conrad's gripping 1907 story *The Secret Agent* has a man blown to pieces in a botched revolutionary bomb attack before World War I here. It's not so far-fetched, as there was an attempt to blow up the Royal Observatory in 1894 and, as recorded in the section on Whitechapel (see page 209), there was a gun-battle with anarchists in 1911. Incidentally, in this book Conrad talks of Greenwich Park station, which sounded like fiction. But it turns out there was one on Royal Hill on a line long vanished, which means yet another abandoned tunnel, under Blackheath on the way to Lewisham.

We go up the hill to the old **Royal Observatory**, a hill which, with its superb view, has for centuries been a great place for Londoners to stroll. Dickens records in his Sketches:

> The chief place of resort in the day-time … is the Park, in which the principal amusement is to drag young ladies up the steep hill which leads to the Observatory, and then drag them down again, at the very top of their speed, greatly to the derangement of their curls and bonnet-caps, much to the edification of the lookers-on from below.

On the flanks of this hill I encountered a young man with a flying saucer model hanging from a long cane by a bit of string. He was waving it around in line with the Greenwich Dome, that great white fried-egg thingy now clearly visible on the North Greenwich peninsula. He didn't mind being photographed but wouldn't give his name. An alien agent? A man making a low-budget sci-fi film? The truth is out there somewhere. Spooky.

The **Dome** was a kind of Millennium exhibitiony circusy thingy (well that was exactly it – you couldn't really say what it was about); it was widely derided, regarded as pointless and inaccessible by those who had never been there and, compared to the 1851 Great Exhibition and the 1951 Festival of Britain, came a poor third in terms of success. The Government's 'Dome Secretary' Peter Mandelson (no, I'm not still on about spooky aliens) was the grandson of Herbert Morrison, the brains behind the 1951 show.

The doomed Dome, which hopefully by the time you read this has found some other use, was never clear of political sniping, yet had actually been supported by all political parties at various times and cost the taxpayer not a penny (it was all funded by National Lottery loot). To be positive, its coming regenerated a polluted, poisonous peninsula, gained Greenwich two 21st-century rail links that wouldn't otherwise have been built and gave possibly six million people a good time (instead of the 12 million expected). Any other country on earth would think six million visitors to a millennium attraction a resounding triumph. I can recall a similar event in Wellington, New Zealand, where as far as I could see, four people and a chihuahua had turned up.

The Dome folly was supposed to be a good thing just because it was big. Big enough to accommodate the Eiffel Tower laid down on its side. They like figures like that round here. Another one is that Canary Wharf, the highest office block you can see across the river, the one with the pyramid top, could be accommodated within the Tube station underneath it. In fact, if the people who messed up Heathrow's new underground railway (which fell in at one point) were in charge, it probably soon will be accommodated within the station. Anyway, if anyone needs to store the Eiffel Tower sideways under cover in London for 25 years, the Dome will be seen as a brilliant piece of foresight. You never know.

MORE WOLFE, HALF OF THE WORLD AND MERIDIAN MADNESS Arriving at Wolfe's statue I found it swamped by a sea of French schoolchildren who lapped up against it giggling and gesticulating, as only they know how, oblivious of the superb view before them. It's even better than the one from across the river looking back. I wonder how they felt, if they knew, about this man Wolfe who denied France Canada. He single-handedly reduced a great nation to second-class status for ever. I refer, of course, to Canada's cuisine … what else?

Talking about status, the meridian line which passes through this observatory – if you go through the little iron gate and along the path on the downhill side of the observatory a few steps there's a brass line in the ground where children can stand with one foot in either hemisphere – provides evidence of Britain's pre-eminence in navigation at the time. Britain got ownership of the prime meridian, 0 degrees, and Greenwich Mean Time, just as in the 20th century, when the US which had taken over the role of super-power, got 1 as their international telephone country calling code. Come to think of it, Britain's reward for inventing post boxes and stamps is that we are the only country that doesn't have to put its name on our stamps, just as Americans don't have to put .usa on the end of their websites. Don't worry, people of Burkina Faso – your time will come.

The **Royal Observatory** (see box for its eccentric history) has long since moved its HQ to Sussex and now conducts its serious stargazing from better-suited viewpoints overseas. The old observatory is now a museum which gives an insight into matters such as the search for means of fixing longitude – upon which thousands of sailors' lives depended and led to the surprise literary hit of 1995, *Longitude* by Dava Sobel (who says British readers are dumbing down?).

Between the brass meridian line and General Wolfe stands a monument to what could in some regards be seen as a final crushing victory for the French. Here there's a set of brass imperial measures pegged out to be used as universal references. It was a long way uphill to come to measure something which, by the way, had to fit between the pegs *exactly*.

Today it's as if Wolfe, Nelson, Trafalgar and Waterloo had never happened. Everyone must use the aforementioned metric system, which is based on some French madman's idea of the distance from the Equator to the North Pole (he was wrong); it's a more logical, but, sadly, a less eccentric one than the imperial one it replaced. There was a human side to the imperial system – a foot was a foot (that tired thing on the end of your leg), and a yard was the distance from the king's nose to his outstretched thumb, but there was also a pleasing insanity about what we called imperial measures. I mean if you defend them, can you work out the cost of 1 stone 9 pounds and 7$\frac{1}{2}$ ounces of kippers at 4 shillings and eightpence farthing a pound? Go on, if you like old measures, just try it. It's near impossible. *Mon dieu, alors*, thank God for the French! And if they always put a dozen bottles, not ten, into a case of wine, who's complaining?

The observatory is the highpoint of the walk, so it's all downhill from here with a relatively short stroll through pleasant parts to the station. There's an optional Blackheath extension, ending at that rather charming village. You could sit here on one of the benches and read about it while resting your weary feet rather than actually do it. Or you could save it for another time.

THE BLACKHEATH EXTENSION: A SPURNED PRINCESS, MYSTERIOUS CAVES, SKATING ON THIN ICE AND CHINESE ECCENTRICITIES

Looking behind the Wolfe statue, you see that the line of Greenwich's great view carries on down Blackheath Avenue to the park gates, beyond which can be seen Blackheath and the church of **All Saints** perfectly aligned. Cosmic. This would be your route to Blackheath station if you fancied striking out – it's perhaps a mile-and-a-half.

In the park itself there's a rather indifferent café on the left of this avenue (in 2001 adequate but uninspiring). On the right of the avenue, about halfway down, there's a path through an ornamental rose garden to the **Ranger's House**, now home to the Wernher Collection of rare treasures (see museums, page 44). On my visit I turned left in front of the Ranger's House which brings you to some unremarkable paving slabs that, unknown to most local people and unsigned in the park, tell the astounding story of a Princess of Wales, spurned by a husband who preferred his mistress, and who was mourned by all London at her emotional funeral. Yes, this is **Princess Caroline's sunken bath**, marked only with a small plaque on the wall, a last relic of this strangest of royal stories (see in full page 262).

Leaving Greenwich Park and heading for that spire of All Saints across Blackheath, you can see why this great open space was used by Londoners for welcoming victorious kings, such as Henry V, home from European wars.

As the route from London to Europe in the days of stagecoaches, Blackheath was a notorious spot for highwaymen, who were often strung up on gibbets to deter others. Samuel Pepys records seeing one such decayed corpse swaying in the wind with the flesh falling from its bones: 'A filthy sight'. The road east from here, Shooters Hill, gave people their first or last view of London and is recalled at the start of Dickens's possibly greatest work (sorry, I can't make my mind up), *A Tale of Two Cities*, and in Byron's poem *Don Juan*.

Hidden under Blackheath are vast networks of underground tunnels for which no known purpose or date exists. There is a similar set at Chiselhurst, Kent, not too far from here. They say you can cross Blackheath from one side to the other without ever coming up on the surface.

Oddly, then, Blackheath has several ponds (you'd think they'd drain away down all those tunnels); and if it is midwinter, youths sometimes skate on them. I wouldn't recommend skating on thin ice at all; I happen to know that the pond a couple of hundred yards to the left of All Saints church – in the angle between

21

Prince of Wales Road and South Row – is at least in part shallow. I fell through the ice here one Boxing Day myself. Just around the corner from the pond, along South Row a little, is the most exquisite and perfect crescent of houses in London, the **Paragon**, well worth a look.

The way down to the village is behind All Saints, down Montpelier Row and Montpelier Vale. If you had heaps of energy, or were car- or bike-borne, there is one more fascinating link with Princess Caroline, in Pagoda Gardens, reached by following the railway on this north side of the tracks to the right (west) up Collins Street, Blazdon Road and Eliot Vale (not down Heath Lane).

This is the eccentric building, **The Pagoda**, built around 1775 for the Duke of Buccleuch; it has a dramatic Chinese-style roof with almost ludicrously upturned corners. This is part of that era's fascination with Chinoiserie which also gave us the much higher pagoda at Kew Gardens, but is of more interest because Princess Caroline came to stay here in 1799 after separating from her husband and before going to live in Greenwich Park where her sunken bath survives.

BACK TO THE STATION AND THE CREAM OF SOCIETY Assuming you intend to visit Blackheath another time, let's return from the observatory over the meridian line and then go downhill to the left and then straight across, crossing the road descending through the park, the Avenue, and leaving by one of the gates beyond into Croom's Hill. Here you might see some fine 17th-, 18th- and 19th-century houses, Wolfe's home at Macartney's House (not open to the public), plus an unusual and splendid **belvedere**, an isolated room set to command a fine view over the wall that had made a garden more private but had cut off the house's view. This room is built on an oblique angle and has a fine moulded ceiling. Have a good gawp, that's what the thing is there for, gawping at you.

Here, too, further down Croom's Hill, is one of London's most eccentric museums, the **London Fan Museum**. A good place to stop on a hot day (see page 41).

Coming out by the theatre, there is a former fine old coaching inn opposite; glancing right up the oddly named Nevada Street you can see a statue of William IV, looking like the total prat that he really was.

Our quickest way to the station is to go left down **Burney Street**, on the far corner of which we come across one of London's more eccentric little parks. This tiny scrap of earth has more monuments than many a large park; there's a marble obelisk-thingy saying 'Built by Greenwich People 1981–82', a plaque saying the Duke of Edinburgh planted an oak tree here in 1982, and yet another plaque raving about a milkman, Dougie Mullins, who was born here. I asked some local people what all the fuss was about, but they didn't know. Please write to me and put me out of my misery. It may be eccentric but why shouldn't milkmen be remembered, as well as the cream of society?

Rounding the corner we're back marvelling again at that staggering Stalinist-fascist Town Hall clock tower and behind it, across the High Road, is Greenwich railway station. Phew!

FURTHER INFORMATION

🚉 From Charing Cross, Cannon Street or Waterloo.
⊖ Central Line to Bank then DLR to Canary Wharf and Cutty Sark.

Charles II, who put Greenwich on the map with its Royal Observatory in 1675 – in fact on every map on this planet, as all longitudes, and indeed time, are measured from Greenwich – was less than generous to his first Astronomer Royal, John Flamsteed.

He paid him just £100 a year and insisted he pay his staff and buy his own telescopes from this amount. He also insisted that architect Christopher Wren (him again) used stones, brick and lead from part of Tilbury Fort further down the river (you could call this recycling). But he did agree that the hill above Greenwich was the very spot for the observatory. This allowed it in the coming centuries to help the mariners in the nearby London Docks, by observing the time precisely and dropping a ball down a flagstaff at exactly 1pm. Then sea captains could set their chronometers to the same precisely measured time, essential for navigation. A gun signal, as at Edinburgh, would have made the signal too inaccurate for this purpose given the relatively slow speed of sound. They weren't too bothered about the faster speed of light then, however, not knowing it had any speed at all. You can still witness the falling of the ball each day.

But is the Prime Meridian, 0 degrees, actually right here where children stand astride a brass line in the path, one foot on either half of the globe?

A big deal was made of the fact that the Millennium Dome had to be in its absurd location on an inaccessible peninsula because it was on the line (it passes up the reach of the river next to the Dome and just clips a corner of the site). But a yachtsman passing the site on the Thames will find that his navigation equipment, based on references from global positioning satellites, says he is on the Meridian 336ft further east. And students of the first Astronomer Royal, John Flamsteed, will find that the first meridian he laid down in 1675 by simply lowering his telescope, is 61ft 3in west of the one used for the millennium celebrations.

The Curator of Astronomy at the Old Royal Observatory at the time of writing, Maria Blyzinsky, told me: 'In fact we have four meridians recorded here, each a little further east as new astronomers built bigger and better telescopes. Halley's, for example, was set up in 1725.' It's the fault of Flamsteed for putting his telescope on the edge of the hill. Later ones had to be behind this.

The meridian line used by the satellite system referred to above was established in 1984 and moves slightly as satellites, wobbling as they orbit the Earth, try to compensate for the globe's imperfections and movements. But for the Millennium celebrations, the 1851 Official Greenwich Meridian established by Sir George Airy in 1851 was the one that counted.

So it had to be on that line. But that gives bags of eccentric possibilities. Why wasn't the Dome at the village of Cold Christmas on the Essex border a few miles due north of here?

Boat From Westminster, Charing Cross and Tower pier, but this will take much longer.
Tourist information ✎ 020 8858 6376
Cutty Sark ✎ 020 8858 3445; www.cuttysark.org.uk
Royal Observatory ✎ 020 8312 6565; www.rog.nmm.ac.uk
National Maritime Museum ✎ 020 8858 4422; www.nmm.ac.uk
St Alfege's church www.st-alfege.org
Fan Museum 12 Croom's Hill; ✎ 020 8858 7879
Emporium ✎ 020 8305 1670
Flying Duck ✎ 020 8858 1964 (even the number is 1960s)
Goddards Pie House ✎ 020 8293 9313
Unique Collections ✎ 020 8395 0867

22

Hammersmith

For too many, Hammersmith is just a place you pass through. By Tube, by river, in the air and, of course, by the trunk roads that have converged here from the four points of the compass since time immemorial. Today, the A4 flyover leading to the M4 and M3 slices though this former village and its busy road junctions and, which motorists on them might reasonably assume, totally ruins the place.

That assumption couldn't be more wrong and it's utterly typical of London that within a stone's throw of this thundering road – virtually beneath it even – you can find delights ranging from bizarre architectural oddities, some of the most wonderful views in London, tales of love, courage, daring, devotion and creation involving death and a princess, numerous fascinating nooks and crannies, and some of the world's best pubs.

Come on a walk around Hammersmith with me and you'll be convinced. But allow yourself plenty of time – it's too good to hurry.

❤ *Hammersmith (either station). You could do it in about 45 minutes flat out, but allow at least a couple of hours to include fascinating pubs, churches and shops. As usual, it's just a format for telling you what's there and some fascinating yarns, so this section is for an enjoyable armchair read, whether or not you walk it.*

Start at **Hammersmith Tube station**; by going anticlockwise we'll save the best stuff till last. When I say start at the Tube, it's daft in itself that the Tubes just fail to connect by about a hundred yards. The Hammersmith and City line station is nicer and, of course, is the one that doesn't head towards the City.

Starting between the two, at the northwest corner of the race track that runs round the Piccadilly and District Line Tube station roundabout (it's so large and incorporates so many roads that we'll call it the Megabout), you'll notice at the corner of King Street and Beadon Road the splendid **Swan pub** with its mosaic sign and over-the-top brickwork; notice also what a pig's ear they have made of the ground floor by renaming it Henry's or Kevin's or something. Never mind, ignore it – there are more splendid, beautiful, charming pubs on this walk than even the late Oliver Reed could have got round in one session. In fact, in 1873 Hammersmith was recorded as having 139 pubs.

Turning down King Street we venture very briefly, I have to say, into multiple-chainstore-land and ghastly concrete shopping centreville, but don't despair – it doesn't last long; notice as we head west how the shops become more and more fascinating. But historic pubs start straight away.

The **Hop Poles** on the left, for example, is where punk pioneer Ian Dury of Blockheads fame used to prop up the bar. If he were here, he would no doubt point out that the bar would have to prop him up now as he died in 1999, but the point of such blockhead remarks is that Hammersmith was, and is, riddled with rock and pop stars who quietly sup pints in the most unassuming places.

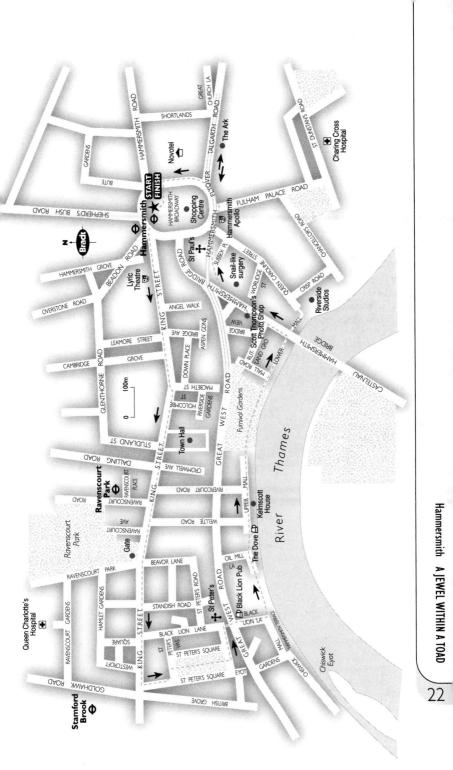

On the right here, invisible amidst the charmless concrete of some shopping mally things, is an amazing architectural survivor. Suspended within all this seventies stuff is the quite beautiful gilt and chandelier and red velvet interior of an entire Victorian theatre moved from nearby. The **Lyric** was designed in 1895 by celebrated theatre designer Frank Matcham. When the theatre was demolished in the 1970s, the lavish interior was carefully taken down, stored for a few years then somehow saved intact within the dull concrete King's Mall shopping centre. It's like cutting open a toad and finding a jewel in it. Plus it's got rather a good caff upstairs.

The old Lyric was originally in nearby Bradmore Grove and had enjoyed a boom in popularity under the manager Nigel Playfair in the 1920s which put Hammersmith on the map for the theatre-going classes, so much so that the humorous magazine *Punch* remarked:

No greater name than Nigel Playfair
Occurs in Thespian lore or myth
'Twas he who first revealed to Mayfair
The whereabouts of Hammersmith.

Soon on the right (after a plaque announcing bizarrely 'Investor in People: Co-operative Funeral Service') is the **Salutation Inn** which dates from 1750 when this was the main road west from the capital. The Queen Mother, reputedly partial to the odd tincture or three herself, gamely pulled a few majestic pints here in 1989. The fabulous early 20th-century tilework is a gem, and the beer is local, from Fuller's brewery just half a mile west on the A4 Great West Road, a place of pilgrimage for real ale fans from around the globe (tours round the brewery can be arranged).

Incidentally, another great brewery stands on the other bank of the Thames, a little further upriver at Mortlake. If these breweries were sited here in West London to draw the massive amounts of water they needed to make beer from the river before it had passed through their customers, it would certainly be true to say that, historically, drinking beer was far safer than drinking water. In those days children were given beer, even at breakfast, and there were many warnings – I can think of one on a tombstone – about the perils of drinking 'small beer', ie: weak brews.

How those Brits built a great city, a global empire and an industrial revolution when they were three sheets to the wind all the time I don't know. But as Victorian cleric Sydney Smith said: 'What two ideas are more inseparable than Beer and Britannia?'

It was at around this point in King Street where the Salutation stands that a creek came all the way up from the river and, difficult though it is to imagine today, those massive spritsail Thames barges could unload right here. Now the creek has been enclosed, although its outlet may be seen from the river. Furnivall Gardens, between here and the river, is laid out where the factories and warehouses were clustered round the wharves of this lost creek.

On the left, opposite the Salutation, we pass one end of the somewhat Stalinist Hammersmith **Town Hall** (by Stalinist I mean the architecture, not the politics;

they're *far* more left-wing than that, silly). Then there's the UGC cinema which, although being a thirties building, stands on the site of one of the earliest cinemas in Britain, dating from 1912. (Hammersmith has been for centuries a place of large-scale entertainment for West London – it still has the Palais, the Apollo, the Riverside Studios, and Olympia.)

Also on the left is some picturesque street clutter: Latin inscriptions about a posh old school (which you can read if you're a Latin lover – nice work if you can get it – or just posh and old); an obelisk which rebels against the traditional uselessness of obelisks by being a drinking fountain (notice the little bowl at the bottom for dogs); a pizza place that looks like it was once a municipal toilet (no jokes, *perlease*); and, tucked behind it, a useful automatic loo.

These are French-inspired automatic galactic cyberspace things which somehow manage to be turned upside down, washed down and disinfected after every user. Just as long as it doesn't happen while you're in it. Whatever they're really called, I prefer to call them Robobogs (imagine Arnie Schwarzenegger snarling 'Half robot, half sanitary ware, all bog') and top marks to Hammersmith for plonking these around the borough and making them free (Stalinists have their uses).

Back on the street, there are suddenly Poles everywhere (not hop poles this time but Polish ones). This is not surprising as this area was virtually the capital of free Poland from the time the post-war victors of World War II carved up Europe in 1945 (no jokes about Stalinists this time; is it not a matter of deep regret, if not shame, that having gone to war supposedly to save Poland from a mad dictator in 1939, we, or perhaps history, handed it over to another one just a few years later?) to when Lech Walesa and Solidarity reclaimed the place for its people. Here, on the right, is **POSK**, the centre for Polish Arts and Culture, where a kind of government in exile kept the flame of freedom burning through all those years.

Not far from here by car on the A40 is the superb Polish war memorial which commemorates the Polish Air Force heroes who fought and died in sorties from these islands in the desperate days of 1940. I went to school near a wartime air base and there were kids there with names which looked to me (in my ignorance) like optician's test cards, evidence that some of these heroes thrived.

On a more cheerful note, here there's Polish food aplenty, Polish arts a-thriving, and much info about Poland today. The Poles are just one of many nationalities who exist and thrive together in this polyglot borough. Here too there is the **Joseph Conrad Library**, a tribute to a Polish master who could write better in his third language than most people, myself of course included, can write in their first.

MASSIVE TESTICLES, STRANGE LEANINGS AND A SHOT GHOST
Soon, tucked away on the left, is possibly the strangest tribute to an MP I can recall. A large bull with massive testicles stands with a wordy tribute to former Hammersmith big cheese **Sir William Bull**. Unless he spent all his time making love to actresses in local flats, or tying himself up in plastic bags here in Hammersmith, like some modern MPs we could mention, then I suppose the massive testicles are irrelevant. The thing, purloined from elsewhere, is merely a rebus, a visual pun on the old chap's name.

If that's not enough bull about Bull, on the right here are some totally over the top gates also dedicated to local Sir William. They lead to **Ravenscourt Park**.

On just a little more, if you can force yourself past the curious curio shops you'll find here, and on the corner of Goldhawk Road at the traffic lights (opposite British Grove) stands an unassuming shop. But look at the brickwork above, a fantasy in terracotta well worth a second glance.

We go no further west lest we venture into Chiswick, but instead turn left down to **St Peter's Square** (the turning before British Grove). At this point, a magic

22

Bizarrely, the unusually elegant Hammersmith Bridge has, four times in the past century, come within an ace of being blown to smithereens, like the bridge in the film *Bridge on the River Kwai*.

Once in the 1930s an IRA bomb was fizzing and spluttering when a passer-by threw it in the river; once when a wartime Nazi bomb fell in the river near the bridge; and once in 1996 when enough IRA Semtex explosive to blow shreds of the bridge all over West London – the largest such bomb yet planted in Britain – failed to detonate properly. A few months later an IRA man was shot dead in a hideout a few hundred yards away.

Finally, it was controversially closed in 1998 for repairs that didn't seem to take place very quickly. At last the bridge was nearly ready. Then Irish terrorists blew up a bit of it again, delaying its re-opening until late 2000. Notices said the closure was due to 'unforeseen circumstances'. Totally predictable circumstances, I'd say.

In the unlikely event that the bridge is still there when you read this, and there aren't any fizzing suitcases visible, it's well worth the walk across. If you look very carefully on the west side handrail, you can see a plaque marking where a hero, Charles Wood, plunged in to save a dying woman, presumably a would-be suicide, and lost his own life somehow in the process.

Now to the extraordinary bridge itself. It is pretty, or pretty ghastly, depending on your view of Victoriana and twiddly bits. The finials on the towers look as if they should turn around while the rest of the contraption does something else (like the breakfast machine in the film *Chitty Chitty Bang Bang*), and it has more outrageous abutments than Dawn French.

Splendid, in its way, it would seem to have granted its designer a kind of immortality (IRA permitting), and indeed in Hammersmith church (St Paul's, which we pass later on the walk) there is a fancy memorial tablet on the wall to bridge builder **W Tierney Clark**, who died in 1852.

It bears a detailed picture of Hammersmith Suspension Bridge and the fine words: 'The great suspension bridge at Pesth in Hungary, those at Hammersmith and Shoreham, and many other works attest to his talent, perseverance and skill and are lasting monuments to his fame.'

But hang on a minute. A close look at his bridge carved on his tomb shows that it is not the current elegant Hammersmith suspension bridge, clearly dated in its arches 1887, but an earlier one which it replaced. This is the same design you may have seen on the Dove pub's wall earlier in the walk round Hammersmith. W Tierney Clark's fame is all but extinguished – so much water under the bridge.

He may have joined Buda and Pest (and the bridge there today indeed directly resembles the drawings of the old Hammersmith Bridge), but only temporarily did the

wand has been waved, for here, just a few feet from the cosmopolitan hubbub of King Street, and a few feet short of the thundering A4 beyond, is an elegant island of total tranquillity, one of London's nicest squares, unknown by those who speed so closely by. Unlike many a central London square of similar elegance, these gardens are open to the public, so one may stroll through them, noting a fine central sculpture, then proceeding to the far end and turning left towards the church of the same name, where a strangely provocative sculpture of a woman resting upon nothing sits half-forgotten to the right.

The church, **St Peter's**, a large 1829 classical job, was too early for the Gothic revival and thus contrasts nicely with St Paul's later in the walk. I wouldn't tarry here unless you love religious wall paintings, of which it offers splendid examples. Perched on its top is an odd, elliptical-section bronze cross.

same for Hammersmith and Barnes. 'Lasting monuments' indeed, although at least Budapest is kinder in naming a street after him.

The creator of the bridge we see today was the great Victorian engineer **Sir Joseph Bazalgette**, who arguably did more for London and left more positive impact on the city than anyone in its history. Victorian London was riddled with disease, much of it, such as cholera, caused by the lack of proper sewage-disposal systems and the consequent pollution of drinking water supplies. The poor drew their water only yards from where others threw their filth. The 'Great Stink' of London's summers was intolerable.

Bazalgette had the vision to build great intercepting sewers going west–east and installed powerful steam-driven pump houses, which allowed water and sewage distribution systems to be completely separated. He was the mastermind behind the simultaneous creation of the great embankments, such as the Victoria Embankment at what is now called Embankment, and the Albert Embankment at Vauxhall. He tamed the river (as his monument on the Victoria Embankment says: 'Flumini Vincula Posuit' – he put chains upon the river) and created not only charming walks along the previously impenetrable riverside, but also useful through routes for the burgeoning traffic and even space for the Tube lines.

Some say by eliminating diseases such as cholera, caused by drinking water contaminated with sewage, Bazalgette saved more lives than any other Victorian, including Florence Nightingale.

If you ever see in the credits after a TV show such as Big Brother 'produced by Bazal Productions', that's Joseph's great-great grandson Peter Bazalgette. Whether there's any connection with sewerage I couldn't say.

So Bazalgette's rebuilding of Tierney Clark's bridge is the one we see today. It's not as wedding-cakey as the prettier Albert Bridge, but like so many Victorian things, it makes a virtue out of necessity in a way we find hard to do today.

And just in case the IRA feel honour bound to blow the thing up properly, get a good look at it now. Perhaps the Mayor of Hammersmith should just fix it with them so that no-one gets hurt. ('How about next Tuesday at 10am?'). Then it could be rebuilt properly.

Even better, if there ever emerges a better way of deciding how we govern these rainswept couple of islands at the edge of the Atlantic of ours than bombing and shooting people who disagree with us, the whole issue could pass into folklore. Then the blowing up of a collapsible bridge could be staged weekly for tourists, theme-park style, with son et lumière – featuring Irish Riverdance girls (rather appropriate) and the usual heartless British toff/idiot (Hugh Grant, possibly) in charge that Hollywood seems to require.

Come on, admit it, there's great potential in that there bridge.

Dive through the subway beneath the A4 and we pop up in Black Lion Lane (of which we saw the other end in King Street). Obviously, many of the streets here have been cut in half, and in a civilised world, not the real one perhaps, it would be the A4 road that went underground.

Soon we reach the **Black Lion** pub on the left, which tells the melancholy tale of the St Peter's haunting. From 1804 onwards, the old St Peter's graveyard was haunted by a frightening ghost on dark nights. One Francis Smith, fed up with his ghoulish next-door neighbour, 'loaded his blunderbuss with shot and himself with ale' and blasted the thing. Sadly, it was not the ghost that the inebriated Smith shot but the white-clothed bricklayer Thomas Millwood, whose body the shocked residents carried to the Black Lion pub.

CRAFTY MORRIS AND THE FIRST WORLDWIDE WEB Now we are entering an area with some quite wonderful 18th-century houses – the tall Hammersmith Terrace between the pub and the river was built in 1750. Here, at the Black Lion steps, before Hammersmith Bridge was built, people needing a boat would shout 'Oars!' Out of the dark and swirling fog a waterman, often half-drunk, would come, water dripping from his oars, to ferry you expertly through the swirling eddies across the Thames to Barnes, or maybe, if he was too far gone, across the River Styx into the underworld.

But cheer up: around the corner are the finest river views you could ask for. Turn left into the **Upper Mall** walkway and head east along the river front.

Looking back along the river westwards there is a view of the island, Chiswick Eyot, not far west and of the sweep of Corney Reach beyond as the loop of the river turns due south. Ahead, to the east, is the elegant Hammersmith Bridge, a picturesque scene that thousands of artists have tried to capture on canvas.

Here, at No 26 Upper Mall, **Kelmscott House** is, where William Morris, thinker, socialist (but not Stalinist), fabric and wallpaper designer par excellence and all-round Arts and Crafts revolutionary, lived and worked from 1878 to 1896, when he died. What a spot to contemplate the world from, with its view of the sweep of the river both ways! You could be envious – particularly when you learn his country house, Kelmscott Manor, much further upriver near Oxford, looked out across the same Thames from where Morris, as he himself remarked, might have contemplated the very same gallons of water he could have seen later at his London house downriver.

Actually, if you delve into the William Morris Society's little museum (open Thursday and Saturday afternoons, 14.00–17.00) you'll find he was much too busy to do that much sitting around. He ran the Kelmscott Press, turning out socialist tracts but with the most wonderful typography. He would have meetings of the angry young men of the day, with people crowding into the coach house of Kelmscott – chaps such as George Bernard Shaw, Sidney Webb and W B Yeats were regulars. Failing that, Morris would march down to Hammersmith Bridge and harangue passers-by.

Several arty printers operated from here at the end of the 19th century and one of them, after a horrendous row over a printing contract, took all the carefully engraved printing plates he'd been commissioned to make to Hammersmith Bridge and threw them off. Now that'd be a find for the metal detectors. Morris's energy was prodigious and his artistic vision rare; his influence in so many fields changed the course of British art. He also found time to write *News From Nowhere* and *The Dream of John Bull*.

When it was his, Morris's house was only a century old (built 1780s) but was already famous for two previous creative geniuses. Sir Francis Ronalds made the first electric telegraph here in 1816; it was eight miles long (unlike the Hammersmith Tube stations, without 100yds missing in the middle). His invention soon transformed the railways, the empire, news gathering, trade, in fact almost everything. Clocks and time zones had to be sorted out. Bristol time was about 12 minutes behind London, for example, before all this. A global wiring up of the very first worldwide web rapidly took hold and started right here.

The house's other illustrious inhabitant was popular children's author George Macdonald (1824–1905).

A PERFECT PUB, GREAT INSPIRATION FOR GREAT MINDS Perhaps these great minds gained inspiration from being across the pathway from **The Dove**, one of the most perfect pubs imaginable. Although a little crowded on summer Saturdays, the pub had just four people in it (including a certain ageing rock star) when I visited on a

November morning when the fire was cheerful in the snug, and the river views from the bar at the back just as good. Don't miss, as I nearly did, the reputed smallest public bar in the world on the right as you come in – it's easy to assume it's a broom cupboard. In here a brass plate marks the high point of a particularly high tide in 1928. No wonder there's not a level floor or straight beam in the place. And have a close look in the first bar by the entrance at the drawings of Hammersmith Bridge for reference later on the walk.

It was originally the Dove Coffee House – they were all the rage in the 18th century; famous ones such as Lloyd's in the City became institutions – and was bought by the aforementioned local brewery Fuller's (Fuller, Smith and Turner) on 23 November 1796. That was more than a century after Charles II and his saucy mistress Nell Gwyn supped here. You can prop up the bar and watch Old Father Thames go by, musing that for more than 200 years – since well before New Zealand was founded and when the United States was a smattering of East Coast settlements – this same, splendid Fuller's beer has cheered many a Londoner at this very same spot. Not that it's been called the Dove ever since. A careless painter painted two Doves on the sign in the 1850s and so it became the Doves until 1948 when a new sign corrected this error.

The Dove also cheered the novelist A P Herbert who loved this spot and thinly disguised the Dove as The Pigeons in his novel *The Water Gipsies*. He lived in Hammersmith Terrace, which we have just walked past, and his portrait is in the Black Lion, another of his favourite pubs.

The poet James Thomson (1700–48) took enough inspiration in the Dove to write the rumbustious *Rule Britannia* in one of its upper rooms. Britannia may have ruled the waves, but waves did for poor Thomson. After a row down the river to Kew, he took a chill and died not knowing half the country and thousands more round the world would bellow his words with gusto on the Last Night of the Proms for centuries to come. Talking of great music, local composer Gustav Holst, whose house can be seen at Barnes on the opposite bank and who wrote *The Planets* suite while music master at St Paul's school, composed the *Hammersmith Suite* in an upstairs room at the Dove.

Dragging ourselves away from this tavern, and continuing along the riverside, there are three more pubs, all good in their own way and superbly situated, along the waterfront, which soon becomes the Lower Mall, before Hammersmith Bridge: the **Old Ship**, the **Rutland** and the **Blue Anchor**, the latter cosy hostelry having been licensed since at least 1722.

Here, the rowing clubs come thick and fast and give drinkers who linger in the pubs by the riverfront something to watch. One of them, Furnivall Sculling Club, is named after local doctor and rowing enthusiast Dr F J Furnivall who outraged some in 1896 by setting up this club for women only initially, although decorum required they had to row their skiffs somehow in long skirts without an ankle being revealed to onlookers!

All along here are beautiful, mainly 18th-century buildings. Now we reach the splendidly over-the-top **Hammersmith Bridge**, a fabulous confection nothing like the one we saw in The

Dove. Its bizarre history is detailed in the box on page 256. It's a pleasant stroll across the bridge and back (if it hasn't been blown up again) and under it at the Hammersmith end.

Beyond you will see the Riverside Studios, where prince of ginger geeks, Chris Evans, made his fortune with *TFI Friday*, a cult post-pub TV show. Further beyond is visible one of the football grounds thick on the ground round here. This one is Fulham's, being not in Fulham but Hammersmith, whereas Chelsea's *is* in Fulham, not Chelsea. I think I've got that right. Same with hospitals: Charing Cross Hospital is here at Hammersmith, but the Hammersmith Hospital is at Wormwood Scrubs. Getting the hang of it?

SYDNEY OPERA COMES TO LONDON AND A RIPPED-OUT HEART One more thing before we leave the river on the road going left from the bridge. This stretch immediately downstream of the bridge was, it is difficult now to believe, once one of London's airports. In 1925 a French company got permission to use the Thames here as an aerodrome and elegant seaplanes would swoop between the towers of Bazalgette's bridge and splash down in the river. Charming, and why not revive it? After all, most great European cities have suitable rivers right in their centre.

Go left up Hammersmith Bridge Road, where there are yet more pubs, and where arty framed photos of a moody Hammersmith Bridge can be bought from eccentric **Scott Thompson's** shop (rarely moody himself, he always likes a chat and one of his regular customers was the aforementioned Ian Dury. More on Scott in box on opposite page).

Soon on the right we find a remarkable small new building – the sail-like, shell-like surgery of Dr Fernandes and partners. Sydney Opera House comes to Hammersmith. It is denying the existence of the thundering adjacent flyover and it somehow contrives to arrange matters so that every one of its rooms has an outside view that doesn't include the flyover. Brilliant (by Guy Greenfield) and, when I saw it, unblemished with graffiti – may it stay that way.

Now walk towards the Gothic 1882 church ahead, **St Paul's**, that provides such a contrast to the giant shoe box of St Peter's, which had not a pointed arch or a spire in sight. Both churches are 19th century but the Gothic revival style of St Paul's couldn't be more different – strange to see how completely styles had changed in only 53 years. The church houses a great organ and offers tremendous recitals from time to time. But St Paul's itself is remarkable more for its astounding contents than for its architecture. A clue is in two street names behind the church: Crispe Road and Caroline Street.

At the back of the nave stands an urn in which Hammersmith bigwig Sir **Nicholas Crispe** requested his heart be put on his death in 1665. The urn is below a bronze bust of 'that glorious martyr Kinge Charles the first of blessed memory' and symbolises Crispe's role as a 'loyall sharer in the sufferings of his late and present majesty'.

Just how loyal can be understood by Crispe's request that on his death his heart be cut out and put in an urn at the foot of a statue of Charles I. He wanted to be for ever at the feet of the king whose head was chopped off by those republican types in 1649. Crispe left money in his will so that someone would take his heart out every year and 'refresh' it with wine to stop it becoming too, well, crisp.

Curiously, the urn is empty. In 1898 the Royalist knight's body was moved to Hammersmith from St Mildred's, Bread Street (in the City of London); someone with a strong stomach took the two-centuries old heart (now thoroughly crisp as the yearly marination ritual had lapsed) from the urn and reunited it with its body in the churchyard where it lies today beneath the thundering A4 flyover. Also in the church, don't miss the telling memorial to the builder of Hammersmith Bridge.

Scott Thompson, the Hammersmith photographer, is fanatical about the Tube. Not so much the routes under the earth as following them on the surface. This he does with London Underground route maps in hand and with the aid of a pipe which he uses like a stethoscope to listen to London's heartbeat and track the tracks. In fact, if you see a man listening to the Tube with a tube, it's Scott. Actually, walking above the tracks may get him there faster than us lot in the trains below.

He's completed his photo survey of the Circle Line (what's above it, that is) and has mounted an exhibition of the results at his gallery at 90 Hammersmith Bridge Road. Which brings us neatly to another of his obsessions: Hammersmith Bridge. His gallery is always stuffed full of pictures of this bridge from every conceivable angle and lighting condition – except perfect lighting. 'I don't want to do a picture-postcard job on the bridge, it's far too wonderful for that,' enthuses Scott. 'When I first saw Hammersmith Bridge I fell in love with it and knew I had to be near it. In fact my gallery is about 100 yards away from the north end. I'd like to be a little closer really.'

The result of Scott's odd approach is that his photos are taken in mist or at night, anything but straightforward pictures.

Scott said he was considering suggesting to Mayor Ken Livingstone that it would be fun for tourists if the pavements were marked with lines with the Tube line colours on above the tracks. 'Well, the Tube map is a convenient fiction really, and the routes are nothing like they appear on the map. It might help people find the nearest Tube station and it would brighten up places like Baker Street to have the various routes in their colours criss-crossing on the streets.'

Even more remarkable is the story of Queen Caroline and the gravestone in the corner nearest the Hammersmith Megabout which tells of the amazing goings-on at her funeral – more dramatic than that, more recent, of the Princess of Wales, but in almost exactly the same circumstances (see box on next page).

Leaving the church, don't cross the hurtling traffic of the Megabout itself but note amidst the cliff-like offices in the middle of it an ancient Georgian brick frontage facing the church. This 1709 baroque front was saved as a mere skin while everything behind it was ripped down for the Centre West reconstruction of 1992.

Pressing on, you'll walk past a huge thirties picture palace, now one of London's leading live stage and music venues, since 1992 named the Apollo, having previously (since 1936) used up most of Britain's cinema names. Formerly it was (in turn) the Gaumont Palace, Gaumont and the Odeon.

Cross busy Fulham Palace Road which leads south from the swirling Megabout, using the underpass unless you wish to join Sir Nicholas and the others in their graveyard.

When you surface on the far side there is a stunning view of the **Ark**, one of London's most imaginative and dramatic modern buildings which avoids the boring cigarette-pack shape of so many glass and steel towers nowadays. The building does indeed loom like a large ship, moored in the city, but the brilliance of its design can perhaps be fully appreciated from many different angles. From the air, its oval shape fits perfectly the hole left by the road flyover on one side and the Tube railway tracks on the south, which curve tightly around it like this: (0). From the ground, pleasing details such as the drain near the front and the rusticated brick texture on the vertical pillars, add a little lightening detail to the looming mass. Inside, it has a massive atrium with dramatic suspended walkways and a strange meeting-room, globe-like thing that apparently hovers in mid-air.

Hammersmith **A JEWEL WITHIN A TOAD**

22

At St Paul's churchyard, right next to Hammersmith's central 'Megabout' and under the thundering A4 flyover, lies a fascinating gravestone you must not miss. It has a poignant, tragic story to tell.

It is the tale of a spurned **Princess of Wales** whose husband, the Prince of Wales, preferred the company of his mistress, a previously married woman, and whose eventual funeral through Kensington, which the authorities tried to downplay, moved the entire population of London to unprecedented public demonstrations of mass emotion.

She was subjected by the Royal Family and the media to constant calumny about her private life, yet was in part the authoress of her own downfall, becoming an adulterer, as her husband certainly was. Towards the end of her life she frequently appeared in public, often scantily clad, with her most unsuitable playboy lover.

When I add that her story explains the presence of Britain's most eccentric building, the oriental fantasy that is the Royal Pavilion at Brighton, it should become clear that we are talking not about the late 20th-century Princess of Wales, Diana, but her early 19th-century counterpart, Caroline, whose name, although totally forgotten by the average Londoner, is at least marked by Queen Caroline Street at this spot in Hammersmith.

In 1795 Caroline of Brunswick married the unpleasantly priggish 'Prinny', the deeply unpopular Prince Regent who was to become George IV. They soon became estranged as the prince spent more and more of his time at a farmhouse near Brighton with a previously married (scandal) Catholic (more scandal) commoner (yet more scandal) woman (well, no scandal about that bit) called Mrs Maria Fitzherbert. In fact Prinny had secretly married Mrs Fitzherbert in 1785, ten years before his therefore bigamous marriage to Caroline. The earlier marriage was declarer invalid.

After the prince's official marriage in 1795, the court put it about that the new Princess of Wales was unfaithful and unhygienic, never changing her undergarments and eating mainly raw onions and garlic. She had consequently the most monstrous breath and bad teeth, one courtier complained.

The unfaithfulness was true but only after she had been shabbily treated by the prince's shameless flaunting of his mistress (is this at all familiar?). Actually she really did go a bit scatty later, travelling with an unsuitable lover to Jerusalem, appearing topless at an Italian ball, that kind of thing.

The prince's claims about her personal hygiene can be seen to be a complete falsehood by travelling to Greenwich Park today where, near the Charlton Way entrance and the Ranger's Lodge, you'll find Princess Caroline's sunken bath, admittedly today looking more like a paved-over sandpit than a bath.

She had moved here to Montague House in 1801, only a few years after arriving in Britain, and when she left to live overseas in 1814, the prince, who loathed the sight of

Built in 1992, it was designed by Ralph Erskine, a British-born Swedish architect, and constructed by Ake Larson, a Swedish developer – which just goes to show that there's a lot more to Swedes than flatpack furniture, sensible cars and root vegetables.

On its eastern side, towards Earl's Court, is the **Lilla Huset** (little house) which was built as Hammersmith Council's pay-off for giving planning permission to the Ark. Of course, if Hammersmith Council really were Stalinists, the 'planning gain' (as the lingo has it) would be to build a private swimming pool for the senior commissars, so they got something right by permitting the building of the Ark and this smaller building which houses the borough's fascinating archives of old documents and photos. By the way, you have to make an appointment to see the archives and specify what you wish to research.

her, had the house flattened. His minions forgot, however, to remove the sunken bath which gave the lie to the story about her personal filth. It was rediscovered in 1909.

The prince, meanwhile, was indulging in the ultimate barn conversion with his Brighton bit on the side. The transformation from tatty old farmhouse to fantasy palace went through a few stages, but the key decision was calling in a builder called John. Not any old John, but John Nash. He who created the breathtaking sweep of Regent Street. Get Nash to tart up your seaside place and you get the most exquisitely eccentric palace of the era – the fabulously oriental Royal Pavilion.

Back to the official royal marriage, and to the Prince and Princess of Wales. When he was being crowned **George IV** on 19 July 1820, Prinny had Caroline shut out of Westminster Abbey. This led to the amazing scene of a legal Queen of England being shut out of her own Coronation. The mob outside were clearly behind Caroline, it was no wonder the doors were barred. It was as dodgy a moment for the monarchy as that one at this very spot in 1997, when Earl Spencer poured scorn on the way another Princess of Wales, Diana, had been treated at her funeral.

Caroline's popularity with Londoners increased in proportion to Prinny's attempts to sideline her. When she died in the following year, on 7 August, said to be heartbroken at being so thoroughly rejected, the government tried to downplay her funeral and stop the procession going up through Kensington. The people wanted her to have a proper funeral, and they marched past Kensington Palace behind the coffin – yes, on the same route taken by the funeral of the recent Princess of Wales.

When troops tried to stop the cortège at Hyde Park Corner, shots rang out and two working men were killed, but the crowd refused to flee and took her coffin through the middle of London to give her due honour, bearing it all the way to a ship which took her to her homeland for interment. You can still see the gravestone of the two men who were killed – carpenter Richard Honey, 36, and bricklayer George Francis, 43 – at St Paul's Church in Hammersmith. It's certainly worth a look for its bitter inscription.

The royal row continued even to her grave. The princess had requested her coffin bear the inscription 'Caroline of Brunswick, the injured Queen of England'. King George IV tried to prevent this being done as 'offensive' but the crowd of supporters insisted the inscription was added. The troops dared not interfere. Again there were fights between her supporters and her detractors at Harwich over the inscription.

Perhaps the oddest thing was that that sorry saga was so soon forgotten. George IV died in 1830 after a few more years of disgusting greed, alcoholism and sloth, slightly bonkers like his father but still wearing a locket with a picture of Mrs Fitzherbert inside it.

One last quotation which is attributed to George IV. On Napoleon's death in 1821, a courtier came to the king and said: 'Great news, Sire, your greatest enemy is dead.' The king replied: 'Is she, by God?'

This, your weary feet will be pleased to hear, is the limit of our walk. We return under the Megabout (or over it) to the Centre West thingy which houses the Tube station and a shopping centre. Its architecture is inoffensively bland (is it post-modern and does that make us post-post-modern and does modern therefore mean ancient?). A fitting location, perhaps, for Coca-Cola's HQ. The Centre West project, including the hugely busy transport interchange costing £20 million, may have been an unremarkable way to spend £85 million, but it was at least finished on time and to budget.

If you leave via the Tube station underneath, there's one more detail to note: the station itself was to have been the architect's answer to the DeLorean car – a sweeping gullwing canopy with no visible supports. Difficult and brilliant, so the

22

last thing you'd do would be to clutter up the platforms with buildings that look as if they support the canopy, right? Wrong. They have completely spoilt the effect with waiting rooms that almost reach the roof. Personally, I'd rather shiver a little and another thing – the canopy is designed so that an out-of-control Tube train driven by a psychopath trying to get to Cuba can smash down one prop without the whole thing coming down. Well, I'd still rather not be there when it's tried out.

So that was Hammersmith with all its fascinating quirks and oddities. If you've got this far, the chances are that you haven't been a victim of violent crime, which at earlier times would have been a strong possibility here.

Hammersmith, as befits anywhere close to London straddling a main road out of town, has always been good for highwaymen and robbers. Dick Turpin was a regular at the Queen's Head on Brook Green.

In the 18th century, before the inception of an organised metropolitan police force, we hear of a fund being collected to give a 'proper reward for the apprehending and convicting of housebreakers, murderers, footpads, robbers of gardens, orchards, poultry etc, as so many daring and atrocious offences have of late been committed'. Even as recently as 1818, local people had to pay for a watch patrol for the village where several murders, robberies and other crimes had recently been committed by gangs of young people completely out of control. Not at all like today, then.

- For Wormwood Scrubs, technically part of Hammersmith, see page 34.

FURTHER INFORMATION

POSK (The Centre for Polish Arts and Culture) 238 King St, Hammersmith, W6; ☎ 020 8741 0398.
The William Morris Society Kelmscott House, 26 Upper Mall, Hammersmith, W6; ☎ 020 8741 3735.
Irish Centre Blacks Rd, Hammersmith, W6; ☎ 020 8563 8232.
Hammersmith Tourist Information opposite St Paul's Church near District Line Tube; ☎ 020 8748 3079.

23

Hampstead

HORRID HISTORY OF HIGHWAYMEN AND HIPPIES

Hampstead, still a charmingly villagey place on the northern heights of London, with long views of the Thames basin in which London sits, and with a long-established source of pure water which attracted the gentry from London for the good of their health, was once an isolated hamlet and haunt of highwaymen such as Dick Turpin.

He famously hung out at the **Spaniards** pub in the 1730s, and was hanged out himself eventually. You can see that where Spaniards Road on the way to Highgate narrowed for the toll gate would be a good spot to hold people up, and the pub long displayed a pistol and bullet of his.

One place Turpin didn't see much of was the village lock-up in **Squire's Mount**, near Well Road. Other notorious local highwaymen included the ladies' heart-throb Duval (see page 99) and Francis Jackson, who was captured after a furious gun-battle on the Heath between his gang and a posse of mounted locals. Five died in the shoot-out, and Jackson was gibbeted in 1674 – that is, strung up in chains between two large trees near **Jack Straw's Castle**, another famous Hampstead pub at the top of Heath Street. It was supposed to deter future highwaymen, but of course it just encouraged them to be more careful.

Today Hampstead is stuffed with literary and intellectual landmarks, including the museumified (that's got the spellchecker to wake up at last) homes of **Keats** (Wentworth Place) and **Freud** (Maresfield Gardens). Less well known but equally fascinating are **Goldfinger's** house at 2 Willow Road and the **Jewish Museum** in East End Road, Finchley.

Although Hampstead was legalised, as it were, by a charter from King Edgar in around 970, Londoners hadn't heard of the tiny hamlet until the Great Plague of 1665, when they fled northwards, and the Great Fire of the following year, which ended the plague but sent carpenters back to the northern heights to hack down the forests for rebuilding timber.

The area's fortunes were further boosted by the 18th-century spa boom, when fashionable London flocked to drink the mineral water that bubbled out of the chalybeate springs here. Hence Flask Walk, Well Road, etc, and the two, rather good, **Flask** pubs (well, you needed a decent drink after quaffing that weird-tasting stuff) at Hampstead and nearby Highgate. The fad for taking the waters drew in the gentry and the riff-raff alike, as we shall discover. The spa craze, of course, created or rebuilt whole towns in the splendid Georgian style – places such as Tunbridge Wells, Cheltenham Spa, Leamington Spa, and of course Bath – but many swore the Hampstead water was the best.

Some of the mineral-rich waters were useless, and others of limited health-giving properties, but at least they didn't kill you, as London water often did. In those days it was delivered around the city by an underground pipe network of hopelessly leaky bored-out elm tree trunks with tapered ends shoved into each other, with supplies taken off in lead pipes at branch holes – hence 'trunk mains' and 'branch pipes', terms still used today. Much of London's water was pumped straight from the terribly polluted Thames.

Incidentally, the strangely-named **Vale of Health** near Jack Straw's Castle is nothing to do with the spa craze. It was an evil-smelling disease-ridden swamp at the time called Hatches Bottom where – surprise, surprise – only the poor lived. It was cleaned up and rebranded at the end of the 18th century.

RADICALS AND ROCK GIANTS Between the two world wars of the 20th century, Hampstead became a magnet for brilliant musicians, architects and artists, all of the leading-edge radical sort: great sculptors and artists Henry Moore, Barbara Hepworth and her husband Ben Nicolson; musicians such as Kathleen Ferrier, American Paul Robeson, William Walton and Sir Thomas Beecham (a great eccentric conductor, see page 191); writers such as H G Wells and – in different periods – Keats, Galsworthy, the comedian Peter Cook, and the du Mauriers.

After World War II Hampstead became a haven for arty radicals who wanted to be Left-wing but not too near the working classes. A funny mixture of bluestockings and bohemians, radicals who sent their children to free-thinking, few rules, no uniform, co-educational schools such as Dartington, Summerhill, Bedales, or indeed Hampstead's own King Alfred's, founded in 1898 by liberal intellectuals who wanted few rules, no religious education, no timetable, and no putting people in sets according to ability. Radical stuff at the time, but by the 1970s just about adopted as national policy. Applied to the masses, it had pretty patchy results.

Rock history fans will know of Hampstead in connection with the **Decca Recording Studios**, although these were in West Hampstead. The first company to issue LPs (long-playing gramophone records) in Britain, Decca brought us artists such as the Rolling Stones, the Small Faces, Billy Fury, Tommy Steele and Tom Jones, but famously turned down The Beatles. The 'Fab Four' were soon recording instead nearby at the **Abbey Road** studios of EMI, which have thrived since 1931. Other Abbey Road artists have included Duran Duran, Pink Floyd and Cliff Richard. Music fans every day visit the famous zebra crossing The Beatles walked across on the front cover of their 'Abbey Road' LP, and write their names on the nearby wall.

Another Hampstead musical connection is that Ian Dury of the Blockheads – 'Hit me with your rhythm stick' – died at his home here in 2000.

In the sixties, hippie culture took a strong hold for a while – there were some characters working for the local paper, the *Hampstead and Highgate Express*, who gave a new meaning to its nickname, the *Ham & High*. Wearing sandals, kaftans and dresses of some sort, incense and drug befuddled chaps would stroll in and out of its offices, putting in Hampsteady articles of great intellectual import. I remember one eccentric middle-aged newspaper executive who moved from the *Ham & High* to a tweedy country newspaper. On seeing a respectable senior besuited court reporter had bought a new car, he slapped him on the back and said: 'Wow! Funky buggy, man!'

Today, the liberal intellectuals of old Hampstead have in many cases matured into a self-appointed group called the 'great and the good' (usually neither, frankly) who sometimes appoint each other to government quangoes to meddle in things they know nothing about, often with disastrous results. Meanwhile the politicians who were the student radicals of that era wear suits and talk about being tough on drugs, only to be reminded of their kaftan-wearing, flat-squatting, joint-smoking Hampstead hippie days by members of the Press with long memories.

Having taken the mickey out of people who richly deserve it, I admit the cannabis clouds have long cleared and that Hampstead retains its previous great charm intact. It has a country-town feel with rows of unspoilt houses dating from the 18th and 19th centuries, a human scale of architecture in a pleasing jumble, and of course it has those terrific south views – standing on Parliament Hill, we are higher than the dome of St Paul's – which remind us that, incredibly, we are only four miles from the centre of Europe's busiest city.

A HAMPSTEAD WALK

Start and finish ❸ *Hampstead (Northern Line), with optional short-cut for those tired by visiting the area's many pubs. Distance 2^1/$_2$ miles; time taken: about 3 hours with browsing. Hilly. Cosmic views.*

Turn right out of Hampstead Tube station (I hope you didn't climb the stairs, it's London's deepest Tube with more than 300 steps; don't worry if you missed the lovely art deco tiled ticket booths, you can see them on the way back). Admire the intricate brickwork and silly Clochemerle-type grandiose clock tower of the former fire station opposite. Going up Heath Street, clock the bijou shops and restaurants, but there's no need to stay too long: there are heaps more to come. Soon there are interesting 18th- and 19th-century houses all around. Poke your head into Back Lane on the right for some. But cross over on the zebra crossing and climb the Holly Bush Steps to the left. Have a poke into the curious **Golden Yard**, a tranquil and pretty haven just a few feet from busy Heath Street. It's named after the Goulding family who lived here when the population of Hampstead numbered around 200. The mass wisteria is superb in late May. At the top of the steps you might want to dodge left around the bend for about 50yds to get the first cosmic view over London and then come back, but we're in fact going right on this lane called Holly Mount which brings us to the **Holly Bush** pub, first of many excellent watering holes.

Whether you go in or not depends on your profession, for on the door it says clearly: 'By popular demand, traffic wardens in uniform or otherwise will not be served in this pub.' Were I a traffic warden (ie: one of London's parking ticket people), that would make me determined to go in plain clothes. In fact to have a meeting of undercover wardens there.

Turn right at the end of this picturesque street and we come on to one of Hampstead's many mini-village greens; turn right again up Holly Bush Hill. The massive pile of masonry opposite was a consumption hospital but is now posh flats, so don't take your massive piles there (unless it's of cash). The views from this ridge must be absolutely splendid. They thought consumptives – those with tuberculosis – needed fresh air (remember pictures of rows of children's beds outdoors?) and they'd certainly have got it here. Not that it did much good. We now turn right up Holly Bush Hill. Before you do, if you're wondering whom the plaque on the house down the long drive opposite commemorates, being so far away, it's Joanna Baillie, Scots poet/dramatist, chum of Keats, Wordsworth, etc.

MAD NAVAL OFFICERS PLUS TRILBYS AND SVENGALIS Crossing the green, one can get a good view of **Romney's House** opposite the hospital – long after being home of George Romney, late 18th-century society portraitist, it belonged to Clough Williams-Ellis, the great eccentric architect who created the fantasy village of

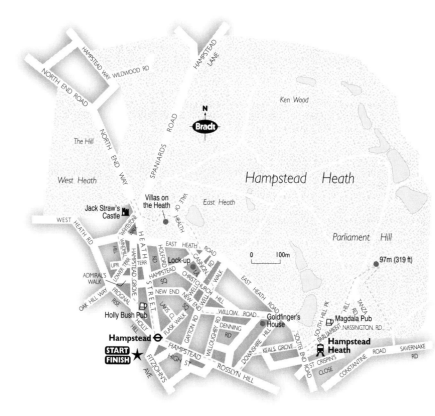

Portmeirion in Wales which (as I say in my book, *Eccentric Britain*) stands out amidst the grim slate and chapel culture like an orange in a slag heap. The Holly Bush pub, by the way, was once the stables for Romney's House.

Going up Holly Bush Hill there's a National Trust house, **Fenton House**, on the left, an unspoilt 17th-century rich merchant's house stuffed with antiques; fine if you are enthusiastic about early porcelain and old keyboard instruments. The gardens are superb and varied but hidden behind that high wall. (Don't people in Hampstead like hiding themselves away? You can see the lovely house and garden on the right better if you stand on those bollardy things.)

Another fabulous house on the right was lived in from 1874 to 1895 by George du Maurier, painter and novelist of that dynasty, who introduced 'svengali' and 'trilby' into the language by the novel of the latter name.

At the rather rural crossroads ahead, go left on Admiral's Walk for a moment to the bend and find **Admiral's House,** which has a roof resembling the deck of a ship, built by a retired sailor who never quite lost his sea-legs. He wasn't an admiral but a mere lieutenant, but what a spot for a look-out with a decent telescope! It was said to be the model for the mad naval officer's house in *My Fair Lady*. I don't know if he ever fired cannon from the deck while his family clung onto precious ornaments downstairs as the house rocked, but I hope so. Naval officers are like that. There was one who lived in a road called The Hatches in Farnham, Surrey. His house was called Batten Down, of course.

The brilliantly eccentric architect Sir George Gilbert Scott who created the mad St Pancras station hotel and the excessive Albert Memorial also lived here.

Back to Hampstead Grove, turn left (on our original direction) and we walk past the ornate gates of the reservoir (1865); if you see a weird thing looking like a **mini-observatory** at the far end, that's because it is. House prices aren't the only astronomical thing round here, North London's highest point is a refreshing 434ft above sea level.

DID DICKENS MEET MARX? SEVERED HEADS AND STRAW MEN Moving on, we pass Whitestone Pond (named after an adjacent milestone) and **Jack Straw's Castle**, where gibbeted highwaymen's bodies would rot in chains. This is a policy the present politician Jack Straw failed to adopt in his 'tough on crime, tough on the causes of crime' (dream on!) period as Home Secretary, but of course the pub's not named after him but after the Jack Straw who led a massive peasants' revolt in 1381, but who ended up, surprise, surprise, with his severed head thrust on a spike on London Bridge. Charles Dickens liked the pub too (it's hard to find one he didn't like, the rascal) and once wrote to a friend:

> You don't feel disposed, do you, to muffle yourself and start off with me for a brisk walk over Hampstead Heath. I know a good 'ouse where we can have a red-hot chop for dinner.

He certainly liked his suppers, and as for red hot, he could have been sitting at the next table to Karl Marx, who, as I remark in the Soho section, liked nothing more than a stroll to this pub. It's a funny-looking place, like a Mississippi stern-wheeler run aground. It was badly bombed in World War II; well, quite well bombed, but you know what I mean.

Beyond here up North End Way is a sign saying Golders Green 3 miles ('to you, two-and-a-half' as the old joke goes – East End rag-trade families who had made good went to live there). The old **Bull & Bush** pub is on the way (for its missing Underground station, see page 95). To the right, Spaniards Road leads to the eponymous **Spaniards Inn**, to the millionaires' row of The Bishops Avenue and to Highgate. But cross the road opposite the Jack Straw by the black signpost and delve down the footpath into the **Vale of Health**, part of the Heath. Plunge down across the open hillside to the Narnian lamppost on the path at the bottom and go left a tad past **Fleet House,** which name reminds us this is the source of that stream that is one of the lost rivers of London (see page 96) that eventually exits under Blackfriars Bridge.

Venture down the path between the houses to take a peek at this delightful sheltered quarter of Hampstead and turn right on another path to come out on another little triangle. The pretty terrace to our left as we come out here are Villas-on-the-Heath and, surprisingly, were home – for a while – to Bengal's greatest poet, Rabindanath Tagore. Go on ahead and keep right by the post box, on the path next to the houses, forking next left at Holly Cottage away from the houses up the asphalted path. Climb the hill to reach East Heath Road at the top. Go left a little and pick up Squires Mount on the far side with its pretty row of cottages, and soon the inviting courtyard on the left. Here, too, is a plaque on **Cannon Hall**, home to actor manager Sir Gerald du Maurier (1873–1934), son of George and father of Daphne, author, as in *Rebecca*. She is the best-known du Maurier today, although not well-enough known to prevent a national newspaper headlining a piece recently 'Du Maurier's Devon' (very alliterative, but it was Cornwall she lived in. Oddly, no-one at all noticed).

WELL, WELL, THE HAMPSTEAD POOR We plunge straight on down the hill (now Cannon Lane) to see the 1730 village lock-up, built into the vast wall of Cannon Hall, where village justice was once dispensed. The Cannon in names hereabouts refer to cannon bollards, a convenient way of disposing of worn-out or obsolete

One of Hampstead's unsung eccentrics is, or rather was, Geoffrey Nathaniel Pyke, a slightly mad inventor whose ideas were so off-beam – crackpot even – they were sometimes rather brilliant.

Born in 1894, he came to the notice of the authorities in World War I when he smuggled himself into Germany to try to be a correspondent reporting from hostile territory for the *Daily Chronicle*. He was nearly shot as a spy, but luckily the Germans saw he was just a daft young man with an over-active imagination. He escaped and his initially puzzled newspaper made him a hero.

But it was in World War II that his at times crazed creations, always with an underlying brilliance, came to the fore. The start of the War caught him trying to run an opinion poll about the threatened conflict with Germany, which he intended to present to Hitler. As a Jew, it was fortunate, to put it mildly, that he got back to Britain before the balloon went up.

He had been inventing things between the Wars – such as a device for saving coal on railway engines by fitting them with lots of cycle pedals – so he was recruited for top secret work. He was asked to draft stratagems for depriving the Germans of the crucial Romanian oil fields. Problem – how to get the commandos in to blow the things up without the guards stopping them. His ideas included:

- Send in dogs disguised as wolves so the guards would run away.
- Start a few fires and then send in teams of agents dressed as Romanian firemen on fake fire engines. The water they pumped on the blaze would have some delayed incendiary bomblets mixed in with it, so things would get worse not better.
- Send in amazingly beautiful whores to distract the guards.
- Send in dogs with brandy flasks around their necks so the guards would be paralysed with drink.

I don't know if the drunken, sex-mesmerised, wolf-chased and half-burned guards would have hated Pyke, thanked him or just shot him. Other ideas of his included marking sabotage equipment in Norway 'Latrines for Officers, Colonels Only' on the basis that rule-bound Germans could never disobey an order and touch the things. Another creative gem was pumping soldiers ashore for invasions inside a pipe. The fluid around the capsules of soldiers in the pipelines could be useful stuff like petrol, he argued.

guns after the Napoleonic wars. (Or so they say. Would you have dragged one all the way to Hampstead from Waterloo to block a road or used a nearby tree stump?)

At the bottom of the road we cross over Well Road into the plunging footpath opposite, Well Passage (not well signed), down to Well Walk which includes the Wells Tavern. (*That's enough wells, Ed.*) As you might have guessed by all this we are nearing the source – literally – of Hampstead's spa craze. Well Walk was where the fashionable flocked to promenade, taste the waters at the pumphouse (where the red-brick house facing you diagonally opposite to the left now stands) and to be made well, well. There's a fountain dedicated to 'Hampstead's poor' at the bottom of the path where we came out and dated 1698, which shows how early Hampstead was in the spa craze. Of course, there are few Hampstead poor to use it today and they'd rather have a designer latte next to them while they beg next to the Tube.

This road is stuffed with connections with the greats of the past – John Constable, whose plaque is opposite, is so famous I don't have to give his profession. (*Was he the first policeman? Ed.*) Then there are writers Keats, D H Lawrence, John Masefield and J B Priestley for starters. We turn right (from the bottom of the path) and go past the Wells Tavern, not a corker. Going on down

Pyke wasn't utterly barking, however. One of his inventions – frozen ice aircraft carriers half-a-mile long and ice-clad warships – actually made some kind of sense. Project Habbakuk was kept secret for many years after the war.

He'd invented Pykrete, a mixture of ice and wood pulp. It was amazingly strong and resistant to melting. He got as far as getting top British commander Lord Mountbatten to show Pykrete to generals at the Allied conference in Quebec during World War II. Mountbatten got a general to swing an axe at a block of ordinary ice and it shattered instantly. Then he took a swing at a similar-sized block of Pykrete and nearly broke his arms as the axe just bounced off. Mountbatten then fired his pistol at the Pykrete and nearly killed another general with the ricochet. The shot hadn't harmed the Pykrete at all. Mountbatten even rushed into Churchill's bathroom, dropped a lump of the stuff into his hot bath and said: 'Look, it doesn't melt' which it didn't.

Churchill was sufficiently taken with the idea to order a 1,000-ton ice aircraft carrier to be built secretly on Patricia Lake, Alberta, Canada, which, being thousands of miles from the sea, would be the last place the enemy would look for such a ship. As predicted by Pyke, the thing didn't melt in the warm summer of 1943 but was kept running, although at considerable cost. So would the unsinkable giant aircraft carriers – floating airfields, nearly – have worked? Had Pyke beaten Titanic's iceberg at its own game? The engineers scaled up the energy requirements for the full-sized thing and discovered the quantities of fuel needed to power the thing would have been astronomical. The D-Day fleets had already been built, so it was too late by then. The cooling system was turned off and the carrier sank to the bottom of the lake where its remains can still be seen by divers.

Of course, being Pyke, he dressed up a great idea with all sorts of insane notions. His huge cork-covered ice ships were to sail into ports and spray everything with supercooled water so the enemy's defences would be frozen solid. Railway tunnels would be blocked with instant ice. Enemy ships would be locked in the stuff. It was science fiction comic stuff, and it didn't help that with his unkempt hair and gabbling speech, Pyke seemed a mad inventor. Nothing more was done about Pykrete ships before the end of the War. Pyke returned to his messy Hampstead flat, dejected; he killed himself in 1948.

here I notice council flats on the right but they had an election placard for Glenda Jackson the well-sculpted, and sometimes naked, actress turned Hampstead MP and government minister for something not too hard.

Here's her name up in lurid red and yellow in the very road where lived Lawrence, author of *Women in Love*, the film of which made her famous – or did she make him famous? Another extraordinary woman lived on the left here: Marie Stopes. She was an early 20th-century feminist, sex educator and birth-control pioneer, setting up clinics for women to receive this kind of advice when the health professionals of the day wouldn't have dreamed of it. She was driven to become great in this way because her own marriage was miserable. I have a theory that many great achievers, such as the fell walker Wainwright, did what they did only because they couldn't stand being at home. Marital bliss has a lot to answer for in preventing greatness. I could have been Bill Bryson by now…

MEET GOLDFINGER, DEAD POETS AND A FIENDISH INSTRUMENT At the – yet another – pleasant triangle we plunge left down Willow Road. Going on down we discover the mildly eccentric fronts to Nos 12, 13 and 14. The 1960s-looking terrace at No 2 is the former home of Goldfinger. No, before you go *Dang-da-da-*

23

Erno Goldfinger, born in Budapest in 1902, who created the ground-breaking houses at 2 Willow Road, Hampstead, grew up in a very different environment to this – the forests of Transylvania. Handsome and charismatic, he studied in Paris and avoided getting in the financial soup by marrying the strikingly beautiful Ursula Blackwell, of the Crosse & Blackwell family. His architectural philosophy was uncompromising and never really fitted in with current fashion. He built this apparently 1960s house in the 1930s when others were building houses covered in white stucco (which he derided as 'kasbah architecture'). His basic belief was that you should show the structure of a building, not hide it. If a house was steel, concrete or brick, let that be seen, don't pretend it's something else, he argued. He was brilliant on details – such as the letter box on 2 Willow Road – and sometimes transparently bad – the bog next to the front door is completely silhouetted at night to the amusement of passers-by. He built tower blocks in the East End and took Ursula and the children to live at the top of one of them, unlike the most hypocritical of his profession who wouldn't dream of living in one of their own ghastly blocks. He built huge government blocks such as those at Elephant & Castle which are perhaps hard for a modern mind to see the merit in. When tower blocks were being derided and demolished in the 1970s, he said the only mistake architects made was not to build them high enough. He certainly showed this with his brilliant and take-no-prisoners **Trellick House** in North Kensington (see page 131).

The tour of his house takes the form of a 15-minute film show about Goldfinger's life in the former garage and then a 40-minute tour, conducted by an expert guide.

dang da dang, Dang-da-da-dang da dang, Doo dah, dang dang dang as in the James Bond theme, it's Goldfinger, as in great architect, not as in Bond villain (see above).

It is a measure of his greatness that this little terrace – now museumified by the National Trust and place of pilgrimage for architecture students worldwide – was actually built in 1939, not 1969. It was way ahead of its time, but like any truly pioneering effort that changes the way we live – such as Letchworth Garden City in Hertfordshire – it becomes boringly normal to those who don't appreciate its significance.

We go on down to join South End Road (note Keats Grove on the right for later) and left into South Hill Park beside Hampstead Heath station, then up Parliament Hill past the **Magdala**, the pub outside which the wronged Ruth Ellis shot her Ruth-less cheating lover and thus became the last woman in Britain to be hanged (see page 29). Those completely out of energy could recharge their batteries here with food and drink while companions do the following loop.

Up to the end of **Parliament Hill** and out on to the Heath and to the 319ft-high summit you'll find the most cosmic views in North London and loads of benches to rest your weary butts on. Light a Du Maurier fag, if you wish. Why on earth don't they cut down those trees that partly obscure the view?

Talking about famous fags – of the American sort – there was a bizarre public health initiative here a few years ago which was aimed at the homosexuals who gather hereabouts at night to indulge in whatever; the trees and bushes here were festooned with glow-in-the-dark condoms like Christmas decorations. It caused much ribaldry and outrage, but perhaps the publicity helped save a life or two from AIDS so I'm not going to make any jokes about it. In the day time, anyhow, the gayest thing you'll see here is a kite being flown higher than the top of St Paul's.

Here, we are between the headwaters of the Tyburn and the Fleet rivers, the source of much terrible history (see *Lost rivers of London*, page 96). At the southern corner in front of us we can see, on a very hot day, a tempting open-air pool (see *London lidos*, page 45).

Actually Hampstead Heath has long been a haunt of interesting people. You might have met in recent years Peter O-Lawrence-of-Arabia Toole learning his lines, or former Labour leader Michael Foot shuffling along in his infamous donkey jacket. There have been more recent sightings of couples copulating in the long grass, model plane nuts, bird-watchers, tai-chi practitioners, flashers showing their all to screaming matrons pushing prams, the odd mugger committing daylight shrubbery, and worse.

All this and what did the authorities stamp down on? A Hampstead bagpipe player named David Brooks, who strode the heath in his tartan and skirled and screeched the dire dirges that only that fiendish instrument of torture can mangle properly. The Corporation of London, which for eccentric reasons runs the Heath although it's miles from the City, discovered that the playing of bagpipes, as a genus of musical instrument, without the Corporation's express consent, was forbidden.

It must have given the lawyers a heap of fun. Much though one might want to release the poor wee timorous beastie of a haggis imprisoned in the bag and making all that wailing noise, are bagpipes musical, m'lud? Are they not an instrument of war and in truth banned as such after the 1745 Jacobite Rebellion?

A man was, after all, executed in 1746 for playing this instrument of war Bonnie Prince Charlie's 1745 insurrection. Did not the Highland regiments march into battle in world wars to the sound of this terrifying instrument? Others argued that they are an instrument of war only *during* a war, and of peace at other times.

Mr Brooks was quoted as saying as Hampstead was torn asunder by the row: 'There are worse things that go on there such as aeroplanes, transistor radios, copulation, rape and the occasional murder. Playing the pipes is one of the lesser offences going on.'

The court case was put off when the Corporation suggested a compromise, and when Mr Brooks had gathered a 1,000-signature petition of support. The Corporation suggested a spot on the Heath about a mile away from the houses – about the ideal distance, some may think. Mr Brooks then received a better offer, with an unlikely endorsement from a visiting God-King.

The Dalai Lama was visiting Alexandra Palace, that massive pile of brickwork near Muswell Hill, for a Tibetan charity evening and praised Mr Brooks's musical contribution. The Council in charge of Ally Pally (as Alexandra Palace is known) was impressed and, being a lefty bunch, saw the music as part of an oppressed minority's culture and stepped in to help. Mr Brooks was offered bagpipe playing room in the grounds of Ally Pally.

So if you see a man on a bike heading east with bagpipes on his back, it's sure to be Mr Brooks, the cockney piper of Hampstead, who was quoted as saying: 'I think I'd go potty without my pipes.' No comment.

Retrace your steps to the edge of the Heath but instead of going back down the same road, take the pleasant broad path on the left down along the backs of the houses and enter Nassington Road at the right, which quickly leads back to the

Magdala and the main road. Go right, uphill a little past the shops on South End Road and left on to Keats Grove. Here on the left is **Keats's House and Museum**. Imagine him in that garden writing '*Ode to a Nightingale*' under that tree. In his short life, didn't he create something far more beautiful than all the other Hampstead writers (discuss; one side of the paper only)? And another thing, if Hampstead was so damn healthy for tuberculosis victims, how come local boys Keats and D H Lawrence coughed their consumptive last at so young an age?

There's a bed in Keats's house (actually the house of his friend Charles Brown who saved his poetry that would otherwise have been lost) with a story to tell. Here, coming back from London on the outside (cheap) seat of a stagecoach, Keats went to bed in a bad way. Brown recalled that Keats coughed and found blood on his pillow. Keats's brother Tom had just died of tuberculosis, so he knew what it meant.

> After regarding it steadfastly, he looked up in my face with a calmness of countenance I can never forget and said: 'I know the colour of that blood – it is arterial blood – I cannot be deceived in that colour – that drop of blood – it is my death warrant.'

Not long after, Lethe-wards he had sunk.

We come out on Downshire Hill, which has an unreasonably unspoilt bunch of Regency houses plus the church of **St John**, very much of its era (1825), all classical and box pews, and not a hint of Gothic revival in sight.

On the left as we go uphill, by the way, is No 9a, a much more radically modern house, made apparently entirely of glass. Carry on up to the main road at the top, Rosslyn Hill, and turn right back towards the Tube, only about a half-mile up this hill. En route, a cornucopia of trendy shops and eating places awaits. Up here by No 6 in Hampstead High Street, as the road here becomes, is a half-mile stone (half a mile from the Whitestone Pond one) and many historic shops, pubs, interesting old yards to the right and left. Don't go straight down the Tube but take a peek down the fascinating side roads and passages such as **Flask Walk** on the right, and, after all the ups and downs, enjoy a well-earned pint or three in the Flask pub.

DEAD INTERESTING HAMPSTEAD: A SHORTER STROLL

Very short walk (about 30 minutes), alternative or additional to the main walk.

If you just want to see 18th-century Hampstead at its unspoiled best, and see the homes and graves of loads of dead celebs, go the other way up Heath Street (left) from the Tube, turning right into Church Row. Here amid quite lovely architecture (did Goldfinger look at any of this?) you can find the homes of George du Maurier (again), Lord Alfred Douglas (Oscar Wilde's fickle lover), writer H G Wells and comic Peter Cook.

Lord Alfred Douglas, aka Bosie, was the one who ruined Oscar Wilde because of their then most illegal gay relationship, Wilde being imprisoned and then fleeing to Paris to die beyond his means. Douglas wrote of Wilde:

> I am passionately fond of him and he of me. There is nothing I would not do for him and if he dies before I do I shall not care to live any longer.

Well, despite these fine words he lived on half a century longer, actually dying in 1945 aged 74; he had an almost conventional married life here in Hampstead, besides bunging down some reasonable lines of verse himself. He ended up a raving Catholic and out-and-out elitist snob. Ironically he too went to jail, for libelling Winston Churchill in 1923. In that case it was a ballad of Wormwood Scrubs, not of Reading Gaol, the prison Wilde had endured half a century before.

H G Wells, former Sussex school teacher and creator of the *War of the Worlds* and *The Time Machine* amidst other fabulous science fiction works, lived here. The writer and strident feminist Rebecca West – oddly that was not her real name but that of a liberated but doomed character she had played in an Ibsen drama and then assumed for herself – was so angry with his writing that she stormed off to see him about it. She ended up having a ten-year affair and a son with him. The perils of literary criticism.

Peter Cook, one-time hilarious partner of Dudley Moore ('Huge great lobsters up Jayne Mansfield's bum' will bring back a few memories), and stalwart of satirical *Private Eye* magazine, is another now-dead resident. The last time I saw Cook was at a Hampshire health farm pushing a bit of lettuce round his plate and looking like he could do with escaping over the wire to the local pub or Little Chef (I've seen them in there). It didn't do any good and he died not long afterwards. And no, I wasn't drying out, just visiting.

At the end of Church Row is **St John's Church**. There's an interesting congregation here in its graveyard and extension: *Hay Wain* painter, **John Constable**, was born in 1776, the year that time ran out for another resident; brilliant clockmaker **John Harrison**, the man who solved the latitude problem. He was a great help to Cook (explorer James, not comedian Peter), who took Harrison's clock around the world, creating whole countries just so we could have someone to play at cricket and rugby; the writer Joanna Baillie (see above); late-Victorian actor Sir Henry Beerbohm Tree; and Michael Llewelyn Davies, one of the lost boys of J M Barrie's *Peter Pan* (see page 100). Plus a Du Maurier or two.

Turn right along Holly Place, right in **Mount Vernon** (where writer Robert Louis Stevenson lived) and right down Holly Hill back to the Tube.

FURTHER INFORMATION

Fenton House (NT) Hampstead Grove, NW3; ✆ 020 7435 3471; www.nationaltrust.org.uk/thameschilterns.
Goldfinger's House (NT) 2 Willow Rd, Hampstead, NW3; ✆ 020 7435 6166; www.nationaltrust.org.uk/thameschilterns. ⊖ Hampstead.
Keats's Museum Wentworth Place, Keats Grove, NW3; ✆ 020 7435 2062. ⊖ Hampstead (Northern Line).
Freud Museum 20 Maresfield Gardens, NW3; ✆ 020 7435 2002. ⊖ Finchley Road.
Jewish Museum 80 East End Rd, Finchley, N3; ✆ 020 8349 1143. ⊖ Finchley Central. Also in Camden at 129–131 Albert St, NW1; ✆ 020 7284 1997; www.jewmusm.ort.org. ⊖ Camden Town.

23

24

Kensington

STRANGE SECRETS BEHIND ALL THE BOLLARDS

It may be an odd thing to say in a guidebook, but here goes. Kensington High Street is a right bore. It's full of international shopping saddos who could be at the same tedious chain stores and burger bars in their home towns, rich Arabs with the women's faces masked over like Ned Kelly on a bad hair day, snobs in their 'Ringe Ravers' trying to be above the throng, and show-offs jogging or rollerblading with great difficulty through the crowds rather than making use of the acres of great parkland at both ends of the street. Harmless, but boring. Forget it.

But within yards of this street, if you plunge through the bollards and away from the crowd, are untold treasures and unique gems, wonderful pubs, eccentric buildings, quiet mews, strange towers, palatial mansions, secret gardens and a seriously cool Arab hall with a tinkling fountain. No crowds, all fascinating, all free, utterly unforgettable. It's there waiting for the in-the-know visitor to discover…

KENSINGTON WALK

Start and finish ❷ *High Street Kensington. Distance 2¹/₂ miles; time taken at least 2 hours. With Campden Hill optional extension.*

DARK SATANIC MILLS AND THE MOUTH OF HELL Leave High Street Kensington Tube station and turn right, past a few shops on crowded pavements and turn right down Derry Street. On the left as we walk down this short street is the former Barkers department store, a fine art deco pile which we can see the front of later, and whose upstairs accommodates the *Daily Mail, Mail on Sunday* and *Evening Standard*, part of the Fleet Street diaspora. On the right is the former Derry & Toms department store which, besides having wonderful ornamentation at the top (we will see this more clearly later from the other side of the road), also has an almost incredible Spanish-style **roof garden** whose trees you can see poking over the parapet. For a free visit to these gardens of the sky, sign in at 99 Kensington High Street, entrance in Derry Street.

We go through the bollards at the end of the road into **Kensington Square**, illustrating again how the atmosphere of London can utterly change in a few yards. Gone is the hurly-burly of the shopping crowds and bustling traffic: all is peace,

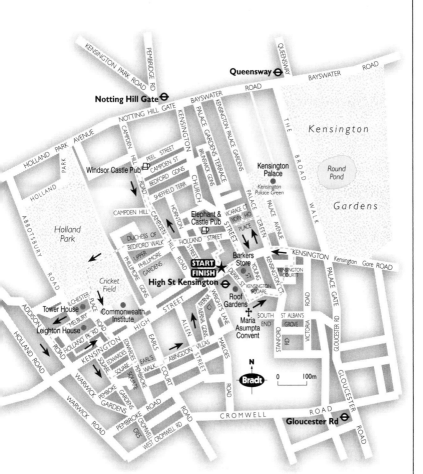

historic charm and leafy gardens. This is in fact one of the oldest squares in London, with some of the buildings dating right back to the 1660 Restoration of the monarchy, and the remainder mostly from the 18th century. You're still not allowed into the gardens, which is either infuriating or intriguing, depending on your mood. This square was laid out in open countryside, south of the country road linking Kensington Palace, as it now is, to the village of Hammersmith where one could take a ferryboat across the Thames. There were no buildings at all to the south, east or west, except farms.

On the right as we enter the square is an old brown plaque – from before the oval, blue ones – to Mrs Patrick Campbell, the great actress and Bernard Shaw's star performer. Indeed, houses throughout the square bear one or more plaques to the great characters who have lived here. By the way, the *Country Life*-reading upper crust of British society (who have homes here as well as country estates) still clings to the practice of naming married women after their husbands – Mrs John Smith, for example. A wife, therefore, has no identity separate from her husband. If you write Mrs Sarah Smith, the toffs assume she's been divorced or widowed. Perhaps they should borrow those Ned Kelly masks which some Arab women wear to cover themselves up completely (a good thing in some cases, you may wickedly think).

Talking about covered-up women, walking ahead to the right-hand corner of the square we see a convent, in full working order despite Henry VIII's best efforts to stamp the things out, and not (as local author William Makepeace Thackeray invented at this spot) a pub. The **Maria Assumpta Convent** is more massive than its frontage here suggests, with gardens going back a long way and including a grotto with a statue of the Virgin Mary. Unfortunately the gardens are just above a cutting holding the world's noisiest underground railway junction, as the trains on the Circle and District lines clatter and bong like insanely demonic *News at Ten* music as they cross each other's tracks and make desperately for their respective tunnel mouths. It's not exactly the mouth of Hell, as Tennyson put it on another occasion, in the days when steam engines belched smoke into pea-soup fogs, it might have seemed it. You can visit the relative paradise of the convent gardens on London Garden Squares Day (when you may also visit the remarkably uninteresting interior of Kensington Square outside the convent, with people playing lutes or weird Indonesian instruments or similar).

Going left along the far side of the square, past the first of many diplomatic buildings on the right, and the home of **John Stuart Mill**, the heavyweight philosopher-economist (1806–73) who was one of the 'dark satanic Mills', I was going to jest, but whom should we find next door – taraa, taraa! – the composer who put those very words to music. Here at No 17 lived **Sir Charles Parry**, whose setting of William Blake's *Jerusalem* to music has produced England's splendid non-royalist alternative national anthem.

I recall a story about one of John Stuart Mill's servants here accepting a manuscript from Carlyle, the somewhat boring Chelsea historian/philosopher, and assuming it to be a supply of fire-lighting paper, gradually burned the lot. I hope she was rewarded with a tip and a day off; pity she didn't burn more of his tedious stuff.

THACKERAY PLAQUERY Reaching the far corner of the square and glancing left up Young Street, which runs back to the High Street up the other side of Barkers, we can see the other pub Thackeray mentions, the Greyhound. Not the one he knew, as that was blown to pieces, not by Irish terrorists but by equally deadly English gas fitters. The Greyhound, by the way – which you needn't visit as there are better pubs later in the walk – is known universally to the hacks of the three newspapers in the Barkers building as the 'Rotty' (short for Rottweiler). Equally, when the same newspapers were in Fleet Street the staff all knew where the Mucky Duck was, but if you were to ask to meet them in the White Swan (its proper name) they wouldn't have had a clue.

We're going straight ahead into **Thackeray Street**, a quiet street justly celebrated for having no connection with Thackeray, and about the only place round here where he didn't live or work. If you want to see real Thackeray plaquery, pop up Young Street to see his yellowbrick house on the left just before Barkers. (There's a story about Thackeray and this house. Some time after he'd left it, he was passing here with his American publisher friend J T Fields. Thackeray remarked to Fields: 'Down on your knees, you rogue, for here *Vanity Fair* was penned, and I will go down with you, for I have a high opinion of that little production myself.')

Thackeray Street harbours poky little odd shops of the kind that the High Street once accommodated before chain stores, with their international dullness, took over. Here is an excellent little café, where I am astonished to be addressed in French by the staff. I ask for things in my poor schoolboy French, but it serves to remind one how polite the French are in their small shops and how rude the majority of the British are. A few doors further on a man is standing in his shop door and shouts across, '*Buon giorno*' at an old widow in black and she replies something about '*bella*' (the weather being good).

The road has a few arty shops including one at the end of the road selling, apparently, obelisks. Let me see, do the shopping list: coffee, soap powder, bog paper, obelisk. Eccentrically useless things, really, although the Obelisk Society, based in this area but not this shop, would not agree; they have an obelisk newsletter, sell obelisk mugs, meet at obscure obsolete obelisks to be obsequious. *(That's enough obfuscation, Ed.)* Bizarre.

Going left at the end of the street, we encounter in **Kensington Court** the Black Forest gateau school of architecture – layered buildings with what looks like icing every few floors, an 1880 building speculation by Albert Grant MP. You can see why Hitler's bombers had such a hard job denting Kensington – they're massive and look difficult to demolish.

Continue right past the massive mansion blocks, and bear right at the end. Now we are in foreign territory, with the interesting combination of Antigua, Mongolia, Belarus and Azerbaijan diplomatic missions all in a row. I hope they have social evenings together; it's possible they aren't *that* diplomatic. The characters engraved in the brass plate of the Mongol horde (well, there are only a few really) are particularly elegant but you have to get close to see them. At the Kensington High Street end of the road, on the right at the corner, four massive black dragons hang on the building for no particular reason. Perhaps it makes the Mongolians feel at home. Isn't Heilong Jiang (Black Dragon river) on their border with China?

The building they are attached to is the **Milestone Hotel**, and if you pop round the corner you can see why. An ancient milestone (not *that* ancient, in fact, as it is iron) says Hounslow 8½, London 1½. But surely we are in the heart of London – why does the milestone record it as being far away? Less than 300 years ago, the few houses of Kensington were isolated from London and reached only by crossing muddy wastes infested with highwaymen.

We go not towards London but left, back across Kensington Court's entrance and down to the pedestrian traffic lights. Ahead of us is a pub, the Goat, that has a tale of the most gruesome murder in living memory attached to it – the acid bath killings (see page 25 for more).

But we cross over by the traffic lights and, going left on the far side, pause by the entrance to **Kensington Gardens** (spiritual home of Peter Pan, to whom there's a memorial here) next to the phone boxes. Look into the quadrangle of grass between the High Street and Kensington Palace beyond the gilt gates at the far side. This was the scene of the most amazing event in London in the past decade – the mass mourning of Princess Diana. If you want to stop and read the still moving story (see page 288) of those few days in 1997, why not grab a bench or a patch of grass in the gardens?

Carrying on past the entrance to the gardens, there's a gate with a long road down to the palace. If you saw the carriage bearing Diana's coffin come out of here that extraordinary day accompanied by a lonely wail from an onlooker, you'll not have forgotten this place.

It would be hard to get a real lion and a unicorn to hold the royal arms, but these stone ones on the gate posts do a good job – the unicorn, if I remember rightly, holding the motto of the Order of the Garter, the eccentric and ancient high order of chivalry based on a female undergarment. Real gas lights add to the atmosphere at night.

Don't go up this narrow road but carry on past the Royal Garden Hotel, with an excellent view of the art deco towers of **Barkers** store ahead. Turn right at the unmarked cobbled road, where there's a watchman in a green box. This is the discreet entrance to London's most exclusive road, Palace Green or **Kensington Palace Gardens** as it becomes. If you haven't got £50 million or so, don't bother house-hunting round here. In fact don't bother anyway, because the powers that be ensure that only sultans or kings (of other countries) or ambassadors get a toehold in this lovely road.

As you pass the gate, note the robo-bollards that protect the road from unauthorised vehicles, rising and falling as required to keep out suicide bombers. The first building on the left is the Israeli embassy and this serves as a reminder of how necessary such precautions are. It was blown up in 1994 and I remember, being in the Barkers building at the time, that the place shook as if hit with a massive demolition ball.

It would be better not to dwell on the security around this embassy today, but it is clearly formidable. The gentleman with a bulge in his pocket isn't necessarily pleased to see you, as Mae West pointed out. Don't make a sudden lunge for the Mars bar inside your jacket. It's a strange thought but by walking the length of this road, you will be on the security video footage of a dozen countries.

On the right, **Kensington Palace** comes into view through the railings. If you don't see bicycles chained to these railings, it is because this practice is thought

unseemly for a royal palace. Militant gay activist Peter Tatchell, who likes to be a pain in the thingy to the establishment, was, for once, not seeking confrontation when he chained his bike up here in 2001. However, when he returned he found it even more padlocked. He had to seek out the palace staff, and I'm told this surreal conversation ensued:

'Her Majesty does not want bicycles chained up to her palaces.'
'There's no notice saying that.'
'Her Majesty does not want notices on her palaces' railings.'

At the far end of this road, with its gorgeous plane trees and huge mansions, is Notting Hill Gate and Bayswater, but we go left opposite the solar-powered parking meter into the passageway with the two wooden bollards.

On the right you encounter a strange noticeboard explaining the arcane workings of the powers-that-be who own the freehold of much of this land: the Crown Estate. When the British moan about the cost of the monarchy, they should come and look at this first. It explains how the billions that the Crown lands earn each year are surrendered to the Government in return for the Civil List expenses for the royal family, a tiny fraction of the estate incomes. A good bargain, most people would agree.

Down at the end of this path we reach **Kensington Church Street** and a good view of **St Mary Abbot's** spire, said to be the tallest on a London parish church.

We cross over by the lights and turn left down the far side, noting the name of Holland Street. The numerous references to Holland around here are connections not with the country but with the place in Norfolk, where the family based at Holland House stately home have their roots. Going down to the corner of Kensington High Street, don't miss an intriguing detail on the opposite corner – the sign of a long disappeared pub, the Civet Cat.

Turning right on to the High Street we can get a good view of the superb 1930s detail on the frieze on the front of **Barkers** across the road, showing the latest steam engines, aeroplanes and similar symbols of modernity, now charmingly dated. Plus the whole building looks like a 1930s radio set. You half expect these vertical windows to light up with station names such as Hilversum and Daventry.

Walking a bit further down, one can see the equally marvellous but totally different detail on the old **Derry & Toms** building, the other side of Derry Street, showing similar scenes of industry plus, high up, signs of the zodiac. From here you can also see a glimpse of the astounding roof gardens mentioned when we passed this on the other side earlier.

We go right up **Kensington Church Walk** and, passing some peaceful gardens, do a right and then a left by the church's west front. As you turn left on the path the building on our right is a school – don't miss the charming figures of a blue-coated boy and girl which appear further along the frontage and were typical of a London school of 200 years ago.

We go on up a Dickensian lane past some odd shops and go left at the end. We are now on Holland Street again. Soon we pass the low-key cottages of Gordon Place – we could be 100 miles from the High Street bustle, couldn't we? On the right the excellent **Elephant and Castle** pub. Unspoiled, good ales, good food, no carpet or jukebox, this presses all the right buttons – for me, at any rate. If only they would chuck out that stupid one-armed bandit that insults the clientele's intelligence (that's because I lost £5 on it!).

Plus, if you like this kind of thing, on the walls in the snug at the far left there's a great collection of *Evening Standard* front pages of the past, including of course Diana's funeral. More fun is the 'exclusive' engraving of the Queen's Coronation dress, and a particularly professional piece of journalism about the first dog in orbit. Clearly the hacks had no idea what the spacecraft looked like – the drawing was hopeless – and only about three facts to go on, but they filed a whole hysterically excited page nonetheless. Brilliant.

We follow Holland Street, past Drayton Mews which were once where the horses and servants for the great houses lived and now are most sought-after and respectable, but retain their original, cobbled and unpretentious appearance.

On the right, as we approach the ghastly red-brick town hall at the end, don't miss the medallion to the Virgin Mary (I think) high up on a gable. It's positioned at exactly the height where a fire insurance mark would have been in the old days (gaining the protection of the private fire brigades) but I suspect this one was invoking a higher authority.

At the end as we come out on the right, is musician Sir Charles Stanford's house, a rare survivor of old, low-rise Kensington before the march of the monstrous mansion blocks which now dominate the area. The town hall seems to have been designed merely to be inoffensive, which in itself offends me, the idea perhaps being that anything built of red brick and at the same height as the surrounding blocks would be acceptable. Let us not intrude on private grief and move straight on.

At the five-way junction ahead, we are, ultimately, going straight ahead, down the **Duchess of Bedford's Walk**. If you wish to do this straight away, skip the next section; do have a look, however, because you may fancy a drink in the pub, and the eccentrics who have lived here are intriguing.

CAMPDEN HILL: STRANGE OLD COWS, A MAHARAJAH, A REAL PAINE This now extremely well-to-do area has in recent centuries contained some very odd properties and strange characters. Indeed, it still does. It also boasts a little gem of a pub.

I'm proposing a brief and rewarding stroll up this hill to take a peek at this odd district. It'll take only 15 minutes there and back, excluding however many hours you stop in the pub. So going right, up Campden Hill Road on its left side, we can see on the right the space known as Observatory Gardens, opposite the college on the left. The view of trees and mansion blocks from this pavement is frequently painted by artists, and frame it with your outstretched arms to imagine why.

On the left is a road, Campden Hill, which we need not take, but a few steps down on the left at No 2 is a house with an interesting history. Typical of many other large houses built for the gentry here in the first half of the 19th century, **Bute House** was built for the flamboyant Marquis of Bute (see Kews, page 180) between 1830 and 1842. We will encounter his eccentric architect later, but one is not able to see much of this house today. It became Blundell House then, as a Nigerian diplomatic building, Abuja House, and the electric security fences etc would even look excessive around Fort Knox.

Going on up Campden Hill Road, we find the **Windsor Castle**, a completely un-messed-up 200-year-old pub without moronic jukeboxes, one-armed bandits, taped music, carpet or any of that nonsense, but original wood interior and a roaring open fire in the winter, and cool ale in the summer. Excellent. Madonna and her hubbie, Guy Ritchie, have been seen in here, but celebs are two-a-penny between Kensington and Notting Hill. I saw that lanky John Cleese outside here once. I just stopped myself yelling 'Basil' in a *Fawlty Towers* falsetto because I expect he's well fed up with it.

The pub's name comes from the fact that you could see Windsor Castle from the upstairs windows before other buildings got in the way. Allegedly. After seven pints you can see the Statue of Liberty.

Another strange story is that a beer drinker once traded a human skeleton here to settle his booze bill. The skeleton was that of Thomas Paine, the philosopher and author of *Rights of Man* who died in America. The beer drinker was the son of William Cobbett, the outspoken MP and social reformer who wrote *Rural Rides* in the early 19th century. It seems Cobbett had earlier had Paine's bones shipped back to England but his wayward son had little respect for them. It is probably true, for there's another record of Paine's stuffed head turning up in various places. Bit of a Paine really, but now we've got used to London beer costing an arm and a leg.

Whether you go into the pub or not, take a peek down Peel Street just past it and to the right. There's a surprisingly long view across London with the Telecom Tower showing how high we are here.

If you took the next left at Aubrey Walk – and I'm instead proposing turning back to the Duchess of Bedford's Walk here – you could walk the length of that to discover a house with a fascinating history. **Aubrey House** is a relic of the days when Campden Hill was an isolated hamlet well outside London. This was a country estate.

Lady Mary Coke, the highly eccentric courtier, diarist and authoress, lived here from 1767 to 1788, this being her country house (she had another in what she considered London). Her cow, Miss Pelham, escaped one day. She wrote:

> Miss Pelham took a frisk this morning, got out of my grounds and went nearly as far as London before I heard of her. I believe she thinks my place too retired, for she was found among a great herd of cattle.

She loved her gardens here and wrote one day:

> Tis a delightful day. I have planted a hundred perannual [sic] flowers that I had this morning from Mr Lee, but my work was twice interrupted by visitors.

She was furious when one day the hunt streamed across her garden and disappeared over the fence into Holland House's grounds. Foxes, however, as we shall see, have a great connection with Holland House.

Lady Mary Coke was for a time a frequent visitor to nearby Kensington Palace where she would play cards with Princess Amelia, but the splendour of the court faded with the death of George II; royalty moved away, leaving it a dusty shell for many years. Lady Mary attended Kensington Church where she frequently and fiercely criticised the sermons.

Daughter of John, Duke of Argyll, she was described in one history as 'this termagent lady'. She had travelled Europe causing ructions wherever she went for no apparent reason.

She claimed to have been driven out of Austria by Empress Maria Theresa and out of France by Queen Marie Antoinette. She started a quarrel with Prime Minister Horace Walpole, who said she 'had a hundred distresses abroad which did not weight a penny together.'

She claimed the Duke of York, brother of George III, was in love with her, but as Walpole said: 'She is like Don Quixote who went in search of adventures, and when she found none, imagined them.' In 1807 she moved to Chiswick, where she had bought the now vanished Manor House, and died four years later 'in a wonderfully uncomfortable manner' half stuck in a recess, surrounded by 'many decrepit pets' and vast heaps of rubbish.

Just to the east of Aubrey House stood **Moray Lodge**, built in 1817, where great men and strange goings-on coincided.

In the 1860s wealthy, art-loving bachelor Arthur J Lewis used to hold entertainments here, plying his male friends with oysters and beer, with theatricals and music all evening. The calibre of guests was such that they included Thackeray (who as we have seen lived nearby), Dickens, Trollope, Arthur Sullivan, George du Maurier, Tattersall (as in horses) and John Millais, the painter who ran off with Mrs Ruskin. The conversation and wit of such illustrious company must have been sparkling: in fact they mostly spent the afternoons drinking beer, and playing billiards and croquet.

The house comes to notice again at the time of the coronation of Edward VII at the beginning of the 20th century. With nearly all the princes and potentates of the world coming to London, finding somewhere to put them all was difficult. The Maharajah of Jaipur was more difficult than most to accommodate, as he had a retinue of 200, and as a devout Hindu needed his own cow and could drink no water that had come through a pipe. Moray Lodge, now empty, was ideal, possessing its own well and gardens big enough to hold a cow and sheds for the staff. Later, in 1940, the balloon literally went up for the Blitz, as some of the barrage balloons were launched from its grounds. Moray Lodge was demolished in 1955. We return down Campden Hill Road to Duchess of Bedford's Walk, now on the right.

ACROSS HOLLAND PARK TO ARTISTIC HEIGHTS
Going down **Duchess of Bedford's Walk**, there are more massive mansion blocks on the right, and not very attractive ones either. Very Kensington, they look more like government ministries than homes. Here I saw a very strangely dressed, over made-up old woman teetering along on high heels clutching trillions of designer bags, Harvey Nicks carriers and Louis Vuitton luggage pieces. She positively *dripped* labels saying 'money, money, money'.

At the end of this walk we go straight ahead through the bollards (the emblem of Kensington, really, a load of old bollards) across a path (watch out for whizzing cyclists) and into Holland Park. The stately home job on the right

24

is only a part of what was once there, the remainder having been bombed to hell in World War II. Built in 1605 for a courtier of James I, it became Holland House in 1768 when Baron Holland bought it. Under his famous son, Charles James Fox, it became the social centre of Whig party intrigue with many a great statesman coming here.

Holland House was bombed severely (as opposed to being bombed politely) in 1940 and only the east wing and the arcades remind us of what a splendid Jacobean pile this must have been. Fox was the family surname, not the title, and when Charles James Fox was himself offered a peerage in later life he said: 'I will not close my politics in that foolish way.'

At the white arch ahead we go left and downhill fast into the artistic world of Melbury Road. We come out on to a bit of road called Ilchester Place, but go straight on down to Melbury Road and turn sharp right into what was once a rather fascinating artistic colony.

A MAD GOTHIC FANTASY AND THE UPPER CRUST Here in **Melbury Road** are a pair of extraordinary houses, the weirdest being the Tower House, on the bend ahead, a six-bedroomed Gothic fantasy which Led Zeppelin's Jimmy Page bought in 1974 (beating, it is said, David Bowie). It has a conical tower, gargoyle, fabulous stained glass and a dark, castle-like interior. The vendor was hell-raising actor Richard Harris, and the buyer had a great interest – academic, no doubt – in black magic, etc. And I don't mean the chocolates.

Tower House

It was built by outrageous Victorian architect/designer William Burges for himself. He was the father of mad Gothic revival extravagances, and reshaped Cardiff Castle for the third Marquess of Bute with quite incredible embellishments, and built the Bavarian fantasy of Castell Coch nearby. He loved high Gothic but didn't want it to be taken too seriously. Gothic could be fun as well as 'churchy', he argued:

> There are some people who … consider medieval art as eminently ecclesiastical, and therefore profoundly serious to be approached with caution, forgetting that mankind has been very much the same in every age, and that our ancestors joked and laughed as much as we do.

Next door (before the Tower House on the same side) was at the time of writing the home of flamboyant film maker, Michael Winner, a deeply eccentric man (praised elsewhere for his memorials to policemen who were killed on duty) who has lived here since 1947 with various consorts such as actress Jenny Seagrove. He has never married but says he's had hundreds of girlfriends.

The director and producer has said he has 87 telephones in this building. He has a Rolls-Royce, is probably worth many millions, and owns quite a few works of art, yet he cheerfully confesses to opening toothpaste tubes at the wrong end, when almost empty, to get a bit more out. He came in for some stick from the *Daily Mail*, at the other end of Kensington High Street, for having a girlfriend in 2000 who was claiming state benefits; in other ways, however, he can be extraordinarily generous, helping out young actors behind the scenes. He once said he doesn't want to live in a tolerant country but an intolerant one, vociferously backing the Tories while they were on top in the 1980s and then switching to Labour just in time for their landslide.

Don't bother trying to break in to steal all that art, by the way. Defences have been stepped up since a very thin burglar slipped through some railings and mingled with guests. Finding a drawer full of Rolex watches, he helped himself. They were all fake, and the household set off in a good old-fashioned hue and cry around the district. This ended with the villain being held down and sat upon outside the Commonwealth Institute nearby. The virtually valueless watches were recovered and the villain escaped or was perhaps let go, even thinner, no doubt. Mr Winner, maker of such successes as *Death Wish* (along with a few not quite so successful movies), gets credited, bizarrely, in certain productions as Arnold Crust Jr. Or just Arnold Crust. No doubt he's the toast of the film industry.

This is not to trivialise the rich heritage of Melbury Road, centre of an area of rich Victorian artists from a time when artists were not poor and struggling but had the mega-rich beating a path to their doors and were heaped with honours – even a peerage for one of the 'Melbury Road set' – by the art-loving establishment. Thus you will see wonderful studio buildings all around this area, with vast acres of glass facing the necessary north (no direct sun, but bags of light).

Winner's own house was built by Victorian painter Sir Luke Fildes, who included an immodestly monogrammed weathervane. Mr Winner suggested to one interviewer that this was 'a little vane', a rather good pun that evidently passed over the interviewer's head, who wrote it as 'vain'. The dates on the blue plaque are a little awry; they should read 1877 to 1924. Edward VII sat in the studio here for a formal portrait, such was Fildes's standing, and described it as 'one of the finest rooms in London' – and he had, after all, seen a few rather fine ones. More recent sitters – in Mr Winner's cinema – have included Lauren Bacall, Marlon Brando, Michael Caine, Charles Bronson, Jeremy Irons and Anthony Hopkins.

Going on down Melbury Road there are more studios and plaques to artists on the left, and reaching the busy Addison Road there's a fine studio house on the opposite side, but avoid crossing the busy road and go left and left again into Holland Park Road, doubling back east into peaceful territory once more.

A MOORISH PARADISE AND SENSUAL WOMEN Here, on the left, is **Leighton House**, the ultimate in fantasy studio-homes in the artists' colony around here. A half-forgotten gem in London from the same era as exotic arabists like Richard Burton (whose strange Arab tent tomb is featured on page 66), this was the home of the great Victorian artist Frederic, Lord Leighton. The creator of the familiar *Flaming June* picture lived at this quite extraordinary house, such an unexpected find in this quiet road. Note the Islamic crescent moon on the dome. Here, for no admission fee, one can experience the heady incense in the exotic, bejewelled Arab hall where Leighton's unique collection of Moorish tilework is brilliantly employed, complete with tinkling fountain and the lofty dome once described as the eighth wonder of the world.

24

Lord Lloyd-Webber and Lady Lucinda Lambton are great fans of what the latter rightly calls 'the secret heart of Kensington'. Leighton, whose career received a huge boost when Queen Victoria bought one of his pictures, was made a peer – the only artist so honoured – shortly before his death in 1896. I sometimes wonder what separates his lifelike nudes, sensually clad in soft fabrics, from soft porn, and of course the answer is his skill. But would he have received as much interest at the time if he had painted sunflowers? As it was, he was the darling of the establishment, although surely not rated among the top ten artists of history today. Have a look at the canvases hanging around Leighton House and decide for youself. For Lady Lucinda's book of toilets, see page 313.

Continuing up Holland Park Road, turn right into Melbury Road and cross Kensington High Street by the traffic lights on your right, turning right at the other side and then left into **Edwardes Square** (or rather the approach road to it). Before plunging down here, take a look at the grand sweep of Earl's Terrace to your left with its lodges at each end. This terrace, recently restored to provide *bijou* homes with underground parking for the mega-rich, is inextricably linked to the strange story of Edwardes Square.

THE FRENCH INVADERS AND THE BATTLE OF EDWARDES SQUARE One of the most enduring urban myths about Kensington, still circulating almost 200 years after local word of mouth started it, is the story of how Edwardes Square, a rather charming backwater off the High Street, was built by a Frenchman with an eye to housing the French army after they had invaded during the Napoleonic wars. Of course, dreams of invasion were sunk during the Battle of Trafalgar (1805) and the Battle of Waterloo (1815), but the story never was true, as the plaque screwed to the charming garden lodge on the far south side of this agreeably low-rise square records.

A French trader from Hammersmith, Louis Changeur, *was* involved in around 1811 in a speculative development, Earl's Terrace, which was the first part of Edwardes Square to be built, opposite the gate to Holland House. With the French – Boney's men – being the bogey men of the era, that was enough to start the rumour mill that hasn't stopped turning yet. But he soon went bankrupt and was out of the picture. Not that it stopped the pub at the southeast corner, the rather good **Scarsdale** (great *cappuccini* and recommended food, good beer and no carpet, jukebox or gaming machine, which by now you will have gathered I disapprove of in a pub, but not over-generous with the ginger beer shandies) from going along with the Battle of Waterloo yarn for many years.

In fact, if you had stood on the north side of Edwardes Square very late at night on 5 November 1805, you would have heard the sounds of hooves and the rattling wheels of a carriage being driven as fast as was possible through the swirling fog eastwards along Kensington High Street. This sound was the death knell for Napoleon's invasion hopes, and ultimately the end of his empire.

The post chaise contained one Royal Navy Lt John Lepenotière who had ridden non-stop for nearly 37 hours from the fast schooner *Pickle* in which he had landed at Falmouth after a nine-day, 1,000-mile dash by sea. He carried the momentous news that the Royal Navy had smashed the combined French/Spanish fleets at Trafalgar, and that Admiral Lord Nelson was dead. Lt Lepenotière had changed horses 21 times on his journey - the last time at Hounslow, a few miles west of here. True, the Napoleonic Wars were to carry on for another ten years, but as with Hitler and the Battle of Britain over a century later, the Continental despot had failed to deal with Britain (and then stupidly attacked Russia), and had thus signed his own regime's death warrant.

The hooves in the fog were beating out the rhythm: 'Europe will be free again, Europe will be free again.'

Oddly there *was*, though totally forgotten today, a battle of Edwardes Square, but it took place a hundred years later, in 1908.

The square itself, finished by 1819, had its own Act of Parliament and its own laws, which included penalties for the beating of carpets outside the house and for the exercising of horses. Residents also had to clean the footpaths outside their houses by 9am; failure to do so could result in a fine or three months' hard labour. Not unreasonable when you think about it.

In 1910 the leases on the houses were due to expire and a speculative firm, Allen Bros, bought the freehold with the aim of flattening Earl's Terrace and building over the garden in the centre of Edwardes Square, thus increasing the rent, and pushing out the remaining tenants.

The residents waited until the firm tried to shut off the gates into the gardens, which they sneakily did while the chairman of the gardens committee was away. He was told and telegraphed back:

> Keep possession of remaining gate; take gate off hinges if necessary; employ
> watchmen day and night to guard.

Every day Allen Bros put up barricades to shut off the gardens. Every day the residents pulled them down. The matter went to the courts and the residents won. It went to appeal and they won again. It went to the House of Lords in January 1912 and they won a third and final time.

This was Edwardes Square's finest hour. A 50ft-high bonfire was made with 40 cartloads of timber, soaked in flammable oil. Decorative lamps were strung all around and some of the residents proceeded round the square with a pipe band, everyone else leaning out of their windows banging gongs, saucepans, baking trays and celebrating their success in saving the square.

After that atypical display of noisy emotion, Edwardes Square returned to its respectable diffidence. Yes, the people of Kensington had rushed to the barricades, but only to make their point politely and firmly with good humour. No bayonets, blazing braziers or republican bare-breasted women here. Or beating carpets outside the house.

A CANNON-BALL FROM HELL AND GOD'S JEWELLERY BOX
Talking about battles, there's a link with one of the worst British military disasters ever (and by God we've had a few of them) in the centre of the square. If you come here on London Garden Squares Day (see page 304), when there'll be access to the rather lovely private gardens in the square, with teas and musicians playing amidst the shrubbery, you'll find a cannon-ball from Balaclava. It was brought here as part of the Victorian fascination with the Charge of the Light Brigade, a monstrous cock-up which – involving as it did, massive heroic and completely pointless sacrifice – was just the sort of thing the British love, or loved. Due to bungled orders, on 25 October 1854 the Light Brigade charged straight into the Russian guns, knowing they would be massacred. As the cannon-balls cut through the ranks, the horses and men re-formed time and time again.

It made a rather good poem and a film. You probably recall the lines:

> Their's not to reason why
> Their's but to do and die
> Into the valley of death
> Rode the six hundred...
> Into the jaws of Death
> Into the mouth of Hell.

Precisely the sort of mawkish morbid melodrama Victorians adored (look at the pleasure they took in the deaths of children in their literature). A more dispassionate judgment came from a French general, Bosquet, who said: *'C'est magnifique, mais ce n'est pas la guerre.'* – 'It's magnificent, but it's not war.'

The Edwardes in Edwardes Square came, like a lot of Edwardes still do, from Wales. William Edwardes (1712–1801), MP for Haverfordwest, owned farmland stretching from what is now Kensington High Street south to Earl's Court and nearly to Fulham Road. He, the first Baron Kensington (an Irish title, oddly), along with the second baron, attempted to make money by property speculation, such as Edwardes Square.

One more thing about Edwardes Square. Its blue plaques tell us a lot about the shortcomings of blue plaques. See page 118 for that story.

Having noted the studios and superb brickwork opposite the lodge, on the south side (some completed in 2006), leave Edwardes Square by the southeast (far left) corner and turn left immediately after the Scarsdale into a path known as Earl's Walk. Along here a couple of Indian bean trees flower spectacularly at certain times, even though one is positioned inconveniently a few inches in front of someone's door. At the end of the road, desist from illegal carpet-beating, as Kensington police station is on our left.

We cross the road to Abingdon Villas opposite and plug on down here, passing the Abingdon restaurant on the right at one crossroads and the **Britannia** pub (recommended, Young's beers) up on the left at the next. We go straight on, however, and then left up Iverna Gardens where the gorgeous London plane trees grow at a slight slant as if they were growing in a canyon, which indeed they are. Here in the quiet square at the end is a charming building: **St Arkis Armenian Church**. This is like a perfect little jewellery box. God's hand, one feels, might come down at any minute, seize the stubby spire of this perfectly symmetrical building and lift off the lid to reveal all kinds of treasures. Quite superb, built in 1922 by Mews & Davis architects; don't miss the Armenian inscription on one of the entrances (in English over another).

Going to the end of Iverna Court, as the road becomes beyond the little square, we're in Wright's Lane. Turn left back into the High Street, turn right and the Tube home is just on the right.

COMPLEX DIANA AND THE UNPALATABLE TRUTH

Sadly, we have been deprived of Kensington's most intriguing resident – Princess Diana. She was a more complex figure than her billions of adoring fans – worshippers, frankly, at some points – ever wanted to believe.

I recall her sitting at the traffic lights here in the crowded High Street in her open top Mercedes preening herself around the time she claimed she wanted less media attention, then turning around and coming back down the busy street. Or taking her sons to McDonald's (it burgers belief, one might say – can you think of a more calculated insult to Prince Charles and all his organic talk-to-vegetables stuff than feeding his sons a Big Mac with fries and Coke?). Or phoning one of the newspapers where I worked to guarantee publicity for one of her 'anonymous' midnight visits to a hospital. Or steering reporters to the friends who would give her side of the story in her marital battles.

On one typically bizarre occasion she was pursuing her vendetta against the nanny of her sons, Tiggy Legge-Bourke. She instructed her staff to provide a quote for a certain newspaper calling Tiggy (are these people grown-ups with names like this?) 'thoughtless, foolish and idiotic' because she had been seen drinking champagne with Prince William, then just 14. Diana was fiercely criticised by the other Press for making such a bitchy attack, so Diana's aides phoned the first newspaper editor back.

They complained: 'How could you do that? It's totally untrue.'

The bemused editor replied: 'But you *know* it's true. You told me yourself two days ago!' Diana had forgotten, or chosen to forget, and was furious. The aides had to follow orders, however insane.

Of course she was also a force for great good in making concern about AIDS respectable, hugging the victims and not treating them like lepers (and the same with lepers), and taking the landmines issue to the world's sitting-rooms via TV as nobody else could have done. Her sincerity shone through on so many occasions. But it just wasn't that simple.

People wanted her to be a sexy version of Mother Teresa – who by coincidence died at about the same time and received only a fraction of the publicity. But she wasn't a saint, she was a modern, mixed-up woman. She died not rushing to some child's surgery or to a landmine or AIDS victim but on yet another huge freebie holiday (the sixth or seventh of that year) with a rich and unsuitable playboy, and because their stupid, irresponsible response to people taking pictures was to drive through a concrete tunnel at perhaps 90mph while not wearing seatbelts. The bodyguard who did put one on survived, you will recall. Typically, Diana had let it be known that she'd arrived in Paris and yet was outraged when the paparazzi – I wouldn't defend their low-life actions for a minute – followed her.

She hated the pressure of the publicity yet could not do without it, for she was as addicted to adoration as the world seemed addicted to her. Do you remember the time she said she would be dropping out of the public eye to lead a reclusive life, with all that head-tilted-on-one-side and doe-eyed sadness? It was a good speech, which attracted much sympathy, and she was probably sincere at the time. How long did it last? Years? Months? No, it was just a few *weeks* before her aides were phoning the Press and tipping them off about her next action.

The Press used her and she used them. The public despised the media yet at the same time lapped up the coverage, buying magazines with her image on the front by the millions and reading every word they could find about her in the newspapers. Woe betide any paper that ignored the latest Diana story: Its sales would fall through the floor. Who was using whom?

Like many people, I despised the paparazzi at the lower end of the business and as a working journalist I'm deeply ashamed of those who printed sneaky pictures. (Remember the shots in the gym, from a secret camera above Diana's exercise machine? Why stop there, why not have a toilet cam, for God's sake? I hope I would have walked out rather than handle those gym pictures.)

But who was buying millions of papers when an exclusive picture was announced, or reading every word of an exclusive interview with someone who betrayed her confidence – the same hypocritical people who condemned it all. I recall saying to a colleague in the year Diana died: 'This story is out of control, it can't go on, it can't get any bigger.' Thanks to global TV and Press picture transmission, more people knew more of Diana's face and her life than *anyone before in history*, and I'm not exaggerating. It was like the adoration of Eva Peron but involving nearly the whole globe, not just one small nation.

True, parts of the Western world were obsessed with Jackie Kennedy just before her husband was killed in 1963, but look how unsophisticated the media were then. One picture a month in most papers, with just a few respectful words. No-one would have dared suggest JFK was a lying philanderer, which we now know he was, and no-one publicly took apart his marriage as they did Diana's, albeit with her help.

The Diana phenomenon was totally different. Many papers had pictures of Diana *every day*, and features thousands of words long analysing her relationships.

Her picture was familiar on TV news in China, Fiji, Arkansas, New Zealand, Japan, Peru, everywhere. It was an inexplicable phenomenon, a kind of global insanity where everyone wanted to believe in a saintly, beautiful superperson who didn't really exist. It couldn't have gone on.

That we are still fascinated by the story was shown in 2007 by Helen Mirren's Oscar win for her portrayal of the Queen in that week (though the film didn't convey the whole picture).

A SCENE THAT MUST BAFFLE CONCEPTION OF THOSE WHO DID NOT WITNESS IT Let
me describe the scene in the square of grass between Kensington Palace and the High Street at midnight, in the few days between the princess's death and her funeral.

It was quite amazing, an experience I'll never, ever forget, and recalling it, writing this book, put me in mind of the day Nelson was mourned at Greenwich nearly 200 years ago. I quote *The Times* man in that case saying the scene 'must baffle conception of those who did not witness it' and this is truly how it seemed that warm September night, but I'll try to unbaffle you.

The reason I went to see the scene at midnight (twice) was because I was working at a nearby newspaper and my shift ended thereabouts. We knew from the words on the pages before us that something truly extraordinary was happening, so we walked up the road to have a look.

The sight that greeted us was something out of the Middle Ages, or out of a great religious film with tens of thousands of extras. Hundreds upon hundreds of people were filing slowly up the road from the Tube and bus stops bearing flowers, cards, messages, pictures of Diana. No-one was talking. Some were, or clearly had been, crying.

The scene in that great grass quadrangle between the High Street and the palace was astonishing. It was packed with tens of thousands of people silently queuing to pay homage to their dead princess: old people, young parents with small children, teenagers.

They shuffled forward in a silent throng, a great line of people five or six deep moving down one path, and leaving in a similar column that must have held many hundreds more. Everywhere there were candles, cards and messages tied to trees, railings, or anything people could find. Oddly, many of the trees had small teddy bears tied to them, I remember, as if a child had been lost. Posters of Diana with heartfelt messages, amateurish poems of obviously strong emotions.

But most amazing was the sea of flowers you could not possibly cross near the great gilt railings of the palace that was her home. In itself this sea of bouquets, messages, candles burning in jars, and tributes seemed to cover hundreds of feet, although my memory may be wrong – the emotion was so overpowering, you could not help but be moved. The far gates were still in the distance when your feet lapped this floral sea of welling emotion.

Flowers at Kensington Palace

This outpouring of silent love and mass devotion was perhaps like a pilgrimage to a great medieval saint's shrine, one where touching the relics would lead to miracles; more accurately, however, it was a moment of unquestioning love and devotion by thousands upon thousands of pilgrims. Those not in the great column pressing and shuffling silently forward stood holding burning tapers, some weeping softly. Amid those thousands of people, the intense feeling was magnified until it was a tangible, irresistible force sweeping around you. It was amazing. You could *not* be neutral.

If at times I comment on Diana's life and death negatively in this book – because I'm trying to tell it how it was, not how we wanted it to be – I don't in any way doubt or belittle the strength of many good people's feelings at that moment. It was an emotional flood-tide that rose to an awful point when the funeral bier left these gates, turning left along the bottom of Hyde Park and proceeding to Westminster Abbey amid quite incredible scenes as thousands of people howled and wept with sorrow.

There was the awe-inspiring moment when her brave sons, her brother, her former husband and her father-in-law fell in behind the coffin. There was that peak of the surging, irresistible tide when Earl Spencer gave his emotional outburst in Westminster Abbey and we had a frightening glimpse, for a second, of what a revolutionary uprising would be like. If he had called the angry crowd listening outside the Abbey to burst in and lynch the Windsors, it is impossible to say where it would all have ended. Such was the anger and grief, and love and hatred in that one explosive moment in history.

I felt a little of that anger directed against myself on a bus in Kensington High Street that week when a colleague unwisely referred to something about our work on a newspaper and one of the bus passengers turned to us and said 'You killed her, you bastards', referring to the paparazzi who chased Diana to her death in that Paris tunnel. 'Get off the bloody bus.' As we did so, shame-faced and frankly a little scared, the bus seethed with the collective fury of the lynch mob.

Then, thankfully, the moment had gone. The cathartic effect of the beautiful funeral did its magic, the tide turned, and the anger ebbed away as powerfully as it had flooded in, laying bare deeper, more lasting emotions. It was quite, quite amazing and people said that nothing like this had ever happened before.

But, astoundingly, it had – almost *exactly the same story,* here in this very same Kensington High Street, with another tragic Princess of Wales, another scene at the Abbey, another angry funeral, less than two centuries before and then totally forgotten about, as I recount in the Hammersmith section (see page 262).

24

25

Wimbledon

A circular walk from Wimbledon station (☒ Waterloo, ⊖ District Line). This gives good views of the most luscious, richest suburbia London can offer, a smattering of the loopy, fascinating, beautiful and unpredictable, including a site where a man set fire to a house containing the king and queen and was rewarded for it, and a decent walk across open countryside. Stout shoes and a stout heart are necessary, for it is 6¹/₂ miles long (4 hours) but suggested short cuts and ways to break it into two easy halves are given, plus advice on buses for the footsore at various points. If you're not a country-walking type, pick out chunks that suit you. Ideal for mountain bikers. I promise not to mention Wombles at any point, or even explain what they are if you're lucky enough not to know.

DIANA SPENCER, THE STAG AND THE TUDORS Leave Wimbledon town centre by turning right out of the station – sneak a look at a rather restrained but effective sculpture-mural on the library's flank in Compton Road on the right, and the grand bank reincarnated as a wine bar opposite – and continue up the main road, turning right into Woodside. Soon we take the second left into Lake Road through some grand gates, past the massive buildings of Queen Alexandra's Court, and the feeling of leafy suburban opulence begins to descend as we ascend. Turn second left again into Church Hill and right into St Mary's Road. In April the magnolias and tulip trees and clouds of cherry blossom all around add broad brushstrokes of brightness to any sunny day.

Coming out at the top we are confronted by our first eccentric building, **Stag Lodge**, which has a massive lead stag on its roof. London has a smattering of loopy lodges, once the entrances to grand houses that have long disappeared, often architectural flourishes in a sea of suburbia which has swamped the rural estates they once served. This one, literally over-the-top in style, was built in 1801 as a gateway for nearby Spencer House, itself demolished in 1949. That's 'Spencer' as in Diana Spencer, late Princess of Wales. The Spencer family's influence around here accounts for the fact that if you came by car you will have passed at least one Spencer Arms pub en route. There are various other oddities surviving from the lost mansion – a former water tower made into a home at Arthur Road, for example. Scrap-metal thieves should note that the valuable lead stag was replaced in 1987 with a less valuable replica.

Resuming our walk along St Mary's Road we plunge down to the right at the mini-roundabout into Church Road. Soon we come to a left fork, Somerset Road, which we will take, but ahead of us between the roads in an ever-widening triangular site is the sprawl of the globally famous **All England Croquet & Lawn Tennis Club**. If you want to visit the Tennis Museum on this site, stay on Church Road and it is soon on the left.

Wimbledon and tennis are inseparable, and for two weeks in June/July this area becomes a Mecca for tennis pilgrims who border on the fanatical (see page 306).

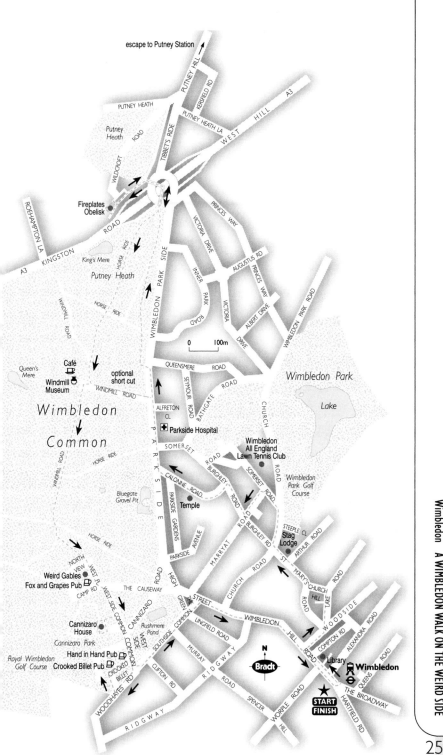

escape to Putney Station

PUTNEY HEATH
Putney Heath
ROAD
Putney Heath

ROEHAMPTON LA
KINGSTON
A3
ROAD
Fireplates Obelisk
King's Mere
HORSE RIDE

Queen's Mere
Café
Windmill Museum
WINDMILL ROAD

Wimbledon
Common
WINDMILL ROAD
HORSE RIDE
Bluegate Gravel Pit
HORSE RIDE
NORTH VIEW
WEST PL
Weird Gables
Fox and Grapes Pub
CAMP RD
THE CAUSEWAY
Cannizaro House
Cannizaro Park
Royal Wimbledon Golf Course
Hand in Hand Pub
Crooked Billet Pub
CROOKED BILLET RD
WOODHAYES RD

PUTNEY HILL
KERSFIELD RD
PUTNEY HEATH LA
TIBBET'S RIDE
WEST HILL
A3

VICTORIA DRIVE
PRINCES WAY
AUGUSTUS RD
PRINCES WAY
ALBERT DRIVE
VICTORIA DRIVE
INNER PARK ROAD
WIMBLEDON PARK ROAD

WIMBLEDON PARK SIDE
HORSE RIDE

0   100m

QUEENSMERE   ROAD
optional short cut

SEYMOUR ROAD
BATHGATE ROAD
ALFRETON CL
Parkside Hospital
SOMERSET ROAD
BURGHLEY ROAD
CHURCH ROAD

Wimbledon
All England
Lawn Tennis Club

SOMERSET ROAD
CALONNE ROAD
PARKSIDE GARDENS
P A R K S I D E
Temple
AVENUE
PARKSIDE
HIGH STREET
ROAD
MARRYAT ROAD
RD BURGHLEY ROAD
CHURCH ROAD

Wimbledon Park
Lake

Wimbledon
Park Golf
Course

STEEPLE CL
Stag Lodge
ARTHUR ROAD
ST MARY'S CHURCH HILL
LAKE ROAD
ALEXANDRA ROAD
WOODSIDE

GREEN
LINGFIELD ROAD
WIMBLEDON
Rushmere Pond
CANNIZARO RD
WEST SIDE COMMON
WEST SIDE COMMON
SOUTHSIDE
MURRAY ROAD
RIDGWAY
CLIFTON ROAD
HILL ROAD
COMPTON RD
QUEENS ROAD

N
Bradt

Library
Wimbledon
THE BROADWAY
HARTFIELD RD
WORPLE ROAD
SPENCER HILL
RIDGWAY

★
START
FINISH

Wimbledon, tennis-wise, stands above all for nice normality and well-behaved middle-class crowds. But that doesn't mean seriously strange things can't happen...

- Californian Jeff Tarango walked off court mid-match in 1995 against Germany's Alex Mronz, complaining that the umpire was biased against him. His wife later punched the official. Shortly before the Wimbledon incident he had bared his bottom at a tournament in Tokyo.
- In 2001 a couple was discovered copulating in one of the staff locker rooms. The ball boys were too young, the straw-hatted and blazered stewards too old ('we're far too crusty for that'), so the prime suspects were the 6,000 young catering workers. It gave Fleet Street tabloids scope for headlines such as 'love match' or 'bonk, bonk off the court', 'mixed doubles'. Or even 'new balls please'.
- In a very hot 1921 Wimbledon quarter-final, Britain's Randolph Lycett demanded champagne. A liveried waiter served him but the alcohol didn't help him much. 'Mr Lycett's distress was obvious,' the newspapers reported. 'He was still capable of making powerful smashes but fell over several times when trying to turn sharply.' Having been in the lead, he lost in the fifth set to a puzzled Japanese opponent.
- Wimbledon had its first Centre Court streaker in 1996 when student Melissa Johnson, 23, leapt over a barrier and ran the length of the court wearing just a

Carrying on, turn left up Marryat Road (we'll encounter this name again later) and you'll notice a narrow footpath on the right just before the houses resume. If it's dryish weather you could take this otherwise muddy path, Dairy Walk, which plunges down and up again and gives more glimpses of Wimbledon tennis on the right. It also evokes the area's rural past with its trees and hints of milk maids toiling up from the dairy with wooden yokes on their shoulders and pails brimming with warm milk. If you do take it – I can *never* resist secretive walks and alleyways – turn left at the top and rejoin the walk by turning right into Calonne Road. However, it is mostly hemmed in by high fences, so I'd stay on the road and see some splendid houses.

Turn right into the dipping Burghley Road and check out the opulent houses. Anywhere in the world these homes would be luxurious. Here in pricey SW19 they're regarded as a rare privilege, but architecturally the best suburbia can offer. Just as with churches, there are really only two British styles (classical and Gothic), so in domestic architecture we offer classical (in its Georgian form) or vernacular (home-grown), of which Tudor, with its beams and exposed brick, is the best-known style. Badly imitated by the ribbon developers near here – for example, along the A3 – with a few black planks tacked on to gables, and rightly despised as pseudo-Tudor, the style done well produces attractive buildings such as **Kimble Wick** on the right as we walk down. Further down the alternative style is reflected in massive pseudo-Georgian houses such as No 42, all discipline and geometric proportions. Which do you prefer? You pays your money (seven figures in this area) and takes your choice.

Of course, all this prim perfection is too much at times. The comic novels of Nigel Williams – such as *The Wimbledon Poisoner, They Came From SW19* and *East of Wimbledon* - poked literary fun at Wimbledon and hit just the right note for some. In fact Williams lives more in Putney. Perhaps we can look forward to *The Putney Chutney Murder*, or *Putney, Lust for Glory* or even, further afield, *24 hours to Tulse Hill* or *How Stands the State of Denmark Hill?*

We turn left up Calonne Road, marvelling at the amount of land that comes with maid's apron during the men's final, raising the flap and showing her all to the players and then turning and doing the same to the Royal Box, to the cheers of the crowd. Mali Vai Washington, who lost to Richard Krajicek, said: 'She lifted up the apron and she was smiling at me. I got flustered.' Well, that was his excuse.

- Just two years after World War II ended, former enemy of the Allies, Austrian player Hans Redl, was back at Wimbledon – and applauded as a hero. He'd lost an arm at the horrendous Battle of Stalingrad, so the rules were changed so he could rest the ball on his racket and flip it in the air to serve. He reached the last 16.

- In 1996 it rained and rained. In July came the unbelievable and unforgettable spectacle of **Cliff Richard** backed by Martina Navratilova, Virginia Wade, Pam Shriver and Gigi Ferna, singing songs such as *We're All Going on a Summer Holiday* for the Centre Court crowd, huddled under umbrellas while the deluge thundered down. The crowd went home happy after one of their best days yet – no tennis, but very British.

- Britain's **Tim Henman**, aching to make Wimbledon history, did so for the wrong reason in 1995 when he lost his temper, and his nice-boy image, when he smashed a ball in anger after losing a point. It accidentally hit ballgirl Caroline Hall, 16, full in the ear. Henman was the first player to be disqualified from Wimbledon, but Caroline got a public apology and a bouquet.

some of these splendid houses (enough for 40 homes in some cases), and come across one of these properties put to startlingly different use.

A STARTLING TEMPLE AND SWINGING HIGHWAYMEN The **Buddhapadipa Temple** is a beautiful, glittering building sitting serenely in a bubble of unlikely oriental tranquillity. The gold-tipped roof glitters like a Bangkok temple and lions and dragons lurk around. The exquisite murals inside are fascinating in their blend of Buddhist teaching and the Western environment.

Respectful visitors are welcome, with shoes removed at the door, but I wouldn't go in wearing a skimpy skirt or a bikini top (actually I wouldn't go in most places wearing those things). Some people do, but Buddhists, even though they enjoy probably the world's most tolerant religion, have their standards.

Clearly the grounds, which include a nursery school, have been converted from the ample gardens of the house that still stands here.

Continuing up Calonne Road we soon reach Parkside, edging the great open space called Wimbledon Common, and turn right along this road. On our left is Windmill Road which gives an opportunity for a short cut, reducing the walk by 1³/₄ miles (2.25km). If taking this, go up Windmill Road to the left to the Mill and pick this walk up below at the section about Duels.

However, you will miss some fascinating features as well as some of the best country walking across the common. Before we come to that, we must follow Parkside to the end. Strike out, as I suggested, for a decent walk, stout of shoe and stout of heart! This is more pleasant if you angle left a little into the woodland after Clockhouse Close, and then walk roughly parallel to the road, passing behind a pond. This is **Seven-Post Pond**, one of ten on the common. It can be mucho muddy along here after wet weather, however.

Surprisingly quickly we reach the corner of the common (technically Putney Heath by now, having crossed a borough boundary where it says Wandsworth on the main road) and a major three-level road junction. Pass under the road, going straight ahead towards Putney. Note the pub-sign-style silhouette of Tibbet the highwayman lurking on a post. This was the first bit of wild country on the important London–Portsmouth Road and many a wealthy man's carriage was held up here. There is a knoll at this end of the common called **Jerry's Hill** where highwayman Jerry Abershaw was hanged and gibbeted – left swinging in chains as a deterrent to others – in 1798.

Having passed under the roundabout, don't carry on straight ahead to Putney; instead, double back left on the path marked with a cycle sign for Roehampton, going back on the far side of the A3. Soon take a path into the woods, to the left keeping closeish to the main road, and look out for a large obelisk. This tells the remarkable story of a man who set fire to a house containing the king and queen and not only got away with it but was richly rewarded.

TRYING TO BURN DOWN A MAD KING AT BREAKFAST David Hartley invited the king and queen to breakfast on this spot in 1774 and while they were eating upstairs tried to burn the house down. Surprisingly, the Fireplates Obelisk here records that he was rewarded with £2,500 from a grateful Parliament and the Freedom of the City of London from the Corporation. George III and Queen Charlotte had agreed to Hartley's daring experiment because he wanted to demonstrate his fireplates which, he claimed, made a fireproof floor. To the great relief of courtiers, he was right.

George III was yet to become completely mad, but if the fireplates had failed Britain might have been even more grateful. The American colonies might not have been lost in the following nine years if a more sane monarch had been on the throne. Come to think of it, maybe the Americans should build Mr Hartley an obelisk too.

Curiously – and I don't suggest walking there right now – there's another isolated loopy lodge about half a mile south of here on Princes Way and it holds metal plaques boasting of its 'fireproof' construction.

And if you're gasping for a drink there's a rather good pub beyond the obelisk, called the **Telegraph**. It is named neither after the newspaper nor the electric message system, but is a relic of an earlier, forgotten chain of semaphore stations (more on page 135).

ESCAPE ROUTE: Those wishing to divide this walk into two smaller chunks could break off here by going back to the roundabout and down Putney Hill, picking up a 14 or 93 bus on the left after the first traffic lights and getting off at the major intersection with traffic lights at the bottom. Putney (≷ to Waterloo) station is just over the lights, East Putney (District Line ⊖) is right at the lights and a few hundred yards along.

Retrace our steps under, and over, the multi-layered road junction, ignoring the paths to the left and taking the one where the sign mentions Kings Mere and Wimbledon. If you've got the right one, you rise slightly to a gravel path and a map of the Common beside it. On the right, by the way, is a clear view of the obelisk we found in the wood, only a few dozen yards away but completely inaccessible from here.

We carry straight on along a path called Ladies Mile, a beautiful country walk on a good day, and increasingly cut off from any hint of town and road.

Wimbledon Common is a great asset to London, just as are the Royal Parks and Hampstead Heath. It is protected by law, governed by the Wimbledon and Putney Commons Act 1871, which provides that it will never be built upon but run for the recreation of the public. Otherwise it would long ago have been developed, such are property pressures round here. It even has its own 'mounties', the Wimbledon Common Rangers, to protect it and enforce what few rules there are. You may see one galloping around. Famous fans of this lovely open space have included local authors Thackeray, Swinburne, Captain Marryat and Lord Baden-Powell, of whom more in a moment.

DUELS, BRACING STUFF FOR BOYS AND GREAT BRITISH BREAKFASTS Soon the sails of **Wimbledon Windmill** come into view and you can see why it was here, high on the heath, ideal for catching the prevailing winds. A white stone on the right as we approach marks our return to the borough of Merton (in the form of Wimbledon Common) from the borough of Wandsworth (that is, Putney Heath). A technicality.

The Wimbledon Windmill Museum, which used to be a set of flats until fairly recently but has been rather well restored with suitable windmilly equipment and exhibits from elsewhere, is usually open on Saturday afternoons, all day Sundays and Bank Holidays. There are also loos here.

This mill was built in 1817 by Charles March, but has been restored half a dozen times since then. There's a good picture of it in working order in the Crooked Billet pub later on.

As a plaque records, Robert Baden-Powell spent a few months here in 1908 writing his classic *Scouting for Boys*, which was the backbone of the worldwide youth movement. What wizard wheezes the Chief Scout dreamed up here nearly 100 years ago are even now directing the lives of youngsters in Wagga Wagga, Kathmandu, Baton Rouge and Penge.

Nowadays, scouting for boys is perhaps a less innocent activity, but the Scout movement, and the Guides, survive, having modified their Edwardian attitudes of healthy outdoor life, self-sufficiency, Christian fellowship and being prepared (for what?) surprisingly little. There was a time during the counter-culture sixties that its uniform, hearty outlook and allegiance to the Queen, etc was scorned as outmoded and militaristic – the ranks of sixers and seconders exactly mirror sergeant and corporal, and the Scout flags sometimes get hung up in churches alongside regimental colours. Certainly any loony-lefty London borough worth its salt in the 1980s would have sooner given money to mad Marxist terrorists than the despised Scouts. In fact in 2001 one London loony borough was at it again, cutting the Scouts' money while throwing cash at some minority stuff.

The Scouts just carried on, taking kids off the streets and teaching them to tie woggles and sheet-bends rather than to nick car stereos and smash up payphones.

A stranger fact of the windmill's history is that the millers in their tower were required to watch for illegal duels on the common. This was a favoured spot for these contests of honour, often involving politicians such as George Canning, shot in the leg in an 1809 duel here with Lord Castlereagh who had sent troops to Holland instead of Portugal which was what Canning intended. Personally, I don't see why politicians shouldn't still settle their differences this way instead of boring us all stupid with their insincerity. It'd make good TV. Mind you, they'd probably cock it up and miss each other, as happened during the duel here between William Pitt the Younger and William Tierney MP. Even so, if you find a gauntlet lying around, *don't* pick it up.

Beside the windmill museum is an excellent and unpretentious café, where on a sunny day one can eat on the terrace. A good, solid, full British breakfast plus a hot drink still gives you change from £5 and probably does wonders for your cholesterol count, if you're from Planet Tharg and need more of it.

To be serious, there was an enlightening study of cholesterol in the diet involving 10,000 Finns. Half were completely deprived of the 'wrong kind' of cholesterol for ten years and half carried on having the full Finnish breakfast. Fascinatingly, although the deprived group had fewer heart attacks it also experienced higher rates of suicide, depression, mental illness and road accidents. That's exactly how I feel about not having a British breakfast when it's on offer. Or to put it another way, going without might not necessarily let you live longer, but it will certainly *feel* like a lot longer.

Back to the path. Continuing along the line we were on, take the wide gravel path through open country. After maybe half a mile, it bends left a little and crosses a bridle path; after another 80yds go left at a path where two short concrete posts are in the ground.

At the end of this pleasant path a Narnian lamppost comes in sight, and we emerge on the corner of West Place and North View. Stroll a few yards to the right down North View to check out the eccentric gables on these last two houses, **Westward Ho** and **Eastward Ho**, probably named after the novel by Charles Kingsley and not the West Country village (which, being Westward Ho!, is the only village in Britain to include punctuation). The gables depict local views.

Continue along West Place past a truly lovely and unpretentious set of cottages, compared to the mansions all around, which includes at No 26 in late May some pleasing mass wisteria with that unique scent the mauve flowers produce. We cross Camp Road and glance down it to yet another historic pub, the **Fox and Grapes**. This is basically unchanged from its 1787 origins (brand new when highwayman Abershaw was arrested).

AN EXTRAVAGANT ITALIAN DUKE AND A TENNIS CHAMP Going on down West Side Common past pompous houses with prominent 'Tradesmen's Entrance' signs (how Hyacinth Bucket), one marvels at the massive piles of masonry and swanky grounds some people have here. Wouldn't it be nice to wander the stupendous grounds of one of these huge houses? A few paces further on and you are offered just that opportunity with the gates of **Cannizaro Park**, named after an Italian duke who lived here, and later home to statesman Henry Dundas Melville (1742–1811).

This is a lovely park whose trees and manicured gardens contrast well with the natural landscape of the Common. It is perhaps worthy of another visit of many hours, particularly in spring when the Friends of Cannizaro Park describe it simply as 'Paradise SW19'. Here there are toilets too.

Pressing on, past the home of Wimbledon's first home-grown tennis champion in 1877, Spencer Gore, we soon reach South Side Common, facing King's College School, and turn right. On the right are two adjacent pubs, oddly both owned by the excellent local brewery, Young's. It is worth first continuing a few yards down the main road to see on the left No 6, once home of the sea-adventure novelist **Captain Frederick Marryat** (1792–1848), a C S Forester or Patrick O'Brian of his day, and creator of the frequently televised *Children of the New Forest*. The peculiar ogee windows give this house a special charm. It is a shape taken from Indian mogul architecture. In India it is called the 'betel' arch because the agreeable shape mimics the leaf of the sacred betel tree. Crossing the road to the little track between some cottages and the houses you can reach the two ancient and pleasant pubs, the **Crooked Billet** and the **Hand in Hand**. The Crooked Billet is the larger, dates from 1509 at least and belonged to the Cromwells – Thomas Cromwell who passed the laws destroying the monasteries in the 1530s, that is. The Hand In Hand is smaller, cosier, and has a children's room. Both do good food.

Now we're heading straight for the station, back up South Side Common along the Common's edge, past even more magnificent mansions and the former home of William Wilberforce, statesman and emancipator of the world's slaves (1759–1833). In Murray Road, to the right, is the childhood home of 20th-century poet **Robert Graves,** who thought Wimbledon Common a poor place, 'neither town nor country'. What did he know?

Graves made the cardinal error, for a war poet, of surviving the trenches. Bad career move. So while Edward Thomas and Wilfred Owen are heroically and tragically frozen in time, poor old Graves had to trudge on through about a dozen different periods of literature, eventually becoming fossilised as a crusty Oxford professor. My eldest brother tells me he dined regularly with Graves at Oxford in the 1960s and the old poet presided over the table wearing a sombrero. He refused to talk about literature and insisted on everyone shutting up while he watched *Maigret* on TV.

Joining the High Street and turning right, the totally exhausted could catch a No 93 bus from the stop across the road down to the station, now three-quarters of a mile (a kilometre) away, mostly downhill. Note the impressive, large, triple-gabled house opposite. A rare Jacobean survivor, **Eagle House** was built in 1613 by East India Company founding member Robert Bell, who made a fortune in the spice trade. It became a boys' school and is now an Islamic cultural centre, maintaining that oriental link.

To the left (back up the High Street) is yet another historic pub, the **Rose and Crown**, from which stage coaches would set off for London, braving the highwaymen. The poets **Leigh Hunt** and **Algernon Swinburne** would meet here; Swinburne, who walked up from Putney, even had a chair named after him. The infant Graves recalled Swinburne as an inveterate patter and kisser of babies such as himself in his pram, and recorded him as 'a public menace' in his memoirs. The Rose and Crown is at the top of Marryat Road, which we saw the other end of an hour or three ago.

We continue on down the High Street, past more food and drink outlets than even George Best and Oliver Reed could have got through in an evening, over two mini-roundabouts and down the hill to Wimbledon station. Phew!

Appendix I

THE ECCENTRIC YEAR

Week by week, the strangest customs of London and its region unfold, only a few of them behind locked doors. Here is your guide to when and where to find the bizarre and inexplicable, plus a reminder for visitors of some rather familiar rituals that Londoners will know and love but, perhaps, have never quite got round to joining in. As events and venues can change over the years, you should check with tourist information centres before making long journeys. Events not open to the public are included because they are unique, fascinating or otherwise eccentric and have stories well worth relating.

JANUARY

I January *Mudathon*: 200-yd dash in often icy conditions through waist-deep oozing mud, at Blackwater River, east of London at Maldon, Essex. Not every year. Sometimes held on 26. December

Mid-January onwards *Chinese New Year:* warm-up in Soho's Chinatown, around Gerrard St, off Leicester Square. Lots of inscrutable but delicious food, processions with dragon-dancing and firecrackers. Actual event not usually till about 13 February. Trouble is, an hour or two later, you feel like another one...

30 January or last Sunday *Royalist army on the march*: 17th-century types march in Cavalier outfits from St James's Palace to Banqueting House, Whitehall, only 360 years too late to stop Charles I having his head chopped off there. Prayers are said at the spot.

FEBRUARY

Shrove Tuesday (date varies, day before Lent starts, related to variable Easter) *Soho Pancake Day Race*: In Carnaby Street, long known for celebrated tossers, and various venues around the capital. Mardi Gras in other Christian countries means fat Tuesday, in the sense that certain foods had to be used up in a feast before the Lenten fast. Shrove Tuesday means 'blessed' or 'shriven' Tuesday, when at noon one would hark to the shriving bell to go to church. One batty lady heard the bell while tossing pancakes (to use up eggs) and ran to the church with pancake and pan. Hence the tradition. For the original race, go to Olney, Buckinghamshire, where it all started in 1445.

Pancake Greaze: At 11.00, a strange procession is seen crossing the medieval Westminster School tucked behind Westminster Abbey. The cook in his white hat and jacket is preceded by the verger, carrying a silver mace. The cook carries a frying pan containing a pancake. In the Great Schoolroom, there is a 16ft-high iron bar which used to mark the division of the Upper and Lower parts of the school. The cook has to toss the pancake over this bar and as it falls on the other side the boys scramble to get a piece in a massive scrum. In fact, the whole school used to take part, which ensured sore heads if not broken limbs. Now representatives of each form do the job. The boy who gets the biggest part receives a guinea from the Dean.

The cook also receives a fee for getting the pancake over in one piece – presumably he can't get to practise much – although it is more than 60 years since the pancake infamously stuck to the bar, requiring a second toss. Not open to the public.

Trail of the Pyx: Held in February or March at the Goldsmiths' Hall, London. The exact and serious purpose of the ancient trial, despite its Peter Pannish name – it dates from at least 1280 – is to provide independent scrutiny of the quality and size of coins of the realm made by the Royal Mint in the previous year. Officers of the Mint are required to place samples in the Pyx (a box) and these are brought before a jury of goldsmiths sworn in by the Queen's Remembrancer (a shadowy figure who appears in the *Horseshoe and Faggot Cutting Ceremony,* see October, page 308). Not open to the public. Also *Great Spitalfields Pancake Race.*

MARCH

Early Sunday *Oranges and Lemons Service:* At St Clement Danes in the Strand. Schoolchildren given one of each (see nursery rhymes, page 71).

21 March *Druids celebrate spring equinox:* Cloaked pagan types meet in Tower Hill, London, to celebrate spring equinox.

Easter (date fixed by Golden Numbers, see Pope for explanation)

Maundy Thursday (three days before Easter) *Royal Maundy Money Distribution:* At Westminster Abbey in even-numbered years, other great cathedrals in odd years. Monarch gives sets of specially minted coins in special purses to as many old people as years of the sovereign's age, travelling by royal train to further cities. The coins are legal tender but rarely spent, as they are much treasured by the families who receive them, which is just as well, as most people would be puzzled to be offered a fourpenny piece.

This is an ancient, complicated and fascinating ceremony for which tickets have to be sought well in advance. The name Maundy Thursday originates from a command, *mandatum* in Latin, from Jesus on the night of the Last Supper. He washed the feet of the apostles and said: 'If I then, your Lord and Master, have washed your feet; ye also ought to wash one another's feet. For I have given you an example, that ye should do as I have done to you.' (John 13: 14–15). Throughout the Middle Ages, monarchs, princes and bishops across Europe treated the poor to feasts and literally washed their feet. English monarchs used also to give their gowns to the poor, but as these were of little use, Elizabeth I substituted purses of coins at the 1572 ceremony at Greenwich Palace. There are records of sovereigns until James II and William III personally washing the feet of the elderly poor. At Somerset House, the records stated that on Maundy Thursday 1685 'our gracious King James the 2nd wash'd, wip'd and kiss'd the feet of 52 poor men with wonderful humility'. In the modern tradition, the washing is merely symbolised by the carrying of nosegays and towels in the procession. The Yeomen of the Guard, the Queen's bodyguard, are also present and two of them carry the great trays on which the purses are piled. Tickets to the ceremony may be obtained from the Abbey or those cathedrals concerned.

Good Friday *Hot Cross Bun Ceremony:* Widow's Son pub, Devons Road, Bow, London E3, noon. A sailor or Wren adds a bun to the somewhat stale collection going back at least 150 years to the time a widow, whose only son was at sea, put out a hot cross bun on Good Friday expecting his return for Easter. He never came back but each year she laid out another, refusing to take any away.

Ascension Day (following Thursday) *Beating the Bounds:* Boys of St Dunstan's beat on the City's boundary markers with willow sticks in an ancient ritual. Starts at 15.00 at All Hallows' by the Tower. For more about bounds and the extraordinary St Clement's ceremonies, etc, see page 105.

APRIL

I April *Police bottom day:* On this day only, before noon, it is customary to pat policemen and policewomen in Trafalgar Square on the bottom, saying: 'It's a fair cop guv, I done it all. I blame it all on society. I was deprived (or depraved in some versions)'. They are supposed to reply 'Irish stew in the name of the law', help you to the ground with their ceremonial stick and award you a ceremonial ride in a car specially decorated with flashing blue lights. See next item before starting this one.

All Fools' Day: The best April Fool yet perpetrated was on 1 April 1698 and made a laughing stock of the gentry of London, great numbers of whom turned up in their carriages and finery at the Tower of London to 'see the lions being washed' as instructed on their gilt-edged invitation cards. A menagerie of animals was kept here at the time, before being transferred to London Zoo in 1831. Londoners still April Fool each other, and newspapers invariably include some completely mad, made up bit of nonsense that's almost credible (actually some of them do this all the year round). The until then very po-faced media started marking All Fools' Day in 1957 when the late broadcaster Richard Dimbleby presented on the BBC TV programme *Panorama* an apparently entirely serious programme about the spaghetti harvest in Italy, including shots of peasants tending their spaghetti trees. But you shouldn't April Fool after midday, otherwise *you're* the fool.

First Saturday (or sometimes last one in March) *The Boat Race:* From Putney to Mortlake. It's a little odd that perhaps quarter of a million people turn out to watch just two boats in a sport few people are interested in – rowing – from two universities most have no connection with over a course they can only see a small part of for a result they will probably miss and aren't particularly interested in. Plus Hammersmith Bridge, which (if the IRA haven't blown it up again) would be the ideal spot to watch from, is usually closed on Boat Race day for some daft reason. But as one Londoner said: 'It's the first day out beside the river in the year, and it's free, so why not if it's a nice day?' The course goes upriver from the University Stone, just upstream of Putney Bridge, to Chiswick Bridge. The pubs such as the Dove, the Rutland and Blue Anchor on the north side, just west of Hammersmith, would be good vantage points, but crowded, ditto the White Hart on the south side a little upriver in Barnes, which has more room and a generous sweep of the river. So well ingrained that in cockney rhyming slang, 'nice girl, pity about the boat [race = face]' means she's ugly but otherwise charming.

April 5 (approx) *Changing of the Quill:* Learned address to statue of 16th-century historian John Stow, including changing the pen in his hand by either the Lord Mayor of London or the Master of the Merchant Taylors' Company, Church of St Andrew Undershaft, London EC3. Every three years (2008, 2011, etc). Open to the public.

2nd Monday (approx) *Beat the Tube race:* The idea of chartered surveyor Richard Guthrie as a tribute to first four-minute-miler, Sir Roger Bannister. You may feel after another ordeal stuck in a crammed Central Line Tube that it would be a stroll to beat the Tube on foot, but in normal service it would not be that easy to outrun a Tube train. A group of determined young professionals, wearing braces and pinstripes, board a Victoria to Wimbledon train, get off at South Kensington and sprint like hell down the Fulham Road to try to get back on it at Fulham Broadway, 1.6 miles and four stops down the line. Few of them make it unless the Tube stops for some inexplicable delay at Earl's Court (now would they do that, I ask you?). An easier course would be to cut across the Circle Line from Farringdon down to Blackfriars where you can virtually see the other end. You could do it on crutches, or pogo sticks and still beat the train. Too easy for Mr Guthrie and his chums …

3rd Sunday *London Marathon:* The world's most popular, 29,000 people pound the pavement for 26 miles from Greenwich to the Mall, many dressed as circus clowns, gorillas, waiters with trays of drinks (glued on), a two-man rhinoceros, etc, but also many serious runners, and almost all raising staggering (and they do at the end) amounts of money for charity. In 2001's race, Angela Stratford ran in her wedding dress, complete with race number of course, and her groom Nigel Jones ran in formal suit (except both dress and trousers were on the short side). They stopped after 25 miles at Cleopatra's Needle on the Embankment and took their vows in front of a Bishop and a crowd of friends. They had met at a running club and she told him that she'd only marry a man who could catch her, so he trained and trained and made the distance. After the service, they continued and finished wearing 'Just Married' placards.

In the following year, a deeply eccentric character called Lloyd Scott set out in a full old-fashioned diving suit including 22lb lead boots. He took six days to finish, gaining the world marathon record (slowest, that is).

April 23 *St George's Day:* On England's national day, the English – who gamely go along with the St Patrick's Day shenanigans about Ireland, or eat a wee haggis beastie on Burns Night for Scotland – eccentrically do precisely nothing. Shakespeare, who contrived not only to be born on St George's Day but patriotically to die on it too, wrote in *Henry V* about the battle of Agincourt:

> I see you stand like greyhounds in the slips,
> Straining upon the start. The game's afoot:
> Follow your spirit; and upon this charge
> Cry 'God for Harry! England and St George!'

He needn't have bothered, frankly. A society dedicated to the saint holds a banquet, certain St George's pubs might offer a free pickled onion or something, but there will be few more St George's flags (red cross on a white background) flying than the usual half-hearted effort. The reason for this is not so much the very eccentric choice of saint – an obscure Palestinian famed for not killing a non-existent beast somewhere far away – as a severe and prolonged lack of oppression of the English, and a healthy suspicion about nationalism unless there's a dire emergency, or it's confined within special occasions such as the Last Night of the Proms or sports internationals. It's no coincidence that the excellent Olivier film of *Henry V* was made during World War II, or that at the end of the war the great national figurehead Churchill was dumped on the political scrapheap. Nationalism is for foreigners.

MAY

Second Saturday *Moon Walk:* Thousands of London lasses brave a cold front, and walk a half or full marathon (13 or 26 miles) around Central London, starting from Battersea Park, in just their bras. Plus trousers or skirts, of course. These bras are decorated with feathers, tinsel, tassels or whatever, and whether the Moon Walk takes place after midnight to spare participants' blushes, to save passing drivers being distracted, or because it's cooler and less crowded, it is one of those strangely life-asserting and courageous events. It is in aid of Breakthrough Breast Cancer and some of the walkers are survivors of that all-too-common disease. The bra firm Playtex gives Wonderbras or Balconette bras to participants, which as *Evening Standard* writer Kate Rew wrote at the 2000 event, would be frankly the last thing you'd want if you'd had a mastectomy or prosthesis. She – the daughter of a survivor of the disease – raised the question of whether it's a stunt in bad taste, but as with all such in-your-face events which raise hundreds of thousands of pounds for research, if the victims and their families join in, one has simply to admire their guts (metaphorically, if not literally). And, as it is after midnight, no-one is forced to see it. There's a minute's silence for the victims of the disease which seems to touch so many families today. For sponsorship and participation details, contact: Walk the Walk, Britannia Wharf, Monument Road, Woking, Surrey GH21 5LW.

Second Sunday *Mr Punch service:* It's almost beyond belief. Dozens of Mr Punches (as in Punch and Judy) sitting in pews in church, listening to a sermon which they subject to irreverent and cheeky interruptions. They hit each other, or their puppetmasters ('professors' is the strict term), for Mr Punch will not sit still. This is the crowded scene at St Paul's church (the actors' church) in Covent Garden where the annual Punch service takes place at 11.30. The day includes a brass band procession of Mr Punches around the area beforehand at 10.30 and a May Fayre including non-stop Punch and Judy performances, and other forms of puppetry, all afternoon. The procession to honour the deeply politically incorrect wife-beater and baby-batterer Mr Punch – Chelmsford and Chesterfield have tried to ban him in recent years – is accompanied, strangely, by his worst enemies, the uniformed bobbies, and includes a toast to the immortal puppet at a plaque to him at St Paul's. This is the very spot where Samuel Pepys made the first recorded sighting of Mr Punch in Britain in May 1662. He wrote (in his own secret code, of course) that he saw '...an Italian puppet play, that is within the rails there, which is very pretty, the best that I ever saw, and great resort of gallants.'

The church is, in the 17th-century fashion, of classical shape with a huge rectangular interior. The architect, the great Inigo Jones, ordered to make it a plain barn to save money, retorted he would make it 'the handsomest barn in England', and he did. For more on this fascinating church, see page 107.

19 May *Beheaded Queen's roses:* Just north of the Tower Green in the Tower of London is the church of, appropriately, St Peter in Chains (or St Peter Ad Vincula). Here an intriguing and strange annual ritual takes place on 19 May, when a florist, acting for a strictly anonymous party, puts a dozen red roses on the grave of Anne Boleyn, Henry VIII's queen, whose head was struck from her body outside the church on the same day in 1536. She protested her love for, and loyalty to, the king with her last words on Tower Green. The blood-red roses have been arriving annually at this sad spot for at least 160 years and are thought to be sent by members of either her family, or possibly the Percys, ancient Dukes of Northumberland, one of whom the king ousted in Anne's affections. The secret admirer has never been identified, although several theories have been advanced.

29 May *Oak Apple Day:* Veteran soldiers at the Christopher Wren-designed Royal Hospital, Chelsea, parade with oak sprigs in their best uniforms and dress the statue of founder Charles II in oak to commemorate his escape in the Civil War by hiding in the Royal Oak. Setting up the hospital for old soldiers was reputedly rollicking royal mistress Nell Gwyn's idea.

JUNE

Early June midweek *Forgotten gems in the shadow of St Paul's:* The City Churches Trust takes guided walks round some of Europe's finest architecture, including some churches normally closed, plus Britain's oldest and lavishly decorated synagogue. A must for Wren and Hawksmoor fans. For details ☎ 020 7626 1555.

Second Sunday *Secret gardens unlocked:* London Garden Squares Day offers a chance to enter hundreds of these intriguing hidden oases of peace and quiet. Tickets for all and details from LHPGT, Duck Island Cottage, St James's Park, London SW1A 2BJ, enclosing £5 and an SAE.

Charlton Horn Fair: There's a lusty origin to this fair in SE7. It dates from when King John had his wicked way with the local miller's wife, and in desperation at facing the cuckolded husband, said the miller could hold an annual fair, which locals naturally called the Horn Fair. It's an ordinary sort of fair today, with stalls and so on, but there's a procession involving King John, the Miller and some horn decorations.

19 June *Garter Ceremony:* At St George's Chapel, Windsor Castle. It is peculiar that the oldest English order of chivalry, the highest such order in the world, revolves around a modest female under-garment, and odd that such Knights of the Round Table-style malarkey carries on in all seriousness in the 21st century. On this day the monarch and 24 Knights of Order of the Garter process with spectacular robes and hats to mark this oldest order of chivalry and a useful, if humble, garment. A few tickets can be booked. Even odder is that the highest and best of the land should parade in what look like Gilbert and Sullivan comic opera outfits of peacock and heron feathers, badges, ribbons and glorified velvet pyjamas (plus of course a prominent garter worn below the left knee) 700 years after its origin, but that's eccentric Britain for you. It originated in 1348 when King Edward III, in picking up a lady's fallen garter at a dance, turned on sniggering noblemen and said in defence of the red-faced lady (possibly the Countess of Salisbury): '*Honi soit qui mal y pense*', now the official motto, meaning: 'Shame on him who thinks bad of it.' The court operated half in Old French at the time and he added in English that he would turn the embarrassing garter into the most honoured garment ever worn, which he did.

The knights have banners which in Arthurian times would have been carried before them into battle but which hang in St George's Chapel, Windsor, where they have their own named stalls. Although generally dukedoms, baronetcies, earldoms or whatever are higher than mere knights, this order is regarded as superceding them all. For example, after Winston Churchill saved the entire world from slavery (not single-handedly, of course), it was suggested that the title Duke of London should be given to him but he asked merely for a 'park for children to play in, that kind of thing'. Later the young Queen Elizabeth offered him Knight of the Garter and he could not resist. Or as he said to a close friend: 'I only accepted because I think she is so splendid.'

June 24 *Knollys Rose Ceremony:* An odd quit-rent, Mansion House, City of London. Every 24 June a single red Knollys Rose is carried on a velvet cushion by churchwardens of All-Hallows-By-The-Tower in the City of London to the Lord Mayor at Mansion House. This quit-rent was a penalty imposed on Sir Robert Knollys in 1381 because he built a gallery bridge between two of his properties – now long gone – across narrow Seething Lane. Naughty man, he's still paying for it six centuries later.

Last Saturday *London Mardi Gras:* Annual festival celebrating gay and lesbian life in London, usually at Finsbury Park. Preceded by a Pride March in Central London. The event is described as a carnival of kitsch with over-dressed drag queens and has major bands performing plus blessings for gay 'marriages'. Tourist chiefs hope the Mardi Gras will become a success à la Sydney, claiming the pink pound is worth £750 million a year, a figure that sounds as if its come from Keith Waterhouse's Department of Guesswork. For further details, see www.londonmardigras.com

Fourth weekend (**approx**) *Small ships race:* The great days of full-rigged sailing ships return to London's waters, in this case the Round Pond in Kensington Gardens, in front of Kensington Palace. Beautiful models with sensational curves – sailing boats, I mean – plus warships with working guns, tugs, fireboats and speedboats take to the waves, and to the deeps if two radio-controlled sets are on the same frequency, as happened recently. The little boats often appear on the Round Pond on other Sundays. The swans, and coots which nest on the lifebuoys, seem unperturbed. A word of advice if you chat to the amiable old coots who sail the things. Not every tall-masted sailing vessel is a ship, that's a particular type. And a barque is not the same as a barquentine. If you don't want a salty sea-dog to fix you with a glittering eye, don't even think about commenting on the rigging. The Round Pond, by the way, isn't round, but then the Derby isn't at Derby but at Epsom, and Leeds Castle is not at Leeds but in Kent. Trinity Square is a crescent and Finsbury Park is, of course, nowhere near Finsbury. Ho hum, you get the idea.

Variable date, every leap year *Dunmow Flitch Trials:* Every fourth year since the 13th century, a flitch of bacon is awarded to a couple who do not repent marriage within a year and a day after a long-winded trial. At Dunmow, Essex, near London Stansted airport. Full details in *Eccentric Britain*.

Last week of June and first of July *Wimbledon tennis:* Like the Proms, a very English event with some fanatical queuers sleeping out all night in Wimbledon Park Road. Tens of thousands of tennis fans, young and old, arrive and leave without the least trouble. When it's crowded in the grounds, the gentle murmur is probably 100,000 middle-class people politely saying 'sorry' as they push past each other. In the Navy, anything that doesn't move gets painted grey (and if it does move, salute it); here everything's a dull matt green, which seems to have a calming effect. No advertising hoardings, everything very restrained and apparently uncommercial. The atmosphere is somehow like a suburban tennis club in Betjeman's *Metroland*, when in fact it's a megamillion pound international media fest.

Once in a blue moon there's a hunky young star such as Borg and a few adolescent tennis groupies will wait by the players' entrance, but it's not really a big deal. They don't push or shove or scream much. The red-top tabloid press whips itself into a frenzy about whoever the latest sexy young female is and endlessly discusses details of their underwear – Kournikova for example – but the true Wimbledon fans wouldn't dream of mentioning such things. Being England, quite often Wimbledon's totally screwed up by rain, in which case tens of thousands of people travel from Cornwall, Carlisle or wherever, politely shuffle around the even more packed grounds, watch ten minutes' play when the rain seems to have stopped, and perhaps participate in a sing-song or, really daring, a small Mexican wave if sitting in one of the big show courts. Then they have their sandwiches and eventually good-naturedly go home without a spot of trouble, saying what a good day out it was. They don't even get their money back if there's some play. Tickets are expensive and for Centre Court vastly oversubscribed. If they were soccer fans they'd have burned Wimbledon down, filled the streets with broken bottles and litter and vandalised the Tube. They're a completely different race, tennis fans. Nice people like Sir Cliff Richard and Sue Barker. For ticket information, ☏ 020 8946 2244. For weird things that happened at Wimbledon, see Wimbledon walk, page 294.

JULY

Mid July (date depends on tides) *Doggett's Coat and Badge Race:* Less well-known than the Oxford and Cambridge boat race, for some reason, but all the more fascinating for its early origins and strange survival. See Southwark walk, page 204.

Second Saturday *Black Cherry Fair:* In Windsor Street, Chertsey, Surrey, on the second Saturday in July. This is ancient, dating from a charter granted by King Henry VI to John de Harmondesworth, Abbot of Chertsey Abbey, and although it originally celebrated St Anne's Day in August, it now coincides with the supposed great Surrey cherry harvest, which of course doesn't exist and would anyway be at a different time of year if it did.

July onwards (until September) *The Proms:* Mostly, but not entirely, in the Royal Albert Hall, the world's biggest and best celebration of classical music, ancient and modern, eagerly followed by the young promenaders who make a gloriously anachronistic, jingoistic extravaganza of the Last Night of the Proms in September. Tickets for that are as hard to come by as those for the Wimbledon tennis final – a lottery based on loyalty to the preceding concerts – but in recent years the thing has also been shown live to a huge crowd in adjacent Hyde Park. Also on TV.

Late July Sunday *Greenwich Mela:* All day, Greenwich, SE7. The largest Asian festival in southeast London, organised by the community, with a wide variety of Asian music, entertainment and stalls. Great food, great music, great clothes.

20/24 July *Swan Upping:* This astonishing and complex ritual starts from the premise that all swans in Britain are royal birds and belong to the Queen. Except those belonging to the

Dyers and Vintners' companies, of course. The ritual involves catching all the swans on the Thames, marking them as to whom they belong (as if it mattered), weeks of work by officials in archaic uniforms swanning about in special boats which is difficult to justify – if, that is, British traditions need any justification other than being traditional. For the full but rather unbelievable story, see page 54.

AUGUST

Last weekend *Notting Hill Carnival:* Held in Portobello Road and Ladbroke Grove, this is always promoted as the biggest street festival in Europe, with up to two million revellers (who counts them?). It is supposed to be where efnic meets yoof, innit, and multicultural London's social mix is celebrated with a Caribbean theme. The reggae is loud, the dancing exuberant, the Jamaican food tasty, the floats and fancy dress spectacular, whatever the weather. Right-wing moaners say that 'multicultural' means whatever your colour, you can still be robbed and stabbed. The police try hard to get it right and are traditionally accused of being too light-handed or heavy-handed or both.

Many of the trendy trust-fund rich kids, film stars and right-on politicos who have colonised once-poor Notting Hill in the last decade find an excuse to go to their country homes that weekend. Then Tory leader William Hague and his then fiancée, Ffion, visited in 1999 and were ridiculed for the white patches on their wrists showing where their watches had been removed to foil the rampant Rolex robbers. Actually you'd be a total prat to wear a watch worth the price of somebody's house to such an event (or, arguably, at all). A further provocative thought: if there were two million loveable cockney football supporters crammed into Notting Hill for a long weekend, what would the death toll be? Twenty stabbings, 70 crushed, three cops killed, four buildings destroyed? Is the gloom-and-doom reporting of this event somewhat exaggerated? Isn't it a little like Christmas, where road deaths are reported with shock-horror headlines even though there are far fewer than those that are ignored on any normal day?

Sunday nearest 24 August *Bartholomew Fair:* The great Bartholomew Fair of the Middle Ages began as a cloth fair but became geared to entertainment with fire-eaters and tightrope walkers, eventually becoming so rowdy that the Victorian authorities suppressed it in 1866. Only 144 years later, in 2000, things were judged calm enough to permit a revival in London's Smithfield. Today the Bartholomew Fair is ironically a restrained and quaint affair, with produce stalls making it something of a market combined with old English fair, an odd contrast with what's happening in Notting Hill at the same time. But, eccentrically, it begins with a flock of sheep being herded across London Bridge. This is a celebration of the ancient rights of the Freemen of the City. The free fair is organised by the Butchers and Drovers Charitable Institution.

SEPTEMBER

First Sunday *Great River Race:* About 200 traditional boats of many different kinds, carefully handicapped against each other, race a gruelling 22 miles right across London from leafy Surrey's elegant Richmond through the heart of government at Westminster and the busy non-stop City to futuristic skylines of Docklands and Island Gardens. It grew out of a challenge in 1987 to beat the winners of Doggett's Coat and Badge (see July). In keeping with the Company of Watermen & Lightermen's traditional role of licensing boatmen who were, when the roads were primitive, the London taxis of the era, a passenger must be carried by each competitor, whatever their style of boat – and that certainly varies, although each must have at least four oars or paddles. They have included in recent years: a Hawaiian outrigger war canoe, Viking longboat, Norwegian scow, Canadian C-8 canoe, Chinese dragonboat, numerous Cornish pilot and other gigs, skiffs, cutters, naval whalers, a magnificent 54ft replica bronze age Greek galley, traditional canvas and tar Irish boats, a new shallop and a Thames wherry (both built specially for the race) and the world's oldest racing rowing boat, the two-centuries-old *Royal Oak* built in Co Down, Northern Ireland. They all take on the Watermen's cutter for the prize, which they keep for a year, of a trophy featuring a real Watermen's Badge (the equivalent of a present-day cabbie's badge) issued to William Savage of Gravesend in 1803. Crews have included policemen, cadets, teenage Sea Scouts, firemen, soldiers and sailors, pub teams of both sexes, along with international entries from America, Canada, Holland, Sweden, France, Germany, Ireland, and the Channel Islands. For details, see www.greatriverrace.co.uk.

Brick Lane Festival: An annual free festival in Brick Lane, E1, with a world music stage, amazing street entertainment, delicious food, craft stalls and a special children's play area. If you've had too much Balti, hail a rickshaw wallah. Celebrates the area's successive waves of immigrant communities: Huguenot, Jewish and, principally, Bangladeshi. See www.bricklanefestival.org.

12 September *Browning remembered:* Browning fans from around the world – that is, admirers of the poet Robert Browning not the equally great, in his way, machine-gun manufacturer – gather at the Browning Chapel at St Marylebone church, on the corner of Marylebone High Street and Marylebone Road. It was here that he and Elizabeth Barrett wed in secret in one of the great love affairs of London literati. People still ask to see the marriage register and buy copies of their certificate.

Third Sunday (approx) *Horseman's Sunday:* Service on horseback, with the minister on horseback too, in St John's, Hyde Park. An annual service where the packed congregation is comprised of dozens of horses sounds too bizarre to be true, but for a sight of a priest in his vestments on horseback intoning to the gathered dozens of horses – or, perhaps, their riders – make the trip to St John's, Hyde Park, in Hyde Park Crescent, W2, at noon. Horseman's Sunday is the occasion when the assembled posse can be seen bursting into a stirring blast of the hymn 'Jerusalem', after a veritable sermon on the mount, before the horses take a trot round the block and then are announced one by one and given a rosette.

Third weekend (approx) *London Open House Day:* Once-a-year access to intriguing buildings of architectural value that are closed to the public for the rest of the year – from futuristic offices to art deco masterpieces, from secret bunkers to private homes to the Bank of England. Fascinating and free. Details, see public libraries or www.londonopenhouse.org.

Late September *Clog and Apron Race:* At the Royal Botanic Gardens at Kew where late each September dozens of horticultural students thus garbed have to clatter their way down the 373yd-long Broad Walk.

OCTOBER

First Sunday *Pearly Harvest Festival:* At St Martin-in-the-Fields, off Trafalgar Square. Lots of folklore cockneys in their strange coats covered with pearly buttons playing ukuleles or just singing their hearts out. More on pearly kings, page 53.

Variable Wednesday *Horseshoe and Faggot Cutting Ceremony:* Deeply bizarre quit-rent, High Court, The Strand, London. This ceremony is unbelievably old and unbelievably meaningless. It must be held on a Wednesday afternoon late each October ('between the morrow of St Michael and the morrow of St Martin'). The City Solicitor cuts hazel rods with two knives, which he then presents to the Queen's Remembrancer, who pronounces 'Good service'. This is the rent for a piece of ground called The Moors at Eardington in Shropshire – or rather it *was* the rent once, but no-one is sure precisely when or which bit of land. Then six very large horseshoes and 61 nails are counted out and the Remembrancer pronounces 'Good number'. This was the rent agreed after Walter le Brun was granted land in 1235 for a forge in St Clement Danes parish, probably where Australia House now stands. The horseshoes are given straight back and kept for next year, as far as I can gather. This little-known event, which you can witness if you apply to the courts, may be the oldest surviving English ceremony, apart from the Coronation. Actually it's deeply bizarre being the Remembrancer for something the purpose of which is totally forgotten. One other duty – he has to receive the Lord Chancellor's Great Seal – a wax one, not a flippered one – when he resigns or dies.

16 October *Lion Sermon:* At St Katharine Cree in Creechurch Lane, in the City. Everyone recalls the Roman slave Androcles who was spared by a lion in the arena because he had once extracted a thorn from its paw. Few recall a London Lord Mayor who, bizarrely, had a similar experience. On every 16 October at 13.00 for more than 350 years, the Lion Sermon has been preached at the church of St Katharine Cree. Sir John Gayer, a trader and outspoken Lord Mayor who was once imprisoned for refusing City money for the Parliamentary army waging civil war, came face-to-face with an enormous lion in the Syrian desert. Perhaps remembering Daniel rather than Androcles, he fell upon his knees and prayed for mercy. The lion came up to him, checked him over and walked off. Oddly, Sir John was Master of the Fishmongers Company, so what he was doing in the desert is anyone's guess. If he did have a box of kippers with him to monger, perhaps it put the lion off. Whatever the explanation, a grateful Sir John gave money to a number of charities, endowed the church to preach his annual sermon, and gave it a splendid font, inscribed with his coat of arms. Cree, incidentally, is not short for creed, as archbishop William Laud wrongly records in his diaries, but for Christchurch, a medieval predecessor.

If you go along and see the wonderful stained-glass windows commemorating the Flower Sermon, I must tell you that this annual colourful honouring of the Sunday School movement had at the time of writing, sadly, fallen into abeyance. But plans are afoot to revive it.

NOVEMBER

5 November *Guy Fawkes Night:* Londoners blow tens of millions of pounds worth of fireworks into the sky to celebrate defeat of the 1605 Gunpowder Plot to blow up Parliament and King James I. Organised displays in various parks, etc, are often on the nearest Saturday. Beefeaters still search the cellars of Parliament on this day, looking for barrels of gunpowder and Catholic conspirators with lanterns in black cloaks.

First Sunday *London to Brighton veteran car run:* Odd in that only cars built before 1 January 1905 are eligible, which means that there are not too many and that their chances of getting to Brighton are a bit ropey. The context of this run was to celebrate the 1896 abolition of the rule whereby a man had to walk in front of any motor car with a red flag, limiting them to about 3mph. Millions of hedgehogs have since flatly denied that this was a good idea. Starts from Hyde Park Corner and ends several hours later in Madeira Drive, Brighton. Thousands of people line the route.

Early November, usually second Saturday *Lord Mayor's Show:* It involves 6,500 participants, both civilian and military, together with 67 floats from organisations across the country, 200 horses, 20 bands and 20 carriages, making a two-and-a-half-mile procession. Ever since 1215, the new Lord Mayor has made his or her way to the Queen's Bench to pledge his allegiance to the Crown. Here you can see the gilded state coach, pikemen in armour and the strange giants Gog and Magog (see *London beasts*, page 155). More info, ☏ 020 7606 3030.

Late November or early December *Royal Smithfield Show:* See below.

DECEMBER

Royal Smithfield Show: Rural beasts and more than 40,000 tweedy folk with straw on their boots take to the streets of London. In fact it's no longer at Smithfield, such is the need to show off the latest combine harvesters, muck spreaders, etc, but is instead at Earl's Court usually in every even-numbered year. Supreme Champion Beast – I can think of a few who might merit that title – was won in 2000 by Danny Boy, a 13-month-old crossbred steer from Balhousie Farm, Carnoustie, Angus. The Limousin/Aberdeen Angus Cross was said by Championship Judge Robert Needham to have 'all the right bits in the right places'. For metaphorical bull**** and muck-spreading, see Fleet Street. Sometimes held in late November.

25 December *Peter Pan Swim:* In the Serpentine lake in Hyde Park. Dozens of men and women vie for the Peter Pan Cup, first presented by author of the children's classic J M Barrie. Everyone has a chance of winning because less able swimmers have a start on the rest. The temperature is usually about 40 degrees Fahrenheit (just above freezing) and as they're a fit and friendly lot there's no need to break the ice. An American visitor who took part in a recent Christmas Day dip quipped: 'I thought it would be really cool ... Just how cool I didn't realise!' A large crowd watches at the usual start time of 09.00 and there are many very fit-looking elderly ladies in the event. In praise of colder women, as it were...

31 December *New Year's Eve:* Celebrations beneath the Christmas tree in Trafalgar Square. For people who have already had too much to drink, there's plenty more to drink in the fountains. Meanwhile various official bodies hurl tens of thousands of pounds worth of fireworks into the sky, oblivious of the fact that it's midwinter and midnight on a rainswept Atlantic island where no sane person would celebrate outside. It's usually a damp squib, with the rockets exploding unseen in the rainclouds.

DAILY

Ceremony of the Keys: Has taken place at the Tower of London every day for more than 700 years. At 21.53, the Chief Warder in Tudor uniform, carrying a lantern and the keys, sets off from the Byward Tower to meet the Escort of the Key all bedecked in Beefeater garb. They tour the various gates, ceremonially locking them. On returning to the Bloody Tower archway, however, the party is challenged by a sentry with the words: 'Halt! Who comes there?' as if he wouldn't know after 700 years.

The reply is bellowed out: 'The Keys.'
'Whose Keys?'
'Queen Elizabeth's Keys.'
'Advance Queen Elizabeth's Keys. All's well.'

The party passes through the arch and the chief warder raises his hat, saying: 'God preserve Queen Elizabeth.' All reply: 'Amen.' A bugler plays the Last Post and the Keys are carried to the Resident Governor of the Tower for the night.

The only time the Keys were late was in September 1941 when the Tower suffered several direct hits from Nazi bombs. It was delayed just half an hour.

Note Admission to the Keys Ceremony is only by written application and invitation. Apply to Ceremony of the Keys, HM Tower of London, EC3N 4AB. For Tower information, ☏ 020 7680 9004.

INFREQUENTLY

Ceremony of the Constable's Dues: This 600-year-old ceremony reiterates the Tower of London's ancient right to tolls from ships wishing to moor close by.

The crew of a visiting Royal Naval vessel, for example, are escorted by Yeoman Warders and a corps of drums to Tower Green, where the Constable of the Tower receives his dues, in this case a barrel of Navy rum.

Any major naval vessel must make this tribute – it happens four or five times a year – and it is far from the only perk of being Constable of the Tower. Never mind company cars, he is also entitled to any cattle, sheep, pigs or horses that fall off London Bridge; a penny for every foot of livestock that falls into the tower moat; and two old pence per pilgrim landing to visit the shrine of St James. Actually, as freemen of the City of London have the legal right to drive sheep across London bridges, and at least one of them occasionally does, this may not be entirely pointless.

The Swearing on the Horns: A strange rite of passage – like that of ship passengers first crossing the Equator – was for people first passing through the inns of Highgate, where there have always been plenty of taverns (19 in 1826, fewer now), being both on the road to the North from London and also a pleasant day's horse ride out from the city to a village high up in clean air. The newcomer is paraded before the pair of cow or stag horns in a pub such as the **Flask**, Highgate West Hill, Highgate, and made to swear an oath vowing never to drink small beer (weak brews, that is) unless he liked it better than strong. Or eat brown bread when he could get white – unless he preferred it. Or make love to the maid when he could get the mistress – unless he preferred her. The sheer nonsense of such a conditional vow gave much opportunity for humour and ribaldry among the coach parties – horse drawn, then motor coaches – that it has never completely died out. After swearing on the horns you have to kiss them, and then can kiss any girl in the pub that you fancy (if she's willing). **The Wrestlers** in North Road has details of the oath displayed and undertook the ceremony twice a year when I was a student. The horns here seem to be antlers of – appropriately – a stag, and their version of the Highgate oath seems to suggest kissing the maid *and* the mistress, if you could get away with it. Byron certainly referred to the ceremony in the 19th century and if you think it's the kind of thing Dickens would have put in *Pickwick Papers,* well Dickens and family stayed next door to **The Red Lion and Sun**, which also regularly ran the ceremony, in 1832. Another pub involved in living memory was the **Gatehouse**. People used to say of a fellow 'he's been sworn at Highgate', which meant he's been around a bit, he's a man of the world.

Serman on the mount:
Horseman's Sunday

Appendix 2

FURTHER READING

I never read a book before reviewing it; it prejudices a man so.

Sydney Smith 1771–1845

Dr Johnson's London by Lisa Picard, Weidenfeld and Nicolson, £20, 2000. ISBN: 0 297 84218 8. Is this a London you recognise? The congestion is appalling and the pollution rising. Vehicles left standing for only an hour are towed away. Wobbly paving slabs squirt black water over your legs when you stand on them. Problems with immigrants, drunkenness, the lottery craze, prostitution … This is 18th-century London and history as it should be told, the history of real life, warts and all, told by someone with wry humour. Worth every penny.

The Oxford Book of London edited by Paul Bailey, OUP, £17.99, 1995. ISBN: 0 19 214192 9. An anthology of extracts from diaries, prose, novels, letters and poems about London from the Middle Ages to the 20th century. A bedside book, containing a few gems, some wit, atmosphere and pathos.

London: The Biography by Peter Ackroyd, Chatto and Windus, £25, 2000. ISBN: 1 85619 716 6. This book by a well-known writer of fiction and non-fiction received quasi-orgasmic rave reviews from fellow literati. Brilliant, as I remark in the section on crime and punishment, in putting together some historical sources to give an apt insight. However, not nearly so dip-in-able as Picard's, and lacking a structure and signposts, making it at times heavy going. At 822 densely printed pages, it's also useful to stop a bog door banging in the wind.

Pubs & Bars, Time Out, £6. ISBN: 0 90344 660 X. It would be difficult to make such a potentially entertaining and lively subject so tedious, but they've done so magnificently. Another ideal bedside book, but only for insomniacs: a few pages of this and you'll be off. Works every time.

Time Out Shopping Guide, £7. ISBN: 0 90344 644 8. Ideal for finding the oddest things, and rather fascinating just to browse. Here's a selection from just the first page of the index: African products, Archery supplies, Art Deco stuff, Binoculars, Boomerangs, Candy-Floss Machines, Chandeliers, Clothes – Teddy Boy. Superb. In fact if you've ever stood there in your Teddy Boy outfit, dodging boomerangs while you fumble for your binoculars to find a candy-floss machine to go with your chandelier – and, frankly, who hasn't? – it's a must.

The History of London in Maps by Felix Barker and Peter Jackson, Barrie & Jenkins, £25, 1990. ISBN 0 7126 3650 1. History, London, maps: if you love two of these topics, you'll find this fascinating; if you love all three, as I do, you'll be in clover and suddenly find it's 04.00 and you have to work tomorrow. You can watch London evolve before your eyes, see schemes that never made it to reality, watch the Zeppelin raids, wander through slums that no longer exist. Plus there are some quite astonishing social revelations (see introduction to my own book).

Walking Notorious London by Andrew Duncan, New Holland, £9.99, 2001. ISBN: 1 85974 464 8. This takes a pedestrian – literally but not literary pedestrian, that is – approach to certain small patches of London looking for murder, gangland violence, the odd well-known political scandal but mainly buckets of sex. Straight sex and very, very deviant sex, and a few cruel punishments meted out too. Not that this suggests anything kinky about Mr Duncan, for he has written several guides for footbound foragers of many different aspects of London. He even has a website, www.andrewduncan.co.uk.

Temples of Convenience by Lucinda Lambton, Pavilion, £9.99, 1995. ISBN: 1862052662. A lavishly illustrated history of lavatories and chamberpots. OK, it's not a lot about London loos (apart from pictures of the priceless ladies' loos at Harrod's, now sadly replaced) but if you are fascinated by the beautiful porcelain contraptions, plus chamber-pots with witty ditties inside (or pictures of Hitler), there's a lot to go on here. I can't help but be amused by picturing the feisty eccentric aristocrat barging her way into men's toilets around the country to examine historic urinals. This picture book is so good that I'd even recommend spending an extra £10 and getting the hardback (ISBN 1-85793-676 0).

The Brookwood Necropolis Railway by John M Clarke, the Oakwood Press, £8.95. ISBN: 0 85361 4717. You travelled only once, then only in one direction. This railway for the dead has a fascination of the Edgar Allan Poe variety, plus the full details of how hearse cars and mourners' carriages were shunted into the afterlife, as it were. A detailed but not too long account of this unique operation. Fascinating.

Poems Not on the Underground, A Parody. Edited by 'Straphanger' (Roger Tagholm), Windrush Press, £5.99, 1996. ISBN: 0 900075 99 6. Sample titles: *Mind the Gap Rap, O Little Town of Basildon,* and *Kubla Khan Takes Junction 31 off the M25.* Hmmmm.

The Battle of Cable Street, The Cable Street Group, £3.95. ISBN: 0 9526827 0 2. When communism met fascism on the streets of the East End and blood flowed, by the people who were there.

The House by the Thames by Gillian Tindall, Chatto & Windus, 2006, £20 or paperback 2007, £8.99. This peculiar and particular biography of just one ancient house – 49 Bankside, mentioned on page 204 – is a delightful and engaging study of this ancient property across the river from St Paul's. It forensically digs down into its history but in doing so tells far more about London's past than many a regular history book. It also explodes the myths oddly attached to this house. Recommended if you like fascinating detail.

FICTION Too wide a field to do justice to, but if you haven't read Dickens's *Our Mutual Friend, Little Dorrit* or *Oliver Twist* plus Conrad's *The Secret Agent*, those are recommended for the 19th century, as are Arthur Conan Doyle's Sherlock Holmes books. For the 20th, Timothy Mo's *Sweet Sour*, and Nick Hornby's books for the end of the century. For the 21st, Monica Ali's *Brick Lane* and *Saturday* by Ian McEwan.

AND FINALLY ... LONDON'S MOST USELESS SIGN In Marylebone tube station, at the end of the platforms, is a sign in old-style tilework announcing 'Great Central'. This railway disappeared not in the 1990s privatisation, not in the 1980s creation of Network Southeast, not in the 1948 nationalisation but in the 1923 grouping of companies by which it became part of the LMS. Its only function today can be to mislead visitors into thinking they can change here for the Central Line, which they can't. And to please those who like historical curiosities ... so let us hope they leave it until 2023 when it will be eccentrically 100 years out of date.

Bradt Travel Guides

Africa	
Africa Overland	£15.99
Benin	£14.99
Botswana: Okavango, Chobe, Northern Kalahari	£15.99
Burkina Faso	£14.99
Cape Verde Islands	£13.99
Canary Islands	£13.95
Cameroon	£13.95
Eritrea	£15.99
Ethiopia	£15.99
Gabon, São Tomé, Príncipe	£13.95
Gambia, The	£13.99
Ghana	£15.99
Johannesburg	£6.99
Kenya	£14.95
Madagascar	£15.99
Malawi	£13.99
Mali	£13.95
Mauritius, Rodrigues & Réunion	£13.99
Mozambique	£13.99
Namibia	£15.99
Niger	£14.99
Nigeria	£15.99
Rwanda	£14.99
Seychelles	£14.99
Sudan	£13.95
Tanzania, Northern	£13.99
Tanzania	£16.99
Uganda	£15.99
Zambia	£15.95
Zanzibar	£12.99

Britain and Europe	
Albania	£13.99
Armenia, Nagorno Karabagh	£14.99
Azores	£12.99
Baltic Capitals: Tallinn, Riga, Vilnius, Kaliningrad	£12.99
Belarus	£14.99
Belgrade	£6.99
Bosnia & Herzegovina	£13.99
Bratislava	£6.99
Budapest	£8.99
Cork	£6.99
Croatia	£13.99
Cyprus see North Cyprus	
Czech Republic	£13.99
Dresden	£7.99
Dubrovnik	£6.99
Eccentric Britain	£13.99
Eccentric Cambridge	£6.99
Eccentric Edinburgh	£5.95
Eccentric France	£12.95
Eccentric London	£13.99
Eccentric Oxford	£5.95
Estonia	£13.99
Faroe Islands	£13.95
Georgia	£14.99
Helsinki	£7.99
Hungary	£14.99
Kiev	£7.95
Kosovo	£14.99

Krakow	£7.99
Latvia	£13.99
Lille	£6.99
Lithuania	£13.99
Ljubljana	£7.99
Macedonia	£14.99
Montenegro	£13.99
North Cyprus	£12.99
Paris, Lille & Brussels	£11.95
Riga	£6.95
River Thames, In the Footsteps of the Famous	£10.95
Serbia	£14.99
Slovakia	£14.99
Slovenia	£12.99
Spitsbergen	£14.99
Switzerland: Rail, Road, Lake	£13.99
Tallinn	£6.99
Ukraine	£14.99
Vilnius	£6.99
Zagreb	£6.99

Middle East, Asia and Australasia	
China: Yunnan Province	£13.99
Great Wall of China	£13.99
Iran	£14.99
Iraq	£14.95
Kabul	£9.95
Maldives	£13.99
Mongolia	£14.95
North Korea	£13.95
Oman	£13.99
Sri Lanka	£13.99
Syria	£14.99
Tibet	£13.99
Turkmenistan	£14.99

The Americas and the Caribbean	
Amazon, The	£14.99
Argentina	£15.99
Bolivia	£14.99
Cayman Islands	£12.95
Costa Rica	£13.99
Chile	£16.95
Eccentric America	£13.95
Eccentric California	£13.99
Falkland Islands	£13.95
Panama	£13.95
Peru & Bolivia: Backpacking and Trekking	£12.95
St Helena	£14.99
USA by Rail	£13.99

Wildlife	
Antarctica: Guide to the Wildlife	£14.95
Arctic: Guide to the Wildlife	£15.99
Galápagos Wildlife	£15.99
Madagascar Wildlife	£14.95
Peruvian Wildlife	£15.99
Southern African Wildlife	£18.95
SriLankan Wildlife	£15.99

Health	
Your Child Abroad: A Travel Health Guide	£10.95

Index